Lecture Notes in Computer Science 8713

Commenced Publication in 1973
Founding and Former Series Editors:
Gerhard Goos, Juris Hartmanis, and Jan van Leeuwen

Organization

Program Committee

Masayuki Abe	NTT Secure Platform Laboratories, Japan
Gail-Joon Ahn	Arizona State University, USA
Mikhail Atallah	Purdue University, USA
Vijay Atluri	Rutgers University, USA
Michael Backes	Saarland University, Germany
Kun Bai	IBM T.J. Watson Research Center, USA
Giampaolo Bella	Universitá di Catania, Italy
Marina Blanton	University of Notre Dame, USA
Kevin Butler	University of Oregon, USA
Zhenfu Cao	Shanghai-Jiao Tong University, PR China
Srdjan Capkun	ETH Zurich, Switzerland
Liqun Chen	Hewlett-Packard Laboratories, UK
Xiaofeng Chen	Xidian University, PR China
Sherman S.M. Chow	Chinese University of Hong Kong, SAR China
Veronique Cortier	CNRS, LORIA, France
Marco Cova	University of Birmingham, UK
Laszlo Csirmaz	Central European University, Budapest, Hungary
Frederic Cuppens	TELECOM Bretagne, France
Nora Cuppens-Boulahia	TELECOM Bretagne, France
Reza Curtmola	New Jersey Institute of Technology, USA
Ozgur Dagdelen	Technische Universität Darmstadt, Germany
Sabrina De Capitani Di Vimercati	Università degli Studi di Milano, Italy
Roberto Di Pietro	Università di Roma Tre, Italy
Claudia Diaz	KU Leuven, Belgium
Josep Domingo-Ferrer	Università Rovira i Virgili, Catalonia
Wenliang Du	Syracuse University, USA
Simon Foley	University College Cork, Ireland
Philip W.L. Fong	University of Calgary, Canada
Sara Foresti	Università degli Studi di Milano, Italy
Keith Frikken	Miami University, Ohio, USA
Dieter Gollmann	Hamburg University of Technology, Germany
Dimitris Gritzalis	Athens University of Economics and Business, Greece
Ehud Gudes	Ben-Gurion University, Israel
Thorsten Holz	Ruhr University Bochum, Germany

Table of Contents – Part II

Table of Contents – Part I

Public-Key Revocation and Tracing Schemes with Subset Difference Methods Revisited

Kwangsu Lee[1], Woo Kwon Koo[1], Dong Hoon Lee[1], and Jong Hwan Park[2]

[1] CIST, Korea University, Korea
{guspin,kwk4386,donghlee}@korea.ac.kr
[2] Sangmyung University, Korea
jhpark@smu.ac.kr

Abstract. *Broadcast encryption* is a very powerful primitive since it can send an encrypted message to a set of users excluding a set of revoked users. *Public-key broadcast encryption (PKBE)* is a special type of broadcast encryption such that anyone can run the encryption algorithm to create an encrypted message by using a public key. In this paper, we propose a new technique to construct an efficient PKBE scheme by using the subset cover framework. First, we introduce a new concept of public-key encryption named *single revocation encryption (SRE)* and propose an efficient SRE scheme in the random oracle model. A user in SRE is represented as a group that he belongs and a member in the group. In SRE, a sender can create a ciphertext for a specified group where one member in the group is revoked, and a receiver can decrypt the ciphertext if he belongs to the group in the ciphertext and he is not revoked in the group. Second, we show that the subset difference (SD) scheme (or the layered subset difference (LSD) scheme) and an SRE scheme can be combined to construct a public-key revocation encryption (PKRE) scheme such that a set of revoked users is specified in a ciphertext. Our PKRE scheme using the LSD scheme and our SRE scheme can reduce the size of private keys and public keys by $\log N$ factor compared with the previous scheme of Dodis and Fazio.

Keywords: Public-key encryption, Broadcast encryption, Traitor tracing, Trace and revoke, Bilinear maps.

1 Introduction

Broadcast encryption, introduced by Fiat and Naor [10], is a mechanism to efficiently send an encrypted message to a set S of receivers by using a broadcast channel. The application of broadcast encryption includes pay-TV systems, DVD content distribution systems, and file systems and many others. Broadcast encryption itself is a very powerful primitive, but the functionality of broadcast encryption can also be increased when it is combined with traitor tracing functionality. Traitor tracing was introduced by Chor, Fiat, and Naor [7], and it enables a tracer to find a traitor who participated the creation of a pirate decoder when a pirate decoder is given to the tracer. Trace and revoke is a mechanism that combines broadcast encryption and traitor tracing, and it first finds a traitor by using the tracing algorithm of traitor tracing and then revoke him by using the encrypt algorithm of broadcast encryption [6, 20, 22].

M. Kutyłowski and J. Vaidya (Eds.): ESORICS 2014, Part II, LNCS 8713, pp. 1–18, 2014.
© Springer International Publishing Switzerland 2014

Public-key broadcast encryption (PKBE) is a special type of broadcast encryption such that anyone can create a ciphertext for a set of receivers by using a publicly known public key. Public-key trace and revoke (PKTR) is a public variant of trace and revoke. There are some general methods for the construction of fully collusion resistant PKBE schemes. The first method is to combine a subset cover scheme in the framework of Naor, Naor, and Lotspiech [20] and an identity-based encryption (IBE) scheme (or a hierarchical IBE (HIBE) scheme) [9, 20, 21]. The PKBE schemes of this method are suitable for the revocation scenario where a small number of users are revoked since the ciphertext size of the schemes is proportional to the size of revoked users. Additionally, this approach also provides the tracing functionality based of the subset cover framework. However, the most efficient scheme of this method suggested by Dodis and Fazio [9] that combines the layered subset difference (LSD) scheme of Halevy and Shamir [16] and the HIBE scheme of Boneh et al. [2] has a demerit such that the size of private keys is $O(\log^{2.5} N)$ and the size of public keys is $O(\log N)$ where N is the total number of users in the system. The second method is to use the power of bilinear groups to reduce the size of ciphertext, and many PKBE schemes were proposed after the work of Boneh, Gentry, and Waters [4, 8, 19]. However, these schemes can not provide the tracing functionality, and the size of public keys is quite large (or the cost of the decryption algorithm is expensive). The third method is to combine a private linear broadcast encryption (PLBE) scheme that was introduced by Boneh, Sahai, and Waters [5] and a PKBE scheme [6, 13, 25]. The main advantage of this approach is that it provides the tracing functionality, but the storage requirement of these schemes are quite large since the size of private keys and public keys of these schemes is $O(\sqrt{N})$ where N is the total number of users in the system.

Reducing the size of private keys is very important since cryptographic key materials are securely stored in an expensive tamper-resistant memory. In case of small devices, the size of (private or public) keys and the cost of decryption operations are critical issues since the manufacturing cost of small devices is limited and the battery is also limited. As far as we know, there is no acceptable PKBE (or PKTR) scheme that can meet this requirements.

1.1   Our Contributions

In this paper, we revisit the method of Dodis and Fazio [9] that combines the SD scheme in the subset cover framework and a variant scheme of IBE to construct an efficient PKBE scheme, and propose a new method for PKBE that can reduce the size of private keys and public keys. The subset cover framework of Naor et al. [20] was very successful to construct broadcast encryption or trace and revoke schemes in the symmetric-key setting [15, 16, 20]. However, these schemes based on the subset cover framework in the public-key setting does not provide the same efficiency parameters as those in the symmetric-key setting since the underlying HIBE scheme multiplies the private key size and the public key size of PKBE by $\log N$ factor [2, 9]. For instance, the PKBE scheme that combines the LSD scheme and the HIBE scheme of Boneh et al. [2] has the ciphertext size of $O(r)$, the private key size of $O(\log^{2.5} N)$, and the public key size of $O(\log N)$.

Table 1. Comparison of public-key broadcast encryption schemes

Scheme	CT Size	SK Size	PK Size	Decrypt Time	Tracing	Assumption
BGW [4]	$O(1)$	$O(1)$	$O(N)$	2P	No	q-Type
BGW [4]	$O(\sqrt{N})$	$O(1)$	$O(\sqrt{N})$	2P	No	q-Type
Delerablée [8]	$O(1)$	$O(1)$	$O(s_{max})$	2P	No	q-Type
LSW [19]	$O(r)$	$O(1)$	$O(1)$	rE + 2P	No	q-Type
NNL [21]	$O(r\log\frac{N}{r})$	$O(\log N)$	$O(1)$	1P	Yes	BDH
DF [9]	$O(r)$	$O(\log^{2.5}N)$	$O(\log N)$	2P	Yes	q-Type
BW [6]	$O(\sqrt{N})$	$O(\sqrt{N})$	$O(\sqrt{N})$	4P	Yes	Static
Ours	$O(r)$	$O(\log^{1.5}N)$	$O(1)$	2E + 2P	Yes	q-Type

N = the maximum number of users, s_{max} = the maximum size of a receiver set,
r = the size of a revoked set, E = exponentiation, P = pairing

To construct an efficient PKBE scheme by using the subset cover framework, we first introduce single revocation encryption (SRE) that can be efficiently combined with the subset difference (SD) scheme, and propose an efficient SRE scheme that is secure in the random oracle model. A user in SRE is represented as a group label and a member label in the group, and a sender can send an encrypted message to one specified group except one member that was revoked in that group. If a user who belongs to the group is not revoked in the group, then he can decrypt the ciphertext by using this private key. Our SRE scheme has the ciphertext size of $O(1)$, the private key size of $O(1)$, and the public key size of $O(1)$, and it is secure in the random oracle model under q-type assumption.

Next, we show that it is possible to construct an efficient public-key revocation encryption (PKRE) scheme such that a set R of revoked users is specified in a ciphertext by combining the SD scheme (or the LSD scheme) and the SRE scheme. Compared to the previous PKBE scheme that combines the LSD scheme and the HIBE scheme of Boneh et al. [2], our proposed PKRE scheme that combines the LSD scheme and our SRE scheme has the shorter size of private keys and public keys. The comparison between previous PKBE schemes and our schemes is given in the Table 1. In the table, the PKBE scheme of Dodis and Fazio is the combination of the LSD scheme and the HIBE scheme of Boneh *et al.* [2], and our PKRE scheme is the combination of the LSD scheme and our SRE scheme.

1.2 Our Technique

The main idea of our PKRE scheme is to invent a new type of public-key encryption (PKE) that has short private key size and can be integrated with the SD scheme of the subset cover framework. In order to understand our technique, we first review the SD scheme of Naor *et al.* [20]. In a full binary tree $\mathcal{T}$, a subtree T_i rooted at a node v_i is defined as the set of all nodes in T_i and a subtree $T_{i,j}$ is defined as the set of nodes in

$T_i - T_j$ where a node v_j is a descendant of a node v_i. In the SD scheme, a user in the SD scheme is assigned to a leaf node in $\mathcal{T}$, and a subset $S_{i,j}$ is defined as the set of leaf nodes in $T_{i,j}$. A user in a leaf node v_u is associated with the set PV_u of subsets $S_{i,j}$ where v_i and v_j are two nodes in the path from the root node of $\mathcal{T}$ to the leaf node v_u. The set S of receivers is associated with the set CV of disjoint subsets $S_{i,j}$ that covers S. If a user u is not revoked, then he can find two subsets $S_{i,j} \in CV$ and $S_{i',j'} \in PV_u$ such that $v_i = v_{i'}$, $d_j = d_{j'}$, and $v_j \neq v_{j'}$ where d_j is the depth of a node v_j. Next, the user can decrypt the ciphertext component that is related with $S_{i,j}$ by using the private key components that are related with PV_u.

One critical condition for the decryption using the SD scheme is that the inequality $v_j \neq v_{j'}$ should be satisfied. For this inequality, Naor *et al.* [20] used the key derivation property of a key assignment algorithm, and Dodis and Fazio [9] used the delegation property of a key generation algorithm in HIBE. To devise a new technique to solve this issue, we look at the IBRE scheme of Lewko, Sahai, and Waters [19]. The notable property of the IBRE scheme is that the decryption is successful only when ID is not equal to ID' where ID is associated with a ciphertext and ID' is associated with a private key. However, the direct combination of this IBRE scheme and the SD scheme is not successful since the IBRE scheme does not support an equality condition. Therefore, we construct an SRE scheme by modifying this IBRE scheme to support two conditions of equality and inequality.

As described in the previous section, a user in SRE is represented as labels (GL, ML) where GL is a group label and ML is a member label in the group, and a sender creates a ciphertext with labels (GL', ML') for all member in the group GL' except the one member ML' in the group. Thus a receiver who has a private key with labels (GL, ML) can decrypt the ciphertext with labels (GL', ML') if $(GL = GL') \wedge (ML \neq ML')$. Therefore, SRE supports the equality of group labels and the inequality of member labels. To integrate the SRE scheme that uses group and member labels (GL, ML) with the SD scheme that uses subsets $S_{i,j}$ in a full binary tree, we need a mapping from the subset $S_{i,j}$ to the labels (GL, ML). A subset $S_{i,j}$ is defined by two nodes v_i, v_j and a subtree T_i is defined by one node v_i. For the mapping function from the subset $S_{i,j}$ to labels (GL, ML), we define the set of all nodes in the subtree T_i that has the same depth as v_j as a one group, and we also define the nodes in the group as the members of the group. That is, if the nodes v_i and v_j of $S_{i,j}$ in the SD scheme have identifiers L_i and L_j respectively, then the labels in the SRE scheme are represented as $GL = L_i \| d_j$ and $ML = L_j$ where d_j is the depth of v_j.

1.3   Related Work

Broadcast Encryption. As mentioned, the concept of broadcast encryption was introduced by Fiat and Naor [10] and broadcast encryption can efficiently send an encrypted message to a set of receivers through a broadcast channel. Many broadcast encryption schemes including the scheme of Fiat and Naor were designed to be secure against a collusion of t users. Naor, Naor, and Lotspiech [20] proposed a general method called the subset cover framework, and they proposed symmetric-key revocation schemes such that a center can broadcast an encrypted message to all users except r number of revoked users. They proposed two broadcast encryption schemes of the subset cover framework, named as the complete subtree (CS) and the subset difference (SD) scheme. Halevy and Shamir [16] proposed the layered subset difference (LSD) scheme and Goodrich *et al.* [15] proposed the stratified subset difference (SSD) scheme.

Public-key broadcast encryption (PKBE) is a special type of broadcast encryption such that anyone can send an encrypted message to a set of receivers through a broadcast channel by using a public key. Naor *et al.* [20] observed that their CS scheme can be combined with the identity-based encryption (IBE) scheme of Boneh and Franklin [3] to reduce the size of public keys in PKBE. Dodis and Fazio [9] showed that the SD scheme (or the LSD scheme) can also be combined with a hierarchical IBE (HIBE) scheme to construct an efficient PKBE scheme. Note that the private key size of this PKBE scheme is larger than that of the original LSD scheme in the symmetric-key setting. Boneh, Gentry, and Waters [4] proposed the first fully collusion-resistant PKBE scheme that has the constant size of ciphertexts based on bilinear groups. Their first PKBE scheme has the ciphertext size of $O(1)$, the private key size of $O(1)$, and the public key size of $O(N)$, and their second PKBE scheme has the ciphertext size of $O(\sqrt{N})$, the private key size of $O(1)$, and the public key size of $O(\sqrt{N})$ where N is the number of users in the system. After the construction of Boneh et al. [4], many other PKBE schemes based on bilinear groups were proposed [8, 14, 19, 23].

Traitor Tracing. The concept of traitor tracing was introduced by Chor, Fiat, and Naor [7] and traitor tracing enables a tracer who is given a pirate decoder to detect at least one user who participated the creation of the pirate decoder. Many traitor tracing schemes were designed to be secure against a collusion of t users. Fully collusion resistant traitor tracing schemes were proposed based on bilinear groups [5, 13, 24]. Abdalla *et al.* [1] proposed the concept of identity-based traitor tracing (IBTT) and constructed an IBTT scheme.

Trace and Revoke. Trace and revoke is broadcast encryption combined with traitor tracing such that it first finds a user whose private key is compromised by using the tracing algorithm of traitor tracing and then it revokes the user by using the revocation algorithm of broadcast encryption [20, 22]. Many trace and revoke schemes were secure against a collusion of t users [22]. Naor *et al.* [20] proposed the first fully collusion resistant trace and revoke schemes by using the general method of the subset cover framework.

Public-key trace and revoke (PKTR) is a special type of trace and revoke such that anyone can trace traitors and revoke the user by using a public key. The PKBE scheme of Dodis and Fazio [9] can also be a PKTR scheme since their scheme also follows the subset cover framework. Boneh and Waters [6] proposed a fully collusion resistant PKTR scheme based on composite order bilinear groups and proved its adaptive security by combining the PKBE scheme of Boneh *et al.* [4] and the traitor tracing scheme of Boneh *et al.* [5]. The efficiency of this scheme was improved by using prime order bilinear groups [13, 25]. Furukawa and Attrapadung [12] proposed a PKTR scheme with short private keys, but the public key size of this is quite large and the security is only proven in the generic group model.

2 Preliminaries

In this section, we briefly review bilinear groups and introduce the complexity assumption of our scheme.

2.1 Bilinear Groups

Let $\mathbb{G}$ and $\mathbb{G}_T$ be multiplicative cyclic groups of prime order p. Let g be a generator of $\mathbb{G}$. The bilinear map $e : \mathbb{G} \times \mathbb{G} \to \mathbb{G}_T$ has the following properties:

1. Bilinearity: $\forall u, v \in \mathbb{G}$ and $\forall a, b \in \mathbb{Z}_p$, $e(u^a, v^b) = e(u, v)^{ab}$.
2. Non-degeneracy: $\exists g$ such that $e(g, g)$ has order p, that is, $e(g, g)$ is a generator of $\mathbb{G}_T$.

We say that $\mathbb{G}, \mathbb{G}_T$ are bilinear groups if the group operations in $\mathbb{G}$ and $\mathbb{G}_T$ as well as the bilinear map e are all efficiently computable.

2.2 Complexity Assumptions

To prove the security of our PKRE scheme, we introduce a new assumption called q-Simplified Multi-Exponent Bilinear Diffie-Hellman (q-SMEBDH) assumption. This q-SMEBDH assumption is derived from the q-Multi-Exponent Bilinear Diffie-Hellman (q-MEBDH) assumption that was introduced by Lewko, Sahai, and Waters [19] with a slight simplification. Our new assumption is secure in the generic group model by using the master theorem of Boneh, Boyen, and Goh [2].

Assumption 1 (q-Simplified Multi-Exponent Bilinear Diffie-Hellman, q-SMEBDH). *Let $(p, \mathbb{G}, \mathbb{G}_T, e)$ be a description of the bilinear group of prime order p with the security parameter λ. Let g be a generator of $\mathbb{G}$. The q-SMEBDH assumption is that if the challenge values*

$$D = ((p, \mathbb{G}, \mathbb{G}_T, e), g, \{g^{a_i}, g^{b/a_i}\}_{1 \leq i \leq q}, \{g^{ba_i/a_j}\}_{1 \leq i,j, i \neq j \leq q}, g^c) \text{ and } T$$

are given, no PPT algorithm $\mathcal{B}$ can distinguish $T = T_0 = e(g, g)^{bc}$ from $T = T_1 = e(g, g)^d$ with more than a negligible advantage. The advantage of $\mathcal{B}$ is defined as $Adv_{\mathcal{B}}^{q\text{-}SMEBDH}(\lambda) = \left| \Pr[\mathcal{B}(D, T_0) = 0] - \Pr[\mathcal{B}(D, T_1) = 0] \right|$ where the probability is taken over the random choice of $a_1, \ldots, a_q, b, c, d \in \mathbb{Z}_p$.

3 Single Revocation Encryption

In this section, we define single revocation encryption (SRE) and the security model of SRE, and then we propose an SRE scheme and prove its security in the random oracle model.

3.1 Definitions

Single revocation encryption (SRE) is a special type of public-key broadcast encryption (PKBE) such that a single user in a group can be revoked. That is, a sender in SRE can securely transmit a message to the members of a specified group except the single revoked member of the group. In SRE, the universe $\mathcal{U}$ is defined as the set of many groups that consist of many members. Note that the maximum number of groups and the maximum number of members in a group is a polynomial number in a security parameter. A center first generates a master key and a public key for SRE by using a setup algorithm, and each user specified by a group label and a member label can receive his private key from the center. To transmit a message, a sender computes a ciphertext by specifying a group label and a revoked member in the group. If a user belongs to the group in the ciphertext and he is not revoked, then he can decrypt the ciphertext by using his private key. The following is the syntax of SRE.

Definition 1 (Single Revocation Encryption). *A SRE scheme for the universe $\mathcal{U}$ of groups and members consists of four algorithms **Setup**, **GenKey**, **Encrypt**, and **Decrypt**, which are defined as follows:*

*   ***Setup**($1^\lambda, \mathcal{U}$). The setup algorithm takes as input a security parameter 1^λ and the universe $\mathcal{U}$ of groups and members. It outputs a master key MK and a public key PK.*
*   ***GenKey**((GL,ML),MK,PK). The key generation algorithm takes as input labels (GL,ML), the master key MK, and the public key PK. It outputs a private key SK for the labels (GL,ML).*
*   ***Encrypt**((GL,ML),M,PK). The encryption algorithm takes as input labels (GL,ML), a message $M \in \mathcal{M}$, and the public key PK. It outputs a ciphertext CT for (GL,ML) and M.*
*   ***Decrypt**(CT,SK,PK). The decryption algorithm takes as input a ciphertext CT for labels (GL,ML), a private key SK for labels (GL′,ML′), and the public key PK. It outputs an encrypted message M or $\bot$.*

*The correctness property of SRE is defined as follows: For all MK,PK generated by **Setup**, any SK_u generated by **GenKey**, and any M, it is required that*

*   *If $(GL = GL') \wedge (ML \neq ML')$, then **Decrypt**(**Encrypt**((GL,ML),M,PP),$SK_{(GL',ML')}$, PK) = M.*
*   *If $(GL \neq GL') \vee (ML = ML')$, then **Decrypt**(**Encrypt**((GL,ML),M,PP),$SK_{(GL',ML')}$, PK) = $\bot$ with all but negligible probability.*

The security property of SRE is defined as indistinguishability. The indistinguishability game of SRE can be similarly defined by modifying the indistinguishability game of PKBE. In this game, an adversary is first given a public key of SRE, and then he can obtain many private keys for labels. In the challenge step, the adversary submits challenge labels and two challenge messages, and then he receives a challenge ciphertext. Finally, the adversary outputs a guess for the random coin that is used to create the challenge ciphertext. If the guess of the adversary is correct, then the adversary wins the game. The following is the formal definition of indistinguishability.

Definition 2 (Indistinguishability). *The indistinguishability property of SRE under a chosen plaintext attack is defined in terms of the following game between a challenger C and a PPT adversary A:*

1. **Setup**: *C runs* **Setup**$(1^\lambda, \mathcal{U})$ *to generate a master key MK and a public key PK. It keeps MK to itself and gives PK to A.*
2. **Query**: *A adaptively requests private keys for labels* $(GL_1, ML_1), \ldots, (GL_q, ML_q)$. *In response, C gives the corresponding private keys* $SK_1, \ldots, SK_q$ *to A by running* **GenKey**$((GL_i, ML_i), MK, PK)$.
3. **Challenge**: *A submits challenge labels* (GL^*, ML^*) *and two messages* M_0^*, M_1^* *with the equal length subject to the restriction: for all* (GL_i, ML_i) *of private key queries, it is required that* $(GL_i \neq GL^*)$ *or* $((GL_i = GL^*) \wedge (ML_i = ML^*))$. *C flips a random coin* $\gamma \in \{0, 1\}$ *and gives the challenge ciphertext* CT^* *to A by running* **Encrypt**$((GL^*, ML^*), M_\gamma^*, PK)$.
4. **Guess**: *A outputs a guess* $\gamma' \in \{0, 1\}$ *of* γ, *and wins the game if* $\gamma = \gamma'$.

The advantage of A is defined as $\mathbf{Adv}_A^{SRE}(\lambda) = \left| \Pr[\gamma = \gamma'] - \frac{1}{2} \right|$ *where the probability is taken over all the randomness of the game. A SRE scheme is indistinguishable under a chosen plaintext attack if for all PPT adversary A, the advantage of A in the above game is negligible in the security parameter* λ.

3.2 Construction

Our SRE scheme is inspired by the IBRE scheme of Lewko, Sahai, and Waters [19] that employs the "two equation" technique. In the two equation technique, a ciphertext is associated with a revoked set $R = \{ID_1, \ldots, ID_r\}$ of users and a user is associated with an identity ID. If a user is not revoked ($ID \neq ID_i$), then he will obtain two independent equations and can decrypt the ciphertext. However, if a user is revoked ($ID = ID_i$), then he will obtain two dependent equations and thus cannot decrypt the ciphertext. Lewko *et al.* [19] constructed a IBRE scheme that has private keys of constant size, public keys of constant size, and ciphertexts of $O(r)$ size. We construct an SRE scheme that enables a sender to broadcast a ciphertext to a given group except a one specified member in the group by slightly modifying the IBRE scheme of Lewko *et al.* First, the IBRE scheme can be modified to revoke a single user instead of multiple users, and then the modified scheme has a private key $SK = (g^\alpha w^r, (hw^{ID})^r, g^{-r})$ and a ciphertext $CT = (e(g,g)^{\alpha t} M, g^t, (hw^{ID})^t)$ where ID is a user identifier. However this modified scheme does not support groups. To support groups, we first represent a user identifier ID as labels (GL, ML) of a group and a member, and use hash functions H_1, H_2 to select unique h, w values for each group. Then the modified scheme has a private key $SK = (g^\alpha H_2(GL)^r, (H_1(GL)H_2(GL)^{ML})^r, g^{-r})$ and a ciphertext $CT = (e(g,g)^{\alpha t}, g^t, (H_1(GL)H_2(GL)^{ML})^t)$ where GL is a group label and ML is a member label.

Let $\mathcal{U} = \{(GL_i, \{ML_j\})\}$ be the universe of groups and members where the maximum number U_g of groups is a polynomial number in a security parameter and the maximum number U_m of members in a group is also a polynomial numbers in a security parameter. Our SRE scheme for the universe $\mathcal{U}$ is described as follows:

SRE.Setup($1^\lambda, \mathcal{U}$): This algorithm first generates the bilinear groups $\mathbb{G}$ of prime order p of bit size $\Theta(\lambda)$. It chooses a random element $g \in \mathbb{G}$. It selects a random exponent $\alpha \in \mathbb{Z}_p$. It outputs a master key $MK = g^\alpha$ and a public key as

$$PK = \Big((p, \mathbb{G}, \mathbb{G}_T, e),\ g,\ H_1, H_2,\ \Omega = e(g,g)^\alpha \Big).$$

SRE.GenKey($(GL, ML), MK, PK$): This algorithm takes as input labels (GL, ML), the master key MK, and the public key PK. It selects a random exponent $r \in \mathbb{Z}_p$ and outputs a private key by implicitly including (GL, ML) as

$$SK_{(GL, ML)} = \Big(K_0 = g^\alpha H_2(GL)^r,\ K_1 = (H_1(GL)H_2(GL)^{ML})^r,\ K_2 = g^{-r} \Big).$$

SRE.Encrypt($(GL, ML), M, PK$): This algorithm takes as input labels (GL, ML), a message $M \in \mathbb{G}_T$, and the public key PK. It chooses a random exponent $t \in \mathbb{Z}_p$ and outputs a ciphertext by implicitly including (GL, ML) as

$$CT_{(GL, ML)} = \Big(C_0 = \Omega^t M,\ C_1 = g^t,\ C_2 = (H_1(GL)H_2(GL)^{ML})^t \Big).$$

SRE.Decrypt($CT_{(GL, ML)}, SK_{(GL', ML')}, PK$): This algorithm takes as input a ciphertext $CT_{(GL, ML)}$, a private key $SK_{(GL', ML')}$, and the public key PK. If $(GL = GL') \wedge (ML \neq ML')$, then it outputs a message as

$$M = C_0 \cdot e(C_1, K_0)^{-1} \cdot (e(C_1, K_1) \cdot e(C_2, K_2))^{1/(ML'-ML)}.$$

Otherwise, it outputs $\bot$.

The correctness of the above SRE scheme is easily verified by the following equation.

$$e(C_1, K_0) / (e(C_1, K_1) \cdot e(C_2, K_2))^{1/(ML'-ML)}$$

$$= e(g^t, g^\alpha H_2(GL)^r) / \Big(e(g^t, (H_1(GL)H_2(GL)^{ML'})^r) \cdot e((H_1(GL)H_2(GL)^{ML})^t, g^{-r}) \Big)^{1/(ML'-ML)}$$

$$= e(g^t, g^\alpha H_2(GL)^r) / \Big(e(g, H_2(GL))^{tr \cdot (ML'-ML)} \Big)^{1/(ML'-ML)}$$

$$= e(g,g)^{\alpha t}.$$

3.3 Security

Theorem 2. *The above SRE scheme is indistinguishable under a chosen plaintext attack in the random oracle model if the q-SMEBDH assumption holds where $U_m \leq q$.*

Proof. Suppose there exists an adversary $\mathcal{A}$ that breaks the indistinguishability game of the SRE scheme with a non-negligible advantage. A simulator $\mathcal{B}$ that solves the q-SMEBDH assumption using $\mathcal{A}$ is given: a challenge tuple $D = ((p, \mathbb{G}, \mathbb{G}_T, e), g, \{g^{a_i}, g^{b/a_i}\}_{1 \leq i \leq q}, \{g^{ba_i/a_j}\}_{1 \leq i,j, i \neq j \leq q}, g^c)$ and T where $T = T_0 = e(g,g)^{bc}$ or $T = T_1 = e(g,g)^d$. Then $\mathcal{B}$ that interacts with $\mathcal{A}$ is described as follows:

Setup: $\mathcal{B}$ first guesses challenge labels (GL', ML') such that ML' is a member of GL'. Next, it initializes two lists H_1-List and H_2-List for random oracles as empty sets. It implicitly sets $\alpha = b$ and creates the public key as $PK = ((p, \mathbb{G}, \mathbb{G}_T, e), g, H_1, H_2, \Omega = e(g^{a_1}, g^{b/a_1}))$.

Query: $\mathcal{A}$ may adaptively request hash queries or private key queries. Let **MemSet**(GL) be a function that takes a group label GL as an input and outputs the set $\{ML_i\}$ of members in the group, $\rho(GL, ML)$ be a function that takes a group label GL and a member label ML as inputs and outputs an index k of the member in the group, and **RevSet**$_{GL', ML'}(GL)$ be a function that outputs **MemSet**(GL) if $GL \neq GL'$ or $\{ML'\}$ if $GL = GL'$. For notational convenience, we use **RevSet**(GL) instead of **RevSet**$_{GL', ML'}(GL)$.

If this is an i-th H_1 hash query on a label GL, then $\mathcal{B}$ handles this query as follows:

1. If there exists a tuple $(GL, -, -)$ in the H_1-List, then it returns $H_1(GL)$ from the H_1-List.
2. It sets $H_1(GL) = \prod_{\forall ML_k \in \mathbf{RevSet}(GL)} (g^{a_{\rho(GL, ML_k)}})^{-ML_k} \cdot g^{h_{1,i}}$ by choosing a random exponent $h_{1,i} \in \mathbb{Z}_p$. Note that if $GL = GL'$, then it sets $H_1(GL') = (g^{a_{\rho(GL, ML_{j'})}})^{-ML'} g^{h_{1,i}}$ since **RevSet**$(GL') = \{ML'\}$ where j' is the index of $ML_{j'}$ such that $ML' = ML_{j'}$.
3. It saves a tuple $(GL, h_{1,i}, H_1(GL))$ to the H_1-List and returns $H_1(GL)$.

If this is a H_2 hash query on a label GL, then $\mathcal{B}$ handles this query as follows:

1. If there exists a tuple $(GL, -, -)$ in the H_2-List, then it returns $H_2(GL)$ from the H_2-List.
2. It sets $H_2(GL) = \prod_{\forall ML_k \in \mathbf{RevSet}(GL)} g^{a_{\rho(GL, ML_k)}} \cdot g^{h_{2,i}}$ by choosing a random exponent $h_{2,i} \in \mathbb{Z}_p$. Note that if $GL = GL'$, then it sets $H_2(GL') = g^{a_{\rho(GL, ML_{j'})}} g^{h_{2,i}}$ since **RevSet**$(GL') = \{ML'\}$ where j' is the index of $ML_{j'}$ such that $ML' = ML_{j'}$.
3. It saves a tuple $(GL, h_{2,i}, H_2(GL))$ to the H_2-List and returns $H_2(GL)$.

If this is a private key query for labels (GL, ML) where $ML = ML_j$ and $\rho(GL, ML) = j$, then $\mathcal{B}$ handles this query as follows:

1. If $(GL = GL') \wedge (ML \neq ML')$, then it aborts since it cannot create a private key.
2. It first retrieves a tuple $(GL, h_{1,i}, H_1(GL))$ for GL from H_1-List and a tuple $(GL, h_{2,i}, H_2(GL))$ for GL from H_2-List.
3. Next, it selects a random exponent $r' \in \mathbb{Z}_p$ and creates a private key $SK_{(GL, ML)}$ by implicitly setting $r = -b/a_{\rho(GL, ML_j)} + r'$ as

$$K_0 = \prod_{\forall ML_k \in \mathbf{RevSet}(GL) \backslash \{ML_j\}} (g^{a_{\rho(GL, ML_k)}/a_{\rho(GL, ML_j)} \cdot b})^{-1} (g^{1/a_{\rho(GL, ML_j)} \cdot b})^{-h_{1,i}} \cdot H_2(GL)^{r'},$$

$$K_1 = \prod_{\forall ML_k \in \mathbf{RevSet}(GL) \backslash \{ML_j\}} (g^{a_{\rho(GL, ML_k)}/a_{\rho(GL, ML_j)} \cdot b})^{ML_k - ML_j} (g^{1/a_{\rho(GL, ML_j)} \cdot b})^{-h_{1,i} - h_{2,i} ML_j}.$$

$$\left(H_1(GL) H_2(GL)^{ML_j} \right)^{r'},$$

$$K_2 = g^{1/a_{\rho(GL, ML_j)} \cdot b} g^{-r'}.$$

Challenge: $\mathcal{A}$ submits challenge labels (GL^*, ML^*) and two messages M_0^*, M_1^*. If $(GL' \neq GL^*) \vee (ML' \neq ML^*)$, then $\mathcal{B}$ aborts the simulation since it failed to guess the challenge labels. Otherwise, $\mathcal{B}$ flips a random coin $\gamma \in \{0,1\}$ internally. Next, it retrieves tuples $(GL^*, h_1^*, H_1(GL^*))$ and $(GL^*, h_2^*, H_2(GL^*))$ from H_1-List and H_2-List respectively. It implicitly sets $t = c$ and creates a challenge ciphertext as

$$C_0 = T \cdot M_\gamma^*, \ C_1 = g^c, \ C_2 = (g^c)^{h_1^* + h_2^* ML^*}.$$

Output: Finally, $\mathcal{A}$ outputs a guess γ'. If $\gamma = \gamma'$, $\mathcal{B}$ outputs 0. Otherwise, it outputs 1.

To finish the proof, we first show that hash outputs, private keys, and the challenge ciphertext are correctly distributed. The hash outputs are correctly distributed since new random elements h_1 and h_2 are chosen for H_1 and H_2 hash queries. The private key is correctly distributed since it satisfies the following equation

$$K_0 = g^\alpha H_2(GL)^r = g^b \Big(\prod_{\forall ML_k \in \mathbf{RevSet}(GL)} g^{a_{\rho(GL,ML_k)}} \cdot g^{h_{1,i}} \Big)^{-b/a_{\rho(GL,ML_j)} + r'}$$

$$= \prod_{\forall ML_k \in \mathbf{RevSet}(GL) \backslash \{ML_j\}} (g^{a_{\rho(GL,ML_k)}/a_{\rho(GL,ML_j)} \cdot b})^{-1} (g^{1/a_{\rho(GL,ML_k)} \cdot b})^{-h_{1,i}} \cdot H_2(GL)^{r'},$$

$$K_1 = \big(H_1(GL) H_2(GL)^{ML_j} \big)^r$$

$$= \Big(\prod_{\forall ML_k \in \mathbf{RevSet}(GL)} (g^{a_{\rho(GL,ML_k)}})^{-ML_k} \cdot g^{h_{1,i}} \cdot$$

$$\Big(\prod_{\forall ML_k \in \mathbf{RevSet}(GL)} g^{a_{\rho(GL,ML_k)}} \cdot g^{h_{2,i}} \Big)^{ML_j} \Big)^{-b/a_{\rho(GL,ML_j)} + r'}$$

$$= \prod_{\forall ML_k \in \mathbf{RevSet}(GL) \backslash \{ML_j\}} (g^{a_{\rho(GL,ML_k)}/a_{\rho(GL,ML_j)} \cdot b})^{ML_k - ML_j} \cdot (g^{1/a_{\rho(GL,ML_j)} \cdot b})^{-h_{1,i} - h_{2,i} ML_j} \cdot$$

$$\big(H_1(GL) H_2(GL)^{ML_j} \big)^{r'},$$

$$K_2 = g^{-r} = g^{b/a_{\rho(GL,ML_j)} - r'} = g^{1/a_{\rho(GL,ML_j)} \cdot b} g^{-r'}.$$

Note that it cannot create a private key for (GL, ML) such that $(GL = GL') \wedge (ML \neq ML')$ since the element g^b cannot be removed because of $\mathbf{RevSet}(GL') \backslash \{ML_j\} = \emptyset$. The challenge ciphertext is also correctly distributed since it satisfies the following equation

$$C_0 = e(g,g)^{\alpha t} M_\gamma^* = e(g,g)^{bc} M_\gamma^*,$$

$$C_1 = g^t = g^c,$$

$$C_2 = (H_1(GL^*) H_2(GL^*)^{ML^*})^t = \big((g^{a_{\rho(GL^*, ML^*)}})^{-ML^*} g^{h_1^*} \cdot (g^{a_{\rho(GL^*, ML^*)}} g^{h_2^*})^{ML^*} \big)^c$$

$$= (g^c)^{h_1^* + h_2^* ML^*}.$$

Finally, we analyze the success probability of the above simulation. Let Good be the event that the simulator successfully guesses the challenge labels. We have that $\Pr[\mathsf{Good}] \geq \frac{1}{U_g \cdot U_m}$. If the event Good occurs, then the simulator does not abort. Therefore, the success probability of the simulation is bounded by $\frac{1}{U_g \cdot U_m}$. This completes our proof. $\qquad\square$

3.4 Discussions

Fast Decryption. The simple decryption algorithm of our SRE scheme requires three pairing operations and a one exponentiation operation. We can improve the performance of the decryption algorithm by modifying the computation of the algorithm as $M = C_0 \cdot e(C_1, K_0^{-1} K_1^{1/(ML'-ML)}) \cdot e(C_2, K_2^{1/(ML'-ML)})$. In this case, the decryption algorithm just consists of two pairing operations and two exponentiation operations.

Chosen-Ciphertext Security. The indistinguishability under a chosen-ciphertext attack (IND-CCA) is similar to the indistinguishability under a chosen-plaintext attack (IND-CPA) except that an adversary is allowed to request decryption queries on ciphertexts. To provide the security of IND-CCA, we can use the transformation of Fujisaki and Okamoto [11] since our scheme is proven in the random oracle model.

Removing Random Oracles. The proposed SRE scheme is only secure when two hash functions H_1 and H_2 are modeled as random oracles. We can easily remove the random oracles by simply selecting random group elements h_i and w_i for $H_1(GL_i)$ and $H_2(GL_i)$ in the public key since the set of group labels is fixed and the total number of group labels is a polynomial number in a security parameter. However, the public key size of this method is quite large.

4 Subset Cover Framework

In this section, we define the subset cover framework and describe the subset difference (SD) scheme. The formal definition of subset cover scheme is given in the full version of this paper [18].

4.1 Full Binary Tree

A full binary tree $\mathcal{T}$ is a tree data structure where each node except the leaf nodes has two child nodes. Let N be the number of leaf nodes in $\mathcal{T}$. The number of all nodes in $\mathcal{T}$ is $2N - 1$ and for any $1 \leq i \leq 2N - 1$ we denote by v_i a node in $\mathcal{T}$. The depth d_i of a node v_i is the length of the path from the root node to the node. The root node is at depth zero. The depth of $\mathcal{T}$ is the length of the path from the root node to a leaf node. A level of $\mathcal{T}$ is a set of all nodes at given depth. For any node $v_i \in \mathcal{T}$, T_i is defined as a subtree that is rooted at v_i. For any two nodes $v_i, v_j \in \mathcal{T}$ such that v_j is a descendant of v_i, $T_{i,j}$ is defined as a subtree $T_i - T_j$, that is, all nodes that are descendants of v_i but not v_j. For any node $v_i \in \mathcal{T}$, S_i is defined as the set of leaf nodes in T_i. Similarly, $S_{i,j}$ is defined as the set of leaf nodes in $T_{i,j}$, that is, $S_{i,j} = S_i \setminus S_j$.

For any node $v_i \in \mathcal{T}$, L_i is defined as an identifier that is a fixed and unique string. The identifier of each node in the tree is assigned as follows: Each edge in the tree is assigned with 0 or 1 depending on whether the edge is connected to its left or right child node. The identifier L_i of a node v_i is defined as the bitstring obtained by reading all the labels of edges in the path from the root node to the node v_i. We define $ID(v_i)$ be a mapping from a node v_i to an identifier L_i. We also define $ID(T_i)$ be a mapping from a subtree T_i to the identifier L_i of the node v_i and $ID(T_{i,j})$ be a mapping from a subtree $T_{i,j}$ to a tuple (L_i, L_j) of identifiers. Similarly, we can define $ID(S_i) = ID(T_i)$ and $ID(S_{i,j}) = ID(T_{i,j})$.

For a full binary tree $\mathcal{T}$ and a subset R of leaf nodes, $ST(\mathcal{T}, R)$ is defined as the Steiner Tree induced by the set R and the root node, that is, the minimal subtree of $\mathcal{T}$ that connects all the leaf nodes in R and the root node. we simply denote $ST(\mathcal{T}, R)$ by $ST(R)$.

4.2 SD Scheme

The subset difference (SD) scheme is the subset cover scheme proposed by Naor *et al.* [20]. We describe the SD scheme with a slight modification for the integration with our SRE scheme.

SD.Setup(N): This algorithm takes as input the maximum number N of users. Let $N = 2^n$ for simplicity. It first sets a full binary tree $\mathcal{T}$ of depth n. Each user is assigned to a different leaf node in $\mathcal{T}$. The collection $\mathcal{S}$ of SD is the set of all subsets $\{S_{i,j}\}$ where $v_i, v_j \in \mathcal{T}$ and v_j is a descendant of v_i. It outputs the full binary tree $\mathcal{T}$.

SD.Assign($\mathcal{T}, u$): This algorithm takes as input the tree $\mathcal{T}$ and a user $u \in \mathcal{N}$. Let v_u be the leaf node of $\mathcal{T}$ that is assigned to the user u. Let $(v_{k_0}, v_{k_1}, \ldots, v_{k_n})$ be the path from the root node v_{k_0} to the leaf node $v_{k_n} = v_u$. It first sets a private set PV_u as an empty one. For all $i, j \in \{k_0, k_1, \ldots, k_n\}$ such that v_j is a descendant of v_i, it adds the subset $S_{i,j}$ defined by two nodes v_i and v_j in the path into PV_u. It outputs the private set $PV_u = \{S_{i,j}\}$.

SD.Cover($\mathcal{T}, R$): This algorithm takes as input the tree $\mathcal{T}$ and a revoked set R of users. It first sets a subtree T as $ST(R)$, and then it builds a covering set CV_R iteratively by removing nodes from T until T consists of just a single node as follows:

1. It finds two leaf nodes v_i and v_j in T such that the least-common-ancestor v of v_i and v_j does not contain any other leaf nodes of T in its subtree. Let v_l and v_k be the two child nodes of v such that v_i is a descendant of v_l and v_j is a descendant of v_k. If there is only one leaf node left, it makes $v_i = v_j$ to the leaf node, v to be the root of T and $v_l = v_k = v$.
2. If $v_l \neq v_i$, then it adds the subset $S_{l,i}$ to CV_R; likewise, if $v_k \neq v_j$, it adds the subset $S_{k,j}$ to CV_R.
3. It removes from T all the descendants of v and makes v a leaf node.

It outputs the covering set $CV_R = \{S_{i,j}\}$.

SD.Match(CV_R, PV_u): This algorithm takes input as a covering set $CV_R = \{S_{i,j}\}$ and a private set $PV_u = \{S'_{i,j}\}$. It finds two subsets $S_{i,j}$ and $S'_{i',j'}$ such that $S_{i,j} \in CV_R$, $S'_{i',j'} \in PV_u$, $i = i'$, $d_j = d_{j'}$, and $j \neq j'$ where d_j is the depth of v_j. If it found two subsets, then it outputs $(S_{i,j}, S'_{i',j'})$. Otherwise, it outputs $\perp$.

Lemma 1 ([20]). *Let N be the number of leaf nodes in a full binary tree and r be the size of a revoked set. In the SD scheme, the size of a private set is $O(\log^2 N)$ and the size of a covering set is at most $2r - 1$.*

5   Revocation Encryption

In this section, we first propose a public-key revocation encryption (PKRE) scheme by combining the SRE scheme and the subset cover scheme, and then we prove its security. The formal definition of PKRE is given in the full version of this paper [18].

5.1   Construction

The basic idea of our PKRE scheme is to combine the SD scheme and the SRE scheme that is a special type of public-key encryption (PKE). The idea of combining the SD scheme with a PKE scheme was introduced by Dodis and Fazio [9]. Dodis and Fazio showed that the key assignment method of Naor *et al.* [20] for the SD scheme can be mimicked by using the delegation property of HIBE. In contrast to the method of Dodis and Fazio, we show that a subset $S_{i,j}$ in the SD scheme can be easily mapped to the group and member labels (GL, ML) of the SRE scheme by using the revocation property of the SRE scheme that can revoke a single member in a group. That is, a subset $S_{i,j}$ in the SD scheme is defined as the set of leaf nodes that belong to T_i but not belong to T_j where T_i and T_j are subtrees with root nodes v_i and v_j respectively. This subset $S_{i,j}$ is represented by two nodes v_i and v_j that have labels L_i and L_j respectively. To map the subset $S_{i,j}$ to labels (GL, ML), we define a group GL as the set of nodes in T_i at the same level as the node v_j and define a revoked member ML as the node v_j.

Before presenting our PKRE scheme, we first define the universe $\mathcal{U}$ of SRE that is derived from a full binary tree $\mathcal{T}$ as follows: Let T_i be a subtree of $\mathcal{T}$ that is rooted at v_i. A single group in $\mathcal{U}$ is defined as a set of nodes that are in the same level of T_i except the level of v_i. Suppose that the tree $\mathcal{T}$ has the number N of leaf nodes. In this case, the maximum number of groups in $\mathcal{U}$ is $N \log N$ and the maximum number of members in a groups is N since the number of internal nodes is $N-1$ and the maximum depth of each subtree is $\log N - 1$. The subset $S_{i,j}$ of the SD scheme that uses $\mathcal{T}$ is easily converted to the labels $(GL = L_i \| d_j, ML = L_j)$ of the SRE scheme where (L_i, L_j) is the identifier of $S_{i,j}$ and d_j is the depth of L_j.

Our PKRE scheme for the set $\mathcal{N} = \{1, \ldots, N\}$ of users is described as follows:

PKRE.Setup($1^\lambda, N$): It first defines a full binary tree $\mathcal{T}$ by running **SD.Setup(N)**. Next, it obtains MK_{SRE} and PK_{SRE} by running **SRE.Setup($1^\lambda, \mathcal{U}$)** where $\mathcal{U}$ is defined from $\mathcal{T}$. It outputs a master key $MK = MK_{SRE}$ and a public key as $PK = (\mathcal{T}, PK_{SRE})$.

PKRE.GenKey(u, MK, PK): This algorithm takes as input a user $u \in \mathcal{N}$, the master key MK, and the public key PK. It first obtains a private set $PV_u = \{S_{i,j}\}$ by running **SD.Assign($\mathcal{T}, u$)**. Let d_j be the depth of a node v_j associated with L_j. For all $S_{i,j} \in PV_u$, it obtains (L_i, L_j) by applying $ID(S_{i,j})$ and computes $SK_{SRE,S_{i,j}}$ by running **SRE.GenKey($(L_i \| d_j, L_j), MK_{SRE}, PK_{SRE}$)**. It outputs a private key as $SK = (PV_u, \{SK_{SRE,S_{i,j}}\}_{S_{i,j} \in PV_u})$.

PKRE.Encrypt(R, M, PK): This algorithm takes as input a revoked set $R \subseteq \mathcal{N}$, a message $M \in \mathbb{G}_T$, and the public key PK. It first finds a covering set $CV_R = \{S_{i,j}\}$ by running **SD.Cover($\mathcal{T}, R$)**. Let d_j be the depth of a node v_j associated with L_j. For all $S_{i,j} \in CV_R$, it obtains (L_i, L_j) by applying $ID(S_{i,j})$ and computes $CT_{SRE,S_{i,j}}$

by running **SRE.Encrypt**$((L_i\|d_j,L_j),M,PK_{SRE})$. It outputs a ciphertext as $CT = (CV_R,\{CT_{SRE,S_{i,j}}\}_{S_{i,j}\in CV_R})$.

PKRE.Decrypt(CT,SK,PK): This algorithm takes as input a ciphertext CT, a private key SK, and the public key PK. It first finds a matching tuple $(S_{i,j},S'_{i,j})$ by running **SD.Match**(CV_R,PV_u). If it found a tuple, then it outputs a message M by running **SRE.Decrypt**$(CT_{SRE,S_{i,j}},SK_{SRE,S'_{i,j}},PK_{SRE})$. Otherwise, it outputs $\perp$.

The correctness of the above PKRE scheme easily follows the correctness of the SD scheme and that of the SRE scheme. If $u \notin R$, then a user u can obtain two subsets $S_{i,j} \in CV_R$ and $S'_{i',j'} \in PV_u$ from a ciphertext CT and his private key SK such that $i = i', d_j = d_{j'}$, and $j \neq j'$ from the correctness of the SD scheme. Next, he can derive two labels $(GL = L_i\|d_j, ML = L_j)$ and $(GL' = L_{i'}\|d_{j'}, ML' = L_{j'})$ for the SRE scheme from the two subsets $S_{i,j}$ and $S'_{i',j'}$ where $(L_i,L_j) = ID(S_{i,j})$ and $(L_{i'},L_{j'}) = ID(S'_{i',j'})$. Note that $L_i = L_{i'}, d_j = d_{j'}$, and $L_j \neq L_{j'}$. Therefore, he can obtains a message M from the correctness of the SRE scheme since $GL = GL'$ and $ML \neq ML'$. If $u \in R$, then a user u cannot obtain two subsets $S_{i,j} \in CV_R$ and $S'_{i',j} \in PV_u$ such that $i = i', d_j = d_{j'}$, and $j \neq j'$ from the correctness of the SD scheme. Note that the correctness property is only satisfied when an honest user simply runs the decryption algorithm of our PKRE scheme.

5.2 Security

Theorem 3. *The above PKRE scheme is indistinguishable under a chosen plaintext attack if the SRE scheme is indistinguishable under a chosen plaintext attack.*

Proof. Suppose that CV_{R^*} is the covering set of the challenge revoked set R^* and the size of CV_{R^*} is w. The challenge ciphertext is described as $CT^* = (CV_R, CT_{SRE,1}, \ldots, CT_{SRE,w})$. The hybrid games $\mathbf{G}_0, \ldots, \mathbf{G}_i, \ldots, \mathbf{G}_w$ for the security proof are defined as follows:

Game $\mathbf{G}_0$: In this game, all ciphertext components $CT_{SRE,j}$ of the challenge ciphertext are encryption on the message M_0^*. That is, the challenge ciphertext CT^* is an encryption on the message M_0^*. Note that this game is the original security game except that the challenge bit γ is fixed to 0.

Game $\mathbf{G}_h$: This game is almost identical to the game $\mathbf{G}_{h-1}$ except the ciphertext component $CT_{SRE,h}$ since $CT_{SRE,h}$ in this game is an encryption on the message M_1^*. Specifically, in this game, the ciphertext component $CT_{SRE,j}$ for $j \leq h$ is an encryption on the message M_1^* and the ciphertext component $CT_{SRE,j}$ for $h < j$ is an encryption on the message M_0^*.

Game $\mathbf{G}_w$: In this game, all ciphertext components $CT_{SRE,j}$ of the challenge ciphertext are encryption on the message M_1^*. That is, the challenge ciphertext CT^* is an encryption on the message M_1^*. Note that this game is the original security game except that the challenge bit γ is fixed to 1.

Let $S_{\mathcal{A}}^{G_h}$ be the event that $\mathcal{A}$ outputs 0 in $\mathbf{G}_h$. In Lemma 2, we prove that it is hard for $\mathcal{A}$ to distinguish $\mathbf{G}_{h-1}$ from $\mathbf{G}_h$ if the SRE scheme is secure. Thus, we have that

$$\Pr[S_{\mathcal{A}}^{G_0}] - \Pr[S_{\mathcal{A}}^{G_w}] = \Pr[S_{\mathcal{A}}^{G_0}] + \sum_{h=1}^{w-1} \left(\Pr[S_{\mathcal{A}}^{G_h}] - \Pr[S_{\mathcal{A}}^{G_h}] \right) - \Pr[S_{\mathcal{A}}^{G_w}]$$

$$\leq \sum_{h=1}^{w} \left| \Pr[S_{\mathcal{A}}^{G_{h-1}}] - \Pr[S_{\mathcal{A}}^{G_h}] \right| \leq 2w \cdot \mathbf{Adv}_{\mathcal{B}}^{SRE}(\lambda).$$

Finally, we obtain the following inequality relation as

$$\mathbf{Adv}_{\mathcal{A}}^{PKRE}(\lambda) \leq \frac{1}{2} \cdot \left| \Pr[S_{\mathcal{A}}^{G_0}] - \Pr[S_{\mathcal{A}}^{G_w}] \right| \leq w \cdot \mathbf{Adv}_{\mathcal{B}}^{SRE}(\lambda).$$

Note that we already have $\mathbf{Adv}^{SRE}(\lambda) \leq N^2 \log N \cdot \mathbf{Adv}^{q\text{-}SMEBDH}(\lambda)$ from Theorem 2 since $U_g \leq N \log N$ and $U_m \leq N$. This completes our proof. □

Lemma 2. *If the SRE scheme is indistinguishable under a chosen plaintext attack, then no polynomial time adversary can distinguish between $\mathbf{G}_{h-1}$ and $\mathbf{G}_h$ with non-negligible advantage.*

The proof of this lemma is given in the full version of this paper [18].

5.3 Discussions

Efficiency. In our PKRE scheme, a public key consists of $O(1)$ group elements, a private key consists of $O(\log^2 N)$ group elements, and a ciphertext consists of $O(r)$ group elements where r is the size of a revoked set. Additionally, the decryption algorithm of our PKRE scheme just requires one decryption operation of the SRE scheme that consists of two pairing operations and two exponentiation operations.

LSD Scheme. We can also combine our SRE scheme with the LSD scheme to construct a PKRE scheme since the LSD scheme is just a special case of the SD scheme. If the LSD scheme is used instead of the SD scheme, then the group elements of a private key can be reduced from $O(\log^2 N)$ to $O(\log^{1.5} N)$ by doubling the number of group elements in a ciphertext.

Chosen-Ciphertext Security. By combining an SRE scheme that provides the IND-CCA security and an one-time signature scheme that provides the strong unforgeability (i.e., an adversary is unable to forge a new signature on the previously signed message.), we can construct a PKRE scheme that achieves the IND-CCA security.

Trace and Revoke. Our PKRE scheme also provides the tracing property since it is derived from the subset cover framework of Naor *et al.* [20]. We omit the description of a tracing algorithm, but it is given in the full version of this paper [18]. Note that the trace and revoke scheme derived from the subset cover framework can only trace to a subset pattern in some colluding scenarios [17].

6 Conclusion

In this paper, we revisited the methodology of the subset cover framework to construct PKRE schemes, and introduced a new type of PKE named single revocation encryption (SRE). We proposed an efficient SRE scheme with the constant size of ciphertexts, private keys, and public keys, and proved its security in the random oracle model under q-type assumption. The SRE scheme may have independent interests. One notable advantage of our SRE scheme is that the PKRE scheme using our SRE scheme maintains the same efficiency parameter as the SD scheme (or the LSD scheme).

There are many interesting problems. The first one is to construct an efficient SRE scheme with short public key without random oracles. We showed that the random oracles in our SRE scheme can be removed. However, this approach has the problem of large public key size. The second one is to reduce the size of private keys. One possible approach is to use the Stratified SD (SSD) scheme of Goodrich et al. [15], but it is not yet known whether the SSD scheme can be applicable in the public-key setting.

Acknowledgements. Kwangsu Lee was supported by Basic Science Research Program through NRF funded by the Ministry of Education (2013R1A1A2008394). Dong Hoon Lee was supported by Mid-career Researcher Program through NRF grant funded by the MEST (2010-0029121). Jong Hwan Park was supported by Basic Science Research Program through NRF funded by the Ministry of Education (2013R1A1A2009524) and the MSIP (Ministry of Science, ICT & Future Planning), Korea in the ICT R&D Program 2014 (KCA-2013-003).

References

1. Abdalla, M., Dent, A.W., Malone-Lee, J., Neven, G., Phan, D.H., Smart, N.P.: Identity-based traitor tracing. In: Okamoto, T., Wang, X. (eds.) PKC 2007. LNCS, vol. 4450, pp. 361–376. Springer, Heidelberg (2007)
2. Boneh, D., Boyen, X., Goh, E.J.: Hierarchical identity based encryption with constant size ciphertext. In: Cramer, R. (ed.) EUROCRYPT 2005. LNCS, vol. 3494, pp. 440–456. Springer, Heidelberg (2005)
3. Boneh, D., Franklin, M.K.: Identity-based encryption from the weil pairing. In: Kilian, J. (ed.) CRYPTO 2001. LNCS, vol. 2139, pp. 213–229. Springer, Heidelberg (2001)
4. Boneh, D., Gentry, C., Waters, B.: Collusion resistant broadcast encryption with short ciphertexts and private keys. In: Shoup, V. (ed.) CRYPTO 2005. LNCS, vol. 3621, pp. 258–275. Springer, Heidelberg (2005)
5. Boneh, D., Sahai, A., Waters, B.: Fully collusion resistant traitor tracing with short ciphertexts and private keys. In: Vaudenay, S. (ed.) EUROCRYPT 2006. LNCS, vol. 4004, pp. 573–592. Springer, Heidelberg (2006)
6. Boneh, D., Waters, B.: A fully collusion resistant broadcast, trace, and revoke system. In: Juels, A., Wright, R.N., di Vimercati, S.D.C. (eds.) ACM Conference on Computer and Communications Security, pp. 211–220. ACM (2006)
7. Chor, B., Fiat, A., Naor, M.: Tracing traitors. In: Desmedt, Y.G. (ed.) Advances in Cryptology - CRYPTO 1994. LNCS, vol. 839, pp. 257–270. Springer, Heidelberg (1994)
8. Delerablée, C.: Identity-based broadcast encryption with constant size ciphertexts and private keys. In: Kurosawa, K. (ed.) ASIACRYPT 2007. LNCS, vol. 4833, pp. 200–215. Springer, Heidelberg (2007)

9. Dodis, Y., Fazio, N.: Public key broadcast encryption for stateless receivers. In: Feigenbaum, J. (ed.) DRM 2002. LNCS, vol. 2696, pp. 61–80. Springer, Heidelberg (2003)
10. Fiat, A., Naor, M.: Broadcast encryption. In: Stinson, D.R. (ed.) Advances in Cryptology - CRYPTO 1993. LNCS, vol. 773, pp. 480–491. Springer, Heidelberg (1994)
11. Fujisaki, E., Okamoto, T.: Secure integration of asymmetric and symmetric encryption schemes. In: Wiener, M. (ed.) CRYPTO 1999. LNCS, vol. 1666, pp. 537–554. Springer, Heidelberg (1999)
12. Furukawa, J., Attrapadung, N.: Fully collusion resistant black-box traitor revocable broadcast encryption with short private keys. In: Arge, L., Cachin, C., Jurdziński, T., Tarlecki, A. (eds.) ICALP 2007. LNCS, vol. 4596, pp. 496–508. Springer, Heidelberg (2007)
13. Garg, S., Kumarasubramanian, A., Sahai, A., Waters, B.: Building efficient fully collusion-resilient traitor tracing and revocation schemes. In: Al-Shaer, E., Keromytis, A.D., Shmatikov, V. (eds.) ACM Conference on Computer and Communications Security, pp. 121–130. ACM (2010)
14. Gentry, C., Waters, B.: Adaptive security in broadcast encryption systems (with short ciphertexts). In: Joux, A. (ed.) EUROCRYPT 2009. LNCS, vol. 5479, pp. 171–188. Springer, Heidelberg (2009)
15. Goodrich, M.T., Sun, J.Z., Tamassia, R.: Efficient tree-based revocation in groups of low-state devices. In: Franklin, M. (ed.) CRYPTO 2004. LNCS, vol. 3152, pp. 511–527. Springer, Heidelberg (2004)
16. Halevy, D., Shamir, A.: The lsd broadcast encryption scheme. In: Yung, M. (ed.) CRYPTO 2002. LNCS, vol. 2442, pp. 47–60. Springer, Heidelberg (2002)
17. Kiayias, A., Pehlivanoglu, S.: Pirate evolution: How to make the most of your traitor keys. In: Menezes, A. (ed.) CRYPTO 2007. LNCS, vol. 4622, pp. 448–465. Springer, Heidelberg (2007)
18. Lee, K., Koo, W.K., Lee, D.H., Park, J.H.: Public-key revocation and tracing schemes with subset difference methods revisited. Cryptology ePrint Archive, Report 2013/228 (2013), http://eprint.iacr.org/2013/228
19. Lewko, A.B., Sahai, A., Waters, B.: Revocation systems with very small private keys. In: IEEE Symposium on Security and Privacy, pp. 273–285. IEEE Computer Society (2010)
20. Naor, D., Naor, M., Lotspiech, J.: Revocation and tracing schemes for stateless receivers. In: Kilian, J. (ed.) CRYPTO 2001. LNCS, vol. 2139, pp. 41–62. Springer, Heidelberg (2001)
21. Naor, D., Naor, M., Lotspiech, J.: Revocation and tracing schemes for stateless receivers. Electronic Colloquium on Computational Complexity (ECCC) (043) (2002)
22. Naor, M., Pinkas, B.: Efficient trace and revoke schemes. In: Frankel, Y. (ed.) FC 2000. LNCS, vol. 1962, pp. 1–20. Springer, Heidelberg (2001)
23. Park, J.H., Kim, H.J., Sung, H.M., Lee, D.H.: Public key broadcast encryption schemes with shorter transmissions. IEEE Trans. Broadcast. 54(3), 401–411 (2008)
24. Park, J.H., Lee, D.H.: Fully collusion-resistant traitor tracing scheme with shorter ciphertexts. Des. Codes Cryptography 60(3), 255–276 (2011)
25. Park, J.H., Rhee, H.S., Lee, D.H.: Fully collusion-resistant trace-and-revoke scheme in prime-order groups. Journal of Communications and Networks 13(5), 428–441 (2011)

NORX: Parallel and Scalable AEAD

Jean-Philippe Aumasson[1], Philipp Jovanovic[2], and Samuel Neves[3]

[1] Kudelski Security, Switzerland
jeanphilippe.aumasson@gmail.com
[2] University of Passau, Germany
jovanovic@fim.uni-passau.de
[3] University of Coimbra, Portugal
sneves@dei.uc.pt

Abstract. This paper introduces NORX, a novel authenticated encryption scheme supporting arbitrary parallelism degree and based on ARX primitives, yet not using modular additions. NORX has a unique parallel architecture based on the monkeyDuplex construction, with an original domain separation scheme for a simple processing of header, payload and trailer data. Furthermore, NORX specifies a dedicated datagram to facilitate interoperability and avoid users the trouble of defining custom encoding and signalling. NORX was optimized for efficiency in both software and hardware, with a SIMD-friendly core, almost byte-aligned rotations, no secret-dependent memory lookups, and only bitwise operations. On a Haswell processor, a serial version of NORX runs at 2.51 cycles per byte. Simulations of a hardware architecture for 180 nm UMC ASIC give a throughput of approximately 10 Gbps at 125 MHz.

Keywords: authenticated encryption, stream cipher, cryptographic sponges.

1 Introduction

We introduce the NORX[1] family of authenticated ciphers, a candidate in the CAESAR competition. NORX uses a parallel and scalable architecture based on the monkeyDuplex construction [1,2], where the parallelism degree and tag size can be tuned arbitrarily. The NORX core is inspired by the ARX primitive ChaCha [3], however it replaces integer addition with the approximation $(a \oplus b) \oplus ((a \wedge b) \ll 1)^2$, with the aim to simplify differential cryptanalysis and improve hardware efficiency. Although, bitwise logic operations are frequently used in cryptographic primitives, we are not aware of any other algorithm using the above approximation of integer addition.

On a Haswell processor (Intel's latest microarchitecture), a *serial* version of NORX achieves 2.51 cycles per byte. For long messages (≥ 4 KiB), our 4-wise parallel version is expected to be four times as fast when run on four cores (that is, more than 5 GiBps at 3.5 GHz).

---

[1] The name stems from "NO(T A)RX" and is pronounced like "norcks".
[2] Derived from the well-known identity $a + b = (a \oplus b) + (a \wedge b) \ll 1$ [4].

M. Kutyłowski and J. Vaidya (Eds.): ESORICS 2014, Part II, LNCS 8713, pp. 19–36, 2014.
© Springer International Publishing Switzerland 2014

In ASIC, NORX's fastest *serial* architecture is expected to achieve a throughput of about 10 Gbps at 125 MHz on a 180 nm technology. As for software implementations, the tunable parallelism allows NORX to reach even higher speeds.

We have not filed and are not aware of patents, patent applications, or other intellectual-property constraints relevant to use of the cipher. The source code of the reference implementation is published under a public domain-like licence (CC0 1.0), see [5].

Outline. Section 2 specifies the NORX family of AEAD schemes, as well as a datagram structure aiming to improve interoperability of NORX implementations. Section 3 describes the expected strength of NORX. Section 4 motivates the design decisions. Section 5 reports on software performance measurements and on preliminary results of a hardware performance evaluation. Finally, Section 6 presents preliminary cryptanalysis results.

2   Specification

2.1   Notations

Hexadecimal numbers are denoted in `typewriter` style, for example $\texttt{ab} = 171$. A *word* is either a 32-bit or 64-bit string, depending on the context. Data streams (as byte arrays) are parsed to word arrays in little-endian order. We denote by $a \parallel b$ the concatenation of strings a and b, by $|x|$ the bit length of x, and by $\mathsf{hw}(x)$ its Hamming weight. We use the standard notations $\neg$, $\wedge$, $\vee$ and $\oplus$ for bitwise negation, `AND`, `OR` and `XOR`; $x \ll n$ and $x \gg n$ for left- and right-shift; $x \lll n$, $x \ggg n$ for left- and right-rotation of x by n bits.

2.2   Generalities

NORX is parameterised by a *word size* of $W \in \{32, 64\}$ bits, a *number of rounds* $1 \le R \le 63$, a *parallelism degree* $0 \le D \le 255$, and a *tag size* $|A| \le 10W$ bits. We denote a NORX instance by NORXW-R-D-$|A|$.

By default NORXW-R-D uses $|A| = 4W$. For example, NORX64-6-1 has $(W, R, D, |A|) = (64, 6, 1, 256)$.

Encryption Interface. NORX encryption takes as input a key K of $4W$ bits, a nonce N of $2W$ bits, and a message $M = H \parallel P \parallel T$ where, H is a *header*, P a *payload*, and T a *trailer*. $|H|$, $|P|$, and $|T|$ are allowed to be 0. NORX encryption produces a ciphertext C, with $|C| = |P|$, and an *authentication tag* A.

Decryption Interface. NORX decryption is similar to encryption: Besides K and N, it takes as input a message $M = H \parallel C \parallel T$, where H and T denote header and trailer, and C the *encrypted payload*, with $|H|$, $|C|$, and $|T|$ are again allowed to be 0. The last component of the input is an authentication tag A. Decryption either returns failure, upon failed verification of the tag, or produces a plaintext P of the same size as C if the tag verification succeeds.

2.3   Layout Overview

NORX relies on the monkeyDuplex construction [1,2], enhanced by the capability of parallel payload processing. The number of parallel encryption lanes L_i is defined by the parameter $0 \le D \le 255$. For the value $D = 1$, the NORX layout is similar to a standard sequential duplex construction, see Figure 1. For $D > 1$, the number of lanes is bounded by the latter value, e.g. for $D = 2$ see Figure 2. If $D = 0$ ("unbounded" parallelism), the number of lanes L_i is bounded by the size of the payload.

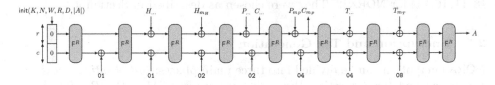

Fig. 1. Layout of NORX with parallelism $D = 1$

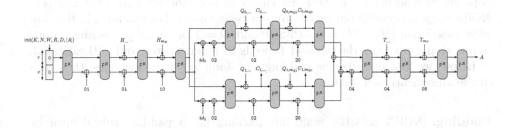

Fig. 2. Layout of NORX with parallelism $D = 2$

The round function F is a permutation of $b = r + c$ bits, where b is called the *width*, r the *rate* (or block length), and c the *capacity*. We call F a *round* and F^R denotes its R-fold iteration. The internal state S of NORX64 has $b = 640 + 384 = 1024$ bits and that of NORX32 has $b = 320 + 192 = 512$ bits. The state is viewed as a concatenation of 16 words, i.e. $S = s_0 \parallel \cdots \parallel s_{15}$, which are conceptually arranged in a 4×4 matrix, where $s_0, \ldots, s_9$ are called the *rate words*, used for data block injection, and $s_{10}, \ldots, s_{15}$ are called the *capacity words*, which remain untouched during absorbing and squeezing.

2.4   The Round Function F

F processes a state S by first transforming its columns with

$$G(s_0, s_4, s_8, s_{12}) \; G(s_1, s_5, s_9, s_{13}) \; G(s_2, s_6, s_{10}, s_{14}) \; G(s_3, s_7, s_{11}, s_{15})$$

and then transforming its diagonals with

$$G(s_0, s_5, s_{10}, s_{15}) \; G(s_1, s_6, s_{11}, s_{12}) \; G(s_2, s_7, s_8, s_{13}) \; G(s_3, s_4, s_9, s_{14})$$

Those two operations are called *column step* and *diagonal step*, as in BLAKE2 [6], and will be denoted by col and diag. The permutation G transforms four words a, b, c, d by computing (top-down, left-to-right):

$$a \longleftarrow (a \oplus b) \oplus ((a \wedge b) \ll 1) \qquad a \longleftarrow (a \oplus b) \oplus ((a \wedge b) \ll 1)$$
$$d \longleftarrow (a \oplus d) \ggg r_0 \qquad\qquad d \longleftarrow (a \oplus d) \ggg r_2$$
$$c \longleftarrow (c \oplus d) \oplus ((c \wedge d) \ll 1) \qquad c \longleftarrow (c \oplus d) \oplus ((c \wedge d) \ll 1)$$
$$b \longleftarrow (b \oplus c) \ggg r_1 \qquad\qquad b \longleftarrow (b \oplus c) \ggg r_3$$

The rotation offsets (r_0, r_1, r_2, r_3) are $(8, 19, 40, 63)$ for NORX64, and $(8, 11, 16, 31)$ for NORX32. They were chosen as described in Section 4.

2.5 Encryption and Tag Generation

NORX encryption can be divided into three main phases: *initialisation, message processing*, and *tag generation*. Processing of a message $M = H \parallel P \parallel T$ is done in one to five steps: *header processing, branching* (for $D \neq 1$ only), *payload processing, merging* (for $D \neq 1$ only), and *trailer processing*. The number of steps depends on whether H, P, or T are empty or not, and whether $D = 1$ or not. NORX skips processing phases of empty message parts. For example, in the simplest case when $|H| = |T| = 0$, $|P| > 0$, and $D = 1$, message processing is done in one step, since only the payload P needs to be encrypted and authenticated.

Below, we first describe the padding and domain separation rules, then each of the aforementioned phases.

Padding. NORX uses the *multi-rate padding* [2], a padding rule defined by $\mathsf{pad}_r : X \longmapsto X \parallel 10^q 1$ with bitstrings X and $10^q 1$, and $q = (-|X| - 2) \bmod r$. This extends X to a multiple of the rate r and guarantees that the last block of $\mathsf{pad}_r(X)$ differs from the all-zero block 0^r. Note, that there are three special cases:

$$q = \begin{cases} r - 2, & \text{if} \quad 0 \equiv |X| \bmod r \\ 0, & \text{if } r - 2 \equiv |X| \bmod r \\ r - 1, & \text{if } r - 1 \equiv |X| \bmod r \end{cases}$$

Domain Separation. NORX performs domain separation by XORing a *domain separation constant* to the least significant byte of s_{15} each time before the state is transformed by the permutation F^R. Distinct constants are used for the different phases of message processing, for tag generation, and in case of $D \neq 1$, for branching and merging steps. Table 1 gives the specification of those constants and Figures 1 and 2 illustrate their integration into the state of NORX.

The domain separation constant used at a particular step is determined by the type of the *next* processing step. The constants are switched together with the steps. For example, as long as the next block is from the header, the domain separation constant 01 is applied. During the processing of the last header block, the constant is switched. If $D = 1$ and the next data block belongs to the payload,

Table 1. Domain separation constants

header	payload	trailer	tag	branching	merging
01	02	04	08	10	20

the new constant is 02. Then, as long as the next block is from the payload, 02 is used, and so on.

For the extra initial and final permutations no domain separation constants are used, which is equivalent to XORing 00 to s_{15}. Additionally, this allows NORX to skip unneeded processing phases, as already discussed above. For the special case $D \neq 1$ and $|P| = 0$ not only payload processing is skipped but also branching and merging phases.

Initialisation. This phase processes a $4W$-bit key $K = k_0 \parallel k_1 \parallel k_2 \parallel k_3$, a $2W$-bit nonce $N = n_0 \parallel n_1$ and the parameters D, R, W and $|A|$.

1. **Basic Setup.** The internal state $S = s_0 \parallel \cdots \parallel s_{15}$ is initialised as

$$\begin{pmatrix} s_0 & s_1 & s_2 & s_3 \\ s_4 & s_5 & s_6 & s_7 \\ s_8 & s_9 & s_{10} & s_{11} \\ s_{12} & s_{13} & s_{14} & s_{15} \end{pmatrix} \longleftarrow \begin{pmatrix} u_0 & n_0 & n_1 & u_1 \\ k_0 & k_1 & k_2 & k_3 \\ u_2 & u_3 & u_4 & u_5 \\ u_6 & u_7 & u_8 & u_9 \end{pmatrix}$$

where u_0 to u_3 are as follows for NORX32 (left) and NORX64 (right):

$$\begin{aligned} u_0 &= \mathtt{243f6a88} & u_0 &= \mathtt{243f6a8885a308d3} \\ u_1 &= \mathtt{85a308d3} & u_1 &= \mathtt{13198a2e03707344} \\ u_2 &= \mathtt{13198a2e} & u_2 &= \mathtt{a4093822299f31d0} \\ u_3 &= \mathtt{03707344} & u_3 &= \mathtt{082efa98ec4e6c89} \end{aligned}$$

The other constants are computed by

$$(u_{4j+4}, u_{4j+5}, u_{4j+6}, u_{4j+7}) = \mathsf{G}(u_{4j}, u_{4j+1}, u_{4j+2}, u_{4j+3})$$

for $j \in \{0, 1\}$. See Section 4 for a discussion on these constants.

2. **Parameter Integration.** The parameters D, R, W and $|A|$ are integrated into the state S by XORing $(R \lll 26) \oplus (D \lll 18) \oplus (W \lll 10) \oplus |A|$[3] to s_{14} followed by an update of S with F^R.

3. **Finalisation.** A domain separation constant v, whose value is determined as shown above, is XORed into s_{15}. Subsequently, S is updated once more by F^R.

Note, that step 1 and part of step 2, namely integration of the parameters, are illustrated as $\mathrm{init}(K, N, W, R, D, |A|)$ in Figures 1 and 2.

---

[3] This layout is used to avoid XOR-collisions between the parameters.

Message Processing. Message processing is the main phase of NORX encryption or decryption. Unless noted otherwise, the value of the domain separation constant v is always determined according to the description above.

1. **Header Processing.** If $|H| = 0$, this step is skipped, otherwise let $\mathsf{pad}_r(H) = H_0 \parallel \cdots \parallel H_{m_H-1}$ denote the padded header data, with r-bit sized header blocks $H_l = h_{l,0} \parallel \cdots \parallel h_{l,9}$ and $0 \leq l \leq m_H - 1$. Then H_l is processed by:

$$s_j \longleftarrow s_j \oplus h_{l,j}, \quad \text{for} \quad 0 \leq j \leq 9$$
$$s_{15} \longleftarrow s_{15} \oplus v$$
$$S \longleftarrow \mathsf{F}^R(S)$$

2. **Branching.** This step is only performed if $D \neq 1$ and $|P| > 0$. In that case, NORX encrypts payload data on parallel *lanes* L_i, with $0 \leq i \leq D - 1$ if $D > 1$, or $0 \leq i \leq \lceil |P| / r \rceil - 1$ if $D = 0$. For each lane L_i, a copy $S_i = s_{i,0} \parallel \cdots \parallel s_{i,15}$ of the state S is created. The *lane number* i and the domain separation constant $v = 02$ are integrated into the least significant bytes of $s_{i,13} \parallel s_{i,14}$ and $s_{i,15}$, respectively. Finally each S_i is updated by F^R. That is, NORX does

$$S_i \longleftarrow S$$
$$(s_{i,14}, s_{i,13}) \longleftarrow (s_{i,14}, s_{i,13}) \oplus (\lfloor i / 2^W \rfloor, i \bmod 2^W)$$
$$s_{i,15} \longleftarrow s_{i,15} \oplus v$$
$$S_i \longleftarrow \mathsf{F}^R(S_i)$$

3. **Payload Processing.** If $|P| = 0$, this step is skipped. Otherwise, payload data is padded using the multi-rate padding and then encrypted. Let $\mathsf{pad}_r(P) = P_0 \parallel \cdots \parallel P_{m_P-1}$, then we distinguish three cases:
   - $D = 1$: This is the standard case, which requires no further modifications.
   - $D > 1$: In this case, a fixed number of lanes L_i is available for payload encryption, with $0 \leq i \leq D - 1$. An r-bit sized block P_j, with $0 \leq j \leq m_P - 1$, is processed by lane L_i if $i \equiv j \bmod D$. In other words, the padded payload blocks are distributed through the lanes in a round-robin fashion.
   - $D = 0$: Here, the number of lanes L_i is determined by the number m_P of padded payload blocks. Each r-bit sized block is processed on its own lane, i.e. block P_i is encrypted on L_i, with $0 \leq i \leq m_P - 1$.

   The data encryption of a single block works equivalently for each value of D, hence we describe it only in a generic way. Again, let $\mathsf{pad}_r(P) = P_0 \parallel \cdots \parallel P_{m_P-1}$ be the padded payload data. To encrypt $P_l = p_{l,0} \parallel \cdots \parallel p_{l,9}$ and get a new ciphertext block $C_l = c_{l,0} \parallel \cdots \parallel c_{l,9}$ the following steps are executed

$$s_j \longleftarrow s_j \oplus p_{l,j}, \text{ for } 0 \leq j \leq 9$$
$$c_{l,j} \longleftarrow s_j$$
$$s_{15} \longleftarrow s_{15} \oplus v$$
$$S \longleftarrow \mathsf{F}^R(S)$$

for $0 \le l < m_P - 1$. For $l = m_P - 1$, the procedure is almost the same, but only a truncated ciphertext block is created such that C has the same length as (unpadded) P. In other words, padding bits are never written to C.

4. **Merging.** This step is only performed if $D \ne 1$ and $|P| > 0$. After processing of P, the states S_i are merged back into a single state S. Then, a domain separation constant v is integrated, and S is updated by F^R:

$$S \longleftarrow \bigoplus_{i=0}^{D-1} S_i$$

$$s_{15} \longleftarrow s_{15} \oplus v$$

$$S \longleftarrow \mathsf{F}^R(S)$$

5. **Trailer Processing.** Digestion of trailer data is done analogously to the processing of header data as already described above. Hence, if $|T| = 0$, trailer processing is skipped. If T is non-empty, let $\mathsf{pad}_r(T) = T_0 \parallel \cdots \parallel T_{m_T-1}$ denote the padded trailer data with r-bit trailer blocks T_l and $0 \le l \le m_T - 1$. A trailer block $T_l = t_{l,0} \parallel \cdots \parallel t_{l,9}$ is then processed by doing the following steps:

$$s_j \longleftarrow s_j \oplus t_{l,j}, \quad \text{for} \quad 0 \le j \le 9$$

$$s_{15} \longleftarrow s_{15} \oplus v$$

$$S \longleftarrow \mathsf{F}^R(S)$$

Tag Generation. NORX generates an authentication tag A by transforming S one last time with F^R and then extracting the $|A|$ least significant bits from the rate words $s_0 \parallel \cdots \parallel s_9$ and setting them as A:

$$S \longleftarrow \mathsf{F}^R(S)$$

$$A \longleftarrow \left(\bigoplus_{i=0}^{9} (s_i \ll W \cdot i) \right) \bmod 2^{|A|}$$

2.6   Decryption and Tag Verification

NORX decryption mode is similar to the encryption mode. The only two differences are described below.

Message Processing. Processing header H and trailer T of $M = H \parallel C \parallel T$ is done in the same way as for encryption. Decryption of the encrypted payload C is achieved as follows:

$$p_{l,j} \longleftarrow s_j \oplus c_{l,j}$$

$$s_j \longleftarrow c_{l,j}$$

$$s_{15} \longleftarrow s_{15} \oplus v$$

$$S \longleftarrow \mathsf{F}^R(S)$$

Like in encryption, as many bits are extracted and written to P as unpadded encrypted payload bits.

Tag Verification. This step is executed after tag generation. Let A and A' denote the *received* and the *generated tag*. If $A = A'$, tag verification succeeds; otherwise it fails, the decrypted payload is discarded and an error is returned.

2.7 Datagrams

Many issues with encryption interoperability are due to ad hoc ways to represent and transport cryptograms and the associated data. For example IVs are sometimes prepended to the ciphertext, sometimes appended, or sent separately. We thus specify datagrams that can be integrated in a protocol stack, encapsulating the ciphertext as a payload. More specifically, we introduce two distinct types of datagrams, depending on whether the parameters of NORX are fixed or need to be signalled in the datagram header.

Fixed Parameters. With *fixed parameters* shared by the parties (for example through the application using NORX), there is no need to include the parameters in the *header of the datagram*. The datagram for fixed parameters thus only needs to contain N, H, C, T, and A, as well as information to parse those elements. It is depicted in Appendix A.

We encode the byte length of H and T on 16 bits, allowing for headers and trailers of up to 64 KiB, a large enough value for most applications. The byte length of C is encoded on 32 bits for NORX32 and on 64 bits for NORX64, which translates to a maximum payload size of 4 GiB and 16 EiB, respectively[4]. Similarly, to frame check sequences in data link protocols, the tag is added as a *trailer of the datagram* specified. The data H, C, and T of the underlying protocol are viewed as the *payload of the datagram*. The default tag length being a constant value of the NORX instance, it needs not be signalled. The length of the datagram header is 28 bytes for NORX64 and 16 bytes for NORX32.

Variable Parameters. In the case of *variable parameters*, the datagram needs to signal the values of W, R, and D. The header is thus extended to encode those values, as specified in Appendix A. To minimize bandwidth, W is encoded on one bit, supporting the two choices 32-bit ($W = 0$) and 64-bit ($W = 1$), R on 7 bits (with the MSB fixed at 0, i.e. supporting up to 63 rounds), and D on 8 bits (supporting parallelization degree up to 255). The datagram header is thus only 2 bytes longer than the header for fixed parameters.

---

[4] Note that NORX is capable of (safely) processing much longer messages; those are just the maximum values when our proposed datagrams are used.

3   Expected Strength

We expect NORX with $R \geq 4$ to provide the maximum security for any AEAD scheme with the same interface (input and output types and lengths). The following requirements should be satisfied in order to use NORX securely:

1. **Unique Nonces.** Each key and nonce pair should not be used to process more than one message.
2. **Abort on Verification Failure.** If the tag verification fails, only an error is returned. In particular, the decrypted plaintext and the wrong tag must not be given as an output and should be erased from memory in a safe way.

We do not make any claim regarding attackers using "related keys", "known keys", "chosen keys", etc. We also exclude from the claims below models where information is "leaked" on the internal state or key.

The security of NORX is limited by the key length (128 or 256 bits) and by the tag length (128 or 256 bits). Plaintext confidentiality should thus have the order of 128 or 256 bits of security. The same level of security should hold for integrity of the plaintext or of associated data (based on the fact that an attacker trying 2^n tags will succeed with probability 2^{n-256}, $n < 256$). In particular, recovery of a k-bit NORX key should require resources ("computations", energy, etc.) comparable to those required to recover the k-bit sized key of an ideal cipher.

Note that NORX restricts the number of messages processed with a given key: in [7] the *usage exponent* e is defined as the value such that the implementation imposes an upper limit of 2^e uses to a given key. NORX sets it to $e_{64} = 128$ for 64-bit and $e_{32} = 64$ for 32-bit, which corresponds in both cases to the size of the nonce. NORX has capacities of $c_{64} = 384$ (64-bit) and $c_{32} = 192$ (32-bit). Hence, security levels of at least $c_{64} - e_{64} - 1 = 384 - 128 - 1 = 255$ bits for NORX64 and $c_{32} - e_{32} - 1 = 192 - 64 - 1 = 127$ bits for NORX32 are expected (see [7]).

Moreover, [8] shows that the NORX mode of operation achieves security levels for authenticity and confidentiality of $\min\{2^{b/2}, 2^c, 2^{|K|}\}$ (recall that $|K| = |A|$), for all $0 \leq D \leq 255$, assuming an ideal underlying permutation F and a nonce respecting adversary.

4   Rationale

The Parallel Duplex Construction. The layout of NORX is based on the monkeyDuplex construction [1,2] enhanced by the capability of parallel payload processing. The *parallel duplex construction* is similar to the tree-hashing mode for sponge functions [9]. It allows NORX to take advantage of multi-core processors and enables high-throughput hardware implementations. Associated data can be authenticated as header and/or trailer data but only on a single lane. We felt that it is not worth the effort to enable processing of H and T in parallel, as they are usually short. The number of lanes is controlled by the parallelism degree $0 \leq D \leq 255$, which is a fixed instance parameter. Hence, two instances with distinct D values cannot decrypt data from each other. Obviously, the same holds for differing W and R values.

To ensure that the payload blocks on parallel lanes are encrypted with distinct key streams, NORX injects a unique id into each of the lanes during the branching phase. Once the parallel payload processing is finished, the states are re-combined in the merging phase and NORX advances to the processing of the trailer (if present) or creation of the authentication tag.

The Permutations G and F. The function G of NORX is inspired by the quarterround function of the stream cipher ChaCha [3]. NORX adopts this core function almost one-to-one, with the only difference being the replacement of the integer addition by $z = (x \oplus y) \oplus ((x \wedge y) \ll 1)$ with n-bit words x, y and z. This operation uses bitwise AND to introduce non-linearity and mimics integer addition of two bit strings x and y with a 1-bit carry propagation. Thus it provides, in addition to non-linearity, also a slight diffusion of bits. Clearly, G is invertible, and thus F is invertible as well.

Number of Rounds. For a higher protection of the key and authentication tag, e.g. against differential cryptanalysis, we chose twice the number of rounds for initialisation and finalisation, compared to the data processing phases. This strategy was previously proposed in [1] and has only minor effects on the overall performance, but increases the security of NORX. The minimal value of $R = 4$ is based on the following observations:

1. The best attacks on Salsa20 and ChaCha [10,11] break 8 and 7 rounds, respectively, which roughly corresponds to 4 and 3.5 rounds of the NORX core. However this is within a much stronger attack model than that provided by the duplex construction of NORX.
2. The preliminary cryptanalysis of NORX as presented in Section 6. The best differentials we were able to find belong to a class of high-probability truncated differentials over 1.5 rounds and a class of impossible differentials over 3.5 rounds. Despite the fact that those differentials cannot be used to mount an attack on NORX, it might be possible to find similar differentials, using more advanced cryptanalytic techniques, which could be used for an attack.

Choice of Constants. The values $u_0, \dots, u_3$ correspond to the first digits of π. The other six constants $u_4, \dots, u_9$ are derived iteratively from $u_0, \dots, u_3$ as described in Section 2.5. Their purpose is to bring asymmetry during initialisation and to limit an attacker's freedom where he might inject differences.

The domain separation constants serve to separate the different processing phases of NORX, which is important for the indifferentiability proofs of the duplex construction [12,2,8]. In addition they help to break the self-similarity of the round function and thus increase the complexity of certain kind of attacks on NORX, like slide attacks (see Section 6.3).

Choice of Rotation Offsets. The rotation offsets as used in F, see Section 2.4, provide a balance between security and efficiency. Their values were selected such that at least two out of four offsets are multiples of 8 and the remaining offsets are odd values of the form $8n \pm 1$ or $8n \pm 3$, with a preference for the first shape. The motivation behind those criteria is as follows: an offset which is a multiple of 8 preserves byte alignment and thus is much faster than an unaligned rotation on many architectures. Many 8-bit microcontrollers have only 1-bit shifts, so for example rotations by 5 bits are particularly expensive. Using aligned rotations, i.e. permutations of bytes, greatly improves the performance of the entire algorithm. Even 64-bit architectures benefit from such aligned rotations, for example when an instruction sequence of two shifts followed by XOR can be replaced by SSSE3's byte shuffling instruction pshufb. Odd offsets break up the byte structure and thus increase diffusion.

To find good rotation offsets and assess their diffusion properties, we used an automated search combined with a simple diffusion metric. The offsets we finally chose achieve full diffusion after F^2 and offer good performance.

Padding Rule. The sponge (or duplex) construction offers protection against generic attacks if the padding rule is sponge-compliant, i.e. if it is injective and ensures that the last block is different from the all-zero block. In [9] it has been proven that the multi-rate padding satisfies those properties. Moreover, it is simple to describe, easy to implement, very efficient and increases the complexity of certain kind of attacks, like slide attacks (see Section 6.3).

5 Performance

NORX was designed to perform well across both software and hardware platforms. This chapter details our implementations and performance results.

5.1 Software

NORX is easily implemented for 32-bit and 64-bit processors, as it works on 32- and 64-bit words and uses only word-based operations (XOR, AND, shifts, and rotations). The specification can directly be translated to code and requires no specific technique such as look-up tables or bitslicing. The core of NORX essentially consists of repeated usage of the G function, which allows simple and compact implementations (e.g., by having only one copy of the G code).

NORX lends itself well to implementations taking advantage of SIMD extensions present in modern processors, such as AVX or NEON. The typical vectorized implementation of NORX, when $D = 1$, works in full rows on the 4×4 state, and computes column and diagonal steps of F in parallel.

Furthermore, constant-time implementations of NORX are straightforward to write, due to the absence of secret-dependent instructions or branchings.

Avoiding Latency. One drawback of G is that it has limited instruction parallelism. In architectures where one is limited by the latency of the G function, an implementer can trade a few extra instructions for reduced latency:

$$
\begin{aligned}
t_0 &\longleftarrow a \oplus b & \quad d &\longleftarrow d \oplus t_0 \\
t_1 &\longleftarrow a \wedge b & \quad d &\longleftarrow d \oplus t_1 \\
t_1 &\longleftarrow t_1 \ll 1 & \quad d &\longleftarrow d \ggg r_0 \\
a &\longleftarrow t_0 \oplus t_1 &
\end{aligned}
$$

This tweak saves up to 1 cycle per instruction sequence, of which there are 4 per G, at the cost of 1 extra instruction. In a sufficiently parallel architecture, this can save at least $4 \times 2 \times R$ cycles, which translates to $6.4R/W$ cycles per byte saved overall.

Results. We wrote portable C reference implementations for both NORX64 and NORX32, as well as optimized versions for CPUs supporting AVX and AVX2 and for NEON-enabled ARMs. Table 2 shows speed measurements on various platforms for messages with varying lengths. The listed CPU frequencies are nominal ones, i.e. without dynamic overclocking features like Turbo Boost, which improves the accuracy of measurements. Furthermore, we listed only those platform-compiler combinations that achieved the highest speeds. Unless stated otherwise we used the compiler flags `-O3 -march=native`.

The top speed of NORX (for $D = 1$), in terms of bytes per second, was achieved by an AVX2 implementation of NORX64-4-1 on a Haswell CPU, listed in Table 2. For long messages ($\geq 4\,\text{KiB}$), it achieves a throughput of about 1.39 GiBps (2.51 cycles per byte at 3.5 GHz). The overhead for short messages (≤ 64 bytes) is mainly due to the initialisation and finalisation rounds (see Figure 1). However, the cost per byte quickly decreases, and stabilizes for messages longer than about 1 KiB.

Note that the speed between reference and optimized implementations differs by a factor of less than 2, suggesting that straightforward and portable implementations will provide sufficient performance in most applications. Such consistent performance reduces development costs and improves interoperability.

5.2   Hardware

Hardware architectures of NORX are efficient and easy to design from the specification: vertical and parallel folding are naturally derived from the iterated and parallel structure of NORX. The cipher benefits from the hardware-friendliness of the function G, which requires only bitwise logical AND, XOR, and bit shifts, and the iterated usage of G inside the core permutation of NORX.

A hardware architecture was designed, supporting parameters $W \in \{32, 64\}$, $R \in \{2, \ldots, 16\}$ and $D = 1$. It was synthesized with the Synopsys Design Compiler for an ASIC using 180 nm UMC technology. The implementation was targeted at high data throughput. The requirements in area amounted to about

Table 2. Software performance of NORX in cycles per byte

Intel Core i7-2630QM at 2.0 GHz						Intel Core i7-4770K at 3.5 GHz					
data length [bytes]		long	1536	576	64	data length [bytes]		long	1536	576	64
NORX64-6-1	Ref	7.69	9.08	11.54	37.75	NORX64-6-1	Ref	6.63	7.77	9.85	32.12
	AVX	4.94	5.90	7.52	24.81		AVX2	3.73	4.47	5.71	19.19
NORX64-4-1	Ref	5.28	6.24	7.94	26.00	NORX64-4-1	Ref	4.50	5.27	6.71	22.06
	AVX	3.28	3.91	5.03	16.69		AVX2	2.51	3.01	3.83	13.06
Intel Core i7-3667U at 2.0 GHz						Samsung Exynos 4412 Prime (Cortex-A9) at 1.7 GHz					
data length [bytes]		long	1536	576	64	data length [bytes]		long	1536	576	64
NORX64-6-1	Ref	7.04	8.32	10.59	34.87	NORX64-6-1	Ref	37.04	44.55	57.99	203.06
	AVX	5.04	6.03	7.71	25.44		NEON	13.17	16.76	23.10	94.56
NORX64-4-1	Ref	4.92	5.86	7.43	24.93	NORX64-4-1	Ref	26.56	32.21	42.35	152.25
	AVX	3.37	4.01	5.16	17.18		NEON	8.94	11.81	16.81	74.12

62 kGE. Simulations for NORX64-4-1 report a throughput of about 10 Gbps (1.2 GiBps), at a frequency of 125 MHz.

A more thorough evaluation of all hardware aspects of NORX is planned for the future. Due to the similarity of NORX to ChaCha and the fact that NORX has only little overhead compared to a blank stream cipher, we expect similar results as presented in [13] for ChaCha.

5.3 Comparison to AES-GCM

AES-GCM, the current de-facto standard for authenticated encryption, achieves very high speeds when the *AES New Instructions* (AES-NI) extension is available. Gueron reports 1.31 cpb for AES256-GCM on a Haswell processor [14]. In that case, NORX is only about half as fast as AES-GCM (the difference is around 1.2 cpb). The situation is different if AES-NI is not available, which is the case for the majority of platforms. We expect that NORX outperforms AES-GCM in these cases. For example, in [15] a constant-time implementation of AES128-GCM is presented, reaching 20.29 cpb on a Nehalem processor, while a vulnerable implementation reaches 10.12 cpb. These speeds are likely to be somewhat better on modern architectures, but certainly not below 3 cpb and especially not for constant-time implementations. On the other hand, NORX was designed to run in constant time, therefore such a protected implementation should have comparable performance to the results presented in Section 5.1.

6   Preliminary Cryptanalysis

This section presents preliminary results on the cryptanalysis of NORX. For a more thorough version, especially with respect to differential and rotational properties, we refer to [16].

6.1   Differential Cryptanalysis

We show how to construct high-probability differentials for the round function F^R when R is small. We focus on NORX64, but similar considerations hold for NORX32.

We consider a simple attack model where the initial state is chosen uniformly at random and where one seeks differences in the initial state that give biased differences in the state obtained after a small number of iterations of F. To find such simple differentials, we decomposed G into two functions G_1 and G_2, i.e. $G = G_2 \circ G_1$, such that G_1 corresponds to the first part of G (i.e. up to the rotation $\ggg r_1$) and G_2 to the second. Then, we analysed the behaviour of G_1 on 1-bit input differences. Exploiting the fact that many differences are deleted by the shift $\ll 1$ when the active bit is in the MSB, we found three high-probability differentials of G with a low-weight output, as shown in Table 3. Extending those differentials to F delays the diffusion by one step. Input differences with other combinations of active MSBs lead to similar output differences, but we found none with a lower or equal Hamming weight as the above. Using the first differential of the above, we derived a truncated differential over 3 steps (i.e. $F^{1.5}$) that has probability 1. This truncated differential can be used to construct an impossible differential over 3.5 rounds for the 64-bit version of F, which is shown in the next part. We expect that advanced search techniques are able to find better differentials for a higher number of rounds of F, e.g. where the sparse difference occurs in a later step than in the first.

Table 3. High-probability, low-weight differentials of G

Input / Output Difference of G	$Pr(\cdot)$
8000000000000000, 8000000000000000, 8000000000000000, 0000000000000000 0000000000000000, 0000000000000001, 8000000000000000, 0000000000000000	1
0000000000000000, 8000000000000000, 8000000000000000, 8000000000000000 8000000000000000, 0000000001000001, 8000000000800000, 0000000000800000	2^{-1}
0000000000000000, 8000000000000000, 8000000000000000, 8000000000000000 8000000000000000, 0000000003000001, 8000000001800000, 0000000000800000	2^{-1}

Impossible Differentials. We show how to construct an impossible differential using the *miss-in-the-middle* approach. In forward direction we use a probability-1 truncated differential over 1.5 rounds with an input difference having active bits in the first 3 MSBs of the input to G in the first column of the state, see Table 3. We set (0000000000000000, 0000000000000000, 8000000000000000, 0000000000000000) as the difference in the third column in backward direction. Applying $F^{1.5}$ to the state in forward direction and $F^{-1.5} \circ col^{-1}$ to the state in backward direction, results in a conflict in the 2nd bit of the 14th word. In forward direction this bit is always 1 and in backward direction it is always 0. We validated the impossible differential empirically in 2^{32} runs, starting in both directions from random states having the above differences. Equivalent impossible differentials can be constructed by varying the columns where the differences are injected. We were unable to construct an impossible differential for more than 3.5 rounds.

Remark. Neither the simple nor the impossible differentials can be used to attack NORX if the attacker is nonce-respecting: first of all the initialisation process prevents an attacker to set the required input difference in forward direction, i.e. active bits in 3 consecutive MSBs of a column. Once the initialisation is finished, the attacker could theoretically set those differences in the first or second column, but it would have no effect, as two states initialised with different nonces have a far too big distance from each other. Additionally the capacity part is completely unknown to the attacker.

6.2   Algebraic Cryptanalysis

Algebraic attacks on cryptographic algorithms discussed in the literature [17,18] target ciphers whose internal state is mainly updated in a linear way and thus exploit a low algebraic degree of the attacked primitive. However, this is not the case for NORX, where the b inner state bits are updated in a strongly non-linear fashion. In the following we briefly discuss the non-linearity properties of NORX, demonstrating why it is unlikely that algebraic attacks can be successfully mounted against the cipher.

We constructed the algebraic normal form (ANF) of G and measured the degree of every of the $4W$ polynomials and the distribution of the monomials. Table 4 reports the number of polynomials per degree for the 32- and 64-bit versions, as well as information on the distribution of monomials.

Table 4. Properties of the ANF of G

	# polynomials by degree						#monomials			
	3	4	5	6	7	8	min	max	avg	median
32-bit	2	6	58	2	8	52	12	489	242	49.5
64-bit	2	6	122	2	8	116	12	489	253	49.5

In both cases most polynomials have degree 5 or 8 and merely 2 have degree 3. Multiplying each of the above values by 4 gives the distribution of degrees of the whole state after a col or diag step. Due to memory constraints, we were unable to construct[5] the ANF for a single full round F, neither for the 64-bit nor for the 32-bit version. In summary, this shows that the state of NORX is updated in a strongly non-linear fashion and due to a rapid degree growth and huge state sizes it is unlikely that algebraic attacks can be successfully used against the AEAD scheme.

6.3   Other Properties

Fixed Points. The G permutation and thus any iteration of the round function F have a trivial distinguisher: the fixed points $G(0) = 0$ and $F^R(0) = 0$. Nevertheless it, seems hard to exploit this property, as hitting the all-zero state is as

---

[5] Using SAGE [19] on a workstation with 64 GiB RAM.

hard as hitting any other arbitrary state. Thus, the ability to hit a predefined state implies the ability to recover the key, which is equivalent to completely breaking NORX. Furthermore, we used the constraint solver STP [20] to prove that there are no further fixed points. For NORX32, the solver was able to show that this is indeed the case, but for NORX64 the proof is a lot more complex. Even after over 1000 hours, STP was unable to finish its computation with a positive or negative result. Therefore, we find it unlikely that there are any other fixed points in NORX64 besides the zero-to-zero point.

Slide Attacks. Slide attacks try to exploit the symmetries that consist of the iteration of a number of identical rounds. To protect sponge constructions against slide attacks, two simple defenses can be found in the literature: [21] proposes to add a non-zero constant to the state just before applying the permutation and [22] recommends to use a message padding, which ensures that the last processed data block is different from the all-zero message. The duplex constructions is derived from sponge functions, hence, the above defenses should hold for the former, too, and thus for NORX. With the domain separation and multi-rate padding both defensive mechanisms are already integrated into NORX.

Rotational Cryptanalysis. NORX includes several defenses against exploitable rotation-invariant behaviour: during state setup 10 out of 16 words are initialised with asymmetric constants, which impedes the occurrence of rotation-invariant behaviour and limits the freedom of an attacker. The non-linear operation of NORX contains a non rotation-invariant bit-shift $\ll 1$, and finally, the duplex construction prevents an attacker from modifying the complete internal state at a given time. He is only able to influence the rate bits, i.e. at most $r = 10W$ bits of the state, and has to "guess" the other $6W$ bits in order to mount an attack.

Acknowledgements. The authors thank Frank K. Gürkaynak, Mauro Salomon, Tibor Keresztfalvi and Christoph Keller for implementing NORX in hardware and for giving insightful feedback from their hardware evaluation. Moreover, the authors would like to thank Alexander Peslyak (Solar Designer), for giving them access to one of his Haswell machines, so that they could test their AVX2 implementations of NORX. Finally, the authors also thank the anonymous reviewers for their efforts and for their very helpful comments regarding this paper.

References

1. Bertoni, G., Daemen, J., Peeters, M., Assche, G.V.: Permutation-based Encryption, Authentication and Authenticated Encryption. Presented at DIAC 2012, Stockholm, Sweden, July 05-06 (2012)

2. Bertoni, G., Daemen, J., Peeters, M., Van Assche, G.: Duplexing the Sponge: Single-Pass Authenticated Encryption and Other Applications. In: Miri, A., Vaudenay, S. (eds.) SAC 2011. LNCS, vol. 7118, pp. 320–337. Springer, Heidelberg (2012)

3. Bernstein, D.J.: ChaCha, a Variant of Salsa20. In: Workshop Record of SASC 2008: The State of the Art of Stream Ciphers (2008), http://cr.yp.to/chacha.html

4. Knuth, D.E.: The Art of Computer Programming. Combinatorial Algorithms, Part 1, vol. 4A. Addison-Wesley, Upper Saddle River (2011), http://www-cs-faculty.stanford.edu/~uno/taocp.html

5. Official website of NORX (2014), https://www.norx.io

6. Aumasson, J.P., Neves, S., Wilcox-O'Hearn, Z., Winnerlein, C.: BLAKE2: Simpler, Smaller, Fast as MD5. In: Jacobson, M., Locasto, M., Mohassel, P., Safavi-Naini, R. (eds.) ACNS 2013. LNCS, vol. 7954, pp. 119–135. Springer, Heidelberg (2013)

7. Bertoni, G., Daemen, J., Peeters, M., Assche, G.V.: On the Security of Keyed Sponge Constructions. Presented at SKEW 2011, Lyngby, Denmark, February 16-17 (2011), http://sponge.noekeon.org/SpongeKeyed.pdf

8. Jovanovic, P., Luykx, A., Mennink, B.: Beyond $2^{c/2}$ Security in Sponge-Based Authenticated Encryption Modes. Cryptology ePrint Archive, Report 2014/373 (2014), http://eprint.iacr.org/2014/373

9. Bertoni, G., Daemen, J., Peeters, M., Assche, G.V.: Cryptographic Sponge Functions (2008), http://sponge.noekeon.org/CSF-0.1.pdf

10. Aumasson, J.-P., Fischer, S., Khazaei, S., Meier, W., Rechberger, C.: New Features of Latin Dances: Analysis of Salsa, ChaCha and Rumba. In: Nyberg, K. (ed.) FSE 2008. LNCS, vol. 5086, pp. 470–488. Springer, Heidelberg (2008)

11. Shi, Z., Zhang, B., Feng, D., Wu, W.: Improved Key Recovery Attacks on Reduced Round Salsa20 and ChaCha. In: Kwon, T., Lee, M.-K., Kwon, D. (eds.) ICISC 2012. LNCS, vol. 7839, pp. 337–351. Springer, Heidelberg (2013)

12. Bertoni, G., Daemen, J., Peeters, M., Van Assche, G.: On the Indifferentiability of the Sponge Construction. In: Smart, N.P. (ed.) EUROCRYPT 2008. LNCS, vol. 4965, pp. 181–197. Springer, Heidelberg (2008)

13. Henzen, L., Carbognani, F., Felber, N., Fichtner, W.: VLSI Hardware Evaluation of the Stream Ciphers Salsa20 and ChaCha, and the Compression Function Rumba. In: 2nd International Conference on Signals, Circuits and Systems 2008, pp. 1–5. IEEE (2008)

14. Gueron, S.: AES-GCM Software Performance on the Current High End CPUs as a Performance Baseline for CAESAR Competition Presented at DIAC 2013, Chicago, USA, August 11-13 (2013), http://2013.diac.cr.yp.to/slides/gueron.pdf.

15. Käsper, E., Schwabe, P.: Faster and Timing-Attack Resistant AES-GCM. Cryptology ePrint Archive, Report 2009/129 (2009), http://eprint.iacr.org/2009/129

16. Jovanovic, P., Neves, S., Aumasson, J.P.: Analysis of NORX. Cryptology ePrint Archive, Report 2014/317 (2014), http://eprint.iacr.org/2014/317

17. Aumasson, J.P., Dinur, I., Henzen, L., Meier, W., Shamir, A.: Efficient FPGA Implementations of High-Dimensional Cube Testers on the Stream Cipher Grain-128. Cryptology ePrint Archive, Report 2009/218

18. Dinur, I., Shamir, A.: Cube Attacks on Tweakable Black Box Polynomials. In: Joux, A. (ed.) EUROCRYPT 2009. LNCS, vol. 5479, pp. 278–299. Springer, Heidelberg (2009)

19. Stein, W.: Sage Mathematics Software. The Sage Development Team (2005–2013), http://sagemath.org

20. Ganesh, V., Govostes, R., Phang, K.Y., Soos, M., Schwartz, E.: STP — A Simple Theorem Prover (2006–2013), http://stp.github.io/stp

21. Gorski, M., Lucks, S., Peyrin, T.: Slide Attacks on a Class of Hash Functions. In: Pieprzyk, J. (ed.) ASIACRYPT 2008. LNCS, vol. 5350, pp. 143–160. Springer, Heidelberg (2008)
22. Peyrin, T.: Security Analysis of Extended Sponge Functions. In: Presented at the ECRYPT Workshop Hash Functions in Cryptology: Theory and Practice, Leiden, The Netherlands (June 4, 2008), http://www.lorentzcenter.nl/lc/web/2008/309/presentations/Peyrin.pdf

A   Datagrams

Representations for the datagrams as introduced in Section 2.7.

- Fixed Parameters:

NORX64	header				payload			trailer
field	N	$|H|$	$|T|$	$|C|$	H	C	T	A
offsets [bytes]	$0 - 15$	$16 - 17$	$18 - 19$	$20 - 27$	$28 - ??$	$?? - ??$	$?? - ??$	$?? - ??$

NORX32	header				payload			trailer
field	N	$|H|$	$|T|$	$|C|$	H	C	T	A
offsets [bytes]	$0 - 7$	$8 - 9$	$10 - 11$	$12 - 15$	$16 - ??$	$?? - ??$	$?? - ??$	$?? - ??$

- Variable Parameters:

NORX64	header						payload			trailer
field	N	$|H|$	$|T|$	$|C|$	$W(1) \| R(7)$	D	H	C	T	A
offsets [bytes]	$0 - 15$	$16 - 17$	$18 - 19$	$20 - 27$	28	29	$30 - ??$	$?? - ??$	$?? - ??$	$?? - ??$

NORX32	header						payload			trailer
field	N	$|H|$	$|T|$	$|C|$	$W(1) \| R(7)$	D	H	C	T	A
offsets [bytes]	$0 - 7$	$8 - 9$	$10 - 11$	$12 - 15$	16	17	$18 - ??$	$?? - ??$	$?? - ??$	$?? - ??$

B   Test Vectors

Test vectors for some instances of NORX are given below. More can be found on the official website [5].

- NORX64:

```
K : 0011223344556677  8899AABBCCDDEEFF  FFEEDDCCBBAA9988  7766554433221100
N : FFFFFFFFFFFFFFFF  FFFFFFFFFFFFFFFF
H : 1000000000000002  3000000000000004
P : 8000000000000007  6000000000000005  4000000000000003  2000000000000001
T :     null
```

NORX64-4-1
```
C : 1B4DCCFF6779A2C3  865464C856BC4B0C  DADBC58565E1690A  2CB12C0BE9D2F045
A : D0CE5276FDEC9F6E  33EE64CE5CCA3ABA  1187C05183464BD0  A0915ECA6FAF8757
```

NORX64-6-1
```
C : 7223675B69C7A934  1EBAB65233E8DC25  AB660E1BF0F3FEE8  71BE33115B333D6D
A : A05D644CCD2C5887  31DE2501AE4FE789  5C153D99943D29A4  98353A0E38D58A93
```

- NORX32:

```
K : 00112233 44556677 8899AABB CCDDEEFF
N : FFFFFFFF FFFFFFFF
H : 10000002 30000004
P : 80000007 60000005 40000003 20000001
T :    null
```

NORX32-4-1
```
C : 1F8F35CD CAFA2A38 724C1417 228732CA
A : 7702CA8A E8BA5210 FD9B73AD C0443A0D
```

NORX32-6-1
```
C : D98EDABA 25C18DD9 A0CA4C36 F73309C6
A : 69872EE5 3DAC068C E8D6D8B3 0A3D2099
```

Even More Practical Secure Logging: Tree-Based Seekable Sequential Key Generators

Giorgia Azzurra Marson[1] and Bertram Poettering[2]

[1] CASED & TU Darmstadt
[2] Information Security Group at Royal Holloway, University of London

Abstract. Sequential key generators produce a forward-secure sequence of symmetric cryptographic keys and are traditionally based on hash chains. An inherent disadvantage of such constructions is that they do not offer a fast-forward capability, i.e., lack a way to efficiently skip a large number of keys—a functionality often required in practice. This limitation was overcome only recently, with the introduction of *seekable sequential key generators* (SSKGs). The only currently known construction is based on the iterated evaluation of a *shortcut one-way permutation*, a factoring-based —and hence in practice not too efficient— building block. In this paper we revisit the challenge of marrying forward-secure key generation with seekability and show that symmetric primitives like PRGs, block ciphers, and hash functions suffice for obtaining secure SSKGs. Our scheme is not only considerably more efficient than the prior number-theoretic construction, but also extends the seeking functionality in a way that we believe is important in practice. Our construction is provably (forward-)secure in the standard model.

Keywords: secured logging, forward security, seekable PRGs.

1 Introduction

Computer log files can be configured to record a large variety of system events that occur on network hosts and communication systems, including users logging on or off, memory resources reaching their capacity, malfunctioning of disk drives, etc. Therefore, log files represent one of the most essential sources of information that support system administrators in understanding the activity of systems and keeping them fully functional. Not less important is the role that log files play in computer forensics: events like login failures and software crashes serve as standard indicators for (attempted) intrusions. Unfortunately, as log files are often recorded locally (i.e., on the monitored machine itself), in many practical cases intruders can a posteriori manipulate the log entries related to their attacks.

Online logging and its disadvantages. In a network environment, one obvious strategy to prevent adversarial tampering of audit logs is to forward log messages immediately after their creation to a remote log sink—in the hope that the attacker cannot also corrupt the latter. Necessary in such a setting is that the

M. Kutyłowski and J. Vaidya (Eds.): ESORICS 2014, Part II, LNCS 8713, pp. 37–54, 2014.
© Springer International Publishing Switzerland 2014

log sink is continuously available, as every otherwise required local buffering of log records would increase the risk that their delivery is suppressed by the adversary. However, in many cases it has to be assumed that the reachability of the log sink can be artificially restrained by the intruder, e.g., by confusing routing protocols with false ARP messages, by sabotaging TCP connections with injected reset packets, by jamming wireless connections, or by directing application-level denial-of-service attacks against the log sink. Independently of these issues, it is inherently difficult to choose an appropriate logging granularity: while the creation of individual records for each established TCP connection, file deletion, or subprocess invocation might be desirable from the point of view of computer forensics, network links and log sinks might quickly reach their capacities if events are routinely reported with such a high resolution. This holds in particular if log sinks serve multiple monitored hosts simultaneously.

Forward-secure cryptography & log file protection. A solution for tamper-resistant log-entry storage that does not require a remote log sink but offers integrity protection via cryptographic means is *secured local logging*. Here, each log entry is stored together with a specific authentication tag that is generated and verified using a secret key. Note that regular message authentication codes (MACs) by themselves seem not to constitute a secure solution: corresponding tags will be forgeable by intruders that succeed in extracting the secret key from the attacked device. Rather, a forward-secure MAC variant is required, as elaborated next.

In a nutshell, a cryptosystem provides *forward security* (FS) if it continues to give meaningful security guarantees after the adversary got a copy of the used keys. A standard example is key exchange: here, all recent security models require established session keys to remain safe when the adversary obtains access to the involved long-term private keys. Likely less known is that the notion of forward security also extends to non-interactive primitives. For instance, in forward-secure public key encryption [1] messages are encrypted in respect to a combination (pk, t), where pk is a public key and $t \in \mathbb{N}$ identifies one out of a set of consecutive time epochs; for each such epoch t, knowledge of a specific decryption key sk_t is necessary for decrypting corresponding ciphertexts. In addition, while by design it is efficiently possible to perform updates $sk_t \mapsto sk_{t+1}$, forward security requires that the reverse mapping be inefficient, i.e., it shall be infeasible to 'go backwards in time'. More precisely, forward security guarantees that plaintexts encrypted for 'expired' epochs remain confidential even if the decryption keys of all later epochs are revealed.

Analogously to the described setting, signatures and authentication tags of the forward-secure variants of signature schemes and MACs, respectively, remain unforgeable for past epochs if only current and future keys are disclosed to the adversary [2,3]. One possible way to obtain such a MAC is to combine a (forward-secure) *sequential key generator* (SKG) with a regular MAC [4,3], where the former can be seen as a stateful *pseudorandom generator* (PRG) that, once initialized with a random seed, deterministically outputs a pseudorandom sequence of fixed-length keys. These keys are then used together with a MAC to ensure unforgeability of messages within the epochs.

The challenge of seekability. Forward-secure SKGs are typically constructed by deterministically evolving an initially random state using a hash chain, i.e., by regularly replacing a 'current' key K_t by $K_{t+1} = H(K_t)$, where H is a cryptographic hash function [4,3]. Although hash chains, in principle, lead to (forward-)secure local logging, they also come with an efficiency penalty on the side of the log auditor: the latter, in order to verify a log record of a certain epoch t, first needs to recover the corresponding key K_t; however, as a high level of security requires a high key update rate, this might involve millions of hash function evaluations. This problem was addressed only recently with the introduction of *seekable sequential key generators* (SSKGs) [5].

We give a rough overview over the ideas in [5]. Essentially, the authors propose a generic construction of an SSKG from a *shortcut one-way permutation* (SCP), a primitive that implements a one-way permutation $\pi \colon D \to D$, for a domain D, with a dedicated shortcut algorithm allowing the computation of the k-fold composition π^k in sublinear time. The concrete SCP considered in [5] is given by the squaring operation modulo a Blum integer N, where applying the shortcut corresponds to reducing a certain exponent modulo $\varphi(N)$. Given an SCP, an SSKG can be obtained by letting its state consist of a single element in D, performing state updates by applying π to this element, and deriving keys by hashing it (more precisely, by applying a random oracle). While it is instructive to observe how the forward security of the SSKG corresponds with the one-wayness of the SCP, and how its seekability is based on the SCP's shortcut property, a notable technical artifact of the squaring-based SCP is that seekability requires knowledge of $\varphi(N)$ while forward security requires this value to be unknown. This dilemma is side-stepped in [5] by giving only the owners of a *seeking key* the ability to fast-forward through the SSKG output sequence.

1.1 Contributions and Organization

The central contribution of this paper is the design of a new seekable sequential key generator. In contrast to the prior SSKG from [5], our scheme relies on just symmetric building blocks; in particular we propose instantiations that exclusively use either PRGs, block ciphers, or hash functions. By consequence, our implementation beats the one from [5] by 1–3 orders of magnitude, on current CPUs. In addition to this efficiency gain, we also identify new and appealing functionality features of our SSKG. In particular, getting rid of the discussed seeking limitations of [5], our scheme allows *every* user to efficiently advance any state by an arbitrary number of epochs. Our SSKG is supported by a security proof in the standard model.

This paper is organized as follows. After starting with preliminaries in Section 2, we formally specify the functionality, syntax, and security requirements of SSKGs in Section 3; this includes a comparison with the (different) formalizations in [5]. In Section 4 we describe our new PRG-based SSKG, including its generalized seekability notion and some possible time-memory trade-offs. Finally, in Section 5, we discuss implementational aspects and efficiency results from our implementation.

1.2 Related Work

The first published work that highlights the importance of *seekability* as a desirable property of sequential key generators in the context of secured local logging is [5,6]. An extensive comparison of the corresponding results with the ones of the current paper can be found in the preceding paragraphs and in Section 3. In the following we discuss further publications on sequential key generation and cryptographic audit log protection. We observe that all considered protocols either are forward-secure or offer seekability, but not both simultaneously.

An early approach towards secured local logging originates from Bellare and Yee [7]; they study the role of forward security in authentication, develop the security notion of *forward integrity*, and realize a corresponding primitive via a PRF chain. Later, the same authors provide the first systematic analysis of forward security in the symmetric setting [3], covering forward-secure variants of pseudorandom generators, symmetric encryption, and MACs, and also providing constructions and formal proofs of security for these primitives.

Shortly after [7], an independent cryptographic scheme specifically targeted at protecting log files was described by Kelsey and Schneier [4,8,9]. Their scheme draws its (forward) security from frequent key updates via iterated hashing, but is not supported by a formal security analysis. A couple of implementations exist, notably the one by Chong, Peng, and Hartel in tamper-resistant hardware [10] and the *logcrypt* system by Holt [11]. The latter improves on [4] by paving the way towards provable security, but also adds new functionality and concepts. Most notable is the suggestion to embed regular metronome entries into log files to thwart *truncation attacks* where the adversary cuts off the most recent set of log entries. Similar work is due to Accorsi [12] who presents *BBox*, a hash-chain-based framework for protecting the integrity and confidentiality of log files in distributed systems.

Ma and Tsudik consider the concept of *forward-secure sequential aggregate authentication* for protecting the integrity of system logs [13,14]. Their constructions build on compact constant-size authenticators with all-or-nothing security (i.e., adversarial deletion of *any* single log message is detected), naturally defend against truncation attacks, and enjoy provable security.

The proposals by Yavuz and Ning [15], and Yavuz, Ning, and Reiter [16], specifically aim at secured logging on constraint devices and support a shift of computation workload from the monitored host to the log auditor. Notably, their key update procedure and the computation of authentication tags takes only a few hash function evaluations and finite field multiplications. In common with the schemes discussed above, their authentication systems are not seekable.

Kelsey, Callas, and Clemm [17] introduced secured logging into the standardization process at IETF. However, their proposal of *signed syslog messages* focuses on remote logging instead of on local logging. Precisely, their extension to the standard UNIX *syslog* facility authenticates log entries via signatures before sending them to a log sink over the network. While this proposal naturally offers seekability, it is bound to the full-time availability of an online log sink.

Indeed, periods where the latter is not reachable are not securely covered, as the scheme is not forward-secure.

2 Preliminaries

We recall basic notions and facts from cryptography, graph theory, and data structures that we require in the course of this paper. Notably, in the section on trees, we define what we understand by the 'co-path' of a node. If not explicitly specified differently, all logarithms are understood to be taken to base 2.

2.1 Pseudorandom Generators

A *pseudorandom generator* (PRG) is a function that maps a random string ('*seed*') to a longer 'random-looking' string. The security property of *pseudorandomness* requires that it be infeasible to distinguish the output of a PRG from random.

Definition 1 (Pseudorandom generator). *For security parameter λ and a polynomial $c\colon \mathbb{N} \to \mathbb{N}^{\geq 1}$, an efficiently computable function $G\colon \{0,1\}^{\lambda} \to \{0,1\}^{\lambda+c(\lambda)}$ is a* pseudorandom generator *if for all efficient distinguishers $\mathcal{D}$ the following advantage function is negligible, where the probabilities are taken over the random choices of s and y, and over $\mathcal{D}$'s randomness:*

$$\mathrm{Adv}_{G,\mathcal{D}}^{\mathrm{PRG}}(\lambda) = \left| \Pr\left[\mathcal{D}(G(s)) = 1 : s \xleftarrow{\$} \{0,1\}^{\lambda} \right] - \Pr\left[\mathcal{D}(y) = 1 : y \xleftarrow{\$} \{0,1\}^{\lambda+c(\lambda)} \right] \right| .$$

2.2 Binary Trees

A *tree* is a simple, undirected, connected graph without cycles. We particularly consider rooted trees, i.e., trees with a distinguished *root* node. The nodes adjacent to the root node are called its *children*; each child can be considered, in turn, the root of a subtree. The *level* L of a node indicates its distance to the root, where we assign level $L = 1$ to the latter. Children of the same node are *siblings* of each other. In this paper we exclusively consider binary trees of constant height H. These are trees in which every node has exactly one sibling, with exception of the root which has no sibling, and where all leaves have the same level $L = H$; such trees have a total of $N = 2^{H} - 1$ nodes. We assume that the children of each node are ordered; we refer to them as 'left' and 'right'. Nodes that have no children are called *leaves*, all other nodes are called *internal*.

We finally define the notion of *co-path* of a node. Let v denote an arbitrary node of a binary tree. Intuitively speaking, the (right) co-path of v is the list of the right siblings of the nodes on the (unique) path connecting the root node with v. For a formal definition, let L denote the level of $v = v_L$ and let $(v_1, \ldots, v_L)$ denote the path that connects the root (denoted here with v_1) with v_L. For each $1 \leq i \leq L$ let $V_i^{\rightarrow}$ be the list of right siblings of node v_i (these lists contain at most one element, and particularly $V_1^{\rightarrow}$ is always empty). We define the co-path of v_L to be the list $V_L^{\rightarrow} \parallel \ldots \parallel V_1^{\rightarrow}$ obtained by combining these lists into a single one using concatenation.

2.3   Stacks and Their Operations

A *stack* is a standard data structure for the storage of objects. Stacks follow the last-in first-out principle: the last element stored in a stack is the first element to be read back (and removed). The following procedures can be used to operate on stacks for storing, reading, and deleting elements. By $\mathbf{Init}(\mathcal{S})$ we denote the initialization of a fresh and empty stack $\mathcal{S}$. To add an element x 'on top of' stack $\mathcal{S}$, operation $\mathbf{Push}(\mathcal{S}, x)$ is used. We write $x \leftarrow \mathbf{Pop}(\mathcal{S})$ for reading and removing the top element of stack $\mathcal{S}$. Finally, with $x \leftarrow \mathbf{Peek}_k(\mathcal{S})$ the k-th element of stack $\mathcal{S}$ can be read without deleting it; here, elements are counted from the top, i.e., $\mathbf{Peek}_1(\mathcal{S})$ reads the top-most element. When using these notations, operations $\mathbf{Init}$, $\mathbf{Push}$, and $\mathbf{Pop}$ are understood to modify their argument $\mathcal{S}$ in place, while $\mathbf{Peek}_k$ leaves it unchanged.

3   Seekable Sequential Key Generators

The main contribution of this paper is a new construction of a *seekable sequential key generator* (SSKG). This cryptographic primitive can be seen as a stateful PRG that outputs a sequence of fixed-length keys—one per invocation. The specific property of *seekability* ensures that it is possible to jump directly to any position in the output sequence. At the same time, the security goal of forward security ensures that keys remain indistinguishable from random even upon corruption of the primitive's state. We next recall the syntactical definition and security properties, (mainly) following the notation from [5]. We defer the exposition of our new scheme to Section 4.

3.1   Functionality and Syntax

Generally speaking, a seekable sequential key generator consists of four algorithms: GenSSKG generates an initial state st_0, the update procedure Evolve maps each state st_i to its successor state st_{i+1}, GetKey derives from any state st_i a corresponding (symmetric) key K_i, and Seek permits to compute any state st_i directly from initial state st_0 and index i. We consider each state associated with a specific period of time, called *epoch*, where the switch from epoch to epoch is carried out precisely with the Evolve algorithm. This setting is illustrated in Figure 1 and formalized in Definition 2.

Definition 2 (Syntax of SSKG). *Let $\ell\colon \mathbb{N} \to \mathbb{N}$ be a polynomial. A seekable sequential key generator with key length ℓ is a tuple* SSKG = {GenSSKG, Evolve, GetKey, Seek} *of efficient algorithms as follows:*

- GenSSKG. *On input of security parameter 1^λ and total number $N \in \mathbb{N}$ of supported epochs, this probabilistic algorithm outputs an initial state st_0.*
- Evolve. *On input of a state st_i, this deterministic algorithm outputs the 'next' state st_{i+1}. For convenience, for $k \in \mathbb{N}$, by Evolve^k we denote the k-fold composition of Evolve, i.e., $\mathsf{Evolve}^k(\mathsf{st}_i) = \mathsf{st}_{i+k}$.*

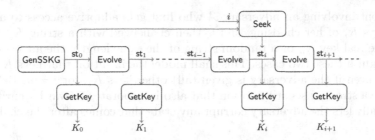

Fig. 1. Illustration of the interplay of the different SSKG algorithms

- GetKey. *On input of state* st_i, *this deterministic algorithm outputs a key* $K_i \in \{0,1\}^{\ell(\lambda)}$. *For* $k \in \mathbb{N}$, *we write* $\mathsf{GetKey}^k(\mathsf{st}_i)$ *for* $\mathsf{GetKey}(\mathsf{Evolve}^k(\mathsf{st}_i))$.
- Seek. *On input of initial state* st_0 *and* $k \in \mathbb{N}$, *this deterministic algorithm returns state* st_k.

Implicit in Definition 2 is the following natural consistency requirement on the interplay of Evolve and Seek algorithms:

Definition 3 (Correctness of SSKG). *A seekable sequential key generator* SSKG *is correct if, for all security parameters* λ, $N \in \mathbb{N}$, $\mathsf{st}_0 \xleftarrow{\$} \mathsf{GenSSKG}(1^\lambda, N)$, *and all* $k \in \mathbb{N}$ *we have*

$$0 \le k < N \quad \Longrightarrow \quad \mathsf{Evolve}^k(\mathsf{st}_0) = \mathsf{Seek}(\mathsf{st}_0, k) \ .$$

Remark 1 (Comparison with the definition from [5]). The syntax specified in Definition 2 does slightly deviate from the one in [5, Definition 3]: firstly, the SSKG setup routine of [5] has a secret 'seeking key' as additional output; it is required as auxiliary input for the Seek algorithm. The necessity of this extra key should be considered an artifact of the number-theory-based construction from [5] (see Section 3.4 for details): the seeking key contains the factorization of the RSA modulus underlying the scheme. As the proposed Evolve algorithm is one-way only if this factorization is not known, the Seek algorithm is available exclusively to those who know the seeking key as a 'trapdoor'. In contrast to that, our syntax for Seek is not only more natural, we also allow *everybody* to use the Seek algorithm to fast-forward efficiently to future epochs. Secondly, in [5] the number of supported epochs does not have to be specified at the time of SSKG initialization; instead, an infinite number of epochs is supported by every instance. We had to introduce this restriction for technical reasons that become clear in Section 4; however, we believe that the requirement of specifying the number of epochs in advance does not constrain the practical usability of our scheme too much: indeed, regarding our scheme from Section 4, instantiations with, say, $N = 2^{30}$ supported epochs are perfectly practical.

3.2 Security Requirements

As the security property of SSKGs we demand indistinguishability of generated keys from random strings of the same length. This is modeled in [5] via an experiment involving an adversary $\mathcal{A}$ who first gets adaptive access to a set of (real) keys K_i of her choosing, and is then challenged with a string K_n^b that is either the real key K_n or a random string of the same length; the adversary has to distinguish these two cases. This shall model the intuition that keys K_n 'look random' even if the adversary is given (all) other keys K_i, for $i \neq n$. Below we formalize a stronger security notion that also incorporates forward security, i.e., additionally lets the adversary corrupt any state that comes after the challenged epoch.

Definition 4 (IND-FS security of SSKG [5]). *A seekable sequential key generator SSKG is indistinguishable with forward security against adaptive adversaries (IND-FS) if, for all efficient adversaries $\mathcal{A} = (\mathcal{A}_1, \mathcal{A}_2)$ that interact in experiments* $\mathrm{Expt}^{\mathsf{IND\text{-}FS},b}$ *from Figure 2 and all $N \in \mathbb{N}$ bounded by a polynomial in λ, the following advantage function is negligible, where the probabilities are taken over the random coins of the experiment (including over $\mathcal{A}$'s randomness):*

$$\mathrm{Adv}^{\mathsf{IND\text{-}FS}}_{\mathsf{SSKG},N,\mathcal{A}}(\lambda) = \left| \Pr\left[\mathrm{Expt}^{\mathsf{IND\text{-}FS},1}_{\mathsf{SSKG},N,\mathcal{A}}(1^\lambda) = 1\right] - \Pr\left[\mathrm{Expt}^{\mathsf{IND\text{-}FS},0}_{\mathsf{SSKG},N,\mathcal{A}}(1^\lambda) = 1\right] \right| .$$

$\mathrm{Expt}^{\mathsf{IND\text{-}FS},b}_{\mathsf{SSKG},N,\mathcal{A}}(1^\lambda)$:

1 $\mathsf{KList} \leftarrow \emptyset$
2 $st_0 \xleftarrow{\$} \mathsf{GenSSKG}(1^\lambda, N)$
3 $(state, n, m) \xleftarrow{\$} \mathcal{A}_1^{\mathcal{O}_{\mathsf{Key}}}(1^\lambda, N)$
4 Abort if not $0 \leq n < m < N$
5 $K_n^0 \xleftarrow{\$} \{0,1\}^{\ell(\lambda)}$
6 $K_n^1 \leftarrow \mathsf{GetKey}^n(st_0)$
7 $st_m \leftarrow \mathsf{Evolve}^m(st_0)$
8 $b' \xleftarrow{\$} \mathcal{A}_2^{\mathcal{O}_{\mathsf{Key}}}(state, st_m, K_n^b)$
9 Abort if $n \in \mathsf{KList}$
10 Return b'

If $\mathcal{A}$ queries $\mathcal{O}_{\mathsf{Key}}(i)$:

1 Abort if not $0 \leq i < N$
2 $\mathsf{KList} \leftarrow \mathsf{KList} \cup \{i\}$
3 $K_i \leftarrow \mathsf{GetKey}^i(st_0)$
4 Answer $\mathcal{A}$ with K_i

Fig. 2. Security experiments for indistinguishability with forward security. The abort operation lets the experiment return 0, disregarding any output of the adversary.

3.3 An Application: Protecting Locally Stored Log Files

Given the definitions from Sections 3.1 and 3.2, the role of SSKGs in the context of secure logging is now immediate: in every epoch i, corresponding key K_i is used to instantiate a message authentication code (MAC) that equips all occurring log messages with an authentication tag. In addition, the Evolve algorithm is regularly invoked to advance from one epoch to the next, burying for all times the previously used keys. In such a setting, an auxiliary copy of initial state st_0 is made available to the log auditor who can use the Seek algorithm to check the integrity of log entries in any order. Clearly, the goal of forward security can be achieved only if the secure erasure of old states is an inherent part of the transition between epochs—for instance using the methods developed in [18].

3.4 Prior Constructions

While general sequential key generators have been considered in a variety of publications [4,9,3,11], the importance of seekability to obtain practical secure logging was only identified very recently [5]. By consequence, we are aware of only a single SSKG that precedes our current work.

Intuitively speaking, the SSKG construction from [5] follows the 'permute-then-hash' paradigm. In more detail, the authors consider so-called *shortcut one-way permutations* $\pi \colon \mathcal{D} \to \mathcal{D}$ that allow the evaluation of the k-fold composition π^k in less than $\mathcal{O}(k)$ time. Given such a primitive, state st_0 consists of a random element $x_0 \in \mathcal{D}$, and keys K_i are computed as $K_i = H(\pi^i(x_0))$, where H is a hash function modeled as a random oracle. The authors propose a number-theory-based shortcut permutation where π implements precisely the squaring operation modulo a Blum integer N; in this case, $\pi^i(x) = x^{2^i} = x^{2^i \bmod \varphi(N)}$ can be evaluated quite efficiently if the factorization of N is known.

4 SSKGs from Pseudorandom Generators

We propose a novel construction of a seekable sequential key generator that assumes only symmetric building blocks. Unlike the scheme in [5] which draws security from shortcut one-way permutations in the random oracle model, our new SSKG assumes just the existence of PRGs, i.e., it relies on a minimal cryptographic assumption. In a nutshell, similarly to the works in [2] and [1] that achieve forward-secure signing and forward-secure public key encryption, respectively, we identify time epochs with the nodes of specially formed trees and let the progression of time correspond to a pre-order visit of these nodes.

4.1 Sequential Key Generator from Binary Trees

From Section 2.2 we know that for any fixed $H \in \mathbb{N}^{\geq 1}$ the binary tree of constant height H has exactly $N = 2^H - 1$ nodes. In our SSKG we identify time epochs with the nodes of such a tree. More precisely, given the pre-order depth-first enumeration $w_0, \ldots, w_{N-1}$ of the nodes (first visit the root, then recursively the left subtree, then recursively the right subtree; cf. Figure 3), we let time epoch i and node w_i correspond.

The idea is to assign to each node w_i a (secret) seed $s_i \in \{0,1\}^\lambda$ from which the corresponding epoch's key K_i and the seeds of all subordinate nodes can be deterministically derived via PRG invocations. Here, exclusively the secret of the root node is assigned at random. Intuitively, pseudorandomness of the PRG ensures that all keys and seeds look random to the adversary.

We proceed with specifying which information the states associated with the epochs shall record. Recall that from each state st_i, $0 \leq i < N$, two pieces of information have to be derivable: the epoch-specific key K_i and the successor state st_{i+1} (and, by induction, also all following states and keys). Clearly, in our construction, the notions of seed and state do not coincide; for instance, in the

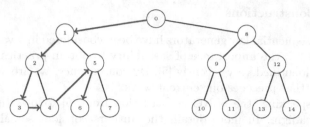

Fig. 3. A binary tree with height $H = 4$ and $N = 2^4 - 1 = 15$ nodes. The latter are numbered according to a pre-order depth-first search, as partially indicated by the arrow from the root node w_0 to node w_6.

tree of Figure 3 key K_9 cannot be computed from just seed s_4. However, if state st_4 contained (s_4, s_5, s_8), then for all $4 \leq i < N$ the keys K_i could be computed from this state. Inspired by this observation, our SSKG stores in each state st_i a collection of seeds, namely the seeds of the roots of the 'remaining subtrees'. The latter set of nodes is precisely what we called in Section 2.2 the *co-path* of node w_i. Intuitively speaking, this construction is forward-secure as each state stores only the minimal information required to compute all succeeding states. In particular, as each node precedes all vertices on its co-path (in the sense of a pre-order visit of the tree), the corresponding key remains secure even if any subsequent epoch's seed is leaked to the adversary.

We present next the algorithms of our SSKG construction. Particularly interesting, we believe, are the details on how the required pre-order depth-first search is implicitly performed by help of a stack data structure.

Construction 1 (TreeSSKG). *Fix a polynomial $\ell \colon \mathbb{N} \to \mathbb{N}$ and a PRG G: $\{0,1\}^\lambda \to \{0,1\}^{2\lambda+\ell(\lambda)}$. For all $s \in \{0,1\}^\lambda$ write $G(s)$ as $G(s) = G_L(s) \,\|\, G_R(s) \,\|\, G_K(s)$ where $G_L(s), G_R(s) \in \{0,1\}^\lambda$ and $G_K(s) \in \{0,1\}^{\ell(\lambda)}$. Assuming the notation for stacks from Section 2.3, the algorithms TreeSSKG = {GenSSKG, Evolve, GetKey, Seek} of our SSKG are defined by Algorithms 1–4 in Figures 4 and 5.*

Let us discuss the algorithms of TreeSSKG in greater detail.

GenSSKG. Besides picking a random seed $s = s_0$ for the root node, Algorithm 1 computes the minimum number $h \in \mathbb{N}$ such that the binary tree of constant height h consists of at least N nodes (cf. Section 2.2). Observe that this tree might have more than N nodes, i.e., more epochs are supported than required. The algorithm stores in state st_0 a stack S that contains only a single element: the pair (s, h). Here and in the following such pairs should be understood as 'seed s shall generate a subtree of height h'.

Evolve. The stack S stored in state st_i generally contains two types of information: the top element is a pair (s, h) associated with the current node w_i, and the remaining elements are associated with the corresponding pairs of the nodes on

w_i's co-path. After taking the current entry (s, h) off the stack, in order to implement the depth-first search idea from Section 4.1, Algorithm 2 distinguishes two cases: if node w_i is an internal node (i.e., $h > 1$), the update step computes the seeds of its two child nodes using PRG G, starting with the right seed as it needs to be prepended to the current co-path. The new seeds $G_L(s)$ and $G_R(s)$ can be considered roots of subtrees of one level less than w_i; they are hence pushed onto the stack with decreased h-value. In the second case, if the current node w_i is a leaf (i.e., $h = 1$), no further action has to be taken: the next required seed is the 'left-most' node on w_i's co-path, which resides on the stack's top position already.

GetKey. Algorithm 3 is particularly simple as it requires only a single evaluation of PRG G. Observe that the **Peek**$_1$ operation leaves its argument unchanged.

Seek. Deriving state st_k from the initial state st_0 via iteratively evoking k times the Evolve procedure is equivalent to visiting all nodes of the tree according to a pre-order traversal until reaching node w_k. However, there is an appealing way to obtain seed s_k more directly, without passing through all the intermediate vertices. The idea is to just walk down the path connecting the root node with w_k. Taking this shortcut decreases the seeking cost to only $\mathcal{O}(\log N)$, as opposed to $\mathcal{O}(N)$. This is the intuition behind the design of our Seek algorithm.

Algorithm 1: GenSSKG	**Algorithm 2:** Evolve	**Algorithm 3:** GetKey
Input: 1^λ, integer N **Output:** initial state st_0 1 **Init**$(\mathcal{S})$ 2 $s \xleftarrow{\$} \{0,1\}^\lambda$ 3 $h \leftarrow \lceil \log_2(N+1) \rceil$ 4 **Push**$(\mathcal{S}, (s,h))$ 5 **return** $\mathcal{S}$ *as* st_0	**Input:** state st_i as $\mathcal{S}$ **Output:** next state st_{i+1} 1 $(s,h) \leftarrow$ **Pop**$(\mathcal{S})$ 2 **if** $h > 1$ **then** 3 $\quad$ **Push**$(\mathcal{S}, (G_R(s), h-1))$ 4 $\quad$ **Push**$(\mathcal{S}, (G_L(s), h-1))$ 5 **return** $\mathcal{S}$ *as* st_{i+1}	**Input:** state st_i as $\mathcal{S}$ **Output:** key K_i 1 $(s,h) \leftarrow$ **Peek**$_1(\mathcal{S})$ 2 $K \leftarrow G_K(s)$ 3 **return** K *as* K_i

Fig. 4. Algorithms GenSSKG, Evolve, and GetKey. Observe that the number of supported epochs is potentially greater than N due to the rounding operation in line 3 of GenSSKG.

Recall that Seek is required to output the whole state st_k, and not just seed s_k. In other words, the execution of the algorithm needs to comprehend the construction of the co-path of node w_k. We provide details on how Algorithm 4 fulfills this task. Our strategy, illustrated in Figure 6, is to walk down the path from the root to node w_k, recording the right siblings of the visited nodes on a stack. During this process, with a variable δ we keep track of the remaining number of epochs that needs to be skipped. This counter is particularly helpful for deciding whether, in the path towards w_k, the left or the right child node have to be taken. Indeed, the number of nodes covered by the left and right subtrees is $2^h - 1$ each; if $\delta \leq 2^h - 1$ then the left child is the next to consider, but

Algorithm 4: Seek	Algorithm 5: SuperSeek
Input: state st_0 as $\mathcal{S}$, integer k	**Input**: state st_i as $\mathcal{S}$, integer k
Output: state st_k	**Output**: state st_{i+k}

Algorithm 4: Seek
1 $\delta \leftarrow k$
2 $(s, h) \leftarrow \textbf{Pop}(\mathcal{S})$
3 **while** $\delta > 0$ **do**
4     $h \leftarrow h - 1$
5   **if** $\delta < 2^h$ **then**
6        $\textbf{Push}(\mathcal{S}, (G_R(s), h))$
7        $s \leftarrow G_L(s)$
8        $\delta \leftarrow \delta - 1$
9   **else**
10        $s \leftarrow G_R(s)$
11        $\delta \leftarrow \delta - 2^h$
12 $\textbf{Push}(\mathcal{S}, (s, h))$
13 **return** $\mathcal{S}$ as st_k

Algorithm 5: SuperSeek
1 $\delta \leftarrow k$
2 $(s, h) \leftarrow \textbf{Pop}(\mathcal{S})$
3 **while** $\delta \geq 2^h - 1$ **do**
4     $\delta \leftarrow \delta - (2^h - 1)$
5     $(s, h) \leftarrow \textbf{Pop}(\mathcal{S})$
6 **while** $\delta > 0$ **do**
7     $h \leftarrow h - 1$
8   **if** $\delta < 2^h$ **then**
9        $\textbf{Push}(\mathcal{S}, (G_R(s), h))$
10        $s \leftarrow G_L(s)$
11        $\delta \leftarrow \delta - 1$
12   **else**
13        $s \leftarrow G_R(s)$
14        $\delta \leftarrow \delta - 2^h$
15 $\textbf{Push}(\mathcal{S}, (s, h))$
16 **return** $\mathcal{S}$ as st_{i+k}

Fig. 5. Algorithms Seek and SuperSeek

the right child has to be recorded for the co-path. On the other hand, if $\delta \geq 2^h$, then the left child can be ignored, the co-path doesn't have to be extended, and the walk towards w_k is continued via the right child. The procedure terminates when for the number of remaining epochs we have $\delta = 0$, which means that we arrived at target node w_k.

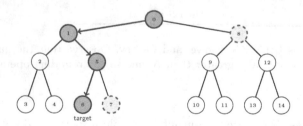

Fig. 6. A visualization of the procedure Seek computing state st_6. As the arrows indicate, the algorithm walks down the path from the root node w_0 to the target node w_6 (thick nodes); simultaneously, it records w_6's co-path, i.e., (w_7, w_8) (dashed nodes).

4.2 Security of Our Tree-Based SSKG

We next formally assess the security of Construction 1. For better legibility, in the following theorem we restrict attention to the setting $N = 2^H - 1$, i.e., where

$\log(N+1)$ is an integer; the extension to the general case is straightforward. We will also shorten the notation for some of the concepts from Definitions 2 and 4 (e.g., we denote $\ell(\lambda)$ simply by ℓ, etc.).

Theorem 1 (Security of TreeSSKG). *Assuming a secure PRG is used, our tree-based SSKG from Construction 1 provides* indistinguishability with forward security (IND-FS). *More precisely, for any efficient adversary $\mathcal{A}$ against the* TreeSSKG *scheme there exist efficient distinguishers $\mathcal{D}_i$ against the underlying PRG such that*

$$\mathrm{Adv}_{N,\mathcal{A}}^{\mathsf{IND\text{-}FS}} \leq 2(N-1) \sum_{i=1}^{\log(N+1)} \mathrm{Adv}_{\mathcal{D}_i}^{\mathsf{PRG}} .$$

Proof (sketch). The security of our scheme follows from the intuition that every SSKG key K_i, for being (part of) the output of a PRG invocation, looks like a random string to any efficient adversary as long as the corresponding seed remains hidden. Recall the IND-FS experiment (cf. Figure 2): the adversary gets state st_m and a challenge K_n^b —either key K_n or a random ℓ-bit string according to the value of b— for integers $n < m$ of her choosing. Although state st_m reveals seed s_m and subsequent seeds, from these seeds none of the preceding states can be computed. In other words, state st_m is of no help to the adversary in distinguishing keys prior to epoch m; in particular, key K_n remains secure.

To formalize this intuition we use game hops to progressively turn the IND-FS experiment into one for which all adversaries have advantage exactly zero. In the first hop we let the challenger guess the epoch $n < N$ corresponding to the challenge key and chosen by the adversary; this reduces the winning probability by a factor of $(N-1)$. Next, let $(v_1, \ldots, v_L)$ be the path from the root $v_1 = w_0$ to node $v_L = w_n$ in the binary tree associated to the SSKG. Starting from the previous game, we consider a hop for all $i = 1, \ldots, L$ by replacing the output of the PRG invocation associated to node v_i by a random $(2\lambda + \ell)$-bit string. Since each of the hops only involves a single PRG invocation, computational indistinguishability of any two consecutive games directly follows from the pseudorandomness of G. Observe that the last hop leads to a game where both K_n^0 and K_n^1 are uniformly chosen at random: here no adversary can do better than guessing. The fact that we lost a factor of $(N-1)$ in the first hop and we have additional $L \leq \log(N+1)$ intermediates games lets us derive the theorem statement.

A detailed proof appers in the full version of this paper [19]. □

4.3   An Enhanced Seeking Procedure

As required by Definition 2, our Seek algorithm allows computing any state st_k given the initial state st_0. Observe, however, that in many applications this initial state might not be accessible; indeed, forward security can be attained only if states of expired epochs are securely erased. From a practical perspective it is hence appealing to generalize the functionality of Seek to allow efficient computation of st_{i+k} from any state st_i, and not just from st_0. We correspondingly extend the notion of SSKG by introducing a new algorithm, SuperSeek, which realizes the Evolve^k functionality for arbitrary starting points; when invoked on input st_0, the new procedure behaves exactly as Seek.

Definition 5 (SSKG with SuperSeek). *A seekable sequential key generator* SSKG *supports* SuperSeek *if it has an auxiliary algorithm as follows:*

- SuperSeek. *On input of a state* st_i *and* $k \in \mathbb{N}$, *this deterministic algorithm returns state* st_{i+k}.

For correctness we require that for all $N \in \mathbb{N}$, *all* $\mathsf{st}_0 \xleftarrow{\$} \mathsf{GenSSKG}(1^\lambda, N)$, *all* $i, k \in \mathbb{N}$, *and* $\mathsf{st}_i = \mathsf{Evolve}^i(\mathsf{st}_0)$ *we have*

$$0 \leq i \leq i + k < N \quad \implies \quad \mathsf{Evolve}^k(\mathsf{st}_i) = \mathsf{SuperSeek}(\mathsf{st}_i, k) \ .$$

Assume a TreeSSKG instance is in state st_i and an application requests it to seek to position st_{i+k}, for arbitrary $0 \leq i \leq i + k < N$. Recall from the discussions in Sections 4.1 that state st_i encodes both the seed s_i and the co-path of node w_i. Recall also that, as a property of the employed pre-order visit of the tree, for each state st_j, $j > i$, the co-path of node w_i contains an ancestor w of w_j. Following these observations, our SuperSeek construction consists of two consecutive phases. For seeking to state st_{i+k}, in the first phase the algorithm considers all nodes on the co-path of w_i until it finds the ancestor w of w_{i+k}. The second phase is then a descent from that node to node w_{i+k}, similarly to what we had in the regular Seek algorithm. In both phases care has to be taken that the co-path of target node w_{i+k} is correctly assembled as part of st_{i+k}. The working principle of our new seeking method is also illustrated in Figure 7. We present explicit instructions for implementing SuperSeek in Figure 5. The first while loop identifies the ancestor w of target node w_{i+k} on w_i's co-path by comparing δ (i.e., the remaining number of epochs to be skipped) with the number of nodes in the subtree where w is the root. The second loop is equivalent to the one from Algorithm 4.

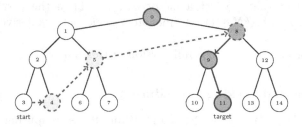

Fig. 7. A visualization of the procedure SuperSeek jumping from epoch 3 to 11. As indicated by the arrows, the algorithm first finds the intersection, here w_8, between the co-path of node w_3 (dashed nodes) and the path that connects the root with the target node w_{11} (thick nodes); from there it proceeds downwards until it reaches node w_{11}.

5 Practical Aspects

In the preceding sections we left open how PRGs can be instantiated in practice; indeed, the well-known recommendations and standards related to symmetric key cryptography exclusively consider block ciphers, stream ciphers, and hash functions. Fortunately, secure PRG instantiations can be boot-strapped from all three named primitives. For instance, a block cipher operated in counter mode can be seen as a PRG where the block cipher's key acts as the PRG's seed. Similar counter-based constructions derived from hash functions or PRFs (e.g., HMAC) are possible. A specific property of PRGs that are constructed by combining a symmetric primitive with a counter is particularly advantageous for efficiently implementing our TreeSSKG scheme. Recall that the PRG used in Construction 1 is effectively evaluated in a blockwise fashion. More precisely, while the PRG is formally defined to output strings of length $2\lambda + \ell(\lambda)$, in our TreeSSKG algorithms it is sufficient to compute only a considerably shorter substring per invocation. This property is perfectly matched by the 'iterated PRGs' proposed above, as the latter allow exactly this kind of evaluation very efficiently.

Implementation. We implemented our TreeSSKG scheme and claim that the level of optimization is sufficient for practical deployment. Our code is written in the C programming language and relies on the OpenSSL library [20] for random number generation and the required cryptographic primitives. We consider a total of four PRG instantiations, using the AES128 and AES256 block ciphers and the MD5 and SHA256 hash functions as described. That is, we have two instantiations at the $\lambda = 128$ security level, and two at the $\lambda = 256$ level.

We experimentally evaluated the performance of our implementation, using the following setup. We generated SSKG instances that support $N = 2^{20} - 1 \approx 10^6$ epochs. We iterated through all epochs in linear order, determining both the average and the worst-case time consumed by the Evolve algorithm. Similarly we measured the average and worst-case time it takes for the Seek algorithm to recover states st_k, ranging over all values $k \in [0, N-1]$. Concerning SuperSeek, we picked random pairs $i, j \in [0, N-1]$, $i < j$, and measured the time required by the algorithm to jump from st_i to st_j. Finally, we performed analogous measurements for GenSSKG and GetKey (here, average and worst-case coincide). The results of our analysis are summarized in Table 1.

For comparison we also include the corresponding timing values of our competitor, the (factoring-based) SSKG from [5][1], for security levels roughly equivalent to ours. We point out that the analogue of GenSSKG from [5] in fact consists of two separate algorithms: one that produces public parameters and an associated 'seeking key', and one that generates the actual initial SSKG state. As any fixed combination of public parameters and corresponding seeking key can be used for many SSKG instances without security compromises, for fairness

---

[1] The reference implementation from [5] can be found at
   http://cgit.freedesktop.org/systemd/systemd/tree/src/journal/fsprg.c.

we decided not to count the generation costs of the former when indicating the GenSSKG performance in Table 1. Instead, we report the results of our timing analysis here as follows: for the costs of parameters and seeking key generation with 2048 bit and 3072 bit RSA moduli we measured $400ms$ and $2300ms$, respectively.

It might be instructive to also study the required state sizes for both our TreeSSKG scheme and the scheme from [5]. In our implementation the (maximum) state size scales roughly linearly in both $\log N$ and the seed length of the used PRG. Concretely, for $N = 2^{20} - 1$ and 128 bit keys (e.g., for AES128- and MD5-based PRGs) the state requires 350 bytes, while for 256 bit security a total of 670 bytes of storage are necessary. In the scheme from [5] the space in the state variable is taken by an RSA modulus N, a value $x \in \mathbb{Z}_N^\times$, a 64 bit epoch counter, and a small header. Precisely, for 2048 and 3072 bit RSA moduli this results in 522 and 778 bytes of state, respectively.

Results and discussion. We discuss the results from Table 1 as follows, beginning with those of our tree-based SSKG (i.e., columns AES128, MD5, AES256, and SHA256). Our first observation is that the GenSSKG time is independent of the respectively used PRG. This is not surprising as the former algorithm never invokes the latter, but spends its time with memory allocation and requesting the random starting seed from OpenSSL's core routines. The timings for Evolve indicate that, as expected, 128-bit cryptographic primitives are faster than 256-bit primitives, and that for a fixed security level the hash-function-based constructions are (slightly) preferable. The hypothesis that the time spent by the individual algorithms is dominated by the internal PRG executions is supported by the observation that the running time of Evolve (on average) and GetKey coincide, and that the worst-case running time of Evolve is twice that value; to see this, recall that Evolve executions perform either two internal PRG invocations or none, and that the average number of invocations is one. We understand that the SuperSeek timings are generally better than the Seek values as the first **while** loop in Algorithm 5 does not comprise a PRG invocation, whereas the second

Table 1. Results of efficiency measurements of our TreeSSKG algorithms when instantiated with different PRGs, and a comparison with the algorithms from [5]. All experiments were performed on an 1.90GHz Intel Core i7-3517U CPU. We used OpenSSL version 0.9.8 for the implementation of our TreeSSKG routines, while for the compilation of the reference code from [5] we used the gcrypt library in version 1.5.0.

	AES128		MD5		[5]/2048 bit	AES256		SHA256		[5]/3072 bit
	[average]	[max]	[average]	[max]		[average]	[max]	[average]	[max]	
GenSSKG	$22\mu s$		$22\mu s$		$27\mu s$	$22\mu s$		$22\mu s$		$38\mu s$
Evolve	$0.2\mu s$	$0.5\mu s$	$0.2\mu s$	$0.4\mu s$	$8\mu s$	$0.5\mu s$	$1\mu s$	$0.4\mu s$	$0.8\mu s$	$13\mu s$
Seek	$7\mu s$	$9\mu s$	$6\mu s$	$7\mu s$	$4.9ms$	$14\mu s$	$18\mu s$	$11\mu s$	$15\mu s$	$12.6ms$
SuperSeek	$6\mu s$	$9\mu s$	$5\mu s$	$7\mu s$	–	$13\mu s$	$18\mu s$	$8\mu s$	$15\mu s$	–
GetKey	$0.2\mu s$		$0.2\mu s$		$12\mu s$	$0.4\mu s$		$0.4\mu s$		$13\mu s$

while loop requires less iterations on average than the corresponding loop in Algorithm 4.

The routines from [5] are clearly outperformed by the ones from our SSKG. Firstly, for the Evolve algorithm our timing values are about 30 times better than those for [5] (recall that the latter's state update involves a modular squaring operation). Similar results show our tree-based GetKey algorithm to be faster, by a factor between 30 and 60, depending on the considered security level. This might be surprising at first sight, as the algorithm from [5] consists of just hashing the corresponding state variable, but presumably the explication for this difference is that [5] operates with considerably larger state sizes than we do. Finally, the superiority of our tree-based construction in terms of efficiency is made even more evident by studying the performance of the seek Seek algorithms, where we can report our routines to be 700–1000 times faster than those from [5], again depending on the security level.

Conclusion

The recently introduced concept of seekable sequential key generator (SSKG) combines the forward-secure generation of sequences of cryptographic keys with an explicit fast-forward functionality. While prior constructions of this primitive require specific number-theoretic building blocks, we show that symmetric tools like block ciphers or hash functions suffice for obtaining secure SSKGs; this leads to impressive performance improvements in practice, by factors of 30–1000, depending on the considered algorithms. In addition to the performance gain, our scheme enhances the functionality of SSKGs by generalizing the notion of seekability, making it more natural and concise, an improvement that we believe is very relevant for applications. Our scheme enjoys provable security in the standard model.

Acknowledgments. The authors thank all anonymous reviewers for their valuable comments. Giorgia Azzurra Marson was supported by CASED and Bertram Poettering by EPSRC Leadership Fellowship EP/H005455/1.

References

1. Canetti, R., Halevi, S., Katz, J.: A forward-secure public-key encryption scheme. Journal of Cryptology 20(3), 265–294 (2007)
2. Bellare, M., Miner, S.K.: A forward-secure digital signature scheme. In: Wiener, M. (ed.) CRYPTO 1999. LNCS, vol. 1666, pp. 431–448. Springer, Heidelberg (1999)
3. Bellare, M., Yee, B.S.: Forward-security in private-key cryptography. In: Joye, M. (ed.) CT-RSA 2003. LNCS, vol. 2612, pp. 1–18. Springer, Heidelberg (2003)
4. Kelsey, J., Schneier, B.: Cryptographic support for secure logs on untrusted machines. In: Proceedings of the 7th USENIX Security Symposium (1998)
5. Marson, G.A., Poettering, B.: Practical secure logging: Seekable sequential key generators. In: Crampton, J., Jajodia, S., Mayes, K. (eds.) ESORICS 2013. LNCS, vol. 8134, pp. 111–128. Springer, Heidelberg (2013)

6. Marson, G.A., Poettering, B.: Practical secure logging: Seekable sequential key generators. Cryptology ePrint Archive, Report 2013/397 (2013), http://eprint.iacr.org/2013/397
7. Bellare, M., Yee, B.S.: Forward integrity for secure audit logs. Technical report (1997)
8. Kelsey, J., Schneier, B.: Minimizing bandwidth for remote access to cryptographically protected audit logs. In: Recent Advances in Intrusion Detection (1999)
9. Schneier, B., Kelsey, J.: Secure audit logs to support computer forensics. ACM Trans. Inf. Syst. Secur. 2(2), 159–176 (1999)
10. Chong, C.N., Peng, Z., Hartel, P.H.: Secure audit logging with tamper-resistant hardware. In: Gritzalis, D., di Vimercati, S.D.C., Samarati, P., Katsikas, S.K. (eds.) SEC. IFIP Conference Proceedings, vol. 250, pp. 73–84. Kluwer (2003)
11. Holt, J.E.: Logcrypt: forward security and public verification for secure audit logs. In: Buyya, R., Ma, T., Safavi-Naini, R., Steketee, C., Susilo, W. (eds.) ACSW Frontiers. CRPIT, vol. 54, pp. 203–211. Australian Computer Society (2006)
12. Accorsi, R.: BBox: A distributed secure log architecture. In: Camenisch, J., Lambrinoudakis, C. (eds.) EuroPKI 2010. LNCS, vol. 6711, pp. 109–124. Springer, Heidelberg (2011)
13. Ma, D., Tsudik, G.: Extended abstract: Forward-secure sequential aggregate authentication. In: 2007 IEEE Symposium on Security and Privacy, May 20-23, pp. 86–91. IEEE Computer Society Press, Oakland (2007)
14. Ma, D., Tsudik, G.: A new approach to secure logging. Trans. Storage 5(1), 2:1–2:2 (2009)
15. Yavuz, A.A., Ning, P.: BAF: An efficient publicly verifiable secure audit logging scheme for distributed systems. In: ACSAC, pp. 219–228. IEEE Computer Society (2009)
16. Yavuz, A.A., Ning, P., Reiter, M.K.: BAF and FI-BAF: Efficient and publicly verifiable cryptographic schemes for secure logging in resource-constrained systems. ACM Trans. Inf. 15(2), 9 (2012)
17. Kelsey, J., Callas, J., Clemm, A.: Signed Syslog Messages. RFC 5848 (Proposed Standard) (May 2010)
18. Gutmann, P.: Secure deletion of data from magnetic and solid-state memory. In: Proceedings of the Sixth USENIX Security Symposium, San Jose, CA, vol. 14 (1996)
19. Marson, G.A., Poettering, B.: Even more practical secure logging: Tree-based seekable sequential key generators. Cryptology ePrint Archive, Report 2014/479 (2014), http://eprint.iacr.org/2014/479
20. Young, E., Hudson, T.: OpenSSL: The Open Source Toolkit for SSL/TLS, http://www.openssl.org

Large Universe Ciphertext-Policy Attribute-Based Encryption with White-Box Traceability

Jianting Ning[1], Zhenfu Cao[1], Xiaolei Dong[1], Lifei Wei[2], and Xiaodong Lin[3]

[1] Department of Computer Science and Engineering,
Shanghai Jiao Tong University, Shanghai 200240, China
{jtning@,zfcao@cs.,dong-xl@cs.}sjtu.edu.cn
[2] College of Information Technology,
Shanghai Ocean University, Shanghai 201306, China
Lfwei@shou.edu.cn
[3] Faculty of Business and Information Technology,
University of Ontario Institute of Technology, Oshawa, Canada
xiaodong.lin@uoit.ca

Abstract. A Ciphertext-Policy Attribute-Based Encryption (CP-ABE) system extracts the decryption keys over attributes shared by multiple users. It brings plenty of advantages in ABE applications. CP-ABE enables fine-grained access control to the encrypted data for commercial applications. There has been significant progress in CP-ABE over the recent years because of two properties called *traceability* and *large universe*, greatly enriching the commercial applications of CP-ABE. Traceability is the ability of ABE to track the malicious users or traitors who intentionally leak the partial or modified decryption keys to others for profits. Nevertheless, due to the nature of CP-ABE, it is difficult to identify the original key owner from an exposed key since the decryption privilege is shared by multiple users who have the same attributes. On the other hand, the property of large universe in ABE proposed by Lewko and Waters enlarges the practical applications by supporting flexible number of attributes. Several systems have been proposed to obtain either of the above properties. However, none of them achieve the two properties simultaneously in practice, which limits the commercial applications of CP-ABE to a certain extent. In this paper, we propose a practical large universe CP-ABE system supporting white-box traceability, which is suitable for commercial applications. Compared to existing systems, our new system has three advantages: (1) The number of attributes is not polynomially bounded; (2) Malicious users who leak their decryption keys could be traced; and, (3) The storage overhead for traitor tracing is constant. We also prove the selective security of our new system in the standard model under "q-type" assumption.

Keywords: Attribute-Based Encryption, Ciphertext-Policy, Large Universe, White-box Traceablity, Commercial Applications.

M. Kutyłowski and J. Vaidya (Eds.): ESORICS 2014, Part II, LNCS 8713, pp. 55–72, 2014.
© Springer International Publishing Switzerland 2014

1   Introduction

In traditional public key encryption, a user is privileged to share his/her data with others in a private manner. The access of a targeted user or device to the shared data is all or nothing. In other words, one can get the entire access capability to the shared data if given the secret key; otherwise, nothing will be revealed. In many cases, however, this may not be true. For example, a user may expect to share his/her data through a more general and expressive way based on the targeted user or device's credentials. To address this issue, Sahai and Waters [1] introduced the notion of Fuzzy Identity-Based Encryption (FIBE). Goyal et al. [2] proposed two complementary forms of Attribute-Based Encryption (ABE) : Key-Policy Attribute-Based Encryption (KP-ABE) and Ciphertext-Policy Attribute-Based Encryption (CP-ABE). In the KP-ABE, users' decryption keys are issued according to an access policy and the cipher-texts are annotated by attributes. In the CP-ABE, users' decryption keys are issued according to the attributes they possess and the encrypting party specifies an access policy for the ciphertexts. A series of KP-ABE or CP-ABE schemes have been proposed [3–13], aiming at better expressiveness, efficiency or security. In particular, large universe and traceability are the two significant progress in ABE, we will discuss following.

Recently, Rouselakis and Waters [11] proposed a new construction and its proof method for Large Universe Attribute-Based Encryption (LU-ABE). In general, an ABE system can be classified to "small universe" and "large universe" constructions. In the "small universe" construction, the attributes are fixed at system setup and the size of the attributes is polynomially bounded, and furthermore the size of public parameters grows linearly with the number of attributes. While in the "large universe" construction, the attributes need not be specified at system setup and the size of the attribute universe is unbounded. The "large universe" construction for ABE system brings an obvious advantage that the designer of the ABE system need not bother to choose a particular bound of the attributes at system setup.

On the other hand, several CP-ABE systems supporting traceability have been proposed [14, 15, 13]. In CP-ABE, each user possesses a set of attributes and can decrypt the ciphertext if his/her attributes satisfy the ciphertext's access policy. This results in an obvious consequence that the encrypter or system does not know who leaks the decryption key to others intentionally. Due to the fact that the attributes are shared by multiple users and different users may have the same subset of attributes, the encrypter or system has no feasible method to trace the suspicious receiver if the the decryption key is leaked. We take Alice (with attributes {Alice, Assistant Professor, Computer Science}) and Bob (with attributes {Bob, Assistant Professor, Computer Science}) as an example. They both have the same decryption key corresponding to attributes {Assistant Professor, Computer Science} and can decrypt such a ciphertext encrypted by the attributes {Assistant Professor, Computer Science}. Suppose no other receiver in the system has both attributes ({Assistant Professor} and {Computer Science}) at the same time. If it happens to exist a user who can decrypt the ciphertext except Alice and Bob, it is significant to find out who leaks such decryption key to him, Alice or Bob? This drawback should be fixed in practice in case of leaking decryption key. It is necessary to add the property of traceability to the original ABE scheme, to identify who exactly leaks the decryption key. The above traceability is called *white-box traceability* [13], which means that any user who leaks his/her decryption key to the third user or device intentionally or unintentionally will be identified. Also note that there exists a relatively stronger notion named *black-box traceability* [16]: the leakage of the user is the decryption equipment instead of its decryption key.

However, there exists no practical traceable CP-ABE system supporting the property of large universe as the (non-traceable) CP-ABE system in [11]. Large universe CP-ABE system with white-box traceability is not yet achieved in practice: (1) The CP-ABE systems supporting traceability proposed in [14, 15, 13] do not support the property of large universe, the attributes need to be fixed at system setup and the size of the attributes is polynomially bounded. Also, public parameters' size grows linearly with the number of attributes. (2) The large universe CP-ABE system proposed in [11] is the first large universe CP-ABE system secure in the standard model; however, it does not support the property of traceability.

A Motivating Story. Consider a commercial application such as a pay-TV system with huge number of users for example. Each user is labeled with lots of related attributes, which are defined as TV channels that the user have ordered. As a versatile one-to-many encryption mechanism, CP-ABE system is quite suitable in this scenario. The pay-TV system provides several TV channels for users, and those who have paid for the TV channels could satisfy the access policy to decrypt the ciphertext and enjoy the ordered TV channels. CP-ABE enables fine-grained access control to the encrypted data according to attributes in users' ordered lists. However, there are two problems with this approach. First, if someone (who does not have the privilege to access to those TV channels) buys the decryption key from the Internet at a lower cost, she/he could also get access to the TV channels. Then who is selling the decryption key? Second, as the TV channels of the pay-TV system expand, an increasing number of new attributes need to be added to the system to describe the new channels. If the number of the attributes exceeds the bound set during the initial deployment of the pay-TV system, then the entire system has to be re-deployed and possibly all its data will have to be re-encrypted [11].

The problems, as described above, are the main obstacles when CP-ABE is implemented in commercial applications such as pay-TV systems and social networks. Due to the nature of CP-ABE, if a malicious user leaks its decryption key to others for profits (such as selling the decryption key on the Internet), it is difficult to find out the original key owner from an exposed key since the decryption key is shared by multiple users who have the same attributes. As such, the pay-TV company will suffer severe financial loss. Thus, it is necessary for the pay-TV system to trace the malicious users who intentionally leak the partial or modified decryption keys. Also, as the pay-TV system expands, an increasing new attributes (which describe new TV channels) have to be added to the system. In previous CP-ABE constructions, the attributes are fixed at system setup and the number of the attributes are bounded. If the bound is not specified large enough, the attributes may exhaust if the number of the users exceeds the threshold and the entire system needs to be completely re-built [11]. On the other hand, if the bound is specified too large, it will increase the storage and communication burden of the entire system due to the corresponding increase of the public parameters' size. Thus, it is necessary for the pay-TV system to support flexible number of attributes. Lastly, since the number of users in a pay-TV system could grow fast, the storage for traceability should not increase linearly with the number of users. Otherwise, the storage for traceability will become relatively huge and exhaust if the users increase dramatically. Thus, the storage for traceability needs to be at a constant level in an ideal case.

1.1 Our Contribution

In this paper, we propose a new large universe CP-ABE system which is white-box[1] traceable on prime order bilinear groups. To the best of our knowledge, this is the first practical CP-ABE system that simultaneously supports the following three properties: white-box traceability, large universe and constant storage for tracing. Compared with other constructions using composite order groups, we build our construction on the efficient prime order bilinear groups. We also prove our new system selectively secure in the standard model.

We solve the obstacles of CP-ABE implementation in the commercial applications such as pay-TV systems and social networks as follows:

1. We achieve the property of white-box traceability in CP-ABE. Our new system can trace the malicious users who may leak the partial or modified decryption keys to others for profits.
2. We obtain the property of large universe in white-box traceable CP-ABE. In our new system attributes need not be fixed at system setup, the attributes' size is not polynomially bounded and the public parameters' size does not grow linearly with the number of attributes.
3. We do not need to maintain an identity table for tracing as used in [13]. Instead, we adopt the Shamir's $(\bar{t}, \bar{n})$ threshold scheme in tracing the malicious users, the storage cost for traceability does not grow linearly with the number of the users, it is constant which only depends on the threshold $\bar{t}$.
4. It yields another result that the stored data for traceability need not be updated when new users are added into the system or malicious users are ejected out of the system, which makes the system more practical for applications.

Table 1 gives the comparison between our work and some other related work.

---

[1] In this paper, we mainly aim to obtain a large universe CP-ABE system with white-box traceability. The realization of black-box traceability for large universe CP-ABE system will be our future work.

Table 1. Comparison with other related work

	[14]	[15]	[13]	[11]	Ours
Large Universe [1]	×	×	×	√	√
Traceability	√	√	√	×	√
Constant Storage for Tracing [2]	√	×	×	–	√
Supporting Any Monotone Access Structures [3]	×	×	√	√	√
Constructed on Prime Order Groups [4]	√	×	×	√	√
Standard Model	×	√	√	√	√

[1] In [14],[15] and [13], their systems only support small universe.
[2] In [15] and [13], the storage for tracing is not constant. In [11], the proposed system does not support traceability.
[3] In [14] and [15], their systems do not support any monotone access structures.
[4] In [15] and [13], their systems are constructed on the composite order groups.

1.2 Our Technique

In this subsection, we briefly introduce the main idea we utilize to realize the properties of large universe and white-box traceability before giving the full details in Section 4.

To realize large universe construction, we adopt the "individual randomness" and "layer" technique from [17, 11]. We use the "layer" technique to encrypt data securely and to be able to decrypt. We employ two "layers" : the "attribute" layer and the "secret sharing" layer, and use a "binder term" to connect these two layers securely. In the "attribute" layer, we utilize u, h terms to provide a Boneh-Boyen-style [18] hash function ($u^A h$). As for the "secret sharing" layer, during KeyGen and Encrypt phases we use w term to hold the secret randomness r and the secret randomness s's shares respectively. Finally, we use the v term to "bind" this two layers together.

To realize traceability, we use the Boneh-Boyen-style signature [18]. Compared with the related work [13], we find that the table T with the tuple identity and its randomness used in [13] grows linearly with the number of the users.[2] With the number of the users in a system scaling large, the corresponding identity table T for traceability will expand as a result, which leads to heavy burden of the storage space for T. Besides, the corresponding cost of searching K' in T during the Trace phase is relatively huge. In this paper, we utilize the Shamir's $(\bar{t}, \bar{n})$ threshold scheme to optimize the property of traceability. We only need store $\bar{t} - 1$ points on a polynomial $f(x)$ at system setup. Consequentially, our storage for traceability does not grow linearly with the number of the users and is a constant.

The main idea of our traceability is as follows.

---

[2] Note that in the extension of [13], it gives another signature scheme for the purpose of removing the identify table T, but unfortunately the new signature scheme is not as efficient as the original one. Besides, it brings some other parameters, which will cause additional computation overhead.

Firstly, the Setup algorithm initializes an instance of Shamir's $(\bar{t}, \bar{n})$ threshold scheme $\mathcal{INS}_{(\bar{t},\bar{n})}$ and keeps a polynomial $f(x)$ and $\bar{t} - 1$ points $\{(x_1, y_1), (x_2, y_2), ..., (x_{\bar{t}-1}, y_{\bar{t}-1})\}$ on $f(x)$ secret. Then we insert c into the decryption key sk during KeyGen phase where $c = Enc_{\bar{k}_2}(x||y), x = Enc_{\bar{k}_1}(id), y = f(x)$.[3] During the Trace phase, the algorithm extracts $(x^* = x', y^* = y')$ from $x'||y' = Dec_{\bar{k}_2}(K')$ in the decryption key sk, and then it checks whether sk is issued by system. If $(x^* = x', y^* = y') \in \{(x_1, y_1), (x_2, y_2), ..., (x_{\bar{t}-1}, y_{\bar{t}-1})\}$, the algorithm computes $Dec_{\bar{k}_1}(x^*)$ to get id to identify the malicious user directly. Otherwise, the algorithm computes the secret of $\mathcal{INS}_{(\bar{t},\bar{n})}$ by interpolating with $\bar{t}-1$ points $\{(x_1, y_1), (x_2, y_2), ..., (x_{\bar{t}-1}, y_{\bar{t}-1})\}$ and (x^*, y^*). If the recovered secret is equal to $f(0)$, the algorithm computes $Dec_{\bar{k}_1}(x^*)$ to get id to identify the malicious user. If the equation fails, sk is not issued by the system. In this way, we could trace the owner of the decryption key. Meanwhile, it brings the benefit that the system only stores $\bar{t} - 1$ points on $f(x)$, and thus the storage for traceability is a constant.

1.3   Related Work

Sahai and Waters introduced the notion of Fuzzy Identity-Based Encryption in [1]. Goyal, Pandey, Sahai and Waters [2] later formalized two notions of ABE: CP-ABE (where user keys are labeled with sets of attributes and ciphertexts are associated with policies) and KP-ABE (where ciphertexts are labeled with sets of attributes and private keys are associated with access structures). Subsequently, many constructions of selectively secure KP-ABE and CP-ABE systems were proposed [3, 4, 19, 4–6, 8, 7, 20]. Many advances have been made for ABE as the following directions: new proof techniques to obtain fully secure [21, 8, 6, 9], decentralizing trust by setting multiple authorities [22–24] and outsourcing computation [25, 26]. The first large universe KP-ABE construction was proposed in [17]. It was built on composite order groups and proved selectively secure in the standard model. Then the first large universe KP-ABE construction on prime order groups was proposed in [27] inspired by the dual pairing vector space framework [28–30]. Recently, the first large universe CP-ABE construction [11] built on prime order bilinear groups was proposed by Rouselakis and Waters. It was proved selectively secure in the standard model under "q-type" assumption. Another branch of ABE research considers the problem of traceability. The notion of accountable CP-ABE was first proposed in [14] to prevent illegal key sharing among colluding users. Then a multi-authority ciphertext-policy (AND gates with wildcard) ABE scheme with accountability was proposed in [15], which allowed tracing the identity of a misbehaving user who leaked the decryption key to others. Liu, Cao and Wong lately proposed a white-box [13] and black-box [16] traceability CP-ABE system which supported policies expressed in any monotone access structures.

---

[3] Note that the tuple (x, y) is a point on $f(x)$

1.4   Organization

Section 2 gives the formal definition of traceable large universe CP-ABE and its security model. Section 3 introduces the background, including the notation, the access policy, the linear secret sharing scheme, the prime order bilinear groups and the assumptions. Section 4 presents the construction of our T-LU-CP-ABE system as well as the security proof. Some extensions of our work are discussed in Section 5. Finally, Section 6 presents a briefly conclusion and foresees our future work.

2   Traceable Large Universe CP-ABE

2.1   Definition

A Traceable Large Universe CP-ABE (T-LU-CP-ABE) system is a CP-ABE system where attributes need not be fixed at system setup and can trace the user by his/her decryption key. We enhance the original large universe CP-ABE system by adding users' identities and a Trace algorithm to it according to [13]. In particular, following the notation of the large universe CP-ABE system introduced in [11], a T-LU-CP-ABE system consists of five algorithms as follows:

- Setup(1^λ) $\to (pp, msk)$: The algorithm takes as inputs a security parameter $\lambda \in \mathbb{N}$ encoded in unary. It outputs the public parameters pp and the master secret key msk. We assume that the description of the attribute universe U is contained in the public parameters.[4] In addition, it initializes an instance of Shamir's $(\bar{t}, \bar{n})$ threshold scheme denoted by $\mathcal{INS}_{(\bar{t},\bar{n})}$.
- KeyGen($1^\lambda, pp, msk, id, S$) $\to sk_{id,S}$: The key generation algorithm takes as inputs the public parameters pp, the master secret key msk and a set of attributes $S \subseteq U$ for a user with identity id. The security parameter in the inputs ensures that it is polynomial time in λ. The algorithm outputs a secret key $sk_{id,S}$ corresponding to S.
- Encrypt($1^\lambda, pp, m, \mathbb{A}$) $\to ct$: The encryption algorithm takes as inputs the public parameters pp, a plaintext message m, and an access structure $\mathbb{A}$ over U. It outputs the ciphertext ct.
- Decrypt($1^\lambda, pp, sk_{id,S}, ct$) $\to m$ or $\bot$: The decryption algorithm takes as inputs the public parameters pp, a secret key $sk_{id,S}$, and a ciphertext ct. It outputs the plaintext m or $\bot$.
- Trace($pp, \mathcal{INS}_{(\bar{t},\bar{n})}, msk, sk$) $\to id$ or $\top$: The tracing algorithm takes as inputs the public parameter pp, an instance of of Shamir's $(\bar{t}, \bar{n})$ threshold scheme $\mathcal{INS}_{(\bar{t},\bar{n})}$, the master secret key msk, and a secret key sk. The algorithm first verifies whether sk is well-formed to determine whether sk needs to be traced. If sk is well-formed and could recover the secret of $\mathcal{INS}_{(\bar{t},\bar{n})}$,

---

[4] In the previous CP-ABE systems, the attribute universe U was one of the arguments in the Setup algorithm. In the large universe case, the attribute universe only depends on the size of the security parameter and the group generation algorithm [11].

the algorithm outputs an identity id implying that sk is linked to id. Otherwise, it outputs a special symbol $\top$ implying that sk does not need to be traced. We define a secret key sk is *well-formed* which means that it passes the *key sanity check* algorithm. The key sanity check is a deterministic algorithm [31, 32], which is used to guarantee the secret key in the well-formed decryption process.

2.2   T-LU-CP-ABE Selective Security

The security model of our T-LU-CP-ABE system is similar to that of the LU-CP-ABE system [11], excepting every key query is companied with an explicit identity. In this subsection we present the definition of selective security for our T-LU-CP-ABE system. It is parameterized by the security parameter $\lambda \in \mathbb{N}$ and is described by a game between an attacker and a challenger. The phases of the game are as follows:

- **Initialization** : The attacker claims the challenge access structure $\mathbb{A}^*$ he will attack, and then sends it to the challenger.
- **Setup** : The challenger runs the $\texttt{Setup}(1^\lambda)$ algorithm and sends the public parameters pp to the attacker.
- **Query Phase 1** : In this phase the attacker can adaptively ask for secret keys for the sets of attributes $(id_1, S_1), (id_2, S_2), ..., (id_{Q_1}, S_{Q_1})$. For each (id_i, S_i) the challenger calls $\texttt{KeyGen}(1^\lambda, pp, msk, id, S) \rightarrow sk_{id,S}$ and sends $sk_{id,S}$ to the attacker. The only restriction is that the attacker can not query the sets that satisfies the challenge access structure $\mathbb{A}^*$, i.e. $\forall_i \in [Q_1] : S_i \notin \mathbb{A}^*$.
- **Challenge** : The attacker declares two equal length messages m_0 and m_1 and sends them to the challenger. The challenge flips a random coin $\beta \in \{0,1\}$ and calls $\texttt{Encrypt}(1^\lambda, pp, m_\beta, \mathbb{A}^*) \rightarrow ct$. It gives ct to the attacker.
- **Query Phase 2** : This is the same as query phase 1. The attacker asks for the secret key for the sets $(id_{Q_1+1}, S_{Q_1+1}), ..., (id_Q, S_Q)$ with the same restriction: $\forall_i \in [Q] : S_i \notin \mathbb{A}^*$.
- **Guess** : The attacker outputs a guess $\beta' \in \{0,1\}$ for β.

The advantage of an attacker is defined to be $Adv = Pr[\beta' = \beta] - 1/2$ in this game.

Definition 1. *A traceable large universe ciphertext-policy attribute-based encryption system is selectively secure if all probabilistic polynomial-time (PPT) attackers have at most negligible advantage in λ in the above security game.*

2.3   Traceability

In this subsection, we give the traceability definition for our T-LU-CP-ABE. It is described by a game between an attacker and a challenger. The phases of the game are as follows:

- **Setup** : Here the challenger calls the Setup(1^λ) algorithm and sends the public parameters pp to the attacker.
- **Key Query** : The attacker submits the sets of attributes $(id_1, S_1), ..., (id_q, S_q)$ to request the corresponding decryption keys.
- **Key Forgery** : The attacker will output a decryption key sk_*. If Trace(pp, $\mathcal{INS}_{(\bar{t},\bar{n})}, msk, sk_*$) $\neq$ T and Trace($pp, \mathcal{INS}_{(\bar{t},\bar{n})}, msk, sk_*$) $\notin \{id_1, ..., id_q\}$, then the attacker wins the game. The advantage of an attacker in this game is defined to be $Pr[Trace(pp, \mathcal{INS}_{(\bar{t},\bar{n})}, msk, sk_*) \notin \{\text{T}, id_1, ..., id_q\}]$.

Definition 2. *A traceable large universe ciphertext-policy attribute-based encryption system is fully traceable if there has no polynomial time attacker have non-negligible advantage in the above game.*

3 Background

3.1 Notation

We define $[l] = \{1, 2, ..., l\}$ for $l \in \mathbb{N}$. By PPT we denote probabilistic polynomial-time. We denote $\mathbb{Z}_p^{l \times n}$ be the set of matrices of size $l \times n$ with elements in $\mathbb{Z}_p$. The set of row vectors of length n (i.e. $\mathbb{Z}_p^{1 \times n}$) and the set of column vectors of length n (i.e. $\mathbb{Z}_p^{n \times 1}$) are the two special subsets. We denote $(s_1, s_2, ..., s_n)$ be a row vector and $(s_1, s_2, ..., s_n)^\perp$ be a column vector. By v_i we denote the i-th element in a vector v. And by Mv we denote the inner product of matrix M with vector v. We define $\mathcal{F}(U_1 \to U_2)$ be the set of functions from set U_1 to U_2.

We denote $GD = (p, \mathbb{G}, \mathbb{G}_T, e)$ be the groups and the bilinear mapping description where $\mathbb{G}$ and $\mathbb{G}_T$ are two multiplicative cyclic groups of prime order p and $e : \mathbb{G} \times \mathbb{G}_T$ is a bilinear map.

3.2 Access Policy

This subsection presents the definition of access structure referred to [33, 11].

Definition 3. *(Access Structure [33]) : Let U denote the attribute universe. A collection $\mathbb{A} \in 2^U$ of non-empty sets of attributes is an access structure on U. The sets in $\mathbb{A}$ are called the authorized sets, and the sets not in $\mathbb{A}$ are called the unauthorized sets. A collection $\mathbb{A} \in 2^U$ is called monotone if $\forall B, C \in \mathbb{A} : if B \in \mathbb{A}$ and $B \subseteq C$, then $C \in \mathbb{A}$.*

The main idea in ABE is that the role of the users is taken by the attributes. Thus, the access structure $\mathbb{A}$ will contain the authorized sets of attributes. For CP-ABE, if a user of the system posses an authorized set of attributes then he can decrypt the ciphertext, otherwise, he can't get any information from ciphertext if the set he possed is unauthorized. In our construction, we restrict our attention to monotone access structure.

3.3 Linear Secret-Sharing Schemes

It is shown in [33] that a linear secret sharing scheme can realize any monotone access structure. In this subsection, we will present the definition of linear secret-sharing scheme (LSSS) referred to [33, 11].

Definition 4. *(Linear Secret-Sharing Schemes (LSSS) [33, 11]). Let U denote the attribute universe and p denote a prime. A secret-sharing scheme $\prod$ with domain of secrets $\mathbb{Z}_p$ realizing access structure on U in called linear (over $\mathbb{Z}_p$) if*

1. The shares of a secret $s \in \mathbb{Z}_p$ for each attribute form a vector over $\mathbb{Z}_p$.

2. For each access structure $\mathbb{A}$ on U, there exists a matrix M with l rows and n columns called the share-generating matrix. For $i = 1, ..., l$, we define a function ρ labels row i of M with attribute $\rho(i)$ from the attribute universe U, i.e. $\rho \in \mathcal{F}([l] \to U)$. When we consider the column vector $\boldsymbol{v} = (s, r_2, ..., r_n)^{\perp}$, where $r_2, ..., r_n \in \mathbb{Z}_p$ are randomly chosen. Then $M\boldsymbol{v} \in \mathbb{Z}_p^{l \times 1}$ is the vector of l shares of the secret s according to $\prod$. The share $(M\boldsymbol{v})_j$ "belongs" to attribute $\rho(j)$, where $j \in [l]$.

As shown in [33], every linear secret-sharing scheme according to the above definition also enjoys the linear reconstruction property, defined as follows: Let $\prod$ be an LSSS for the access structure $\mathbb{A}$, $S \in \mathbb{A}$ be any authorized set and let $I \subset \{1, 2, ..., l\}$ be defined as $I = \{i \in [l] \wedge \rho(i) \in S\}$. Then, there exist constants $\{\omega_i \in \mathbb{Z}_p\}_{i \in I}$ such that for any valid shares $\{\lambda_i = (M\boldsymbol{v})_i\}_{i \in I}$ of a secret s according to $\prod$, then $\sum_{i \in I} \omega_i \lambda_i = s$. Additionally, it is shown in [33] that these constants $\{\omega_i\}_{i \in I}$ can be found in time polynomial in the size of the share-generating matrix M. On the other hand, for any unauthorized set S', no such constants $\{\omega_i\}$ exist.

Also note that if we encode the access structure as a monotonic Boolean formula over attributes, there exists a generic algorithm by which we can generate the corresponding access policy in polynomial time [33, 24].

In our construction, an LSSS matrix (M, ρ) will be used to express an access policy associated to a ciphertext.

3.4 Prime Order Bilinear Groups

Let $\mathbb{G}$ and $\mathbb{G}_T$ be two multiplicative cyclic groups of prime order p. Let g be a generator of $\mathbb{G}$ and $e : \mathbb{G} \times \mathbb{G} \to \mathbb{G}_T$ be a bilinear map. The bilinear map e has the following properties:

1. Bilinearity: $\forall u, v \in \mathbb{G}$ and $a, b \in \mathbb{Z}_p$, we have $e(u^a, v^b) = e(u, v)^{ab}$.
2. Non-degeneracy: $e(g, g) \neq 1$.

We say that $\mathbb{G}$ is a bilinear group if the group operations in $\mathbb{G}$ and the bilinear map $e : \mathbb{G} \times \mathbb{G} \to \mathbb{G}_T$ can both be computed efficiently. Notice that the map $e(\cdot, \cdot)$ is symmetric since $e(g^a, g^b) = e(g, g)^{ab} = e(g^b, g^a)$.

3.5 Assumptions

We adopt the "q-type" assumption of [11] as this construction's assumption.

Assumption 1 ("q-type" assumption [11]). *We define the q-type problem as follows. Initially choose a group generation algorithm with input the security parameter, pick a random group element $g \in \mathbb{G}$, and $q+2$ random exponents $d, s, b_1, b_2, ..., b_q \in \mathbb{Z}_p$. If the attacker is given the group description $(p, \mathbb{G}, \mathbb{G}_T, e)$ and $\boldsymbol{y}$ including the following terms:*

$$g, g^s$$
$$g^{d^i}, g^{b_j}, g^{sb_j}, g^{d^i b_j}, g^{d^i/b_j^2} \quad \forall(i,j) \in [q,q]$$
$$g^{d^i/b_j} \quad \forall(i,j) \in [2q,q] \text{ with } i \neq q+1$$
$$g^{d^i b_j/b_{j'}^2} \quad \forall(i,j,j') \in [2q,q,q] \text{ with } j \neq j'$$
$$g^{sd^i b_j/b_{j'}}, g^{sd^i b_j/b_{j'}^2} \quad \forall(i,j,j') \in [q,q,q] \text{ with } j \neq j',$$

it is hard for the attacker to distinguish $e(g,g)^{sd^{q+1}} \in \mathbb{G}_T$ from an element which is randomly chosen from $\mathbb{G}_T$.

   An algorithm $\mathcal{A}$ that outputs $\beta \in \{0,1\}$ has advantage ϵ in solving the above assumption if $|\Pr[\mathcal{A}(\boldsymbol{y}, e(g,g)^{sd^{q+1}}) = 0] - \Pr[\mathcal{A}(\boldsymbol{y}, R) = 0]| \geq \epsilon$.

Definition 5. *We say that the q-type assumption holds if no PPT algorithm has a non-negligible advantage in solving the q-type problem.*

We define our l-SDH assumption according to [18, 31].

Assumption 2. *(l-SDH assumption [18, 31]) : Let $\mathbb{G}$ be a bilinear group of prime order p and g be a generator of $\mathbb{G}$, the l-Strong Diffie-Hellman (l-SDH) problem in $\mathbb{G}$ is defined as follows: given a $(l+1)$-tuple $(g, g^x, g^{x^2}, ..., g^{x^l})$ as inputs, output a pair $(c, g^{1/(c+x)}) \in \mathbb{Z}_p \times \mathbb{G}$. An algorithm $\mathcal{A}$ has advantage ϵ in solving l-SDH in $\mathbb{G}$ if $Pr[\mathcal{A}(g, g^x, g^{x^2}, ..., g^{x^l}) = (c, g^{1/(c+x)})] \geq \epsilon$, where the probability is over the random choice of x in $\mathbb{Z}_p^*$ and the random bits consumed by $\mathcal{A}$.*

Definition 6. *We say that the (l, t, ϵ)-SDH assumption holds in $\mathbb{G}$ if no t-time algorithm has advantage at least in solving the l-SDH problem in $\mathbb{G}$.*

3.6   Shamir's $(\bar{t}, \bar{n})$ Threshold Scheme

It is well known for Shamir's $(\bar{t}, \bar{n})$ threshold scheme [34] (or Shamir's secret sharing scheme) in cryptography. The essential idea of that scheme is that $\bar{t}$ points on a $\bar{t} - 1$ degree curve are sufficient to confirm such a curve, that is, $\bar{t}$ points are enough to determine a $\bar{t} - 1$ degree polynomial. For a $(\bar{t}, \bar{n})$ threshold scheme, a secret can be divided into $\bar{n}$ parts (or even more), which are sent to each participant a unique part. All of them can be used to reconstruct the secret. Suppose that the secret is assumed to be an element in a finite field $\mathbb{F}_p^*$. Choose $\bar{t} - 1$ random coefficients $a_1, a_2, \cdots, a_{\bar{t}-2} \in \mathbb{F}_p$ and $a_{\bar{t}-1} \in \mathbb{F}_p^*$ and set the secret in the constant term a_0. Note that, we have such a polynomial: $f(x) = a_0 + a_1 x + a_2 x^2 + \cdots + a_{\bar{t}-1} x^{\bar{t}-1}$. Every participant is given a point (x, y) on the above curve, that is, the input to the polynomial x and its output $y = f(x)$. Given a subset with any $\bar{t}$ points, we can recover the constant term a_0 using the Lagrange interpolation.

4   Our T-LU-CP-ABE System

In this section we propose the construction of our new large universe CP-ABE system with white-box traceability.

4.1   Construction

- $\texttt{Setup}(1^\lambda) \to (pp, msk)$: The algorithm runs the group generator algorithm $\mathfrak{g}(1^\lambda)$ and gets the groups and the bilinear mapping description $GD = (p, \mathbb{G}, \mathbb{G}_T, e)$, where $(\mathbb{G}, \mathbb{G}_T)$ are groups of order p and e is the bilinear mapping. Let $U = \mathbb{Z}_p$ be the attribute universe. The algorithm randomly chooses $g, u, h, w, v \in \mathbb{G}$ and $\alpha, a \in \mathbb{Z}_p$. Besides, the algorithm chooses a probabilistic encryption scheme (Enc, Dec) [35] from a binary string to $\mathbb{Z}_p^*$ with different secret key $\bar{k}_1, \bar{k}_2$. Furthermore, it initializes an instance of Shamir's $(\bar{t}, \bar{n})$ threshold scheme $\mathcal{INS}_{(\bar{t}, \bar{n})}$ [5] [34] and keeps $f(x)$ [6] and $\bar{t} - 1$ points $\{(x_1, y_1), (x_2, y_2), ..., (x_{\bar{t}-1}, y_{\bar{t}-1})\}$ secret. It sets $(GD, g, u, h, w, v, g^a, e(g, g)^\alpha)$ as pp and $(\alpha, a, \bar{k}_1, \bar{k}_2)$ as msk.

- $\texttt{KeyGen}(1^\lambda, pp, msk, id, S = \{A_1, A_2, ..., A_k\} \subseteq \mathbb{Z}_p) \to sk_{id,S}$: The algorithm computes: $x = Enc_{\bar{k}_1}(id), y = f(x), c = Enc_{\bar{k}_2}(x||y)$. Note that the computing result c is not distinguished from a random number [7]. And it randomly chooses $r, r_1, r_2, ...r_k \in \mathbb{Z}_p$. The decryption key $sk_{id,S}$ is set as follows:

$$\langle K = g^{\alpha/(a+c)} w^r, K' = c, L = g^r, L' = g^{ar},$$
$$\{K_{\tau,1} = g^{r_\tau}, K_{\tau,2} = (u^{A_\tau} h)^{r_\tau} v^{-(a+c)r}\}_{\tau \in [k]}\rangle$$

- $\texttt{Encrypt}(1^\lambda, pp, m \in \mathbb{G}_T, (M, \rho) \in (\mathbb{Z}_p^{l \times n}, \mathcal{F}([l] \to \mathbb{Z}_p))) \to ct$: The algorithm takes the public parameters pp, a plaintext message m and randomly chooses $\overrightarrow{y} = (s, y_2, ..., y_n)^{\perp} \in \mathbb{Z}_p^{n \times 1}$, where s is the random secret to be shared according to Subsection 3.3. It gets the vector of the shares $\overrightarrow{\lambda} = (\lambda_1, \lambda_2, ..., \lambda_l)$ by computing the inner product $\lambda_i = M_i \overrightarrow{y}$, where M_i is the i-th row of M. Then it randomly picks l exponents $t_1, t_2, ..., t_l \in \mathbb{Z}_p$. The ciphertext ct is set as follows:

$$\langle (M, \rho), C = m \cdot e(g, g)^{\alpha s}, C_0 = g^s, C_0' = g^{as},$$
$$\{C_{i,1} = w^{\lambda_i} v^{t_i}, C_{i,2} = (u^{\rho(i)} h)^{-t_i}, C_{i,3} = g^{t_i}\}_{i \in [l]}\rangle$$

It outputs the ciphertext ct.

---

[5] In our system, it requires $\bar{n}$ is greater than the number of the total users.

[6] If all of the users register and get the secret keys at the beginning of system initialization, the system could secretly store $f(0)$ instead of the polynomial $f(x)$ since the storage for $f(x)$ is much larger than that of $f(0)$.

[7] Due to the definition of probabilistic encryption, x is not distinguished from a random number. In addition, f is linear function and thus y is also a random number. Therefore, c, combined with x and y and through a probabilistic encryption, can also be a random number.

- $\texttt{Decrypt}(1^\lambda, pp, sk_{id,S}, ct) \to m$ or $\perp$: The algorithm first computes the set of rows in M that produces a share to attributes in S, that is, $I = \{i : \rho(i) \in S\}$. If the attribute set S is not an authorized set of the access policy, then it cannot satisfy the access structure of (M, ρ), the algorithm outputs $\perp$. Otherwise, the algorithm lets $\{\omega_i \in \mathbb{Z}_p\}_{i \in I}$ be a set of constants such that $\sum_{i \in I} \omega_i M_i = (1, 0, ..., 0)$, where M_i is the matrix M's i-th row. Note that $\sum_{i \in I} \omega_i \lambda_i = s$ if the attribute set S is authorized, and there may exists other different ways to choose the values of ω_i to satisfy this. Then it computes:

$$E = e(K, C_0^{K'} C_0') = e(g,g)^{\alpha s} e(w,g)^{(a+c)sr}$$

$$D = \prod_{i \in I} (e(L^{K'} L', C_{i,1}) e(K_{\tau,1}, C_{i,2}) e(K_{\tau,2}, C_{i,3}))^{\omega_i} = e(g,w)^{(a+c)rs}$$

$$F = E/D = e(g,g)^{\alpha s}$$

where τ is the attribute $\rho(i)$'s index in S (it depends on i). It outputs the plaintext $m = C/F$.

Correctness:

$$F = \frac{E}{D} = \frac{e(g,g)^{\alpha s} e(w,g)^{(a+c)sr}}{\prod_{i \in I} D_1 \cdot D_2 \cdot D_3 \cdot D_4 \cdot D_5} = \frac{e(g,g)^{\alpha s} e(w,g)^{(a+c)sr}}{e(g,w)^{(a+c)r \sum_{i \in I} \omega_i \lambda_i}} = e(g,g)^{\alpha s}$$

where

$$D_1 = e(g,w)^{(a+c)r\lambda_i \omega_i}, \quad D_2 = e(g,v)^{(a+c)rt_i \omega_i}, \quad D_3 = e(g, u^{\rho(i)}h)^{-r_\tau t_i \omega_i},$$
$$D_4 = e(u^{\rho(i)}h, g)^{r_\tau t_i \omega_i}, \quad D_5 = e(v,g)^{-(a+c)rt_i \omega_i}.$$

- $\texttt{Trace}(pp, \mathcal{INS}_{(\bar{t},\bar{n})}, msk, sk) \to id$ or $\top$: If the sk is not in the form of $sk = (K, K', L, L', \{K_{\tau,1}, K_{\tau,2}\}_{\tau \in k})$ and can not pass the key sanity check, the algorithm will output $\top$. Otherwise, sk is a well-formed decryption key, and the algorithm will do as follows:

(1) The algorithm extracts $(x^* = x, y^* = y)$ from $x||y = Dec_{\bar{k}_2}(K')$ in sk.
(2) If $(x^* = x, y^* = y) \in \{(x_1, y_1), (x_2, y_2), ..., (x_{\bar{t}-1}, y_{\bar{t}-1})\}$, the algorithm computes $Dec_{\bar{k}_1}(x^*)$ to get id to identify the malicious user (with id). Otherwise, go to (3).
(3) The algorithm recovers the secret a_0^* of $\mathcal{INS}_{(\bar{t},\bar{n})}$ by interpolating with $\bar{t} - 1$ points $\{(x_1, y_1), (x_2, y_2), ..., (x_{\bar{t}-1}, y_{\bar{t}-1})\}$ and $(x^* = x, y^* = y)$. If $a_0^* = f(0)$, it computes $Dec_{\bar{k}_1}(x^*)$ to get id to find out the malicious user. Otherwise, the algorithm outputs $\top$.

Key Sanity Check: $K' \in \mathbb{Z}_p^*, K, L, L', K_{i,1}, K_{i,2} \in \mathbb{G}$ [8].

---

[8] Here only a brief check is needed.

4.2 Selective Security Proof

In the selective security proof, although we can proof that directly based on the Assumption 1 as [11] does, for simplicity, we will reduce the selective security of our T-LU-CP-ABE system to that of Rouselakis and Waters's system in [11] which is proved selectively secure under Assumption 1.

For simplicity, we denote by $\Sigma_{lucpabe}$, $\Sigma_{tlucpabe}$ the LU-CP-ABE system in [11] and our system respectively. Note that the security model of our system $\Sigma_{tlucpabe}$ is almost same with that of the system $\Sigma_{lucpabe}$ in [11], excepting every key query is companied with an explicit identity.

Lemma 1. *[11] If the assumption 1 holds, then the LU-CP-ABE system $\Sigma_{lucpabe}$ is selectively secure.*

Selective security of our new T-LU-CP-ABE:

Lemma 2. *If the LU-CP-ABE system $\Sigma_{lucpabe}$ is selectively secure in the game of [11], then our new T-LU-CP-ABE system $\Sigma_{tlucpabe}$ is selectively secure in the game of Subsection 2.2.*

Due to space limitations, we refer the interested reader to the full version [36] of this paper for the proof of this lemma.

Theorem 1. *If Assumption 1 holds, then our T-LU-CP-ABE system is selectively secure.*

Proof : It follows directly from Lemma 1 and Lemma 2.

4.3 Traceability Proof

In this subsection, we will give the traceability proof of our T-LU-CP-ABE system based on l-SDH assumption. We use a proof method from [18] and [13].

Theorem 2. *If the l-SDH assumption holds, then our T-LU-CP-ABE system is fully traceable provided that $q < l$.*

Due to space limitations, we refer the interested reader to the full version [36] of this paper for the proof of this theorem.

5 Extensions

5.1 Transform from One-Use T-LU-CP-ABE to Multi-Use T-LU-CP-ABE

The construction in our system is a *one-use* T-LU-CP-ABE construction. Since the ρ in our system is an injective function for each access policy associated to a ciphertext. During the row label of the share-generating matrix, the attributes are only used once. This kind of construction is called one-use CP-ABE.

We can extend our new T-LU-CP-ABE system to a *multi-use* system using the encoding technique in [6]: we take k copies of each attribute A instead of a single attribute. Then we have new "attributes": $\{A : 1, ..., A : k\}$. Now we can label a row of the access matrix $\mathbb{A}$ with $\{A : i\}$. Thus the attribute can be used multiple times. Note that the size of the public parameters do not grow linearly with the number of the involved attributes, so that the size of the public parameters will remain the same size under this transformation. Besides the access matrix's size does not change under this transformation either, thus the size of the ciphertext also remains the same size. This makes our T-LU-CP-ABE system more suitable for commercial applications.

5.2   Revocable T-LU-CP-ABE

Through our new T-LU-CP-ABE system proposed in this paper, it is easy to trace the malicious user who leak his/her decryption key for benefits. This evokes another significant issue to be considered: how to revoke the malicious users. Several work has focused on designing revocable ABE [37, 10]. With the technology of ciphertext delegation and piecewise key generation introduced in [10], we can achieve a revocable T-LU-CP-ABE construction. Furthermore, since we make use of the Shamir's $(\bar{t}, \bar{n})$ threshold scheme in the Trace algorithm, the system only need store $\bar{t} - 1$ tuples in system for tracing, rather than an identify table T which contains all users' identifies. This brings an obvious advantage that the system need not update the identify table T when some users are revoked.

6   Conclusion and Future Work

In this work, we have presented a practical large universe CP-ABE system supporting white-box traceability. Specifically, we have achieved the property of white-box traceability in CP-ABE, which could trace the malicious users leaking the partial or modified decryption keys to others for profits. We have also obtained the property of large universe in white-box traceable CP-ABE where the attributes' size is unbounded and the public parameters' size does not grow linearly with the number of attributes. In addition, we optimize the system in tracing the malicious users to cut down the storage cost for traceability and to make the system efficient in the user revocation. Based on the above advantages, our new system could be applied to many scenarios such as pay-TV systems and social networks. As far as we known, this is the first practical CP-ABE system that simultaneously supports white-box traceability and large universe. We have also proved our new system selectively secure in the standard model.

In our future work, we will focus on the stronger notion for traceability named black-box traceability. In that scenario, the malicious users leak their decryption devices instead of decryption keys. Specifically, the malicious users could hide the decryption algorithm by tweaking it, as well as the decryption keys. In this case, due to the fact that the decryption keys and decryption algorithm are both not well-formed, the new system supporting white-box traceability in this paper will fail. It will be our future work to obtain a large universe CP-ABE system, which supports black-box traceability.

There is another important issue about public auditing we need to pay attention to. Suppose a user Bob is identified as a malicious user by the system, but claims to be innocent and framed by the system. It is a big problem to judge whether Bob is in fact innocent or not. In this case, the suspected user does not trust the system and the system needs to provide some evidence persuasive enough to prove that the suspected user is guilty. To address this issue, a public auditor which is played by a trusted third party needs to be introduced. However, the suspected user does not want the public auditor to know the private information since in the `Trace` phase the auditor will obtain Bob's decryption keys and be able to decrypt all the data that Bob has. Achieving a traceable large universe CP-ABE system with public auditors is still an open problem, and we will keep working on it.

Acknowledgements. We are grateful to the anonymous reviewers for their invaluable suggestions. This work is supported by the National Natural Science Foundation of China (Grant No. 61371083, 61373154 and 61033014), the Prioritized Development Projects of the Specialized Research Fund for the Doctoral Program of Higher Education of China (Grant No. 20130073130004) and the Natural Science Foundation of Shanghai of Yang-Fan Plan (Grant No. 14YF1410400).

References

1. Sahai, A., Waters, B.: Fuzzy identity-based encryption. In: Cramer, R. (ed.) EUROCRYPT 2005. LNCS, vol. 3494, pp. 457–473. Springer, Heidelberg (2005)
2. Goyal, V., Pandey, O., Sahai, A., Waters, B.: Attribute-based encryption for fine-grained access control of encrypted data. In: Proceedings of the 13th ACM Conference on Computer and Communications Security, pp. 89–98. ACM (2006)
3. Bethencourt, J., Sahai, A., Waters, B.: Ciphertext-policy attribute-based encryption. In: IEEE Symposium on Security and Privacy, SP 2007, pp. 321–334. IEEE (2007)
4. Ostrovsky, R., Sahai, A., Waters, B.: Attribute-based encryption with non-monotonic access structures. In: Proceedings of the 14th ACM Conference on Computer and Communications Security, pp. 195–203. ACM (2007)
5. Goyal, V., Jain, A., Pandey, O., Sahai, A.: Bounded ciphertext policy attribute based encryption. In: Aceto, L., Damgård, I., Goldberg, L.A., Halldórsson, M.M., Ingólfsdóttir, A., Walukiewicz, I. (eds.) ICALP 2008, Part II. LNCS, vol. 5126, pp. 579–591. Springer, Heidelberg (2008)
6. Lewko, A., Okamoto, T., Sahai, A., Takashima, K., Waters, B.: Fully secure functional encryption: Attribute-based encryption and (hierarchical) inner product encryption. In: Gilbert, H. (ed.) EUROCRYPT 2010. LNCS, vol. 6110, pp. 62–91. Springer, Heidelberg (2010)
7. Waters, B.: Ciphertext-policy attribute-based encryption: An expressive, efficient, and provably secure realization. In: Catalano, D., Fazio, N., Gennaro, R., Nicolosi, A. (eds.) PKC 2011. LNCS, vol. 6571, pp. 53–70. Springer, Heidelberg (2011)

8. Okamoto, T., Takashima, K.: Fully secure functional encryption with general relations from the decisional linear assumption. In: Rabin, T. (ed.) CRYPTO 2010. LNCS, vol. 6223, pp. 191–208. Springer, Heidelberg (2010)

9. Lewko, A., Waters, B.: New proof methods for attribute-based encryption: Achieving full security through selective techniques. In: Safavi-Naini, R., Canetti, R. (eds.) CRYPTO 2012. LNCS, vol. 7417, pp. 180–198. Springer, Heidelberg (2012)

10. Sahai, A., Seyalioglu, H., Waters, B.: Dynamic credentials and ciphertext delegation for attribute-based encryption. In: Safavi-Naini, R., Canetti, R. (eds.) CRYPTO 2012. LNCS, vol. 7417, pp. 199–217. Springer, Heidelberg (2012)

11. Rouselakis, Y., Waters, B.: Practical constructions and new proof methods for large universe attribute-based encryption. In: Proceedings of the 2013 ACM SIGSAC Conference on Computer & Communications Security, pp. 463–474. ACM (2013)

12. Hohenberger, S., Waters, B.: Attribute-based encryption with fast decryption. In: Kurosawa, K., Hanaoka, G. (eds.) PKC 2013. LNCS, vol. 7778, pp. 162–179. Springer, Heidelberg (2013)

13. Liu, Z., Cao, Z., Wong, D.S.: White-box traceable ciphertext-policy attribute-based encryption supporting any monotone access structures. IEEE Transactions on Information Forensics and Security 8(1), 76–88 (2013)

14. Li, J., Ren, K., Kim, K.: A2be: Accountable attribute-based encryption for abuse free access control. IACR Cryptology ePrint Archive 2009, 118 (2009)

15. Li, J., Huang, Q., Chen, X., Chow, S.S., Wong, D.S., Xie, D.: Multi-authority ciphertext-policy attribute-based encryption with accountability. In: Proceedings of the 6th ACM Symposium on Information, Computer and Communications Security, pp. 386–390. ACM (2011)

16. Liu, Z., Cao, Z., Wong, D.S.: Blackbox traceable cp-abe: how to catch people leaking their keys by selling decryption devices on ebay. In: Proceedings of the 2013 ACM SIGSAC Conference on Computer & Communications Security, pp. 475–486. ACM (2013)

17. Lewko, A., Waters, B.: Unbounded hibe and attribute-based encryption. In: Paterson, K.G. (ed.) EUROCRYPT 2011. LNCS, vol. 6632, pp. 547–567. Springer, Heidelberg (2011)

18. Boneh, D., Boyen, X.: Short signatures without random oracles. In: Cachin, C., Camenisch, J.L. (eds.) EUROCRYPT 2004. LNCS, vol. 3027, pp. 56–73. Springer, Heidelberg (2004)

19. Cheung, L., Newport, C.: Provably secure ciphertext policy abe. In: Proceedings of the 14th ACM Conference on Computer and Communications Security, pp. 456–465. ACM (2007)

20. Attrapadung, N., Libert, B., de Panafieu, E.: Expressive key-policy attribute-based encryption with constant-size ciphertexts. In: Catalano, D., Fazio, N., Gennaro, R., Nicolosi, A. (eds.) PKC 2011. LNCS, vol. 6571, pp. 90–108. Springer, Heidelberg (2011)

21. Lewko, A., Waters, B.: New techniques for dual system encryption and fully secure hibe with short ciphertexts. In: Micciancio, D. (ed.) TCC 2010. LNCS, vol. 5978, pp. 455–479. Springer, Heidelberg (2010)

22. Chase, M.: Multi-authority attribute based encryption. In: Vadhan, S.P. (ed.) TCC 2007. LNCS, vol. 4392, pp. 515–534. Springer, Heidelberg (2007)

23. Chase, M., Chow, S.S.: Improving privacy and security in multi-authority attribute-based encryption. In: Proceedings of the 16th ACM Conference on Computer and Communications Security, pp. 121–130. ACM (2009)

24. Lewko, A., Waters, B.: Decentralizing attribute-based encryption. In: Paterson, K.G. (ed.) EUROCRYPT 2011. LNCS, vol. 6632, pp. 568–588. Springer, Heidelberg (2011)

25. Parno, B., Raykova, M., Vaikuntanathan, V.: How to delegate and verify in public: Verifiable computation from attribute-based encryption. In: Cramer, R. (ed.) TCC 2012. LNCS, vol. 7194, pp. 422–439. Springer, Heidelberg (2012)

26. Green, M., Hohenberger, S., Waters, B.: Outsourcing the decryption of abe ciphertexts. In: USENIX Security Symposium, p. 3 (2011)

27. Lewko, A.: Tools for simulating features of composite order bilinear groups in the prime order setting. In: Pointcheval, D., Johansson, T. (eds.) EUROCRYPT 2012. LNCS, vol. 7237, pp. 318–335. Springer, Heidelberg (2012)

28. Okamoto, T., Takashima, K.: Homomorphic encryption and signatures from vector decomposition. In: Galbraith, S.D., Paterson, K.G. (eds.) Pairing 2008. LNCS, vol. 5209, pp. 57–74. Springer, Heidelberg (2008)

29. Okamoto, T., Takashima, K.: Hierarchical predicate encryption for inner-products. In: Matsui, M. (ed.) ASIACRYPT 2009. LNCS, vol. 5912, pp. 214–231. Springer, Heidelberg (2009)

30. Okamoto, T., Takashima, K.: Fully secure functional encryption with general relations from the decisional linear assumption. In: Rabin, T. (ed.) CRYPTO 2010. LNCS, vol. 6223, pp. 191–208. Springer, Heidelberg (2010)

31. Goyal, V.: Reducing trust in the pkg in identity based cryptosystems. In: Menezes, A. (ed.) CRYPTO 2007. LNCS, vol. 4622, pp. 430–447. Springer, Heidelberg (2007)

32. Goyal, V., Lu, S., Sahai, A., Waters, B.: Black-box accountable authority identity-based encryption. In: Proceedings of the 15th ACM Conference on Computer and Communications Security, pp. 427–436. ACM (2008)

33. Beimel, A.: Secure schemes for secret sharing and key distribution. PhD thesis, Israel Institute of Technology, Technion, Haifa, Israel (1996)

34. Shamir, A.: How to share a secret. Communications of the ACM 22(11), 612–613 (1979)

35. Goldwasser, S., Micali, S.: Probabilistic encryption. Journal of Computer and System Sciences 28(2), 270–299 (1984)

36. Ning, J., Cao, Z., Dong, X., Wei, L., Lin, X.: Large universe ciphertext-policy attribute-based encryption with white-box traceability. Cryptology ePrint Archive, Report 2014/471 (2014), http://eprint.iacr.org/

37. Qian, J.L., Dong, X.L.: Fully secure revocable attribute-based encryption. Journal of Shanghai Jiaotong University (Science) 16, 490–496 (2011)

PPDCP-ABE: Privacy-Preserving Decentralized Ciphertext-Policy Attribute-Based Encryption

Jinguang Han[1], Willy Susilo[2], Yi Mu[2], Jianying Zhou[3], Man Ho Au[2]

[1] Jiangsu Provincial Key Laboratory of E-Business, Nanjing University of Finance and Economics, Nanjing, Jiangsu 210003, China
[2] School of Computer Science and Software Engineering, University of Wollongong, Wollongong, NSW 2522, Australia
[3] Infocomm Security Department, Institute for Infocomm Research, 1 Fusionopolis Way, Singapore 138632, Singapore
jghan22@gmail.com, {wsusilo,ymu,aau}@uow.edu.au, jyzhou@i2r.a-star.edu.sg

Abstract. Cipher-policy attribute-based encryption (CP-ABE) is a more efficient and flexible encryption system as the encryptor can control the access structure when encrypting a message. In this paper, we propose a privacy-preserving decentralized CP-ABE (PPDCP-ABE) scheme where the central authority is not required, namely each authority can work independently without the cooperation to initialize the system. Meanwhile, a user can obtain secret keys from multiple authorities without releasing his global identifier (GID) and attributes to them. This is contrasted to the previous privacy-preserving multi-authority ABE (PPMA-ABE) schemes where a user can obtain secret keys from multiple authorities with them knowing his attributes and a central authority is required. However, some sensitive attributes can also release the user's identity information. Hence, contemporary PPMA-ABE schemes cannot fully protect users' privacy as multiple authorities can cooperate to identifier a user by collecting and analyzing his attributes. Therefore, it remains a challenging and important work to construct a PPMA-ABE scheme where the central authority is not required and both the identifiers and the attributes are considered.

Keywords: CP-ABE, decentralization, privacy.

1 Introduction

In network society, users can be identified by their distinct attributes. For example, European electronic identity cards often contain the attributes: nationality, sex, civil status, hair and eye color, and applicable minority status. These attributes are either binary or discrete numbers from a pre-defined finite sets [1]. Especially, they are very privacy-sensitive and require a selective disclosure of one while hiding others completely; otherwise, a user can be identified and impersonated by collecting and analyzing his attributes.

In practical applications, we often share data with some expressive attributes without knowing who will receive it. To resolve this problem, Sahai and Waters

M. Kutyłowski and J. Vaidya (Eds.): ESORICS 2014, Part II, LNCS 8713, pp. 73–90, 2014.
© Springer International Publishing Switzerland 2014

[2] introduced the seminal concept of attribute-based encryption (ABE). In this new encryption system, there is a central authority who monitors the universal attributes and distributes secrete keys to users accordingly. A user can decrypt a ciphertext if and only if there is a match between the attributes which he holds and the attributes listed in the ciphertext. Since it can protect the confidentiality of sensitive data and express flexible access control, ABE schemes have been focused extensively [3–8].

To reduce the trust on the central authority, Chase [9] proposed a multi-authority ABE (MA-ABE) scheme where multiple authorities must cooperate with the central authority to initialize the system. Then, Lewko and Waters [10] proposed a new MA-ABE scheme called decentralized CP-ABE (DCP-ABE) where multiple authorities can work independently without a central authority or any cooperation among them.

1.1   Privacy in Multi-Authority Attribute-Based Encryption

In an MA-ABE scheme, malicious users may combine their secret keys to create a new secret key if the multiple authorities work independently [9]. For example, suppose that there is a ciphertext which can be decrypted by the attributes monitored by the authorities A_1 and A_2. If Alice obtains secret keys from A_1 and Bob obtains secret keys from A_2, they can collaborate to decrypt the ciphertext. To overcome this hurdle, each user in the system [9] must be designated an unique global identifier (GID) which is known by each authority. When generating secret keys for the user, the authorities tie them to his GID.

Privacy issues in MA-ABE are the primary concern of users as the authorities can personate the target user if they know his attributes. Some schemes towards solving this problem have been proposed, but they cannot provide a complete solution, because, in all these schemes, only the privacy of the GID has been considered. Currently, there is no any scheme addressing the privacy issue of the attributes in MA-ABE schemes. However, it is extremely important as a user can be identified by some sensitive attributes. For example, suppose that the Head of the Department of Computer Science is Bob. Given two sets of attributes S_1={Position="Header", Department="CS", Sex="Male"} and S_2= {Position="PhD Student", Department="CS", Sex="Male"}, we can guess S_1 is the attributes of Bob even if we do not know his GID. This clearly shows that controlled release of sensitive attributes is necessary.

1.2   Our Contributions

In this paper, we propose a privacy-preserving decentralized CP-ABE (PPDCP-ABE) scheme. In our scheme, any authority can dynamically join or leave the system, and there is no any requirement for the central authority or interactions among multiple authorities. As a notable feature, each authority can work independently, while other authorities do not need to change their secret keys and reinitialize the system when an authority joins or leaves the system. Each authority monitors a set of attributes and distributes secret keys to users accordingly. To resist the collusion attacks, user's secret keys are tied to his GID. Especially, a user can obtain secret keys for his attributes from multiple authorities without revealing any information about his GID and attributes to the authorities. Therefore, it provides stronger privacy compared to the previous PPMA-ABE schemes where only the identifier is protected. To encrypt a message, the encryptor selects an access structure for each authority and encrypts the message under them so that only the users whose attributes satisfy all the access structures can decrypt the ciphertext and obtain the plaintext. Compared to the existing decentralized ABE scheme [10] which was constructed in the random oracle model, our scheme is designed in the standard model. To the best of our knowledge, it is the *first* PPDCP-ABE scheme where both the identifiers and attributes are considered.

1.3   Organization

The remainder of this paper is organized as follows. In Section 2, the related work is introduced. We describe the preliminaries which are used throughout this paper in Section 3. In Section 4, we first construct a DCP-ABE scheme, and then propose a privacy-preserving key extract algorithm for it. Finally, Section 5 concludes this paper.

2   Related Work

In this section, the related work is introduced.

2.1   Attribute-Based Encryption

Introduced by Sahai and Waters [2], attribute-based encryption (ABE) is a new encryption system where both the ciphertext and the secret key are labeled with a set of attributes. A user can decrypt a ciphertext if and only if there is a match between the attributes listed in the ciphertext and the attributes held by the user. Currently, ABE schemes can be classified into two types: key-policy ABE (KP-ABE) and cipher-policy ABE (CP-ABE).

KP-ABE. In these schemes, an access structure is embedded in the secret keys, while the ciphertext is associated with a set of attributes [2, 9, 11, 5, 6, 12].

CP-ABE. In these schemes, the secret keys are associated with a set of attributes, while an access structure is embedded in the ciphertext [3, 4, 13].

In CP-ABE schemes, the encryptor can freely determine the access structure, while, in KP-ABE schemes, it is decided by the authority.

2.2   Multi-Authority Attribute-Based Encryption

In the work [2], Sahai and Waters left an open problem, namely how to construct an ABE scheme where the secret keys can be obtained from multiple authorities so that users can reduce the trust on the central authority. Chase [9] answered this question affirmatively by proposing an MA-ABE scheme. The technical hurdle in designing an MA-ABE scheme is to resist the collusion attacks. To overcome this hurdle, GID was introduced to tie all the user's secret keys together. In [9], there is a central authority, and multiple authorities must interact to initialize the system.

Based on the distributed key generation (DKG) protocol [14] and the joint zero secret sharing (JZSS) protocol [15], Lin *et al.* [16] proposed an MA-ABE scheme where the cental authority is not required. To initialize the system, the multiple authorities must cooperatively execute the DKG protocol and the JZSS protocol twice and k times, respectively, where k is the degree of the polynomial selected by each authority. Each authority must maintain $k + 2$ secret keys. This scheme is k-resilient, namely the scheme is secure if and only if the number of the colluding users is no more than k, and k must be fixed in the setup stage.

Müller *et al.* [17] proposed a distributed CP-ABE scheme which was proven to be secure in the generic group [3], instead of reducing to a complexity assumption. Furthermore, a central authority is required to generate the global key and issue secret keys to users.

Liu *et al.* [18] proposed a fully secure multi-authority CP-ABE scheme in the standard model. This scheme was derived from the CP-ABE scheme [7]. In this scheme, there are multiple central authorities and attribute authorities. The central authorities issue identity-related keys to users, while the attribute authorities issue attribute-related keys to users. Prior to possessing attribute keys from the attribute authorities, the user must obtain secret keys from the multiple central authorities. This MA-ABE scheme was designed in the composite order ($N = p_1 p_2 p_3$) bilinear group.

Lekwo and Waters [10] proposed a new MA-ABE scheme named decentralizing CP-ABE (DCP-ABE) scheme. This scheme improved the previous MA-ABE schemes that require collaborations among multiple authorities to conduct the system setup. In this scheme, no cooperation between the multiple authorities is required in the setup stage and the key generation stage, and there is no central authority. Notably, an authority in this scheme can join or leave the system freely without reinitializing the system. The scheme was constructed in the composite order ($N = p_1 p_2 p_3$) bilinear group, and achieves full (adaptive) security in the random oracle model. They also pointed out two methods to create a prime order group variant of their scheme. Nevertheless, the authorities can collect a user's attributes by tracing his GID.

Considering the privacy issues in MA-ABE schemes, Chase and Chow proposed [11] a new MA-ABE scheme which improved the previous scheme [9] and removed the need of a central authority. In previous MA-ABE schemes [9, 16], to obtain the corresponding secret keys, a user must submit his GID to each authority. So, multiple authorities can cooperate to collect the user's attributes by it. In [11], Chase and Chow provided an anonymous key issuing protocol for the GID where the 2-party secure computing technique is employed. As a result, a group of authorities cannot cooperate to pool the users attributes by tracing his

GID. However, the multiple authorities must collaborate to setup the system. Furthermore, each pair of authorities must execute the 2-party key exchange protocol to share the seeds of the selected pseudo random functions (PRFs) [19]. This scheme is $N - 2$ tolerant, namely the scheme is secure if and only if the number of the corrupted authorities is no more than $N - 2$, where N is the number of the authorities in the system. Although the authorities cannot know any information about the user's GID, they can know the user's attributes. Chase and Chow [11] also left an open challenging research problem on how to construct a privacy-preserving MA-ABE scheme without the need of cooperations among authorities.

Li [20] proposed a multi-authority CP-ABE (MACP-ABE) scheme with accountability, where the anonymous key issuing protocol [11] was employed. In this scheme, a user can be identified when he shared his secret keys with others. Notably, the multiple authorities must initialize the system interactively.

Recently, Han *et al.* [12] proposed a privacy-preserving decentralized KP-ABE (PPDKP-ABE) scheme. In this scheme, multiple authorities can work independently without any cooperation. Especially, the central authority is not required and a user can obtain secret keys from multiple authorities without releasing anything about his GID to them. Qian *et al.* [21] proposed a privacy-preserving decentralized CP-ABE (PPDCP-ABE) scheme which can support simple access structures. Nevertheless, similar to that in [11], the authorities in these schemes can know the user's attributes.

2.3   Anonymous Credential

In an anonymous credential system [22], an identity provider can issue a credential to a user, which includes the user's pseudonym and attributes. By using it, the user can prove in zero knowledge to a third party that he obtains a credential containing the given pseudonym and attributes without releasing any other information. In a multiple-show credential system [23], a credential can be demonstrated an arbitrary number of times, and cannot be linked to each other.

Therefore, in our construction, we assume that each user has obtained an anonymous credential including his GID and attributes. Then, he can prove in zero knowledge to the multiple authorities that he has a GID and holds the corresponding attributes using the anonymous credential technique.

3   Preliminaries

In this section, we introduce the preliminaries used throughout this paper.

In the remainder, by $\alpha \xleftarrow{\$} A$, we denote that α is selected from A randomly. Especially, $\alpha \xleftarrow{\$} A$ stands for that α is selected from A uniformly at random if A is a finite set. By $|A|$, we denote the cardinality of a finite set A. A function $\epsilon : \mathbb{Z} \to R$ is negligible if for any $z \in \mathbb{Z}$ there exists a k such that $\epsilon(x) < \frac{1}{x^z}$ when $x > k$. By $A(x) \to y$, we denote that y is computed by running the algorithm A with input x. $\mathcal{KG}(1^\kappa)$ denotes a secret-public key pair generator which takes as input a security parameter 1^κ and outputs a secret-public key pair. We denote $\mathbb{Z}_p$ as a finite field with prime order p. Finally, by $R \xrightarrow{r} S$ and $R \xleftarrow{s} S$, we denote that the party R sends r to the party S and the party S sends s to the party R, respectively.

3.1 Complexity Assumption

Let $\mathbb{G}$ and $\mathbb{G}_\tau$ be two cyclic groups with prime order p, and g be a generator of $\mathbb{G}$. A map $e : \mathbb{G} \times \mathbb{G} \to \mathbb{G}_\tau$ is a bilinear group if the following properties can be satisfied:

1. Bilinearity. For all $a, b \in \mathbb{Z}_p$ and $u, v \in \mathbb{G}$, $e(u^a, v^b) = e(u^b, v^a) = e(u, v)^{ab}$.
2. Nondegeneracy. $e(g, g) \neq 1_\tau$ where 1_τ is the identity of the group $\mathbb{G}_\tau$.
3. Computability. For all $u, v \in \mathbb{G}$, there exists an efficient algorithm to compute $e(u, v)$.

Let $\mathcal{GG}(1^\kappa)$ be a bilinear group generator, which takes as input a security parameter 1^κ and outputs a bilinear group $(e, p, \mathbb{G}, \mathbb{G}_\tau)$ with prime order p and a bilinear map $e : \mathbb{G} \times \mathbb{G} \to \mathbb{G}_\tau$.

Definition 1. (q-Strong Diffie-Hellman (q-SDH) Assumption [24]) *Let $x \xleftarrow{\$} \mathbb{Z}_p$, $\mathcal{GG}(1^\kappa) \to (e, p, \mathbb{G}, \mathbb{G}_\tau)$ and g be a generator of $\mathbb{G}$. Given a $(q+1)$-tuple $\overrightarrow{y} = (g, g^x, g^{x^2}, \cdots, g^{x^q})$, we say that the q-SDH assumption holds on $(e, p, \mathbb{G}, \mathbb{G}_\tau)$ if no probabilistic polynomial-time adversary $\mathcal{A}$ can output $(c, g^{\frac{1}{x+c}})$ with the advantage*

$$Adv_\mathcal{A} = \Pr[\mathcal{A}(\overrightarrow{y}) \to (c, g^{\frac{1}{x+c}})] \geq \epsilon(k)$$

where $c \in \mathbb{Z}_p$ and the probability is token over the random choices $x \xleftarrow{\$} \mathbb{Z}_p$ and the random bits consumed by $\mathcal{A}$.

Definition 2. (Decisional q-Parallel Bilinear Diffie-Hellman Exponent (q-PBDHE) Assumption [8]) *Let $a, s, b_1, \cdots, b_q \xleftarrow{\$} \mathbb{Z}_p$, $\mathcal{GG}(1^\kappa) \to (e, p, \mathbb{G}, \mathbb{G}_\tau)$ and g be a generator of $\mathbb{G}$. Given a tuple $\overrightarrow{y} =$*

$$g, g^s, g^a, \cdots, g^{(a^q)}, g^{(a^{q+2})}, \cdots, g^{(a^{2q})}$$

$$\forall_{1 \leq j \leq q} \quad g^{s \cdot b_j}, g^{\frac{a}{b_j}}, \cdots, g^{(\frac{a^q}{b_j})}, g^{(\frac{a^{q+2}}{b_j})}, \cdots, g^{(\frac{a^{2q}}{b_j})}$$

$$\forall_{1 \leq j,k \leq q, k \neq j} \quad g^{\frac{a \cdot s \cdot b_k}{b_j}}, \cdots, g^{(\frac{a^q \cdot s \cdot b_k}{b_j})},$$

we say that the decisional q-PBDHE assumption hold on $(e, p, \mathbb{G}, \mathbb{G}_\tau)$ if no probabilistic polynomial-time adversary $\mathcal{A}$ can distinguish $(\overrightarrow{y}, e(g, g)^{a^{q+1}s})$ from $(\overrightarrow{y}, R)$ with the advantage

$$Adv_\mathcal{A} = \left| \Pr[\mathcal{A}(\overrightarrow{y}, e(g, g)^{a^{q+1}s}) = 1] - \Pr[\mathcal{A}(\overrightarrow{y}, R) = 1] \right| \geq \epsilon(k),$$

where $R \xleftarrow{\$} \mathbb{G}_\tau$ and the probability is token over the random choices of $a, s, b_1, \cdots, b_q \xleftarrow{\$} \mathbb{Z}_p$ and the bits consumed by $\mathcal{A}$.

3.2 Building Blocks

In this paper, the following building blocks are adopted.

Definition 3. (Access Structure [25]) *Let* $\mathcal{P} = (P_1, P_2, \cdots, P_n)$ *be n parties. A collection* $\mathbb{A} \subseteq 2^{\{P_1, P_2, \cdots, P_n\}}$ *is monotonic if $B \in \mathbb{A}$ and $B \subseteq C$, then $C \in \mathbb{A}$. An access structure (respectively monotonic access structure) is a collection (respectively monotonic collection) $\mathbb{A}$ of the non-empty subset of $(P_1, P_2, \cdots, P_n)$, i.e., $\mathbb{A} \subseteq 2^{\{P_1, P_2, \cdots, P_n\}} \setminus \{\phi\}$. A set P is called an authorized set if $P \in \mathbb{A}$; otherwise P is an unauthorized set.*

Definition 4. (Linear Secret Sharing Schemes [25]) *A secret sharing scheme $\prod$ over a set of parties $\mathcal{P}$ is called linear (over $\mathbb{Z}_p$) if it satisfies the following properties:*

1. *The shares for each party form a vector over $\mathbb{Z}_p$.*

2. *For $\prod$, there is a matrix M with ℓ rows and n columns called the share-generating matrix. For $x = 1, 2, \cdots, \ell$, the ith row is labeled by a party $\rho(i)$ where $\rho : \{1, 2, \cdots, \ell\} \to \mathbb{Z}_p$. When we consider the vector $\overrightarrow{v} = (s, v_2, \cdots, v_n)$, where $s \in \mathbb{Z}_p$ is the secret to be shared and $v_2, \cdots, v_n \in \mathbb{Z}_p$ are randomly selected, then $M \overrightarrow{v}$ is the vector of the ℓ shares according to $\prod$. The share $M_i \overrightarrow{v}$ belongs to the party $\rho(i)$, where M_i is the ith row of M.*

Linear reconstruction property. Let S be an authorized set and $\mathcal{I} = \{i | \rho(i) \in S\}$. Then, there exist constants $\{\omega_i \in \mathbb{Z}_p\}_{i \in \mathcal{I}}$ such that, for any valid shares λ_i according to $\prod$, we have $\sum_{i \in \mathcal{I}} \omega_i \lambda_i = s$. The constants $\{\omega_i\}_{i \in \mathcal{I}}$ can be computed in polynomial time with the size of share-generating matrix M.

Commitment Schemes. A commitment scheme consists of the following algorithms.

Setup(1^κ) $\to$ *params*. This algorithm takes as input a security parameter 1^κ, and outputs the public parameters *params*.

Commit(*params*, m) $\to$ (*com*, *decom*). This algorithm takes as input the public parameters *params* and a message m, and outputs a commitment *com* and a decommitment *decom*. *decom* can be used to decommit *com* to m.

Decommit(*params*, m, *com*, *decom*) $\to \{0, 1\}$. This algorithm takes as input the public parameters *params*, the message m, the commitment *com* and the decommitment *decom*, and outputs 1 if *decom* can decommit *com* to m; otherwise, it outputs 0.

A commitment scheme should provide two properties: *hiding* and *binding*. The hiding property requires that the message m keeps unreleased until the user releases it later. The binding property requires that only the value *decom* can be used to decommit the commitment *com* to m.

In this paper, we use the Pedersen commitment scheme [26] which is a perfectly hiding commitment scheme and is based on the discrete logarithm assumption. This scheme works as follows. Let $\mathbb{G}$ be a cyclic group with prime order p, and $g_0, g_1, \cdots, g_k$ be generators of $\mathbb{G}$. To commit a tuple of messages $m_1, m_2, \cdots, m_k$, the user selects $r \xleftarrow{\$} \mathbb{Z}_p$, and computes $R = g_0^r g_1^{m_1} g_2^{m_2} \cdots g_k^{m_k}$. Then, the user can use r to decommit the commitment R.

Proof of Knowledge. We use the notion introduced by Camenisch and Stadler [27] to prove statements about discrete logarithm. By

$$\text{PoK}\left\{(\alpha, \beta, \gamma) : y = g^\alpha h^\beta \wedge \tilde{y} = \tilde{g}^\alpha \tilde{h}^\gamma\right\},$$

we denote a zero knowledge proof of knowledge of integers α, β and γ such that $y = g^\alpha h^\beta$ and $\tilde{y} = \tilde{g}^\alpha \tilde{h}^\gamma$ hold on the group $\mathbb{G} = \langle g \rangle = \langle h \rangle$ and $\tilde{\mathbb{G}} = \langle g \rangle = \langle h \rangle$, respectively. Conventionally, the values in the parenthesis denote the knowledge that is being proven, while the rest of the values are known by the verifier. There exists an extractor that can be used to rewind the knowledge from the successful prover.

Set-Membership Proof. Camenisch *et al.* [28] proposed a set membership proof scheme. This scheme works as follows. Let $\mathcal{GG}(1^\kappa) \rightarrow (e, p, \mathbb{G}, \mathbb{G}_\tau)$, and g, h be generators of $\mathbb{G}$.

1. The verifier picks up $x \xleftarrow{\$} \mathbb{Z}_p$, and computes $Y = g^x$ and $T_i = g^{\frac{1}{x+i}}$ for $i \in \Phi$, where $\Phi \subseteq \mathbb{Z}_p$ is a finite set. Then, it sends $\{Y, (T_i)_{i \in \Phi}\}$ to the prover.
2. To prove $\sigma \in \Phi$, the prover selects $v, s, t, r, k \xleftarrow{\$} \mathbb{Z}_p$, and computes $C = g^\sigma h^r$, $D = g^s h^k$, $V = g^{\frac{v}{x+\sigma}}$ and $A = e(V, g)^{-s} \cdot e(g, g)^t$. Then, it sends (C, D, V, A) to the verifier.
3. The verifier selects $c \xleftarrow{\$} \mathbb{Z}_p$, and sends it to the prover.
4. The prover computes $z_\sigma = s - c\sigma$, $z_r = k - cr$ and $z_v = t - cv$, and sends (z_σ, z_k, z_t) to the verifier.
5. The verifier verifies $D \stackrel{?}{=} C^c g^{z_\sigma} h^{z_r}$ and $A \stackrel{?}{=} e(Y, v)^c \cdot e(V, g)^{-z_\sigma} \cdot e(g, g)^{z_r}$.

Theorem 1. *This protocol is a zero-knowledge argument of set-membership proof for a set Φ if the $|\Phi|$-SDH assumption holds on the bilinear group $(e, p, \mathbb{G}, \mathbb{G}_\tau)$ [28].*

3.3 DCP-ABE: Decentralized Cipher-Policy Attribute-Based Encryption

A DCP-ABE scheme consists of the following five algorithms.

Global Setup(1^κ) $\rightarrow$ *params*. The global setup algorithm takes as input a security parameter 1^κ, and outputs the public parameter *params*. Suppose that there are N authorities $\{\breve{A}_1, \breve{A}_2, \cdots, \breve{A}_N\}$, and each authority $\breve{A}_i$ monitors a set of attributes $\tilde{A}_i$. Each user U has a unique global identifier GID_U and holds a set of attributes $\tilde{U}$.

Authority Setup(1^κ) $\rightarrow (SK_i, PK_i)$. Each authority $\breve{A}_i$ takes as input the security parameter 1^κ, and runs the authority setup algorithm to generate its secret-public key pair (SK_i, PK_i), where $\mathcal{KG}(1^\kappa) \rightarrow (SK_i, PK_i)$.

Encrypt$(params, \mathcal{M}, (M_i, \rho_i, PK_i)_{i\in\mathcal{I}}) \to CT$. The encryption algorithm takes as input the public parameter $params$, a message $\mathcal{M}$, a set of access structures $(M_i, \rho_i)_{i\in\mathcal{I}}$ and a set of public keys $(PK_i)_{i\in\mathcal{I}}$, and outputs the ciphertext CT.

KeyGen$(params, SK_i, GID_U, \tilde{U} \cap \tilde{A}_i) \to SK_U^i$. Each authority $\check{A}_i$ runs the key generation algorithm with inputs of the public parameter $params$, his secret key SK_i, a user's global identifier GID_U and a set of attributes $\tilde{U} \cap \tilde{A}_i$ to generate a secret key SK_U^i for U.

Decrypt$(params, GID, (SK_U^i)_{i\in\mathcal{I}}, CT) \to \mathcal{M}$. The decryption algorithm takes as input the public parameter $params$, the user's globe identifier GID_U, the secret keys $(SK_U^i)_{i\in\mathcal{I}}$ and the ciphertext CT, and outputs the message $\mathcal{M}$.

Definition 5. *A decentralized cipher-policy attribute-based encryption is correct if*

$$\Pr\left[\begin{array}{l|l} \text{Decrypt}(params, & \text{Global Setup}(1^\kappa) \to params; \\ GID, (SK_U^i)_{i\in\mathcal{I}}, & \text{Authority Setup}(1^\kappa) \to (SK_i, Pk_i); \\ CT) \to \mathcal{M} & \text{Encrypt}(params, \mathcal{M}, (M_i, \rho_i, PK_i)_{i\in\mathcal{I}}) \to CT; \\ & \text{KeyGen}(params, SK_i, GID_U, \tilde{U} \cap \tilde{A}_i) \to SK_U^i \end{array}\right] = 1$$

where the probability is token over the random bits consumed by all the algorithms in the scheme.

3.4 Security Model of Decentralized Cipher-Policy Attribute-Based Encryption

We use the following game to define the security model of DCP-ABE schemes, which is executed between a challenger and an adversary $\mathcal{A}$. This model is called selective-access structure model, and is similar to that introduced in [9, 11, 12, 10, 8].

Initialization. The adversary $\mathcal{A}$ submits a list of corrupted authorities $\mathfrak{A} = \{\check{A}_i\}_{i\in\mathcal{I}}$ and a set of access structures $\mathbb{A} = \{M_i^*, \rho_i^*\}_{i\in\mathcal{I}^*}$, where $\mathcal{I} \subseteq \{1, 2, \cdots, N\}$ and $\mathcal{I}^* \subseteq \{1, 2, \cdots, N\}$. There should be at lease an access structure $(M^*, \rho^*) \in \mathbb{A}$ which cannot be satisfied by the attributes monitored by the authorities in $\mathfrak{A}$ and the attributes selected by $\mathcal{A}$ to query secrete keys.

Global Setup. The challenger runs the Global Setup algorithm to generate the public parameters $params$, and sends them to $\mathcal{A}$.

Authority Setup. There are two cases.

1. For the authority $\check{A}_i \subseteq \mathfrak{A}$, the challenger runs the Authority Setup algorithm to generate the secret-public key pair (SK_i, PK_i), and sends them to $\mathcal{A}$.
2. For the authority $\check{A}_i \nsubseteq \mathfrak{A}$, the challenger runs the Authority Setup algorithm to generate the secret-public key pair (SK_i, PK_i), and sends the public key PK_i to $\mathcal{A}$.

Phase 1. $\mathcal{A}$ can query secret key for a user U with an identifier GID_U and a set of attributes $\tilde{U}$. The challenger runs the KeyGen algorithm to generate a secret key SK_U, and sends it to $\mathcal{A}$. This query can be made adaptively and repeatedly.

Challenge. $\mathcal{A}$ submits two messages $\mathcal{M}_0$ and $\mathcal{M}_1$ with the same length. The challenger flips an unbiased coin with $\{0,1\}$, and obtains a bit $b \in \{0,1\}$. Then, the challenger runs $\mathsf{Encrypt}(parmas, \mathcal{M}_b, (M_i^*, \rho^*, PK_i)_{i \in \mathcal{I}^*})$ to generate the challenged ciphertext CT^*, and sends CT^* to $\mathcal{A}$.

Phase 2. Phase 1 is repeated.

Guess. $\mathcal{A}$ outputs his guess b' on b. $\mathcal{A}$ wins the game if $b' = b$.

Definition 6. (*Selective-Access Structure Secure DCP-ABE (IND-sAS-CPA)*) *A decentralized cipher-policy attribute-based encryption (DCP-ABE) scheme is $(T, q, \epsilon(\kappa))$ secure in the selective-access structure model if no probably polynomial-time adversary $\mathcal{A}$ making q secret key queries can win the above game with the advantage*

$$Adv_{\mathcal{A}}^{DCP-ABE} = \left| \Pr[b' = b] - \frac{1}{2} \right| > \epsilon(\kappa)$$

where the probability is token over all the bits consumed by the challenger and the adversary.

3.5 PPDCP-ABE: Privacy-Preserving Decentralized Cipher-Policy Attribute-Based Encryption

A PPDCP-ABE has the same algorithms Global Setup, Authority Setup, Encrypt and Decrypt with the DCP-ABE scheme. The main difference is that we replace the KeyGen algorithm with a privacy-preserving key generation algorithm PP-KeyGen. Considering privacy issues, the authorities cannot know both the user's identifier and attributes in PPDCP-ABE schemes. This is motivated by the blind IBE schemes [29, 30]. The PPKeyGen algorithm is formally defined as follows.

$\mathsf{PPKeyGen}(U(params, GID_U, \tilde{U}, PK_i, decom_i, (decom_{i,j})_{a_{i,j} \in \tilde{U} \cap \tilde{A}_i}) \leftrightarrow \breve{A}_i(params, SK_i, PK_i, com_i, (com_{i,j})_{a_{i,j} \in \cap \tilde{A}_i})) \rightarrow (SK_U^i, \mathsf{empty})$. This is an interactive algorithm executed between a user U and an authority $\breve{A}_i$. U runs the commitment algorithm $\mathsf{Commit}(params, GID_U) \rightarrow (com_i, decom_i)$ and $\mathsf{Commit}(params, a_{i,j}) \rightarrow (com_{i,j}, decom_{i,j})$ for the attribute $a_{i,j} \in \tilde{U} \cap \tilde{A}_i$, and sends $(com_i, (com_{i,j})_{a_{i,j} \in \cap \tilde{A}_i})$ to the authority $\breve{A}_i$. Then, U and $\breve{A}_i$ take as input $(params, GID_U, \tilde{U}, PK_i, decom_i, (decom_{i,j})_{a_{i,j} \in \tilde{U} \cap \tilde{A}_i})$ and $(params, SK_i, PK_i, com_i, (com_{i,j})_{a_{i,j} \in \cap \tilde{A}_i})$, respectively. If $\mathsf{Decommit}(params, GID_U, com_i, dcom_i) = 1$ and $\mathsf{Decommit}(params, a_{i,j}, com_{i,j}, decom_{i,j}) = 1$, this algorithm outputs a secret key SK_U^i for U and an empty bit empty for $\breve{A}_i$; otherwise, it outputs $(\bot, \bot)$ to indicate that there are error messages.

3.6   Security Model of Privacy-Preserving Decentralized Cipher-Policy Attribute-Based Encryption

Now, we define the security of a PPDCP-ABE scheme, which informally is any IND-sAS-CPA-secure DCP-ABE scheme with a privacy-preserving key extract algorithm PPKeyGen that satisfies two properties: *leak-freeness* and *selective-failure blindness*. Leak-freeness requires that by executing the algorithm PPKey-Gen with honest authorities, the malicious user cannot know anything which it cannot know by executing the algorithm KeyGen with the authorities. Selective-failure blindness requires that malicious authorities cannot know anything about the user's identifier and his attributes, and cause the PPKeyGen algorithm to selectively fail depending on the user's identifier and his attributes. These two properties can be formalized by using the following games.

Leak-Freeness. This game is defined by a real world experiment and an ideal world experiment.

Real World Experiment. Runs the Global Setup algorithm and Authority Setup algorithm. As many as the distinguisher $\mathcal{D}$ wants, the malicious user $\mathcal{U}$ chooses a global identifier $GID_{\mathcal{U}}$ and a set of attributes $\tilde{\mathcal{U}}$, and executes PPKeyGen($U(params, GID_{\mathcal{U}}, \tilde{\mathcal{U}}, PK_i, decom_i, (decom_{i,j})_{a_{i,j} \in \tilde{\mathcal{U}} \cap \tilde{A}_i}) \leftrightarrow \breve{A}_i(params, SK_i,$
$PK_i, com_i, (com_{i,j})_{a_{i,j} \in \cap \tilde{\mathcal{U}} \cap \tilde{A}_i})) \to (SK_{\mathcal{U}}^i, \text{empty})$ with $\breve{A}_i$.

Ideal World Experiment. Runs the Global Setup algorithm and Authority Setup algorithm. As many as the distinguisher $\mathcal{D}$ wants, the malicious user $\bar{U}$ chooses a global identifier $GID_{\bar{U}}$ and a set of attributes $\tilde{\tilde{U}}$, and requires a trusted party to obtain the output of KeyGen($params, SK_i, GID_{\bar{U}}, \tilde{\tilde{U}} \cap \tilde{A}_i) \to SK_{\bar{U}}^i$.

Definition 7. *An algorithm* PPKeyGen($U \leftrightarrow \breve{A}_i$) *associated with a DCP-ABE scheme* $\prod$ = (GlobalSetup, AuthoritySetup, Encrypt, KeyGen, Decrypt) *is leak-free if for all efficient adversary* $\mathcal{U}$, *there exists a simulator* $\bar{U}$ *such that, for the security parameter* 1^κ, *no distinguisher* $\mathcal{D}$ *can distinguish whether* $\mathcal{U}$ *is playing in the real world experiment or in the ideal world experiment with non-negligible advantage.*

Selective-Failure Blindness. This game is formalized as follows.

1. The malicious authority $\mathcal{A}_i$ outputs his public key PK_i and two pairs of globe identifiers and attribute sets $(GID_{U_0}, \tilde{U}_0)$ and $(GID_{U_1}, \tilde{U}_1)$.
2. A random bit $b \in \{0, 1\}$ is selected.
3. $\mathcal{A}_i$ is given comments

$$\left\{ com_b, (com_{i,j})_{a_{i,j} \in \tilde{U}_b \cap \tilde{A}_i} \right\} \quad \text{and} \quad \left\{ com_{1-b}, (com_{i,j})_{a_{i,j} \in \tilde{U}_{1-b} \cap \tilde{A}_i} \right\},$$

and can black-box access oracles $U(params, GID_{U_b}, \tilde{U}_b, PK_i, decom_b,$
$(decom_{i,j})_{a_{i,j} \in \tilde{U}_b \cap \tilde{A}_i})$ and $U(params, GID_{U_{1-b}}, \tilde{U}_{1-b}, PK_i, decom_{1-b},$
$(decom_{i,j})_{a_{i,j} \in \tilde{U}_{1-b} \cap \tilde{A}_i}).$
4. The algorithm U outputs the secret keys $SK_{U_b}^i$ and $SK_{U_{1-b}}^i$, respectively.

5. If $SK^i_{U_b} \neq \perp$ and $SK^i_{U_{1-b}} \neq \perp$, $\mathcal{A}_i$ is given $(SK^i_{U_b}, SK^i_{U_{1-b}})$; if $SK^i_{U_b} \neq \perp$ and $SK^i_{U_{1-b}} = \perp$, $\mathcal{A}_i$ is given $(\epsilon, \perp)$; if $SK^i_{U_b} = \perp$ and $SK^i_{U_{1-b}} \neq \perp$, $\mathcal{A}_i$ is given $(\perp, \epsilon)$; if $SK^i_{U_b} = \perp$ and $SK^i_{U_{1-b}} = \perp$, $\mathcal{A}_i$ is given $(\perp, \perp)$.
6. $\mathcal{A}_i$ outputs his guess b' on b. $\mathcal{A}_i$ wins the game if $b' = b$.

Definition 8. *An algorithm* PPKeyGen$(U \leftrightarrow \breve{A}_i)$ *associated to a DCP-ABE scheme* $\prod =$ (Global Setup, Authority Setup, Encrypt, KeyGen, Decrypt) *is selective-failure blind if no probably polynomial-time adversary $\mathcal{A}_i$ can win the above game with the advantage $Adv^{SFB}_{\mathcal{A}_i} = \left| \Pr[b' = b] - \frac{1}{2} \right| > \epsilon(\kappa)$, where the probability is token over the bits consumed by all the algorithms and the adversary.*

Definition 9. *A privacy-preserving decentralized cipher-policy attribute-based encryption (PPDCP-ABE) scheme $\widetilde{\prod} =$ (Global Setup, Authority Setup, Encrypt, PPKeyGen, Decrypt) is secure if and only if the following conditions are satisfied:*

1. *$\prod =$ (Global Setup, Authority Setup, Encrypt, KeyGen, Decrypt) is a secure DCP-ABE in the selective-access structures model;*
2. *the PPKeyGen algorithm is both leak-free and selective-failure blind.*

4 Our Constructions

In this session, we first construct a DCP-ABE scheme, and then propose a privacy-preserving key extract protocol for it.

4.1 DCP-ABE: Decentralized Cipher-Policy Attribute-Based Encryption

Overview. Suppose that there are N authorities $\{\breve{A}_1, \breve{A}_2, \cdots, \breve{A}_N\}$ in the scheme, and each authority $\breve{A}_i$ monitors a set of attributes $\tilde{A}_i$ for $i = 1, 2, \cdots, N$. $\breve{A}_i$ generates his secret-public key pair $\mathcal{KG}(1^\kappa) \to (SK_i, PK_i)$. For each attribute $a_{i,j} \in \tilde{A}_i$, $\breve{A}_i$ chooses a random number $z_{i,j} \xleftarrow{\$} \mathbb{Z}_p$. Then, the public key is computed as $Z_{i,j} = g^{z_{i,j}}$ and the authentication tag is computed as $T_{i,j} = h^{z_{i,j}} g^{\frac{1}{\gamma_i + a_{i,j}}}$ where γ_i is the partial secret key of $\breve{A}_i$. $T_{i,j}$ can be used to convince $\breve{A}_i$ that the attribute $a_{i,j}$ is monitored by him without revealing it.

To encrypt a message $\mathcal{M}$ under the attributes monitored by the authorities $\{\breve{A}_j\}_{j \in \mathcal{I}}$, the encryptor selects a random number $s_j \xleftarrow{\$} \mathbb{Z}_p$ and an access structure (M_j, ρ_j) for each $\breve{A}_j$. Then, it splits s_j into shares $\lambda_{j,i}$ according to the LSSS technique. Finally the message $\mathcal{M}$ is blinded with $\prod_{j \in \mathcal{I}} e(g, g)^{\alpha_j s_j}$.

To resist the collusion attack, when generating a secret key for a user U with GID μ and a set of attributes $\tilde{U}$, $\breve{A}_i$ chooses two random numbers $(t_{U,i}, w_{U,i}) \xleftarrow{\$} \mathbb{Z}_p$. Specifically, $t_{U,i}$ is used to tie the user's attribute keys to his GID by computing $\mathfrak{g}^{t_{U,i}} \mathfrak{g}^{\frac{\beta_i + \mu}{t_{U,i}}}$ where β_i is the partial secret key of $\breve{A}_i$, and

$w_{U,i}$ is used to randomize the public keys by computing $(F_x = Z_x^{w_{U,i}})_{a_x \in \tilde{U} \cap \breve{A}_i}$.
Then, $\breve{A}_i$ can generate a secret key for U by using his secret key and $(t_{U,i}, w_{U,i})$.

To decrypt a ciphertext, each $e(g,g)^{\alpha_j s_j}$ must be recovered. If the attributes in $\tilde{U}$ satisfy the access structures $(M_j, \rho_j)_{j \in \mathcal{I}}$, the user can use his secret keys and the corresponding ciphertexte elements to reconstruct $e(g,g)^{\alpha_j s_j}$, and obtain $\mathcal{M}$.

Our DCP-ABE scheme is described in Fig.1.

Correctness. Our scheme in Fig. 1 is correct as we have

$$\prod_{j \in \mathcal{I}} e(K_j, X_j) = \prod_{j \in \mathcal{I}} e(g^{\alpha_j} g^{x_j w_{U,j}} \mathfrak{g}^{t_{U,j}} \mathfrak{g}^{\frac{\beta_j + \mu}{t_{U,j}}}, g^{s_j}) =$$

$$\prod_{j \in \mathcal{I}} e(g,g)^{\alpha_j s_j} \cdot e(g,g)^{x_j w_{U,j} s_j} \cdot e(g,\mathfrak{g})^{t_{U,j} s_j} \cdot e(g,\mathfrak{g})^{\frac{\beta_j s_j}{t_{U,j}}} \cdot e(g,\mathfrak{g})^{\frac{\mu s_j}{t_{U,j}}},$$

$$\prod_{j \in \mathcal{I}} e(R_j, E_j) \cdot e(R_j, Y_j)^\mu = \prod_{j \in \mathcal{I}} e(g^{\frac{1}{t_{U,j}}}, B_j^{s_j}) \cdot e(g^{\frac{1}{t_{U,j}}}, \mathfrak{g}^{s_j})^\mu =$$

$$\prod_{j \in \mathcal{I}} e(g^{\frac{1}{t_{U,j}}}, \mathfrak{g}^{\beta_j s_j}) \cdot e(g^{\frac{1}{t_{U,j}}}, \mathfrak{g}^{s_j})^\mu = \prod_{j \in \mathcal{I}} e(g,\mathfrak{g})^{\frac{\beta_j s_j}{t_{U,j}}} \cdot e(g,\mathfrak{g})^{\frac{\mu s_j}{t_{U,j}}},$$

$$\prod_{j \in \mathcal{I}} e(L_j, X_j) = e(g,g)^{t_{U,j} s_j},$$

$$\prod_{j \in \mathcal{I}} \prod_{i=1}^{\ell_j} \left(e(C_{j,i}, P_j) \cdot e(D_{j,i}, F_{\rho_j(i)}) \right)^{\omega_{j,i}} =$$

$$\prod_{j \in \mathcal{I}} \prod_{i=1}^{\ell_j} \left(e(g g^{x_j \lambda_{j,i}} Z_{\rho_j(i)}^{-r_{j,i}}, g^{w_{U,j}}) \cdot e(g^{r_{j,i}}, Z_{\rho_j(i)}^{w_{U,j}}) \right)^{\omega_{j,i}} =$$

$$\prod_{j \in \mathcal{I}} e(g,g)^{x_j w_{U,j} \sum_{i=1}^{\ell_j} \omega_{j,i} \lambda_{j,i}} = \prod_{j \in \mathcal{I}} e(g,g)^{x_j w_{U,j} s_j}.$$

Therefore,

$$\frac{C_0 \cdot \prod_{j \in \mathcal{I}} e(L_j, X_j) \cdot e(R_j, E_j) \cdot e(R_j, Y_j)^\mu}{\prod_{j \in \mathcal{I}} e(K_j, X_j)} \cdot \prod_{j \in \mathcal{I}} \prod_{i=1}^{\ell_j} \left(e(C_{j,i}, P_j) \cdot e(D_{j,i}, F_{\rho_j(i)}) \right)^{\omega_{j,i}}$$
$$= \mathcal{M}.$$

Theorem 2. *Our decentralized cipher-policy attribute-based encryption (DCP-ABE) is $(T, q, \epsilon(k))$ secure in the selective-access structure model if the $(T', \epsilon'(k))$-decisional q-PBDHE assumption holds on $(e, p.\mathbb{G}, \mathbb{G}_\tau)$, where $T' = T + \mathcal{O}(T)$ and $\epsilon'(\kappa) = \frac{1}{2}\epsilon(\kappa)$.*

The proof of this theorem is referred to the full version of this paper [31].

4.2 Privacy-Preserving Key Extract Protocol

In this session, we propose a privacy-preserving key extract protocol for the DCP-ABE scheme described in Fig. 1.

Overview. In Fig. 1, to generate a secret key for a user U, the authority $\breve{A}_i$ selects two random numbers $(t_{U,i}, w_{U,i})$, and uses them to tie the user's secret keys to his GID. If $\breve{A}_i$ records $(t_{U,i}, w_{U,i})$, he can compute $\mathfrak{g}^\mu = \left(\frac{K_i}{g^{\alpha_i} g^{x_i w_{U,i}} \mathfrak{g}^{t_{U,i}}} \right)^{t_{U,i}} \mathfrak{g}^{-\beta_i}$ and $(Z_x = F_x^{\frac{1}{w_{U,i}}})_{a_x \in \tilde{U} \cap \breve{A}_i}$. Hence, he can know the user's GID and attributes. Therefore, in order to protect the privacy of the user's GID and attributes, $(t_{U,i}, w_{U,i})$ should be computed using the 2-party secure computing technique.

Global Setup. This algorithm takes as input a security parameter 1^κ, and outputs a bilinear group $\mathcal{GG}(1^\kappa) \rightarrow (e, p, \mathbb{G}, \mathbb{G}_\tau)$. Let g, h and $\mathfrak{g}$ be generators of the group $\mathbb{G}$. Suppose that there are N authorities $\{\breve{A}_1, \breve{A}_2, \cdots, \breve{A}_N\}$, and $\breve{A}_i$ monitors a set of attributes $\tilde{A}_i = \{a_{i,1}, a_{i,2}, \cdots, a_{i,q_i}\}$ where $a_{i,j} \in \mathbb{Z}_p$ for $i = 1, 2, \cdots, N$ and $j = 1, 2, \cdots, q_i$. The public parameters are $PP = (g, h, \mathfrak{g}, e, p, \mathbb{G}, \mathbb{G}_\tau)$.

Authorities Setup. Each authority $\breve{A}_i$ selects $\alpha_i, x_i, \beta_i, \gamma_i \xleftarrow{\$} \mathbb{Z}_p$, and computes $H_i = e(g,g)^{\alpha_i}$, $A_i = g^{x_i}$, $B_i = \mathfrak{g}^{\beta_i}$, $\Gamma_i^1 = g^{\gamma_i}$ and $\Gamma_i^2 = h^{\gamma_i}$, where $i = 1, 2, \cdots, N$. For each attribute $a_{i,j} \in \tilde{A}_i$, $\breve{A}$ chooses $z_{i,j} \xleftarrow{\$} \mathbb{Z}_p$, and computes $Z_{i,j} = g^{z_{i,j}}$ and $T_{i,j} = h^{z_{i,j}} g^{\frac{1}{\gamma_i + a_{i,j}}}$. Then, $\breve{A}$ publishes the public key $PK_i = \left\{ H_i, A_i, B_i, (\Gamma_i^1, \Gamma_i^2), (T_{i,j}, Z_{i,j})_{a_{i,j} \in \tilde{A}_i} \right\}$, and keeps the master secrete key as $SK_i = (\alpha_i, a_i, \beta_i, \gamma_i, (z_{i,j})_{a_{i,j} \in \tilde{A}_i})$.

Encryption. To encrypt a message $\mathcal{M} \in \mathbb{G}_\tau$, this algorithm works as follows. Let $\mathcal{I}$ be a set which consists of the indexes of the authorities whose attributes are selected to encrypt $\mathcal{M}$. For each $j \in \mathcal{I}$, this algorithm first selects an access structures (M_j, ρ_j) and a vector $\overrightarrow{v_j} = (s_j, v_{j,2}, \cdots, v_{j,n_j})$, where $s_j, v_{j,2}, \cdots, v_{j,n_j} \xleftarrow{\$} \mathbb{Z}_p$ and M_j is an $\ell_j \times n_j$ matrix. Then, it computes $\lambda_{j,i} = M_j^i \overrightarrow{v}_j$, where M_j^i is the corresponding ith row of M_j. Finally, it selects $r_{j,1}, r_{j,2}, \cdots, r_{j,\ell_j} \xleftarrow{\$} \mathbb{Z}_p$, and computes

$$C_0 = \mathcal{M} \cdot \prod_{j \in \mathcal{I}} e(g,g)^{\alpha_j s_j}, \ \{X_j = g^{s_j}, \ Y_j = \mathfrak{g}^{s_j}, \ E_j = B_j^{s_j}\}_{j \in \mathcal{I}}$$

$$\left((C_{j,1} = g^{x_j \lambda_{j,1}} Z_{\rho_j(1)}^{-r_{j,1}}, \ D_{j,1} = g^{r_{j,1}}), \ \cdots, \ (C_{j,\ell_j} = g^{x_j \lambda_{j,\ell_j}} Z_{\rho_j(\ell_j)}^{-r_{j,\ell_j}}, \ D_{j,\ell_j} = g^{r_{j,\ell_j}}) \right)_{j \in \mathcal{I}}$$

The ciphertext is $CT = \left\{ C_0, \ (X_j, \ Y_j, \ E_j, \ (C_{j,1}, \ D_{j,1}), \ \cdots, \ (C_{j,\ell_j}, \ D_{j,\ell_j}))_{j \in \mathcal{I}} \right\}$.

KeyGen. To generate secret keys for a user U with GID μ and a set of attributes $\tilde{U} \bigcap \tilde{A}_i$, $\breve{A}_i$ selects $t_{U,i}, w_{U,i} \xleftarrow{\$} \mathbb{Z}_p$, and computes $K_i = g^{\alpha_i} g^{x_i w_{U,i}} \mathfrak{g}^{t_{U,i}} \mathfrak{g}^{\frac{\beta_i + \mu}{t_{U,i}}}$, $P_i = g^{w_{U,i}}$, $L_i = g^{t_{U,i}}$, $L_i' = h^{t_{U,i}}$, $R_i = g^{\frac{1}{t_{U,i}}}$, $R_i' = h^{\frac{1}{t_{U,i}}}$ and $(F_x = Z_x^{w_{U,i}})_{a_x \in \tilde{U} \bigcap \tilde{A}_i}$. The secret keys for U are $SK_U^i = \left\{ K_i, P_i, L_i, L_i', R_i, R_i', (F_x)_{a_x \in \tilde{U} \bigcap \tilde{A}_i} \right\}$.

Decryption. To decrypt a ciphertext CT, this algorithm computes

$$\frac{C_0 \cdot \prod_{j \in \mathcal{I}} e(L_j, X_j) \cdot e(R_j, E_j) \cdot e(R_j, Y_j)^\mu \cdot \prod_{j \in \mathcal{I}} \prod_{i=1}^{\ell_j} \left(e(C_{j,i}, P_j) \cdot e(D_{j,i}, F_{\rho_j(i)}) \right)^{\omega_{j,i}}}{\prod_{j \in \mathcal{I}} e(K_j, X_j)}$$

$$= \mathcal{M}$$

where $\{\omega_{j,i} \in \mathbb{Z}_p\}_{i=1}^{\ell_j}$ are a set of constants such that $\sum_{i=1}^{\ell_j} \omega_{j,i} \lambda_{j,i} = s_j$ if $\{\lambda_{j,i}\}_{i=1}^{\ell_j}$ are valid shares of the secret value s_j according to the access structure (M_j, ρ_j).

Fig. 1. Decentralized Cipher-Policy Attribute-based Encryption

$U(PP, PK_i, \mu, a_x \in \tilde{U} \bigcap \tilde{A}_i)$

1. Selects $k_1, k_2, d_1, d_2 \xleftarrow{\$} \mathbb{Z}_p$
and sets $d_u = d_1 d_2$.
Computes
$\Theta_1 = A_i^{d_1}, \Theta_2 = g^{d_u}$,
$\Theta_3 = h^{k_1} \mathfrak{g}^{\mu}, \Theta_4 = \Theta_3^{k_2}$,
$\Theta_5 = B_i^{k_2}, \Theta_6 = \mathfrak{g}^{\frac{1}{k_2}}$,
$(\Psi_x^1 = T_x^{d_u}, \Psi_x^2 = Z_x^{d_u})_{a_x \in \tilde{U} \bigcap \tilde{A}_i}$
and $\Sigma_U = \mathsf{PoK}\{(k_1, k_2, d_1, d_u, \mu,$
$(a_x \in \tilde{U} \bigcap \tilde{A}_i)) : \Theta_1 = A_i^{d_1} \wedge$
$\Theta_2 = g^{d_u} \wedge \Theta_3 = h^{k_1} \mathfrak{g}^{\mu}, \wedge$
$\Theta_4 = \Theta_3^{k_2} \wedge \Theta_5 = B_i^{k_2} \wedge$
$e(\Theta_5, \Theta_6) = e(B_i, \mathfrak{g}) \wedge$
$(\wedge \frac{e(\Gamma_i^1, \Psi_x^1)}{e(\Gamma_i^2, \Psi_x^2)} = e(g, \Psi_x^1)^{-a_x}.$
$\wedge e(h, \Psi_x^2)^{a_x} \cdot e(g, g)^{d_u})_{a_x \in \tilde{U} \bigcap \tilde{A}_i}\}$

$\xrightarrow[\Theta_5, \Psi_x^1, \Psi_x^2, \Sigma_U]{\Theta_1, \Theta_2, \Theta_3, \Theta_4}$

3. Computes $K_i = \frac{K_i'}{\Upsilon_4^{k_1 k_2}}, P_i = \Upsilon_5^{d_1}$, $\xleftarrow[\Upsilon_5, K_i', \Phi_x, \Sigma_{A_i}]{\Upsilon_1, \Upsilon_2, \Upsilon_3, \Upsilon_4}$

$L_i = \Upsilon_1^{\frac{1}{k_2}}, R_i = \Upsilon_2^{k_2}, R_i' = \Upsilon_4^{k_2}$ and
$\left(F_x = \Phi_x^{\frac{1}{d_2}} \right)_{a_x \in \tilde{U} \bigcap \tilde{A}_i}$

$\breve{A}_i(PP, PK_i, SK_i)$

2. Selects $c_u, e_u \xleftarrow{\$} \mathbb{Z}_p$ and
computes $\Upsilon_1 = g^{c_u}, \Upsilon_2 = g^{\frac{1}{c_u}}$,
$\Upsilon_3 = h^{c_u}, \Upsilon_4 = h^{\frac{1}{c_u}}, \Upsilon_5 = g^{e_u}$,
$K_i' = g^{\alpha_i} \Theta_1^{e_u} \Theta_6^{c_u} (\Theta_4 \Theta_5)^{\frac{1}{c_u}}$,
$(\Phi_x = (\Psi_x^2)^{e_u})_{a_x \in \tilde{U} \bigcap \tilde{A}_i}$ and
$\Sigma_{A_i} = \mathsf{PoK}\{(\alpha_i, c_u, e_u) :$
$e(\Upsilon_1, \Upsilon_2) = e(g, g) \wedge \Upsilon_1 = g^{c_u} \wedge$
$\Upsilon_2 = g^{\frac{1}{c_u}} \wedge \Upsilon_3 = h^{c_u} \wedge \Upsilon_4 = h^{\frac{1}{c_u}}$
$e(\Upsilon_3, \Upsilon_4) = e(h, h) \wedge \Upsilon_5 = g^{e_u} \wedge$
$K_i' = g^{\alpha_i} \Theta_1^{e_u} \Theta_6^{c_u} (\Theta_4 \Theta_5)^{\frac{1}{c_u}}$
$\wedge (\wedge (\Phi_x = (\Psi_x^2)^{e_u})_{a_x \in \tilde{U} \bigcap \tilde{A}_i}\}.$

Fig. 2. PPKeyGen: Privacy-Preserving Key Generation Protocol

First, U chooses $(k_1, k_2, d_1, d_2) \xleftarrow{\$} \mathbb{Z}_p$. It uses (k_1, k_2) to commit his GID and (d_1, d_2) to commit his attributes and the corresponding authentication tags. Then, U proves in zero knowledge to $\breve{A}_i$ that he knows the GID, and the attributes for which he is obtaining secret keys are monitored by $\breve{A}_i$. $\breve{A}_i$ checks the proof. If it fails, $\breve{A}_i$ aborts. Otherwise, $\breve{A}_i$ chooses $(c_u, e_u) \xleftarrow{\$} \mathbb{Z}_p$ and generates a secret key for U by using his secret key, the elements from U and (c_u, e_u). Furthermore, $\breve{A}_i$ proves in zero knowledge that he knows the secret key and (c_u, e_u); Finally, U can compute his real secret key by (k_1, k_2, d_1, d_2) and the elements from $\breve{A}_i$.

Actually, by executing the 2-party secure computing protocol, U and $\breve{A}_i$ co-operatively compute $w_{U,i} = e_u d_1$ and $t_{U,i} = \frac{c_u}{k_2}$, where (d_1, k_2) are from U and (c_u, e_u) are from $\breve{A}_i$. Therefore, from the view of $\breve{A}_i$, the secret key computed by U is indistinguishable from the random elements in $\mathbb{G}$.

The privacy-preserving key extract protocol is described in Fig. 2.

Correctness. Let $w = d_1 e_u$ and $t = \frac{c_u}{k_2}$. The secret keys generated in Fig. 2 are correct as the following equations hold.

$$K_i = \frac{K_i' \Upsilon^{\frac{1}{k_2}}}{\Upsilon_4^{k_1 k_2}} = \frac{g^{\alpha_i} \Theta_1^{e_u} (\Theta_4 \Theta_5)^{\frac{1}{c_u}} \mathfrak{g}^{\frac{c_u}{k_2}}}{\Upsilon_4^{k_1 k_2}} = \frac{g^{\alpha_i} A_i^{d_1 e_u} ((\mathfrak{h}^{k_1} \mathfrak{g}^{\mu})^{k_2} B_i^{k_2})^{\frac{1}{c_u}} \mathfrak{g}^{\frac{c_u}{k_2}}}{\mathfrak{h}^{\frac{k_1 k_2}{c_u}}}$$

$$= \frac{g^{\alpha_i} g^{x_i d_1 e_u} \mathfrak{h}^{\frac{k_1 k_2}{c_u}} \mathfrak{g}^{\frac{k_2 (\beta_i + \mu)}{c_u}} \mathfrak{g}^{\frac{c_u}{k_2}}}{\mathfrak{h}^{\frac{k_1 k_2}{c_u}}} = g^{\alpha_i} g^{x_i w} \mathfrak{g}^t \mathfrak{g}^{\frac{\beta_i + \mu}{t}},$$

$$P_i = \Upsilon_6^{d_1} = g^{d_1 e_u} = g^w, \quad L_i = \Upsilon_1^{\frac{1}{k_2}} = g^{\frac{c_u}{k_2}} = g^t,$$

$$R_i = \Upsilon_2^{k_2} = g^{\frac{k_2}{c_u}} = g^{\frac{1}{t}}, \quad R_i' = \Upsilon_4^{k_2} = h^{\frac{k_2}{c_u}} = h^{\frac{1}{t}},$$

and

$$F_x = \Phi_x^{\frac{1}{d_2}} = (\Psi_x^2)^{\frac{e_u}{d_2}} = Z_x^{\frac{d_u e_u}{d_2}} = Z_x^{d_1 e_u} = Z_x^w.$$

Theorem 3. *The privacy-preserving key extract protocol in Fig. 2 is both leak-free and selective-failure blind under the q-SDH assumption, where* $q = max\{q_1, q_2, \cdots, q_N\}$.

The proof of this theorem is referred to the full version of this paper [31].

By **Theorem** 2 and **Theorem** 3, we have the following theorem.

Theorem 4. *Our privacy-preserving decentralized cipher-policy attribute-based encryption (PPDCP-ABE) scheme* $\prod$ = (Global Setup, Authority Setup, Encrypt, PPKeyGen, Decrypt) *is secure in the selective-access structure model under the decisional q-PBDHE assumption and q-SDH assumption.*

5   Conclusion

Decentralized ABE scheme is more efficient and flexible encryption system as it dose not require a central authority nor the cooperation among multiple authorities. Considering to reduce the trust on the authorities, some privacy-preserving MA-ABE schemes have been proposed. However, in these schemes, only the privacy of the GID was considered. In this paper, we proposed a PPDCP-ABE scheme where both the privacy of the GID and the attributes are concerned. Especially, the user can convince the authorities that the attributes for which he is obtaining secret keys are monitored by them. Therefore, our scheme provides a perfect solution for the privacy issues in MA-ABE schemes.

Acknowledgement. We would like to thank the anonymous reviewers for useful comments. The first author was partially supported by National Natural Science Foundation of China (Grant No. 61300213), National Center for International Joint Research on E-Business Information Processing (Grant No. 2013B01035) and A Project Funded by the Priority Academic Program Development of Jiangsu Higher Education Institutions(PAPD). The second author was partially supported by Australia Research Council Discovery Project (DP130101383).

References

1. Bichsel, P., Camenisch, J., Groβ, T., Shoup, V.: Anonymous credentials on a standard java card. In: Al-Shaer, E., Jha, S., Keromytis, A.D. (eds.) CCS 2009, pp. 600–610. ACM (2009)
2. Sahai, A., Waters, B.: Fuzzy identity-based encryption. In: Cramer, R. (ed.) EUROCRYPT 2005. LNCS, vol. 3494, pp. 457–473. Springer, Heidelberg (2005)
3. Bethencourt, J., Sahai, A., Waters, B.: Ciphertext-policy attribute-based encryption. In: IEEE S& P 2007, pp. 321–334. IEEE (2007)
4. Cheung, L., Newport, C.: Provably secure ciphertext policy ABE. In: Ning, P., di Vimercati, S.D.C., Syverson, P.F. (eds.) CCS 2007, pp. 456–465. ACM (2007)
5. Goyal, V., Pandey, O., Sahai, A., Waters, B.: Attribute-based encryption for fine-grained access control of encrypted data. In: Juels, A., Wright, R.N., di Vimercati, S.D.C. (eds.) CCS 2006, pp. 89–98. ACM (2006)
6. Ostrovsky, R., Sahai, A., Waters, B.: Attribute-based encryption with non-monotonic access structures. In: Ning, P., di Vimercati, S.D.C., Syverson, P.F. (eds.) CCS 2007, pp. 195–203. ACM (2007)
7. Lewko, A., Okamoto, T., Sahai, A., Takashima, K., Waters, B.: Fully secure functional encryption: Attribute-based encryption and (hierarchical) inner product encryption. In: Gilbert, H. (ed.) EUROCRYPT 2010. LNCS, vol. 6110, pp. 62–91. Springer, Heidelberg (2010)
8. Waters, B.: Ciphertext-policy attribute-based encryption: An expressive, efficient, and provably secure realization. In: Catalano, D., Fazio, N., Gennaro, R., Nicolosi, A. (eds.) PKC 2011. LNCS, vol. 6571, pp. 53–70. Springer, Heidelberg (2011)
9. Chase, M.: Multi-authority attribute based encryption. In: Vadhan, S.P. (ed.) TCC 2007. LNCS, vol. 4392, pp. 515–534. Springer, Heidelberg (2007)
10. Lewko, A., Waters, B.: Decentralizing attribute-based encryption. In: Paterson, K.G. (ed.) EUROCRYPT 2011. LNCS, vol. 6632, pp. 568–588. Springer, Heidelberg (2011)
11. Chase, M., Chow, S.S.: Improving privacy and security in multi-authority attribute-based encryption. In: Al-Shaer, E., Jha, S., Keromytis, A.D. (eds.) CCS 2009, pp. 121–130. ACM (2009)
12. Han, J., Susilo, W., Mu, Y., Yan, J.: Privacy-preserving decentralized key-policy attribute-based encryption. IEEE Transactions on Parallel and Distributed Systems 23(11), 2150–2162 (2012)
13. Herranz, J., Laguillaumie, F., Ràfols, C.: Constant size ciphertexts in threshold attribute-based encryption. In: Nguyen, P.Q., Pointcheval, D. (eds.) PKC 2010. LNCS, vol. 6056, pp. 19–34. Springer, Heidelberg (2010)
14. Gennaro, R., Jarecki, S., Krawczyk, H., Rabin, T.: Secure distributed key generation for discrete-log based cryptosystems. In: Stern, J. (ed.) EUROCRYPT 1999. LNCS, vol. 1592, pp. 295–310. Springer, Heidelberg (1999)
15. Gennaro, R., Jarecki, S., Krawczyk, H., Rabin, T.: Robust threshold dss signatures. In: Maurer, U.M. (ed.) Advances in Cryptology - EUROCRYPT 1996. LNCS, vol. 1070, pp. 354–371. Springer, Heidelberg (1996)
16. Lin, H., Cao, Z., Liang, X., Shao, J.: Secure threshold multi authority attribute based encryption without a central authority. In: Chowdhury, D.R., Rijmen, V., Das, A. (eds.) INDOCRYPT 2008. LNCS, vol. 5365, pp. 426–436. Springer, Heidelberg (2008)
17. Müller, S., Katzenbeisser, S., Eckert, C.: Distributed attribute-based encryption. In: Lee, P.J., Cheon, J.H. (eds.) ICISC 2008. LNCS, vol. 5461, pp. 20–36. Springer, Heidelberg (2009)

18. Liu, Z., Cao, Z., Huang, Q., Wong, D.S., Yuen, T.H.: Fully secure multi-authority ciphertext-policy attribute-based encryption without random oracles. In: Atluri, V., Diaz, C. (eds.) ESORICS 2011. LNCS, vol. 6879, pp. 278–297. Springer, Heidelberg (2011)

19. Naor, M., Pinkas, B., Reingold, O.: Distributed pseudo-random functions and KDCs. In: Stern, J. (ed.) EUROCRYPT 1999. LNCS, vol. 1592, pp. 327–346. Springer, Heidelberg (1999)

20. Li, J., Huang, Q., Chen, X., Chow, S.S.M., Wong, D.S., Xie, D.: Multi-authority ciphertext-policy attribute-based encryption with accountability. In: Cheung, B.S.N., Hui, L.C.K., Sandhu, R.S., Wong, D.S. (eds.) ASIACCS 2011, pp. 386–390. ACM (2011)

21. Qian, H., Li, J., Zhang, Y.: Privacy-preserving decentralized ciphertext-policy attribute-based encryption with fully hidden access structure. In: Qing, S., Zhou, J., Liu, D. (eds.) ICICS 2013. LNCS, vol. 8233, pp. 363–372. Springer, Heidelberg (2013)

22. Camenisch, J., Lysyanskaya, A.: An efficient system for non-transferable anonymous credentials with optional anonymity revocation. In: Pfitzmann, B. (ed.) EUROCRYPT 2001. LNCS, vol. 2045, pp. 93–118. Springer, Heidelberg (2001)

23. Persiano, G., Visconti, I.: An efficient and usable multi-show non-transferable anonymous credential system. In: Juels, A. (ed.) FC 2004. LNCS, vol. 3110, pp. 196–211. Springer, Heidelberg (2004)

24. Boneh, D., Boyen, X.: Short signatures without random oracles. In: Cachin, C., Camenisch, J.L. (eds.) EUROCRYPT 2004. LNCS, vol. 3027, pp. 56–73. Springer, Heidelberg (2004)

25. Beime, A.: Secure Schemes for Secret Sharing and Key Distribution. Phd thesis, Israel Institute of Technology, Technion, Haifa, Israel (1996)

26. Pedersen, T.P.: Non-interactive and information-theoretic secure verifiable secret sharing. In: Feigenbaum, J. (ed.) Advances in Cryptology - CRYPTO 1991. LNCS, vol. 576, pp. 129–140. Springer, Heidelberg (1992)

27. Camenisch, J., Stadler, M.: Efficient group signature schemes for large groups. In: Kaliski Jr., B.S. (ed.) Advances in Cryptology - CRYPTO 1997. LNCS, vol. 1294, pp. 410–424. Springer, Heidelberg (1997)

28. Camenisch, J., Chaabouni, R., Shelat, A.: Efficient protocols for set membership and range proofs. In: Pieprzyk, J. (ed.) ASIACRYPT 2008. LNCS, vol. 5350, pp. 234–252. Springer, Heidelberg (2008)

29. Camenisch, J., Kohlweiss, M., Rial, A., Sheedy, C.: Blind and anonymous identity-based encryption and authorised private searches on public key encrypted data. In: Jarecki, S., Tsudik, G. (eds.) PKC 2009. LNCS, vol. 5443, pp. 196–214. Springer, Heidelberg (2009)

30. Green, M., Hohenberger, S.: Blind identity-based encryption and simulatable oblivious transfer. In: Kurosawa, K. (ed.) ASIACRYPT 2007. LNCS, vol. 4833, pp. 265–282. Springer, Heidelberg (2007)

31. Han, J., Susilo, W., Mu, Y., Zhou, J., Au, M.H.: PPDCP-ABE: Privacy-Preserving Decentralized Cipher-Policy Attribute-Based Encryption, Cryptology ePrint Archive: Report 2014/470, http://eprint.iacr.org/2014/470

Practical Direct Chosen Ciphertext Secure Key-Policy Attribute-Based Encryption with Public Ciphertext Test

Weiran Liu[1,2], Jianwei Liu[1,3], Qianhong Wu[1,3], Bo Qin[2], and Yunya Zhou[1]

[1] School of Electronic and Information Engineering, Beihang University, Beijing
liuweiran900217@gmail.com, {liujianwei,qianhong.wu}@buaa.edu.cn
[2] School of Information, Renmin University of China, Beijing
bo.qin@ruc.edu.cn
[3] The Academy of Satellite Application, Beijing

Abstract. We propose a direct Key-Policy Attribute-Based Encryption (KP-ABE) scheme with semantic security against adaptively chosen ciphertext attacks (CCA2) in the standard model. Compared with its counterpart with security against chosen-plaintext attacks (CPA), the cost of our scheme is only a Chameleon hash. In contrast to the Boyen-Mei-Waters shrink approach from CPA-secure $(l+1)$-Hierarchical Identity Based Encryption $((l+1)$-HIBE) to CCA2-secure l-HIBE, our approach only adds one on-the-fly dummy attribute. Further, our approach only requires that the underlying ABE is selectively secure and allows public ciphertext test. A major obstacle for the security proof in this scenario is that the simulator cannot prepare the challenge ciphertext associated with the on-the-fly dummy attribute due to the selective security constraint. We circumvent this obstacle with a Chameleon hash. Technically, unlike existing use of Chameleon hash in (online/offline) signature applications, our work shows Chameleon hash can also have unique applications in encryption schemes.

Keywords: Attribute-Based Encryption, Chameleon Hash, Chosen Ciphertext Security.

1 Introduction

Attribute-Based Encryption (ABE) allows an encryptor to share data with users according to specified access policies. ABE can be classified into two categories, Key-Policy ABE (KP-ABE) [21] and Ciphertext-Policy ABE (CP-ABE) [3]. In KP-ABE, secret keys are associated with access policies and ciphertexts are associated with sets of attributes. One can decrypt if and only if the set of attributes specified in the ciphertext satisfies the access policy in his/her secret key. In contrast, the CP-ABE ciphertexts are associated with access policies and the secret keys specify sets of attributes. Due to its capability of providing fine-grained access control over encrypted data, ABE is extensively applied for many cloud storage applications [17, 29, 32].

M. Kutyłowski and J. Vaidya (Eds.): ESORICS 2014, Part II, LNCS 8713, pp. 91–108, 2014.
© Springer International Publishing Switzerland 2014

Semantic security against adaptively chosen ciphertext attacks (CCA2) is widely recognized as a standard security notion for cryptosystems against active attacks. ABE is usually suggested to enforce fine-grained access control on outsourced data in cloud storage and computing applications. In such applications, active attackers who can modify ciphertexts in storage or in transit may reveal useful information from sensitive data even if the employed ABE system is chosen plaintext (CPA) secure. Thus, it is desirable to deploy CCA2-secure ABE to defend against such strong attackers.

There are some ABE schemes that can be shown CCA2 security in the standard model. They are reasonably less efficient than their CPA-secure counterparts. Some of them involve the one-time signature cryptographic primitives [16, 21, 33]. However, one-time signatures either have high storage or high computational cost. Specifically, one-time signature schemes based on cryptographic hash functions involve long public keys and signatures; and the one-time signature schemes based on number-theoretic assumptions have the advantage of short public keys and signatures, but yield expensive computational cost. Some other CCA2-secure ABE schemes are with the restriction of only supporting single threshold access policies [15, 20], which is inconvenient when the system is required to support complicated access policies.

It is preferable to construct CCA2-secure ABE from CPA-secure ones by directly using the underlying ABE structures and requiring no extra inefficient cryptographic primitives. In 2006, Boyen *et al.* [6] introduced a shrink approach that can directly obtain CCA2-secure l-Hierarchical Identity-Based Encryption (HIBE) from CPA-secure $(l + 1)$-HIBE. By setting $l = 0$, their approach can directly obtain CCA2-secure Public Key Encryption (PKE) from CPA-secure Identity-Based Encryption (IBE). The key point is to first hash the intermediate ciphertext components independent of the identity to obtain a dummy identity, and then generate the final ciphertext using the dummy "identity". A natural question is whether we can construct a direct CCA2-secure ABE by applying their approach.

Issues in Direct CCA2-Secure ABE. There are three main issues in constructing CCA2-secure ABE using the Boyen-Mei-Waters approach.

Arbitrary-Attributes Requirement. Similarly, the hash output may be treated as an attribute in a direct CCA2-secure construction. However, the hash output cannot be controlled. This implies that the underlying ABE needs to have the property of "large universe", i.e., supporting arbitrary strings as attributes.

Delegatability Obstacle. The Boyen-Mei-Waters approach leverages the delegatability of (H)IBE systems. Specifically, one encrypts to the "hash identity" at a lower level than all users who can delegate a key to this hash identity for ciphertext validity test. This is the reason why their shrink approach converts a $(l + 1)$-HIBE to be a CCA2-secure l-HIBE, and converts a CPA-secure IBE to be a CCA2-secure PKE. A straightforward application of their approach in ABE settings requires the underlying CPA-secure ABE allows to delegate a key to arbitrary attributes. However, the only ABE scheme due to Deng *et al.* [19] allowing hierarchical attributes cannot support arbitrary attributes.

Full Identity/Attribute Security Obstacle. If the (H)IBE system is of only selective-identity security, instead of full-identity security, then by applying Boyen-Mei-Waters approach one obtains a CCA2-secure (H)IBE Key Encapsulation Mechanism (KEM), instead of a fully functional encryption system. The main obstacle for fully functional encryption is that in the security proof, due to the selective security constraint, the simulator cannot prepare the challenge ciphertext associated with the hashed "identity". The same problem occurs in direct construction of CCA2-secure ABE if the underlying CPA-secure ABE has only selective security. It is challenging to obtain direct CCA2-secure ABE schemes from ABE schemes with selective CPA-security.

Our Contributions. We propose a direct publicly verifiable CCA2-secure KP-ABE scheme in the standard model. We achieve this goal by addressing the above issues in direct CCA2-secure KP-ABE construction. We exploit a recent CPA-secure KP-ABE one [30] with the property of "large universe". This property addresses the *Arbitrary-Attributes Requirement*.

We add one on-the-fly dummy attribute in our construction, instead of extending one attribute hierarchy. The on-the-fly dummy attribute is computed by hashing the intermediate ciphertext components independent of the specified attribute set. The other ciphertext components are generated by the new attribute set containing the dummy attribute. In the decryption procedure, the receiver can validate the ciphertext with the dummy attribute. This approach circumvent the *Delegatability Obstacle* with only a marginal cost, i.e., by adding constant size ciphertext components related to the dummy attribute. Further more, the ciphertext validity test only involves public information. This public ciphertext test property is enjoyable and allows a third party, e.g., a gateway or firewall, to filter encrypted spams in some applications.

Our proposal is a fully functional CCA2-secure ABE scheme, instead of a CCA2-secure KEM scheme, although the underlying ABE is only selectively secure. We circumvent the obstacle in the security proof by replacing a regular hash with a Chameleon hash. The cost to achieve CCA2 security from CPA security is only a Chameleon hash. The Chameleon hash plays a critical role in the security proof. Specifically, the universal forgeability (w.r.t. the hash trapdoor holder) of the Chameleon hash allows the simulator to prepare the challenge ciphertext associated with the hashed "attribute" even if the underlying ABE has only selective security. Technically, our constructions illustrate novel and unique applications of Chameleon hash in encryption systems, in contrast to previous main use of Chameleon hash in (online/offline) signature applications [1, 11, 14].

Related Work. ABE was introduced by Sahai and Waters [31]. Goyal *et al.* extended the idea and distinguished KP-ABE and CP-ABE. The KP-ABE and CP-ABE systems were then respectively proposed by Goyal *et al.* [21] and Bethencourt *et al.* [3] that support monotonic access policies. Fully secure constructions in the standard model were first provided by Okamoto *et al.* [27] and Lewko *et al.* [23]. Many other ABE schemes have been further proposed to gain more preferable properties, such as hierarchical ABE (allowing users with attributes of higher hierarchy to delegate keys to lower levels) [17], "non-monotonic access policies" (supporting general access structures with negation boolean formulas) [26], "large universe" [24, 25, 28, 30], and "multiple central authorities" (there exists multiple authenticated PKGs in ABE) [8, 9, 24]. The latest work [18] on ABE achieves black-box traitor tracing in which a tracing algorithm can be invoked to find the secret keys leaked for illegal access to encrypted data.

Several ABE systems have been proposed with CCA2 security in the standard model. The KP-ABE scheme proposed by Goyal *et al.* [21] can be converted to have CCA2 security by revising the Canetti-Halevi-Katz approach [7] from CPA-secure IBE [5] to CCA2-secure PKE schemes at the cost of one-time signatures. Cheung *et al.* [16] leveraged the Canetti-Halevi-Katz approach [7] in CP-ABE to construct a CCA2-secure CP-ABE. Yamada *et al.* [33] introduced a generic construction to transform CPA-secure ABE to CCA2-secure ones if the involved ABE schemes satisfy either delegatability or verifiability. The above CCA2-secure ABE schemes involve one-time signatures. Chen *et al.* [15] and Ge *et al.* [20] recently constructed direct CCA2-secure ABE without one-time signatures, with a restriction on only supporting threshold access policies.

Paper Organization. The rest of the paper is organized as follows. In Sec. 2, we review prime-order bilinear groups, the number-theoretic assumption we use, and the background information about access structures, linear secret-sharing schemes and Chameleon hash functions. Sec. 3 formalizes KP-ABE and their CCA2 security definitions. We propose our practical CCA2-secure KP-ABE with detailed analyses in Sec. 4, followed by concluding remarks in Sec. 5.

2   Preliminaries

2.1   Notations

We use $[a, b]$ to denote the set $\{a, a + 1, \cdots, b\}$ containing consecutive integers. We write $[a]$ as shorthand for $[1, a]$ if no ambiguities are caused. For a set S, its cardinality is denoted by $|S|$. We denote $s_1, s_2, \cdots, s_n \overset{R}{\leftarrow} S$ for $n \in \mathbb{N}$ to show that $s_1, \cdots, s_n$ is chosen uniformly at random from S. We use $\mathbb{Z}_p^{m \times n}$ to denote the matrices of m rows and n columns with entries in $\mathbb{Z}_p$. Specifically, the row vectors and column vectors are denoted by $\mathbb{Z}_p^{1 \times n}$ and $\mathbb{Z}_p^{m \times 1}$ respectively. For the given two vectors $\vec{v}, \vec{w}$ of any type, we denote by v_i the i-th entry in $\vec{v}$, and by $\langle \vec{v}, \vec{w} \rangle$ the inner product of the two vectors.

2.2   Bilinear Groups and Computational Assumption

Our scheme is built on prime-order bilinear groups which can be efficiently generated by a generator $\mathcal{G}$ with a security parameter λ. The bilinear group system can be represented as tuple $(p, \mathbb{G}, \mathbb{G}_T, e)$, where p is a large prime, $\mathbb{G}$ and $\mathbb{G}_T$ are two cyclic groups of order p, and a bilinear map $e : \mathbb{G} \times \mathbb{G} \to \mathbb{G}_T$ satisfying three properties. (1) *Bilinearity*: for all $g, h \in \mathbb{G}$ and $a, b \in \mathbb{Z}_p$, $e(g^a, h^b) = e(g, h)^{ab}$; (2)*Non-degeneracy*: there exists at least an element $g \in \mathbb{G}$ such that $e(g, g)$ has order p in $\mathbb{G}_T$; (3) *Computability*: there exists an efficient algorithm (in polynomial time with respect to λ) to compute the bilinear pairing $e(u, v)$ for all $u, v \in \mathbb{G}$. Although our scheme is built from above symmetric pairing groups, the constructions do not rely on the symmetric property of the bilinear groups and can be easily extended to asymmetric pairing groups.

The security of our scheme relies on a weak version of the Decisional Bilinear Diffie-Hellman Assumption (wDBDH), introduced by Rouselakis and Waters [30], reviewed as follows.

Let $(p, \mathbb{G}, \mathbb{G}_T, e) \leftarrow \mathcal{G}(1^\lambda)$ be the description of the bilinear groups that is outputted by the group generator $\mathcal{G}$. Let $g \xleftarrow{R} \mathbb{G}$ be a random generator of $\mathbb{G}$. Then, choose $q + 3$ random exponents $x, y, z, b_1, b_2, \cdots, b_q \xleftarrow{R} \mathbb{Z}_p$. The q-wDBDH problem in $\mathbb{G}$ is to determine whether the given element $T \in \mathbb{G}_T$ equals $e(g, g)^{xyz}$, or a random element in $\mathbb{G}_T$ by taken the input as

$$
D \leftarrow \begin{pmatrix}
g, g^x, g^y, g^z, g^{(xz)^2} & \\
g^{b_i}, g^{xzb_i}, g^{xz/b_i}, g^{x^2 zb_i}, g^{y/b_i^2}, g^{y^2/b_i^2} & i \in [q] \\
g^{xzb_i/b_j}, g^{yb_i/b_j^2}, g^{xyzb_i/b_j}, g^{(xz)^2 b_i/b_j} & i \in [q], j \in [q], i \neq j
\end{pmatrix}
$$

The advantage of an algorithm $\mathcal{A}$ that outputs $b \in \{0, 1\}$ in solving q-wDBDH in $\mathbb{G}$ is defined as

$$
Adv_\mathcal{A}(\lambda) = \left| \Pr\left[\mathcal{A}\left(D, T = e(g, g)^{xyz}\right) = 1\right] - \Pr\left[\mathcal{A}\left(D, T \xleftarrow{R} \mathbb{G}_T\right) = 1\right] \right| - \frac{1}{2}
$$

Definition 1. *We say that the (ϵ, q)-weak Decisional Bilinear Diffie-Hellman Assumption in $\mathbb{G}$ holds if no polynomial time algorithm has at least a non-negligible advantage $Adv_\mathcal{A}(\lambda) \geq \epsilon$ in solving the q-wDBDH problem in $\mathbb{G}$.*

2.3 Access Structures and Linear Secret Sharing Schemes

Definition 2. *(Access Structure [2]) Let $\mathcal{U}$ be a set of parties. A collection $\mathbb{A} \subseteq 2^\mathcal{U}$ is monotone if for all $B \in \mathbb{A}$: if $B \in \mathbb{A}$ and $B \subseteq C$, then $C \in \mathbb{A}$. An access structure (monotone access structure) on $\mathcal{U}$ is a collection (monotone collection) $\mathbb{A}$ of non-empty subsets of $\mathcal{U}$, i.e., $\mathbb{A} \subseteq 2^\mathcal{U} \setminus \{\emptyset\}$. The sets in $\mathbb{A}$ are called the authorized sets, and the sets not in $\mathbb{A}$ are called the unauthorized sets.*

In Attribute-Based Encryption systems, the roles of the parties are taken by the attributes in the attribute universe $\mathcal{U}$. Therefore, the access structure $\mathbb{A}$ will contain the authorized sets of attributes. We restrict the access structure to monotone access structure. However, it is possible to realize general access structure from a monotone one by having the not of an attribute as a separate attribute altogether [3, 21], at a cost of doubling the total number of attributes in the system.

Definition 3. *(Linear Secret Sharing Schemes (LSSS) [2, 30]) Let $\mathcal{U}$ be the attribute universe. A secret sharing scheme $\prod$ with domain of secrets $\mathbb{Z}_p$ for realizing access structure on $\mathcal{U}$ is linear if*

1. *The shares of a secret $s \in \mathbb{Z}_p$ for each attribute form a vector over $\mathbb{Z}_p$.*
2. *For each access structure $\mathbb{A}$ on $\mathcal{U}$, there exists a share-generating matrix $M \in \mathbb{Z}_p^{l \times n}$ for $\prod$. For all $i \in [l]$, we define the function $\rho(i)$ that labels the i-th row of M with attributes from $\mathcal{U}$, i.e., $\rho(i) : i \to \mathcal{U}$. When we consider the column vector $\vec{v} = (s, r_2, r_3, \cdots, r_n)^{\mathrm{T}}$, where $r_2, \cdots, r_n \xleftarrow{R} \mathbb{Z}_p$, then $M\vec{v} \in \mathbb{Z}_p^{l \times 1}$ is the vector of l shares of the secret s according to $\prod$. The share $(M\vec{v})_i$ belongs to the attribute $\rho(i)$ for $i \in [l]$.*

From now on, we refer to the tuple (M, ρ) as the access structure $\mathbb{A}$ encoded by the LSSS-policy. As pointed out by Beimel [2], all secret sharing schemes should satisfy the following requirements:

1. *Reconstruction Requirement.* The secret can be reconstructed efficiently for authorized sets.
2. *Security Requirement.* It is hard to reveal any partial information about the secret for any unauthorized sets.

These two requirements are used in our setting. Let $\mathcal{S}$ denote an authorized set for the access structure $\mathbb{A}$ encoded by the LSSS-policy (M, ρ), where $M \in \mathbb{Z}_p^{l \times n}$ and $\rho : [l] \to \mathcal{U}$. We define $I_{\mathcal{S}} \subseteq [l]$ as $I_{\mathcal{S}} = \{i : \rho(i) \in \mathcal{S}\}$. On one hand, the *Reconstruction Requirement* states that there exists constants $\{\omega_i \in \mathbb{Z}_p\}_{i \in I}$ such that for any valid shares $\{\lambda_i = (M\vec{v})_i\}_{i \in I}$ of a secret s according to $\prod$, we have $\sum_{i \in I} \omega_i \lambda_i = s$. Additionally, the constants $\{\omega_i\}_{i \in I}$ can be generated in time polynomial in the size of the share-generating matrix M [2]. On the other hand, the *Security Requirement* states that for any unauthorized sets $\mathcal{S}'$ for the access structure $\mathbb{A}$, such constants $\{\omega_i\}$ do not exist. We define $I_{\mathcal{S}'} \subseteq [l]$ as $I_{\mathcal{S}'} = \{i : \rho(i) \in \mathcal{S}'\}$. In this case, there exists a vector $\vec{\omega} = (\omega_1, \cdots, \omega_n) \in \mathbb{Z}_p^{1 \times n}$, such that $\langle \vec{M_i}, \vec{\omega} \rangle = 0$ for all $i \in I_{\mathcal{S}'}$ and ω_1 can be any non zero element in $\mathbb{Z}_p$, where $\vec{M_i}$ is the i-th row of the secret-generating matrix M.

2.4 Chameleon Hash

Our scheme exploits the so-called Chameleon hash functions which were first introduced by Krawczyk and Rabin [22], further refined respectively by Ateniese et al. [1] and by Chen et al. [10–14]. A Chameleon hash has a key pair (pk_{ch}, sk_{ch}). Anyone who knows the public key pk_{ch} can efficiently compute the hash value for any given input. Meanwhile, there exists an efficient algorithm for the holder of the secret key sk_{ch} to find collisions for every given input, but anyone who does not have sk_{ch} cannot compute the collisions for any given input. Formally, a Chameleon hash function consists of three polynomial time algorithms:

– $(sk_{ch}, pk_{ch}) \leftarrow \mathbf{KeyGen_{ch}}(1^\lambda)$. The algorithm $\mathbf{KeyGen_{ch}}$ takes the security parameter $\lambda \in \mathbb{N}$ as input, and outputs a pair containing a Chameleon hash secret key and a public key (sk_{ch}, pk_{ch}).

- $H_m \leftarrow$ **Hash$_{ch}$**(pk_{ch}, m, r_{ch}). The algorithm **Hash$_{ch}$** takes as inputs the Chameleon hash public key pk_{ch}, a message m, and an auxiliary random parameter r_{ch}. It outputs the hashed value H_m.
- $r'_{ch} \leftarrow$ **UForge$_{ch}$**(sk_{ch}, m, r_{ch}, m'). The algorithm **UForge$_{ch}$** takes as inputs the Chameleon hash secret key sk_{ch}, a message m with its auxiliary random parameter r_{ch} for perviously calculating its Chameleon hash value H_m, and another message $m' \neq m$. The algorithm outputs another auxiliary random parameter r'_{ch} such that $H_m =$ **Hash$_{ch}$**$(pk_{ch}, m, r_{ch}) =$ **Hash$_{ch}$**$(pk_{ch}, m', r'_{ch}) = H_{m'}$.

A Chameleon hash function should satisfy the following security requirements.

1. *Collision Resistance.* There is no efficient algorithm that takes as input the Chameleon hash public key pk_{ch} to find two pairs (m, r_{ch}), (m', r'_{ch}) where $m \neq m'$, such that **Hash$_{ch}$**$(pk_{ch}, m, r_{ch}) =$ **Hash$_{ch}$**(pk_{ch}, m', r'_{ch}) except with negligible probability.
2. *Uniformity.* All messages m induce the same probability distribution on $H_m \leftarrow$ **Hash$_{ch}$**(pk_{ch}, m, r_{ch}) for r_{ch} chosen uniformly at random.

3   Key-Policy Attribute-Based Encryption

A KP-ABE system consists of four polynomial time algorithms defined as follows.

- $(pp, msk) \leftarrow$**Setup**(1^λ). The algorithm **Setup** only takes the security parameter $\lambda \in \mathbb{N}$ as input. It outputs a master secret key msk and a public parameter pp. We assume that the description of the attribute universe $\mathcal{U}$ is also included in the public parameter pp.
- $sk_{\mathbb{A}} \leftarrow$**KeyGen**$(pp, msk, \mathbb{A})$. The algorithm **KeyGen** takes as inputs the public parameter pp, the master secret key msk, and an access structure $\mathbb{A}$. It outputs a secret key $sk_{\mathbb{A}}$ associated with the access structure $\mathbb{A}$.
- $ct_{\mathcal{S}} \leftarrow$**Encrypt**$(pp, m, \mathcal{S})$. The algorithm **Encrypt** takes as inputs the public parameter pp, a message m in the plaintext space $\mathcal{M}$, and a set of attributes $\mathcal{S}$ on the attribute universe $\mathcal{U}$. The algorithm outputs the ciphertext $ct_{\mathcal{S}}$ for m associated with the attribute set $\mathcal{S}$.
- $m \leftarrow$**Decrypt**$(pp, sk_{\mathbb{A}}, ct_{\mathcal{S}})$. The algorithm **Decrypt** takes as inputs the public parameter pp, a secret key $sk_{\mathbb{A}}$ associated with an access structure $\mathbb{A}$, and a ciphertext $ct_{\mathcal{S}}$ for a message $m \in \mathcal{M}$ associated with an attribute set $\mathcal{S}$. It returns m.

A KP-ABE system is correct if for all $(pp, msk) \leftarrow$ **Setup**(1^λ), all $sk_{\mathbb{A}} \leftarrow$ **KeyGen**$(pp, msk, \mathbb{A})$, all $m \in \mathcal{M}$, and all $ct_{\mathcal{S}} \leftarrow$ **Encrypt**$(pp, m, \mathcal{S})$ with $\mathcal{S} \subseteq \mathcal{U}$, if $\mathcal{S}$ satisfies $\mathbb{A}$, then **Decrypt**$(pp, sk_{\mathbb{A}}, ct_{\mathcal{S}}) = m$.

We next define the indistinguishability against chosen ciphertext attacks in KP-ABE systems. In this security model, the adversary is allowed to obtain the secret keys associated with any access structure $\mathbb{A}$ of its choice and to issue decryption queries for its chosen ciphertexts, provided that the adversary does not query for the secret keys with access structures that can be satisfied by the challenge attribute set $\mathcal{S}^*$, or for the challenge ciphertext of one of its chosen message. We require that even such an adversary cannot distinguish the encrypted messages.

Formally, the selective chosen attribute set and chosen ciphertext security model is defined through a game played by an adversary and a challenger. Both of them are given the security parameter λ as input.

- **Init.** The adversary $\mathcal{A}$ commits to a challenge attribute set $\mathcal{S}^*$ and sends it to the challenger.
- **Setup.** The challenger gives the public parameter pp to the adversary $\mathcal{A}$.
- **Phase 1.** The adversary $\mathcal{A}$ adaptively issues two kinds of queries:
  - Secret key query for an access structure $\mathbb{A}$ that is not satisfied by the challenge attribute set $\mathcal{S}^*$. The challenger generates a secret key for $\mathbb{A}$ and gives it to the adversary.
  - Decryption query for the ciphertext $ct_\mathcal{S}$ with an attribute set $\mathcal{S}$. The challenger responds by constructing an access structure $\mathbb{A}$ satisfied by the attribute set $\mathcal{S}$, and running **KeyGen**$(pp, msk, \mathbb{A})$ to generate a secret key $sk_{\mathbb{A}}$. It then runs **Decrypt**$(pp, sk_{\mathbb{A}}, ct_\mathcal{S})$ to decrypt the ciphertext $ct_\mathcal{S}$ and returns the resulting message to the adversary.
- **Challenge.** When adversary $\mathcal{A}$ decides that **Phase 1** is over, it outputs two equal-length messages m_0 and m_1 on which it wishes to challenge. The challenger flips a random coin $b \in \{0, 1\}$ and encrypts m_b under the challenge attribute set $\mathcal{S}^*$. It returns the challenge ciphertext ct^* to $\mathcal{A}$.
- **Phase 2.** The adversary $\mathcal{A}$ further adaptively issues two kinds of queries:
  - Secret key query for access structures $\mathbb{A}$ that is not satisfied by the challenge attribute set $\mathcal{S}^*$.
  - Decryption query for the ciphertext $ct_\mathcal{S}$ with a constraint that $ct_\mathcal{S} \neq ct^*$.

  The challenger responds the same as in **Phase 1**.
- **Guess.** Finally, the adversary $\mathcal{A}$ outputs a guess $b' \in \{0, 1\}$ and wins in the game if $b = b'$.

The advantage of such an adversary $\mathcal{A}$ in attacking the KP-ABE system with security parameter λ is defined as $Adv_{\mathcal{A}}^{\text{KP-ABE}}(\lambda) = \left| \Pr[b' = b] - \frac{1}{2} \right|$.

Definition 4. *A KP-ABE system is selective chosen attribute set and chosen ciphertext secure if for any probabilistic polynomial time adversary $\mathcal{A}$, the advantage of breaking the security game defined above is at most a negligible function.*

4   Direct CCA2-Secure KP-ABE with Public Verifiability

4.1   Basic Ideas

We first provide an overview of the construction. We exploit specific ciphertext structure in the ABE scheme in [30] and address the three issues shown in Sec. 1 to obtain a practical CCA2-secure KP-ABE scheme in the standard model.

1. Our construction is based on a recent KP-ABE system [30]. The CCA2-secure IBE schemes [6] exploits a specific structure of the underlying IBE ciphertext [4] including Decision Diffie-Hellman (DDH) tuple, i.e., $(g, g^r, h \cdot u^{ID}, (h \cdot u^{ID})^r)$, where ID is the target identity. The KP-ABE system [30] contains a DDH ciphertext tuple and allows arbitrary attributes, which addresses the arbitrary attribute requirement.
2. Instead of extending an attribute hierarchy in ABE, our construction adds one on-the-fly dummy attribute used for ciphertext validation in the decryption procedure. We split the original attribute universe into two parts, one for regular attribute universe $\mathcal{U}$, the other for verification universe $\mathcal{V}$ for the on-the-fly attributes. This trick ensures that the dummy attributes will only be used for ciphertext validation, and allows us to circumvent the arbitrary attribute delegation obstacle.
3. We exploit Chameleon hash $\mathbf{Hash_{ch}}$ to solve the problem that the simulator cannot in advance know the challenge on-the-fly dummy attribute in the security proof. In the **Setup** phase, the simulator generates a temporary message and calls $\mathbf{Hash_{ch}}$ to obtain the on-the-fly dummy attribute. When learning the actual challenge message in the **Challenge** phase, the simulator replaces the temporary message to the actual message, while keeping the dummy attribute unchanged by using the "universe collision" property of Chameleon hash. In the adversary's view, the Chameleon hash function keeps collision resistant since it does not know the Chameleon hash secret key.

4.2 Our Construction

Let $\mathcal{U} = \left[0, \frac{p-1}{2}\right]$ be the regular attribute universe, and $\mathcal{V} = \left[\frac{p+1}{2}, p-1\right]$ the verification universe. Note that $\mathcal{U} \cap \mathcal{V} = \emptyset$, and $\mathcal{U} \cup \mathcal{V} = \mathbb{Z}_p$, where $\mathbb{Z}_p$ is the original attribute universe in Rouselakis-Waters KP-ABE. Our CCA2-secure KP-ABE scheme works as follows.

- **Setup**(1^λ). Run $(p, \mathbb{G}, \mathbb{G}_T, e) \leftarrow \mathcal{G}(1^\lambda)$ to generate a prime p, two groups $\mathbb{G}, \mathbb{G}_T$ of order p, and a bilinear map $e : \mathbb{G} \times \mathbb{G} \to \mathbb{G}_T$. A secure Chameleon hash function $\mathbf{Hash_{ch}}: \{0, 1\}^* \to \left[\frac{p+1}{2}, p-1\right]$ with an auxiliary parameter universe $\mathcal{R}$ is also employed in the scheme. Then, select a random generator $g \xleftarrow{R} \mathbb{G}$, random elements $h, u, w \xleftarrow{R} \mathbb{G}$, and a random exponent $\alpha \xleftarrow{R} \mathbb{Z}_p$. The algorithm calls $(sk_{ch}, pk_{ch}) \leftarrow \mathbf{KeyGen_{ch}}(1^\lambda)$ to obtain a (sk_{ch}, pk_{ch}) pair for the Chameleon hash. The public parameter is $pp \leftarrow (\mathbf{Hash_{ch}}, \mathcal{R}, pk_{ch}, g, h, u, w, e(g, g)^\alpha)$. The master secret key is $msk \leftarrow (\alpha)$.

- **KeyGen**$(pp, msk, (M, \rho))$. For generating a secret key for an access structure encoded by the LSSS-policy (M, ρ), where $M \in \mathbb{Z}_p^{l \times n}$ and $\rho : [l] \to \left[0, \frac{p-1}{2}\right]$, the key generation algorithm first picks $n - 1$ random exponents $y_2, \cdots, y_n \xleftarrow{R} \mathbb{Z}_p$, and constructs the vector $\vec{y} = (\alpha, y_2, \cdots, y_n)^\mathrm{T}$. Then, the vector of the shares $\vec{\lambda}$ can be computed by the key generation algorithm as $\vec{\lambda} = (\lambda_1, \lambda_2, \cdots, \lambda_l)^\mathrm{T} = M\vec{y}$. The algorithm next picks

l random exponents $t_1, t_2, \cdots, t_l \xleftarrow{R} \mathbb{Z}_p$. For every $i \in [l]$, it calculates
$K_{i,0} = g^{\lambda_i} w^{t_i}, K_{i,1} = (h \cdot u^{\rho(i)})^{-t_i}, K_{i,2} = g^{t_i}$. The secret key is

$$sk_{(M,\rho)} \leftarrow ((M,\rho), \{K_{i,0}, K_{i,1}, K_{i,2}\}_{i \in [l]})$$

- **Encrypt**$(pp, m, \mathcal{S})$. Given the attribute set $\mathcal{S} = \{A_1, A_2, \cdots, A_\kappa\}$, where $\kappa = |\mathcal{S}|$, the algorithm first picks $\kappa + 2$ random exponents $s, r_0, r_1, \cdots, r_\kappa \xleftarrow{R} \mathbb{Z}_p$. It then computes $C = m \cdot e(g,g)^{\alpha s}, C_0 = g^s, C_{0,1} = g^{r_0}$, and for every $i \in [\kappa], C_{i,1} = g^{r_i}, C_{i,2} = (h \cdot u^{A_i})^{r_i} w^{-s}$. It picks a parameter $r_{ch} \xleftarrow{R} \mathcal{R}$ and sets $V = \mathbf{Hash_{ch}}(pk_{ch}, pk_{ch} \| C \| C_0 \| C_{0,1} \| C_{1,1} \| C_{2,1} \| \cdots \| C_{\kappa,1}, r_{ch}) \in \mathcal{V}$. The $C_{0,2}$ component can be computed as $C_{0,2} = (h \cdot u^V)^{r_0} w^{-s}$. The algorithm finally outputs the ciphertext associated with the attribute set $\mathcal{S}$ as

$$ct_\mathcal{S} \leftarrow (\mathcal{S}, r_{ch}, C, C_0, C_{0,1}, C_{0,2}, \{C_{i,1}, C_{i,2}\}_{i \in [\kappa]}).$$

- **Decrypt**$(pp, sk_{(M,\rho)}, ct_\mathcal{S})$. Before decrypting $ct_\mathcal{S}$, the algorithm first calculates $V = \mathbf{Hash_{ch}}(pk_{ch}, pk_{ch} \| C \| C_0 \| C_{0,1} \| C_{1,1} \| C_{2,1} \| \cdots \| C_{\kappa,1}, r_{ch})$, where $\kappa = |\mathcal{S}|$. Then, it verifies whether the ciphertext is legitimate by testing whether the following equation holds for each $i \in [\kappa]$

$$e(g, C_{i,2}) \overset{?}{=} e(C_{i,1}, h \cdot u^{A_i}) / e(C_0, w) \tag{1}$$

It additionally tests whether the following equation holds

$$e(g, C_{0,2}) \overset{?}{=} e(C_{0,1}, h \cdot u^V) / e(C_0, w) \tag{2}$$

Note that the above ciphertext validity test can be done publicly since it only involves public parameter pp and ciphertext $ct_\mathcal{S}$.

If any equality does not hold, the ciphertext is invalid and the decryption algorithm outputs $\perp$. Otherwise, the algorithm calculates the row set of M that provides the share to attributes in the given attribute set $\mathcal{S}$, i.e., $I = \{i : \rho(i) \in \mathcal{S}\}$. Then, it computes the constants $\{\omega_i \in \mathbb{Z}_p\}_{i \in I}$ such that $\sum_{i \in I} \omega_i \overrightarrow{M_i} = (1, 0, \cdots, 0)$, where $\overrightarrow{M_i}$ is the i-th row of the share-generating matrix M. We note that the constants $\{\omega_i \in \mathbb{Z}_p\}_{i \in I}$ can be found in polynomial time for all $\mathcal{S}$ that satisfies the access structure [2]. Finally, the message m can be recovered by computing

$$B = \prod_{i \in I} (e(K_{i,0}, C_0) e(K_{i,1}, C_{j,1}) e(K_{i,2}, C_{j,2}))^{\omega_i}$$

where j is the index of the attribute $\rho(i)$ in $\mathcal{S}$ that is depended on i, and computing $m = C/B$.

Consistency. If the ciphertext is associated with the attribute set $\mathcal{S}$, then for every $i \in [\kappa]$ where $\kappa = |\mathcal{S}|$, we have that

$$e(g, C_{i,2}) = e\left(g, (h \cdot u^{A_i})^{r_i} w^{-s}\right) = e\left(g, (h \cdot u^{A_i})^{r_i}\right) \cdot e(g, w^{-s})$$

$$= e(g^{r_i}, h \cdot u^{A_i}) \cdot e(g^{-s}, w) = \frac{e(g^{r_i}, h \cdot u^{A_i})}{e(g^s, w)} = \frac{e(C_{i,1}, h \cdot u^{A_i})}{e(C_0, w)}$$

Accordingly, Equation (1) holds. With the similar procedure shown above, Equation (2) holds for the valid on-the-fly dummy attribute

$$V = \mathbf{Hash_{ch}}\,(pk_{ch}, pk_{ch}\|C_0\|C_{1,1}\|C_{2,1}\|\cdots\|C_{\kappa,1}, r_{ch})$$

Also, if the attribute set $\mathcal{S}$ of the ciphertext $ct_{\mathcal{S}}$ satisfies the access structure encoded by the LSSS-policy (M, ρ), then $\sum_{i\in I} \omega_i \lambda_i = \alpha$. Since j is the index of the attribute $\rho(i)$ in $\mathcal{S}$, we have that $\rho(i) = A_j$. Therefore

$$
\begin{aligned}
B &= \prod_{i\in I} \left(e\left(K_{i,0}, C_0\right) e\left(K_{i,1}, C_{j,1}\right) e\left(K_{i,2}, C_{j,2}\right) \right)^{\omega_i} \\
&= \prod_{i\in I} \left(e\left(g^{\lambda_i} w^{t_i}, g^s\right) e\left(\left(h\cdot u^{\rho(i)}\right)^{-t_i}, g^{r_j} \right) e\left(g^{t_i}, \left(h\cdot u^{A_j}\right)^{r_j} w^{-s} \right) \right)^{\omega_i} \\
&= \prod_{i\in I} \left(e\left(g^{\lambda_i}, g^s\right) e\left(w^{t_i}, g^s\right) e\left(g^{t_i}, w^{-s}\right) \right)^{\omega_i} \\
&= \prod_{i\in I} \left(e\left(g^{\lambda_i}, g^s\right) \right)^{\omega_i} = e(g, g^s)^{\sum_{i\in I} \omega_i \lambda_i} = e(g, g)^{\alpha s}
\end{aligned}
$$

Thus, we have that $C/B = m\cdot e(g,g)^{\alpha s}/e(g,g)^{\alpha s} = m$.

Public Verifiability. Our scheme is a publicly verifiable CCA2-secure KP-ABE, since the above ciphertext validity test only involves public parameter pp and ciphertext $ct_{\mathcal{S}}$. This property is useful to build advanced Attribute-Based cryptography protocols, e.g., ciphertext filtering KP-ABE, in which anyone (e.g., a gateway of a firewall) can verify whether the ciphertext is encrypted by the specified access structure to filter spams (i.e., invalid ciphertexts) without requiring the secret keys of the receivers.

4.3   Performance Analysis

Table 1 compares our CCA2-secure KP-ABE with the underlying Rouselakis-Waters CPA-secure KP-ABE. In the table, the secret key $sk_{(M,\rho)}$ is associated with the LSSS-policy (M, ρ) with $M \in \mathbb{Z}_p^{l\times n}$, and the ciphertext $ct_{\mathcal{S}}$ is associated with the attribute set $\mathcal{S}$ with $\kappa = |\mathcal{S}|$. We denote τ_e as one exponent operation in $\mathbb{G}$ and $\mathbb{G}_T$, τ_m as one multiplication operation in $\mathbb{G}$ and $\mathbb{G}_T$, τ_p as one pairing operation time, and τ_h as one Chameleon hash operation time.

From Table 1, it can be seen that the additional overheads for CCA2-security are considerably low. Specifically, the secret key size in our CCA2-secure KP-ABE scheme remain the same as that of the underlying Rouselakis-Waters KP-ABE scheme [30]. For a ciphertext associated with arbitrary number of attributes, only two more group elements in $\mathbb{G}$ are added. The encryption algorithm needs only one more hash operation, three more exponent operations in $\mathbb{G}$ and two more multiplication operation in $\mathbb{G}$.

Table 1. Comparisons among Rouselakis-Waters KP-ABE and our KP-ABE

	Rouselakis-Waters ABE	Our KP-ABE
Security	CPA-secure	CCA2-secure
pp Size	5	$5 + |pk_{ch}|$
$sk_{(M,\rho)}$ Size	$3l + |(M,\rho)|$	$3l + |(M,\rho)|$
ct_S Size	$3\kappa + 2$	$3\kappa + 4 + |r_{ch}|$
KeyGen Time	$5l \cdot \tau_e + 2l \cdot \tau_m$	$5l \cdot \tau_e + 2l \cdot \tau_m$
Encrypt Time	$(3\kappa + 2) \cdot \tau_e + (2\kappa + 1) \cdot \tau_m$	$(3\kappa + 5) \cdot \tau_e + (2\kappa + 3) \cdot \tau_m + \tau_h$

We note that the work in [16] also exploits dummy attributes to achieve CCA2-secure ABE. In [16], signatures are added to CPA-secure ABE for validating ciphertext in decryption. Each bit of the verification keys K_v is treated as an attribute, which introduces $|K_v|$ dummy attributes. In contrast, we only introduce one dummy attribute. Our approach is compact and efficient.

4.4 Security Analysis

The Chameleon hash is critical in our proof. In the **Init** phase, the simulator chooses a random challenge message m^* and an auxiliary parameter r^* to construct the challenge on-the-fly dummy attribute V^*. In the **Challenge** phase, given the challenge messages m_0, m_1, the simulator obtains a collision pair (m_b^*, r_b^*) such that $\mathbf{Hash_{ch}}(pk_{ch}, m^*, r^*) = \mathbf{Hash_{ch}}(pk_{ch}, m_b^*, r_b^*) = V^*$ to make the challenge on-the-fly dummy attribute V^* unchanged. This approach allows the simulator in advance obtain the challenge dummy attribute. Since all challenge attributes can be obtained in the **Setup** phase, the simulator can correctly play the selective security game with the adversary.

Formally, the selective chosen attribute set and chosen ciphertext security result is guaranteed by Theorem 1.

Theorem 1. *Let $\mathbb{G}$ be a group of prime order p equipped with an efficient bilinear map $e : \mathbb{G} \times \mathbb{G} \to \mathbb{G}_T$. Our KP-ABE scheme is selective chosen attribute set and chosen ciphertext secure if the $(\epsilon, q+1)$-wDBDH assumption holds in $\mathbb{G}$, the employed Chameleon hash function is secure, and the challenge attribute set S^* that the adversary commits to satisfies that $|S^*| \leq q$.*

Proof. Suppose that there exists an algorithm $\mathcal{A}$ that has advantage ϵ to break our KP-ABE system in the security game defined in Sec. 3. We construct an algorithm $\mathcal{B}$ that can solve the $(q+1)$-wDBDH problem in $\mathbb{G}$. The input of the algorithm $\mathcal{B}$ is the challenge tuple (D, T) of the $(q+1)$-wDBDH problem. Algorithm $\mathcal{B}$ interacts with $\mathcal{A}$ as follows.

Init. Algorithm $\mathcal{A}$ sends the challenge set $S^* = \{A_1^*, A_2^*, \cdots, A_\kappa^*\}$ to $\mathcal{B}$.

Setup. Algorithm $\mathcal{B}$ sets the public parameter pp as follows. It randomly chooses $\widetilde{u} \xleftarrow{R} \mathbb{Z}_p$ and sets

$$(g, u, w, e(g,g)^\alpha) = (g, g^{\widetilde{u}} \cdot \prod_{i \in [\kappa+1]} g^{y/b_i^2}, g^x, e(g^x, g^y))$$

It then sets $C_0^* = g^s = g^z$, $C_{0,1}^* = g^{r_0} = g^{b_{\kappa+1}}$, and $C_{i,1}^* = g^{r_i} = g^{b_i}$ for all $i \in [\kappa]$. It next chooses a secure Chameleon hash function $\mathbf{Hash_{ch}} : \{0,1\}^* \to \left[\frac{p+1}{2}, p-1\right]$ with an auxiliary parameter universe $\mathcal{R}$ and runs $(sk_{ch}, pk_{ch}) \leftarrow \mathbf{KeyGen_{ch}}(1^\lambda)$. Algorithm $\mathcal{B}$ picks a random auxiliary parameter $r_{ch}^* \xleftarrow{R} \mathcal{R}$, a random challenge message $m^* \xleftarrow{R} \mathbb{G}_T$, sets $C^* = m^* \cdot T$, and calls $\mathbf{Hash_{ch}}$ to calculate $V^* = \mathbf{Hash_{ch}}(pk_{ch}, C^*, r_{ch}^*)$. Finally, algorithm $\mathcal{B}$ picks a random exponent $\widetilde{h} \xleftarrow{R} \mathbb{Z}_p$ and sets

$$h = g^{\widetilde{h}} \cdot \prod_{i \in [\kappa+1]} g^{xz/b_i} \cdot \prod_{i \in [\kappa]} \left(g^{y/b_i^2}\right)^{-A_i^*} \left(g^{y/b_{\kappa+1}^2}\right)^{-V^*}$$

The public parameter is $pp \leftarrow (\mathbf{Hash_{ch}}, \mathcal{R}, pk_{ch}, g, h, u, w, e(g,g)^\alpha)$ and $\mathcal{B}$ is implicitly set $msk \leftarrow (xy)$ and $s \leftarrow z$, which $\mathcal{B}$ cannot know their values from D. Note also that sk_{ch} and r_{ch}^* is kept secret by $\mathcal{B}$.

Phase 1. Algorithm $\mathcal{A}$ adaptively issues two kinds of queries.

Secret Key Queries: Secret key query for a LSSS-policy (M, ρ) for which the challenge set $\mathcal{S}^*$ is not authorized. Suppose that $M \in \mathbb{Z}_p^{l \times n}$ and $\rho : [l] \to \left[0, \frac{p-1}{2}\right]$. According to *security requirement* of LSSS that has previously shown in Sec. 2.3, algorithm $\mathcal{B}$ can use linear algebra to generate a vector $\overrightarrow{\omega} = (\omega_1, \omega_2, \cdots, \omega_n)^{\mathrm{T}} \in \mathbb{Z}_p^n$ satisfying that $\omega_1 = 1$ and $\langle \overrightarrow{M_i}, \overrightarrow{\omega} \rangle = 0$ for all $i \in [l]$ such that $\rho(i) \in \mathcal{S}^*$. Then, algorithm $\mathcal{B}$ randomly chooses $\widetilde{y}_2, \widetilde{y}_3, \cdots, \widetilde{y}_n \xleftarrow{R} \mathbb{Z}_p$ and implicitly sets $\overrightarrow{y} = xy\overrightarrow{\omega} + (0, \widetilde{y}_2, \widetilde{y}_3, \cdots, \widetilde{y}_n)^{\mathrm{T}} = (xy, \widetilde{y}_2 + \omega_2, \widetilde{y}_3 + \omega_3, \cdots, \widetilde{y}_n + \omega_n)^{\mathrm{T}}$. For all $i \in [l]$, we have the following two cases:

1. $i \in [l]$ such that $\rho(i) \in \mathcal{S}^*$. In this case, we have that $\omega_1 = 1$ and $\langle \overrightarrow{M_i}, \overrightarrow{\omega} \rangle = 0$. Therefore, the share λ_i is $\lambda_i = \langle \overrightarrow{M_i}, \overrightarrow{y} \rangle = \langle \overrightarrow{M_i}, xy\overrightarrow{\omega} + (0, \widetilde{y}_2, \widetilde{y}_3, \cdots, \widetilde{y}_n)^{\mathrm{T}} \rangle = xy \cdot 0 + \langle \overrightarrow{M_i}, (0, \widetilde{y}_2, \cdots, \widetilde{y}_n)^{\mathrm{T}} \rangle$, where we set $\widetilde{\lambda}_i = \langle \overrightarrow{M_i}, (0, \widetilde{y}_2, \cdots, \widetilde{y}_n)^{\mathrm{T}} \rangle$ that can be calculated by $\mathcal{B}$. Algorithm $\mathcal{B}$ can finally pick a random exponent $\widetilde{t}_i \xleftarrow{R} \mathbb{Z}_p$, and outputs $K_{i,0} = g^{\widetilde{\lambda}_i} w^{\widetilde{t}_i}$, $K_{i,1} = \left(h \cdot u^{\rho(i)}\right)^{-\widetilde{t}_i}$, $K_{i,2} = g^{\widetilde{t}_i}$.

2. $i \in [l]$ such that $\rho(i) \notin \mathcal{S}^*$. In this case, we have that $\langle \overrightarrow{M_i}, \overrightarrow{\omega} \rangle \neq 0$. The share λ_i is also formed as $\lambda_i = \langle \overrightarrow{M_i}, \overrightarrow{y} \rangle = xy \cdot \langle \overrightarrow{M_i}, \overrightarrow{\omega} \rangle + \langle \overrightarrow{M_i}, (0, \widetilde{y}_2, \cdots, \widetilde{y}_n)^{\mathrm{T}} \rangle = xy \cdot \langle \overrightarrow{M_i}, \overrightarrow{\omega} \rangle + \widetilde{\lambda}_i$, where $xy \cdot \langle \overrightarrow{M_i}, \overrightarrow{\omega} \rangle \neq 0$. Algorithm $\mathcal{B}$ next picks a random $\widetilde{t}_i \xleftarrow{R} \mathbb{Z}_p$ to implicitly set t_i as

$$t_i = -y\langle \overrightarrow{M_i}, \overrightarrow{\omega} \rangle + \sum_{j \in [\kappa]} \frac{xzb_j \langle \overrightarrow{M_i}, \overrightarrow{\omega} \rangle}{\rho(i) - A_j^*} + \frac{xzb_{\kappa+1} \langle \overrightarrow{M_i}, \overrightarrow{\omega} \rangle}{\rho(i) - V^*} + \widetilde{t}_i$$

Since $\rho(i) \notin \mathcal{S}^*$, we have that $\rho(i) - A_j^* \neq 0$ for all $j \in [k]$. Also, $\rho(i) \in \left[0, \frac{p-1}{2}\right]$ while $V^* \in \left[\frac{p+1}{2}, p-1\right]$ so that $\rho(i) - V^* \neq 0$. Therefore, t_i can be well-defined and it is properly distributed due to the randomness of $\widetilde{t}_i$. The first component $K_{i,0}$ can be calculated as

$$
K_{i,0} = g^{\lambda_i} w^{t_i} = g^{xy \cdot W_i + \widetilde{\lambda}_i} \cdot w^{-y \cdot W_i + \left(\sum\limits_{j \in [\kappa]} \frac{xzb_j \cdot W_i}{\rho(i) - A_j^*} \right) + \frac{xzb_{\kappa+1} \cdot W_i}{\rho(i) - V^*} + \widetilde{t}_i}
$$
$$
= g^{\widetilde{\lambda}_i} \cdot w^{\widetilde{t}_i} \cdot \prod_{j \in [\kappa]} \left(g^{x^2 zb_j} \right)^{\frac{W_i}{\rho(i) - A_j^*}} \cdot \left(g^{x^2 zb_{\kappa+1}} \right)^{\frac{W_i}{\rho(i) - V^*}}
$$

where we denote $W_i = \langle \vec{M}_i, \vec{\omega} \rangle$. Accordingly, $K_{i,1}$ can be calculated as

$$
K_{i,1} = \left(u^{\rho(i)} h \right)^{-t_i} = \left(g^{\rho(i)\widetilde{u} + \widetilde{h}} \prod_{k \in [\kappa+1]} g^{\frac{\rho(i)y}{b_k^2} + \frac{xz}{b_k}} \prod_{k \in [\kappa]} \left(g^{\frac{y}{b_k^2}} \right)^{-A_k^*} \left(g^{\frac{y}{b_{\kappa+1}^2}} \right)^{-V^*} \right)^{yW_i}
$$
$$
\cdot \left(g^{\rho(i)\widetilde{u} + \widetilde{h}} \prod_{k \in [\kappa+1]} g^{\frac{\rho(i)y}{b_k^2} + \frac{xz}{b_k}} \prod_{k \in [\kappa]} \left(g^{\frac{y}{b_k^2}} \right)^{-A_k^*} \left(g^{\frac{y}{b_{\kappa+1}^2}} \right)^{-V^*} \right)^{-\sum\limits_{j \in [\kappa]} \frac{xzb_j \cdot W_i}{\rho(i) - A_j^*}}
$$
$$
\cdot \left(g^{\rho(i)\widetilde{u} + \widetilde{h}} \prod_{k \in [\kappa+1]} g^{\frac{\rho(i)y}{b_k^2} + \frac{xz}{b_k}} \prod_{j \in [\kappa]} \left(g^{\frac{y}{b_k^2}} \right)^{-A_k^*} \left(g^{\frac{y}{b_{\kappa+1}^2}} \right)^{-V^*} \right)^{-\frac{xzb_{\kappa+1} \cdot W_i}{\rho(i) - V^*} - \widetilde{t}_i}
$$
$$
= (g^y)^{W_i \left(\rho(i)\widetilde{u} + \widetilde{h} \right)} \prod_{k \in [\kappa]} \left(g^{\frac{y^2}{b_k^2}} \right)^{W_i(\rho(i) - A_k^*)} \left(g^{\frac{y^2}{b_{\kappa+1}^2}} \right)^{W_i(\rho(i) - V^*)}
$$
$$
\cdot \prod_{j \in [\kappa+1]} \left(g^{xzb_j} \right)^{\frac{-W_i(\rho(i)\widetilde{u} + \widetilde{h})}{\rho(i) - A_j^*}} \left(g^{xzb_{\kappa+1}} \right)^{\frac{-W_i \cdot (\rho(i)\widetilde{u} + \widetilde{h})}{\rho(i) - V^*}}
$$
$$
\cdot \prod_{\substack{j \in [\kappa] \\ k \in [\kappa+1]}} \left(g^{\frac{(xz)^2 b_j}{b_k}} \right)^{-\frac{W_i}{\rho(i) - A_j^*}} \prod_{k \in [\kappa+1]} \left(g^{(xz)^2 b_{\kappa+1}/b_k} \right)^{-\frac{W_i}{\rho(i) - V^*}} \left(u^{\rho(i)} h \right)^{-\widetilde{t}_i}
$$
$$
\cdot \left(\prod_{\substack{j,k \in [\kappa] \\ j \neq k}} \left(g^{\frac{xyzb_j}{b_k^2}} \right)^{\frac{\rho(i) - A_k^*}{\rho(i) - A_j^*}} \prod_{j \in [\kappa]} \left(g^{\frac{xyzb_j}{b_{\kappa+1}^2}} \right)^{\frac{\rho(i) - V^*}{\rho(i) - A_j^*}} \left(\prod_{k \in [\kappa]} g^{\frac{xyzb_{\kappa+1}}{b_k^2}} \right)^{\frac{\rho(i) - A_k^*}{\rho(i) - V^*}} \right)^{-W_i}
$$

Similarly, the third component $K_{i,2}$ is formed as

$$
K_{i,2} = g^{t_i} = g^{-y \cdot W_i + \left(\sum\limits_{j \in [\kappa]} \frac{xzb_j \cdot W_i}{\rho(i) - A_j^*} \right) + \frac{xzb_{\kappa+1} \cdot W_i}{\rho(i) - V^*} + \widetilde{t}_i}
$$
$$
= (g^y)^{-W_i} \cdot \prod_{j \in [\kappa]} \left(g^{xzb_j} \right)^{\frac{W_i}{\rho(i) - A_j^*}} \cdot \left(g^{xzb_{\kappa+1}} \right)^{\frac{W_i}{\rho(i) - V^*}} \cdot g^{\widetilde{t}_i}
$$

Therefore, all components in $sk_{(M,\rho)}$ can be computed by $\mathcal{B}$. Hence, algorithm $\mathcal{B}$ can generate the secret key for the issued access structure (M, ρ) and correctly response to $\mathcal{A}$'s request.

Decryption Queries: Decryption query for the ciphertext $ct_{\mathcal{S}}$ associated with an attribute set $\mathcal{S} = \{A_1, \cdots, A_{|\mathcal{S}|}\}$. Algorithm $\mathcal{B}$ first computes

$$V = \mathbf{Hash}_{\mathbf{ch}} \left(pk_{ch}, pk_{ch} \| C \| C_0 \| C_{1,1} \cdots \| C_{|\mathcal{S}|,1}, r_{ch} \right)$$

and determines whether the ciphertext is valid by checking Equation (1) for all $i \in [|\mathcal{S}|]$ and Equation (2). If one of the equalities does not hold, the ciphertext is invalid and $\mathcal{B}$ returns with $\bot$. Otherwise:

1. $\mathcal{S} \nsubseteq \mathcal{S}^*$. In this case, algorithm $\mathcal{B}$ can construct an access structure (M, ρ) such that $\mathcal{S}$ satisfies (M, ρ) but $\mathcal{S}^*$ does not (For example, an access structure $(A_1 \wedge A_2 \wedge \cdots \wedge A_{|\mathcal{S}|})$). Since $\mathcal{S}^*$ cannot be authorized by (M, ρ), algorithm $\mathcal{B}$ can run the same algorithm described in secret key query phase to generate a well-formed secret key $sk_{(M,\rho)}$ for that access structure and decrypt by running $\mathbf{Decrypt}(pp, sk_{(M,\rho)}, ct_{\mathcal{S}})$.

2. $\mathcal{S} \subseteq \mathcal{S}^*$ and $V \neq V^*$. Algorithm $\mathcal{B}$ is unable to construct any secret keys for an access structure (M, p) for which $\mathcal{S}^*$ is not authorized. However, note that the ciphertext is additional encrypted by a on-the-fly dummy attribute V. When $V \neq V^*$, algorithm can generate a secret key for the access structure $(M = (1), \rho(1) = V)$. This secret key is indeed an invalid secret key in the actual system, since $V \notin \left[0, \frac{p-1}{2}\right]$ so that V is not in the attribute universe $\mathcal{U}$. However, algorithm $\mathcal{B}$ can use such a key to decrypt the issued ciphertext. Note that $\mathcal{A}$ cannot distinguish which key $\mathcal{B}$ uses to decrypt. Hence, the decryption result is a well-formed message.

3. $\mathcal{S} \subseteq \mathcal{S}^*$ and $V = V^*$. In this case, algorithm $\mathcal{B}$ is unable to respond. It terminates the simulation with $\mathcal{A}$, outputs a random bit $b \in \{0, 1\}$ and halts. Since the Chameleon hash function $\mathcal{B}$ employs satisfies the properties of *collision resistance* and *uniformity* for anyone without sk_{ch}, this case happens with negligible probability $1/|\mathcal{V}| = 2/(p-1)$.

Challenge. Algorithm $\mathcal{A}$ submits two equal-length messages $m_0, m_1 \in \mathbb{G}_T$ to $\mathcal{B}$. Algorithm $\mathcal{B}$ flips a random coin $b \in \{0, 1\}$. The first component C_0^* of the challenge ciphertext is previously computed as $C_0^* = g^s = g^z$ in **Setup** phase, so is $C_{i,1}^* = g^{r_i} = g^{b_i}$ for each $i \in [\kappa]$. Algorithm $\mathcal{B}$ sets

$$C_{i,2}^* = \left(h \cdot u^{A_i^*} \right)^{r_i} w^{-s} = g^{b_i \left(\widetilde{u} A_i^* + \widetilde{h} \right)} \prod_{j \in [\kappa+1]} g^{\frac{xzb_j}{b_j}} \prod_{j \in [\kappa]} g^{\frac{yb_i \left(A_i^* - A_j^* \right)}{b_j^2}} \cdot g^{\frac{yb_i \left(A_i^* - V^* \right)}{b_{\kappa+1}^2}}$$

$$= \left(g^{b_i} \right)^{\widetilde{u} A_i^* + \widetilde{h}} \cdot \prod_{\substack{j \in [\kappa+1] \\ j \neq i}} g^{\frac{xzb_j}{b_j}} \prod_{\substack{j \in [\kappa] \\ j \neq i}} g^{\frac{yb_i \left(A_i^* - A_j^* \right)}{b_j^2}} \cdot g^{\frac{yb_i \left(A_i^* - V^* \right)}{b_{\kappa+1}^2}}$$

for each $i \in [\kappa]$. For the on-the-fly dummy attribute V^*, algorithm $\mathcal{B}$ sets

$$C_{0,1}^* = g^{b_{\kappa+1}}, C_{0,2}^* = \left(g^{b_{\kappa+1}} \right)^{\widetilde{u} V^* + \widetilde{h}} \cdot \prod_{j \in [\kappa]} g^{\frac{xzb_{\kappa+1}}{b_j}} \prod_{j \in [\kappa]} g^{\frac{yb_{\kappa+1} \left(V^* - A_j^* \right)}{b_j^2}}$$

To keep the on-the-fly dummy attribute V^* unchanged, algorithm $\mathcal{B}$ sets $C_b^* = m_b \cdot T$ and runs $r_b^* \leftarrow$ $\mathbf{UForge_{ch}}(sk_{ch}, C^*, r_{ch}^*, pk_{ch} \| C_b^* \| C_0^* \| C_{0,1}^* \| C_{1,1}^* \| \cdots \| C_{\kappa,1}^*)$. Note that the functionality of $\mathbf{UForge_{ch}}$ ensures

$$V^* = \mathbf{Hash_{ch}}(pk_{ch}, pk_{ch} \| C_b^* \| C_0^* \| C_{0,1}^* \| C_{1,1}^* \| C_{2,1}^* \| \cdots \| C_{\kappa,1}^*, r_b^*)$$

Algorithm $\mathcal{B}$ responses $ct^* = \left(\mathcal{S}^*, r_b^*, C_b^*, C_0^*, C_{0,1}^*, C_{0,2}^*, \{C_{i,1}^*, C_{i,2}^*\}_{i \in [\kappa]} \right)$ to $\mathcal{A}$.

Phase 2. Algorithm $\mathcal{B}$ processes as in **Phase 1** to response two kinds of queries issued from $\mathcal{A}$.

Guess. Finally, adversary $\mathcal{A}$ outputs a guess $b' \in \{0,1\}$. Algorithm $\mathcal{B}$ also outputs b' to answer the $(q+1)$-wDBDH problem. If $T = e(g,g)^{xyz} = e(g,g)^{\alpha s}$, then $\mathcal{B}$ plays the proper security game with $\mathcal{A}$ since the ct^* is a valid ciphertext for the message m_b. In this case, the advantage of algorithm $\mathcal{A}$ is ϵ. On the other hand, if $T \xleftarrow{R} \mathbb{G}_T$, then ct^* is a ciphertext for the random message chosen in $\mathbb{G}_T$ so that the advantage of $\mathcal{A}$ is exactly 0. Therefore, if $\mathcal{A}$ has advantage $Adv_{\mathcal{A}}^{\text{KP-ABE}}(\lambda) = \epsilon$ in breaking our KP-ABE scheme, then $\mathcal{B}$ can determine the distribution of T with advantage $Adv_{\mathcal{B}}(\lambda) \geq \epsilon - \frac{2}{p-1}$. $\square$

5   Conclusion

We proposed a direct construction of fully functional CCA2-secure KP-ABE scheme. Compared with the underlying CPA-secure one, our scheme only introduces the cost of a Chameleon hash. Furthermore, our scheme allows public ciphertext validity test. Technically, in contrast existing Chameleon hash applications to signatures, our construction illustrates novel applications of Chameleon hashes in construction and security proofs of encryption schemes.

Acknowledgments and Disclaimer. We appreciate the anonymous reviewers for their valuable suggestions. We especially thank Willy Susilo for his many helps on preparing the final version of the paper. Dr. Bo Qin is the corresponding author. This paper is partially supported by the National Key Basic Research Program (973 program) through project 2012CB315905, by the Natural Science Foundation through projects 61272501, 61173154, 61370190 and 61003214, by the Fundamental Research Funds for the Central Universities, and the Research Funds(No. 14XNLF02) of Renmin University of China, by the Open Research Fund of Beijing Key Laboratory of Trusted Computing and by the Open Research Fund of The Academy of Satellite Application.

References

1. Ateniese, G., de Medeiros, B.: On the key exposure problem in Chameleon hashes. In: Blundo, C., Cimato, S. (eds.) SCN 2004. LNCS, vol. 3352, pp. 165–179. Springer, Heidelberg (2005)

2. Beimel, A.: Secure schemes for secret sharing and key distribution. PhD thesis, Israel Institute of Technology, Technion, Haifa, Israel (1996)
3. Bethencourt, J., Sahai, A., Waters, B.: Ciphertext-policy attribute-based encryption. In: IEEE S&P 2007, pp. 321–334. IEEE Press, USA (2007)
4. Boneh, D., Boyen, X.: Efficient selective-ID secure identity-based encryption without random oracles. In: Cachin, C., Camenisch, J.L. (eds.) EUROCRYPT 2004. LNCS, vol. 3027, pp. 223–238. Springer, Heidelberg (2004)
5. Boneh, D., Franklin, M.: Identity-based encryption from the Weil pairing. In: Kilian, J. (ed.) CRYPTO 2001. LNCS, vol. 2139, pp. 213–229. Springer, Heidelberg (2001)
6. Boyen, X., Mei, Q., Waters, B.: Direct chosen ciphertext security from identity-based techniques. In: ACM CCS 2005, pp. 320–329. ACM Press, New York (2005)
7. Canetti, R., Halevi, S., Katz, J.: Chosen-ciphertext security from identity-based encryption. In: Cachin, C., Camenisch, J.L. (eds.) EUROCRYPT 2004. LNCS, vol. 3027, pp. 207–222. Springer, Heidelberg (2004)
8. Chase, M., Chow, S.S.M.: Improving privacy and security in multi-authority attribute-based encryption. In: ACM CCS 2009, pp. 121–130. ACM Press, New York (2009)
9. Chase, M.: Multi-authority attribute based encryption. In: Vadhan, S.P. (ed.) TCC 2007. LNCS, vol. 4392, pp. 515–534. Springer, Heidelberg (2007)
10. Chen, X., Zhang, F., Kim, K.: Chameleon hashing without key exposure. In: Zhang, K., Zheng, Y. (eds.) ISC 2004. LNCS, vol. 3225, pp. 87–98. Springer, Heidelberg (2004)
11. Chen, X., Zhang, F., Susilo, W., Mu, Y.: Efficient generic on-line/off-line signatures without key exposure. In: Katz, J., Yung, M. (eds.) ACNS 2007. LNCS, vol. 4521, pp. 18–30. Springer, Heidelberg (2007)
12. Chen, X., Zhang, F., Susilo, W., Tian, H., Li, J., Kim, K.: Identity-based chameleon hash scheme without key exposure. In: Steinfeld, R., Hawkes, P. (eds.) ACISP 2010. LNCS, vol. 6168, pp. 200–215. Springer, Heidelberg (2010)
13. Chen, X., Zhang, F., Tian, H., Wei, B., Kim, K.: Discrete logarithm based Chameleon hashing and signatures without key exposure. Computers and Electrical Engineering 37(4), 614–623 (2011)
14. Chen, X., Zhang, F., Tian, H., Wei, B., Susilo, W., Mu, Y., Lee, H., Kim, K.: Efficient generic on-line/off-line (threshold) signatures without key exposure. Information Sciences 178(21), 4192–4203 (2008)
15. Chen, C., Zhang, Z., Feng, D.: Efficient ciphertext policy attribute-based encryption with constant-size ciphertext and constant computation-cost. In: Boyen, X., Chen, X. (eds.) ProvSec 2011. LNCS, vol. 6980, pp. 84–101. Springer, Heidelberg (2011)
16. Cheung, L., Newport, C.: Provably secure ciphertext policy ABE. In: ACM CCS 2007, pp. 456–465. ACM Press, New York (2007)
17. Deng, H., Wu, Q., Qin, B., Chow, S.S., Domingo-Ferrer, J., Shi, W.: Tracing and revoking leaked credentials: Accountability in leaking sensitive outsourced data. In: ACM ASIACCS 2014, pp. 425–443. ACM Press, New York (2014)
18. Deng, H., Wu, Q., Qin, B., Mao, J., Liu, X., Zhang, L., Shi, W.: Who is touching my cloud? ESORICS 2014, To Appear (2014)
19. Deng, H., Wu, Q., Qin, B., Domingo-Ferrer, J., Zhang, L., Liu, J., Shi, W.: Ciphertext-policy hierarchical attribute-based encryption with short ciphertexts. Information Sciences 275, 370–384 (2014)

20. Ge, A.J., Zhang, R., Chen, C., Ma, C.G., Zhang, Z.F.: Threshold ciphertext policy attribute-based encryption with constant size ciphertexts. In: Susilo, W., Mu, Y., Seberry, J. (eds.) ACISP 2012. LNCS, vol. 7372, pp. 336–349. Springer, Heidelberg (2012)
21. Goyal, V., Pandey, O., Sahai, A., Waters, B.: Attribute-based encryption for fine-grained access control of encrypted data. In: ACM CCS 2006, pp. 89–98. ACM Press, New York (2006)
22. Krawczyk, H., Rabin, T.: Chameleon hashing and signatures. In: NDSS 2000, pp. 143–154. The Internet Society, San Diego (2000)
23. Lewko, A., Okamoto, T., Sahai, A., Takashima, K., Waters, B.: Fully secure functional encryption: Attribute-based encryption and (hierarchical) inner product encryption. In: Gilbert, H. (ed.) EUROCRYPT 2010. LNCS, vol. 6110, pp. 62–91. Springer, Heidelberg (2010)
24. Lewko, A., Waters, B.: Decentralizing attribute-based encryption. In: Paterson, K.G. (ed.) EUROCRYPT 2011. LNCS, vol. 6632, pp. 568–588. Springer, Heidelberg (2011)
25. Lewko, A., Waters, B.: Unbounded HIBE and attribute-based encryption. In: Paterson, K.G. (ed.) EUROCRYPT 2011. LNCS, vol. 6632, pp. 547–567. Springer, Heidelberg (2011)
26. Ostrovsky, R., Sahai, A., Waters, B.: Attribute-based encryption with non-monotonic access structures. In: ACM CCS 2007, pp. 195–203. ACM Press, New York (2007)
27. Okamoto, T., Takashima, K.: Fully secure functional encryption with general relations from the decisional linear assumption. In: Rabin, T. (ed.) CRYPTO 2010. LNCS, vol. 6223, pp. 191–208. Springer, Heidelberg (2010)
28. Okamoto, T., Takashima, K.: Fully secure unbounded inner-product and attribute-based encryption. In: Wang, X., Sako, K. (eds.) ASIACRYPT 2012. LNCS, vol. 7658, pp. 349–366. Springer, Heidelberg (2012)
29. Qin, B., Wang, H., Wu, Q., Liu, J., Domingo-Ferrer, D.: Simultaneous authentication and secrecy in identity-based data upload to cloud. Cluster Computing 16(4), 845–859 (2013)
30. Rouselakis, Y., Waters, B.: Practical constructions and new proof methods for large universe attribute-based encryption. In: ACM CCS 2013, pp. 463–474. ACM Press, New York (2013)
31. Sahai, A., Waters, B.: Fuzzy identity-based encryption. In: Cramer, R. (ed.) EUROCRYPT 2005. LNCS, vol. 3494, pp. 457–473. Springer, Heidelberg (2005)
32. Wang, Y., Wu, Q., Wong, D.S., Qin, Q., Chow, S.S.M., Liu, Z., Tan, X.: Offloading provable data Possession by securely outsourcing exponentiations in single untrusted program model. ESORICS 2014, To Appear (2014)
33. Yamada, S., Attrapadung, N., Hanaoka, G., Kunihiro, N.: Generic constructions for chosen-ciphertext secure attribute based encryption. In: Catalano, D., Fazio, N., Gennaro, R., Nicolosi, A. (eds.) PKC 2011. LNCS, vol. 6571, pp. 71–89. Springer, Heidelberg (2011)

Privacy-Preserving Auditing
for Attribute-Based Credentials

Jan Camenisch, Anja Lehmann, Gregory Neven, and Alfredo Rial

IBM Research – Zurich, Rüschlikon, Switzerland
{jca,anj,nev,lia}@zurich.ibm.com

Abstract. Privacy-enhancing attribute-based credentials (PABCs) allow users to authenticate to verifiers in a data-minimizing way, in the sense that users are unlinkable between authentications and only disclose those attributes from their credentials that are relevant to the verifier. We propose a practical scheme to apply the same data minimization principle when the verifiers' authentication logs are subjected to external audits. Namely, we propose an extended PABC scheme where the verifier can further remove attributes from presentation tokens before handing them to an auditor, while preserving the verifiability of the audit tokens. We present a generic construction based on a signature, a signature of knowledge and a trapdoor commitment scheme, prove it secure in the universal composability framework, and give an efficient instantiation based on the strong RSA assumption in the random-oracle model.

Keywords: Attribute-based credentials, audits, universal composability, privacy-enhancing technologies.

1 Introduction

Privacy-enhancing attribute-based credentials (PABC) [1], also known as anonymous credentials [2, 3] or minimal-disclosure tokens [4], are cryptographic mechanisms to perform data-minimizing authentication. They allow users to obtain credentials from an issuer, by which the issuer assigns a list of certified attribute values to the user. Users can then use these credentials to authenticate to verifiers, but have the option to disclose only a subset of the attributes; all non-disclosed attributes remain hidden from the verifier. Moreover, different authentications are unlinkable, in the sense that a verifier cannot tell whether they were performed by the same or by different users. PABCs offer important privacy advantages over other attribute certification schemes, which usually either employ a central authority that is involved in every authentication and therefore forms a privacy bottleneck (e.g., SAML, OpenID, or Facebook Connect), or force users to disclose all of their attributes (e.g., X.509 certificates [5]).

But sometimes, attributes travel beyond the verifier. Verifiers may be subjected to external audits to check that access was only granted to entitled users. For example, government authorities may require a video streaming service to

M. Kutyłowski and J. Vaidya (Eds.): ESORICS 2014, Part II, LNCS 8713, pp. 109–127, 2014.

prove that age-restricted movies were streamed exclusively to viewers of the required age, or film distributors may require it to prove that films were only streamed to residents of geographic areas for which it bought the rights. It makes perfect sense to extend the data minimization principle to auditors as well: why should auditors be handed any user attributes that are not relevant to the audit? Can one design a scheme where verifiers can further "maul" authentication tokens so that some of the disclosed attributes are blinded, yet keeping the audit token verifiable under the issuer's public key?

Trivial Constructions. Current PABC schemes do not allow for such functionality, or at least not efficiently. Presentation tokens usually consist of non-malleable non-interactive zero-knowledge proofs. In theory, one can always rely on generic zero-knowledge techniques [6] to prove knowledge of a valid presentation token for a subset of the disclosed attributes, but such proofs will be prohibitively expensive in practice. If the number of disclosed attributes is small, or the combination of attributes required by the auditor is known upfront, the user can generate multiple separate presentation tokens, one for the verifier and one for each of the auditors. This solution does not scale, however: if there are m disclosed attributes and the audited combination is not known upfront, the user would have to prepare 2^m presentation tokens.

Our Contributions. We present an efficiently auditable PABC scheme, meaning the size of authentication tokens as well as audit tokens stays linear in the number of attributes. Just like many PABC schemes, credentials in our construction are signatures on blocks of messages, where each message block encodes an attribute value. A presentation token is computed with an efficient signature of knowledge [7] of a valid credential that reveals only part of the message blocks. The basic idea of our construction is that, rather than simply revealing the disclosed attribute values, the user commits to them and creates a signature of knowledge of a valid credential for the same values as those that he committed to. The opening information of all commitments is handed to the verifier, who can check that they contain the claimed attribute values, but in the auditing phase, the verifier only forwards the opening information of the transferred attributes to the auditor, together with the user's original signature of knowledge.

We prove our construction secure in the universal composability (UC) framework [8], which guarantees that our protocol can be securely composed with itself as well as with other protocols in arbitrary environments. Given the several iterations that it took to define the security of basic signatures in this framework [9–11], defining security for a complicated primitive like ours is a delicate balancing act. We elaborately motivate our design choices for our ideal functionality in Section 3, in the hope that it can be of independent interest as a source of inspiration for future signature variants with privacy features.

Related Work. There are several proposals for dedicated signature schemes that allow the receiver of a signed message to reduce the amount of information in the message while retaining the ability to verify the corresponding signature.

Those are known as homomorphic [12], sanitizable [13–15], redactable [16], or content extracting signatures [17]. Other constructions, described e.g. in [18, 19] even allow more advanced operations on the signed data.

Those mechanisms do not yield straightforward constructions of our primitive as they only consider modifications of signed *messages*, whereas our scheme has to work with *presentation tokens* which itself are already derived from signed credentials. The crucial difference between signed messages and presentation tokens is that the latter should not be usable by a cheating verifier to impersonate the user at other verifiers. Therefore, the simple scheme where the credential and presentation token are redactable signatures on the list of attributes and where the presentation token can be further redacted by the verifier does not work.

Another related line of work conducts research on delegatable anonymous credentials [20], structure-preserving signatures [21], and commuting signatures [22]. The former allow credentials to be repetitively delegated while hiding the identity of the delegators. The latter two are more general signature schemes where the public key, the signed message, and the signature are all in the same mathematical group, and that among other things can be used to build delegatable credentials. Even though verifiable auditing is a sort of delegation, none of these primitives achieves the goals that we set out, as they cannot bind attributes to a delegatable credential.

2   System Overview

A privacy-preserving audit protocol consists of four parties: an auditor $\mathcal{R}$, an issuer $\mathcal{I}$, verifiers $\mathcal{V}_1, \ldots, \mathcal{V}_J$, and users $\mathcal{U}_1, \ldots, \mathcal{U}_N$. The interaction between the parties is as follows. First, in the *issuing phase*, a user $\mathcal{U}_n$ gets credentials that certify her attributes from the issuer $\mathcal{I}$. A credential consists of L attributes $(a_1, \ldots, a_L)$. In the *presentation phase*, $\mathcal{U}_n$ sends a presentation token to a verifier $\mathcal{V}_j$. In each presentation token, $\mathcal{U}_n$ chooses which attributes are revealed to $\mathcal{V}_j$ and, moreover, which of those attributes can further be revealed to the auditor $\mathcal{R}$. The indexes of the attributes that are only revealed to $\mathcal{V}_j$ are included in a set F, and the indexes of the attributes that are revealed to $\mathcal{V}_j$ and that can also be revealed to $\mathcal{R}$ are included in a set D. We call the attributes given by D *transferable*, while the ones given by F are *non-transferable*. In the *audit phase*, $\mathcal{V}_j$ reveals to $\mathcal{R}$ (a subset of) the transferable attributes, whose indexes are included in a subset T such that $T \subseteq D$.

3   Security Definition of Privacy-Preserving Audits

3.1   Universally Composable Security

The universal composability framework [23] is a general framework for analyzing the security of cryptographic protocols in arbitrary composition with other protocols. The security of a protocol φ is analyzed by comparing the view of an environment $\mathcal{Z}$ in a real execution of φ against that of $\mathcal{Z}$ when interacting with an ideal functionality $\mathcal{F}$ that carries out the desired task. The environment $\mathcal{Z}$ chooses the inputs of the parties and collects their outputs. In the real world, $\mathcal{Z}$ can communicate freely with an adversary $\mathcal{A}$ who controls the network as well as any corrupt parties. In the ideal world, $\mathcal{Z}$ interacts with dummy parties, who simply relay inputs and outputs between $\mathcal{Z}$ and $\mathcal{F}$, and a simulator $\mathcal{S}$. We say that a protocol φ securely realizes $\mathcal{F}$ if $\mathcal{Z}$ cannot distinguish the real world from the ideal world, i.e., $\mathcal{Z}$ cannot distinguish whether it is interacting with $\mathcal{A}$ and parties running protocol φ or with $\mathcal{S}$ and dummy parties relaying to $\mathcal{F}_\varphi$.

When describing ideal functionalities, we use the following conventions: The identity of an ITM instance (ITI) consists of a party identifier *pid* and a session identifier *sid*. An instance of $\mathcal{F}$ with session identifier *sid* only accepts inputs from and passes outputs to machines with the same session identifier *sid*. When describing functionalities, the expressions "output to $\mathcal{P}$" and "on input from $\mathcal{P}$", where $\mathcal{P}$ is a party identity *pid*, mean that the output is passed to and the input is received from party $\mathcal{P}$ only. Communication between ITIs with different party identifiers takes place over the network which is controlled by the adversary, meaning that he can arbitrarily delay, modify, drop, or insert messages.

When we say that $\mathcal{F}$ *sends m to $\mathcal{S}$ and waits for m' from $\mathcal{S}$*, we mean that $\mathcal{F}$ chooses a unique execution identifier, saves its current state, and sends m together with the identifier to $\mathcal{S}$. When $\mathcal{S}$ invokes a dedicated resume interface with a message m' and an execution identifier, $\mathcal{F}$ looks up the execution state associated to the identifier and continues running its program where it left off using m'.

Our protocol makes use of the standard functionalities $\mathcal{F}_{\mathrm{REG}}$ [23] for key registration, $\mathcal{F}_{\mathrm{SMT}}$ for secure message transmission [23], and $\mathcal{F}_{\mathrm{CRS}}^{\mathcal{D}}$ [23] for common reference strings with distribution $\mathcal{D}$. Descriptions and realizations of all these functionalities can be found in the literature.

We also use the non-standard anonymous secure message transmission functionality $\mathcal{F}_{\mathrm{ASMT}}$ given in Figure 1. The literature provides a fair number of protocols that provide some form of anonymous communication. These include some onion routing protocols for which ideal functionalities have been defined [24, 25]. Their functionalities are quite complex, as they model the various imperfections of the protocols, in particular, what routing information an adversary learns. This information depends heavily on how messages are routed, how many other users currently use the channel, how many nodes are controlled by the adversary, etc. Indeed, the modeling and realizations of anonymous communication is an active field of research. Now, if we had used one of these functionalities for our protocols, we would have had to model all these imperfections in our ideal functionality $\mathcal{F}_{\mathrm{AUD}}$ as well. We consider such modeling orthogonal to our protocol and our goals and therefore choose to assume ideal anonymous communication where the adversary only learns that some message is sent (and is allowed to deny its delivery) but does not learn the identities of the sender and the receiver.

Functionality $\mathcal{F}_{\text{ASMT}}$

Parameterized by a leakage function $l : \{0,1\}^* \rightarrow \{0,1\}^*$, $\mathcal{F}_{\text{ASMT}}$ works as follows:

1. On input (send, sid, m) from a party $\mathcal{T}$, execute the following program:
   - If $sid \neq (\mathcal{R}, sid')$, exit the program.
   - Send (send, sid', $l(m)$) to $\mathcal{S}$.
   - Wait for a message (send, sid') from $\mathcal{S}$.
   - Send (sent, sid, m) to $\mathcal{R}$.

Fig. 1. The ideal functionality of anonymous secure message transmission

3.2 Ideal Functionality of Privacy-Preserving Audits

We describe our ideal functionality $\mathcal{F}_{\text{AUD}}$ of privacy-preserving audits in Figure 2. We assume static corruptions, meaning that the adversary decides which parties to corrupt at the beginning of the game but cannot corrupt additional parties once the protocol is running. $\mathcal{F}_{\text{AUD}}$ employs the following tables:

Table 1. Tbl_1 stores entries of the form $[\mathcal{U}_n, \langle a_l \rangle_{l=1}^L]$ associating a user $\mathcal{U}_n$ to her attributes $\langle a_l \rangle_{l=1}^L$, or of the form $[\mathcal{S}, \langle a_l \rangle_{l=1}^L]$ if the credential was issued to a corrupt user.

Table 2. Tbl_2 stores entries of the form $[\mathcal{V}_j, D, F, \langle a_l \rangle_{l \in D \cup F}, msg, tid]$ associating verifiers $\mathcal{V}_j$ to the information of previous presentation phases.

Table 3. Tbl_3 stores entries of the form $[audtok, \mathcal{V}_j, D, F, T, \langle a_l \rangle_{l \in T}, msg, v]$, associating audit tokens to the data used to compute or verify the token, plus $v \in \{\text{valid}, \text{invalid}\}$ indicating whether the token is valid.

To shorten the description, we assume that the functionality proceeds only if the incoming messages are well-formed. That is, for presentation, audit, and verify messages, $\mathcal{F}_{\text{AUD}}$ continues only if $D \cap F = \emptyset$, $D \subseteq [1, L]$, $F \subseteq [1, L]$, and $sid = (\mathcal{I}, sid')$ holds. For the audit and verify messages, $\mathcal{F}_{\text{AUD}}$ additionally checks that $T \subseteq D$.

The functionality assumes certified identities of all users, verifiers, and the signer (cf. the discussion on public keys below). We now discuss the four interfaces of the ideal functionality $\mathcal{F}_{\text{AUD}}$ given in Figure 2.

The issue interface is called by the issuer with the user identity and the attributes in the to-be-issued credential, meaning that the issuer is aware of which attributes he issues to which user. The simulator indicates when the issuance is to be finalized by sending a (issue, sid) message. At this point, the issuance is recorded in Table 1. If the user is honest, the issuance is recorded under the correct user's identity; any instantiating protocol will have to set up an authenticated channel to the user to ensure this in the real world. If the user is corrupt, the credential is recorded as belonging to the simulator, modeling that corrupt users may pool their credentials. Note that the simulator is not given the issued attribute values, so the real-world protocol must hide these from the adversary.

The present interface lets a user $\mathcal{U}_n$ present a subset of attributes to a verifier $\mathcal{V}_j$. Honest users can only show combinations of attributes that appear in

---

Functionality $\mathcal{F}_{\text{AUD}}$

1. On input (issue, $sid, \mathcal{U}_n, \langle a_l \rangle_{l=1}^L$) from $\mathcal{I}$:
   - If $sid \neq (\mathcal{I}, sid')$ then exit the program.
   - Send (issue, $sid, \mathcal{U}_n$) to $\mathcal{S}$ and wait for (issue, sid) from $\mathcal{S}$.
   - If $\mathcal{U}_n$ is honest then store $[\mathcal{U}_n, \langle a_l \rangle_{l=1}^L]$ in Tbl_1, else store $[\mathcal{S}, \langle a_l \rangle_{l=1}^L]$.
   - Output (issue, $sid, \langle a_l \rangle_{l=1}^L$) to $\mathcal{U}_n$.

2. On input (present, $sid, \mathcal{V}_j, D, F, \langle a_l \rangle_{l \in D \cup F}, msg$) from $\mathcal{U}_n$:
   - Continue only if one of the following conditions is satisfied:
     - there exist $[\mathcal{U}_n', \langle a_l' \rangle_{l=1}^L] \in \text{Tbl}_1$ s.t. $a_l' = a_l \; \forall l \in D \cup F$ where $\mathcal{U}_n' = \mathcal{U}_n$ if $\mathcal{U}_n$ is an honest user, or $\mathcal{U}_n' = \mathcal{S}$ if $\mathcal{U}_n$ is corrupt,
     - $\mathcal{U}_n$ and $\mathcal{I}$ are both corrupt.
   - Send (present, $sid, \mathcal{V}_j$) to $\mathcal{S}$ and wait for (present, sid) from $\mathcal{S}$.
   - Increment the token identifier $tid(\mathcal{V}_j) = tid(\mathcal{V}_j) + 1$.
   - Store $[\mathcal{V}_j, D, F, \langle a_l \rangle_{l \in D \cup F}, msg, tid(\mathcal{V}_j)]$ in Tbl_2.
   - Output (tokrec, $sid, D, F, \langle a_l \rangle_{l \in D \cup F}, msg, tid(\mathcal{V}_j)$) to $\mathcal{V}_j$.

3. On input (auditgen, $sid, D, F, T, \langle a_l \rangle_{l \in T}, msg, tid$) from $\mathcal{V}_j$:
   - Continue only if one of the following conditions is satisfied:
     - $\mathcal{V}_j$ and $\mathcal{I}$ are both corrupt,
     - $\mathcal{V}_j$ is corrupt and there exists $[\mathcal{S}, \langle a_l' \rangle_{l=1}^L] \in \text{Tbl}_1$ s.t. $a_l' = a_l \; \forall l \in T$,
     - there exist $[\mathcal{V}_j, D, F, \langle a_l'' \rangle_{l \in D \cup F}, msg, tid] \in \text{Tbl}_2$ s.t. $a_l'' = a_l \; \forall l \in T$.
   - Send the message (auditgen, $sid, \mathcal{V}_j, D, F, T, \langle a_l \rangle_{l \in T}, msg, tid$) to $\mathcal{S}$ and wait for (auditgen, $sid, audtok$) from $\mathcal{S}$.
   - Store $[audtok, \mathcal{V}_j, D, F, T, \langle a_l \rangle_{l \in T}, msg, \texttt{valid}]$ in Tbl_3.
   - Output (audrec, $sid, audtok$) to $\mathcal{V}_j$.

4. On input (auditvf, $sid, audtok, \mathcal{V}_j, D, F, T, \langle a_l \rangle_{l \in T}, msg$) from a party $\mathcal{P}$:
   - Send (auditvf, $sid, audtok, \mathcal{V}_j, D, F, T, \langle a_l \rangle_{l \in T}, msg$) to $\mathcal{S}$ and wait for (auditvf, sid, w) from $\mathcal{S}$.
   - If there exists $[audtok, \mathcal{V}_j, D, F, T, \langle a_l \rangle_{l \in T}, msg, u] \in \text{Tbl}_3$ then set $v = u$. *(Completeness/Consistency)*
   - Else, set $v = w$ only if one of the following conditions is satisfied *(Unforgeability)*:
     - $\mathcal{V}_j$ and $\mathcal{I}$ are both corrupt,
     - $\mathcal{V}_j$ is corrupt and there exists $[\mathcal{S}, \langle a_l' \rangle_{l=1}^L] \in \text{Tbl}_1$ or $[\mathcal{V}_j, D, F, \langle a_l' \rangle_{l \in D \cup F}, msg, tid] \in \text{Tbl}_2$ such that $a_l' = a_l \; \forall l \in T$,
     - there exists $[audtok', \mathcal{V}_j, D, F, T, \langle a_l \rangle_{l \in T}, msg, \texttt{valid}] \in \text{Tbl}_3$.
   - Otherwise, set $v = \texttt{invalid}$.
   - Store $[audtok, \mathcal{V}_j, D, F, T, \langle a_l \rangle_{l \in T}, msg, v]$ in Tbl_3.
   - Output (audvf, sid, v) to $\mathcal{P}$.

Fig. 2. The ideal functionality $\mathcal{F}_{\text{AUD}}$ and its four interfaces

a credential issued to that user. If the issuer is honest, but the user is corrupt, then the presented attributes must be part of a credential issued to some corrupt user, not necessarily $\mathcal{U}_n$ itself. Upon receiving a message (present, sid) from $\mathcal{S}$, the presented attributes and the associated message are recorded in Table 2. The table also contains the identity of the verifier to whom the attributes were presented. Finally, the verifier is informed about the revealed attributes and the message. Note that neither the verifier nor the simulator learns the identity of the user who initiated the presentation protocol, which guarantees that presentation protocols are anonymous. Of course, one requires some form of anonymous communication between the user and the verifier to achieve this.

To generate and verify audit tokens, $\mathcal{F}_{\mathrm{AUD}}$ offers two interfaces: the auditgen interface to create audit tokens, and the auditvf to verify audit tokens. Honest verifiers can only create audit tokens that can be derived from presentations that they have seen, as recorded in Table 2. If the verifier is corrupt, but the issuer is honest, the verifier can additionally create tokens that can be derived from any credentials issued to a corrupt user, as recorded in Table 1. If the verifier and the issuer are both corrupt, then the adversary can generate any audit tokens that he wants. Unlike credentials and presentations, audit tokens have an actual bit string representations in our functionality that can be verified by anyone, not just by a dedicated auditor. We follow Canetti's signature functionality [11] by letting the simulator determine the value of the audit token. Note that the simulator is only given the values of the transferred attributes T, which guarantees that audit tokens do not reveal any information about the non-transferred attributes. The functionality registers the token as valid in Table 3 and returns it to the verifier.

Any party can verify an audit token through the auditvf interface. The functionality enforces consistency through Table 3, guaranteeing that verification of the same audit token for the same parameters always returns the same result. Note that this also enforces completeness, i.e., that honestly generated tokens verify correctly, because honestly generated tokens are recorded in Table 3 as valid. When the issuer is honest, the functionality enforces unforgeability by rejecting all audit tokens that the adversary should not be able to create. If in the real world the adversary manages to come up with a valid forgery, then the environment will be able to notice a difference between the real and the ideal world by verifying the token. Tokens are considered forgeries when they could not have been derived from any credentials issued to corrupt users in Table 1, from any presentation to a corrupt verifier $\mathcal{V}_j$ in Table 2, or from any honestly generated audit tokens in Table 3. Note that in the latter condition, the honestly generated token $audtok'$ may be different from the verified token $audtok$. This models conventional (i.e., non-strong) unforgeability: if the environment previously obtained any token that is valid for the same parameters, then the current token is no longer considered a forgery.

Public Keys. We define our functionality $\mathcal{F}_{\mathrm{AUD}}$ so that, rather than providing a binding to the public key of the issuer, audit tokens provide a direct binding to the issuer's identity, much like Canetti's certified signature functionality $\mathcal{F}_{\mathrm{CERT}}$

provides a direct binding to the signer's identity [11]. Similarly, presentation protocols are bound directly to verifiers' identities rather than their public keys. This greatly simplifies the description of our functionality because we do not have to model public keys of issuers and verifiers, and we do not have to specify how the various interfaces behave when called with incorrect public keys. Indeed, when tokens are bound directly to party identities, public keys become an implementation detail of the protocol. This of course comes at a price: in order to satisfy the functionality, our protocol must rely on an underlying public-key infrastructure to bind public keys to party identities.

Session Identifiers. The restriction that the issuer's identity $\mathcal{I}$ must be included in the session identifier $sid = (\mathcal{I}, sid')$ guarantees that each issuer can initialize its own instance of the functionality. In applications where the issuer is to remain anonymous, the issuer identity could be replaced with a unique pseudonym.

Representations of Credentials, Presentations, and Audit Tokens. The issuing phase depicted in Figure 2 does not expose any bit string representation for credentials to the environment, but merely records which attributes are issued to which user. Just like public keys, credentials are thereby reduced to implementation details that remain internal to the state of honest parties. Unlike public keys, however, this is not just an easy way to simplify our functionality, but is actually crucial to the unforgeability guarantee. Namely, our functionality imposes unforgeability of audit tokens by letting the verification interface reject tokens that the environment should not have been able to produce, including tokens that could have been derived from honest users' credentials, but not from corrupt users' credentials. However, if the functionality were to output actual credentials to honest users, the environment could itself derive valid audit tokens from these credentials, which the functionality would have to accept. Similarly, the presentation phase in Figure 2 merely records which combinations of attributes were shown to which verifier, without exposing a cryptographic token of that presentation to the environment.

Linkability of Audit Tokens. An audit token can be linked to the presentation token from which it was computed. For each verifier $\mathcal{V}_j$, each presentation phase is given a unique identifier $tid(\mathcal{V}_j)$, and this identifier is passed to the functionality when creating an audit token through the auditgen interface. The functionality also passes $tid(\mathcal{V}_j)$ to the simulator when it is asked to create the actual token, so that the simulator can create an audit token that respects the linkability to the corresponding presentation token. The simulator still does not get any information about the non-transferred attributes, however.

4   Preliminaries

This section describes the cryptographic primitives our realization of $\mathcal{F}_{\mathrm{AUD}}$ uses.

4.1 Trapdoor Commitment Schemes

A non-interactive commitment scheme consists of algorithms CSetup, Com and VfCom. CSetup(1^k) generates the parameters of the commitment scheme par_c, which include a description of the message space $\mathcal{M}$. Com(par_c, x) outputs a commitment com to x and auxiliary information $open$. A commitment is opened by revealing ($x, open$) and checking whether VfCom($par_c, com, x, open$) outputs 1 or 0. A commitment scheme should fulfill the correctness, hiding and binding properties. Correctness requires that VfCom accepts all commitments created by algorithm Com, i.e., for all $x \in \mathcal{M}$

$$\Pr \left[\begin{array}{c} par_c \leftarrow \mathsf{CSetup}(1^k); \ (com, open) \leftarrow \mathsf{Com}(par_c, x): \\ 1 = \mathsf{VfCom}(par_c, com, x, open) \end{array} \right] = 1 .$$

The hiding property ensures that a commitment com to x does not reveal any information about x, whereas the binding property ensures that com cannot be opened to another value x'.

Definition 1 (Hiding Property). *For any PPT adversary $\mathcal{A}$, the hiding property is defined as follows:*

$$\Pr \left[\begin{array}{l} par_c \leftarrow \mathsf{CSetup}(1^k); \\ (x_0, x_1, st) \leftarrow \mathcal{A}(par_c); \\ b \leftarrow \{0,1\}; \ (com, open) \leftarrow \mathsf{Com}(par_c, x_b); \\ b' \leftarrow \mathcal{A}(st, com): \\ x_0 \in \mathcal{M} \ \wedge \ x_1 \in \mathcal{M} \ \wedge \ b = b' \end{array} \right] \leq \frac{1}{2} + \epsilon(k) .$$

Definition 2 (Binding Property). *For any PPT adversary $\mathcal{A}$, the binding property is defined as follows:*

$$\Pr \left[\begin{array}{l} par_c \leftarrow \mathsf{CSetup}(1^k); \ (com, x, open, x', open') \leftarrow \mathcal{A}(par_c): \\ x \in \mathcal{M} \ \wedge \ x' \in \mathcal{M} \ \wedge x \neq x' \wedge \ 1 = \mathsf{VfCom}(par_c, com, x, open) \\ \wedge \ 1 = \mathsf{VfCom}(par_c, com, x', open') \end{array} \right] \leq \epsilon(k) .$$

A trapdoor commitment scheme [26, 27] is a commitment scheme where there exists trapdoor information that allows to open commitments to any value.

Definition 3 (Trapdoor Property). *There exist polynomial-time algorithms CSimSetup and ComOpen, where CSimSetup on input 1^k outputs parameters par_c with trapdoor td_c such that: (1) par_c are indistinguishable from those produced by CSetup, and (2) for any $x, x' \in \mathcal{M}$*

$$\left| \Pr \left[\begin{array}{l} (par_c, td_c) \leftarrow \mathsf{CSimSetup}(1^k); \ (com, open') \leftarrow \mathsf{Com}(par_c, x'); \\ open \leftarrow \mathsf{ComOpen}(par_c, td_c, x, x', open'): \ 1 = \mathcal{A}(par_c, td_c, com, open) \end{array} \right] \right.$$
$$\left. - \ \Pr \left[\begin{array}{c} (par_c, td_c) \leftarrow \mathsf{CSimSetup}(1^k); (com, open) \leftarrow \mathsf{Com}(par_c, x): \\ 1 = \mathcal{A}(par_c, td_c, com, open) \end{array} \right] \right| \leq \epsilon(k).$$

4.2   Signature Schemes

A signature scheme consists of the algorithms KeyGen, Sign, and VfSig. Algorithm KeyGen(1^k) outputs a secret key sk and a public key pk, which include a description of the message space $\mathcal{M}$. Sign(sk, m) outputs a signature s on message $m \in \mathcal{M}$. VfSig(pk, s, m) outputs 1 if s is a valid signature on m and 0 otherwise. This definition can be extended to blocks of messages $\bar{m} = (m_1, \ldots, m_n)$. A signature scheme must fulfill the correctness and existential unforgeability properties [28].

4.3   Signatures of Knowledge

Let $\mathcal{L}$ be an NP language defined by a polynomial-time computable relation R as $\mathcal{L} = \{x | \exists w : (x, w) \in R\}$. We call x a statement in the language $\mathcal{L}$ and w with $(x, w) \in R$ a witness for x. A signature of knowledge (SK) [29, 7] for $\mathcal{L}$ consists of the following algorithms:

SKSetup(1^k). Output parameters par_s, which include a description of the message space $\mathcal{M}$.

SKSign(par_s, R, x, w, m). If $(x, w) \in R$, output a signature of knowledge σ on the message m with respect to statement x, else output $\bot$.

SKVerify(par_s, R, x, m, σ). If σ is a valid signature of knowledge on the message m with respect to statement x, output 1, else output 0.

Correctness ensures that SKVerify accepts the signatures of knowledge generated by SKSign. More formally, for any $(x, w) \in R$ and any $m \in \mathcal{M}$, we require

$$\Pr \left[\begin{array}{c} par_s \leftarrow \mathsf{SKSetup}(1^k); \ \sigma \leftarrow \mathsf{SKSign}(par_s, R, x, w, m) : \\ 1 = \mathsf{SKVerify}(par_s, R, x, m, \sigma) \end{array} \right] = 1 \; .$$

To obtain efficient instantiations in the random-oracle model, we adopt the signature of knowledge definitions of Benhamouda et al. [36], which are a random-oracle adaptation of those of Chase and Lysyanskaya [7].

Definition 4 (Simulatability and Extractibility). *There exists a stateful simulation algorithm* SKSim *that can be called in three modes. When called as* $(par_s, st) \leftarrow$ SKSim(setup, 1^k), *it produces simulated parameters* par_s, *possibly keeping a trapdoor in its internal state* st. *When run as* $(h, st') \leftarrow$ SKSim(ro, q, st), *it produces a response* h *for a random oracle query* q. *When run as* $(\sigma, st') \leftarrow$ SKSim(sign, R, x, m, st), *it produces a simulated signature of knowledge* σ *without using a witness.*

For ease of notation, let SKSimRO(q) *be an oracle that returns the first part of* SKSim(ro, q, st) *and let* SKSimSign(R, x, w, m) *be an oracle that returns the first part of* SKSim(sign, R, x, m, st) *if* $(x, w) \in R$ *and returns* $\bot$ *otherwise, while a synchronized state is kept for* SKSim *across invocations. H denotes a hash function, which is modeled as a random oracle. The algorithms satisfy the following properties:*

- Simulatability: *No adversary can distinguish whether it is interacting with a real random oracle and signing oracle, or with their simulated versions. Formally, for all PPT $\mathcal{A}$ there exists a negligible function ϵ such that*

$$\left| \Pr[(par_s, st) \leftarrow \mathsf{SKSim}(\mathtt{setup}, 1^k), b \leftarrow \mathcal{A}^{\mathsf{SKSimRO},\mathsf{SKSimSign}}(par_s) : b = 1] \right.$$
$$\left. - \Pr[par_s \leftarrow \mathsf{SKSetup}(1^k), b \leftarrow \mathcal{A}^{H,\mathsf{SKSign}}(par_s) : b = 1] \right| \leq \epsilon(k) .$$

- Extractability: *The only way to produce a valid signature of knowledge is by knowing a witness. Formally, for all PPT $\mathcal{A}$ there exists an extractor $\mathsf{SKExt}_{\mathcal{A}}$ and a non-negligible function p such that*

$$\Pr\left[\begin{array}{c} (par_s, st) \leftarrow \mathsf{SKSim}(\mathtt{setup}, 1^k), \\ (R, x, m, \sigma) \leftarrow \mathcal{A}^{\mathsf{SKSimRO},\mathsf{SKSimSign}}(par_s; \rho_{\mathcal{A}}), \\ w \leftarrow \mathsf{SKExt}_{\mathcal{A}}(par_s, R, x, m, \sigma, \rho_\mathsf{S}, \rho_{\mathcal{A}}) : \\ \mathsf{SKVerify}(par_s, R, x, m, \sigma) = 1 \wedge (R, x, m) \notin Q \wedge (x, w) \notin R \end{array} \right] \geq \epsilon(k) ,$$

where Q is the set of queries (R, x, m) that $\mathcal{A}$ submitted to its $\mathsf{SKSimSign}$ oracle, and where ρ_S and $\rho_{\mathcal{A}}$ are the random tapes of the simulator and the adversary, respectively.

5 Construction of Privacy-Preserving Audits

The high-level idea of our protocol is as follows: a user $\mathcal{U}_n$ can obtain credentials from an issuer $\mathcal{I}$, where credentials are signed sets of attributes. From a credential the user can subsequently derive a presentation token which discloses attributes a_l for $l \in D$ in a transferable way to the verifier, and attributes a_l for $l \in F$ in a non-transferable way. To this end, the user first creates a commitment and opening $(com_l, open_l)$ for each disclosed attribute a_l with $l \in D \cup F$. He then generates a signature of knowledge σ, proving that he has a valid credential for all the committed values. To further ensure that the signature cannot be used in a different context, e.g., by a malicious party trying to impersonate an honest user, the signature signs a message which contains the verifier identifier and a fresh *nonce* chosen by the user. The entire presentation token then consists of the signature of knowledge σ, the commitments $\langle com_l \rangle_{l \in D \cup F}$ and openings $\langle open_l \rangle_{l \in D \cup F}$ for all disclosed attributes, and the random *nonce*.

The verifier $\mathcal{V}_j$ can check the correctness of such a token by verifying the signature of knowledge and verifying whether the commitments com_l open to the correct values a_l for all $l \in D \cup F$. If that is the case, the verifier stores the token and will not accept any further token that signs the same *nonce*.

When the verifier wants to derive an audit token from the presentation token and to transfer attributes $T \subseteq D$ to the auditor, he simply reuses the presentation token with the modification that he only includes the openings for the subset of transferred attributes into the audit token. The verifier further adds a signature s, where he signs the redacted presentation token with his own signing key. This ensures that a malicious user cannot bypass an honest verifier and directly create an audit token by himself.

An auditor can verify an audit token by verifying the correctness of the forwarded signature of knowledge σ, the correct opening of all commitments for the transferred attributes and the verifier's signature s.

5.1   Our Realization of $\mathcal{F}_{\text{AUD}}$

Our protocol uses a trapdoor commitment scheme (CSetup, Com, VfCom), and two signature schemes, one for the issuer (KeyGen$_{\mathcal{I}}$, Sign$_{\mathcal{I}}$, VfSig$_{\mathcal{I}}$) and one for the verifier (KeyGen$_{\mathcal{V}}$, Sign$_{\mathcal{V}}$, VfSig$_{\mathcal{V}}$). Both signature schemes follow the standard signature definition given in Section 4.2 and can be instantiated with the same construction. However, as the issuer's signature also serves as witness in a signature of knowledge scheme (SKSetup, SKSign, SKVerify) it might be beneficial to choose a signature scheme for (KeyGen$_{\mathcal{I}}$, Sign$_{\mathcal{I}}$, VfSig$_{\mathcal{I}}$) that already comes with efficient protocols for such proofs. Furthermore, the issuer's signature scheme must allow signing blocks of messages, whereas for the verifier's scheme only a single message needs to be signed.

For simplicity, it is assumed that all issuers and verifiers in the scheme have registered public keys. That is, the issuer and verifiers generate their signing keys as $(ipk, isk) \leftarrow$ KeyGen$_{\mathcal{I}}(1^k)$ and $(vpk_j, vsk_j) \leftarrow$ KeyGen$_{\mathcal{V}}(1^k)$ respectively and register their public keys with $\mathcal{F}_{\text{REG}}$. We further assume that all parties fetch the necessary parameters and public keys by invoking the corresponding functionalities. That is, the system parameters (par_s, par_c) with $par_s \leftarrow$ SKSetup(1^k) and $par_c \leftarrow$ CSetup(1^k) are obtained via $\mathcal{F}_{\text{CRS}}^{\mathcal{D}}$, and the public keys of the verifiers and issuer can be retrieved via the $\mathcal{F}_{\text{REG}}$ functionality. Note that the issuer identity $\mathcal{I}$ is part of the session identifier $sid = (\mathcal{I}, sid')$ that is contained in every message. Each verifier maintains a list of nonces L_{nonce} which is initially set to $\mathsf{L}_{nonce} := \emptyset$ and will be filled with nonces of verified presentation tokens, which is used to guarantee a one-time showing for each token. The communication between the different parties is done over ideal functionalities $\mathcal{F}_{\text{SMT}}$ in the issuing phase and $\mathcal{F}_{\text{ASMT}}$ in the presentation phase.

As in the ideal functionality $\mathcal{F}_{\text{AUD}}$, the parties in our protocol only proceed if the incoming messages are well-formed, i.e., for the presentation, audit and verify messages the respective party only continues if $D \cap F = \emptyset$, $D \subseteq [1, L]$, $F \subseteq [1, L]$ and $sid = (\mathcal{I}, sid')$. For the audit and verify messages, the verifier and auditor further check that $T \subseteq D$.

Issuance. On input (issue, $sid, \mathcal{U}_n, \langle a_l \rangle_{l=1}^L$) where $sid = (\mathcal{I}, sid')$, the issuer $\mathcal{I}$ executes the following program with the user $\mathcal{U}_n$:

Step I1 – Issuer $\mathcal{I}$ generates and sends credential:

a) Generate credential as $cred \leftarrow$ Sign$_{\mathcal{I}}(isk, \langle a_l \rangle_{l=1}^L)$.
b) Set $sid_{\text{SMT}} := (\mathcal{U}_n, sid, sid'')$ for a fresh sid'' and send (send, $sid_{\text{SMT}}, (\langle a_l \rangle_{l=1}^L, cred)$) to $\mathcal{F}_{\text{SMT}}$.

Step I2 – User $\mathcal{U}_n$ verifies and stores credential:

a) Upon receiving (sent, $sid_{\text{SMT}}, (\langle a_l \rangle_{l=1}^L, cred)$) from $\mathcal{F}_{\text{SMT}}$, verify that $1 \leftarrow$ VfSig$_{\mathcal{I}}(ipk, cred, \langle a_l \rangle_{l=1}^L)$ and abort if the verification fails.

b) Store $(\langle a_l \rangle_{l=1}^{L}, cred)$ and output $(\mathsf{issue}, sid, \langle a_l \rangle_{l=1}^{L})$.

Presentation. On input $(\mathsf{present}, sid, \mathcal{V}_j, D, F, \langle a_l \rangle_{l \in D \cup F}, msg)$, the user $\mathcal{U}_n$ executes the following program with verifier $\mathcal{V}_j$.

Step P1 – User $\mathcal{U}_n$ creates a presentation token:

a) Retrieve the credential $(\langle a_l' \rangle_{l=1}^{L}, cred)$ where $a_l' = a_l$ for all $l \in D \cup F$. Abort if no such credential exists.

b) Create a signature of knowledge of a valid credential w.r.t. committed attributes and bound to a nonce:

- Compute $(com_l, open_l) \leftarrow \mathsf{Com}(par_c, a_l) \; \forall l \in D \cup F$.
- Choose a random nonce $nonce \in \{0,1\}^k$ and set $m := (msg, \mathcal{V}_j, nonce)$.
- Prepare a signature of knowledge for the statement that a valid credential is known which contains the same attribute values as the commitments. That is, set the relation to $R :=$

$$(1 = \mathsf{VfSig}_{\mathcal{I}}(ipk, cred, \langle a_l \rangle_{l=1}^{L}) \; \wedge$$
$$1 = \mathsf{VfCom}(par_c, a_l, com_l, open_l) \; \forall l \in D \cup F),$$

and set the statement and witness to $x := (ipk, \langle com_l \rangle_{l \in D \cup F}, par_c, D, F)$, $w := (cred, \langle a_l \rangle_{l=1}^{L}, \langle open_l \rangle_{l \in D \cup F})$.
- Generate the signature of knowledge as $\sigma \leftarrow \mathsf{SKSign}(par_s, R, x, w, m)$.

c) Compose and send the presentation token:

- Set $sid_{\mathrm{ASMT}} := (\mathcal{V}_j, sid, sid'')$ for a fresh sid'' and send $(\mathsf{send}, sid_{\mathrm{ASMT}}, (\langle a_l \rangle_{l \in D \cup F}, D, F, msg, nonce, \langle com_l \rangle_{l \in D \cup F}, \langle open_l \rangle_{l \in D \cup F}, \sigma))$ to $\mathcal{F}_{\mathrm{ASMT}}$.

Step P2 – Verifier $\mathcal{V}_j$ verifies the presentation token:

a) Upon receiving a message given by $(\mathsf{sent}, sid_{\mathrm{ASMT}}, (\langle a_l \rangle_{l \in D \cup F}, D, F, msg, nonce, \langle com_l \rangle_{l \in D \cup F}, \langle open_l \rangle_{l \in D \cup F}, \sigma))$ from $\mathcal{F}_{\mathrm{ASMT}}$, verify that $nonce \notin \mathsf{L}_{nonce}$ and abort otherwise.

b) Verify signature of knowledge and commitments:

- Set the tuple (R, x, m) similarly as in Step P1(b) and check that $1 = \mathsf{SKVerify}(par_s, R, x, m, \sigma)$.
- Verify that $1 = \mathsf{VfCom}(par_c, a_l, com_l, open_l)$ for all $l \in D \cup F$. Abort if a verification fails.

c) Store token and nonce and end:

- Set the token-identifier to $tid := tid + 1$ and $\mathsf{L}_{nonce} := \mathsf{L}_{nonce} \cup nonce$.
- Store $(\langle a_l \rangle_{l \in D \cup F}, D, F, msg, nonce, \langle com \rangle_{l \in D \cup F}, \langle open_l \rangle_{l \in D \cup F}, \sigma, tid)$.
- Output $(\mathsf{tokrec}, sid, D, F, \langle a_l \rangle_{l \in D \cup F}, msg, tid)$.

Audit Token Generation. On input $(\mathsf{auditgen}, sid, D, F, T, \langle a_l \rangle_{l \in T}, msg, tid)$, the verifier $\mathcal{V}_j$ executes the following program.

a) Retrieve the tuple $(\langle a_l' \rangle_{l \in D \cup F}, D, F, msg, nonce, \langle com \rangle_{l \in D \cup F}, \langle open_l \rangle_{l \in D \cup F}, \sigma, tid)$ such that $a_l' = a_l$ for all $l \in T$. Abort if no such tuple exists.

b) Sign the redacted token information as

$$s \leftarrow \mathsf{Sign}_{\mathcal{V}}(vsk_j, (\langle com_l \rangle_{l \in D \cup F}, \langle open_l \rangle_{l \in T}, \sigma, T)).$$

c) Set the audit token to $audtok := (\langle com_l \rangle_{l \in D \cup F}, \langle open_l \rangle_{l \in T}, \sigma, nonce, s)$ and end with output $(\mathsf{audrec}, sid, audtok)$.

Audit Token Verification. On input the message (auditvf, sid, $audtok$, $\mathcal{V}_j$, D, F, T, $\langle a_l \rangle_{l \in T}$, msg), the auditor $\mathcal{R}$ executes the following program. Whenever a verification step fails, the auditor ends with output (audvf, sid, invalid).

a) Parse token as $audtok = (\langle com_l \rangle_{l \in D \cup F}, \langle open_l \rangle_{l \in T}, \sigma, nonce, s)$.
b) Verify that $1 = \mathsf{VfSig}_\mathcal{V}(vpk_j, s, (\langle com_l \rangle_{l \in D \cup F}, \langle open_l \rangle_{l \in T}, \sigma, T))$.
c) Set (R, x, m) as in Step P1(b) and verify that $1 = \mathsf{SKVerify}(par_s, R, x, m, \sigma)$.
d) Verify that $1 = \mathsf{VfCom}(par_c, a_l, com_l, open_l)$ for all $l \in T$.
e) If all checks succeeded, output (audvf, sid, valid).

5.2   Security Analysis

Our protocol is secure in the UC model based on the security properties of the underlying building blocks.

Theorem 1. *The above construction securely implements* $\mathcal{F}_{\text{AUD}}$ *in the* $\mathcal{F}_{\text{REG}}$, $\mathcal{F}_{\text{SMT}}$, $\mathcal{F}_{\text{CRS}}^\mathcal{D}$, *and* $\mathcal{F}_{\text{ASMT}}$-*hybrid model if the underlying trapdoor commitment scheme is hiding and binding, the underlying signature schemes are existentially unforgeable, and the signature of knowledge scheme is simulatable and extractable.*

A full proof of the above theorem is given in the full version of this paper [30]. Below, we summarize the sequence of games that leads to an indistinguishable simulation of our protocol.

Game 0: This is the original game where the simulator lets all honest parties run the real protocol based on the inputs from the environment and the network communication controlled by the adversary. The simulator also executes the code of the ideal functionalities $\mathcal{F}_{\text{REG}}$, $\mathcal{F}_{\text{SMT}}$, $\mathcal{F}_{\text{CRS}}^\mathcal{D}$, and $\mathcal{F}_{\text{ASMT}}$.

Game 1: When an honest verifier receives a presentation token from an honest user, the verifier skips the check that the nonce is fresh. This game deviates from the previous one whenever an honestly generated nonce collides with any previously seen nonce, which for a total of N received presentations happens with probability at most $N(N+1)/2^k$.

Game 2: This game maintains tables Tbl_1 with the credentials that were issued to corrupt users, Tbl_{2a} with the presentation tokens sent by honest users to a corrupt verifier, Tbl_{2b} with the presentation tokens received by honest verifiers from corrupt users, and Tbl_3 with the audit tokens created by honest verifiers. When an honest user computes a presentation token for an honest verifier $\mathcal{V}_j$, the simulator adds an entry of the form $[\bot, \ldots, \bot, tid(\mathcal{V}_j)]$ to Tbl_{2b}. These changes do not affect the environment's view at all.

Game 3: This game replaces the common parameters for the commitment and the signature of knowledge schemes with simulated parameters, so that the simulator knows the corresponding trapdoors. The change is indistinguishable by the simulatability of the signature of knowledge scheme and by the trapdoor property of the commitment scheme.

Game 4: Whenever an honest issuer sends a credential to an honest user, the simulated user submits a string of zeroes of the correct length to $\mathcal{F}_{\text{SMT}}$ instead of a real credential. Likewise, an honest user submits a string of zeroes to $\mathcal{F}_{\text{ASMT}}$ when it performs a presentation to an honest verifier. Since $\mathcal{F}_{\text{SMT}}$ and $\mathcal{F}_{\text{ASMT}}$ only leak the length of the transmitted message, these changes do not affect the environment's view.

Game 5: When an honest user sends a presentation token to a corrupt verifier, the simulator uses SKSim to generate the signature of knowledge σ. Similarly, when an honest verifier is asked to compute an audit token from a presentation token that originates from an honest user and where Tbl_{2b} stores $[\perp, \ldots, \perp, tid]$, this game builds the audit token based on a simulated presentation token. That is, it simulates the signature of knowledge, computes the rest according to the protocol, and then updates the entry in Tbl_{2b} to contain σ as well as all commitments and openings. The indistinguishability follows from the simulatability of the signature of knowledge scheme.

Game 6: When an honest verifier computes an audit token from a presentation token that originates from an honest user but where a complete entry in Tbl_{2b} exists (i.e., another audit token based on the same presentation token was already produced), it uses the trapdoor of the commitment scheme to compute the opening, rather than using the *open* value stored in Tbl_{2b}. This game hop is indistinguishable by the trapdoor property of the commitment scheme.

Game 7: If an honest verifier is instructed to compute an audit token for a presentation token from an honest user and for which Tbl_{2b} stores $[\perp, \ldots, \perp, tid]$, this game replaces all commitments for values that are *not* disclosed with commitments to random values. Note that, by the previous game, commitments which are opened only in a subsequent audit token are opened to the required value using the trapdoor. This game is indistinguishable from the previous one by the hiding property of the commitment scheme.

Note that at this point, all presentations and audit tokens are simulated based only on information that is given to the adversary by $\mathcal{F}_{\text{AUD}}$.

Game 8: When a corrupt user sends a valid presentation token to an honest verifier for attribute values that were never issued to a corrupt user as recorded in Tbl_1, the simulator aborts. This game hop is indistinguishable if the issuer's signature scheme is unforgeable, the signature of knowledge is extractable, and the commitment scheme is binding.

Game 9: When any honest party is instructed to verify a valid audit token for an honest verifier $\mathcal{V}_j$ that the verifier never created, then abort. By the unforgeability of the verifier's signature scheme, this only happens with negligible probability.

Game 10: When any honest party is instructed to verify a valid audit token for a corrupt verifier $\mathcal{V}_j$ that cannot have been derived from credentials issued to honest users (as recorded in Tbl_1), nor from presentations by honest users to $\mathcal{V}_j$ (as recorded in Tbl_{2a}), then abort. This happens with negligible probability by the extractability of the signature of knowledge, the binding property of the commitment scheme, and the unforgeability of the issuer's signature scheme.

6   Instantiation of Privacy-Preserving Audits

We recall the Damgård-Fujisaki commitment scheme, which securely instantiates the algorithms (CSetup, Com, VfCom, CSimSetup, ComOpen) described in Section 4.1 under the strong RSA assumption. Let l_n be the bit-length of the RSA modulus n and l_r be the bit-length of a further security parameter, both are functions of k. Typical values are $l_n = 2048$ and $l_r = 80$.

CSetup(1^k). Compute a safe RSA modulus $\tilde{n}$ of length l_n, i.e., such that $\tilde{n} = pq$, $p = 2p' + 1$, $q = 2q' + 1$, where p, q, p', and q' are primes. Pick a random generator $h \in QR_{\tilde{n}}$ and random $\alpha \leftarrow \{0,1\}^{l_n+l_r}$ and compute $g \leftarrow h^\alpha$. Output the commitment parameters $par_c = (g, h, \tilde{n})$.

Com(par_c, x). Pick random $open \leftarrow \{0,1\}^{l_n+l_r}$, set $com \leftarrow g^x h^{open}$ (mod $\tilde{n}$), and output the commitment com and the auxiliary information $open$.

VfCom($par_c, com, x, open$). On inputs x and $open$, compute $com' \leftarrow g^x h^{open}$ mod $\tilde{n}$ and output 1 if $com = com'$ and 0 otherwise.

CSimSetup(1^k). Run CSetup and output par_c and α as trapdoor.

ComOpen($com, x_1, open_1, x_2, td_c$). Compute $open_2 = open_1 + \alpha(x_1 - x_2)$.

We employ the Camenisch-Lysyanskaya signature scheme [31] to implement the issuer signature scheme (KeyGen$_\mathcal{I}$, Sign$_\mathcal{I}$, VfSig$_\mathcal{I}$). This signature scheme is existentially unforgeable against adaptive chosen message attacks [28] under the strong RSA assumption.

Let ℓ_m, ℓ_e, ℓ_n, and ℓ_r be system parameters determined by a function of k, where ℓ_r is a security parameter and the meaning of the others will become clear soon. We denote the set of integers $\{-(2^{\ell_m} - 1), ..., (2^{\ell_m} - 1)\}$ by $\pm\{0,1\}^{\ell_m}$. Elements of this set can thus be encoded as binary strings of length ℓ_m plus an additional bit carrying the sign, i.e., $\ell_m + 1$ bits in total.

KeyGen$_\mathcal{I}$(1^k). On input 1^k, choose an ℓ_n-bit safe RSA modulus $n = pq$. Choose, uniformly at random, $R_1, \ldots, R_L, S, Z \in QR_n$. Output the public key $(n, R_1, \ldots, R_L, S, Z)$ and the secret key $sk \leftarrow p$.

Sign$_\mathcal{I}$($sk, \langle m_1, \ldots, m_L \rangle$). The message space is the set $\{(m_1, \ldots, m_L) : m_i \in \pm\{0,1\}^{\ell_m}\}$. On input $m_1, \ldots, m_L$, choose a random prime number e of length $\ell_e > \ell_m + 2$, and a random number v of length $\ell_v = \ell_n + \ell_m + \ell_r$. Compute $A \leftarrow (Z/(R_1^{m_1} \ldots R_L^{m_L} S^v))^{1/e}$ mod n. Output the signature (e, A, v).

VfSig$_\mathcal{I}$($pk, s, \langle m_1, \ldots, m_L \rangle$). To verify that the tuple (e, A, v) is a signature on message $\langle m_1, \ldots, m_L \rangle$, check that the statements $Z \equiv A^e R_1^{m_1} \ldots R_L^{m_L} S^v$ (mod n), $m_i \in \pm\{0,1\}^{\ell_m}$, and $2^{\ell_e} > e > 2^{\ell_e-1}$ hold.

For the realization of signatures of knowledge we use generalized Schnorr proof protocols [33, 29, 34]. We describe how to instantiate the signature of knowledge scheme for the relation we require in our protocol, i.e., for

$$R := \{1 = \mathsf{VfSig}_\mathcal{I}(ipk, cred, \langle a_l \rangle_{l=1}^L) \;\; \wedge$$
$$1 = \mathsf{VfCom}(par_c, a_l, com_l, open_l) \; \forall l \in D \cup F\}.$$

with $x := (ipk, \langle com_l \rangle_{l \in D \cup F}, par_c, D, F)$ and $w := (cred, \langle a_l \rangle_{l=1}^L, \langle open_l \rangle_{l \in D \cup F})$

where *cred* is a CL-signature (e, A, v) as defined above. It is a secure signature of knowledge in the random-oracle model under the strong RSA assumption (the proof is straightforward and is given in the full version of this paper [30]).

SKSetup(1^k). There are no separate system parameters for the signature of knowledge scheme.

SKSign(par_s, R, x, w, m). Randomize the credential (contained in w): choose random $v' \in_R \{0,1\}^{\ell_v}$ and compute $A' \leftarrow AS^{v'}$ and $v^* \leftarrow v - v'e$. Compute

$$\pi \leftarrow SPK\{(e, v^*, \langle a_l \rangle_{l=1}^L, \rangle_{o_l \langle l \in D \cup F}) : \bigwedge_{\forall l \in D \cup F} com_l = g^{a_l} h^{o_l} \pmod{\tilde{n}}$$

$$\wedge Z = A'^e R_1^{a_1} \dots R_L^{a_L} S^{v^*} \pmod{n} \wedge a_i \in \pm\{0,1\}^{\ell_m} \wedge 2^{\ell_e} > e > 2^{\ell_e - 1}\}(m)$$

and output $\sigma \leftarrow (A', \pi)$. For the realization of the non-interactive proof of knowledge π we refer to Camenisch et al. [29, 34].

SKVerify($par_s, R, x, m, (A', \pi)$). This algorithm verifies if π is correct.

The signature of knowledge simulator SKSimSign will make use of the random oracle and the honest-verifier zero-knowledge property of the generalized Schnorr proofs. One can get rid of the random oracle with alternative techniques [35]. SKExt works by rewinding the adversary to obtain, with non-negligible probability, all attributes, the opening information of all commitments, and the credential (CL-signature).

Efficiency. We obtain a rough estimate of the efficiency of our protocol by counting only multi-exponentiations modulo n or $\tilde{n}$. Computation of a presentation for our protocol takes each of the user and the verifier $2(\#D + \#F) + L + 2$ multi-exponentiations modulo $\tilde{n}$. Auditing a token costs only a single standard signature, while verifying an audit token involves one standard signature verification and $\#D + \#F + \#T + L + 2$ multi-exponentiations modulo $\tilde{n}$. In terms of bandwidth, a presentation consumes, apart from the length of the revealed attributes, $2\ell_n + \ell_m + \ell_e + 4k + 3\ell_r + L(\ell_m + k + \ell_r) + (\#D + \#F)(3\ell_n + k + 3\ell_r)$ bits. An audited token takes $2\ell_n + \ell_m + \ell_e + 4k + 3\ell_r + L(\ell_m + k + \ell_r) + (\#D + \#F)(2\ell_n + k + 2\ell_r) + \#T(\ell_n + \ell_r)$ bits plus the length of a standard signature.

7 Conclusion

Data minimization is a basic privacy principle in authentication mechanisms. In this paper, we show that data minimization does not need to stop at the verifier: using our auditable PABC scheme, the information revealed in a presentation token can be further reduced when forwarding it to an auditor, all while preserving the verifiability of the audit token. In our construction, presentations and audit tokens are anonymous in the sense that neither of them can be linked to the user or credential from which they originated. Audited tokens can be linked to the presentation from which they were derived. This can be used as a feature when the verifier must be unable to inflate the number of presentations that it performed, but it may also be a privacy drawback. We leave open the construction of a scheme satisfying a stronger privacy notion with fully unlinkable audit tokens.

Acknowledgement. This work was supported by the European Community through the Seventh Framework Programme (FP7), under grant agreements n°257782 for the project ABC4Trust and n°318424 for the project FutureID.

References

1. Camenisch, J., Krontiris, I., Lehmann, A., Neven, G., Paquin, C., Rannenberg, K., Zwingelberg, H.: H2.1 – abc4trust architecture for developers. ABC4Trust Heartbeat H2.1 (2011), https://abc4trust.eu
2. Chaum, D.: Security without identification: Transaction systems to make big brother obsolete. Communications of the ACM 28(10), 1030–1044 (1985)
3. Camenisch, J., Lysyanskaya, A.: A signature scheme with efficient protocols. In: Cimato, S., Galdi, C., Persiano, G. (eds.) SCN 2002. LNCS, vol. 2576, pp. 268–289. Springer, Heidelberg (2003)
4. Brands, S.A.: Rethinking Public Key Infrastructures and Digital Certificates: Building in Privacy. MIT Press, Cambridge (2000)
5. Adams, C., Farrell, S.: Rfc 2510, x. 509 internet public key infrastructure certificate management protocols. Internet Engineering Task Force (1999)
6. Goldreich, O., Micali, S., Wigderson, A.: Proofs that yield nothing but their validity or all languages in NP have zero-knowledge proof systems. Journal of the ACM 38(3), 691–729 (1991)
7. Chase, M., Lysyanskaya, A.: On signatures of knowledge. In: Dwork, C. (ed.) CRYPTO 2006. LNCS, vol. 4117, pp. 78–96. Springer, Heidelberg (2006)
8. Canetti, R.: Universally composable security: A new paradigm for cryptographic protocols. In: 42nd FOCS, pp. 136–145. IEEE Computer Society Press (October 2001)
9. Canetti, R.: Universally composable signature, certification, and authentication. In: IEEE CSFW-17. IEEE Computer Society (2004)
10. Backes, M., Hofheinz, D.: How to break and repair a universally composable signature functionality. In: Zhang, K., Zheng, Y. (eds.) ISC 2004. LNCS, vol. 3225, pp. 61–72. Springer, Heidelberg (2004)
11. Canetti, R.: Universally composable signatures, certification and authentication. IACR Cryptology ePrint Archive, Report 2003/239 (2003)
12. Johnson, R., Molnar, D., Song, D.X., Wagner, D.: Homomorphic signature schemes. In: Preneel, B. (ed.) CT-RSA 2002. LNCS, vol. 2271, pp. 244–262. Springer, Heidelberg (2002)
13. Ateniese, G., Chou, D.H., de Medeiros, B., Tsudik, G.: Sanitizable signatures. In: de Capitani di Vimercati, S., Syverson, P.F., Gollmann, D. (eds.) ESORICS 2005. LNCS, vol. 3679, pp. 159–177. Springer, Heidelberg (2005)
14. Brzuska, C., Fischlin, M., Lehmann, A., Schröder, D.: Unlinkability of sanitizable signatures. In: Nguyen, P.Q., Pointcheval, D. (eds.) PKC 2010. LNCS, vol. 6056, pp. 444–461. Springer, Heidelberg (2010)
15. Brzuska, C., Fischlin, M., Freudenreich, T., Lehmann, A., Page, M., Schelbert, J., Schröder, D., Volk, F.: Security of sanitizable signatures revisited. In: Jarecki, S., Tsudik, G. (eds.) PKC 2009. LNCS, vol. 5443, pp. 317–336. Springer, Heidelberg (2009)
16. Brzuska, C., Busch, H., Dagdelen, O., Fischlin, M., Franz, M., Katzenbeisser, S., Manulis, M., Onete, C., Peter, A., Poettering, B., Schröder, D.: Redactable signatures for tree-structured data: Definitions and constructions. In: Zhou, J., Yung, M. (eds.) ACNS 2010. LNCS, vol. 6123, pp. 87–104. Springer, Heidelberg (2010)

17. Steinfeld, R., Bull, L., Zheng, Y.: Content extraction signatures. In: Kim, K.-c. (ed.) ICISC 2001. LNCS, vol. 2288, pp. 285–304. Springer, Heidelberg (2002)
18. Ahn, J.H., Boneh, D., Camenisch, J., Hohenberger, S., Shelat, A., Waters, B.: Computing on authenticated data. In: Cramer, R. (ed.) TCC 2012. LNCS, vol. 7194, pp. 1–20. Springer, Heidelberg (2012)
19. Bellare, M., Neven, G.: Transitive signatures based on factoring and RSA. In: Zheng, Y. (ed.) ASIACRYPT 2002. LNCS, vol. 2501, pp. 397–414. Springer, Heidelberg (2002)
20. Belenkiy, M., Camenisch, J., Chase, M., Kohlweiss, M., Lysyanskaya, A., Shacham, H.: Randomizable proofs and delegatable anonymous credentials. In: Halevi, S. (ed.) CRYPTO 2009. LNCS, vol. 5677, pp. 108–125. Springer, Heidelberg (2009)
21. Abe, M., Fuchsbauer, G., Groth, J., Haralambiev, K., Ohkubo, M.: Structure-preserving signatures and commitments to group elements. In: Rabin, T. (ed.) CRYPTO 2010. LNCS, vol. 6223, pp. 209–236. Springer, Heidelberg (2010)
22. Fuchsbauer, G.: Commuting signatures and verifiable encryption. In: Paterson, K.G. (ed.) EUROCRYPT 2011. LNCS, vol. 6632, pp. 224–245. Springer, Heidelberg (2011)
23. Canetti, R.: Universally composable security: A new paradigm for cryptographic protocols. In: FOCS, pp. 136–145. IEEE Computer Society (2001)
24. Backes, M., Goldberg, I., Kate, A., Mohammadi, E.: Provably secure and practical onion routing. In: IEEE CSF-25, pp. 369–385. IEEE Press
25. Camenisch, J., Lysyanskaya, A.: A formal treatment of onion routing. In: Shoup, V. (ed.) CRYPTO 2005. LNCS, vol. 3621, pp. 169–187. Springer, Heidelberg (2005)
26. Brassard, G., Chaum, D., Crépeau, C.: Minimum disclosure proofs of knowledge. J. Comput. Syst. Sci. 37(2), 156–189 (1988)
27. Fischlin, M.: Trapdoor Commitment Schemes and Their Applications. PhD thesis, Goethe Universität Frankfurt (2001)
28. Goldwasser, S., Micali, S., Rivest, R.: A digital signature scheme secure against adaptive chosen-message attacks. SIAM J. Comput. 17(2), 281–308 (1988)
29. Camenisch, J., Stadler, M.: Efficient group signature schemes for large groups (extended abstract). In: Kaliski Jr., B.S. (ed.) CRYPTO 1997. LNCS, vol. 1294, pp. 410–424. Springer, Heidelberg (1997)
30. Camenisch, J., Lehmann, A., Neven, G., Rial, A.: Privacy-preserving auditing for attribute-based credentials. IACR Cryptology ePrint Archive, Report 2014/468
31. Camenisch, J., Lysyanskaya, A.: A signature scheme with efficient protocols. In: Cimato, S., Galdi, C., Persiano, G. (eds.) SCN 2002. LNCS, vol. 2576, pp. 268–289. Springer, Heidelberg (2003)
32. Camenisch, J., Shoup, V.: Practical verifiable encryption and decryption of discrete logarithms. In: Boneh, D. (ed.) CRYPTO 2003. LNCS, vol. 2729, pp. 126–144. Springer, Heidelberg (2003)
33. Schnorr, C.-P.: Efficient identification and signatures for smart cards (abstract) (rump session). In: Quisquater, J.-J., Vandewalle, J. (eds.) Advances in Cryptology - EUROCRYPT 1989. LNCS, vol. 434, pp. 688–689. Springer, Heidelberg (1990)
34. Camenisch, J., Kiayias, A., Yung, M.: On the portability of generalized schnorr proofs. In: Joux, A. (ed.) EUROCRYPT 2009. LNCS, vol. 5479, pp. 425–442. Springer, Heidelberg (2009)
35. Damgård, I.: Efficient concurrent zero-knowledge in the auxiliary string model. In: Preneel, B. (ed.) EUROCRYPT 2000. LNCS, vol. 1807, pp. 418–430. Springer, Heidelberg (2000)
36. Benhamouda, F., Camenisch, J., Krenn, S., Lyubashevsky, V., Neven, G.: Improved Zero-Knowledge Proofs for Lattice Encryption Schemes, Linking Classical and Lattice Primitives, and Applications (2014) (unpublished manuscript)

What's the Gist?
Privacy-Preserving Aggregation of User Profiles

Igor Bilogrevic[1], Julien Freudiger[2], Emiliano De Cristofaro[3], and Ersin Uzun[2]

[1] Google, Switzerland*
[2] PARC, USA
[3] University College London, UK*

Abstract. Over the past few years, online service providers have started gathering increasing amounts of personal information to build user profiles and monetize them with advertisers and data brokers. Users have little control of what information is processed and are often left with an *all-or-nothing* decision between receiving free services or refusing to be profiled. This paper explores an alternative approach where users only disclose an *aggregate model* – the "gist" – of their data. We aim to preserve data utility and simultaneously provide user privacy. We show that this approach can be efficiently supported by letting users contribute encrypted and differentially-private data to an aggregator. The aggregator combines encrypted contributions and can only extract an aggregate model of the underlying data. We evaluate our framework on a dataset of 100,000 U.S. users obtained from the U.S. Census Bureau and show that (i) it provides accurate aggregates with as little as 100 users, (ii) it can generate revenue for both users and data brokers, and (iii) its overhead is appreciably low.

Keywords: Privacy, Secure Computation, Differential Privacy, User Profiling.

1 Introduction

The digital footprint of Internet users is growing at an unprecedented pace, driven by the pervasiveness of online interactions and large number of posts, likes, check-ins, and content shared everyday. This creates invaluable sources of information that online service providers use to profile users and serve targeted advertisement. This economic model, however, raises major privacy concerns [1,2,3] as advertisers might excessively track users, data brokers might illegally market consumer profiles [4], and governments might abuse their surveillance power [5,6] by obtaining datasets collected for other purposes (i.e., monetization). Consequently, consumer advocacy groups are promoting policies and legislations providing greater control to users and more transparent collection practices [7,3].

Along these lines, several efforts – such as OpenPDS, personal.com, Sellbox, and Handshake – advocate a novel, user-centric paradigm: users store their personal information in "data vaults", and directly manage with whom to share their data. This approach has several advantages, namely, users maintain data ownership (and may

---

* Work done, in part, while authors were at PARC.

M. Kutyłowski and J. Vaidya (Eds.): ESORICS 2014, Part II, LNCS 8713, pp. 128–145, 2014.
© Springer International Publishing Switzerland 2014

monetize their data), while data brokers and advertisers benefit from more accurate and detailed personal information [8,9]. Nevertheless, privacy still remains a challenge as users need to trust data vaults operators and relinquish their profiles to advertisers [10,11].

To address such concerns, the research community has proposed to maintain data vaults on user devices and share data in a privacy-preserving way. Prior work can be grouped into three main categories: (1) serving ads locally, without revealing any information to advertisers/data brokers [12,13,14]; (2) relying on a trusted third party to anonymize user data [15,16]; and (3) relying on a trusted third party for private user data aggregation [17,18,19]. Unfortunately, these approaches suffer from several limitations. First, localized methods prevent data brokers and advertisers from obtaining user statistics. Second, anonymization techniques provide advertisers with significantly reduced data utility and are prone to re-identification attacks [20]. Finally, existing private aggregation schemes rely on a trusted third party for differential privacy (e.g., a proxy [19], a website [17], or mixes [18]; also, aggregation occurs after decryption, thus making it possible to link contributions and users.

Motivated by the above challenges, this paper proposes a novel approach to privacy-preserving aggregation of user data. Rather than contributing data *as-is*, users combine their data into *an aggregate model* – the "gist." Intuitively, users contribute encrypted and differentially-private data to an aggregator that extracts a statistical model of the underlying data (e.g., probability density function of the age of contributing users). Our approach addresses issues with existing work in that it does not depend on a third-party for differential privacy, incurs low computational overhead, and addresses linkability issues between contributions and users. Moreover, we propose a metric to dynamically value user statistics according to their inherent amount of "valuable" information (i.e., sensitivity): for instance, aggregators can assess whether age statistics in a group of participants are more sensitive than income statistics. To the best of our knowledge, our solution provides the first privacy-preserving aggregation scheme for personal data monetization.

Our contributions can be summarized as follows:

1. We design a privacy-preserving framework for monetizing user data, where users trade an aggregate of their data instead of actual values.
2. We define a measure of the sensitivity of different data aggregates. In particular, we adopt the information-theoretic Jensen-Shannon divergence [21] to quantify the distance between the actual distribution of a data attribute, and a distribution that does not reveal actionable information [22], such as the uniform distribution.
3. We show how to rank aggregates based on their sensitivity, i.e., we design a dynamic valuation scheme based on how much information an aggregate leaks.

We evaluate our privacy-preserving framework on a real, anonymized dataset of 100,000 US users (obtained by the Census Bureau) with different types of attributes. Our results show that our framework (i) provides accurate aggregates with as little as 100 participants, (ii) generates revenue for users and data aggregators depending on the number of contributing users and sensitivity of attributes, and (iii) has low computational overhead on user devices (0.3 ms for each user, independently of the number of participants). In summary, our approach provides a novel perspective to the privacy-preserving monetization of personal data, and finds a successful balance between data accuracy for advertisers, privacy protection for users, and incentives for data aggregators.

Paper Organization. The rest of the paper is organized as follows. Next section introduces the system architecture and the problem statement. Then, Section 3 presents our framework and Section 4 reports on our experimental evaluation. After reviewing related work in Section 5, we conclude the paper in Section 6.

2   System Architecture

This section introduces the problem definition and presents participating entities.

2.1   Problem Statement

We consider a system comprised of three entities: A set of users $\mathbb{U} = \{1, \ldots, N\}$, a data aggregator $\mathbb{A}$, and a customer $\mathbb{C}$. The system architecture is illustrated in Fig. 1. Customers query the data aggregator for user information, while users contribute their personal information to the data aggregator. The aggregator acts as a proxy between users and customers by aggregating (and monetizing) user data. The main goal of this paper is to propose practical techniques to aggregate and monetize user personal data in a privacy-preserving way, i.e., without revealing personal information to other users or third parties.

2.2   System Model

Users. We assume that users store a set of personal attributes such as age, gender, and preferences locally. Each user $i \in \mathbb{U}$ maintains a profile vector $\mathbf{p_i} = [x_{i,1}, \ldots, x_{i,K}]$, where $x_{i,j} \in \mathcal{D}$ is the value of attribute j and $\mathcal{D}$ is a suitable domain for j. For example, if j represents the age of user i, then $x_{i,j} \in \{1, \ldots, M_j\}$, $M_j = 120$, and $\mathcal{D} \subset \mathbb{N}$.

In practice, users can generate their personal profiles manually, or leverage profiles maintained by third parties. Several social networks allow subscribers to download their online profile. A Facebook profile, for example, contains numerous Personally Identifiable Information (PII) items (such as age, gender, relationships, location), preferences (movies, music, books, tv shows, brands), media (photos and videos) and social interaction data (list of friends, wall posts, liked items).

Following the results of recent studies on user privacy attitudes [23,10,8], we assume that each user i can specify a privacy-sensitivity value $0 \le \lambda_{i,j} \le 1$ for each attribute j. A large $\lambda_{i,j}$ indicates high privacy sensitivity (i.e., lower willingness to disclose). In practice, $\lambda_{i,j}$ can assume a limited number of discrete values, which could represent the different levels of sensitivity according to Westin's Privacy Indexes [24].

We assume that users want to monetize their profiles while preserving their privacy. For instance, users may be willing to trade an *aggregate* of their online behavior, such as the *frequency* at which they visit different *categories* of websites, rather than the exact time and URLs.

Finally, we assume that user devices can perform cryptographic operations consisting of multiplications, exponentiations, and discrete logarithms.

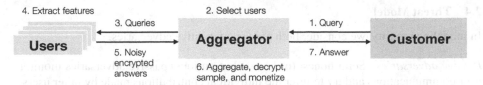

Fig. 1. System architecture and basic protocol. Users contribute encrypted profiles to the aggregator. The aggregator combines encrypted profiles and obtains plaintext data models, which it monetizes with customers.

Data Aggregator. A data aggregator $\mathbb{A}$ is an untrusted third-party that performs the following actions: (1) it collects encrypted attributes from users, (2) it aggregates contributed attributes in a privacy-preserving way, and (3) it monetizes users' aggregates according to the amount of "valuable" information that each attribute conveys.

We assume that users and $\mathbb{A}$ sign an agreement upon user registration that authorizes $\mathbb{A}$ to access the aggregated results (but not users' actual attributes), to monetize them with customers, and to take a share of the revenue from the sale. It also binds $\mathbb{A}$ to redistribute the rest of the revenue among contributing users.

Customer. We consider a customer $\mathbb{C}$ willing to obtain aggregate information about users and to pay for it. $\mathbb{C}$ can have commercial contracts with multiple data brokers. Similarly, a data aggregator can have contracts with multiple customers. $\mathbb{C}$ interacts with a data aggregator $\mathbb{A}$ and does not communicate directly with users. $\mathbb{C}$ obtains available attributes, and initiates an aggregation by querying the data aggregator for specific attributes.

2.3 Applications

The proposed system model is well-suited to many real-world scenarios, including market research and online tracking use cases. For instance, consider a car dealer $\mathbb{C}$ that wants to assess user preferences for car brands, their demographics, and income distributions. A data aggregator $\mathbb{A}$ might collect aggregate information about a representative set of users $\mathbb{U}$ and monetize it with the car dealer $\mathbb{C}$. Companies such as Acxiom currently provide this service, but raise privacy concerns [25]. Our solution enables such companies to collect aggregates of personal data instead of actual values and reward users for their participation.

Another example is that of an online publisher (e.g., a news website) $\mathbb{C}$ that wishes to know more about its online readership [17]. In this case, the aggregator $\mathbb{A}$ is an online advertiser that collects information about online users $\mathbb{U}$ and monetizes it with online publishers.

Finally, our proposed model can also be appealing to data aggregators in healthcare [26]. Healthcare data is often fragmented in silos across different organizations and/or individuals. An healthcare aggregator $\mathbb{A}$ can compile data from various sources and allow third parties $\mathbb{C}$ to buy access to the data. At the same time, data contributors ($\mathbb{U}$) receive a fraction of the revenue. Our approach thwarts privacy concerns and helps with the pricing of contributed data.

2.4   Threat Model

In modeling security, we consider both passive and active adversaries.

Passive adversaries. Semi-honest (or honest-but-curious) passive adversaries monitor user communications and try to infer the individual contributions made by other users. For instance, users may wish to obtain attribute values of other users; similarly, data aggregators and customers may try to learn the values of the attributes from aggregated results. A passive adversary executes the protocol correctly and in the correct order, without interfering with inputs or manipulating the final result.

Active adversaries. Active (or malicious) adversaries can deviate from the intended execution of the protocol by inserting, modifying or erasing input or output data. For instance, a subset of malicious users may collude with each other in order to obtain information about other (honest) users or to bias the result of the aggregation. To achieve their goal, malicious users may also collude with either the data aggregator or with the customer. Moreover, a malicious data aggregator may collude with a customer in order to obtain private information about the user attributes.

3   Monetizing User Profiles with Privacy

We outline and formalize the data monetization framework, which consists of a protocol that is executed between users $\mathbb{U}$, a data aggregator $\mathbb{A}$ and a customer $\mathbb{C}$. We first provide an intuitive description and then detail each individual component.

3.1   High-Level Description

We propose a protocol where users trade personal attributes in a privacy-preserving way, in exchange for (possibly) monetary retributions. Intuitively, there are two possible modes of implementations: *interactive* and *batch*.

In interactive mode, a customer initiates a query about specific attributes and users. The aggregator selects users matching the query, collects encrypted replies, computes aggregates, and monetizes them according to a pricing function.

In batch mode, users send their encrypted profile, containing personal attributes, to the data broker. The aggregator combines encrypted profiles, decrypts them, obtains aggregates for each attribute, and ranks attributes based on the amount of "valuable" information they provide. A customer is then offered access to specific attributes. Without loss of generality, hereafter we describe the interactive mode.

Initialization: The data aggregator $\mathbb{A}$ and users $i \in \mathbb{U}$ engage in a secure key establishment protocol to obtain individual random secret keys s_j, where s_0 is only known to $\mathbb{A}$ and s_i ($\forall i \in \mathbb{U}$) is only known to user i, such that $s_0 + s_1 + \ldots + s_N = 0$ (this condition is required for the data aggregation described hereafter). Any secure key establishment protocol or trusted dealer can be used in this phase to distribute the secret keys, as long as the condition on their sum is respected. The initialization phase is the same as in [27]. Each user i generates its profile vector $\mathbf{p_i} \in \mathcal{D}^K$ containing personal attributes $j \in \{1, \ldots, K\}$.

1. **Customer Query:** A customer queries the aggregator. The query contains information about the type of aggregates and users. In practice, it could be formatted as an SQL query.
2. **User Selection:** The aggregator selects users based on the customer query. To do so, we consider that users shared some basic information with the aggregator, such as their demographics. Another option is for the aggregator to forward the customer query to users, and let users decide whether to participate or not.
3. **Aggregator Query:** The aggregator forwards the customer's query to the users, together with a public feature extraction function f.
4. **Feature Extraction:** Each user i can optionally execute a public feature extraction function $f : \mathcal{D}^K \rightarrow \mathcal{O}^L$ on $\mathbf{p_i}$, where L is the dimension of the output feature space $\mathcal{O}$, thus resulting in a feature vector $\mathbf{f_i}$. In our implementation, we consider a simple function that extracts the value of an attribute and its square.
5. **Encryption and Obfuscation:** Each user adds noise to $\mathbf{f_i}$, obtaining $\widehat{\mathbf{f_i}}$, and encrypts it. Encryption and obfuscation provide strong guarantees both in terms of data confidentiality and differential privacy [28]. Each user sends the encrypted vector $\mathcal{E}(\widehat{\mathbf{f_i}})$ to $\mathbb{A}$.
6. **Aggregation, Decryption, and Pricing:** $\mathbb{A}$ combines all $\mathcal{E}(\widehat{\mathbf{f_i}})$ and decrypts the result, generating a 2-tuple $(V_j, W_j) \in \mathbb{R}^2$ for each attribute j. These tuples are used to approximate the probability density function of attributes across users. $\mathbb{A}$ uses (V_j, W_j) to create a discrete sampled probability distribution function $d\mathcal{N}_j$ for each attribute j. $\mathbb{A}$ then computes a distance measure $d_j = d(d\mathcal{N}_j, d\mathcal{U}_j) \in [0, 1]$ between $d\mathcal{N}_j$ and $d\mathcal{U}_j$, where $d\mathcal{U}_j$ is a discrete uniform distribution in the interval $[m_j, M_j]$. A small/large distance corresponds to an attribute with low/high information "value", as described later in the text.

   $\mathbb{A}$ determines the cost $Cost(j)$ of each attribute j by taking into account both the distances d_j, the number of contributing users, and the price per attribute.
7. **Answer:** $\mathbb{A}$ sends a set of 2-tuples $\{(d_{\rho_z}, Cost(\rho_z))\}_{\rho_z=1}^K$ to $\mathbb{C}$, which selects aggregates to purchase. After the purchase, $\mathbb{A}$ obtains a share of the total sale revenue and equally distributes the remainder to users.

3.2 Detailed Description

We detail the functions and primitives for the aggregation and monetization of user data. In this paper, we compute aggregates by estimating the probability density function (pdf) of user attributes. We use the Gaussian approximation to estimate pdfs for two reasons. First, existing work shows that this will lead to precise aggregates with few users. The CLT [29,30] states that the arithmetic mean of a sufficiently large number of independent random variables, drawn from distributions of expected value μ and variance σ^2, will be approximately normally distributed $\mathcal{N}(\mu, \sigma^2)$. Second, a Gaussian pdf $\mathcal{N}$ is fully defined by two parameters and thus we do not need additional coordination among users (after the initialization phase). For information leakage ranking, we use a well-established information-theoretic distance function.

For conciseness, we focus on the description of privacy-preserving aggregation and pricing (phases 4 to 6, i.e., feature extraction, encryption, aggregation and ranking).

With respect to the initialization and query forwarding phases (1-3), our method is general enough and can be adapted to any specific implementation.

Phase 4-5: Feature Extraction and Encryption. Each user i generates a profile vector $\mathbf{p_i} = [x_{i,1}, \ldots, x_{i,K}]$. Each attribute j takes value $x_{i,j} \in \{m_j, \ldots, M_j\}$, where $m_j, M_j \in \mathbb{Z}_p$ are the minimum and maximum value. Note that as in [27], computations are in cyclic group $\mathbb{Z}_p$ of prime order p. The aggregator also chooses a generator g at random, such that $g \in \mathbb{Z}_p$, and H is a Hash function. Remember that in practice, a user can derive $\mathbf{p_i}$ either from an existing online profile (e.g., Facebook) or by manually entering values $x_{i,j}$. In our evaluation, we use values from the U.S. Census Bureau [31,32].

We consider a simple feature extraction f that consists in providing x_j and computing x_j^2. Obviously, other feature extraction method may contribute higher-order moments or simply combine attributes together to obtain richer x_j's.

To guarantee (ϵ, δ)-Differential Privacy, each user i adds noise $r_{i,j}, o_{i,j}$ to attribute values sampled from a symmetric Geometric distribution according to Algorithm 1 in [27]. In particular, in the following we add noise to both $x_{i,j}$ and $x_{i,j}^2$, as they will be subsequently combined to obliviously compute the parameters of the model that underlies the actual data:

$$\widehat{x_{i,j}} = x_{i,j} + r_{i,j} \mod p$$

and

$$\widehat{x_{i,j}}^{(2)} = x_{i,j}^2 + o_{i,j} \mod p$$

where p is the prime order [27].

With $\widehat{x_{i,j}}$ and $\widehat{x_{i,j}}^{(2)}$, each user generates the following encrypted vectors $(\mathbf{c_i}, \mathbf{b_i})$:

$$\mathbf{c_i} = \begin{pmatrix} c_{i,1} \\ c_{i,2} \\ \vdots \\ c_{i,K} \end{pmatrix} = \begin{pmatrix} g^{\widehat{x_{i,1}}} H(t)^{s_i} \\ g^{\widehat{x_{i,2}}} H(t)^{s_i} \\ \vdots \\ g^{\widehat{x_{i,K}}} H(t)^{s_i} \end{pmatrix}, \quad \mathbf{b_i} = \begin{pmatrix} b_{i,1} \\ b_{i,2} \\ \vdots \\ b_{i,K} \end{pmatrix} = \begin{pmatrix} g^{\widehat{x_{i,1}}^{(2)}} H(t)^{s_i} \\ g^{\widehat{x_{i,2}}^{(2)}} H(t)^{s_i} \\ \vdots \\ g^{\widehat{x_{i,K}}^{(2)}} H(t)^{s_i} \end{pmatrix}$$

Each user i then sends $(\mathbf{c_i}, \mathbf{b_i})$ to $\mathbb{A}$. Note that the encryption scheme guarantees that $\mathbb{A}$ is unable to decrypt the vectors $(\mathbf{c_i}, \mathbf{b_i})$. However, thanks to its own secret share s_0, $\mathbb{A}$ can decrypt aggregates as explained hereafter.

Phase 6: Privacy-Preserving Aggregation and Pricing. To compute the sample mean $\widehat{\mu_j}$ and variance $\widehat{\sigma_j^2}$ without having access to the individual values $\widehat{x_{i,j}}, \widehat{x_{i,j}}^{(2)}$ of any user i, $\mathbb{A}$ first computes intermediate 2-tuple (V_j, W_j):

$$V_j = H(t)^{s_0} \Pi_{i=1}^N c_{i,j} = H(t)^{\sum_{k=0}^N s_k} g^{\sum_{i=1}^N \widehat{x_{i,j}}} = g^{\sum_{i=1}^N \widehat{x_{i,j}}}$$

$$W_j = H(t)^{s_0} \Pi_{i=1}^N b_{i,j} = H(t)^{\sum_{k=0}^N s_k} g^{\sum_{i=1}^N \widehat{x_{i,j}}^{(2)}} = g^{\sum_{i=1}^N \widehat{x_{i,j}}^{(2)}}$$

To obtain $(\widehat{\mu_j}, \widehat{\sigma_j^2})$, $\mathbb{A}$ takes the discrete logarithm base g of (V_j, W_j):

$$\widehat{\mu_j} = \frac{\log_g(V_j)}{N} = \frac{\sum_{i=1}^{N} \widehat{x_{i,j}}}{N}$$

$$\widehat{\sigma_j^2} = \frac{\log_g(W_j)}{N} - \widehat{\mu_j}^2 = \frac{\sum_{i=1}^{N} \widehat{x_{i,j}}^{(2)}}{N} - \widehat{\mu_j}^2$$

Finally, using the derived $(\widehat{\mu_j}, \widehat{\sigma_j^2})$, $\mathbb{A}$ computes the Normal *pdf* approximation $\mathcal{N}_j \sim \mathcal{N}(\widehat{\mu_j}, \widehat{\sigma_j^2})$ for each attribute j.

Ranking. In order to estimate the amount of "valuable" information (i.e., sensitivity) that each attribute leaks, we propose to measure the *distance* (i.e., divergence) between the Normal approximation $\mathcal{N}_j$ and the Uniform distribution $\mathcal{U}$. This makes sense because divergence measures distance between distributions: By comparing $\mathcal{N}_j$ to the Uniform, we measure how much information $\mathcal{N}_j$ leaks compared to the distribution $\mathcal{U}$ that leaks the least amount of information [33]. This approach applies to a variety of computing scenarios. For example, a related concept was studied in [22,34] for measuring the "interestingness" of textual data by comparing it to an expected model, usually with the Kullback-Liebler (KL) divergence.

To the best of our knowledge, we are the first to explore this approach in the context of information privacy. Instead of the KL divergence, we rely on the Jensen-Shannon (JS) divergence for two reasons: (1) JS is a symmetric and (2) bounded equivalent of the KL divergence. It is defined as:

$$JS(u, q) = \frac{1}{2} KL(u, m) + \frac{1}{2} KL(q, m) = H(\frac{1}{2}u + \frac{1}{2}q) - \frac{1}{2}H(u) - \frac{1}{2}H(q)$$

where $m = u/2 + q/2$ and H is the Shannon entropy. As JS is in $[0, 1]$ (when using the logarithm base 2), it quantifies the relative distance between $\mathcal{N}_j$ and $\mathcal{U}_j$, and also provides absolute comparisons with distributions different from the uniform.

As JS operates on discrete values, $\mathbb{A}$ must first discretize distributions $\mathcal{N}_j$ and $\mathcal{U}_j$. Given the knowledge of intervals $\{m_j, \ldots, M_j\}$ for each attribute j, we can use Riemann's centered sum to approximate a definite integral, where the number of approximation bins is related to the accuracy of the approximation. We choose the number of bins to be $M_j - m_j$, and thus guarantee a bin width of 1. We approximate $\mathcal{N}_j$ by the discrete random variable $d\mathcal{N}_j$ with the following probability mass function:

$$\mathbf{Pr}(d\mathcal{N}_j) = \begin{pmatrix} Pr(x_j = m_j) \\ Pr(x_j = m_j + 1) \\ \vdots \\ Pr(x_j = M_j) \end{pmatrix} = \begin{pmatrix} pdf_j(\frac{1}{2}(m_j + m_j - 1)) \\ pdf_j(\frac{1}{2}(m_j + 1 + m_j)) \\ \vdots \\ pdf_j(\frac{1}{2}(M_j + M_j - 1)) \end{pmatrix}$$

where pdf_j is the probability density function $\mathcal{N}_j$ and $x_j \in \{m_j, \ldots, M_j\}$. We then normalize $\mathbf{Pr}(d\mathcal{N}_j)$ such that $\sum_k Pr(x_j = k) = 1$, for each j. For the uniform distribution $\mathcal{U}_j$, the discretization to $d\mathcal{U}_j$ is straightforward, i.e., $\mathbf{Pr}(d\mathcal{U}_j) = (1/(M_j - m_j), \ldots, 1/(M_j - m_j))^T$, where $\dim(d\mathcal{U}_j) = M_j - m_j$.

$\mathbb{A}$ can now compute distances $d_j = JS(\mathrm{d}\mathcal{N}_j, \mathrm{d}\mathcal{U}_j) \in [0,1]$ and rank attributes in increasing order of information leakage such that $d_{\rho_1} \leq d_{\rho_2} \leq \ldots \leq d_{\rho_K}$, where $\rho_1 = \arg\min_j d_j$ and ρ_z (for $2 \leq z \leq K$) are defined as $\rho_z = \arg\min_{j \neq \{\rho_k\}_{k=1}^{z-1}}(d_j)$

At this point, $\mathbb{A}$ computed the 3-tuple $(d_{\rho_j}, \widehat{\mu_j}, \widehat{\sigma_j^2})$ for each attribute j. Each user i can now decide whether it is comfortable sharing attribute j given distance d_j and privacy sensitivity $\lambda_{i,j}$. To do so, each user i sends $\lambda_{i,j}$ to $\mathbb{A}$ for comparison. $\mathbb{A}$ then checks which users are willing to share each attribute j and updates the ratio $\gamma_j = S_j/N$, where S_j is the number of users that are comfortable sharing, i.e., $S_j = |\{i \in \mathbb{U} \text{ s.t. } d_j \leq 1 - \lambda_{i,j}\}|$. In practice, $\mathbb{A}$ could then use the majority rule to decide whether or not to monetize attribute j.

Pricing. After this ranking phase, the data broker $\mathbb{A}$ concludes the process with the pricing and revenue phases. Prior work shows that users assign unique monetary value to different types of attributes depending on several factors, such as offline/online activities [10], type of third-parties involved [10], privacy sensitivity [23], amount of details and fairness [8].

We measure the value of aggregates depending on their sensitivity, the number of contributing users, and the cost of each attribute. Without loss of generality, we estimate the value of an aggregate j using the following linear model:

$$Cost(j) = Price(j) \cdot d_j \cdot N$$

where $Price(j)$ is the monetary value that users assign to attribute j. Without loss of generality, we assume in our pricing scheme a relative value of 1 for each attribute. Existing work discussed the value of user attributes, and estimated a large range from \$ 0.0005 to \$33 [10,35] highlighting the difficulty in determining a fixed price. In practice, this is likely to change depending on the monetization scenario.

$\mathbb{A}$ then sends the set of 2-tuples $\{(d_{\rho_z}, Cost(\rho_z))\}_{\rho_z=1}^K$ to $\mathbb{C}$. Based on the tuples, $\mathbb{C}$ selects the set $\mathbb{P}$ of attributes it wishes to purchase. After the purchase is complete, $\mathbb{A}$ re-distributes revenue R among users and itself, according to the agreement stipulated with the users upon their first registration with $\mathbb{A}$.

We consider a standard revenue sharing monetization scheme, where the revenue is split among users and the data aggregator (i.e., aggregator takes commissions):

$$R(\mathbb{A}) = \sum_{j \in \mathbb{P}} \omega_j \cdot Cost(j), \qquad R(i) = \frac{1}{N} \sum_{j \in \mathbb{P}} (1 - \omega_j) \cdot Cost(j), \qquad \forall i \in \mathbb{U}$$

where ω_j is the commission percentage of $\mathbb{A}$. This system is popular in existing aggregating schemes [26], credit-card payments, and online stores (e.g., iOS App Store). We assume a fixed ω_j for each attribute j.

4   Evaluation

To test the relevance and the practicality of our privacy-preserving monetization solution, we measure the quality of aggregates, the overhead, and generated revenue. In particular, we study how the number of protocol participants and their privacy sensitivities affect the accuracy of the Gaussian approximations, the computational performance, the amount of information leaked for each attribute, and revenue.

Table 1. Summary of the U.S. Census dataset used for the evaluation. We considered three types of attributes (level of income, education and age), which reflect different types of sample distributions (as shown in Fig. 2).

		Number of randomly selected users in the dataset					
		10	100	1k	10k	50k	100k
Income	μ	6.50	9.72	10.30	10.87	10.83	10.89
	σ	19.17	18.70	20.04	17.05	16.72	16.52
	(m_j, M_j)	(1, 10)	(1, 15)	(1, 15)	(1, 16)	(1, 16)	(1, 16)
Educ.	μ	5.70	7.23	10.29	10.38	10.21	10.18
	σ	15.57	7.07	7.96	7.68	7.73	7.63
	(m_j, M_j)	(1, 9)	(1, 12)	(1, 15)	(1, 16)	(1, 16)	(1, 16)
Age	μ	38.10	35.40	41.91	42.44	41.49	39.79
	σ	252.54	502.79	563.32	546.40	553.68	539.60
	(m_j, M_j)	(11, 67)	(1, 85)	(0, 85)	(0, 85)	(0, 85)	(0, 85)

4.1 Setup

We consider secret shares in $\mathbb{Z}_p$ where p is a 1024 bits modulus, the number of users $N \in [10, 100000]$, and each user i with profile $\mathbf{p_i}$. We implemented our privacy-preserving protocol in Java, and rely on public libraries for secret key initialization, for multi-threading decryption, and on the MALLET [36] package for computation of the JS divergence.

We run our experiments on a machine equipped with Mac OSX 10.8.3, dual-core Core i5 processor, 2.53 GHz, and 8 GB RAM. Measurements up to 100 users are averaged over 300 iterations, and the rest (from 1k to 100k users) are averaged over 3 iterations due to large simulation times.

We populate user profiles with U.S. Census Bureau information [31,32]: We obtained anonymized offline and online attributes about 100,000 people. We pre-processed the acquired data by removing incomplete profiles (i.e., some respondents prefer not to reveal specific attributes).

Without loss of generality, we focus on three types of offline attributes: Yearly *income* level, *education* level and *age*. We selected these attributes because (1) a recent study [10] shows that these attributes have high monetary value (and thus privacy sensitivity), and (2) they have significantly different distributions across users. This allows us to compare retribution models, and measure the accuracy of the Gaussian approximation for a variety of distributions.

Table 1 shows the mean and standard deviation for the three considered attributes with a varying number of users. Note that the provided values for *income* and *education* use a specific scale defined by the Census Bureau. For example, a value of 1 and 16 for *education* correspond to "Less than 1st grade" and "Doctorate", respectively.

We could consider other types of attributes as well, such as internet, music and video preferences from alternative sources, such as Yahoo Webscope [37]. Although an exhaustive comparison of the monetization of all different attributes is an exciting perspective, it is out of the scope of this paper and we leave this for future work.

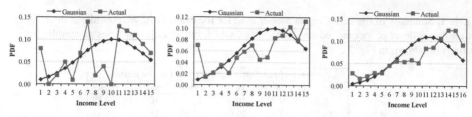

(a) Attribute *income*, sampled from 100 users (left), 1k users (middle) and 100k users (right).

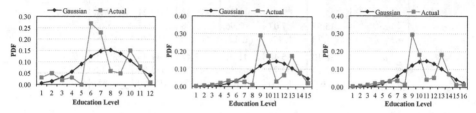

(b) Attribute *education*, sampled from 100 users (left), 1k users (middle) and 100k users (right).

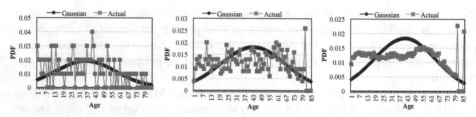

(c) Attribute *age*, sampled from 100 users (left), 1k users (middle) and 100k users (right).

Fig. 2. Gaussian approximation vs. actual distribution for each considered attribute

4.2   Results

We evaluate four aspects of our privacy-preserving scheme: model accuracy, information leakage, overhead and pricing.

Model Accuracy. In our proposal, we approximate empirical probability density functions with Gaussian distributions. The accuracy of approximations is important to assess the relevance of derived data models. In Fig. 2, we compare the actual distribution of each attribute with their respective Gaussian approximation and vary the number of users from 100 to 100,000. Note that in order to compare probabilities over the domain $[m_j, M_j]$, we scaled both the actual distribution and the Gaussian approximation such that their respective sums over that domain are equal to one. We observe that, visually, the Gaussian approximation captures general trends in the actual data.

We measure the accuracy of the Gaussian approximation in more details with the JS divergence (Fig. 3a). We observe that with 100 users, the approximation reaches a plateau for *education*, whereas *income* and *age* require 1k users to converge. For the two latter attributes, the approximation accuracy triples when increasing from 100 to 1k users. Moreover, as the number of user increases, the fit of the Gaussian model for *income* and *age* is two times better (JS of 0.05 bits) than for *education* (JS of 0.1 bits).

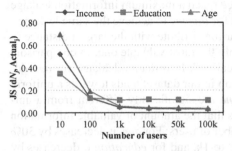

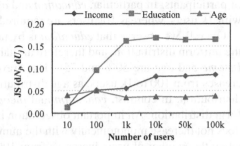

(a) Divergence between the Gaussian approximation and the actual distribution of each attribute j, computed as the $JS(\mathrm{d}\mathcal{N}_j, \mathrm{Actual}_j)$. Lower values indicate better accuracy.

(b) Information leakage for each type of attribute j (income, education and age), defined as $JS(\mathrm{d}\mathcal{N}_j, \mathrm{d}\mathcal{U}_j)$. Lower values indicate smaller information leaks.

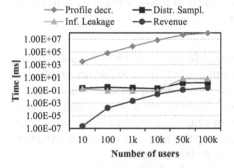

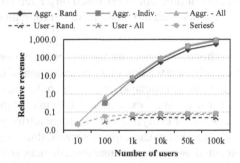

(c) Performance measurements for each of the four phases of the protocol performed by the data broker.

(d) Relative revenue (per attribute) for each user $i \in \mathbb{U}$ and the data aggregator $\mathbb{A}$, assuming that an attribute is valued at 1.

Fig. 3. Results of the evaluation of the proposed framework on the U.S. Census dataset

The main reason is that *education* has more data points with large differences between actual and approximated distributions than *income* and *age* (as shown in Fig. 2).

These results indicate that, for non-uniform distributions, the Gaussian approximation is accurate with a relatively small number of users (about 100). It is interesting to study this result in light of the Central Limit Theorem (CLT). Remember that the CLT states that the arithmetic mean of a sufficiently large number of variables will tend to be normally distributed. In other words, a Gaussian approximation quickly converges to the original distribution and this confirms the validity of our experiments. This also means that $\mathbb{C}$ can obtain accurate models even if it requests aggregates about small groups of users. In other words, collecting data about more than 1k users does not significantly improve the accuracy of approximations, even for more extreme distributions.

Information Leakage. We compare the divergence between Gaussian approximations and uniform distributions to measure the information leakage of different attributes. Fig. 3b shows the sensitivity for each attribute with a varying number of users. We observe that the amount of information leakage stabilizes for all attributes after a given number of participants. In particular, *education* and *age* reach a maximum information leakage with 1k users, whereas 10k users are required for *income* to achieve the same leakage.

Overall, we observe that *education* is by far the attribute with the largest distance to the uniform distribution, and therefore arguably the most valuable one. In comparison, *Income* and *age* are 50% and 75% less "revealing". Information leakage for *age* decreases from 100 to 1k users, as age distribution in our dataset tends towards a uniform distribution. In contrast, *education* and *income* are significantly different from a uniform distribution. An important observation is that the amount of valuable information does not increase monotonically with the number of users: For *age*, it decreases by 30% when the number of users increases from 100 to 1k, and for *education* it decreases by 3% when transitioning from 10k to 50k users.

These findings show that larger user samples do not necessarily provide better discriminating features. This also shows that users should not decide whether to participate in our protocol solely based on a fixed threshold over total participants, as this may prove to leak slightly more private information.

Overhead. We measure the computation overhead for both users and the data broker. For each user, we find that one execution of the protocol requires 0.284 ms (excluding communication delays), out of which 0.01 ms are spent for the profile generation, 0.024 ms for the feature extraction, 0.026 ms for the differential-privacy noise addition, and 0.224 ms for encryption of the noisy attribute. In general, user profiles are not subject to change within short time intervals, thus suggesting that user-side operations could be executed on resource-constrained devices such as mobile phones.

From Fig. 3c, observe that the data broker requires about one second to complete its phases when there are only 10 users, 1.5 min with 100 users, 15 min with 1k users, and 27.7 h for 100k users. Note, however, that running times can be remarkably reduced using algorithmic optimization and parallelization, which is part of our future work. In our results, decryption is the most time-consuming operation for the data broker as it incurs ($O(N \cdot M_j)$): this could be reduced to $O(\sqrt{N \cdot M_j})$ by using the Pollard's Rho method for computing the discrete logarithm [38]. Also, decryption can be speedup up by splitting decryption operations across multiple machines (i.e., the underlying algorithm is highly-parallelizable).

Pricing. Recall that the price of an attribute aggregate depends on the number of contributing users, the amount of information leakage, and the cost of the attribute. We consider that each attribute j has a unit cost of 1 and the data broker takes a commission ω_j. We consider three types of privacy sensitivities λ: (i) a uniform random distribution of privacy sensitivities $\lambda_{i,j}$ for each user i and for each attribute j, (ii) an individual privacy sensitivity λ_i for each user (same across different attributes), and (iii) an all-share scenario ($\lambda_i = 0$ and all users contribute). The commission percentage is set to $\omega_j = \omega = 0.1$.

Fig. 3d shows the average revenue generated from one attribute by the data broker and by users. We observe that user revenue is small and does not increase with the number of participants. In contrast, the data broker revenue increases linearly with the number of participants. In terms of privacy sensitivities, we observe that with higher privacy sensitivities ($\lambda_i > 0$), fewer users contribute, thus generating lower revenue overall and per user. For example, users start earning revenue with 10 participants in the all-share scenario, but more users are required to start generating revenue if users adopt higher privacy sensitivities.

We observe that users are incentivized to participate as they earn some revenue (rather than not benefiting at all), but the generated revenue does not generate significant income, thus, it might encourage user participation from "biased" demographics (e.g., similar to Amazon Mechanical Turk). In contrast, the data broker has incentives to attract more users, as it revenue increases with the number of participants. However, customers are incentivized to select fewer users because cost increases with the number of users, and 100 users provide as good an aggregate as 1000 users. This is an intriguing result, as it encourages customers to focus on small groups of users representative of a certain population category.

4.3 Security

Passive adversaries. To ensure privacy of the personal user attributes, our framework relies on the security of the underlying encryption and differential-privacy methods presented in [27]. Hence, no passive adversary (a user participating in the monetization protocol, the data aggregator or an external party not involved in the protocol) can learn any of the user attributes, assuming that the key setup phase has been performed correctly and that a suitable algebraic group (satisfying the DDH assumption) with a large enough prime order (1024 bits or more) has been chosen.

Active adversaries. As per [27], our framework is resistant to collusion attacks among users and between a subset of users and the data broker, as each user i encrypts its attribute values with a unique and secret key s_i. However, pollution attacks, which try to manipulate the aggregated result by encrypting out-of-scope values, can affect the aggregate result of our protocol. Nevertheless, such attacks can be mitigated by including, in addition to encryption, range checks based on efficient (non-interactive) zero-knowledge proofs of knowledge [39,40,41]: each user could submit, in addition to the encrypted values, a proof that such values are indeed in the plausible range specified by the data aggregator. However, even within a specific range, a user can manipulate its contributed value and thus affect the aggregate. Although nudging users to reveal their true attribute value is an important challenge, it is outside of the scope of this paper.

5 Related Work

Our work builds upon two main domains, in order to provide the privacy and incentives for the users and data aggregators: (1) privacy-preserving aggregation [42,27,43,44], and (2) privacy-preserving monetization of user profiles [15,12,16,14]. Hereafter we discuss these two sets of works.

5.1 Privacy-Preserving Aggregation

Erkin and Tsudik [42] design a method to perform privacy-preserving data aggregation in the smart grid. Smart meters jointly establish secret keys without having to rely on a trusted third party, and mask individual readings using a modified version of the Paillier encryption scheme [45]. The aggregator then computes the sum of all readings without seeing individual values. Smart meters must communicate with each other, thus limiting this proposal to online settings. Shi et al. [43] compute the sum of different inputs based on data slicing and mixing with other users, but have the same limitation: all participants must actively communicate with each other during the aggregation.

Another line of work [18,19] introduces privacy-preserving aggregation by combining homomorphic encryption and differential privacy, i.e., users encrypt their data with the customer public key and send it to a trusted aggregator. The aggregator adds differential noise to encrypted values (using the homomorphic property), and forwards the result to the customer. The customer decrypts contributions and computes desired aggregates. These proposals, however, suffer from a number of shortcomings as: (i) they rely on a trusted third party for differential privacy; (ii) they require at least one public key operation per single bit of user input, and one kilobit of data per single bit of user answer, or rely on XOR encryption; and (iii) contributions are linkable to users as aggregation occurs after decryption.

The work by Shi et al. [27] supports computing the sum of different inputs in a privacy-preserving fashion, without requiring communication among users, nor repeated interactions with a third party. It also provides differential privacy guarantees in presence of malicious users, and establishes an upper bound on the error induced by the additive noise. This work formally shows that a Geometric distribution provides (ϵ, δ)-differential privacy (DD) in $\mathbb{Z}_p$. We extend the construction in [27] to support the privacy-preserving computation of probability distributions (in addition to sums). Intuitively, we use the proposed technique to compute the parameters of Gaussian approximations in a privacy-preserving way. As we maintain the same security assumptions, our framework preserves provable privacy properties. As part of future work, we intend to explore the properties of regression modeling and privacy-preserving computation of regression parameters [46,44], in addition to distributions.

5.2   Privacy-Preserving Monetization

Previous work investigated two main approaches to privacy-preserving Online Behavioral Advertisement (OBA). The first approach minimizes the data shared with third parties, by introducing local user profile generation, categorization, and ad selection [17,12,13,14]. The second approach relies on anonymizing proxies to shield users' behavioral data from third parties, until users agree to sell their data [15,16].

Toubiana et al. [14] propose to let users maintain browsing profiles on their device and match ads with user profiles, based on a cosine-similarity measure between visited websites meta-data (title, URL, tags) and ad categories. Users receive a large number of ads, select appropriate ones, and share selected ads with ad providers (not revealing visited websites nor user details). Guha et al. [12] propose to do the ad matching with an anonymization proxy instead. Although the cost of such system is estimated at $0.01/user per year, such solution demands significant changes from web browser vendors and online advertisers. Akkus et al. propose to let users rely on the website publisher to anonymize their browsing patterns *vis-à-vis* the ad-provider. Their protocol introduces significant overhead: The website publisher must repeatedly interact with each visitor and forward encrypted messages to the ad-provider.

Instead of local profiles, Riederer et al. [16] propose a fully centralized approach, where an anonymization proxy mediates interactions between users and website publishers. The proxy releases the mapping between IP addresses and long-term user identifiers only after users agree to sell their data to a customer, thus allowing the customer to link different visits by the same users. However, users have to entrust a third party with their personal information.

In contrast, our framework does not rely on any additional user-side software, does not impose computationally expensive cryptographic computation on user devices, and prevents the customer from learning individual user data.

6   Conclusion

As the amount and sensitivity of personal data shared with service providers increases, so do privacy concerns. Users usually have little control over what information is processed by service providers and how it is monetized with advertisers. Our work offers a privacy-preserving alternative where users only disclose an aggregate model of their profiles, by means of encrypted and differentially private contributions. Our solution tackles trust and incentive challenges: rather than selling data *as-is*, users trade a *model* of their data. Users also monetize their profiles by dynamically assessing the value of data aggregates. To this end, we use an information-theoretic measure to compute the amount of valuable information provided to advertisers.

We evaluate our framework on a real and anonymized dataset with more than 100,000 users (obtained from the U.S. Census Bureau) and show, with an experimental evaluation, that our solution (i) provides accurate aggregates with as little as 100 users, (ii) introduces low overhead for both users (less than 1ms on commodity hardware) and data aggregators, and (iii) generates revenue for both users and aggregators.

As part of future work, we plan to enhance our scheme with new features, including fault-tolerant aggregation [47] to allow users to join/leave dynamically and range checks for the encrypted user attributes, based on efficient zero-knowledge proofs, against active pollution attacks. Users could also contribute higher order moments (e.g., x^3 or x^4) for the aggregator to obtain more precise approximations using moment-generating functions (an alternative to *pdf*s). Finally, we intend to investigate schemes for targeting ads to users contributing data to the aggregation, by allowing the aggregator to select specific subgroups of users according to the customer's target population.

References

1. ComRes: Big Brother Watch Online Privacy Survey (2013), http://www.comres.co.uk/polls/Big_Brother_Watch_Online_Privacy_Survey.pdf
2. Flood, G.: Online Privacy Worries Increasing Worldwide. InformationWeek (2013), http://www.informationweek.co.uk/security/privacy/online-privacy-worries-increasing-worldw/240153200

3. Tanzina Vega, E.W.: U.s. agency seeks tougher consumer privacy rules. The New York Times (2012), http://nyti.ms/GQQCrY
4. Wyatt, E.: U.S. Penalizes Online Company in Sale of Personal Data. The New York Times (2012), http://nyti.ms/OsDrgI
5. Gellman, B., Poitras, L.: US Intelligence Mines Data from Internet Firms in Secret Program. The Washington Post (2013), http://wapo.st/J2gkLY
6. Greenwald, G., MacAskill, E.: NSA Prism program taps in to user data of Apple, Google and others. The Guardian (2013), http://www.theguardian.com/world/2013/jun/06/us-tech-giants-nsa-data
7. Natasha: Congress to examine data sellers. The New York Times (2012), http://nyti.ms/Pewbq1
8. Malheiros, M., Preibusch, S., Sasse, M.A.: "Fairly truthful": The impact of Perceived Effort, Fairness, Relevance, and Sensitivity on Personal Data Disclosure. In: Huth, M., Asokan, N., Čapkun, S., Flechais, I., Coles-Kemp, L. (eds.) TRUST 2013. LNCS, vol. 7904, pp. 250–266. Springer, Heidelberg (2013)
9. Tunner, A.: Bizarro World of Hilarious Mistakes Revealed In Long Secret Personal Data Files Just Opened. Forbes, http://onforb.es/1rZ5PZQ (2013)
10. Carrascal, J.P., Riederer, C., Erramilli, V., Cherubini, M., de Oliveira, R.: Your Browsing Behavior for a Big Mac: Economics of Personal Information Online. In: WWW (2013)
11. Singel, R.: Encrypted E-Mail Company Hushmail Spills to Feds (2007), http://www.wired.com/threatlevel/2007/11/encrypted-e-mai/
12. Guha, S., Cheng, B., Francis, P.: Privad: practical privacy in online advertising. In: NSDI (2011)
13. Mohan, P., Nath, S., Riva, O.: Prefetching Mobile Ads: Can Advertising Systems Afford It? In: EuroSys (2013)
14. Toubiana, V., Narayanan, A., Boneh, D., Nissenbaum, H., Barocas, S.: Adnostic: Privacy preserving targeted advertising. In: NDSS (2010)
15. Backes, M., Kate, A., Maffei, M., Pecina, K.: Obliviad: Provably secure and practical online behavioral advertising. In: IEEE Security and Privacy (2012)
16. Riederer, C., Erramilli, V., Chaintreau, A., Krishnamurthy, B., Rodriguez, P.: For Sale: Your Data: By: You. In: HotNets (2011)
17. Akkus, I.E., Chen, R., Hardt, M., Francis, P., Gehrke, J.: Non-tracking Web Analytics. In: ACM CCS (2012)
18. Chen, R., Akkus, I.E., Francis, P.: SplitX: High-performance Private Analytics. In: ACM SIGCOMM (2013)
19. Chen, R., Reznichenko, A., Francis, P., Gehrke, J.: Towards statistical queries over distributed private user data. In: NSDI (2012)
20. Narayanan, A., Shmatikov, V.: Robust de-anonymization of large sparse datasets. In: IEEE Security and Privacy (2008)
21. Lin, J.: Divergence measures based on the shannon entropy. IEEE TIT 37(1) (1991)
22. Feldman, R., Dagan, I.: Knowledge Discovery in Textual Databases. In: KDD (1995)
23. Aperjis, C., Huberman, B.A.: A market for unbiased private data: Paying individuals according to their privacy attitudes. ArXiv Report 1205.0030 (2012)
24. Kumaraguru, P., Cranor, L.F.: Privacy Indexes: A Survey of Westins Studies. Institute for Software Research International (2005)
25. Singer, N.: Mapping, and sharing, the consumer genome. The New York Times (2012), http://nyti.ms/LcBw0g
26. DataCommons: Partner Organizations Helping to Advance Healthcare (2014), http://mydatacommons.org
27. Shi, E., Chan, T.H.H., Rieffel, E.G., Chow, R., Song, D.: Privacy-Preserving Aggregation of Time-Series Data. In: NDSS (2011)

28. Dwork, C.: Differential privacy. In: Bugliesi, M., Preneel, B., Sassone, V., Wegener, I. (eds.) ICALP 2006, Part II. LNCS, vol. 4052, pp. 1–12. Springer, Heidelberg (2006)
29. Laplace, P.S.: Mémoire sur les approximations des formules qui sont fonctions de très-grands nombres, et sur leur application aux probabilités. Baudouin (1810)
30. Rice, J.A.: Mathematical statistics and data analysis. Wadsworth & Brooks/Cole (1988)
31. U.S. Census Bureau: DataFerrett Analysis and Extraction Tool, http://dataferrett.census.gov
32. U.S. Government: The home of the U.S. Government's open data, www.data.gov
33. Hamilton, H.J., Hilderman, R.J., Cercone, N.: Attribute-oriented induction using domain generalization graphs. In: IEEE ICTAI (1996)
34. Hilderman, R.J., Hamilton, H.J., Barber, B.: Ranking the interestingness of summaries from data mining systems. In: FLAIRS Conference (1999)
35. Olejnik, L., Minh-Dung, T., Castelluccia, C.: Selling Off Privacy at Auction. In: NDSS (2014)
36. McCallum, A.K.: Mallet: A machine learning for language toolkit (2002), http://mallet.cs.umass.edu
37. Yahoo Labs: Webscope, http://webscope.sandbox.yahoo.com
38. Pollard, J.M.: Monte carlo methods for index computation. Mathematics of Computation 32(143) (1978)
39. Blum, M., Feldman, P., Micali, S.: Non-interactive zero-knowledge and its applications. In: ACM STOC (1988)
40. Boudot, F.: Efficient proofs that a committed number lies in an interval. In: Preneel, B. (ed.) EUROCRYPT 2000. LNCS, vol. 1807, pp. 431–444. Springer, Heidelberg (2000)
41. Lipmaa, H.: On diophantine complexity and statistical zero-knowledge arguments. In: Laih, C.-S. (ed.) ASIACRYPT 2003. LNCS, vol. 2894, pp. 398–415. Springer, Heidelberg (2003)
42. Erkin, Z., Tsudik, G.: Private computation of spatial and temporal power consumption with smart meters. In: Bao, F., Samarati, P., Zhou, J. (eds.) ACNS 2012. LNCS, vol. 7341, pp. 561–577. Springer, Heidelberg (2012)
43. Shi, J., Zhang, R., Liu, Y., Zhang, Y.: Prisense: Privacy-preserving Data Aggregation in People-Centric Urban Sensing Systems. In: IEEE INFOCOM (2010)
44. Xing, K., Wan, Z., Hu, P., Zhu, H., Wang, Y., Chen, X., Wang, Y., Huang, L.: Mutual privacy-preserving regression modeling in participatory sensing. In: IEEE INFOCOM (2013)
45. Paillier, P.: Public-key Cryptosystems Based on Composite Degree Residuosity Classes. In: Stern, J. (ed.) EUROCRYPT 1999. LNCS, vol. 1592, pp. 233–238. Springer, Heidelberg (1999)
46. Ahmadi, H., Pham, N., Ganti, R., Abdelzaher, T., Nath, S., Han, J.: Privacy-aware regression modeling of participatory sensing data
47. Chan, T.-H.H., Shi, E., Song, D.: Privacy-preserving stream aggregation with fault tolerance. In: Keromytis, A.D. (ed.) FC 2012. LNCS, vol. 7397, pp. 200–214. Springer, Heidelberg (2012)

Challenging Differential Privacy: The Case of Non-interactive Mechanisms

Raghavendran Balu[1], Teddy Furon[1], and Sébastien Gambs[1,2]

[1] Inria Rennes Bretagne-Atlantique, France
[2] Université de Rennes 1 / IRISA, France
{rbalu,teddy.furon}@inria.fr, sgambs@irisa.fr

Abstract. In this paper, we consider personalized recommendation systems in which before publication, the profile of a user is sanitized by a non-interactive mechanism compliant with the concept of differential privacy. We consider two existing schemes offering a differentially private representation of profiles: BLIP (BLoom-and-flIP) and JLT (Johnson-Lindenstrauss Transform). For assessing their security levels, we play the role of an adversary aiming at reconstructing a user profile. We compare two inference attacks, namely *single* and *joint* decoding. The first one decides of the presence of a single item in the profile, and sequentially explores all the item set. The latter strategy decides whether a subset of items is likely to be the user profile, and considers all the possible subsets. Our contributions are a theoretical analysis as well as a practical implementation of both attacks, which were evaluated on datasets of real user profiles. The results obtained clearly demonstrates that joint decoding is the most powerful attack, while also giving useful insights on how to set the differential privacy parameter ϵ.

Keywords: Differential privacy, Joint decoding.

1 Introduction

Most of the social applications, like recommender systems or private matching, require computing some kind of pairwise similarity between the profiles of different users. Some of the challenges that such systems face include privacy and scalability issues. For instance, privacy concerns arise naturally due to the potentially sensitive nature of profiles, and some users may even refuse to participate if they have no guarantees on the privacy of their profiles.

To address these concerns, the concept of differential privacy [1] has been introduced by Dwork in the context of private analysis on statistical databases and has known a widespread adoption in the privacy community. In a nutshell, the main privacy guarantee provided by differential privacy is that for any computation that will be performed on the database, adding or removing a single row from the database will not significantly change the probability of a particular output. Usually, the database is composed of the collection of the individuals' data, and differential privacy protects the privacy of a particular individual,

M. Kutyłowski and J. Vaidya (Eds.): ESORICS 2014, Part II, LNCS 8713, pp. 146–164, 2014.

which corresponds to a row of the database. In contrast in our context, the "database" is actually the profile of an individual (*e.g.*, composed of the items he has liked) and therefore the guarantees provided by differential privacy applies to the protection of the items contained in the profile.

One of the usual limits of differential privacy is that each time a differentially private computation takes place, the user loses a little bit of privacy (as measured by the value of the privacy parameter ϵ). Therefore, if this computation takes place too many times, the user may spend all his privacy budget and remains with no privacy left. The adversary is then able to reconstruct almost entirely the user's profile. One possible approach to solve this problem is to sanitize the profile of a user with a non-interactive mechanism compliant with the concept of differential privacy before his publication. In particular, this paper investigates the privacy guarantees offered by two non-interactive mechanisms offering a differentially private representation of profiles: BLIP (BLoom-and-flIP) [2] and JLT (Johnson-Lindenstrauss Transform) [3].

In this paper, we propose two inference attacks that help to assess the privacy guarantee provided by the BLIP and JLT mechanisms. We provide an analysis of the utility and the protection offered by BLIP and JLT against these attacks, by deriving theoretical bounds on the resulting approximation error generated by a specific value of the privacy parameter. Furthermore, we evaluate experimentally the trade-off between privacy and utility achieved by these mechanisms. These attacks helps to better understand the privacy guarantees offered by a differentially-private mechanism, while also enabling the privacy practitioner to tune ϵ experimentally.

A detailed survey on inference attacks on sanitized data can be found in [4] and [5]. Common attacks include eigen-analysis [6,7], MAP estimation [7], Independent Component Analysis (ICA) [8] and distribution analysis [9]. MAP estimation and ICA make direct assumptions on the distribution of the original data, whereas distribution analysis and our approach estimate it from publicly available information. In addition, eigen-analysis makes even stronger assumptions on the representation of data and thus is not generic enough to apply to representations studied in this paper. Furthermore, the possibility of using probabilistic inference techniques to attack sanitized histogram data has been illustrated in [10] and [11]. In these works, bounds of records count are estimated from histogram of attributes coming from a Markov Chain Monte Carlo (MCMC) simulation. This line of work is different from our approach aiming at reconstructing a user profile from perturbed data. Application of probabilistic inference techniques for parameter estimation on differentially private data is illustrated in [12]. In this work, the authors have also experimentally validated their approach using MCMC on parameter estimation of logistic regression and probabilistic inference of principal components. Although their objective was not directly the reconstruction of data, their approach demonstrates that probabilistic inference is possible on differentially private data.

The outline of the paper is the following. First in Section 2, we give an overview of the concept of differential privacy. Then, we describe two non-interactive differentially private mechanisms in Sections 3 and 4 that have been recently proposed: BLIP (*BLoom-and-fIIP*) [2] and one based on the *Johnson-Lindenstrauss Transform* (JLT in short) [3]. These mechanisms transform the profile of a user into a compact representation that estimate the similarity between profiles while hiding the presence or absence of a particular item in the profile (in the sense of differential privacy). Afterwards in Section 5, we provide a theoretical analysis showing that the joint decoding strategy is more powerful than the single decoding strategy in reconstructing the profile of a user. Finally in Section 6, we propose a tractable implementation of this strategy based on the MCMC algorithm before reporting in Section 7 the results on two real datasets.

2   Differential Privacy

In this paper, we are interested in a strong privacy notion called *differential privacy* [1]. Differential privacy aims at providing strong privacy guarantees with respect to the input of some computation by randomizing the output of this computation, and this independently of the auxiliary information that the adversary might have gathered. In our setting, the input of the computation is the profile of a user and the randomized output will be a perturbed version of a compact representation of this profile (*e.g.*, a Bloom filter or a random projection).

Two profiles $\mathbf{x}$ and $\mathbf{x}'$ are said to *differ in at most one element* or said to be *neighbors* if they are equal except for possibly one entry.

Definition 1 (Differential privacy [13]). *A randomized function $\mathcal{F} : \mathcal{D}^n \to \mathcal{D}^n$ is ϵ-differentially private, if for all neighboring profiles $\mathbf{x}, \mathbf{x}' \in \mathcal{D}^n$ and for all $\mathbf{t} \in \mathcal{D}^n$:*

$$\mathbb{P}[\mathcal{F}(\mathbf{x}) = \mathbf{t}] \leqslant e^\epsilon \cdot \mathbb{P}[\mathcal{F}(\mathbf{x}') = \mathbf{t}] \ .$$

This probability is taken over all the coin tosses of $\mathcal{F}$ and e is the base of the natural logarithm.

The parameter ϵ is public and may take different values depending on the application (for instance it could be 0.1, 0.25, 1.5 or even 10). The smaller the value of ϵ, the higher the privacy but also as a consequence the higher the impact might be on the utility of the resulting output. A relaxed notion differential privacy called (ϵ,δ)-differential privacy [14], can be seen as a probabilistic variant in which the guarantees of differential privacy hold with probability of $1 - \delta$.

Originally, differential privacy was developed within the context of private data analysis and the main guarantee is that if a differentially private mechanism is applied on a dataset composed of the personal data of individuals, no output would become significantly more (or less) probable whether or not a *single* participant contributes to the dataset. This means that observing the output of the mechanism only gains negligible information about the presence (or absence) of a particular individual in the database. This statement is a statistical property about the behavior of the mechanism (*i.e.*, function) and holds independently of the auxiliary knowledge that the adversary might have gathered.

More specifically, even if the adversary knows the whole database but one individual row, a mechanism satisfying differential privacy still protects the privacy of this individual row. In our setting, the database that we want to protect is the profile of a user and the objective of a differentially private mechanism is to hide the presence or absence of a particular item in the profile.

Dwork, McSherry, Nissim and Smith have designed a generic technique, called the *Laplacian mechanism* [13], that achieves ϵ-differential privacy for a function f by adding random noise to the true answer of f before releasing it. Subsequently, McSherry and Talwar have proposed the *exponential mechanism* [15] which unlike the Laplacian mechanism that works only for functions with numerical output, provides differential privacy for functions whose output is more structured (*e.g.*, graphs or trees). Both previous mechanisms (*i.e.*, Laplacian and Exponential mechanisms) are *interactive* as they require a two-way communication protocol between the curator (the entity in charge of the database) and the client performing the query. Therefore, the curator has to be online in order to receive the query and prepare the associate response to this query.

On the other hand, a *non-interactive* mechanism computes some function from the original database and releases it once and for all, which corresponds to a one-way communication protocol. The output released by the non-interactive mechanism can later be used by anyone to compute the answer to a particular class of queries (usually not just a single specific query), without requiring any further interactions with the curator. It is important to understand that the answer is computed from the output released by the non-interactive mechanism, thus after publishing this output the curator can go offline. One particular type of non-interactive mechanism is the *generation of a synthetic dataset* that allows the answer to certain class of queries (but not necessarily all) to be approximated. Examples of non-interactive mechanisms for differential privacy include [16,17].

In the next sections, we describe two non-interactive mechanisms that have recently been proposed. The first mechanism is based on randomizing a Bloom filter representation of the profile [2] while the second relies on the application of the Johnson-Lindenstrauss transform and the addition of noise [3]. Both mechanisms preserve some global properties such as the ability to compute a distance between two profiles while hiding the details of the profiles themselves.

3 BLIP

The main objective of BLIP [2] is to prevent the adversary from learning the presence (or absence) of an item in the profile of a user by observing the Bloom filter representation of this profile. Our theoretical analysis provided in Section 5 is based on the model of profiles and the BLIP sanitization described thereafter.

3.1 Setup of BLIP

The setup that we consider for the theoretical analysis is the following. We assume that a profile P is a list of c items randomly picked from a set of $N \in$

$\mathbb{N}^\star$ possible items: $P = \{j_1, \ldots, j_c\}$. We denote the set of items by $[N]$, with $[N] \triangleq \{1, \ldots, N\}$ and the set of all possible profiles by $\mathcal{P}$. This set is a subset of the power set of $[N]$ and we have $|\mathcal{P}| = \binom{N}{c}$. For the moment, we make the assumption that c is publicly known, but this hypothesis will be lifted later by inferring this value directly from the Bloom filter.

The profile is first encoded in the form of a Bloom filter, which is a binary string of L bits. Each item $j \in P$ is hashed through K different hash functions $(h_1, \ldots, h_K)$. Each hash function yields a position $h_k(j)$ in the Bloom filter, pseudo-randomly selected based on the identifier of the item j. One simple technique to implement this is to rely on K cryptographic hash functions modulo L. We call the codeword $\mathbf{X}_j$ associated to item j the following string of L bits:

$$X_j(\ell) = \begin{cases} 1 \text{ if } \exists k \in [K] \text{ such that } h_k(j) = \ell, \\ 0 \text{ otherwise.} \end{cases} \tag{1}$$

The Bloom filter associated to the profile $P = \{j_1, \ldots, j_c\}$ is denoted by $\mathbf{B}_P$ and computed as the aggregation of the codewords:

$$\mathbf{B}_P = \mathbf{X}_{j_1} \vee \ldots \vee \mathbf{X}_{j_c}, \tag{2}$$

in which $\vee$ denotes the bit-wise (inclusive) OR operator. Our presentation of Bloom filters is different than usual to stress the link with our general problem.

The BLIP mechanism adds noise to the Bloom filter representation of a profile before publishing it. We denote the output of BLIP by $\tilde{\mathbf{B}}_P$:

$$\tilde{\mathbf{B}}_P = \mathbf{B}_P \oplus \mathbf{N}, \tag{3}$$

in which $\oplus$ corresponds to the bit-wise logical (exclusive) XOR operator and $\mathbf{N} \in \{0,1\}^L$ is a random binary string of size L, whose symbols are *i.i.d.* (independent and identically distributed) as a Bernoulli distribution $\mathcal{B}(p_\epsilon)$ (*i.e.*, $N(\ell) \in \{0,1\}$ and $\mathbb{P}[N(\ell) = 1] = p_\epsilon, \forall \ell \in [L]$). Alaggan, Gambs and Kermarrec [2] proved that the BLIP mechanism ensures ϵ-differential privacy for the items of the profile if

$$p_\epsilon = 1/(1 + e^{\epsilon/K}). \tag{4}$$

3.2   The Simple Model

We assume that the hash functions produce independently random outputs, which means that the probability that $h_k(j)$ "points" to a given index is $1/L$. This assumption implies that the bits of the codewords can be modeled as independent Bernoulli random variables: $X_j(\ell) \sim \mathcal{B}(p), \forall (j, \ell) \in [N] \times [L]$ with

$$p \triangleq \mathbb{P}[X_j(\ell) = 1] = 1 - \left(1 - \frac{1}{L}\right)^K. \tag{5}$$

For a random P composed of c items, we have $B_P(\ell) \sim \mathcal{B}(\pi_c), \forall \ell \in [L]$, with

$$\pi_c \triangleq \mathbb{P}[B_P(\ell) = 1] = 1 - (1 - p)^c = 1 - \left(1 - \frac{1}{L}\right)^{cK}. \tag{6}$$

As for the BLIP, $\tilde{\mathbf{B}}_P$ contains i.i.d. random symbols $\tilde{B}_P(\ell) \sim \mathcal{B}(\tilde{\pi}_c)$ with

$$\tilde{\pi}_c \triangleq \mathbb{P}[\tilde{B}_P(\ell) = 1] = (1 - p_\epsilon)\pi_c + p_\epsilon(1 - \pi_c). \tag{7}$$

3.3   More Complex Models

This subsection presents two possible extensions of the simple model, in which we no longer assume that c is fixed in advance and publicly known.

To account for this, we introduce the probability $\mathbb{P}[|P| = c]$, in which $|P|$ denotes the number of items in P. Then, we have to replace π_c by:

$$\pi_c \to \pi = \sum_{c>0} \pi_c \mathbb{P}[|P| = c]. \tag{8}$$

This new expression leads to $\tilde{\pi} = (1 - p_\epsilon)\pi + p_\epsilon(1 - \pi)$. Not knowing c may not be a big challenge for the adversary because he can easily infer the number of items in a profile. The quantity $\omega(\tilde{\mathbf{B}}_P)/L$, in which $\omega(.)$ is the Hamming weight of a binary string (the number of bits set to one), is an unbiased estimator of $\tilde{\pi}_c$. Inverting (7) is possible when $p_\epsilon \neq 1/2$ (*i.e.* , $\epsilon > 0$) since p_ϵ is public:

$$\hat{\pi}_c = \frac{\omega(\tilde{\mathbf{B}}_P)/L - p_\epsilon}{1 - 2p_\epsilon}, \tag{9}$$

which in turn gives an estimator $\hat{c}$ by inverting (6). In the same way, a confidence interval for $\tilde{\pi}_c$ based on $\omega(\tilde{\mathbf{B}}_P)/L$ yields a confidence interval $[c_{\min}, c_{\max}]$ on c.

An even more refined model consists in taking into account the popularity of the items. Indeed, popular items impact the Bloom filter by ensuring that some of its bits are more likely to be set to one. To tackle this issue, we still pretend that the bits are independent but distributed according their own Bernoulli law: $B_P(\ell) \sim \mathcal{B}(\pi(\ell))$, $\forall \ell \in [L]$. The same model holds for the BLIP symbols: $\tilde{B}_P(\ell) \sim \mathcal{B}(\tilde{\pi}(\ell))$, with $\tilde{\pi}(\ell) = (1 - p_\epsilon)\pi(\ell) + p_\epsilon(1 - \pi(\ell))$.

4   JLT

Kenthapadi and co-authors [3] proposed another mechanism to prevent the adversary from learning the presence (or absence) of an item in the profile, although their scheme tackles a different data type (*i.e.*, real vector). In the sequel, we denote this proposal by JLT because it is based on the Johnson-Lindenstrauss Transform.

4.1   Description

The profile is encoded in the form of a real vector of length L as follows. A codeword $\mathbf{X}_j$ associated to item j is a real vector. Its L components have been independently and identically drawn such that $X_j(i) \stackrel{i.i.d.}{\sim} \mathcal{N}(0, 1/L)$, $\forall (i, j) \in [L] \times N$. The codebook $(\mathbf{X}_1, \mathbf{X}_2, \cdots, \mathbf{X}_N)$ is generated once for all and is public.

Profile P is encoded into vector $\mathbf{Y}_P = \sum_{j \in P} \mathbf{X}_j$, then the user adds a noise $\mathbf{N}$ (private data) before publishing $\tilde{\mathbf{Y}}_P = \mathbf{Y}_P + \mathbf{N}$. The authors of [3] recommend a white Gaussian noise: $N(i) \overset{i.i.d.}{\sim} \mathcal{N}(0, \sigma^2)$. According to [3, Lemma 2], if

$$L \geq 2(\log(N) + \log(2/\delta)), \quad \sigma \geq \frac{4}{\epsilon}\sqrt{\log(1/\delta)} \text{ and } \epsilon < \log(1/\delta) \quad (10)$$

then this mechanism complies with (ϵ, δ)-differential privacy (for $0 < \delta < 1$).

4.2   A Simple Probabilistic Model

The adversary does not know the profile P and therefore he models the observation $\tilde{\mathbf{Y}}_P$ as a white Gaussian noise since $\tilde{\mathbf{Y}}_P$ is the sum of $c+1$ white Gaussian noises. As these patterns are statistically independent, their powers sum up so that $\tilde{Y}_P(i) \overset{i.i.d.}{\sim} \mathcal{N}(0, \sigma^2 + c/L)$. We assume now that σ^2 is a recommended noise power, and thus that it is a public parameter. This allows the adversary to estimate the number of items in profile P in the following manner:

$$\hat{c} = \frac{L}{L-1}\sum_{i=1}^{L} \tilde{Y}_P(i)^2 - L\sigma^2. \quad (11)$$

Consider now the case in which the adversary knows that the item j is in the profile. This knowledge stems into a refined statistical model of the observation: $\tilde{Y}_P(i) \overset{i.i.d.}{\sim} \mathcal{N}(X_j(i), \sigma^2 + (c-1)/L)$. In the same way, knowing the profile P ends up with $\tilde{Y}_P(i) \overset{i.i.d.}{\sim} \mathcal{N}\left(\sum_{j \in P} X_j(i), \sigma^2\right)$.

5   Theoretical Analysis

In this section, we propose two decoders that can be used by an adversary to reconstruct the profile of a given user out of his public representation. This analysis is detailed for the BLIP mechanism, but similar concepts hold for the JLT scheme. The expressions of the information theoretical quantities are given in Appendix A for BLIP and Appendix B for JLT.

5.1   Single Decoder

From the observation of one BLIPed representation $\tilde{\mathbf{b}}$, the adversary would like to infer which item belongs to the original profile. The adversary can conduct this inference by analyzing the L symbols of $\tilde{\mathbf{b}}$ and making an hypothesis test about the presence of item j in the underlying profile.

- $\mathcal{H}_0$: Item j is not in the profile, which means that the observed BLIP symbols are statistically independent from the symbols of codeword $\mathbf{X}_j$: $\mathbb{P}[\tilde{B}_P(\ell), X_j(\ell)] = \mathbb{P}[\tilde{B}_P(\ell)]\mathbb{P}[X_j(\ell)], \forall \ell \in [L]$.

– $\mathcal{H}_1$: Item j belongs to P, and thus there is a slight dependency between the symbols of the observed BLIP and that of codeword $\mathbf{X}_j$: $\mathbb{P}[\tilde{B}_P(\ell), X_i(\ell)] = \mathbb{P}[\tilde{B}_P(\ell)|X_i(\ell)]\mathbb{P}[X_i(\ell)], \forall \ell \in [L]$.

For a given item, this test may make two types of error: 1) False positive rate α_1: The probability of detecting the presence of an item that does not belong to the profile; 2) False negative rate α_2: The probability of missing the presence of an item that belongs to the profile. Information theory gives an upper bound on the performance of the test thanks to the Stein's lemma. More precisely, for a given α_2, the probability of false positive cannot be lower than

$$\alpha_1 \geq e^{-(I(\tilde{\mathbf{B}}_P;\mathbf{X})+1)/(1-\alpha_2)}, \tag{12}$$

in which $I(\tilde{\mathbf{B}}_P; \mathbf{X})$ is the mutual information between a BLIPed filter and the codeword of an item of the profile.

This test concerns a particular item, but an adversary that wants to reconstruct the whole profile needs to repeat it for the whole ensemble of size N. This repetition increases the global probability of false positive η_1:

$$\eta_1 = 1 - (1 - \alpha_1)^{N-c} \lesssim N\alpha_1, \tag{13}$$

in which we assume that $N\alpha_1 \ll 1$ and $c \ll N$. η_1 is the probability that at least one item not in the profile is detected as belonging to the profile. At the end, for targeted error probabilities (α_2, η_1), inequality (12) constraints the size of the item ensemble the adversary can deal with:

$$\log(N) \leq \frac{I(\tilde{\mathbf{B}}_P; \mathbf{X})}{1 - \alpha_2} + \log \eta_1. \tag{14}$$

The last inequality stresses the important role of $I(\tilde{\mathbf{B}}_P; \mathbf{X})$. Appendices A and B provide expressions of this quantity for the BLIP and JLT mechanisms.

5.2   Joint Decoder

Let us consider another strategy. From the observation $\tilde{b}$, the adversary would like to test whether P was the original profile that gave birth to this BLIPed representation. The difference with the previous approach is that the presence of items are not tested independently but jointly, hence the name "joint decoder".

Basically, the analysis is the same as previously except that the information theoretic quantity is now $I(\tilde{\mathbf{B}}_P; P) = I(\tilde{\mathbf{B}}_P; (\mathbf{X}_{j_1}, \ldots, \mathbf{X}_{j_c}))$ and that the ensemble of profiles is much bigger. Roughly, $\log(|\mathcal{P}|) \approx c \log N$, thus we have:

$$\log(N) \leq \frac{I(\tilde{\mathbf{B}}_P; P)}{c(1 - \alpha_2)} + \log \eta_1. \tag{15}$$

Stated differently, the performance of this approach is driven by the quantity $I(\tilde{\mathbf{B}}_P; P)/c$. Theorem [18, Eq. (3.4)] states that $I(\tilde{\mathbf{B}}_P; (\mathbf{X}_{j_1}, \ldots, \mathbf{X}_{j_c}))/c \geq$

$I(\tilde{\mathbf{B}}_P; \mathbf{X}_j)$, which means that considering the items jointly yields better performances. Appendices A and B provide expressions of this quantity for respectively the BLIP and JLT mechanisms. For this first scheme, subsection A.2 shows that the difference $I(\tilde{\mathbf{B}}_P; (\mathbf{X}_{j_1}, \dots, \mathbf{X}_{j_c}))/c - I(\tilde{\mathbf{B}}_P; \mathbf{X}_j)$ can be be substantial for practical setups. We also provide upper bounds simply depending on ϵ.

6   Practical Decoders

The previous section can be summarized as follows: joint decoding is theoretically more powerful than single decoding. However, no complexity argument has been so far taken into account. This section deals with this issue by proposing practical implementations of a single and a joint decoder. Again, we take the example of BLIP but our approach is more generic as it works also with JLT.

6.1   Single Decoders

In practice, a single decoder computes from the observed BLIPed profile a score s_j for any item $j \in [N]$, which reflects the likelihood of belonging to the profile (i.e., the most likely item has the highest score). The score is compared to a threshold to decide whether or not the item should be included in the reconstructed profile. The complexity of this single decoder is $O(N)$ since it is exhaustive and goes through all the possible items.

As a practical implementation, we propose the Maximum Likelihood decoder in which the score $s_j = \log \frac{\mathbb{P}[\tilde{\mathbf{B}}_P = \tilde{b} | j \in P]}{\mathbb{P}[\mathbf{B}_P = \tilde{b}]}$ equals, by independence of the symbols:

$$s_j = n_{11} \log \frac{1 - p_\epsilon}{\tilde{\pi}} + n_{01} \log \frac{p_\epsilon}{1 - \tilde{\pi}}, \quad \text{with:} \tag{16}$$

$$n_{11} = |\{\ell \in [L] | \tilde{b}(\ell) = 1 \text{ AND } X_j(\ell) = 1\}|, \tag{17}$$

$$n_{01} = |\{\ell \in [L] | \tilde{b}(\ell) = 0 \text{ AND } X_j(\ell) = 1\}|. \tag{18}$$

This decoder is derived from models that are more realistic in which $\pi_c \approx \pi_{c-1} \approx \pi$, so that the score of item j only takes into account the $(n_{11} + n_{01})$ symbols in which $X_j(\ell) = 1$ (i.e., at most K symbols over L).

6.2   Joint Decoder

In practice, a joint decoder computes from the observed BLIPed filter a score for any profile $P' \in \mathcal{P}$, which reflects the likelihood that P' is the true profile. This score is computed by taking into account L symbols but the complexity of a joint decoder is proportional to $|\mathcal{P}|$ (i.e., $O(N^c)$), which is computationally expensive. Yet, there exists at least three possible approaches that approximate joint decoding with a reasonable complexity: 1) Monte Carlo Markov Chain (MCMC) [19,20], 2) Belief Propagation Decoder [21] and 3) Joint Iterative Decoder [22].

In this paper, we investigate the first approach. The MCMC decoder is based on two key ideas. First, it receives as input an observed BLIPed filter $\tilde{\mathbf{b}}$ and then creates a Markov Chain that will be used to sample profiles according to the posterior distribution $\mathbb{P}[P|\tilde{\mathbf{b}}]$. This sampling requires a burn-in period after which the Markov Chain has converged. Once this convergence has occurred, it samples profiles with the targeted posterior distribution. During a second phase, some profiles are sampled and statistics are computed such as the marginal a posteriori distribution $\hat{\mathbb{P}}[j \in P|\tilde{\mathbf{b}}]$ that item j belongs to the true profile.

Posterior distribution. The objective is to sample profiles according to the posterior distribution $\mathbb{P}[P|\tilde{\mathbf{b}}]$, which can be written as:

$$\mathbb{P}[P|\tilde{\mathbf{b}}] = \frac{\mathbb{P}[\tilde{\mathbf{B}}_P = \tilde{\mathbf{b}}|P]\mathbb{P}[P]}{\mathbb{P}[\tilde{\mathbf{B}}_P = \tilde{\mathbf{b}}]}. \tag{19}$$

In this equation, $\mathbb{P}[P]$ is the a priori probability of P. To simplify our presentation, we consider only the simple model exposed in Section 3.2. We denote by $|P|$ the size of profile P (*i.e.*, the number of his items), and we set by $\mathbb{P}[P] = 0$ if $|P| \neq c$, and $1/|\mathcal{P}|$ otherwise. Any profile is equally likely provided it has exactly c items. When we use more realistic models in our experimental work, the prior will be substantially different. We denote by $\omega(\mathbf{B})$ the Hamming weight of a binary vector $\mathbf{B}$ (*i.e.*, the number of bits set to 1). The probability $\mathbb{P}[\tilde{\mathbf{B}}_P = \tilde{\mathbf{b}}|P] = \mathbb{P}[\mathbf{N} = \mathbf{B}_P \oplus \tilde{\mathbf{b}}]$ has the following expression

$$\mathbb{P}[\tilde{\mathbf{B}}_P = \tilde{\mathbf{b}}|P] = p_\epsilon^{\omega(\mathbf{B}_P \oplus \tilde{\mathbf{b}})}(1 - p_\epsilon)^{L - \omega(\mathbf{B}_P \oplus \tilde{\mathbf{b}})}. \tag{20}$$

The evaluation of the last quantity $\mathbb{P}[\tilde{\mathbf{B}}_P = \tilde{\mathbf{b}}]$ in (19) is more involved:

$$\mathbb{P}[\tilde{\mathbf{B}}_P = \tilde{\mathbf{b}}] = \sum_{P \in \mathcal{P}} \mathbb{P}[\tilde{\mathbf{B}}_P = \tilde{\mathbf{b}}|P]\mathbb{P}[P]. \tag{21}$$

It requires a screening of $\mathcal{P}$, which is intractable for large c and N, which is why we will rely on the Markov chain.

Markov Chain. A Markov Chain is an iterative process with an internal state (*i.e.*, a profile in our case) taking value $P^{(t)}$ at iteration t. The next iteration draws a new state $P^{(t+1)}$ according to a transition probability distribution $\mathbb{P}[P^{(t+1)}|P^{(t)}]$. The Markov Chain is initialized randomly at state $P^{(0)}$. The probability distribution of transitions is crafted with care to enforce a convergence of the distribution of sampled profile $P^{(t)}$ to the posterior $\mathbb{P}[P|\tilde{\mathbf{b}}]$ of (19) as $t \to \infty$ (see Section 6.3). In practice, the convergence occurs after the first T iterations, the so-called burn-in period. Once this period has passed, it means that the Markov Chain has forgotten its starting point (*i.e.*, the samples are now independent of $P^{(0)}$) and that the distribution of the sample profiles has converged.

Monte Carlo method. After the burn-in period, the Markov Chain keeps on sampling for M more iterations. The marginal a posteriori probabilities are then estimated by a Monte Carlo method, which computes the empirical frequency that item j is present in sample $P^{(t)}$:

$$\hat{\mathbb{P}}[j \in P|\tilde{\mathbf{b}}] = |\{t \in [T+1, T+M]|j \in P^{(t)}\}|/M. \tag{22}$$

From these estimations, several post-processing are possible such as:

- inferring the most likely items of the true profile by ranking them in decreasing marginal probabilities,
- reconstructing the profile as the set of items whose marginal probability is above a given threshold,
- reconstructing the profile as the set of items with highest marginal.

6.3   Transition Probabilities

Algorithmic coding of a profile. Section 3.3 describes how to infer from the observed BLIP a maximum number $c_{\max}$ of items of the corresponding profile. In this algorithm, we code a profile as a vector of $c_{\max}$ components taking values in $[N] \cup \{0\}$. Some of these components may take the value "0" meaning an "empty item", while the others have different values (*i.e.*, there is no pair of non-zero components with the same value). For instance, for $c_{\max} = 5$, $P = (0, 3, 2, 0, 4)$ represents the profile of 3 items: #2, #3 and #4.

We define $\mathcal{V}(P_0, i)$ as the neighborhood of profile P_0 in the following manner:

$$\mathcal{V}(P_0, i) = \{P \in \mathcal{P}|P(k) = P_0(k) \quad \forall k \neq i\}. \tag{23}$$

This neighborhood profile is the set of all profiles whose coding differs at most from the i-th component. Note that $P_0 \in \mathcal{V}(P_0, i)$. If $P_0(i) = 0$, this neighborhood comprises profiles having at most one more item. Otherwise if $P_0(i) > 0$, this neighborhood contains profiles having at most one different item (*i.e.*, $P_0(i)$ is substituted by another item) and one profile having one less item (*i.e.*, item $P_0(i)$ is substituted by 0, the "empty item").

Multi-stage Gibbs sampling. Instead of computing the transition probabilities for all the possible profiles, we restrict the transitions to the neighborhood of the actual state. At the iteration $t+1$, an integer i is first uniformly drawn in $[c_{\max}]$ that indicates the subset $\mathcal{V}(P^{(t)}, i)$. Then, the following transition probability distribution is computed: $\forall P \in \mathcal{V}(P^{(t)}, i)$

$$\mathbb{P}[P^{(t+1)} = P|P^{(t)}] = \frac{\mathbb{P}[\tilde{\mathbf{B}}_P = \tilde{\mathbf{b}}|P]\mathbb{P}[P]}{\sum_{P' \in \mathcal{V}(P^{(t)}, i)} \mathbb{P}[\tilde{\mathbf{B}}_{P'} = \tilde{\mathbf{b}}|P']\mathbb{P}[P']} \tag{24}$$

Iteration $t+1$ ends by randomly drawing state $P^{(t+1)}$ from this distribution.

This choice of probabilistic transitions is called a multi-stage Gibbs sampler with random scan [23, Alg. A.42]. It guarantees that the law of sampled

Table 1. Datasets characteristics

	Nb of users	Training set size	Testing set size	N	c_{avg}	Sparsity %
Digg	531	331	200	1237	317	25.63%
MovieLens	943	600	343	1682	106	6.30%

profiles converges to the stationary distribution $\mathbb{P}[P|\tilde{\mathbf{b}}]$, which legitimates our approach [23, Sect. 10.2.1]. The unknown multiplicative constant $\mathbb{P}[\tilde{\mathbf{B}}_P = \tilde{\mathbf{b}}]$ in (19) has disappeared in the ratio. This transition probability distribution only depends on the priors $\mathbb{P}[P]$ (which depends on the mathematical model of a profile), and the conditional probabilities $\mathbb{P}[\tilde{\mathbf{B}}_P = \tilde{\mathbf{b}}|P]$ (which depends on the privacy-preserving mechanism). For instance, for the JLT mechanism, $\mathbb{P}[\tilde{\mathbf{Y}}_P = \tilde{\mathbf{y}}|P] \propto \exp(-\|\tilde{\mathbf{y}} - \sum_{j \in P} \mathbf{X}_j\|^2/2\sigma^2)$.

7 Experiments

7.1 Setup

In this section, we test the inference attacks designed on two real datasets: Digg and MovieLens. The Digg dataset has been collected on a social news aggregator and the profile of a user is composed of the news he has read. The MovieLens dataset is a snapshot from a movie recommendation site and in this dataset the profile of a user is composed of the movies he likes. For the experiments, we split both datasets into two parts : the training set and the testing set. The characteristics of these datasets are summarized in Table 1, in which c_{avg} is the average number of items per profile and sparsity is the average occupancy of items among the user profiles.

During the experiments, we assume that the adversary has access to some raw profiles of users to estimate the item priors (i.e., popularities of items). This is similar to assuming that the adversary has access to some global information about the general distribution of items in the population. We rely on the training dataset for computing the frequencies of items while the testing dataset is used solely for evaluating the performance of the attacks. In terms of parameters, for BLIP we set the number of hash functions $K = 20$ and the number of bits of the representation to $L = 5,000$. The values of ϵ are from the set $\{59, 28, 17, 8, 6, 5, 3, 2, 0\}$, which equivalently translate to the corresponding flipping p_ϵ from the range $\{0.05, 0.2, 0.3, 0.4, 0.42, 0.44, 0.46, 0.48, 0.5\}$. For the JLT scheme, we set the size of the representation L to $1,000$. L is set to a lower value as the representation, a dense real vector, is richer than the binary version of BLIP. The privacy parameter ϵ takes value in the set $\{600, 6, 3, 2, 1, 0.75, 0.5, 0.25, 0.1\}$, which translates into a noise level σ in $\{0, 1, 2, 3, 6, 8, 12, 24, 61\}$.

For MCMC, we used a burn-in period of $T = 1,000$ samples and estimation sample size of $M = 19,000$ for all the experiments. In practice, we observed that the performance is not very sensitive to the burn-in period length. As with other

MCMC based approaches proper initialization for sampling is highly desirable for a faster convergence to the stationary distribution. We used the input public representation of the profile to estimate $\hat{c}$ and started with $\hat{c}$ random items. A poor estimation of $\hat{c}$ has to be traded-off with a longer burn-in period. We also prefilter items that are to be tested against the public profile for joint decoder, to reduce the search space. To realize this, we first predict the $f \times \hat{c}$ most probable items for a given profile ($f \in [2,6]$) using single decoder and then run the joint decoder on the filtered items to return $\hat{c}$ items. This prefiltering decreases significantly the running time of the algorithm without impacting the prediction as only unlikely items will not be considered by the joint decoder.

7.2 Reconstruction Attacks

We benchmark four attacks that produce a score per item:

- The single decoder described in [2].
- The popularity-based attack in which the score of an item is its prior estimated from the training data, independent of the given public representation.
- Our MCMC joint decoder with and without priors (i.e., with flat priors) in which the scores are the estimated marginal a posteriori probabilities.

Reconstruction $\hat{P}$ is then the list of the top $\hat{c}$ items ranked based on their scores.

We measure the performance of a reconstruction attack by computing the cosine similarity between the reconstruction $\hat{P}$ and the true profile P as expressed in (25) for all the profiles of the testing set.

$$\cos(P, \hat{P}) = \frac{|P.\hat{P}|}{|P||\hat{P}|} \tag{25}$$

Afterwards, we compute the following statistics: average, the 10% and the 90% quantiles of the cosine similarities.

The plots in Figure 1 show that the performance of the reconstruction attack is better for high values of ϵ while it degrades as $\epsilon \to 0$. In this case, $p_\epsilon \to 0.5$ and every profile becomes equiprobable so that inferring the original profile becomes impossible. In addition, $\hat{c}$ depends on ϵ and low value results in a poor estimation of $\hat{c}$, which impacts the similarity measure as only top $\hat{c}$ items of the prediction is considered in the reconstructed profile. As the estimation of $\hat{c}$ is performed similarly for all the four attacks, the performance drop is common to all of them. Overall the performance of our MCMC attack is better than the single decoder of [2] for almost all ϵ values over the two datasets. Another way to see this is to find the range of ϵ in which a given attack performs worse than the baseline (i.e., the popularity-based attack). For instance, by setting $\epsilon = 8$, the designer is sure that the single attack is no longer a threat. However, a skilled adversary can reconstruct almost 50% of the profile thanks to our MCMC attack.

Taking into account the prior of items improves the efficiency in the reconstruction significantly, provided that the estimation is reliable. This improvement is clearly observed on the MovieLens dataset. As for the Digg setup, priors of the training set do not generalized to the test set, hence they do not help much. We conducted the same experiment with the JLT scheme. The figure is not included in the paper due to a lack of space, but the results that we obtained are very close from the one of BLIP and thus we can draw the same conclusions.

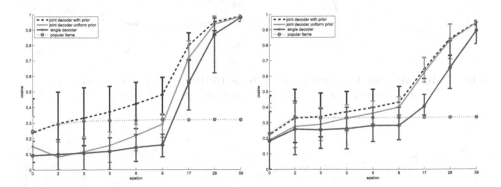

Fig. 1. Values of the cosine similarity (average, 10% quantile and 90% quantile) of BLIP for MCMC with prior, with no prior and single decoding for various ϵ on Movielens (left) and Digg (right) dataset

7.3   Identifying the Presence of an Item

When ϵ is very small, Figure 1 clearly shows that the adversary cannot hope to reconstruct the full profile. In this situation, we evaluate the prediction of top R items, with $R \ll c$, as another assessment of the privacy guarantees. The success is measured in terms of the mean Average Precision at R (mAP@R) given in (26), which is the mean over the Q profiles in the test dataset of the average of the precisions at rank $1 \leq r \leq R$. The precision(r) refers to the fraction of correct items out of the top r predicted items. The mAP is sensitive to the order of the correct results and is a better gauge of the quality of a ranking.

$$\text{mAP@}K = \frac{1}{Q} \sum_{q=1}^{Q} \left(\frac{1}{R} \sum_{r=1}^{R} \text{precision}_q(r) \right). \tag{26}$$

The characteristics of mAP@R depicted in Figure 2 are almost similar to the exact reconstruction measurement. Even if the exact reconstruction of profile is hardly possible for a given ϵ, predicting the top R items work. For instance, the maximum reconstruction for $\epsilon = 0$ for Movielens is 0.23 whereas the mean average precision is close to 0.5. The same conclusion holds for the Digg dataset.

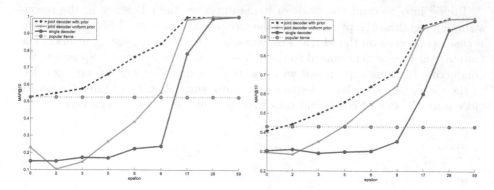

Fig. 2. Mean Average Precision for $R = 10$ for BLIP for MCMC with prior, with no prior and single decoding for various ϵ on Movielens (left) and Digg (right) dataset

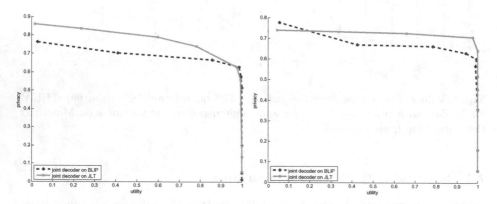

Fig. 3. Utility against privacy for BLIP and JLT for various ϵ on Movielens (left) and Digg (right) datasets

7.4   Utility-Privacy Trade-Off

Finally, we also studied the achievable trade-off between privacy and utility. Since BLIP and JLT are used for similarity estimation, we quantify the utility in terms of the recall, which is defined as the probability of identifying the k-nearest neighbors (we set $k = 10$ in our experiments). In this experiment, we measure privacy as $1 - \cos(P, \hat{P})$ (see (25)) based on the joint decoder. Figure 3 illustrates the utility-privacy trade-off obtained for various ϵ. The trade-off is almost similar on the two datasets. The privacy preserving properties of JLT transform is slightly better than BLIP, at least for the parameters we used in our simulation. This difference in performance is due partially to the representation superiority of dense real vector over binary vector. However, BLIP offers a more compact representation of the profile (5,000 bits versus 1,000 scalars). The plot is helpful in fixing ϵ giving good utility without compromising much on privacy.

8   Conclusion

In differential privacy, the trade-off between utility and privacy is set by the parameter ϵ. However, being able to choose an appropriate value for this parameter is still an open research question, which has not been deeply investigated, with a few exceptions [24,25]. In this paper, we have made a step forward to answer this question by proposing two generic inference attacks, namely single and joint decoding, whose objective is to reconstruct the profile of a user out of a differentially-private representation produced through a non-interactive mechanism. The first inference attack decides of the presence of a single item and sequentially explores all the item set, while the latter strategy decides whether a subset of items is likely to be the user profile and considers all possible subsets.

We have evaluated the effectiveness of the attack on two schemes producing differentially private representations: BLIP (BLoom-and-flIP) [2] and JLT (Johnson-Lindenstrauss Transform) [3]. Our theoretical analysis as well as the experimental results clearly shows that joint decoding is more powerful than single decoding. Overall, we believe that this attack helps better understanding the privacy guarantees offered by a wide class of differentially-private mechanisms (interactive or not) as well as for the privacy practitioner to tune experimentally ϵ to ensure the maximum utility without compromising much on privacy.

References

1. Dwork, C.: Differential privacy. In: Bugliesi, M., Preneel, B., Sassone, V., Wegener, I. (eds.) ICALP 2006, Part II. LNCS, vol. 4052, pp. 1–12. Springer, Heidelberg (2006)
2. Alaggan, M., Gambs, S., Kermarrec, A.-M.: BLIP: Non-interactive Differentially-Private Similarity Computation on Bloom Filters. In: Richa, A.W., Scheideler, C. (eds.) SSS 2012. LNCS, vol. 7596, pp. 202–216. Springer, Heidelberg (2012)
3. Kenthapadi, K., Korolova, A., Mironov, I., Mishra, N.: Privacy via the johnson-lindenstrauss transform. arXiv preprint arXiv:1204.2606 (2012)
4. Liu, K., Giannella, C., Kargupta, H.: A survey of attack techniques on privacy-preserving data perturbation methods. In: Privacy-Preserving Data Mining. Advances in Database Systems, vol. 34, pp. 359–381. Springer (2008)
5. Chen, K., Liu, L.: A survey of multiplicative perturbation for privacy-preserving data mining. In: Privacy-Preserving Data Mining, pp. 157–181. Springer (2008)
6. Guo, S., Wu, X.: On the use of spectral filtering for privacy preserving data mining. In: ACM Symp. on Applied Computing, pp. 622–626 (2006)
7. Huang, Z., Du, W., Chen, B.: Deriving private information from randomized data. In: ACM SIGMOD Int. Conf. on Management of Data, pp. 37–48. ACM (2005)
8. Guo, S., Wu, X.: Deriving private information from arbitrarily projected data. In: Zhou, Z.-H., Li, H., Yang, Q. (eds.) PAKDD 2007. LNCS (LNAI), vol. 4426, pp. 84–95. Springer, Heidelberg (2007)
9. Agrawal, D., Aggarwal, C.C.: On the design and quantification of privacy preserving data mining algorithms. In: 20th ACM SIGMOD-SIGACT-SIGART Symp. on Principles of Database Systems, pp. 247–255 (2001)
10. Diaconis, P., Sturmfels, B.: Algebraic algorithms for sampling from conditional distributions. The Annals of Statistics 26(1), 363–397 (1998)

11. Dobra, A.: Measuring the disclosure risk for multi-way tables with fixed marginals corresponding to decomposable log-linear models. Technical report (2000)
12. Williams, O., McSherry, F.: Probabilistic inference and differential privacy. In: Advances in Neural Information Processing Systems, pp. 2451–2459 (2010)
13. Dwork, C., McSherry, F., Nissim, K., Smith, A.: Calibrating noise to sensitivity in private data analysis. In: Halevi, S., Rabin, T. (eds.) TCC 2006. LNCS, vol. 3876, pp. 265–284. Springer, Heidelberg (2006)
14. Dwork, C., Kenthapadi, K., McSherry, F., Mironov, I., Naor, M.: Our data, ourselves: Privacy via distributed noise generation. In: Vaudenay, S. (ed.) EURO-CRYPT 2006. LNCS, vol. 4004, pp. 486–503. Springer, Heidelberg (2006)
15. McSherry, F., Talwar, K.: Mechanism design via differential privacy. In: IEEE Symposium on Foundations of Computer Science, pp. 94–103 (2007)
16. Beimel, A., Nissim, K., Omri, E.: Distributed private data analysis: Simultaneously solving how and what. In: Wagner, D. (ed.) CRYPTO 2008. LNCS, vol. 5157, pp. 451–468. Springer, Heidelberg (2008)
17. Li, Y.D., Zhang, Z., Winslett, M., Yang, Y.: Compressive mechanism: utilizing sparse representation in differential privacy. CoRR abs/1107.3350 (2011)
18. Moulin, P.: Universal fingerprinting: capacity and random-coding exponents. arXiv:0801.3837 (January 2008)
19. Knill, E., Schliep, A., Torney, D.C.: Interpretation of pooling experiments using the Markov chain Monte Carlo method. J. Comput. Biol. 3(3), 395–406 (1996)
20. Furon, T., Guyader, A., Cerou, F.: Decoding fingerprints using the Markov Chain Monte Carlo method. In: IEEE Int. Work. on Information Forensics and Security (WIFS), pp. 187–192 (2012)
21. Sejdinovic, D., Johnson, O.: Note on noisy group testing: asymptotic bounds and belief propagation reconstruction. In: Proc. 48th Allerton Conf. on Commun., Control and Computing, Monticello, IL, USA (October 2010) arXiv:1010.2441v1
22. Meerwald, P., Furon, T.: Toward practical joint decoding of binary Tardos fingerprinting codes. IEEE Trans. on Inf. Forensics and Security 7(4), 1168–1180 (2012)
23. Robert, C., Casella, G.: Monte Carlo statistical methods. Springer (2004)
24. Lee, J., Clifton, C.: How much is enough? Choosing ϵ for differential privacy. In: Lai, X., Zhou, J., Li, H. (eds.) ISC 2011. LNCS, vol. 7001, pp. 325–340. Springer, Heidelberg (2011)
25. Alvim, M.S., Andrés, M.E., Chatzikokolakis, K., Palamidessi, C.: On the relation between differential privacy and quantitative information flow. In: Aceto, L., Henzinger, M., Sgall, J. (eds.) ICALP 2011, Part II. LNCS, vol. 6756, pp. 60–76. Springer, Heidelberg (2011)

A   Appendix A: BLIP Mechanism

A.1   Single and Joint Decoding

We have $I(\tilde{\mathbf{B}}_P; \mathbf{X}) = H(\tilde{\mathbf{B}}_P) - H(\tilde{\mathbf{B}}_P|\mathbf{X})$, in which H is the (Shannon) entropy of a random variable. With the simple model detailed in Section 3.2, we get that

$$I(\tilde{\mathbf{B}}_P; \mathbf{X}) = L(h_b(\tilde{\pi}_c) - (1-p)h_b(\tilde{\pi}_{c-1}) - ph_b(p_\epsilon)), \qquad (27)$$

with $h_b(p)$ the entropy of a Bernoulli distribution $\mathcal{B}(p)$ (in hats):

$$h_b(p) \triangleq -p\log(p) - (1-p)\log(1-p) = h_b(1-p). \qquad (28)$$

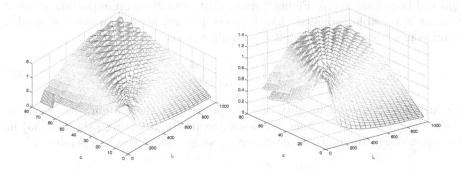

Fig. 4. (Left): Mutual information of the joint decoder $I(\tilde{\mathbf{B}}_P; P)/c$ in nats as a function of (c, L). (Right): Difference $I(\tilde{\mathbf{B}}_P; P)/c - I(\tilde{\mathbf{B}}_P; X)$ in nats as a function of (c, L).

The probabilities $\tilde{\pi}_c$ and $\tilde{\pi}_{c-1}$ appear in (27) because we assume that the profiles are of identical size c. When considering more complex but also more practical models, this difference vanishes as $\tilde{\pi}_c$ and $\tilde{\pi}_{c-1}$ are replaced by $\tilde{\pi}$:

$$I(\tilde{\mathbf{B}}_P; \mathbf{X}) \approx Lp(h_b(\tilde{\pi}) - h_b(p_\epsilon)). \tag{29}$$

As for the joint decoding, Bloom filter being a deterministic process, we write:

$$I(\tilde{\mathbf{B}}_P; P) = I(\tilde{\mathbf{B}}_P; \mathbf{B}_P) = H(\tilde{\mathbf{B}}_P) - H(\tilde{\mathbf{B}}_P | \mathbf{B}_P)$$
$$= H(\tilde{\mathbf{B}}_P) - H(\mathbf{N}) = L(h_b(\tilde{\pi}_c) - h_b(p_\epsilon)). \tag{30}$$

A.2 Comments

Example. Figure 4 (left) shows $I(\tilde{\mathbf{B}}_P; P)/c$ as a function of c and L. From a particular (c, L), we set

$$K = \left\lfloor \log(2)\frac{L}{c} \right\rfloor, \tag{31}$$

which is the recommended number of hash functions in Bloom filter design, and we apply the model of Section 3.2 with $\epsilon = 20$. For a given c, too small L means too few observed symbols for reliably estimating the profile. Too large L implies a big K and therefore, p_ϵ tends to $1/2$ according to (4). Figure 4 (right) shows that $I(\tilde{\mathbf{B}}_P; P)/c - I(\tilde{\mathbf{B}}_P; \mathbf{X})$ can be substantial: a joint decoding allows the adversary to tackle up to 3.5 (*i.e.* $e^{1.25}$) times more items.

Upper bounds. As $\epsilon \to 0$, $p_\epsilon \to 1/2$ as well as $\tilde{\pi}$, so that $I(\tilde{\mathbf{B}}_P; \mathbf{X}) \to 0$ and also $I(\tilde{\mathbf{B}}_P; P) \to 0$. When $\epsilon = 0$, observing the BLIP is useless since it brings no information. In this situation, neither the single nor the joint decoding can do anything. We can bound the quantity in common in both expressions as follows:

$$h_b(\tilde{\pi}_c) - h_b(p_\epsilon) \leq \log(2) - h_b(p_\epsilon) \leq \log(2) - \log\left(1 + e^{\epsilon/K}\right) + \frac{\epsilon}{K}\frac{e^{\epsilon/K}}{1 + e^{\epsilon/K}}$$
$$\leq \frac{\epsilon}{K}\frac{e^{\epsilon/K}}{1 + e^{\epsilon/K}} \leq \frac{\epsilon}{K}. \tag{32}$$

Typical Bloom filter setup. Figure 4 shows that estimating an important number of items is possible provided that L grows linearly with c. Indeed, it is also common practice in the design of Bloom filter to set:

$$L = \left\lceil -c\frac{\log(P_{fp})}{(\log 2)^2} \right\rceil, \tag{33}$$

in which P_{fp} is the probability of false positive of the Bloom filter (*i.e.*, to detect the presence of an item not belonging to P). Inserting (31) and (33) in the expression of the mutual informations, we get quantities independent of c:

$$\frac{1}{c}I(\tilde{\mathbf{B}}_P; P) \sim -\frac{\log(P_{fp})}{\log(2)}\left(1 - \frac{1}{\log(2)}h_b\left((1 + 2^{\frac{\epsilon}{-\log(P_{fp})}})^{-1}\right)\right), \tag{34}$$

$$I(\tilde{\mathbf{B}}_P; \mathbf{X}) \sim \log(2).\frac{1}{c}I(\tilde{\mathbf{B}}_P; P). \tag{35}$$

This shows that if the Bloom filter is properly designed, the power of the attack does not depend on c but solely on the values of $-\log(P_{fp})$ and ϵ. Moreover, the joint decoder is $1/\log(2) \sim 1.44$ more "powerful" than the single decoder.

B   Appendix B: JLT Mechanism

The same analysis holds for the JLT representation described in Section 4. The main difference lies in the fact that we manipulate differential entropies because the JLT representation is a real vector. The quantities at stake respectively for the single and joint decoders are upper bounded, thanks to conditions (10)

$$I(\tilde{\mathbf{Y}}_P; \mathbf{X}) = \frac{L}{2}\log\left(1 + \frac{1}{(c-1) + L\sigma^2}\right) \leq \frac{\epsilon}{32 + 2\epsilon(c-1)L}, \tag{36}$$

$$\frac{I(\tilde{\mathbf{Y}}_P; P)}{c} = \frac{L}{2c}\log\left(1 + \frac{c}{L\sigma^2}\right) \leq \frac{\epsilon}{32}, \tag{37}$$

Optimality and Complexity of Inference-Proof Data Filtering and CQE[*]

Joachim Biskup[1], Piero A. Bonatti[2], Clemente Galdi[2], and Luigi Sauro[2]

[1] Fakultät für Informatik, TU Dortmund
[2] Dip. Ing. Elet. e Tecnologie dell'Informazione, Università di Napoli Federico II

Abstract. The ample literature on confidentiality-preserving data publishing – and controlled query evaluation (CQE) in particular – leaves several questions open. Are the greedy data-filtering algorithms adopted in the literature maximally cooperative? Can novel secure view formats or answer distortion methods improve security or cooperativeness? What is the inherent complexity of confidentiality-preserving data publishing under different constraints, such as cooperativeness and availability? Can the theoretical results on CQE be systematically extended to more general settings? In this paper we answer the above questions using a completely generic, abstract data filtering framework, independent from any syntactic details and data source encodings, and compatible with all possible distortion methods. Some of the main results are: Refusal-based filterings can be adopted as a normal form for all kinds of filterings; greedy refusal-based filterings are optimal; cooperativeness checks and some availability checks are coNP-hard in the simplest case.

Keywords: Controlled query evaluation, Maximally cooperative filterings, Refusals and lies.

1 Introduction

The studies on confidentiality-preserving data publishing introduced a variety of inference-proof, data filtering methods, including controlled query evaluation (CQE) as a special case [1–4]. The main goal is protecting confidentiality from inferences that exploit a mix of background knowledge and data source answers. In CQE, confidentiality is protected by *refusing* to answer some queries, by *lying*, and by a combination of these two approaches. Data filtering can be *dynamic* or *static*. Dynamic approaches process a stream of queries one by one, and aim at answering each query correctly whenever the previous answers allow. Static approaches, instead, construct a secure view of the data source before publishing it. Many works focussed on databases [1–4]; later studies have been extended to knowledge bases, where inferences can naturally be automated using standard semantic web technology [5, 6]. This substantial body of works analyzes in depth the properties of various query distortion methods (including refusals, lies, and

---

[*] This work has been partially supported by the Italian projects PRIN *Security Horizons* and PON *SmartHealth 2.0*, and by the German DFG under grant SFB 876/A5.

M. Kutyłowski and J. Vaidya (Eds.): ESORICS 2014, Part II, LNCS 8713, pp. 165–181, 2014.

combined methods) and their mutual relationships. Despite this, several open questions remain:

1. Most of the static and dynamic CQE methods in the literature construct secure views by processing a query sequence in a greedy fashion. Since greedy algorithms, in general, do not yield an optimal solution, there is no guarantee of obtaining a *maximally cooperative* confidentiality protection mechanism, that maximizes the amount of correct information disclosed while protecting confidentiality. In this paper, we are going to prove that greedy refusal-based CQE is optimal (w.r.t. different filtering methods, too), while greedy lie-based CQE is not.

2. The inherent complexity of inference-proof data filtering is not yet known. It clearly depends on the languages used to describe data sources and formulate queries. However, even if these languages were tractable (or could be processed with an oracle), how much additional complexity would be caused by confidentiality-preserving query processing? We are going to investigate this issue with a fully generic account of deterministic, inference-proof data filtering that abstracts away all the details about syntax and distortion methods. In this framework, the computational complexity of secure, inference-proof query answering will be investigated under different constraints (e.g. maximal cooperativeness and selected query preservation, that is, *availability*).

3. In principle, there is no a priori bound to the range of answer distortion methods applicable to inference-proof data filtering. Could a novel answer transformation method improve confidentiality or cooperativeness? With the help of the abstract data filtering framework we shall answer this question by showing that every protection method can be turned into an equivalent refusal-based CQE method. Also lying and combined CQE approaches can be reduced to pure refusal-based methods, which means that for a smart, informed attacker there are no real lies.

As a further advantage, the abstract data-filtering framework applies to data sources of different nature, including databases, RDF stores, OWL ontologies, and their respective query languages, just to name a few. So, our results apply to a wide range of information and knowledge systems.

The paper is organized as follows: We start with a brief summary of the literature on inference-proof query answering and CQE (Sec. 2), then introduce the abstract framework and prove the reducibility of all deterministic data-filtering mechanisms to essentially equivalent refusal-based methods (Sec. 3). The complexity analysis is carried out in Sec. 4, followed by a security and optimality analysis of (the abstract versions of) the greedy CQE mechanisms based on refusals and lies introduced in [3] (Sec. 5). Finally, Sec. 6 is devoted to a discussion of the paper's results and future work.

2   Related Work

The systematic studies of inference-proof, secure query answering based on refusals date back at least to [7]. The confidentiality criterion introduced in that paper is based on the indistinguishability of each information system that entails a secret S from at least another information system that does not entail S. The same criterion has been systematically adopted later in the literature on CQE and is embraced by the abstract framework introduced in the following section.[1] Analogous criteria had already been adopted for addressing information flow control (e.g. [8]) and inference control problems in non-logical, operational settings (cf. the *non-interference* property [9]). A general overview of inference control can be found in [10, Chapter 4]; [1] surveys a number of deterministic and probabilistic privacy-preserving methods.

Lie-based approaches are implicit in cover stories and polyinstantiation [11, 12] and have been explicitly studied in a logical, epistemic framework in [13]. However, that paper did not address the indistinguishability-based security criterion of [7].

A first comparison of lies and refusals in terms of that criterion, published in [2], has been later extended to more general policies and assumptions about user knowledge in [3]. A hybrid CQE method that combines lies and refusals is analyzed and compared with "pure" approaches in [4]. These works focus on dynamic CQE, that will be formalized in the abstract framework in Sec. 5. Lies, refusals and combined methods were essentially regarded as incomparable methods, from an information disclosure perspective; with lies, the first answer distortion may occur earlier, but from that point on the other methods may obfuscate incomparable sets of answers. With the help of a novel, absolute cooperativeness criterion, we shall prove in Sec. 5 that dynamic refusal-based CQE converges to a maximally cooperative set of views, while the lie-based version does not.

The representation and query language investigated in the earliest CQE papers is propositional logic. First-order databases and open queries have been dealt with in [14, 15]. In both cases, open queries are reduced to propositional queries. CQE methods have been further extended to handle updates in [16]. Efficient implementations have been studied in [17].

Along the years, CQE has been extended from relational databases to more general kinds of data sources, such as incomplete databases (e.g. [15]) and OWL ontologies [5, 6]. The results of [14] are relevant to knowledge bases, too, since they apply to rich description logics such as $\mathcal{ALCIO}$ with boolean role operators.

3   The Abstract Data Filtering Framework

Let $\mathscr{D}$ be a set of *data sources*.[2] They can be queried by means of a set of *boolean queries* $\mathscr{B} \subseteq \mathscr{P}(\mathscr{D})$.[3] The set $\mathscr{B}$ represents the query language, abstracting away its syntax. A data source $d \in \mathscr{D}$ is meant to satisfy a query $Q \in \mathscr{B}$ iff

---

[1] More precisely, the abstract framework adopts the confidentiality criterion for *known potential secrets*, cf. [3].

[2] To help intuition, the reader may assume that data sources are database instances, or knowledge bases.

[3] $\mathscr{P}(X)$ denotes the powerset of X.

$d \in Q$ (in other words a query Q is identified with the set of data sources that satisfy it). For all queries $Q \in \mathscr{B}$, $\bar{Q}$ denotes its complement ($\bar{Q} = \mathscr{D} \setminus Q$).

Restricting the query language to boolean queries helps in abstracting away query language syntax and data source structure; it is not a severe restriction, since open queries can be reduced to suitable sets of boolean queries (cf. [14, 15]). In general, $\mathscr{B}$ does not equal $\mathscr{P}(\mathscr{D})$, because the query language may not be expressive enough to encode all boolean properties. In a propositional framework, where $\mathscr{D}$ is a finite set of interpretations and queries are propositional formulae, $\mathscr{B}$ would cover all $\mathscr{P}(\mathscr{D})$.

If two real-world data sources answer each possible query in the same way, then—from a confidentiality perspective—they are equivalent, and can be regarded as a single entity in the abstract framework. Accordingly, for all $d_1, d_2 \in \mathscr{D}$ such that $d_1 \neq d_2$, we assume that there exists a query $Q \in \mathscr{B}$ that is satisfied by exactly one of d_1 and d_2 (formally, $Q \cap \{d_1, d_2\} \neq \emptyset$ and $\{d_1, d_2\} \not\subseteq Q$).

The abstract framework further comprises a nonempty set of secrets $\mathscr{S} \subseteq \mathscr{B}$. We assume that for all $S \in \mathscr{S}$, $\mathscr{D} \not\subseteq S$, otherwise S could not be kept confidential because all data sources would satisfy it (like a tautology). Note that this framework, based on boolean queries, can represent k-anonymity as a special case:

Example 1. Each row $\langle I_1, \ldots, I_n \rangle$ in a k-anonymized table with attributes $\langle A_1, \ldots, A_n \rangle$ is like a boolean statement:

"*there exist $\geq k$ individuals such that $A_1 \in I_1, \ldots, A_n \in I_n$*"

where $I_1, \ldots, I_n$ represent abstracted values such as incomplete birthdates, salary ranges, and so on. Similarly, secrets are boolean queries like:

"*there exist x individuals, $0 < x < k$, such that $A_1 \in I_1, \ldots, A_n \in I_n$*".   □

Secrets are protected by computing *filtered views* of the data sources, by means of a filtering function $f : \mathscr{D} \to \mathscr{V}$. In general, we place no restriction on $\mathscr{V}$, that is, on the structure of filtered views, so as to cover all possible query modification methods (refusals, lies, and more).

For example, the filterings based on refusal can be represented by setting $\mathscr{V} = \mathscr{P}(\mathscr{D})$; the answer to a query Q evaluated against $f(d)$ is "yes" if $f(d) \subseteq Q$ (i.e., all data sources in $f(d)$ satisfy Q), "no" if $f(d) \subseteq \bar{Q}$ (i.e., none of the data sources in $f(d)$ satisfy Q), and "query refused" otherwise. Since refusal-based CQE is not allowed to lie, refusal-based filterings satisfy the property $d \in f(d)$, for all data sources d, which guarantees that the real data source d is compatible with all the answers computed against the filtering. The filterings based on lies can be encoded in a similar way, with the restriction that $f(d)$ is always a singleton (so there are no refused answers). Differently from refusals, a data source d is not guaranteed to belong to $f(d)$. In combined methods, $f(d)$ may contain multiple data sources (i.e., some queries may be refused) none of which is d (that is, some answers may be lies).

Definition 1. *Two data sources d and d' are* indistinguishable with respect to f *iff $f(d) = f(d')$. In this case, we write $d \sim_f d'$.*

Note that $\sim_f$ is an equivalence relation. The equivalence class of a data source d in $\sim_f$ will be denoted by $[d]_f$. We denote with $[\cdot]_f$ the function that maps each $d \in \mathscr{D}$ on $[d]_f$.

The following definition of secure filtering generalizes the notion of confidentiality adopted in the CQE literature. A smart, informed attacker, who knows the protection method f, given an output $v \in \mathscr{V}$, may invert f and compute the set $f^{-1}(v) = \{d \mid f(d) = v\}$. If all $d \in f^{-1}(v)$ satisfy a secret $S \in \mathscr{S}$ (that is, $f^{-1}(v) \subseteq S$), then the attacker can reliably conclude that the data source being protected with f satisfies the secret. Therefore, for all $v \in \mathscr{V}$, $f^{-1}(v)$ should not be included in any secret S. Note that $d \in f^{-1}(v)$ iff $f^{-1}(v) = [d]_f$, so the above confidentiality criterion becomes:

Definition 2. *A filtering f is* secure *(i.e. confidentiality preserving) iff for all datasets $d \in \mathscr{D}$ and all secrets $S \in \mathscr{S}$, $[d]_f \not\subseteq S$.*[4]

Example 2. Suppose that the data source instances are the interpretations of the propositional language with propositional symbols p and q, and that queries are propositional formulae. This setting can be represented in the abstract framework as follows. Interpretations can be represented by the subsets of $\{p, q\}$, so let $\mathscr{D} = \mathscr{P}(\{p, q\})$. There are 16 different queries up to logical equivalence. Each sentence φ can be represented by $\{d \in \mathscr{D} \mid d \models \varphi\}$, so $\mathscr{B} = \mathscr{P}(\mathscr{D})$. Assume that p is the only secret. The corresponding query is $S = \{\{p\}, \{p, q\}\}$ and $\mathscr{S} = \{S\}$. A possible filtering $f : \mathscr{D} \to \mathscr{P}(\mathscr{D})$ is $f(d) = \{d\}$. This filtering answers each query Q honestly: $f(d) \subseteq Q$ iff $d \in Q$. This filtering is not secure, because f is a bijection, therefore, for all $d \in S$, $[d]_f = \{d\} \subseteq S$. Another possible filtering with the same type is $g(d) = \{d \setminus \{p\}\}$. This filtering sometimes lies, for instance $g(\{p, q\}) = \{\{q\}\} \subseteq \{\emptyset, \{q\}\}$ which, in logical terms, means that g answers "yes" to query $\neg p$, although $\{p, q\} \models p$. This filtering is secure: for all $d \in \mathscr{D}$, $d \setminus \{p\} \in [d]_g$ so $[d]_g \not\subseteq S$.   □

The abstract framework highlights that confidentiality does not depend on the structure and nature of the filtered views (i.e., it does not depend on $\mathscr{V}$). Indeed, from Def. 2 we easily get:

Proposition 1. *A filtering f is secure iff $[\cdot]_f$ is secure.*

Therefore, every secure filtering f can be replaced with the "standard" filtering $[\cdot]_f$, preserving confidentiality. Note that $[\cdot]_f$ has the same type as refusal filterings ($[\cdot]_f : \mathscr{D} \to \mathscr{P}(\mathscr{D})$), and that for all $d \in \mathscr{D}$, $d \in [d]_f$, which implies that the filtering $[\cdot]_f$ never lies (see the discussion before Def. 1). Consequently, $[\cdot]_f$ is in all respects a refusal-based filtering, and the above proposition actually says that *every secure filtering can be equivalently replaced with a refusal filtering*, as far as the confidentiality criterion is the one formalized in Def. 2.

---

[4] This definition corresponds to the preservation of *potential secrets*, as opposed to *secrecies* [3]. The latter would require both $[d]_f \not\subseteq S$ and $[d]_f \not\subseteq \bar{S}$. Clearly, secrecies can be simulated with potential secrets by including in $\mathscr{S}$ both S and $\bar{S}$, so Definition 2 provides the most general formulation.

Alternative secure filterings can be compared based on the accuracy of the answers they return. Again, accuracy is measured in terms of the inferences that a smart, informed user can draw from the filtered view: the smallest $f^{-1}(v)$, the largest the set of queries that can be answered using $f^{-1}(v)$ (i.e., those whose answer is invariant over $f^{-1}(v)$). Using the relationships between f^{-1} and $[\cdot]_f$, the above accuracy criterion can be formalized as follows:

Definition 3. *A filtering f is* more cooperative *than a filtering g iff for all $d \in \mathscr{D}$, $[d]_f \subseteq [d]_g$. If f_1 is more cooperative than f_2 then we write $f_1 \succeq f_2$. If $f_1 \succeq f_2$ and $f_2 \not\succeq f_1$, then we write $f_1 \succ f_2$.*

Maximally cooperative filterings are called *optimal.*

Definition 4. *A secure filtering f is* optimal *iff there exists no secure filtering f' such that $f' \succ f$.*

Example 3. The filtering g defined in Example 2 is optimal. It partitions $\mathscr{D}$ in two equivalence classes: $\{\emptyset, \{p\}\}$ and $\{\{q\}, \{p, q\}\}$. Each filtering $h \succ g$ must split either the former or the latter class. In the first case, one of the equivalence classes induced by h is $\{p\} \subseteq S$. In the other case, one of the new equivalence classes is $\{p, q\} \subseteq S$. So h cannot possibly be secure. $\square$

Proposition 2. *Let $g = [\cdot]_f$ be the standard refusal-based filtering corresponding to f. Then f is optimal iff g is.*

Proof. Note that if $g = [\cdot]_f$, then for all $d \in \mathscr{D}$, $[d]_f = [d]_g$. The proposition immediately follows. $\square$

Summarizing, the standard refusal-based filtering $[\cdot]_f$ induced by *any* filtering f preserves f's security and optimality properties. Thus, standard refusal based filterings can be adopted as a sort of normal form for arbitrary filterings, as far as the reference criteria are those formalized by Def. 2 and Def. 4.

4   Complexity

In this section we present some relevant decision problems related to secure data filtering, and study their computational complexity. We are primarily interested in checking whether confidentiality preservation is intrinsically intractable under different constraints, abstracting away the additional complexity of specification and query languages. We shall choose problem size measures accordingly. Let us start by introducing the decision problems of interest:

Definition 5. *Let f range over filtering functions with type $\mathscr{D} \to \mathscr{V}$, where $\mathscr{V}$ is an arbitrary set of views. Consider the following decision problems:*

Security checking: *Given f and $\mathscr{S}$, decide whether f is a secure filtering;*
Optimal security checking: *Given f and $\mathscr{S}$, decide whether f is an optimal secure filtering;*

Pointwise availability: *Given $\mathscr{D}$, a data source $d \in \mathscr{D}$, and a boolean query $Q \subset \mathscr{D}$, decide whether there exists a secure filtering f such that $[d]_f \subseteq Q$ iff $d \in Q$;*

Global availability: *Given $\mathscr{D}$ and a boolean query $Q \subset \mathscr{D}$, decide whether there exists a secure filtering f such that for all $d \in \mathscr{D}$, $[d]_f \subseteq Q$ iff $d \in Q$.*

In other words, the two availability problems aim at preserving confidentiality without modifying the answers to the given query Q. The goal of pointwise availability is preserving Q over a single data source of interest d (e.g. the actual data source being protected). The goal of global availability is preserving Q across *all* possible datasets, which may be useful in the presence of updates, that may transform the current data source d into a member of another equivalence class.

Complexity will be analyzed under the following assumptions: *(i)* $\mathscr{D}$ is finite[5] and $\mathscr{S} = \{S_1, \ldots, S_n\}$; *(ii)* secrets are not violated a priori, that is, for all $1 \le i \le n$, $S_i \subset \mathscr{D}$; *(iii)* $\mathscr{V}$ contains at least two views, $|\mathscr{V}| \ge 2$. If a filtering f is part of a problem instance, then it is encoded by its *graph*.[6] This encoding ensures that f and $[\cdot]_f$ can be computed in polynomial time.

Our complexity results make use of the following classical NP-complete problem [18]:

Definition 6 (Set Splitting Problem). *Let $\{C_1, \ldots, C_m\}$ be a collection of subsets of a ground set G. Decide whether there exists a bipartition (G_1, G_2) of G such that for each $1 \le i \le m$, $C_i \not\subseteq G_1$ and $C_i \not\subseteq G_2$.*

Theorem 1. *Security checking and global availability are in P. Pointwise availability is NP-complete whereas optimal security checking is coNP-complete.*

Proof. Security checking. It suffices to check that for each $S \in \mathscr{S}$ and for all $d \in \mathscr{D}$, $[d]_f \not\subseteq S$. Since $[d]_f$ can be computed in polynomial time, security checking can be solved in polynomial time w.r.t. $|\mathscr{D}|$.

Global availability. Let f_Q be a *characteristic filtering* of Q, that is: $f_Q(d) = v_1$, if $d \in Q$, $f_Q(d) = v_2$, otherwise (where v_1 and v_2 are two distinct views in $\mathscr{V}$). The filtering f_Q induces a bipartition of $\mathscr{D}$ in two equivalence classes Q and $\overline{Q} = \mathscr{D} \setminus Q$. Let f be a filtering such that for all $d \in \mathscr{D}$, $[d]_f \subseteq Q$ iff $d \in Q$. Clearly, if $d \in Q$, then $[d]_f \subseteq Q$, whereas if $d \notin Q$ then $[d]_f \subseteq \overline{Q}$, that is $f_Q \preceq f$. Consequently, if f is secure, then also f_Q is secure. It follows that the global availability problem can be answered by checking whether f_Q is secure. Since security checking is tractable, global availability is tractable, too.

Optimal security checking. By the results of Sec. 3, f is not optimal iff there exists a secure, standard refusal-based filtering $[\cdot]_g \succ f$. The filtering $[\cdot]_g$ can be guessed in polynomial time, and checking that it is secure and that $[\cdot]_g \succ f$ is in P, too. Therefore, checking that f is not optimal is in NP.

---

[5] This assumption applies directly to propositional frameworks such as those adopted in [2–4]. However, also first-order database frameworks and open queries can be reduced to a propositional model, see for example [17].

[6] Recall that the graph of f is $\{ (d, f(d)) \mid d \in \mathscr{D} \}$.

Hardness is proved by reducing the set splitting problem to the problem of checking that a degenerate filtering f (i.e. a constant filtering, inducing a single equivalence class) is not optimal. Given an instance $\langle G, \{C_1, \ldots, C_m\}\rangle$ of the set splitting problem, let $\mathscr{D} = G$ and $\mathscr{S} = \{\bar{C}_1, \ldots, \bar{C}_m\}$ where for each $1 \leq i \leq m$, $\bar{C}_i = \mathscr{D} \setminus C_i$. Now f is not optimal iff there exists a secure filtering g such that $g \succ f$. Since f is degenerate, this is equivalent to say that there exist a secure filtering g and a dataset d such that $[d]_g \subset \mathscr{D}$. Consider the filtering g' such that for all $d' \in \mathscr{D}$, $g'(d') = v_1$ if $d' \in [d]_g$, and $g'(d') = v_2$ if $d' \notin [d]_g$ (where v_1 and v_2 are two distinct views). Notice that (i) $g' \succ f$, (ii) g' induces a bipartition (G_1, G_2) of G such that $G_1 = [d]_g$ and $G_2 = \mathscr{D} \setminus [d]_g$, (iii) since g is secure and $g \succeq g'$, g' is secure as well, that is for each $1 \leq i \leq m$, $G_1 \not\subseteq \bar{C}_i$ and $G_2 \not\subseteq \bar{C}_i$. This is equivalent to say that $C_i \not\subseteq G_1$ and $C_i \not\subseteq G_2$. It follows that f is not optimal iff there exists a set splitting (G_1, G_2) for $\{C_1, \ldots, C_m\}$.

Pointwise availability. Given a query Q and a dataset d, let f be a filtering such that $[d]_f \subseteq Q$ iff $d \in Q$. Consider two distinct views $v_1, v_2 \in \mathscr{V}$ and a filtering f' such that for all $d' \in \mathscr{D}$ $f'(d') = v_1$ if $d' \in [d]_f$, and $f'(d') = v_2$, otherwise. Clearly, $f' \preceq f$, therefore if f is secure, then f' is secure as well. This means that in order to check pointwise availability it suffices to guess in linear time a subset $Q' \subseteq Q$ if $d \in Q$ (resp. $\overline{Q'} \subseteq \overline{Q}$ if $d \notin Q$) and check whether the characteristic filtering $f_{Q'}$ (resp. $f_{\overline{Q'}}$) is secure. Since security checking is in P, pointwise availability is in NP.

Hardness is proved by reducing the set splitting problem to pointwise availability. That is, given an instance of the set splitting problem, we transform it into an instance of the pointwise availability problem such that there exists a secure filtering f for the latter iff there exists a bipartition for the former.

Given an instance $\langle G, \{C_1, \ldots, C_m\}\rangle$ of the set splitting problem, we construct an instance $(\mathscr{D}, d, Q, \mathscr{S})$ for the pointwise availability problem as follows: let $\mathscr{D} = G \cup \{d_0\}$, where $d_0 \notin G$, $d \in G$, $Q = G$ and $\mathscr{S} = \{S_0, S_1, \ldots, S_m\}$ where $S_0 = \{d_0\}$ and for each $1 \leq i \leq m$, $S_i = (Q \setminus C_i) \cup \{d_0\}$. By applying the same argument as for optimal security checking, it can be proved that there exists a secure filtering f for $\mathscr{S}$ such that $[d]_f \subseteq Q$ iff there exists a secure filtering f' that induces a bipartition of $\mathscr{D}$ in two equivalent classes $H_1 = [d]_f$ and $H_2 = \mathscr{D} \setminus [d]_f$. By definition f' is secure iff for all $0 \leq i \leq m$, $H_1 \not\subseteq S_i$ and $H_2 \not\subseteq S_i$. In particular, we have that $H_2 \not\subseteq S_0$ implies that $H_2 \cap Q \neq \emptyset$, therefore $G_1 = H_1$ and $G_2 = H_2 \setminus \{d_0\}$ are a bipartition of G.

Finally, we have that, for all $1 \leq i \leq m$ (i) $G_1 = H_1 \not\subseteq S_i = (G \setminus C_i) \cup \{d_0\} \iff C_i \cap G_2 \neq \emptyset$ and (ii) $H_2 \not\subseteq S_i \iff C_i \cap G_1 \neq \emptyset$. The two latter relations are equivalent to $C_i \not\subseteq G_1$ and $C_i \not\subseteq G_2$, which means that (G_1, G_2) is a set splitting for $\{C_1, \ldots, C_m\}$. $\square$

4.1   Poly-Time Computability of Optimal Filterings

There exist special cases in which optimal filterings can be computed in polynomial time. Let us start by introducing some terminology.

We call a data source d *free* if it does not belong to any secret (in logical terms, all secrets are false in d). Furthermore, we say that a secret S *exclusively includes* d if d belongs to S and it does not belong to any other secret $S' \neq S$ (in logical terms, the only secret satisfied by d is S).

An optimal filtering f secure for a set of m secrets $\mathscr{S} = \{S_0, \ldots, S_{m-1}\}$ can be easily constructed if the sets S_i are non-overlapping (i.e. secrets are mutually inconsistent) and at least m free data sources $d_0, \ldots, d_{m-1}$ are available. To prove this, consider a filtering f in which equivalence classes are obtained as follows: for each $d_i \in \{d_0, \ldots, d_{m-1}\}$, let $[d_i]_f = S_i \cup \{d_i\}$; for each $d \notin \cup_{i=0}^{m-1} S_i \cup \{d_0, \ldots, d_{m-1}\}$ let $[d]_f = \{d\}$. It is easy to see that this filtering function is secure, since no $[d_i]_f$ is included in any secret S_j. Optimality follows immediately by observing that every partition of $[d_i]_f$ contains a subset of S_i, and hence it induces a non-secure filtering.

Another assumption (perhaps more frequently satisfied in practice) under which optimal filterings can be found in polynomial time is the following: each S_i exclusively includes at least one data source[7] and a sufficient number of free data sources exist. The exact number k of free data sources is specified in the next theorem, and is bounded by the number of secrets.

Theorem 2. *Let $\mathscr{S} = \{S_0, \ldots, S_{m-1}\}$ and assume that each S_i exclusively includes at least one data source. Furthermore, let k be the number of secrets that exclusively include exactly one data source. If there exist at least k distinct, free data sources, then an optimal secure filtering f for $\mathscr{S}$ can be computed in polynomial time.*

Proof. For each $i = 0, \ldots, m-1$, let $S_i = C_i \cup E_i$, where C_i are the data sources that S_i shares with the other secrets in $\mathscr{S}$, while E_i contains the data sources that exclusively belong to S_i. By hypothesis, $|E_i| \geq 1$. If $|E_i| > 1$, let $S'_i = S_i$, otherwise, let $S'_i = C_i \cup E_i \cup \{d'_i\}$, where each d'_i is a distinct, free data source. Clearly the total number of free data sources used to construct the sets S'_i is k. Observe that, for each i, there exist at least two data sources, $\{d_i, d'_i\} \subseteq S'_i$, that belong neither to S'_j nor to S_j, for each $j \neq i$. Let $\mathscr{D}_S = \cup_{i=0}^{m-1} S'_i$.

Define $f : \mathscr{D} \to \mathscr{D}$ as follows:

- $\forall d \in \delta_0 \stackrel{def}{=} (S'_0 \setminus \{d'_0\}) \cup \{d'_1\}$, let $f(d) = d'_1$
- $\forall d \in \delta_i \stackrel{def}{=} (S'_i \setminus \cup_{j<i} \delta_j) \cup \{d'_{i+1 \bmod m}\}$, with $1 \leq i \leq m-1$, let $f(d) = d'_{i+1 \bmod m}$
- $\forall d \in \mathscr{D} \setminus \mathscr{D}_S$, let $f(d) = d$

Note that $d_i \in S_i$ while d'_i may or may not belong to S_i. Furthermore, $d_i \in \delta_i$ while $d'_i \in \delta_{i-1}$, with the special case $d'_0 \in \delta_{m-1}$. This implies, $d'_i \notin \delta_i$ and $\delta_i \subseteq S_i \cup \{d'_{i+1 \bmod m}\}$.

First we show that f is secure for $\mathscr{S}$. For each δ_i we have: (a) $d_i \in \delta_i$, and (b) $d'_{i+1 \bmod m} \in \delta_i$. By (a), since d_i exclusively belongs to S_i, it follows that $\delta_i \not\subseteq S_j$ for each $j \neq i$. By (b), since $d'_{i+1 \bmod m}$ either exclusively belongs to $S_{i+1 \bmod m}$

---

[7] In logical terms, this means that each secret must be consistent with the negation of all the other secrets, that is, a kind of logical independence between secrets.

or is a free data source, it follows that, $\delta_i \not\subseteq S_i$. Finally, for each $d \in \mathscr{D} \setminus \mathscr{D}_S$ and for all i, $[d]_f \cap S_i = \emptyset$. This proves security.

Concerning optimality, assume per absurdum that there exists a secure filtering function $g \succ f$. By definition, for each $d \in \mathscr{D}$, $[d]_g \subseteq [d]_f$ where the containment is strict for at least one data source. Clearly, for each $d \in \mathscr{D} \setminus \mathscr{D}_S$ it holds that $[d]_g = [d]_f = \{d\}$. Therefore, there exists $d \in \mathscr{D}_S$ such that $[d]_g \subset [d]_f$ which means that g partitions $[d]_f$ into at least two parts, say $[d_1]_g$ and $[d_2]_g$. Since $[d]_f = \delta_i \subseteq S_i \cup \{d'_{i+1 \bmod m}\}$ it holds that either $[d_1]_g \subseteq S_i$ or $[d_2]_g \subseteq S_i$, i.e. g is not a secure filtering for $\mathscr{S}$. □

5 Greedy CQE and Optimality

A dynamic CQE method [3, 4] is a greedy algorithm that answers a given (possibly infinite) sequence of queries $Q_1, Q_2, \ldots, Q_i, \ldots$, in the order they are presented, and for each Q_i returns the correct answer whenever this is safe with respect to how $Q_1, \ldots, Q_{i-1}$ have been answered. The decision of whether the correct answer to the current query can be safely returned is based on a boolean *censor function* that given a data source, the knowledge disclosed by the previous answers (traditionally called *log*), and the current query Q_i, returns *true* iff the answer to Q_i needs to be modified to preserve confidentiality. Formally, the type of the censor function is $\mathscr{D} \times \mathscr{P}(\mathscr{D}) \times \mathscr{B} \to \{true, false\}$. The second parameter of the censor encodes the log as the set of all the data sources that answer the previous queries as observed in the history.

In the literature, answers are modified by rejecting the query (refusals), changing the result (lies), and combinations thereof. In the abstract framework, the filterings produced by dynamic CQE will be represented as functions $f : \mathscr{D} \to \mathscr{P}(\mathscr{D})$, adopting the convention that the answer to a query Q evaluated against $f(d)$ is "yes" if $f(d) \subseteq Q$ (i.e., all data sources in $f(d)$ satisfy Q), "no" if $f(d) \subseteq \bar{Q}$ (i.e., none of the data sources in $f(d)$ satisfy Q), and "query refused" otherwise.

Greedy approaches have also been used to statically construct secure views. See for example [5], where a selected sequence of queries is pre-processed using the same greedy approach sketched above; the sequence of answers is used to construct a secure knowledge base view.

In the following, we assume that $\mathscr{B}$ is denumerable, since greedy filtering constructions need to iteratively process all possible queries.

5.1 Greedy CQE Based on Refusals

When confidentiality is protected with refusals, the decision of whether the current query should be answered or refused is based on the *refusal censor* function. The original, logic-based formulation of the refusal censor is: if either the correct answer to the current query Q_i or its negation (together with the previous answers) implies a secret, then the query must be refused. In the abstract framework, this definition becomes:

$$cen_r(d, L, Q) = \begin{cases} true & \text{if for some } S \in \mathscr{S}, \text{ either } L \cap Q \subseteq S \text{ or } L \cap \bar{Q} \subseteq S; \\ false & \text{otherwise.} \end{cases}$$

Since this censor does not depend on d we shall omit the first argument and write $cen_r(L, Q)$. The log, for a given $d \in \mathcal{D}$, is maintained as follows:

$$L_{i+1}(d) = \begin{cases} L_i(d) & \text{if } cen_r(L_i(d), Q_{i+1}) = true & \text{(refusal);} \\ L_i(d) \cap Q_{i+1} & \text{if } cen_r(L_i(d), Q_{i+1}) = false \text{ and } d \in Q_{i+1} & \text{(yes);} \\ L_i(d) \cap \bar{Q}_{i+1} & \text{if } cen_r(L_i(d), Q_{i+1}) = false \text{ and } d \in \bar{Q}_{i+1} & \text{(no).} \end{cases}$$

The initial log $L_0(d)$ represents the background knowledge of the user. For simplicity, in our abstract framework, we assume that such background knowledge is already captured by $\mathcal{D}$ and assume that $L_0(d) = \mathcal{D}$. Note that at each step, the log represents the conjunction of answers that have been returned up to that point.

Now a *greedy refusal filtering* f_r can be defined as follows: given any enumeration $Q_1, Q_2, \ldots, Q_i, \ldots$ of $\mathcal{B}$, and the corresponding sequence of logs $\langle L_i(d) \rangle_i$,

$$f_r(d) = \bigcap_i L_i(d).$$

Greedy CQE methods have been proved to be secure *at all finite prefixes of the query sequence* (cf. [3, Def. 1]), while the above greedy refusal filtering (as well as the greedy lying filtering defined in the next section) captures the limit of the logs $L_i(d)$. In order to prove security at the limit, we need to assume that the query language is *compact* like first-order logic.[8] In the abstract framework, compactness is defined as follows:

Definition 7. $\mathcal{B}$ is compact *if for all (possibly infinite) $\mathcal{B}' \subseteq \mathcal{B}$ and for all $Q \in \mathcal{B}$, $\bigcap\{Q' \mid Q' \in \mathcal{B}'\} \subseteq Q$ only if there exists a finite $\mathcal{B}'' \subseteq \mathcal{B}'$ such that $\bigcap\{Q'' \mid Q'' \in \mathcal{B}''\} \subseteq Q$.*

Theorem 3. *If $\mathcal{B}$ is compact, then greedy refusal filterings are secure.*

Proof. Suppose that the greedy refusal filtering f_r generated by some query sequence $\langle Q_i \rangle_i$ is not secure, and let d be a data source such that $[d]_{f_r} \subseteq S$, for some secret $S \in \mathcal{S}$. By definition, $f_r(d)$ is the intersection of the non-refused queries of $\mathcal{B}$, therefore, by compactness, there is a log $L_k(d)$ such that $L_k(d) \subseteq S$. Without loss of generality, let k be the minimal such index. This implies that Q_k is not refused, otherwise $L_k(d) = L_{k-1}(d)$, contradicting the minimality of k. Then, either $L_k(d) = L_{k-1}(d) \cap Q_k \subseteq S$ or $L_k(d) = L_{k-1}(d) \cap \bar{Q}_k \subseteq S$; in both cases, $cen_r(L_{k-1}, Q_k) = true$. But then Q_k should be refused—a contradiction. $\square$

Greedy refusal filterings can be proved to be optimal under mild hypotheses:

1. $\mathcal{B}$ is closed under finite set union, finite intersection, and complement. In logical terms: Queries are closed under negation and under finite conjunction and disjunction.

---

[8] First-order logic's compactness states that if an infinite set of sentences T entails a sentence φ, then some finite subset of T must entail φ, too.

2. The set of secrets $\mathcal{S}$ is finite.

First we need a simple technical lemma that confirms that greedy refusal filterings tell no lies:

Lemma 1. *For all $d \in \mathcal{D}$, $d \in f_r(d)$.*

Proof. It suffices to prove, by induction on i, that for all non-negative integers i, $d \in L_i(d)$. The base case is trivial, since $L_0(d) = \mathcal{D}$. The induction step is a straigthforward consequence of the induction hypothesis ($d \in L_{i-1}(d)$) and the definition of $L_i(d)$.   □

Theorem 4. *If the above two hypotheses hold, than every greedy refusal filtering f_r is optimal.*

Proof. Suppose not, which implies that for some $d \in \mathcal{D}$, its equivalence class $[d]_{f_r}$ can be split into two nonempty partitions D and E both of which intersect the complements of all secrets. In other words, assuming that $\mathcal{S} = \{S_1, \ldots, S_n\}$, there must be data sources $d_i \in D \cap \bar{S}_i$ and $e_i \in E \cap \bar{S}_i$ ($1 \le i \le n$). Since for all $i = 1, \ldots, n$, d_i and e_i belong to $[d]_{f_r}$ by assumption (that is, $f_r(d_i) = f_r(e_i) = f_r(d)$), Lemma 1 implies:

$$\{d_1, \ldots, d_n, e_1, \ldots, e_n\} \subseteq f_r(d). \tag{1}$$

Recall that all distinct data sources can be distinguished with some query and $\mathcal{B}$ is closed under complements. So, for each pair d_i, e_j there exists a query $Q_{i,j}$ such that $d_i \in Q_{i,j}$ and $e_i \in \bar{Q}_{i,j}$. Moreover, since $\mathcal{B}$ is closed under finite unions and intersections, it contains the query:

$$Q^* = \bigcup_{i=1}^{n} \bigcap_{j=1}^{n} Q_{i,j},$$

that has the property of containing all d_i and none of the e_i ($1 \le i \le n$). Now let Q_k be the element in the enumeration of $\mathcal{B}$ such that $Q_k = Q^*$. By definition, $L_{k-1}(d_1) \supseteq f_r(d_1) = f_r(d)$, therefore – using the property of Q^* and (1) – $\{d_1, \ldots, d_n\} \subseteq L_{k-1}(d_1) \cap Q_k$ and $\{e_1, \ldots, e_n\} \subseteq L_{k-1}(d_1) \cap \bar{Q}_k$. It follows that $cen_r(L_{k-1}(d_1), Q_k) = false$. But then, by definition, $L_k(d_1) = L_{k-1}(d_1) \cap Q_k$, and hence $f_r(d_1)$ does not contain any of the e_i. Since $f_r(d_1) = f_r(d)$, this contradicts (1).   □

Theorem 4 can be proved also under a different, alternative hypothesis: namely, that the query language is expressive enough to capture all possible sets of information sources (as it happens in finite propositional frameworks).

Theorem 5. *If $\mathcal{B} = \mathcal{P}(\mathcal{D})$, then greedy refusal filterings are optimal.*

Proof. Similar to the proof of Theorem 4. The query Q^* containing $d_1, \ldots, d_n$ and none of $e_1, \ldots, e_n$ exists by hypothesis.   □

5.2   Greedy CQE Based on Lies

When confidentiality is protected with lies, the decision of whether the true answer to the current query should be returned is based on the *lie censor* function. Its logic-based definition is: if the honest answer to the current query Q_i (together with the previous answers) entails a disjunction of secrets, then lie. The corresponding definition in the abstract framework is:

$$cen_l(d, L, Q) = \begin{cases} true \text{ if } d \in Q \text{ and } L \cap Q \subseteq \bigcup\{S \mid S \in \mathscr{S}\}; \\ true \text{ if } d \in \bar{Q} \text{ and } L \cap \bar{Q} \subseteq \bigcup\{S \mid S \in \mathscr{S}\}; \\ false \text{ otherwise.} \end{cases}$$

The log, for a given $d \in \mathscr{D}$, is maintained as follows:

$$L_{i+1}(d) = \begin{cases} L_i(d) \cap Q_{i+1} \text{ if } cen_l(d, L_i(d), Q_{i+1}) = false \text{ and } d \in Q_{i+1} & \text{(yes)}; \\ L_i(d) \cap \bar{Q}_{i+1} \text{ if } cen_l(d, L_i(d), Q_{i+1}) = false \text{ and } d \in \bar{Q}_{i+1} & \text{(no)}. \\ L_i(d) \cap Q_{i+1} \text{ if } cen_l(d, L_i(d), Q_{i+1}) = true \text{ and } d \in \bar{Q}_{i+1} & \text{(lie)}. \\ L_i(d) \cap \bar{Q}_{i+1} \text{ if } cen_l(d, L_i(d), Q_{i+1}) = true \text{ and } d \in Q_{i+1} & \text{(lie)}. \end{cases}$$

Now *greedy lying filterings* f_l can be defined analogously to greedy refusal filterings: given any enumeration $Q_1, Q_2, \ldots, Q_i, \ldots$ of $\mathscr{B}$, and the corresponding sequence of logs $L_i(d)$, let $f_r(d) = \bigcap_i L_i(d)$.

Since the invariant preserved by the lying censor is stronger than the invariant maintained by the refusal censor, security can only be guaranteed if the disjunction of all secrets is not trivially violated a priori, that is, if $\mathscr{D} \nsubseteq \bigcup\{S \mid S \in \mathscr{S}\}$.

Theorem 6. *If $\mathscr{B}$ is compact and closed under complements, and if $\mathscr{D} \nsubseteq \bigcup\{S \mid S \in \mathscr{S}\}$, then greedy lying filterings are secure.*

Proof. Suppose that the greedy lying filtering f_l generated by some query sequence $\langle Q_i \rangle_i$ is not secure, and let d be a data source such that $[d]_{f_l} \subseteq S$, for some secret $S \in \mathscr{S}$. By definition, $f_l(d)$ is an intersection of queries (and complements thereof, that are in $\mathscr{B}$ as well), therefore, by compactness, there is a log $L_i(d)$ such that $L_i(d) \subseteq S \subseteq \bigcup\{S \mid S \in \mathscr{S}\}$. Let k be the minimal index such that $L_k(d) \subseteq \bigcup\{S \mid S \in \mathscr{S}\}$. This implies that $cen_l(d, L_{k-1}(d), Q_k) = true$, and that both $L_{k-1}(d) \cap Q_k \subseteq \bigcup\{S \mid S \in \mathscr{S}\}$ and $L_{k-1}(d) \cap \bar{Q}_k \subseteq \bigcup\{S \mid S \in \mathscr{S}\}$ hold. But then $L_{k-1}(d) \subseteq \bigcup\{S \mid S \in \mathscr{S}\}$, contradicting the minimality of k. $\square$

Using (a) the definition of the logs, and (b) the assumption that two distinct data sources can be distinguished by at least one query, it can be proved that:

Proposition 3. *If $\mathscr{D} \nsubseteq \bigcup\{S \mid S \in \mathscr{S}\}$, then $f_l(d)$ is a singleton.*

Proof. (Sketch) It can be proved by induction that $L_i(d) \nsubseteq \bigcup\{S \mid S \in \mathscr{S}\}$, for all $i \geq 0$. In particular, this ensures that $f_l(d)$ is nonempty. Now assume that $f_l(d)$ contains two different data sources d_1 and d_2. There must be a query Q_k in the enumeration of $\mathscr{B}$ that contains exactly one of d_1 and d_2. Then, by definition, $L_{k+1}(d)$ must not contain both, and the same holds for $f_l(d) \subseteq L_{k+1}(d)$ (a contradiction). $\square$

The above proposition makes it explicit that lying filterings answer *all* queries (not always truthfully), as required by cover stories. Note that queries are answered as if d were the member of $f_l(d)$.

Theorem 7. *Greedy lying filterings are not optimal, in general, even if the hypotheses of Theorem 4 and Theorem 5 hold.*

Proof. Take the abstract version of the propositional framework with secrets $\{p, q\}$ and background knowledge $r \to p \vee q$. Formally, let $\mathscr{D} = \mathscr{P}(\{p, q, r\}) \setminus \{\{r\}\}$, $\mathscr{B} = \mathscr{P}(\mathscr{D})$, and $\mathscr{S} = \{S_p, S_q\}$, where $S_p = \{d \in \mathscr{D} \mid p \in d\}$ and $S_q = \{d \in \mathscr{D} \mid q \in d\}$. For all enumerations of $\mathscr{B}$, the corresponding lying filtering f_l maps all d onto $\{\emptyset\}$, that is, f_l induces a single equivalence class and for all data sources d, $f_l'(d) = \emptyset$ (the data source where p, q, r are false). The optimal filtering, instead, yields two equivalence classes containing the data sources that include r and those that don't (respectively), that is, (in propositional terms) the refusal filtering permits to answer the queries r and $\neg r$ correctly.   □

Suboptimal filterings (that in some sense mean less cooperative answers) are the price to pay for cover stories, that is, the cost of avoiding explicit, visible answer distortions (such as refusals). As we pointed out, this requires protecting *disjunctions* of secrets (encoded by unions of secrets in the abstract framework) rather than individual secrets ([3, Prop. 4] shows why this is necessary). Not surprisingly, the need of preserving this stronger variant makes the lying filtering less cooperative.

In the previous works on CQE, the lack of an independent notion of filtering optimality prevented a thorough comparison of lying and refusal-based methods. It was only established that on a same query sequence, the lying method starts distorting queries before the refusal method, but after the first distortion the answers returned by the two methods are incomparable, in general. Thanks to our completely abstract notions of filtering and optimality (that are compatible with all possible output domains $\mathscr{V}$), now we know that refusal-based CQE is at least as cooperative as any other deterministic data-filtering method, including those that do not fall within the category of CQE.

6   Discussion and Future Work

The abstract framework introduced in Sec. 3 covers all the concrete, deterministic data-filtering mechanisms introduced in the literature, and more. It is largely independent from any syntactic detail of the query languages; it makes no assumption on the structure of data sources, that may be standard relational database instances, XML documents, RDF/OWL knowledge bases, and so on; it makes no assumption on the structure of secure views, that may be thought of as incomplete databases, sets or sequences of query answers, labelled knowledge bases, as in [19, 20], and so forth. In particular, the generic representation of secure views covers answer distortion mechanisms different from the standard approaches based on refusal and lies (e.g. partial or "blurred" answers that are neither a "yes" nor a "no", such as returning birth year instead of a full birth date).

At this abstraction level, it is possible to compare very different mechanisms (static, dynamic, based on different answer distortion methods) in terms of the amout of information they disclose, that is, in terms of the mechanism's cooperativeness. It is also possible to define an optimality criterion (corresponding to maximal cooperativeness).

We showed that each of the above different mechanisms f can be associated to a refusal-based censor $[\cdot]_f$ that conveys to a smart, informed user exactly the same amount of information as f, and hence preserves important properties such as security and optimality (cf. Prop. 1 and Prop. 2). This result generalizes to the above variety of settings the analysis of unreliable answers (sometimes called potential lies) [3, Sec. 3.3 and Theorem 13]. Of course, this does not mean that lies can be simply replaced by refusals: cover stories are incompatible with refusals, and although a smart user who knows the protection method f may tell which answers are unreliable as if they were refused, the system should not be allowed to reject any query. The issue of the value and function of the verbatim meaning of answers will be dealt with in an extended version of this paper. The standardized representation of filterings as refusal-based filterings may also become a useful tool for proving general properties of CQE methods.

We proved further nice properties of refusal filterings. Under mild assumptions ($\mathscr{B}$ should be compact and $\mathscr{S}$ finite), greedy, refusal-based CQE remains secure at the limit of the query sequence (Theorem 3), and the disclosed information converges to an optimal (maximally cooperative) secure filtering (cf. Theorems 4 and 5). On the contrary, the greedy lying filtering is not optimal, in general (Theorem 7). The consequences are novel: previously, refusal and lies were simply considered incomparable protection methods. Non-optimality depends on the need of protecting the union of all secrets—which is known to be an essential prerequisite to the security of lie-based CQE. The study of optimality with respect to this stronger constraint will be a subject of future work.

We introduced a few interesting decision problems related to CQE: Security checking (i.e. checking whether a given filtering f is secure); Optimal security checking (which further checks whether f is optimal); Pointwise and Global availability (that check whether there is a way of preserving confidentiality that preserves the answers to a given query Q). The inherent complexity of these problems has been analyzed assuming that the list of possible data sources is part of the input and that the given filterings are computable in polynomial time, in order to remove all the complexity related to the structure of data sources and the filtering method. In this setting, security checking and global availability are in P, while pointwise availability and optimal security are hard (NP and coNP-complete, respectively), as proved in Theorem 1. Interestingly, preserving a query Q in a single, given data source (if at all possible) is harder than preserving Q in *all* data sources, because in the latter case it is easier to detect that the problem has no solution. These results tells us that in no concrete framework the pointwise availability problem and the optimal security checking problem can be tractable. The construction of optimal secure filterings becomes easier in some cases, e.g. when secrets satisfy a certain degree of logical independence (Theorem 2). Moreover, greedy refusal-based filterings constitute a method for approximating an optimal secure filtering on a query-by-query basis (Theorem 4). We are planning to investigate the above decision problems in more concrete settings and derive specific complexity bounds. We are also going to extend our results to availability problems where multiple queries must be simultaneously preserved.

References

1. Fung, B.C.M., Wang, K., Chen, R., Yu, P.S.: Privacy-preserving data publishing: A survey of recent developments. ACM Comput. Surv. 42(4) (2010)
2. Biskup, J.: For unknown secrecies refusal is better than lying. Data Knowl. Eng. 33(1), 1–23 (2000)
3. Biskup, J., Bonatti, P.A.: Lying versus refusal for known potential secrets. Data Knowl. Eng. 38(2), 199–222 (2001)
4. Biskup, J., Bonatti, P.A.: Controlled query evaluation for known policies by combining lying and refusal. Ann. Math. Artif. Intell. 40(1-2), 37–62 (2004)
5. Bonatti, P.A., Sauro, L.: A confidentiality model for ontologies. In: [21], pp. 17–32
6. Grau, B.C., Kharlamov, E., Kostylev, E.V., Zheleznyakov, D.: Controlled query evaluation over OWL 2 RL ontologies. In: [21], pp. 49–65
7. Sicherman, G.L., de Jonge, W., van de Riet, R.P.: Answering queries without revealing secrets. ACM Trans. Database Syst. 8(1), 41–59 (1983)
8. Denning, D.E.: A lattice model of secure information flow. Commun. ACM 19(5), 236–243 (1976)
9. Goguen, J.A., Meseguer, J.: Security policies and security models. In: IEEE Symposium on Security and Privacy, pp. 11–20 (1982)
10. Biskup, J.: Security in Computing Systems - Challenges, Approaches and Solutions. Springer (2009)
11. Lunt, T.F.: Polyinstantiation: An inevitable part of a multilevel world. In: CSFW, pp. 236–238. IEEE Computer Society (1991)
12. Sandhu, R.S., Jajodia, S.: Polyinstantiation for cover stories. In: Deswarte, Y., Quisquater, J.-J., Eizenberg, G. (eds.) ESORICS 1992. LNCS, vol. 648, pp. 307–328. Springer, Heidelberg (1992)
13. Bonatti, P.A., Kraus, S., Subrahmanian, V.S.: Foundations of secure deductive databases. IEEE Trans. Knowl. Data Eng. 7(3), 406–422 (1995)
14. Biskup, J., Bonatti, P.A.: Controlled query evaluation with open queries for a decidable relational submodel. Ann. Math. Artif. Intell. 50(1-2), 39–77 (2007)
15. Biskup, J., Tadros, C., Wiese, L.: Towards controlled query evaluation for incomplete first-order databases. In: Link, S., Prade, H. (eds.) FoIKS 2010. LNCS, vol. 5956, pp. 230–247. Springer, Heidelberg (2010)
16. Biskup, J., Gogolin, C., Seiler, J., Weibert, T.: Inference-proof view update transactions with forwarded refreshments. Journal of Computer Security 19(3), 487–529 (2011)
17. Biskup, J., Hartmann, S., Link, S., Lochner, J.H.: Efficient inference control for open relational queries. In: Foresti, S., Jajodia, S. (eds.) Data and Applications Security XXIV. LNCS, vol. 6166, pp. 162–176. Springer, Heidelberg (2010)

18. Garey, M.R., Johnson, D.S.: Computers and Intractability: A Guide to the Theory of NP-Completeness. Freeman & Co., New York (1979)
19. Baader, F., Knechtel, M., Peñaloza, R.: A generic approach for large-scale ontological reasoning in the presence of access restrictions to the ontology's axioms. In: Bernstein, A., Karger, D.R., Heath, T., Feigenbaum, L., Maynard, D., Motta, E., Thirunarayan, K. (eds.) ISWC 2009. LNCS, vol. 5823, pp. 49–64. Springer, Heidelberg (2009)
20. Knechtel, M., Stuckenschmidt, H.: Query-based access control for ontologies. In: Hitzler, P., Lukasiewicz, T. (eds.) RR 2010. LNCS, vol. 6333, pp. 73–87. Springer, Heidelberg (2010)
21. Alani, H., et al. (eds.): ISWC 2013, Part I. LNCS, vol. 8218. Springer, Heidelberg (2013)

New Insight to Preserve Online Survey Accuracy and Privacy in Big Data Era

Joseph K. Liu[1], Man Ho Au[2,4], Xinyi Huang[3,*], Willy Susilo[4],
Jianying Zhou[1], and Yong Yu[4,5]

[1] Infocomm Security Department, Institute for Infocomm Research, Singapore
{ksliu,jyzhou}@i2r.a-star.edu.sg
[2] Department of Computing, The Hong Kong Polytechnic University, Hong Kong
allen.au@gmail.com
[3] Fujian Provincial Key Laboratory of Network Security and Cryptology, School of
Mathematics and Computer Science, Fujian Normal University, Fuzhou, China
xyhuang81@gmail.com
[4] Centre for Computer and Information Security Research, School of Computer
Science and Software Engineering, University of Wollongong, Australia
{aau,wsusilo,yyong}@uow.edu.au
[5] School of Computer Science and Engineering, University of Electronic Science and
Technology of China, Chengdu, China
yyucd2012@gmail.com

Abstract. An online survey system provides a convenient way for people to conduct surveys. It removes the necessity of human resources to hold paper surveys or telephone interviews and hence reduces the cost significantly. Nevertheless, accuracy and privacy remain as the major obstacles that need additional attention. To conduct an accurate survey, privacy maybe lost, and vice versa. In this paper, we provide new insight to preserve these two seeming contradictory issues in online survey systems especially suitable in big data era. We propose a secure system, which is shown to be efficient and practical by simulation data. Our analysis further shows that the proposed solution is desirable not only in online survey systems but also in several potential applications, including E-Voting, Smart-Grid and Vehicular Ad Hoc Networks.

Keywords: Online Survey, Privacy, Big Data.

1 Introduction

Privacy has always been considered as a significant issue in our daily life. As an age-old concern, it is not unique in the digital world but the advances in digital technologies have brought an array of new privacy challenges. The granularity (or depth) of information captured in the digital world and the rapid information

* Xinyi Huang is supported by Distinguished Young Scholars Fund of Department of Education, Fujian Province, China (JA13062) and Fok Ying Tung Education Foundation (Grant No. 141065).

M. Kutyłowski and J. Vaidya (Eds.): ESORICS 2014, Part II, LNCS 8713, pp. 182–199, 2014.

dissemination facilitated by the Internet are factors that contribute most to those new privacy concerns.

Online Survey System. One of the situations that privacy plays an important factor is an online survey system. An online survey system (e.g., Kwik Survey [1], My3q [2] or Survey Monkey [3]) is an Internet surveying technique in which the interviewee follows a script provided in a website. The questionnaires are created in a program for creating web interviews. The program allows for the questionnaire to contain pictures, audio and video clips, or links to different web pages. The website is able to customize the flow of the questionnaire based on the answers provided, as well as information already known about the participant. It is considered to be a cheaper way of conducting surveys since it does not require any human resources to conduct surveys or telephone interview. With the increasing use of the Internet, online questionnaires have become a popular way of collecting information. The design of an online questionnaire often has an effect on the quality of data gathered. There are many factors in designing an online questionnaire, and issues including guidelines, available question formats, administration, *accuracy* and *privacy* should be carefully addressed. Here we focus on the last two factors.

A survey form may collect the interviewee's personal particulars, such as sex, age, salary range and interest. Such information may be very useful for the interviewer to conduct a survey with accurate information. However, the interviewer has no way to verify the authenticity of this information. For example, a 15 years old boy may say that "she" is a 50 years old woman earning one million US dollars per annual. This may not be possible if a face-to-face survey or telephone interviewing survey is carried out, or at least to some certain extent. Nevertheless, in a virtual world such as Internet, anonymity without authentication means the source is highly questionable. Furthermore, this 15 years old boy may fill in the online survey multiple times. Next time he may pretend he is a retired 80 years old man. There is no way to verify whether these 2 different surveys are from the same source or not.

Digital signature provides an easy and convenient way to authenticate the message sender in the Internet. By digitally signing a message (the survey), the verifier (the interviewer) can be convinced that the sender is a person with true particulars provided. Using the above example, assume Bob is that 15 years old boy. If he signs the survey, the interviewer may check his certificate (or identity if ID-based signature [4] is used) to find out his personal information from the certificate authority (or private key generator for ID-based signature). He cannot pretend to be another person. If he conducts the survey more than once, it will be easily detected since the signature contains the information of the signer.

It seems that digital signature can easily solve the problem of *accuracy*. However, on the other side, signing the survey means the loss of privacy. In reality, many users are not willing to reveal their real identities to interviewers due to privacy concerns. If it is a compulsory requirement for conducting the survey, they will decline the survey invitation. It maybe the main reason that many existing online survey systems do not compulsorily require interviewees to input their real identifying information (or no need to verify their information, e.g., no email validation is required).

Contributions. In this paper, we provide a new insight to preserve accuracy and privacy in online survey systems. We propose a new system which provides the following desirable features:

1. **Authentication**: It allows only those authenticated or qualified users to take part into the survey.
2. **Anonymity**: No one knows the identity of the user who has submitted the survey.
3. **Detection of double submission**: No one can submit more than once in a single survey event without being detected.
4. **Unlinkability**: Given two surveys from two different events, no one can tell whether they are from the same user.
5. **Constant Complexity**: The complexity of our system is independent to the total number of users in the system. Thus it is particularly suitable for any system with large user database in the **big data analytic era**.

We provide a concrete instantiation of our system. Further, we show our system to be efficient and practical by some simulation data analysis.

We believe our proposed system can fully resolve the contradiction between accuracy and privacy in online survey system. We also suggest other practical applications that can employ our system with only slightly modification required.

Organization. The rest of this paper is organized as follows. Some related works will be given in Section 2. Section 3 reviews the preliminaries required in this paper. In Section 4 we give an overview of our scheme, which is followed by detail description in Section 5. We present other applications that can deploy our primitive in Section 6 and conclude our paper in Section 7.

2   Related Works

There are many ways to resolve the contradiction between user privacy and data accuracy. Several solutions have been proposed and notable examples include ring signatures [5, 6] and group signatures [7, 8]. In ring signatures, one can spontaneously form a group of possible signers and sign on behalf of the group anonymously. One can also use group signatures to sign on behalf of a group of possible signers, but group signatures require an initial group setup procedure performed by the group manager who can revoke the anonymity of any group signer.

Attribute-Based Signatures [9–12] (or, ABS for short) is another primitive proposed to provide signer anonymity. As a versatile primitive, ABS allows an entity to sign a message with fine-grained control over identifying information. A valid ABS signature attests to the fact that "A single user, whose attributes satisfy the predicate, has endorsed the message". Ring signatures and group

signatures are then comparable to special cases of ABS, in which the only allowed predicates are disjunctions over the universe of attributes (identities). In
ABS, each entity possesses a set of attributes and a key-authority generates
the associated private keys, with which one can sign a message with a predicate satisfied by his/her attributes. The signature reveals no more than the fact
that a single user with some set of attributes satisfying the predicate has at-
tested to the message. In particular, ABS does not provide any information on
the particular set of attributes used to satisfy the predicate. For example, an
"(Engineer, Department A)" or an "(Engineer, Department B)" can independently
generate an ABS to assure the recipient that the signature was produced by an
"Engineer" without disclosing the department information. Furthermore, users
of ABS cannot collude to pool their attributes together (which separates ABS
from mesh signatures): It is never possible for an "(Engineer, Department A)"
and an "(Auditor, Department B)" to collude and generate an ABS satisfying the
predicate "(Auditor, Department A)".

Yet all these solutions cannot resolve the contradiction. They are not practical
enough to be used in an online survey system. For example, in a ring signature,
it requires the signer to know all other members within the group. It is obvious
impossible for an interviewee to know all other interviewee in a survey. For group
signature, the properties of the group have to be fixed at the beginning. That is,
assume we need to conduct a survey for female engineers aged between 20-25.
Such a group has been formed (thus a group manager needs to distribute user
secret keys for every user). Later on, another survey for British engineers ages
between 20-25 will be conducted. Although there are some overlaps between
these two groups of people, the secret key (obtained from the first group) cannot
be reused, even for the same person since the properties of the group are fixed.
In other words, for every single survey, it is required for the group manager to
generate a new set of secret keys to every user. It is again impractical.

ABS seems to be the nearest solution. It provides user privacy. At the same
time, it also authenticates the signers for some attributes at a flexible way.
For example, assume Alice is a "female" "engineer" working in "Department
A". Now there is a survey for all engineers in Department A. Those eligible
interviewee including Alice can use their attribute "(Engineer, Department A)"
to sign the survey. Later on, another survey for all female staff in department
will be conducted. Alice can reuse her secret key but on a different attribute set
"(Female, Department A)" to sign the survey. Different from ring signature, she
does not need to know who else users will participate the survey. Also different
from group signature, she does not need to obtain a different secret key for a
different survey.

There is just one problem that ABS cannot resolve. Since ABS is anonymous,
by no mean the verifier knows whether Alice has conducted twice or more in a
survey, as depicted in Fig 1. In the Internet world, the situation is even worse.
There are many programming scripts that can automatically submit online form.
By using these scripts, one can submit a thousand of online forms in a very short

period of time. The result will then be heavily biased. No existing designs of ABS can detect this kind of behavior.

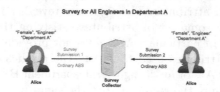

Fig. 1. Undetectable Double Submission Using Ordinary ABS

It is fair to say no existing solutions can perfectly resolve the contradiction in an online survey system.

3 Preliminaries

3.1 Mathematical Definitions

Bilinear Maps. Let $\mathbb{G}_1, \mathbb{G}_2, G_T$ be cyclic (multiplicative) groups of order p, where p is a prime. Let g be a generator of $\mathbb{G}_1$, and h be a generator of $\mathbb{G}_2$. Then $\hat{e} : \mathbb{G}_1 \times \mathbb{G}_2 \to \mathbb{G}_T$ is a bilinear map if $\hat{e}(g, h)$ is a generator of G_T, and $\hat{e}(g^a, h^b) = \hat{e}(g, h)^{ab}$ for all $a, b \in \mathbb{Z}_p$.

Mathematical Hard Problem. The security of our construction depends on the hardness of the following problem:

Definition 1 (Decisional Diffie-Hellam Problem (DDH).). *On input g, g^a, $g^b, Z \in \mathbb{G}$, decide whether $Z = g^{ab}$ or just a random element in $\mathbb{G}$. The DDH assumption states that the DDH problem is hard for any polynomial-time bounded algorithm.*

3.2 Monotone Span Programs

Let $\Upsilon : \{0,1\}^n \to \{0,1\}$ be a monotone boolean function. A monotone span program for Υ over a field $\mathbb{F}$ is an $\ell \times t$ matrix $\mathbf{M}$ with entries in $\mathbb{F}$, along with a labeling function $a : [\ell] \to [n]$ that associates each row of $\mathbf{M}$ with an input variable of Υ, that for every $(x_1, ..., x_n) \in \{0,1\}^n$, satisfies the following:

$$\Upsilon(x_1, ..., x_n) = 1 \iff \exists \boldsymbol{v} \in \mathbb{F}^{1 \times \ell} \text{ such that}$$
$$\boldsymbol{v}\mathbf{M} = [1, 0, 0, ..., 0], \text{ and } (\forall i : x_{a(i)} = 0 \Rightarrow v_i = 0).$$

In other words, $\Upsilon(x_1, ..., x_n) = 1$ if and only if the rows of $\mathbf{M}$ indexed by $\{i | x_{a(i)} = 1\}$ span the vector $[1, 0, 0, ..., 0]$. We call ℓ the length and t the width of the span program, and $\ell + t$ the size of the span program.

Readers may refer to [11] for the details.

4 Overview

4.1 Basic Idea

There are three entities in our system:

- Attribute Authority (AA): It is responsible for setting up the public parameters and issuing user secret keys for various attributes. In practice, it can be a government authority, computer service centre of an university or human resources department of a company.
- User: Any entity who has a user secret key is an user. A user can have different attributes.
- Survey Centre (SC): It is an organization to organize a survey. It is responsible to define the required policy of the survey, to collect the survey from users and to verify the result.

Basically our system is an ABS scheme. Each user generates an ABS using his own attributes required by the current survey. However, due to the unlinkability property of an ABS scheme, it is not suitable to be used directly, since a user may submit the survey more than once. We modify an ABS scheme from [11] by adding linkability to it. That is, any verifier is able to detect whether two signatures are generated by the same user within a single survey. Yet any user that generates two signatures in two different surveys cannot be linked. The survey centre can discard any double-submitted survey to maintain the accuracy of the result.

4.2 Assumptions

We assume each user communicates with SC through an anonymous channel [13, 14] or uses some IP-hiding technology. We also assume that the user keeps his secret key in a safe place. This can be achieved by some external means, such as keeping the secret key in a device to be always in possession or set it to be password-protected. When considering some attacks such as IP hijacking, distributed denial-of-service attack, man-in-the-middle attack etc., it is out of the scope of this paper.

4.3 Threat Model

In this sytem, we consider the following attacks:

1. (Unforgeability Attack:) The attacker acts as an unauthorized user (who does not possess the required attributes) who tries to submit a survey to the SC for being accepted.
2. (Anonymity Attack:) The attacker acts as the AA colluded with the SC who tries to find out the identity of the user of a particular submission.
3. (Linkability Attack:) The attacker acts as an authorized user who tries to submit more than one survey to the SC for being accepted in a single survey event.

4. (Unlinkability (for different users) Attack:) The attacker acts as an authorized user who tries to submit some surveys to link with other surveys submitted by honest users. The attack may have intention to do so in order to remove other undesirable results submitted by other users.

4.4 Notations

Notations used in our system are summarized in Table 1.

Table 1. Frequently Used Notations

TPK	system parameters
APK	public key of the AA
ASK	master secret key of the AA
$\mathbb{A}$	universe of attributes
$\mathcal{A}$	an attribute set of a user
USK	user secret key
m	data or the content of a survey
$event$	the description of a particular survey event
Υ	policy of the survey
σ	signature of the survey

5 Details of Our Online Survey System

5.1 The Construction

Our system consists of different phases. The detailed step-by-step construction of each phase is given in the framed box.

Setup. The AA defines all system parameters and generates the public key and a master secret key.

Details: The AA first generates the system parameters as follows:

1. Let $\hat{e} : \mathbb{G}_1 \times \mathbb{G}_2 \to \mathbb{G}_T$ be a bilinear map (defined in Section 3.1) such that $|\mathbb{G}_1| = |\mathbb{G}_2| = |\mathbb{G}_T| = p$ for some prime p. Let g, G be generators of $\mathbb{G}_1$ and $\mathfrak{g}, \mathfrak{h}, h, h_0, \ldots, h_{t_{max}}, H$ be generators of $\mathbb{G}_2$. The value t_{max} is the maximum width of the monotone span programs as defined in Section 3.2. Let $\mathbb{A} = \mathbb{Z}_p^*$ be the universe of attributes.
2. Assume the DDH problem (defined in Section 3.1) is hard in $\mathbb{G}_1$ and $\mathbb{G}_2$. Let $\mathcal{G} : \{0,1\}^* \to \mathbb{G}_1$, $\mathcal{H} : \{0,1\}^* \to \mathbb{Z}_p$ be hash functions that will be modeled as random oracles. The system parameters TPK is $(\mathbb{G}_1, \mathbb{G}_2, \mathbb{G}_T, \hat{e}, p, g, G, \mathfrak{g}, \mathfrak{h}, h, h_0, \ldots, h_{t_{max}}, H, \mathcal{H}, \mathcal{G})$.

Then it generates the public and master secret keys as follows:

1. Choose $a_0, a, b, c \in_R \mathbb{Z}_p$. Compute: $C = g^c$, $A_0 = h_0^{a_0}$, $A_j = h_j^a$, $B_j = h_j^b$ for $j = 1, \ldots, t_{max}$.
2. Choose $s, v, w, z \in_R \mathbb{Z}_p$. Compute $U = G^s, V = H^v, W = H^w, Z = H^z$.
3. Set the public key APK as $(C, A_0, \{A_j, B_j\}_{j=1}^{t_{max}}, U, V, W, Z)$ and the master secret key ASK as (a, a_0, b, s, v, w, z). Publish both APK and TPK while keep ASK secret.

User Key Generation. The AA issues user secret key to each user, according to different attributes each user possesses. This is an interactive protocol between each user and the AA.

Details:

1. The user with an attribute set $\mathcal{A} \in \mathbb{A}$ randomly selects $L, r_L \in \mathbb{Z}_p$ and computes $C_L = \mathfrak{g}^L \mathfrak{h}^{r_L} \in \mathbb{G}_2$ and sends C_L to the AA.
2. The AA randomly chooses $K_{base} \in_R \mathbb{G}_1$, $r \in_R \mathbb{Z}_p$ and uses the master secret key ASK to compute: $K_0 = K_{base}^{\frac{1}{a_0}}$, $K_u = K_{base}^{\frac{1}{a+bu}}$ $\forall u \in \mathcal{A}$, $R = G^r$, $S = G^{z-rv} K_{base}^{-w}$, $T = (HC_L^{-s})^{\frac{1}{r}}$.
3. The AA returns K_{base}, K_0, $\{K_u\}_{u \in \mathcal{A}}$, R, S, T to the user.
4. The user parses his user secret key $SK_{\mathcal{A}}$ as $(K_{base}, K_0, \{K_u\}_{u \in \mathcal{A}}, R, S, T, L, r_L)$.

Survey Submission. The SC defines a survey event and a policy such that only those users that fulfill the policy with their attributes can participate this survey. The user submits the survey data together with the corresponding signature signed with his user secret key through an anonymous channel to the SC.

Details: Let m be the data and *event* be the description of this survey. For a given policy Υ such that if a user with an attribute set $\mathcal{A}$ fulfills this policy, we have $\Upsilon(\mathcal{A}) = 1$. First convert the policy to its corresponding monotone span program $\mathcal{M} \in \mathbb{Z}_p^{\ell \times t}$ (defined in Section 3.2), with row labeling function $u : [\ell] \to \mathbb{A}$ and the vector v that corresponds to the satisfying assignment of $\mathcal{A}$. The user executes the following steps with his user secret key $SK_{\mathcal{A}}$:

1. Compute $\mu = \mathcal{H}(m||\Upsilon)$ and $\tau = \mathcal{G}(event)^L$.
2. Pick $r_0 \in_R \mathbb{Z}_p^*$, $r_1, \ldots, r_\ell \in_R \mathbb{Z}_p$ and compute $Y = K_{base}^{r_0}$, $W = K_0^{r_0}$, $S_i = (K_{u(i)}^{v[i]})^{r_0} (Cg^\mu)^{r_i} (\forall i \in [\ell])$, $P_j = \prod_{i=1}^{\ell} (A_j B_j^{u(i)})^{\mathcal{M}_{ij} \cdot r_i} (\forall j \in [t])$.
3. Compute Π_τ as a non-interactive zero-knowledge proof-of-knowledge of the values $(R, S, T, K_{base}, r_0, L, r_L)$ satisfying the following relation:

$$\hat{e}(R, V)\hat{e}(S, H)\hat{e}(K_{base}, W) = \hat{e}(G, Z) \quad \wedge$$
$$\hat{e}(R, T)\hat{e}(U, \mathfrak{g}^L \mathfrak{h}^{r_L}) = \hat{e}(G, H) \quad \wedge$$
$$Y = K_{base}^{r_0} \quad \wedge$$
$$\tau = \mathcal{G}(event)^L.$$

The details of Π_τ are shown in Appendix A.
4. Submit the survey data m with its signature $\sigma = \left(Y, W, \{S_i\}_{i \in [\ell]}, \{P_j\}_{j \in [t]}, \tau, \Pi_\tau\right)$ to the SC.

Validity Checking. Upon received the survey, the SC checks its validity. The checking consists of two parts. In the first part, it verifies the signature to see whether it is generated by a qualified user. In the second part, it checks whether this user has submitted another survey before. Note that the user is not allowed to submit more than one survey, no matter the content is the same or not.

Details: Upon received the data m and the signature σ, the SC executes the followings:

1. Signature Verification:
   (a) Convert the policy Υ such that $\Upsilon(\mathcal{A}) = 1$ to its corresponding monotone span program $\mathcal{M} \in \mathbb{Z}_p^{\ell \times t}$, with row labeling function $u : [\ell] \to \mathbb{A}$.
   (b) Compute $\mu = \mathcal{H}(m || \Upsilon)$ and check if $\hat{e}(W, A_0) \stackrel{?}{=} \hat{e}(Y, h_0)$ and

$$\prod_{i=1}^{\ell} \hat{e}(S_i, (A_j B_j^{u(i)})^{\mathcal{M}_{i,j}}) \stackrel{?}{=}$$

$$\begin{cases} \hat{e}(Y, h_1)\hat{e}(Cg^\mu, P_1), & \text{for } j = 1. \\ \hat{e}(Cg^\mu, P_j), & \text{for } j > 1. \end{cases}$$

   (c) Checks if Π_τ is a valid proof. The verification of Π_τ is also shown in Appendix A.
   If all equalities hold and the proof is correct, it outputs ACCEPT and proceeds to the second part. Otherwise it outputs REJECT.
2. Double Submission Checking: The SC extracts τ from σ and checks its database whether any other signatures for this survey *event* also contain the the same τ. If yes, that means the user has double submissions. It then outputs REJECT. Otherewise, it outputs ACCEPT and stores the data and signature into its database.

5.2   Security Analysis

To explain the security of our online survey system, we first present our design philosophy in details. As discussed in Section 2, the primitive attribute-based signature (ABS) is the closest solution to our problem. Thus, it is natural to construct our system from an existing ABS. An ABS is a tuple of five algorithms, namely, TSetup, ASetup, AttrGen, Sign, Ver, which are briefly reviewed below for completeness. Interested readers may refer to [11] for their formal definitions.

- TSetup is responsible for system parameters creation.
- ASetup is the process of creating the master key of the attribute authority.
- AttrGen is invoked to certify the attribute of a user.
- Sign is responsible for signature generations.
- Ver is responsible for signature verifications.

It is straightforward to observe the correspondence of an ABS and an online survey system. The Setup procedure of our system consists of TSetup and ASetup. User Key generation procedure corresponds to AttrGen. For survey submission, the user submits the survey response together with an ABS-signature generated from Sign. Finally, the validity checking is realized by verifying the ABS-signature on the survey response, that is, an invocation of the algorithm Ver.

The security properties of any ABS, namely, unforgeability and perfect privacy would protect the online survey system from unforgeability, anonymity and linkability attack. Unfortunately, such a system will be vulnerable under unlinkability attack. The reason is obvious, since an authorized user can submit the survey response together with a freshly generated attribute-based signature repeatedly without being detected. This lead to our approach, which is to restrict the number of times a signing key can be used for each survey *event*.

Our idea is to require that for each signature, the signer is required to attach with a piece of information called tag, which is a pseudo-random function on input of *event* and a secret that is known only to the user. If the user is in possession of one single secret, for each event, he/she can only create one tag without being detected. At the same time, since the secret is known only to the user, no one will be able to trace this user given tag.

The final issue is to bind the user secret to his/her signing key. With this binding, one authorized user can only to use the specific signing key. We introduce the technique of "certified signing key". Specifically, for each attribute-based signing key issued to an authorized user, the attribute authority also generates a standard signature on the signing key together with the commitment of the user secret. This standard signature is used to certify that this specific signing key is generated directly from the attribute authority and binds the signing key to this specific user secret. At the same time, the user secret is not revealed to the attribute authority due to the hiding property of the commitment scheme.

Finally, whenever the user uses his/her signing key, a zero-knowledge proof will be attached. The zero-knowledge proof serves as an evidence that the attribute-based signature is created from a "certified" signing key and that the tag is generated correct from *event* and the committed user secret.

Notes on Our Practical System. Our online survey system is built following the above framework using the ABS from [11]. The standard signature scheme used to certify the signing key together with the committed user secret is the signature scheme from [15]. The user secret is just a random element from $L \in \mathbb{Z}_p$ for some prime p and that the commitment scheme is the well-known Pedersen commitment. The pseudo-random function on the user secret and *event* was defined as: $\mathcal{F} : L, event \mapsto \mathcal{G}(event)^L$.

It can be seen easily that the user secret key $(K_{base}, K_0, \{K_u\}_{u \in \mathcal{A}}, R, S, T, L, r_L)$ in our system can be classified into three groups.

1. ABS signing key. $(K_{base}, K_0, \{K_u\}_{u \in \mathcal{A}})$ is exactly a signing key from the ABS scheme due to [11]
2. User secret: (L). The Pedersen commitment of the user secret is $C_L = \mathfrak{g}^L \mathfrak{h}^{r_L}$ and thus r_L is the randomness used in the commitment.

3. Certification of the signing key. (R, S, T, L) is the standard signature (of the scheme [15]) on the tuple (K_{base}, C_L).

Note that we have simplified the process of "certified signing key" by signing K_{base} and C_L since each signing key is uniquely determined by the value K_{base}.

The role of the zero-knowledge proof Π_τ in the survey submission can be explained easily after this classification. It states that the generator of the ABS signature is in possession of a user secret L and that the tag τ is created correctly from τ. In addition, the generator of the signature is creating this signature from a "certified signing key" (i.e., he/she is in possession of a standard signature (R, S, T, L) on the tuple (K_{base}, C_L) and that K_{base} is used in this ABS signature creation and C_L is a commitment of L).

Now we are ready to give a security argument based on the threat model defined in Section 4.3.

1. **Security against Unforgeability Attack.** Each survey response has to be accompanied with a properly created attribute-based signature. In our system only authorized users are issued the signing keys. If the ABS scheme from [11] is unforgeable, our system is secure against unforgeability attack.
2. **Security against Anonymity Attack.** The only information related to the survey participant is the ABS signature, the zero-knowledge proof Π_τ and the tag τ. Due to the perfect privacy of the ABS scheme from [11], the ABS part leaks no information about the actual participant. The zero-knowledge proof Π_τ (details are given in the Appendix), a standard non-interactive Σ-protocol, leaks no information due to its zero-knowledgeness (in the random oracle model). Finally, the tag τ itself is created from $\mathcal{G}(event)^L$. Since L is never shown in plain and is protected by the perfect hiding property of the Pedersen commitment, it again leaks no information about the survey participant. In fact, our construction provides a stronger level of privacy. Specifically, if the user never participate in the same survey more than once, his participation across different surveys are not relatable under the decisional Diffie-Hellman assumption. That is, given $event_1, event_2, \mathcal{G}(event_1)^L$ and a value τ^*, it is computationally hard to tell if $\tau^* = \mathcal{G}(event_2)^L$ or not. Recall that our system is built on bilinear groups with pairing $\hat{e} : \mathbb{G}_1 \times \mathbb{G}_2 \to \mathbb{G}_T$ such that the DDH problem is hard in both $\mathbb{G}_1$ and $\mathbb{G}_2$.
3. **Security against Linkability Attack.** Each authorized user in our system is given only one "certified signing key" only and thus for each survey, he or she can only generate one unique tag τ. This is due to the fact that the non-interactive zero-knowledge proof Π_τ is sound (i.e. the attacker cannot produce a fake proof) and the signature from [15] is unforgeable (i.e. the attacker cannot produce a fake certified signing key).
4. **Unlinkability (for different users) Attack.** Two surveys are linked if they share the same tag τ. In order to use a tag, the attacker has to produce the zero-knowledge proof Π_τ. That is, the attacker either produces a fake proof or has to know the value of L that is used to generate τ. The former

is computationally impossible under the soundness property of the zero-knowledge proof Π_τ. The latter is computationally impossible under the discrete logarithm assumption.

5.3 A Practical Example

Here we briefly describe how to deploy our system in a company. Assume there is a multinational corporation ABC, which is working in the cosmetics business arena. The human resources department (HR) acts as the AA to carry out the **Setup** phase. When a new staff joins this corporation, the HR issues his/her secret key by executing **User Key Generation** phase. The attribute set may contain the following items: sex, marital status, location, date of birth and department. Suppose the marketing department of ABC intends to introduce a new night cream product into its Japanese market product line. Part of the feasibility study involves conducting an online survey to find out the preference of Japanese women in the Japanese market. As a preliminary step, the marketing department would like to conduct the survey to the staff of ABC before gathering responses from the public. To do this, firstly the marketing department will act as the SC. In this scenario, the targets are very clear, namely Japanese female staffs. All the Japanese female staffs can use their secret key to sign the completed online form by using **Survey Submission** algorithm using the attribute "female" and "Japanese". The signed and completed form may be sent back to the server through an anonymous channel. The marketing department executes **Validity Checking** to check the validity of each survey. It discards any survey which has not been signed by the attribute "female" and "Japanese", and those who are linked (that means duplicated copies).

5.4 Performance Analysis

Generic Analysis. We give the performance analysis of our concrete instantiation described in Section 5.1. We first give a generic analysis, which varies for different attribute sets and signing policies. We only count the time required for exponentiation and pairing. Other operations such as hashing, group addition, integer addition/multiplication etc. are insignificant compared with exponentiation and pairing. For exponentiation, we further optimize for those bases which

Table 2. Operations required

	ASetup	AttrGen	Sign	Verify
Group $\mathbb{G}_1$ / $\mathbb{G}_2$ exponentiation (pre-processed)	$6 + 2\,t_{max}$	3	12	0
Group $\mathbb{G}_1$ / $\mathbb{G}_2$ exponentiation (no pre-processed)	0	$2 + |\mathcal{A}|$	$2 + 2\,\ell + t\ell$	$6 + t\ell$
Group $\mathbb{G}_T$ exponentiation (pre-processed)	0	0	7	7
Group $\mathbb{G}_T$ exponentiation (no pre-processed)	0	0	0	2
Pairing (1 element is a constant)	0	0	0	$5 + t$
Pairing (both elements are not constant)	0	0	0	$2 + t\ell$

are constant. It allows the use of some pre-processed data for faster computation. For pairing, we also optimize for those such that one of the pairing elements is a constant. We put our analyzed result in Table 2. We use t_{max} to represent the maximum width of the monotone span program, $|\mathcal{A}|$ to represent the number of attributes a user has, t and ℓ to represent the width and length of the monotone span program converted from the signing claim policy respectively.

Concrete Example. Next we analyze the efficiency of our scheme using the simulation result from jPBC [16] for the following devices:

- A desktop equiped with Intel(R) Core(TM)2 Quad CPU Q6600 2.40GHz, 3 GB RAM, Ubuntu 10.04 as the simulation device.

We measured the performance using a 160-bit secret key in elliptic curve cryptosystem (ECC). It is generally believed that a 160-bit secret key in ECC provides stronger security than a 1024-bit key in RSA. We use the example described in Section 5.3 to illustrate the exact running time and communication overhead. In the example, we assume the following attributes:

- Sex: {Male}, {Female}
- Marriage Status: {Single}, {Married}, {Divoice}
- Office Location: {United States}, {United Kingdom}, {Australia}, {Japan}, {China}
- Year of Bith: {≤ 1960}, {1961 − 1970}, {1971 − 1980}, {1981 − 1990}, {> 1990}
- Department: {Sales}, {Finance}, {Logistic}, {Human Resources}

Now it plans to carry out some surveys based on the following different cases:

1. All staffs who are based in Japan.
2. All Female staffs who are Married.
3. All Male staffs who are based in Australia and working in the Sales department.
4. All Female staffs who are Single, born after 1990 and based in Japan.
5. All Male staffs who are Married, based in United States, born between 1971-1980 are working in the Finance department.
6. All staffs who are based in either Australia or China and working in the Sales department.
7. All Female staffs who are based in United Kingdom and working in either Finance or Human Resources department.

Table 3. Performance

Case	Size of APK	Ur. Key Gen. running time	Size of se. key	Survey Subm. running time	Size of signature	Val. Check running time
1				127.052	480	225.915
2				182.828	520	333.185
3				350.156	560	506.893
4	880	138.667	220	517.484	600	747.12
5				721.996	640	1053.839
6				294.38	540	399.65
7				443.116	580	606.631

The simulation result is shown in Table 3. The unit for running time is ms while the unit for public parameter APK, secret key and signature is $byte$.

6   Other Applications

We note that the protocol described in this paper is specifically designed for online survey systems. However, we do not eliminate the possibility to apply our scheme (or modified version) in other environments if they find it suitable. We list some of the potential applications:

Electronic Voting (E-Voting) [17–22] is introduced to replace existing punched-card and mechanical voting systems. With e-voting, one can cast ballots from the comfort of his/her home or from mobile devices like cellular phones or iPads, and this is a great convenience to people, especially those disabled and aging population. On the other hand, e-voting also introduces a wide range of privacy and security issues. As an example, tallying authorities want to be assured that a ballot is from a voter satisfying certain requirements and any eligible voter can vote only once (to eliminate double-voting), but due to privacy concerns voters want to prevent tallying authorities from telling who they are.

One of the solutions is using linkable ring signatures [23–29]. Like normal ring signatures, linkable ring signatures provide signer anonymity but one can verify whether or not two ring signatures were signed using the same key. In the scenario of e-voting, the voter first creates a group of eligible voters and then produces a linkable ring signature on the ballot. Such a signature ensures the tallying authority that the ballot is from an eligible person in the group but does not tell who the actual voter is, due to the anonymity of ring signatures. Any double voting will be detected since the signature is linkable.

E-voting based on linkable ring signature has demonstrated several practice-friendly properties, but a closer look discovers a subtle issue to be addressed, namely how to tell if someone else is eligible for the voting when one forms a group of eligible persons. This issue can be easily solved in some cases, e.g., "any female staff is eligible for voting", but not if the requirements include "anyone with monthly income less than \$1,000". It is very unlikely that such privacy information is publicly known, or an entity wants to share it with others. In such cases, it would be difficult to form a group with a large number of eligible persons, and this could put the privacy of the actual voter at risk.

Another disadvantage of linkable ring signature based e-voting system is the requirement for voters to know the identities or public keys of all eligible voters, especially in the case when the number of voters is very large. It is certainly a desirable choice if one can vote anonymously without the need to find other eligible persons, and this reminds us of attribute-based signatures. Each entity in attributed-based signatures is given a private key according to the attributes he/she possesses. One can use the private key to sign the ballot, and the result-ing signature only shows that it is from a person satisfying certain attributes (e.g., the voting requirements). Compared with ring signatures, the advantage of attribute-based signatures is that there is no need to form a group of eligible persons, and thus issues like "Does Alice satisfy voting requirements?" are eliminated. However, we still need to detect double-voting if attribute-based signatures are used in e-voting, and this would require the linkability in ABS.

<u>Smart Grid</u> [30] is a form of electricity network utilizing modern digital technology. The most distinctive feature in smart grid is its two-way capabilities for data communication: Not only the grid controller can issue commands to intelligent devices, consumers and devices can also send data to grid controllers. This feature brings controllers and consumers with an in-depth insight of energy usage, which would lead to a more efficient electricity system.

Attribute-based signature seems to be a promising approach to address the aforementioned issue. Each entity is given a private key according to the attributes he/she possesses. One can sign the energy consumption data using his/her own private key, and such a signature can convince the service provider that the data is from a person satisfying certain attributes, without the need to seek other consumers with similar attributes. It is a natural requirement that each data is counted only once in statistical reports, and an attribute-based signature scheme with linkability will better suit that situation. More importantly, smart grid usually comprises big data for analysis. Attribute-based protocol allows a constant complexity for authentication, which is independent to the number of users in the system. Thus it is particularly suitable in this scenario.

<u>Vehicular Ad Hoc Networks (VANETs)</u> allow wireless communications between vehicles and roadside infrastructures. Chen *et al.* [31] addressed the problem of reliability of information exchange between vehicles. Suppose that a car driver Bob receives a message from another vehicle reporting some traffic jam a few miles away, he has no idea whether the message is true or not. At the beginning, he attempts to ignore it. But shortly after that he receives several messages (say n) reporting the same traffic jam. If this number n is a reasonably large number and these messages are sent by n different vehicles, this information is likely to be true, as it seems unlikely that any n vehicles would collude to lie. However, all these messages are sent anonymously due to privacy concern, how can Bob find out whether n received messages are sent by n different legitimate vehicles without discovering the identities of these vehicles? The authors proposed a solution using Threshold Anonymous Announcement (TAA) service.

TAA allows every vehicle to obtain a token from a trusted party. One may broadcast an anonymous message to other vehicles signed by this token so that anyone received this broadcast message may know that it is from a legitimate vehicle yet the identity is unknown. At the same time, TAA provides linkability. That is, if a vehicle sends the same message twice, the receiver will be able to know these two messages are sent by the same vehicle. So it is easy to distinguish whether n messages are from n different vehicles. However, their scheme only provides linkability to the same message from the same signer. If the signer slightly changes the message, e.g., change from "The city area is very congested now." to "Now the city area is very congested.", they appear as two different messages and thus cannot be linked. That is, a receiver cannot distinguish whether these two messages are sent by the same signer.

Using linkable ring signature may resolve this issue, because linkable ring signature provides event-based linkability. In a single event (e.g., traffic congestion announcement in the city area), any two signatures generated by the same singer will be linked, no matter the two signed messages are the same or not. Nevertheless, linkable ring signature requires the signer to know the identities of all legitimate vehicles in the area, which is impossible. An event linkable attribute-based signature provides a better solution because it does not require anyone to know other legitimate vehicles, while providing event-based (instead of message-based) linkability. Simultaneously anonymity of the signer is also preserved.

7 Conclusion

In this paper, we provided a new insight to preserve accuracy and privacy in online survey systems simultaneously. The new insight comes from our proposed system. We proved the security of it. The performance analysis is also given to show that our system is efficient and practical. In addition to online survey systems, we further suggested several other applications that can make use of our new system, including e-voting, smart-grid and vehicular ad hoc networks. We believe our system is particular suitable for handling big data as the complexity remains constant, regardless to the number of users.

References

1. Kwik Survey: KwikSurveys: Offical Free online survey and questionnaire tool, http://www.kwiksurveys.com/
2. My3q: FREE Online Survey Questionnaire Research by my3q, http://www.my3q.com/
3. Survey Monkey: SurveyMonkey: Free online survey software and questionnaire tool, http://www.surveymonkey.com/
4. Shamir, A.: Identity-Based Cryptosystems and Signature Schemes. In: Blakely, G.R., Chaum, D. (eds.) Advances in Cryptology - CRYPTO 1984. LNCS, vol. 196, pp. 47–53. Springer, Heidelberg (1985)
5. Rivest, R.L., Shamir, A., Tauman, Y.: How to Leak a Secret. In: Boyd, C. (ed.) ASIACRYPT 2001. LNCS, vol. 2248, pp. 552–565. Springer, Heidelberg (2001)
6. Boyen, X.: Mesh Signatures. In: Naor, M. (ed.) EUROCRYPT 2007. LNCS, vol. 4515, pp. 210–227. Springer, Heidelberg (2007)
7. Chaum, D., van Heyst, E.: Group Signatures. In: Davies, D.W. (ed.) Advances in Cryptology - EUROCRYPT 1991. LNCS, vol. 547, pp. 257–265. Springer, Heidelberg (1991)
8. Ateniese, G., Camenisch, J., Joye, M., Tsudik, G.: A Practical and Provably Secure Coalition-Resistant Group Signature Scheme. In: Bellare, M. (ed.) CRYPTO 2000. LNCS, vol. 1880, pp. 255–270. Springer, Heidelberg (2000)
9. Shahandashti, S.F., Safavi-Naini, R.: Threshold Attribute-Based Signatures and Their Application to Anonymous Credential Systems. In: Preneel, B. (ed.) AFRICACRYPT 2009. LNCS, vol. 5580, pp. 198–216. Springer, Heidelberg (2009)

10. Li, J., Au, M.H., Susilo, W., Xie, D., Ren, K.: Attribute-Based Signature and Its Applications. In: Feng, D., Basin, D.A., Liu, P. (eds.) ASIACCS, pp. 60–69. ACM (2010)

11. Maji, H.K., Prabhakaran, M., Rosulek, M.: Attribute-Based Signatures. In: Kiayias, A. (ed.) CT-RSA 2011. LNCS, vol. 6558, pp. 376–392. Springer, Heidelberg (2011)

12. Okamoto, T., Takashima, K.: Efficient Attribute-Based Signatures for Non-Monotone Predicates in the Standard Model. In: Catalano, D., Fazio, N., Gennaro, R., Nicolosi, A. (eds.) PKC 2011. LNCS, vol. 6571, pp. 35–52. Springer, Heidelberg (2011)

13. Okamoto, T.: Receipt-Free Electronic Voting Schemes for Large Scale Elections. In: Christianson, B., Crispo, B., Lomas, M., Roe, M. (eds.) Security Protocols 1997. LNCS, vol. 1361, pp. 25–35. Springer, Heidelberg (1998)

14. Juels, A., Catalano, D., Jakobsson, M.: Coercion-resistant electronic elections. In: WPES 2005, pp. 61–70. ACM Press (2005)

15. Abe, M., Groth, J., Haralambiev, K., Ohkubo, M.: Optimal Structure-Preserving Signatures in Asymmetric Bilinear Groups. In: Rogaway, P. (ed.) CRYPTO 2011. LNCS, vol. 6841, pp. 649–666. Springer, Heidelberg (2011)

16. Lynn, B.: The Java Pairing Based Cryptography Library, jPBC (2010), http://libeccio.dia.unisa.it/projects/jpbc/

17. Chaum, D.: Untraceable Electronic Mail, Return Addresses, and Digital Pseudonyms. Communications of the ACM 24(2), 84–88 (1981)

18. Fujioka, A., Okamoto, T., Ohta, K.: A Practical Secret Voting Scheme for Large Scale Election. In: Zheng, Y., Seberry, J. (eds.) AUSCRYPT 1992. LNCS, vol. 718, pp. 244–260. Springer, Heidelberg (1993)

19. Benaloh, J., Tuinstra, D.: Receipt-Free Secret-Ballot Elections (Extended Abstract). In: STOC 1994: Proceedings of the Twenty-sixth Annual ACM Symposium on Theory of Computing, pp. 544–553. ACM Press (1994)

20. Hirt, M., Sako, K.: Efficient Receipt-Free Voting Based on Homomorphic Encryption. In: Preneel, B. (ed.) EUROCRYPT 2000. LNCS, vol. 1807, pp. 539–556. Springer, Heidelberg (2000)

21. Groth, J.: A Verifiable Secret Shuffle of Homomorphic Encryptions. In: Desmedt, Y.G. (ed.) PKC 2003. LNCS, vol. 2567, pp. 145–160. Springer, Heidelberg (2002)

22. Liu, J.K., Wong, D.S.: A Restricted Multi-show Credential System and its Application on E-Voting. In: Deng, R.H., Bao, F., Pang, H., Zhou, J. (eds.) ISPEC 2005. LNCS, vol. 3439, pp. 268–279. Springer, Heidelberg (2005)

23. Liu, J.K., Wei, V.K., Wong, D.S.: Linkable Spontaneous Anonymous Group Signature for Ad Hoc Groups (Extended Abstract). In: Wang, H., Pieprzyk, J., Varadharajan, V. (eds.) ACISP 2004. LNCS, vol. 3108, pp. 325–335. Springer, Heidelberg (2004)

24. Liu, J.K., Wong, D.S.: Enhanced security models and a generic construction approach for linkable ring signature. Int. J. Found. Comput. Sci. 17(6), 1403–1422 (2006)

25. Au, M.H., Liu, J.K., Susilo, W., Yuen, T.H.: Certificate based (linkable) ring signature. In: Dawson, E., Wong, D.S. (eds.) ISPEC 2007. LNCS, vol. 4464, pp. 79–92. Springer, Heidelberg (2007)

26. Chow, S.S.M., Liu, J.K., Wong, D.S.: Robust Receipt-Free Election System with Ballot Secrecy and Verifiability. In: NDSS. The Internet Society (2008)

27. Yuen, T.H., Liu, J.K., Au, M.H., Susilo, W., Zhou, J.: Efficient linkable and/or threshold ring signature without random oracles. Comput. J. 56(4), 407–421 (2013)

28. Au, M.H., Liu, J.K., Susilo, W., Yuen, T.H.: Secure id-based linkable and revocable-iff-linked ring signature with constant-size construction. Theor. Comput. Sci. 469, 1–14 (2013)
29. Liu, J.K., Au, M.H., Susilo, W., Zhou, J.: Linkable ring signature with unconditional anonymity. IEEE Trans. Knowl. Data Eng. 26(1), 157–165 (2014)
30. of Standards, N.I., Technology: NIST IR 7628: Guidelines for Smart Grid Cyber Security. Technical report (2010), http://csrc.nist.gov/publications/PubsNISTIRs.html
31. Chen, L., Ng, S.L., Wang, G.: Threshold Anonymous Announcement in VANETs. IEEE Journal on Selected Areas in Communications 29(3), 605–615 (2011)

A   Details of Π_τ

Π_τ can be constructed in the random oracle model using 19 elements.

Let $\mathfrak{g}_1, \mathfrak{g}_2$ be generators of $\mathbb{G}_1$ and $\mathfrak{h}_1, \mathfrak{h}_2$ be generators of $\mathbb{G}_2$. They can be regarded as part of TPK. The signer randomly chooses $x_1, \ldots, x_6 \in_R \mathbb{Z}_p$, computes: $X_1 = \mathfrak{g}_1^{x_1}\mathfrak{g}_2^{x_2}$, $X_2 = R\mathfrak{g}_1^{x_2}$, $X_3 = S\mathfrak{g}_1^{x_3}$, $X_4 = \mathfrak{g}_1^{x_4}\mathfrak{g}_2^{x_5}$, $X_5 = K_{base}\mathfrak{g}_1^{x_5}$, $Y_1 = T\mathfrak{h}_1^{x_6}$. The signer also randomly chooses $\rho_1, \ldots, \rho_{13} \in_R \mathbb{Z}_p$ and computes: $\mathfrak{T}_1 = \mathfrak{g}_1^{\rho_1}\mathfrak{g}_2^{\rho_2}$, $\mathfrak{T}_2 = \mathfrak{g}_1^{\rho_4}\mathfrak{g}_2^{\rho_5}$, $\mathfrak{T}_3 = X_1^{-\rho_6}\mathfrak{g}_1^{\rho_7}\mathfrak{g}_2^{\rho_8}$, $\mathfrak{T}_4 = X_4^{-\rho_{11}}\mathfrak{g}_1^{\rho_9}\mathfrak{g}_2^{\rho_{10}}$, $\mathfrak{T}_5 = \hat{e}(\mathfrak{g}_1, V)^{\rho_2} \cdot \hat{e}(\mathfrak{g}_1, H)^{\rho_3} \cdot \hat{e}(\mathfrak{g}_1, W)^{\rho_5}$, $\mathfrak{T}_6 = \hat{e}(X_2, \mathfrak{h}_1)^{-\rho_6} \cdot \hat{e}(\mathfrak{g}_1, Y_1)^{-\rho_2} \cdot \hat{e}(\mathfrak{g}_1, \mathfrak{h}_1)^{\rho_8} \cdot \hat{e}(U, \mathfrak{g})^{\rho_{12}} \cdot \hat{e}(U, \mathfrak{h})^{\rho_{13}}$, $\mathfrak{T}_7 = X_5^{\rho_{11}}\mathfrak{g}_1^{-\rho_{10}}$, $\mathfrak{T}_8 = \mathcal{G}(event)^{\rho_{12}}$. Then, the signer computes $k = \mathcal{H}(\mathfrak{T}_1 \ldots || \mathfrak{T}_8 || X_1 || \ldots || X_5 || Y_1 || m || event || \Upsilon)$ and computes: $z_1 = \rho_1 - kx_1$, $z_2 = \rho_2 - kx_2$, $z_3 = \rho_3 - kx_3$, $z_4 = \rho_4 - kx_4$, $z_5 = \rho_5 - kx_5$, $z_6 = \rho_6 - kx_6$, $z_7 = \rho_7 - kx_1x_6$, $z_8 = \rho_8 - kx_2x_6$, $z_9 = \rho_9 - kx_4r_0$, $z_{10} = \rho_{10} - kx_5r_0$, $z_{11} = \rho_{11} - kr_0$, $z_{12} = \rho_{12} - kL$, $z_{13} = \rho_{13} - kr_L$. Parse Π_τ as $(k, X_1, \ldots, X_5, Y_1, z_1, \ldots, z_{12})$. It consists of 5 elements in $\mathbb{G}_1$, one element in $\mathbb{G}_2$ and 13 elements of $\mathbb{Z}_p$.

To verify Π_τ, the verifier computes: $\mathfrak{T}_1' = X_1^k\mathfrak{g}_1^{z_1}\mathfrak{g}_2^{z_2}$, $\mathfrak{T}_2' = X_4^k\mathfrak{g}_1^{z_4}\mathfrak{g}_2^{z_5}$, $\mathfrak{T}_3' = X_1^{-z_6}\mathfrak{g}_1^{z_7}\mathfrak{g}_2^{z_8}$, $\mathfrak{T}_4' = X_4^{-z_{11}}\mathfrak{g}_1^{z_9}\mathfrak{g}_2^{z_{10}}$, $\mathfrak{T}_5' = \left(\frac{\hat{e}(X_2, V)\hat{e}(X_3, H)\hat{e}(X_5, W)}{\hat{e}(G, Z)}\right)^k \cdot \hat{e}(\mathfrak{g}_1, V)^{z_2} \cdot \hat{e}(\mathfrak{g}_1, H)^{z_3} \cdot \hat{e}(\mathfrak{g}_1, W)^{z_5}$, $\mathfrak{T}_6' = \left(\frac{\hat{e}(G, H)}{\hat{e}(X_2, Y_1)}\right)^k \hat{e}(X_2, \mathfrak{h}_1)^{-z_6} \hat{e}(\mathfrak{g}_1, Y_1)^{-z_2} \cdot \hat{e}(\mathfrak{g}_1, \mathfrak{h}_1)^{z_8} \hat{e}(U, \mathfrak{g})^{z_{12}} \hat{e}(U, \mathfrak{h})^{z_{13}}$, $\mathfrak{T}_7' = Y^k X_5^{z_{11}}\mathfrak{g}_1^{-z_{10}}$, $\mathfrak{T}_8' = \tau^k \mathcal{G}(event)^{z_{12}}$. Accept the proof if and only if:

$$k \overset{?}{=} \mathcal{H}(\mathfrak{T}_1' \ldots || \mathfrak{T}_8' || X_1 || \ldots || X_5 || Y_1 || m || event || \Upsilon).$$

Software Countermeasures for Control Flow Integrity of Smart Card C Codes

Jean-François Lalande[1,3], Karine Heydemann[2], and Pascal Berthomé[3]

[1] Inria, Supélec, CNRS, Univ. Rennes 1, IRISA, UMR 6074
35576 Cesson-Sévigné, France
jean-francois.lalande@insa-cvl.fr
[2] Sorbonne Universités, UPMC, Univ. Paris 06, CNRS, LIP6, UMR 7606
75005 Paris, France
karine.heydemann@lip6.fr
[3] INSA Centre Val de Loire, Univ. Orléans, LIFO, EA 4022
18022 Bourges, France
pascal.berthome@insa-cvl.fr

Abstract. Fault attacks can target smart card programs in order to disrupt an execution and gain an advantage over the data or the embedded functionalities. Among all possible attacks, control flow attacks aim at disrupting the normal execution flow. Identifying harmful control flow attacks as well as designing countermeasures at software level are tedious and tricky for developers. In this paper, we propose a methodology to detect harmful intra-procedural jump attacks at source code level and to automatically inject formally-proven countermeasures. The proposed software countermeasures defeat 100% of attacks that jump over at least two C source code statements or beyond. Experiments show that the resulting code is also hardened against unexpected function calls and jump attacks at assembly level.

Keywords: control flow integrity, fault attacks, smart card, source level.

1 Introduction

Smart cards or more generally secure elements are essential building blocks for many security-critical applications. They are used for securing host applications and sensitive data such as cryptographic keys, biometric data, pin counters, etc. Malicious users aim to get access to these secrets by performing attacks on the secure elements. Fault attacks consists in disrupting the circuit's behavior by using a laser beam or applying voltage, clock or electromagnetic glitches [5,6,24]. Their goal is to alter the correct progress of the algorithm and, by analyzing the deviation of the corrupted behavior with respect to the original one, to retrieve the secret information [14]. For java card, fault attacks target particular components of the virtual machine [3,4,9].

Many protections have therefore been proposed to counteract attacks. Fault detection is generally based on spatial, temporal or information redundancy at hardware or software level. In java card enabled smart cards, software components of the virtual machine can perform security checks [18,20,10].

M. Kutyłowski and J. Vaidya (Eds.): ESORICS 2014, Part II, LNCS 8713, pp. 200–218, 2014.

In practice, developers of security-critical applications often manually add countermeasures into an application code. This operation requires knowledge about the target code vulnerabilities. Both these tasks are time-consuming with direct impact on the certification of the product. One harmful consequence of fault attacks is control flow disruption which may bypass some implemented countermeasures. It is difficult for programmers to investigate all possible control flow disruption in order to detect sensitive parts of the code and then investigate how to add countermeasures inside these sensitive parts. Moreover, secure smart cards have strong security requirements that have to be certified by an independent qualified entity before being placed on the market. Certification can rely on a review of source code and the implemented software countermeasures. The effectiveness of software security countermeasures is then guaranteed by the use of a certified compiler [21]. Injecting control flow integrity checks at compile time would require to certify the modified compiler. To avoid this difficult and expensive task, countermeasures must be designed and inserted at a high code level.

In this paper, we propose a full methodology 1) to detect harmful attacks that disrupt the control flow of native C programs executed on a secure element and 2) to automatically inject formally verified countermeasures into the code. In the first step of our methodology, the set of harmful attacks is determined through an exhaustive search relying on a classification of attack effects from a functional point of view. The identified harmful attacks can be visualized spatially in order to identify the affected functions and to precisely locate the corresponding sensitive code regions. Following our methodology, a tool automatically injects countermeasures into the code to be protected without any direct intervention of a developer. The countermeasure scheme proposed in this paper operates at function level. Countermeasures rely on counters that are incremented and checked throughout execution enabling detection of any attack that disrupts control flow by not executing at least two adjacent statements of the code. The effectiveness of the proposed countermeasure scheme has been formally verified: any attack that jumps over more than two C statements is detected. This is confirmed by experimental results for three well-known encryption algorithms and additionally results show that 1) attacks are much more difficult to perform on the secured code and that 2) attacks trying to call an unexpected function are detected.

The paper is organized as follows: Section 2 discusses related work. Section 3 gives an overview of our methodology detecting application weaknesses and automatically securing an application code. Section 4 details the detection of weaknesses and visualization. Section 5 and 6 respectively presents the countermeasures for hardening a code against control flow attacks and the formal approach used for verifying their correctness. Section 7 presents experimental results.

2   Related Work

This section discusses work related to fault models before presenting previously proposed countermeasures for smart card and control flow integrity.

2.1   Fault Models

Countermeasures are necessarily designed with respect to a fault model specifying the type of faults an attacker is able to carry out [27]. Elaborating a fault model requires analysis of the consequences of physical attacks and modeling them at the desired level (architectural level, assembly code level, source code level). Consequences of fault attacks, at program level, include the processing of corrupted values by the program, a corrupted program control flow or a corrupted program as a result of changed instructions. In this paper, we focus on attacks that impact control flow of native C programs.

Several works [24,2] have shown that attacks can induce instruction replacements. For example, electromagnetic pulse injections can induce a clock glitch on the bus during transmission of instruction from the Flash memory resulting in an instruction replacement [24]. Such an instruction replacement can provoke a control flow disruption in the two following cases:

1. The evaluation of a condition is altered, by the replacement of one instruction involved in the computation, causing the wrong branch to be taken. Inverting the condition of a conditional branch instruction by only replacing the opcode in the instruction encoding has the same consequence.
2. The replacement of a whole instruction by a jump at any location of the program. The executed instruction becomes a jump to an unexpected target [9,24]. The same effect is obtained if the target address of a jump is changed by corrupting the instruction encoding or, in case of indirect jump, if computation of the target address is disrupted. This also happens if the program counter becomes the destination operand of the replacing instruction, *e.g.* an ALU instruction such a `PC = PC +/- cst` which are the most likely to succeed into a correct jump.

In this paper, we consider jump attacks as described in the second case just above.

2.2   Code Securing and Control Flow Securing

Code securing techniques can be applied to the whole application or only to specific parts. Securing only sensitive code regions requires to know weaknesses which need to be strengthened for a given fault model. When considering some convenient fault models or when varying input, tractable static analysis, such as taint analysis, can be used to infer the impact of a fault on control flow [12] or to detect missing checks [29]. To the best of our knowledge, no previous work has considered a jump attack fault model probably due to its complexity: all possible jumps from one point of the program to another point have to be considered.

Protections against control flow attacks depend then on the nature of the attacks. If the evaluation of a condition involved in a conditional branch is disrupted at runtime, recovering techniques must strengthen the condition computation. This can be achieved by inserting redundancy and appropriate checks [5]. Countermeasures designed for ensuring control flow integrity or code integrity often rely on signature techniques or on checks to ensure the validity of accesses to the instruction memory or of the target address of jump instructions.

Signature techniques typically rely on an offline computation of a checksum for each basic block. At runtime, the protected code recomputes the checksum of the basic block being executed and compares with the expected result. Dedicated hardware [28,15] can be used to compute signatures dynamically. However, solutions requiring hardware modification are unpractical for smart cards. Several works proposed to integrate the checks at software level [26,13,16]. Oh et al. [26] only checks the destinations of all jumps. Bletsch et al. [8] focus on return-oriented attacks. Abadi et al. [1] proposed a broader method for ensuring control flow integrity which checks for both the source and the destination of jumps. However, this approach relies on a new machine instruction.

For javacard enabled smart card, software components of the virtual machine can perform security checks. Basic block signature computations and checks can then be carried out by the virtual machine, as proposed by [18]. A transition automaton, in which each state corresponds to a basic block and each transition corresponds to allowed control flow, can also be built by analyzing the bytecode [10]. Calls to `setState()`, added to the source code, instruct the virtual machine to check the integrity of the control flow by comparing the current state with the allowed ones according to the automaton. The virtual machine can also check the validity of the bytecode address to avoid the execution of any bytecode stored outside the applet currently being executed [20]. However, a small jump inside the allowed bytecode, for example inside a function, would not be detected and might have serious consequences for security. These java card approaches rely on the ability to perform runtime checks during the interpretation of the bytecode. For native programs, it is mandatory to include any software countermeasure inside the code, as proposed in [26,13,16].

Approaches that verify the direction or the target address of branches or jumps only harden the control flow integrity at basic blocks boundaries. This is not sufficient to cover physical faults that cause an unconditional jump from an instruction inside a basic block to another instruction inside another basic block. The approach proposed in this paper enforces the control flow integrity with a granularity of one C statement, which is finer than basic block granularity.

Two previously proposed approaches also use a step counter to protect a code region [10,25]. The former targets computation disruption while the latter combined counters with a signature approach at assembly level to ensure tolerance to hardware fault. The use of a certified compiler requires to work at the source code level as proposed in this paper. Our approach, based on counters, is similar to the intra basic block approach of [25] for securing sequential code. But our approach operates at higher code level and is able to harden control flow of high level constructs.

Thus, in the specific context of smart cards or secure elements, to the best of our knowledge, no research work has proposed formally verified and experimentally evaluated countermeasures at C level that ensure control flow integrity in the presence of jump attacks during native execution.

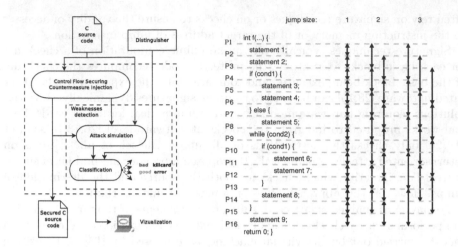

Fig. 1. Code securing methodology   **Fig. 2.** Injection of jump attacks at C level

3   Weakness Detection and Code Securing; Overview

This section gives an overview of our methodology, supported by tools and represented in Figure 1, to help developers to improve the security of smart card C codes subject to physical attacks inducing jumps. Our approach starts with a functional C code of the application. A distinguisher is necessary in order to discriminate between an execution that gives advantage to an attacker and an execution that does not. The full code security analysis and securing methodology can be split into two main steps.

The first step identifies the weaknesses in the code by simulating all possible attacks during code execution. The output of all these executions is passed to a classification tool that classifies attacks as harmful or as harmless. We refer to these classes as *bad* and *good*, respectively. While the bad class contains all attacks that give advantages to the attacker, the good class is the set of attacks that have no effect from a security point of view.

The second step consists in hardening the code. It relies on automated injection of countermeasures that ensure control flow integrity for any function that has been successfully attacked in the first step. The design of the countermeasures is detailed in Section 5 and the verification of their correctness is explained in Section 6. Note that, once a code has been secured, the evaluation of the efficiency of the implemented countermeasures or the identification of remaining weaknesses can be achieved by returning to the weaknesses detection step.

We have also implemented a visualization tool offering a graphical representation of the attacks classification and enabling to have a look at the code regions corresponding to harmful attacks.

4   Detection of Weaknesses and Visualization

In this section, we describe the part of our methodology that identifies harmful attacks. The identification of weaknesses is carried out by simulating, classifying and visualizing physical attacks at source code level.

4.1   Simulation of Attacks

Motivations to work at source code level. As code securing is often performed at source level by developers, simulating attacks at this level allows to identify the harmful ones as well as the code regions that should be secured. Simulating attacks at assembly level would require to match assembly instructions with the source code which is not trivial [7]. Furthermore, assembly programs are tightly coupled to specific architectures. Thus, simulating attacks at assembly programming limits portability. It is also time-consuming. Indeed, simulation of attack injection at the source code level speeds up the detection of weaknesses compared to injection at assembly level due to the lower number of source statements. However, jump attacks that start/arrive inside a C statement cannot be simulated at C level [7]. Nevertheless, it is helpful to detect as many weaknesses as possible at source code level, and as we show in the experimental results, working at this level enables to strengthen code security by making successful attacks very difficult to perform.

Simulation of C level attacks. In order to discover harmful attacks, we simulate jump attacks using software hacks at C level, as proposed in [7]. For each function of the application, all possible intra-procedural jump attacks that jump backward or forward C statements are injected at source level. Figure 2 illustrates all possible jumps within a function, sorted according to their distance expressed in statements. Statements in this context are C statements such as assignments, conditional expressions (*e.g.* if (cond1) or while(cond2)) and also any bracket or syntactic elements (*e.g.* }else{ or the bracket between P14 to P15) that impact control flow.

4.2   Classification of Simulated Attacks

The benefits of an attack differ depending on the application and the context of its use. A successful attack may break data confidentiality (by forcing a leak of sensitive data such as an encryption key or a PIN code) or may break the integrity of an application (by corrupting an embedded service). In order to cover the various benefits for an attacker in a general way, our methodology requires a distinguisher to be provided. This distinguisher must be able to classify as bad any execution where an attack has succeeded in breaking the expected security property of the code. Other attacks can be assigned to the good class. A finer classification of the effects of an attack can be achieved by providing a more precise distinguisher. In the remainder of the paper, we consider four different classes: *bad*: during execution a benefit has been obtained by the attacker; *good*:

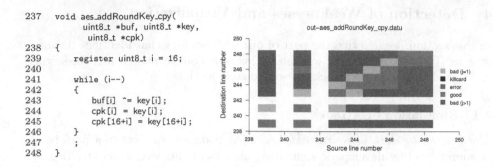

```
237    void aes_addRoundKey_cpy(
              uint8_t *buf, uint8_t *key,
              uint8_t *cpk)
238    {
239        register uint8_t i = 16;
240
241        while (i--)
242        {
243            buf[i] ^= key[i];
244            cpk[i] = key[i];
245            cpk[16+i] = key[16+i];
246        }
247        ;
248    }
```

Fig. 3. Result of weakness detection for the aes_addRoundKey_cpy function

the behavior of the application remains unchanged; *error* or *timeout*: the program has seemed to not terminate and has to be killed or finished with an error message, a signal (SIGSEGV, SIGBUS, ...) or crashes; *killcard*: a countermeasure has detected an attack and has triggered a security protection to terminate the program and possibly to destroy the card. We assume that no benefit can be obtained by an erroneous or endless execution, so both *error* and *timeout* cases are distinguished from *bad* cases in the remainder of the paper. If an error is preceded by a gain, such as a leak of sensitive information, the distinguisher must be able to discriminate between these attack effects.

4.3   Weaknesses Analysis and Visualization

Since our securing scheme operates at function level, the detection of weaknesses aims at identifying harmful attacks at source code level in order to identify the functions to be secured. Thus, any function that, when attacked, exhibits a *bad* case is considered for the countermeasure injection. The tools supporting our methodology offer a visualization tool that can be used by a security expert or a developer to quickly understand which variables and functionalities are involved in the generation of harmful attacks by analyzing the jumped part of the code.

The visualization tool builds a graphical representation of the results of the identification of weaknesses by drawing a square at the coordinate (source_line, target_line) using the color associated to its class. To illustrate this, consider the function aes_addRoundKey_cpy of an implementation of AES-256 [22] in C, used later in experiments, given in Figure 3. The distinguisher considers as *bad* any execution producing incorrect encrypted data, representing the attacker's ability to disrupt the encryption. The visualization of the weaknesses is illustrated in the right part of Figure 3. All except one forward jump generate a *bad* case (orange squares correspond to a jump size of one statement, red squares to a larger jump distance). Analyzing statements impacted by these harmful attacks shows that the whole loop body, hence the whole function, must be secured.

```
#define DECL_INIT(cnt, x) int cnt; if ((cnt = x) != x) killcard();
#define CHECK_INCR(cnt, x) cnt = (cnt == x ? cnt +1 : killcard());
#define CHECK_INCR_FUNC(cnt1, x1, cnt2, x2) cnt1 = ((cnt1 == x1) && (cnt2 == x2) ? cnt1 +
    1 : killcard());
#define CHECK_END_IF_ELSE(cnt_then, cnt_else, b, x, y) if (! ((cnt_then == x && cnt_else
    == 0 && b) || (cnt_else == y && cnt_then == 0 && !b))) killcard();
#define CHECK_END_IF(cnt_then, b, x) if ( ! ( (cnt_then == x && b) || (cnt_then == 0 && !
    b) ) ) killcard();
#define CHECK_INCR_COND(b, cnt, val, cond) (b = (((cnt)++ != val) ? killcard() : cond))
#define RESET_CNT(cnt_while, val) cnt_while = !(cnt_while == 0 || cnt_while == val) ?
    killcard() : 0;
#define CHECK_LOOP_INCR(cnt, x, b) cnt = (b && cnt == x ? cnt +1 : killcard());
#define CHECK_END_LOOP(cnt_while, b, val) if ( ! (cnt_while == val && !b) ) killcard();
```

Fig. 4. Security macros used for control flow securing

5   Countermeasure for C Code Securing

In this section, we present the countermeasures we have designed to detect jump attacks with a distance of at least two C statements. These countermeasures deal with the different high-level control-flow constructs such as straight line flow, if-then-else and loops. Countermeasures are presented in C-style in Appendix A and use the macros shown in Figure 4. Note that all macros are expanded to only one line of source code.

5.1   Protection of a Function and Straight-Line Flow of Statements

To secure the control flow integrity of a whole function or a whole block of straight-line statements, our securing scheme uses a dedicated counter. Each function or each block of sequential code has its own counter to ensure its control flow integrity. Counters are incremented after each C statements of the original source code using the CHECK_INCR macro. Before any incrementation, a check of the expected value of the counter is performed. When a check fails, a handler named, killcard() as the one used in smart card community, stops the execution.

To ensure control flow integrity, checks and incrementations of counters need to be nested. Consider the example in Figure 5 that illustrates the countermeasure for a function g with a straight-line control flow composed of N statements. The dedicated statement counter cnt_g is declared and initialized outside the function, i.e., in any function f calling g prior to each call to g. The initialization associated to the counter declaration is *surrounded* by two checks and incrementations of the counter cnt_f dedicated to the block of the function f where g is called. Moreover, the initialization value is different for each function which enables the detection of any call to another function as shown in the experiments. A reference to the counter cnt_g is passed to g as an extra parameter. Upon return from g, a check of the values of both counters cnt_f and cnt_g is performed in order to detect any corruption of the flow inside the function g. This way, any jump to the beginning of the function is detected inside the called

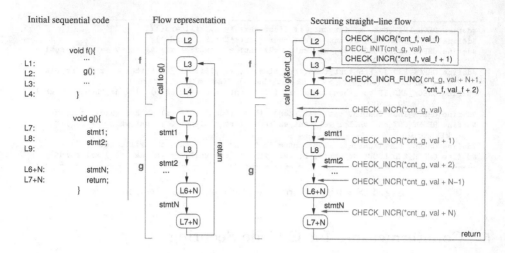

Fig. 5. Securing function call and straight-line flow

function g. Any jump to the end of a function is caught when the control flow returns to the calling function. The nesting of counter checks is at the core of our countermeasure scheme ensuring control flow integrity.

5.2   Conditional if-then and if-then-else Constructs

High level conditional control flow refers to if-then or if-then-else constructs, illustrated by the example on the left part of Figure 6. The securing scheme for conditional flow is illustrated in the right part of the Figure. For such a construct, our securing scheme requires 2 counters cnt_then and cnt_else (for the control flow integrity of each branch of the conditional construct) and one extra variable b to hold the value of the condition of the conditional flow. Declarations and initializations of cnt_then, cnt_else and b are performed outside the if-then-else block. Similar to functions or straight-line blocks, these new statements are interleaved with checks and incrementations of the counter cnt used for the control flow of the surrounding block. This is performed by the additionnal statements in the red box on the upper right part of Figure 6.

The condition evaluation in the secured version is performed through the macro CHECK_INCR_COND: if the counter cnt for the flow integrity of the surrounding block holds the expected value, cnt is incremented and the condition is evaluated. Thus, any jump attack over the condition evaluation is detected after the if-then-else construct, when checking the cnt counter. The extra variable b is set to the value of the condition, in order to be able to distinguish, after the execution of the if-then-else construct, which branch has been taken. Both counters dedicated to the conditional branches are then checked according to the value of b. This is performed by the code corresponding to the CHECK_END_IF_ELSE

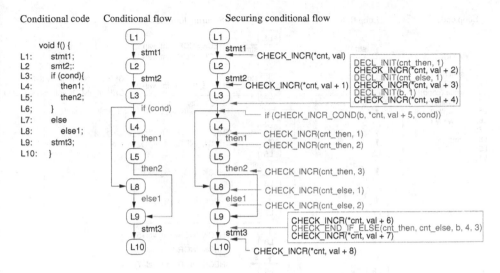

Fig. 6. Securing conditional control flow

macro inserted between two checks of the counter `cnt`. Again, this nesting of counter checks is at the core of the effectiveness of our countermeasure scheme.

5.3   Loop Constructs

We have also designed a countermeasure scheme for loops. Due to lack of space, we only present `while` loops. Any other loop constructs (`for`, `do while`) can be rewritten into a `while` construct. The left part of Figure 7 shows a `while` loop and the corresponding control flow between statements `stmt_1`, `stmt_2` and `stmt_3` of the surrounding sequential code. Our countermeasure scheme uses one counter, `cnt_while`, for securing the control flow of the loop body. Similar to conditional constructs, our countermeasure scheme requires an extra variable `b` to hold the value of the loop condition. The variable `b` is needed at the end of the loop to verify correct execution of the loop body and correct termination of the loop. This is performed by the `CHECK_END_LOOP` macro which is surrounded by `CHECK_INCR` of the counter `cnt`. The `b` variable is declared and initialized outside the loop as for the other constructs. The initial value must be `true`: if an attack jumps over the loop, `b` holds `true` and the `CHECK_END_LOOP` macro, checking for `b` being `false` after the loop, detects the attack. The `cnt_while` counter is reset before each initial iteration using the `RESET_CNT(cnt_while, val)` macro with `val` being the final value of the counter after one iteration. The reset is performed only if `cnt_while` is equal to 0 or to the value `val` that is expected after one complete iteration. As a jump from the end of the loop to the beginning of the body would result in a correct value for `cnt_while` that is reset before each new iteration, the first check inside the loop body of the while counter is guarded with `b` to detect a jump attack leading to an additional

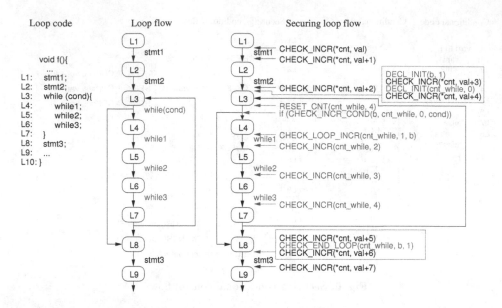

Fig. 7. Securing loop control flow

iteration of the loop. Moreover, the evaluation of the condition (that may update an induction variable) is performed along with a check and an incrementation of the counter `cnt_while` using the `CHECK_INCR_COND` macro. Hence, any attack that jumps over the evaluation of the condition of the loop will then be detected inside the loop.

We have also designed a countermeasure scheme for other C constructs such as `switch case`, `break`, multiple `return`s, `goto`. Due to space limitations and their absence in applications we have considered, they are not presented here.

6   Formal Verification of Countermeasures

Formal verification of our securing scheme helped us designing effective countermeasures and gives strong confidence in their effectiveness against attacks. In this section, we present the models used for program execution from a control flow point of view and for jump attacks, as well as properties to check to ensure the control flow integrity of a secured program execution even in presence of attacks. The verification of the correctness of the secured code is based on an equivalence checking with the original code.

6.1   Code Representation and Decomposition for CFI Verification

From a control flow perspective, a program execution can be viewed as the execution of a sequence of statements. A high-level program can be represented as a transition system whose states are defined by the values of variables of the program (contents of the memory) and of the program counter whose value specifies a source code line in the C program. Any transition mimics the state transformation induced by the execution of an individual statement: updating the program counter and potentially changing variables or the contents of memory. Figure 8 illustrates the representation of a program as a transition system.

A program can be decomposed into functions, and any function body can be decomposed into top-level code regions containing either only straight-line statements or a single control flow construct (loops or if-then-else). Sequential execution of these regions guarantees that, if the control flow integrity is ensured at the end of a code region, the following code region starts with a correct input from a control flow point of view. Thus, the integrity of the control flow of both code regions can be proven by proving the control flow integrity of each code region. Our countermeasure scheme relies on securing each control flow construct (function call/sequential code, if-then-else, while constructs) nested with few straight-line statements of the surrounding block. Then, our approach consists in verifying separately for each control flow construct enclosed with straight-line statements of the surrounding block that all possible executions of the secured version are stopped by a countermeasure in presence of harmful attacks or their control flow is upstanding with respect to the initial code.

As control flow constructs can be nested, many combinations of control flow constructs could be modeled. However, any control flow construct can be viewed as a single statement which is correctly executed or not. Thus, in the models used for verification of our countermeasures, we only consider straight-line statements inside control flow constructs. The idea is that, if properties hold for each individual construct, they hold for all of their combinations.

6.2   Models for Verification of Control Flow Integrity

State machine model. To model and verify the integrity of the control flow, we associate to each statement stmt_i of the original code of a function α a dedicated verification counter denoted cntv_αi. In the remainder of the paper, we refer to such counters as *statement counter*. We model the execution of a statement stmt_i by incrementing its associated statement counter cntv_αi.

Then, the execution of a sequence of statements is modeled by a transition system TS, defined by $TS = \{S, T, S_0, S_f, L\}$, where S is the set of states, T the set of transitions $T : S \to S$, S_0 and S_f are the subsets of S containing the initial states and final states respectively. The final states from S_f are absorbing states. A state from S is defined by the value of the program counter and the value of statement counters associated to every statement of the initial code. L is a set of labels corresponding to the possible values of the program counter, *i.e.* line numbers in the source code. Initial states are states with a program counter value equal to the first line of the modeled code and where all statement counters hold 0. Any transition from T is defined by the effect of the statement stmt_i associated to the program counter value. Transitions change the program counter value to the next line number to be executed and increment the

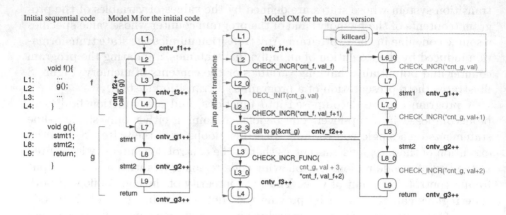

Fig. 8. Compact representation of TS for a function call and straight-line statements

statement counter `cntv_`αi associated to `stmt_i` of function α. A jump attack, as considered, can only corrupt the program counter. Thus, for such attacks, modeling the memory and other registers is not relevant.

To prove that our countermeasure scheme for a construct c is robust against a jump attack and that its secured version is equivalent to the initial one, we build two transition systems: one for the initial control-flow construct named M(c) and another one for the version including countermeasures named CM(c). Figure 8 illustrates a compact representation of both transition systems for a generic example code with a call to a function composed of straight-line statements. In a secured version, checks may result in a call to `killcard()`. Hence, there is an additional program counter value denoted `killcard` in any CM(c). All states with this program counter value are final. All transitions labeled with a countermeasure macro may change the program counter to `killcard`. Due to the high number of such transitions, only a subset is represented in order to keep the Figure readable.

Jump attack model. A jump attack is equivalent to the modification of the program counter with an unexpected value. As our countermeasures are effective against attacks that jump at least two lines, we add faulty transitions between every pair of states of CM(c) separated by at least one line of C. These transitions only update the program counter. The green arrows in CM(c) in Figure 8 illustrate all possible jump attacks occurring at line 3 of the code. As we assume that only a single fault can occur, every fault transition is guarded with a boolean indicating that a fault has already occurred.

6.3   Specification of Control Flow Integrity and Equivalence Checking

To perform the verification of the control flow integrity and the correctness of a secured code, we connect the two transition systems M(c) and CM(c) in order to force the input (such as condition value, iteration counts), if any, to be identical. The model checker builds a product of both models. We explain in this section, the properties to verify on this product.

To verify the correctness of the secured code, in the presence or absence of an attack, we need to prove that:

1. Any path in M(c) or CM(c) reaches a final absorbing state.
2. The statement counter values in any final correct state in CM(c) (with a program counter value different from killcard) are equal to the statement counter values in final states of M(c).
3. In CM(c) at any time and in any path, counters cntv_αi and cntv_α(i+1) for two adjacent statements stmt_i and stmt_i+1 in a straight-line flow respects $1 \geq$ cntv_αi $\geq$ cntv_α(i+1) ≥ 0 or execution will reach a final state with the killcard value for the program counter.

Property 2 ensures the right execution counts of statements in CM(c) if the execution reaches a correct final state. Property 3 checks that line i is always executed before line i+1 and after line i-1 or the execution will reach a killcard state. By transitivity, this property, if verified by all statement counters, ensures that in a straight-line flow, the statement of line k is always executed after line i and before line l with i < k < l both in M(c) and CM(c). Hence, Property 3 ensures the right order of execution of statements.

For a conditional flow or for a loop, Properties 1 and 2 are the same but the Property 3 changes slightly. For a conditional flow, such as the example in Figure 6, Property 3 specifies that at any time in an execution path that reaches a correct final state 1) the straight-line flow before and after the branches, condition included, is correct and 2) inside both branches, condition included, the straight-line flow is correct. Property 2 ensures that only one branch is executed. For a while loop as in Figure 7, Property 3 says that at any time in an execution that reaches a correct final state 1) the statements before and after the loop (condition excluded) are executed only once and in order; 2) the condition is never executed before its preceding statements, 3) statements inside the loop, condition included, are executed in order but their execution counts is not limited. Property 2 ensures the right number of iterations and Property 3 ensures the right control flow during execution.

We have chosen the Vis model checker [11] to prove the effectiveness of our countermeasure scheme. After modeling all the constructs given in this section and expressing the properties in CTL, all properties hold.

7 Experimental Results

We implemented all software components[1] presented in Figure 1. The counter-measures for control flow securing as well as the jump attacks for the detection of weaknesses are injected using a python C parser that manipulates the C instructions. For the experiments, we considered three well-known encryption algorithms available in C: AES [22], SHA [17] and Blowfish [17].

---

[1] A demonstration video is available at: http://dai.ly/x205n3x

Table 1. Jump attack classification for original and secured version (+ CM)

	BAD size > 1	BAD size = 1	GOOD	KILLCARD	ERROR	TOTAL
C JUMP ATTACKS	Attacking all functions at C level for all transient rounds					
AES	7786 29%	1104 4.2%	17372 65%		108 0.4%	26370
AES + CM	0	528 0.2%	18015 5.3%	318972 94%	1 0.0%	337516
SHA	32818 75%	1528 3.5%	8516 19%		412 1.0%	43274
SHA + CM	0	1149 0.3%	5080 1.2%	421200 98%	261 0.1%	427690
Blowfish	70086 32%	3550 1.7%	134360 62%		5725 2.7%	213721
Blowfish + CM	0	2470 0.2%	331664 23%	1060156 75%	6065 0.4%	1400355
ASM JUMP ATTACKS	Attacking the aes_encrypt function at ASM level for the first transient round					
aes_encrypt	1566 82.8%	36 1.9%	179 9.4%		111 5.9%	1892
aes_encrypt + CM	627 0.2%	21 0%	63040 20.2%	239303 78.4%	2264 0.7%	305255
ASM CALL ATTACKS	Attacking all function calls at ASM level for the first transient round					
AES	249 59.3%		139 33.1%		32 5%	420
AES + CM	0		21 5%	398 94.8%	1 0.2%	420
SHA	35 48.7%		13 18%		24 33.3%	72
SHA + CM	0		8 11.1%	61 84.7%	3 4.2%	72
Blowfish	9 21.4%		18 42.9%		15 35.7%	42
Blowfish + CM	0		18 42.9%	17 40.5%	7 16.6%	42

First, we simulated all the intra-procedural jump attacks at C level for each function (such as in Figure 2). A simulated attack is transient and triggered once during execution. However, using the gcov tool to determine how many times each line is executed, we simulated all possible instances of jump attacks from a Line i to a Line j. In all our experiments, the distinguisher classifies as *bad* any attack that provokes program termination with corrupted output. The second column of Table 1 shows that all attacks with a jump distance greater than or equal to two C statements are captured by our countermeasures. For example, 32 818 jump attacks were harmful for SHA whereas none was for its secured version (SHA + CM). The number of attacks jumping only one C statements is also reduced (third column). More important, the ratio of the remaining jump attacks of size one becomes very low ($\leq 0.3\%$). For example, for AES the *bad* cases of size one decrease from 33.2% to 0.2%.

Also, we simulated all possible intra-procedural jump attacks at assembly level targeting the aes_encrypt function of AES executed by an ARM Cortex-M3 processor. We used the Keil ARM-MDK compiler and Keil simulator [19] for the replacement of any instruction by a jump anywhere into the same function. We considered only one function due to a very long simulation time (3 weeks), highlighting the benefits to perform the attack simulation at source level. Results are presented in the ASM JUMP ATTACKS section of Table 1. The harmful attacks in the secured version represent only 40% of the ones in the original code: our countermeasures enable to defeat 60% of the attacks on this example. Moreover, only 0.2% of attacks give advantage to the attacker while 78.4% are detected. Thanks to the frequent checks added by our countermeasures, the harmful attacks are much harder to perform on the secured code. It shows our countermeasures are effective while being implemented at source code level.

Table 2. Size and overhead for original and secured version (+ CM)

	x86					ARM-V7M		
	Simulation time	Size		Execution time		Size		Execution time	
		bytes	overhead	time	overhead	bytes	overhead	time	overhead
AES	27m	17 996		1.27 ms		4216		38.3 ms	
AES + CM	9h 46m	30 284	(+68%)	2.61 ms	(+106%)	15 696	(+272%)	191.7 ms	(+400.5%)
SHA	1h 18m	13 235		1.47 μs		3184		106.5μs	
SHA + CM	16h 52m	21 702	(+64%)	2.81 μs	(+91%)	7752	(+143%)	499.1μs	(+368%)
Blowfish	5h 52m	30 103		47.6 μs		6292		3.02 ms	
Blowfish + CM	3d 6h 19m	46 680	(+55%)	70.6 μs	(+48%)	16 396	(+161%)	6.3 ms	(+109%)

Finally, we simulated attacks that call an unexpected function instead of the expected one for all the benchmarks using the Keil simulator. Results, presented in the ASM CALL ATTACKS section of Table 1, show that all harmful attacks are captured and many harmless attacks are also detected. Thus, our countermeasures are also very effective against unexpected function calls.

Table 2 reports code sizes as well as execution times of both the original version and the secured one, for a x86 target machine and a cortex-M3 processor. For the x86 platform, the execution time overhead ranges from +59% (blowfish) up to +106% (AES). For the embedded ARM processor, the overhead is higher as the simpler processor does not exploit instruction level parallelism. The highest overhead is also achieved for AES (+400%). As all functions of our benchmarks exhibit vulnerabilities, they were all fully secured by our methodology. We will consider in future work how to achieve at least the same level of security without fully securing sensitive functions. However, as a smart card is primarily the host of sensitive operations, ensuring the required security level is crucial. Full code securing often implies such a high overhead [23,25].

8 Conclusion

This paper has presented a methodology to automatically secure any C application with formally verified countermeasures at source level. Results has shown that these countermeasures defeat 100% of C jump attacks with a distance of two statements or beyond. Moreover, our countermeasures are able to capture all unexpected function calls. They also have been able to reduce significantly the number of attacks injected at assembly level: for the studied function, 60% of the assembly jump attacks were eliminated. Future work will address the optimization of countermeasure injection according to the weaknesses detection step. If harmless attacks are found inside a function, countermeasures might be adapted accordingly to reduce their cost while preserving their effectiveness.

References

1. Abadi, M., Budiu, M., Erlingsson, U., Ligatti, J.: Control-flow integrity. In: Atluri, V., Meadows, C., Juels, A. (eds.) 12th ACM Conference on Computer and Communications Security, pp. 340–353. ACM Press, Alexandria (2005)

2. Balasch, J., Gierlichs, B., Verbauwhede, I.: An in-depth and black-box characterization of the effects of clock glitches on 8-bit MCUs. In: Breveglieri, L., Guilley, S., Koren, I., Naccache, D., Takahashi, J. (eds.) The 8th Workshop on Fault Diagnosis and Tolerance in Cryptography, pp. 105–114. IEEE Computer Society Press, Nara (2011)

3. Barbu, G., Duc, G., Hoogvorst, P.: Java card operand stack: fault attacks, combined attacks and countermeasures. In: Prouff, E. (ed.) CARDIS 2011. LNCS, vol. 7079, pp. 297–313. Springer, Heidelberg (2011)

4. Barbu, G., Thiebeauld, H., Guerin, V.: Attacks on java card 3.0 combining fault and logical attacks. In: Gollmann, D., Lanet, J.-L., Iguchi-Cartigny, J. (eds.) CARDIS 2010. LNCS, vol. 6035, pp. 148–163. Springer, Heidelberg (2010)

5. Barenghi, A., Breveglieri, L., Koren, I., Naccache, D.: Fault Injection Attacks on Cryptographic Devices: Theory, Practice, and Countermeasures. Proceedings of the IEEE 100(11), 3056–3076 (2012)

6. Barenghi, A., Trichina, E.: Fault attacks on stream ciphers. In: Joye, M., Tunstall, M. (eds.) Fault Analysis in Cryptography. Information Security and Cryptography, pp. 239–255. Springer, Heidelberg (2012)

7. Berthomé, P., Heydemann, K., Kauffmann-Tourkestansky, X., Lalande, J.F.: High level model of control flow attacks for smart card functional security. In: 7th International Conference on Availability, Reliability and Security, AReS 2012, pp. 224–229. IEEE Computer Society, Prague (2012)

8. Bletsch, T., Jiang, X., Freeh, V.: Mitigating code-reuse attacks with control-flow locking. In: Zakon, R.H., McDermott, J.P., Locasto, M.E. (eds.) 27th Annual Computer Security Applications Conference, pp. 353–362. ACM Press, Orlando (2011)

9. Bouffard, G., Iguchi-Cartigny, J., Lanet, J.L.: Combined software and hardware attacks on the java card control flow. In: Prouff, E. (ed.) CARDIS 2011. LNCS, vol. 7079, pp. 283–296. Springer, Heidelberg (2011)

10. Bouffard, G., Thampi, B.N., Lanet, J.-L.: Detecting laser fault injection for smart cards using security automata. In: Thampi, S.M., Atrey, P.K., Fan, C.-I., Perez, G.M. (eds.) SSCC 2013. CCIS, vol. 377, pp. 18–29. Springer, Heidelberg (2013)

11. Brayton, R., et al.: Vis: A system for verification and synthesis. In: Alur, R., Henzinger, T.A. (eds.) CAV 1996. LNCS, vol. 1102, pp. 428–432. Springer, Heidelberg (1996), http://vlsi.colorado.edu/~vis/

12. Ceara, D.: Detecting Software Vulnerabilities - Static Taint Analysis. Bsc thesis, Universitatea Politehnica Bucuresti, Verimag (2009)

13. Chen, Y., Venkatesan, R., Cary, M., Pang, R., Sinha, S., Jakubowski, M.H.: Oblivious hashing: A stealthy software integrity verification primitive. In: Petitcolas, F.A.P. (ed.) IH 2002. LNCS, vol. 2578, pp. 400–414. Springer, Heidelberg (2003)

14. Dehbaoui, A., Mirbaha, A.-P., Moro, N., Dutertre, J.-M., Tria, A.: Electromagnetic glitch on the AES round counter. In: Prouff, E. (ed.) COSADE 2013. LNCS, vol. 7864, pp. 17–31. Springer, Heidelberg (2013)

15. Fiskiran, A.M., Lee, R.B.: Runtime execution monitoring (REM) to detect and prevent malicious code execution. In: IEEE International Conference on Computer Design: VLSI in Computers and Processors, pp. 452–457. IEEE Computer Society, San Jose (2004)

16. Goloubeva, O., Rebaudengo, M., Reorda, M.S., Violante, M.: Soft-error detection using control flow assertions. In: 18th International Symposium on Defect and Fault Tolerance in VLSI Systems, pp. 581–588. IEEE Computer Society, Boston (2003)

17. Guthaus, M.R., Ringenberg, J.S., Ernst, D., Austin, T.M., Mudge, T., Brown, R.B.: MiBench: A free, commercially representative embedded benchmark suite. In: 4th Annual Workshop on Workload Characterization, pp. 3–14. IEEE Computer Society, Austin (2001), http://www.eecs.umich.edu/mibench/
18. Iguchi-cartigny, J., Lanet, J.L.: Evaluation of Countermeasures Against Fault Attacks on Smart Cards. International Journal of Security and Its Applications 5(2), 49–60 (2011)
19. Keil: Keil uVision for ARM processors (2012), http://www.keil.com/support/man_arm.htm
20. Lackner, M., Berlach, R., Raschke, W., Weiss, R., Steger, C.: A defensive virtual machine layer to counteract fault attacks on java cards. In: Cavallaro, L., Gollmann, D. (eds.) WISTP 2013. LNCS, vol. 7886, pp. 82–97. Springer, Heidelberg (2013)
21. Leroy, X.: Formal certification of a compiler back-end or: programming a compiler with a proof assistant. In: Morrisett, J.G., Jones, S.L.P. (eds.) 33rd ACM Symposium on Principles of Programming Languages, pp. 42–54. ACM Press, Charleston (2006)
22. Levin, I.: A byte-oriented AES-256 implementation (2007), http://www.literatecode.com/aes256
23. Moro, N., Heydemann, K., Encrenaz, E., Robisson, B.: Formal verification of a software countermeasure against instruction skip attacks. Journal of Cryptographic Engineering, 1–12 (2014)
24. Moro, N., Dehbaoui, A., Heydemann, K., Robisson, B., Encrenaz, E.: Electromagnetic Fault Injection: Towards a Fault Model on a 32-bit Microcontroller. In: Workshop on Fault Diagnosis and Tolerance in Cryptography, pp. 77–88. IEEE Computer Society, Santa Barbara (2013)
25. Nicolescu, B., Savaria, Y., Velazco, R.: SIED: Software implemented error detection. In: 18th International Symposium on Defect and Fault Tolerance in VLSI Systems, pp. 589–596. IEEE Computer Society, Boston (2003)
26. Oh, N., Shirvani, P., McCluskey, E.: Control-flow checking by software signatures. IEEE Transactions on Reliability 51(1), 111–122 (2002)
27. Verbauwhede, I., Karaklajić, D., Schmidt, J.M.: The fault attack jungle - a classification model to guide you. In: Breveglieri, L., Guilley, S., Koren, I., Naccache, D., Takahashi, J. (eds.) 8th Workshop on Fault Diagnosis and Tolerance in Cryptography, pp. 3–8. IEEE Computer Society, Nara (2011)
28. Xia, Y., Liu, Y., Chen, H., Zang, B.: CFIMon: Detecting violation of control flow integrity using performance counters. In: Swarz, R.S., Koopman, P., Cukier, M. (eds.) IEEE/IFIP International Conference on Dependable Systems and Networks, pp. 1–12. IEEE Computer Society, Boston (2012)
29. Yamaguchi, F., Wressnegger, C., Gascon, H., Rieck, K.: Chucky: exposing missing checks in source code for vulnerability discovery. In: Sadeghi, A.R., Gligor, V.D., Yung, M. (eds.) ACM Conference on Computer and Communications Security, Berlin, Germany, pp. 499–510 (November 2013)

A   Countermeasures Securing Codes

This section presents the implementation of the countermeasures of Figure 5, 6 and 7 using the macros of Figure 4.

The implementation of countermeasures for function calls and sequence of statements are shown in the two listings below. The statement counter cnt_g for a function g must be initialized with a value different that the one for all other functions in order to capture jump attacks that try to call another function. Moreover, the range of values taken by the statement counter of a function must be different from the ones of other functions in order to detect inter-procedural jumps.

```
int g(int n, int m, int * cnt_g){
CHECK_INCR(*cnt_g, 8)
statement;
CHECK_INCR(*cnt_g, 9)
...
CHECK_INCR(*cnt_g, 10)
statement;
CHECK_INCR(*cnt_g, 11)
return res;
}
```

```
int f(int * cnt_f){
...
CHECK_INCR(*cnt_f, 15)
// initialization value ≠ for each func.
DECL_INIT(cnt_g, 8)
CHECK_INCR(*cnt_f, 16)
x = g(p, q, &cnt_g)
CHECK_INCR_FUNC(*cnt_f, 17, cnt_g, 12);
...
}
```

The listings below illustrate the implementation of the countermeasures for an if construct (left) and for a while construct (right). The while construct example contains the statements to be inserted to handle a `for` construct for the initialization of the induction variable and its incrementation.

```
...
CHECK_INCR(*cnt, 8)
statement;
CHECK_INCR(*cnt, 9)
DECL_INIT(cnt_then, 1)
CHECK_INCR(*cnt, 10)
DECL_INIT(cnt_else, 1)
CHECK_INCR(*cnt, 11)
DECL_INIT(b, 1)
CHECK_INCR(*cnt, 12)
if (CHECK_INCR_COND(b, *cnt, 13, cond))
{
    CHECK_INCR(cnt_then, 1)
    statement;
    CHECK_INCR(cnt_then, 2)
    ...
    CHECK_INCR(cnt_then, 4)
}
else
{
    CHECK_INCR(cnt_else, 1)
    statement;
    CHECK_INCR(cnt_else, 2)
    ...
    CHECK_INCR(cnt_else, 6)
}
CHECK_INCR(*cnt, 14)
CHECK_END_IF_ELSE(cnt_then, cnt_else, b, 5,
    7)
CHECK_INCR(*cnt, 15)
statement;
```

```
...
CHECK_INCR(*cnt, 8)
statement;
CHECK_INCR(*cnt, 9)
DECL_INIT(b, 1)
CHECK_INCR(*cnt, 10)
DECL_INIT(cnt_while, 1)
CHECK_INCR(*cnt, 11)
// optional induction variable
// initialization statement for a for
CHECK_INCR(cnt, 12)
while: {
    RESET_CNT(cnt_while, 8)
    if (! CHECK_INCR_COND(b, cnt_while,
        0, cond)) goto next;
    CHECK_LOOP_INCR(cnt_while, 1, b)
    statement;
    CHECK_INCR(cnt_while, 2)
    statement;
    CHECK_INCR(cnt_while, 3)
    ...
    CHECK_INCR(cnt_while, 6)
    // optional incrementation statement
    // for a for
    CHECK_INCR(cnt_while, 7)
    goto while;
}
next:
CHECK_INCR(*cnt, 13)
CHECK_END_LOOP(cnt_while, b, 1)
CHECK_INCR(*cnt, 14)
statement;
```

LeakWatch: Estimating Information Leakage from Java Programs

Tom Chothia[1], Yusuke Kawamoto[2],[*], and Chris Novakovic[1]

[1] School of Computer Science, University of Birmingham, UK
[2] INRIA Saclay & LIX, École Polytechnique, France

Abstract. Programs that process secret data may inadvertently reveal information about those secrets in their publicly-observable output. This paper presents LeakWatch, a quantitative information leakage analysis tool for the Java programming language; it is based on a flexible "point-to-point" information leakage model, where secret and publicly-observable data may occur at any time during a program's execution. LeakWatch repeatedly executes a Java program containing both secret and publicly-observable data and uses robust statistical techniques to provide estimates, with confidence intervals, for min-entropy leakage (using a new theoretical result presented in this paper) and mutual information. We demonstrate how LeakWatch can be used to estimate the size of information leaks in a range of real-world Java programs.

Keywords: Quantitative information flow, statistical estimation, Java, mutual information, min-entropy leakage.

1 Introduction

An information leak occurs when a passive observer learns something about a system's secret data by observing its public outputs. Information leaks may be a side effect of a correctly-functioning system, and pose no real threat to security (e.g., a rejected guess of a secret, high-entropy password leaks some information: that this value is not the correct password). Larger information leaks, on the other hand, may lead to a complete breakdown of security (e.g., a flawed random number generator may give an observer all the information they need to guess important secret values). It is therefore important for a designer or analyst of a system to know exactly where information leaks occur and to be able to quantify them.

Information theory is a useful mechanism for providing quantitative bounds on what an attacker can learn. The attacker's uncertainty about a system's secret data is usually represented as Shannon entropy [1], and the reduction in uncertainty about the secret data is represented using a measure such as the mutual information of the secret data and publicly-observable data [2], or the

---

[*] Work by Yusuke Kawamoto was supported by a postdoc grant funded by the IDEX Digital Society project.

M. Kutyłowski and J. Vaidya (Eds.): ESORICS 2014, Part II, LNCS 8713, pp. 219–236, 2014.

min-entropy leakage from the secret data to the publicly-observable data [3]. Although the bounds provided by these measures are meaningful, it is tedious to manually compute them; there is therefore a need for tools that automatically and robustly detect information leakage vulnerabilities in software.

This paper presents LeakWatch, a quantitative information leakage analysis tool for the Java programming language. It is based on a "point-to-point" information leakage model in which secret and publicly-observable data may occur at any time during the program's execution, including inside complex code structures such as branches and nested loops. This model, which we developed previously using a semantics based on discrete-time Markov chains [4], is particularly well-suited to analysing complex programs where secret and publicly-observable data may occur at any point: if secret and publicly-observable values are "tagged" using the secret and observe commands respectively, it measures how much information a passive attacker with knowledge of the program's source code learns about the secret values by examining the observable values.

Given a Java program whose source code has been annotated with the positions where its secret and publicly-observable data occurs, LeakWatch repeatedly executes it, recording the occurrences of secret and public data, and then performs robust statistical tests to detect whether an information leak is present and, if so, estimate the size of the leak. We note that this relies on the analyst correctly identifying which values in their program should be kept secret and which other values might be observable to an attacker, but, assuming this is done correctly (a reasonable assumption for most programs), LeakWatch can be used to verify whether the program is secure, or whether it contains an information leak that could lead to an attack.

LeakWatch uses previous techniques [5,6] for estimating mutual information and a new technique for estimating min-entropy leakage. These are brute-force approaches for probabilistic systems; i.e., we must run the program enough times to collect sampled data for every possible secret value. If the systems we target were deterministic, we could compute the information leakage precisely; however, since they are probabilistic, we use these statistical estimation techniques to distinguish a real information leak from noise in the measurements and to place bounds on the possible leakage.

We note that this estimation technique is quite different from those that estimate mutual information or min-entropy leakage with sampled data for only *some* of the possible secrets (e.g., [7]). These results often require additional assumptions about the distribution of the secret values, which we do not make, and may only work for non-probabilistic systems. Practically, we can analyse systems containing tens (or, in some cases, hundreds) of thousands of secret and observable values that occur with a non-negligible probability, and in which each trial run of the system is independent and identically distributed. We show that this provides interesting results for complex systems.

We present new results for calculating when enough samples have been collected for our estimates to be accurate, and handling user (but not attacker) input to a system. We provide a full Java-based implementation of our analysis method, and illustrate its power with three realistic security-themed examples.

Other tools, such as QUAIL [8], QIF [9] and our earlier CH-IMP implementation [4], compute the leakage from small formal models of programs. A key difference in this work is that we target full Java programs, at the cost of estimating leakage instead of computing it precisely.

There are other information leakage tools built on model checkers for C and Java [10,11,12]. They require the secret values to be inputs to the program and the observable values to be the program's final outputs; they are also restricted to the subset of the language's syntax supported by the model checker. LeakWatch has neither of these constraints.

In summary, our main contributions are the following:

a) a new result for estimating min-entropy leakage from trial runs of systems, as well as providing confidence intervals for those estimates using χ^2 tests;
b) a technique that, given certain assumptions, ensures we have enough samples to estimate information leakage from trial runs of a system;
c) LeakWatch, a robust information leakage analysis tool that can estimate mutual information and min-entropy leakage in Java programs; LeakWatch is freely available at [13], with full documentation and a range of sample Java programs.

The rest of the paper is organised as follows. In Section 2 we introduce relevant theoretical background information. In Section 3 we show a new theoretical result for estimating min-entropy leakage and its confidence interval from trial runs of a system. In Sections 4 and 5 we discuss LeakWatch's design and implementation respectively. In Section 6 we show three examples of LeakWatch being used to uncover information leakage vulnerabilities in real-world Java programs.

2   Background

2.1   Leakage Measures and Estimating Mutual Information

Our approach assumes that trial runs of the system are independent and identically distributed; the analyst must verify that this is the case. We also assume the system has probabilistic behaviour: each run results in some secret values $x \in \mathcal{X}$ occurring from some probability distribution X, and some observable behaviour $y \in \mathcal{Y}$ occurring from some probability distribution Y. Then, for each run of the system, the probability of the secrets x occurring and the attacker observing y is given by the joint probability distribution $p(x, y)$. The question we wish to answer is "how much does an attacker learn about the value of the secret from the observable behaviour of the system?".

We use two popular measures of information leakage: mutual information and min-entropy leakage. Mutual information is given by the equation

$$I(X;Y) = \sum_{x \in \mathcal{X}, y \in \mathcal{Y}} p(x,y) \log_2 \left(\frac{p(x,y)}{p(x)p(y)} \right) \tag{1}$$

and tells us how much information, in bits, we learn about X by observing Y. Min-entropy leakage is given by the equation

$$\mathcal{L}(X;Y) = \log_2 \sum_{y \in \mathcal{Y}} \max_{x \in \mathcal{X}} p(x,y) - \log_2 \max_{x \in \mathcal{X}} \sum_{y \in \mathcal{Y}} p(x,y) \qquad (2)$$

and tells us how difficult it is for the attacker to guess the secret values in one attempt, given the observable behaviour. We refer the reader to [2] for a more in-depth evaluation of mutual information and min-entropy leakage as information leakage measures.

From trial runs of a system we can estimate the joint distribution $\hat{p}(x,y)$ and the distributions $\hat{p}(x)$ and $\hat{p}(y)$; we can use these distributions in Equation 1 to estimate the mutual information $\hat{I}(X;Y)$. To find bounds on the true mutual information of the secret and observable values in a system, we need to know how $\hat{I}(X;Y)$ relates to $I(X;Y)$. We have shown previously [14] how these values are related when the distribution on secrets is known and we estimated $\hat{p}(y|x)$; however, this case is different, in that we are also estimating $\hat{p}(x)$. This case has been studied by Moddemeijer [5] and Brillinger [6], who found that:

Theorem 1. *When $I(X;Y) = 0$, for a large number of samples n, $2n\hat{I}(X;Y)$ will be drawn from a χ^2 distribution with $(\#\mathcal{X} - 1)(\#\mathcal{Y} - 1)$ degrees of freedom; i.e., $\hat{I}(X;Y)$ has an average value of $(\#\mathcal{X} - 1)(\#\mathcal{Y} - 1)/2n$ and variance $(\#\mathcal{X} - 1)(\#\mathcal{Y} - 1)/2n^2$.*

Theorem 2. *When $I(X;Y) > 0$, for a large number of samples n, the estimates $\hat{I}(X;Y)$ will be drawn from a distribution with mean $I(X;Y) + (\#\mathcal{X} - 1)(\#\mathcal{Y} - 1)/2n + O\left(\frac{1}{n^2}\right)$ and variance*

$$\frac{1}{n} \left(\sum_{x,y} p(x,y) \log^2 \left(\frac{p(x,y)}{p(x)p(y)} \right) - \left(\sum_{x,y} p(x,y) \log \left(\frac{p(x,y)}{p(x)p(y)} \right) \right)^2 \right) + O\left(\frac{1}{n^2}\right).$$

Using these results, we first test a $\hat{I}(X;Y)$ value against the χ^2 distribution from Theorem 1; if it is consistent with the 95% confidence interval for this distribution, we conclude that there is no evidence of an information leak in our sampled data. If $\hat{I}(X;Y)$ is inconsistent with the distribution from Theorem 1, we conclude that there is evidence of an information leak in our sampled data and use Theorem 2 to calculate a confidence interval for the leakage.

In both cases "a large number of samples" means enough samples to ensure that every $\hat{p}(x,y)$ is close to $p(x,y)$, so it is important to note that this is a brute-force approach that requires many more samples than the product of the number of secret and observable values. The contribution of the estimation results is to allow us to analyse systems that behave probabilistically.

The $O(n^{-2})$ term in Theorem 2 is an infinite sum on descending powers of n. This term is a result of using the Taylor expansion of entropy and conditional entropy. To make use of Theorem 2 we require enough samples for the $O(n^{-2})$ term to be small. This will always be the case for a sufficiently large n, and we address how to tell when n is large enough in Section 4.1. In practice, these results let us analyse systems with tens of thousands of unique secrets and observables.

2.2   Our Information Leakage Model

Our tool uses a "point-to-point" information leakage model, which tells us how much an attacker learns about a secret value at a particular point in a program from the program's observable outputs. This model is particularly well-suited to analysing entire programs (rather than code fragments), and it is a generalisation of the more common model of information flow that measures the leakage from high-level secret inputs of a function to its low-level public outputs [15]. It is important to note that our information flow model measures the information leakage from the value of variable at a particular point in the program. This differs from (e.g.) the Jif [16] information flow model, which ensures that no value stored in a high-level variable ever affects the value stored in a low-level variable. We have previously [4] developed a formal model of this information leakage, showed that it can be computed precisely for a simple probabilistic language using discrete-time Markov chains and that it can be estimated from trial runs of a program.

The LeakWatch API provides the command secret(v1) to denote that the current value of the variable v1 should be kept secret, and observe(v2) to denote that v2 is a value the attacker can observe; it is up to the analyst to decide where to place these commands. We then measure the information leakage from occurrences of v1 to occurrences of v2.

For example, consider a Java card game program in which a Card object (theirCard) is drawn from a deck and sent over an insecure socket to an opposing player. Another Card object (ourCard) is drawn from the deck and stored locally; the opponent is then given the opportunity to make a bet based on the value of theirCard. If an analyst wanted to estimate how much information a remote attacker learns about ourCard from theirCard, the code could be annotated as:

```
Card theirCard = deck.drawCard();
LeakWatchAPI.observe(theirCard);
opponent.writeToSocket(theirCard);
Card ours = deck.drawCard();
LeakWatchAPI.secret(ours);
if (opponent.placedBet()) determineWinner();
```

This would, for example, alert the analyst to a badly-implemented random number generator in the deck-shuffling algorithm that allows the opposing player to predict the value of the next card dealt from the deck, giving them an unfair advantage when deciding whether to bet.

We note that our measure of information leakage only tells us what a passive attacker learns about the secret values by examining the observable values; it does not measure how easy the secret value is to guess (e.g., because it has low entropy). Therefore, the leakage measurement is only useful when there is uncertainty about the secret values. This could be due to secret values being randomly-generated numbers, or programs exhibiting unpredictable behaviour such as process scheduling or network timing. In cases where the secret is an input to the system, code can be added to generate a truly random value for the secret and then measure the leakage to the observable values. We give examples illustrating all of these cases in Section 6 and on the LeakWatch web site [13].

3   Estimating Min-Entropy Leakage

Our mutual information estimation result calculates the exact distribution of
the estimates and so lets us calculate exact confidence intervals; obtaining a
similar result for min-entropy leakage is difficult because of the maximum in
its definition. So, to allow us to calculate this popular leakage measure, we find
upper and lower bounds for a (more than) 95% confidence interval.

The estimation gives a point estimate of the leakage $\mathcal{L}(X;Y)$ from a distribution X on secret values to a distribution Y on observable values, and its (more
than) 95% confidence interval. We do not know the exact distribution X, so we
estimate it from the trial run data. Since we do not know the exact joint probability distribution $p(x,y)$ for the system, we first calculate the empirical joint
distribution from the trial runs. Let L be the total number of trial runs, and
$\hat{s}(x,y)$ be the frequency of (i.e., the number of trial runs with) a secret $x \in \mathcal{X}$
and an observable $y \in \mathcal{Y}$; then the empirical probability of having a secret x and
an observable y is defined by $\frac{\hat{s}(x,y)}{L}$. Also, let $\hat{u}(x)$ be the frequency of a secret
$x \in \mathcal{X}$; i.e., $\hat{u}(x) = \sum_{y \in \mathcal{Y}} \hat{s}(x,y)$; then we calculate the empirical probability of
seeing x as $\frac{\hat{u}(x)}{L}$. Using these empirical distributions we obtain a point estimate
$\widehat{\mathcal{L}}(X;Y)$ of the min-entropy leakage:

$$\widehat{\mathcal{L}}(X;Y) = -\log_2 \max_{x \in \mathcal{X}} \frac{\hat{u}(x)}{L} + \log_2 \sum_{y \in \mathcal{Y}} \max_{x \in \mathcal{X}} \frac{\hat{s}(x,y)}{L}.$$

Given L independent and identically distributed trial runs, the frequency $\hat{s}(x,y)$
follows the binomial distribution $B(L, p(x,y))$, where $p(x,y)$ is the *true* joint
probability of a secret x and an observable y occurring. We note that we cannot
treat each of the empirical joint probabilities as independently sampled from a
binomial distribution, because together they must sum to 1. Instead, we perform
Pearson's χ^2 tests [17,18] for a large number L of trial runs.

The estimation of a confidence interval is based on the fact that, with a high
probability, each observed frequency $\hat{s}(x,y)$ is close to the "expected frequency"
$p(x,y)L$, where $p(x,y)$ is the true probability we want to estimate. By applying
χ^2 tests, we evaluate the probability that the observed frequencies $\hat{s}(x,y)$ come
from the joint probability distributions $p(x,y)$. Given the observed frequencies
$\hat{s}(x,y)$ and the expected frequencies $p(x,y)L$, the χ^2 test statistics is defined by:

$$\chi^2 = \sum_{x \in \mathcal{X}, y \in \mathcal{Y}} \frac{(\hat{s}(x,y) - p(x,y)L)^2}{p(x,y)L}.$$

Since the joint probability distribution is regarded as a one-way table in this
setting, the χ^2 test statistics follows the χ^2 distribution with $(\#\mathcal{X} \cdot \#\mathcal{Y}) - 1$
degrees of freedom. We denote by $\chi^2_{(0.05,k)}$ the test statistics with upper tail area
0.05 and k degrees of freedom.

The goal of our new method is to obtain a (more than) 95% confidence interval of the min-entropy leakage $\mathcal{L}(X;Y)$ between the secret and observable

distributions X, Y. To obtain this, we estimate the 95% confidence intervals of the min-entropy $H_\infty(X) = -\log_2 \max_{x \in \mathcal{X}} p(x)$ and the conditional min-entropy $H_\infty(Y|X) = -\log_2 \sum_{y \in \mathcal{Y}} \max_{x \in \mathcal{X}} p(x, y)$ respectively.

We first present a method for obtaining the confidence interval of the conditional min-entropy $H_\infty(Y|X)$. Given L independent and identically distributed trial runs of the system, we obtain the observed frequencies $\hat{s}$. Then we construct expected frequencies $s_{\max}$ that give the largest *a posteriori* vulnerability $\sum_{y \in \mathcal{Y}} \max_{x \in \mathcal{X}} p(x, y)$ among all expected frequencies that satisfy: $\chi^2_{(0.05, \#\mathcal{X}\#\mathcal{Y}-1)} = \sum_{x \in \mathcal{X}, y \in \mathcal{Y}} \frac{(\hat{s}(x,y) - s_{\max}(x,y))^2}{s_{\max}(x,y)}$. More specifically, $s_{\max}$ is constructed from $\hat{s}$ by increasing only the maximum expected frequencies $\max_{x \in \mathcal{X}} \hat{s}(x, y)$ and by decreasing others, while keeping the total number of frequencies as L; i.e., $\sum_{x \in \mathcal{X}, y \in \mathcal{Y}} s_{\max}(x, y) = L$. From $s_{\max}$ we calculate the empirical distribution $P^{\text{post}}_{\max}[x, y] = \frac{s_{\max}(x,y)}{L}$. Next, we construct expected frequencies $s_{\min}$ that give the smallest *a posteriori* vulnerability. Keeping the total number of frequencies as L, we repeatedly decrease the current maximum expected frequency and increase the smallest frequencies until we obtain $\chi^2_{(0.05, \#\mathcal{X}\#\mathcal{Y}-1)} = \sum_{x \in \mathcal{X}, y \in \mathcal{Y}} \frac{(\hat{s}(x,y) - s_{\min}(x,y))^2}{s_{\min}(x,y)}$. Then we calculate the corresponding distribution $P^{\text{post}}_{\min}$. From $P^{\text{post}}_{\max}$ and $P^{\text{post}}_{\min}$ we obtain the following confidence interval of the conditional min-entropy:

Lemma 1. *The lower and upper bounds for the 95% confidence interval of the conditional min-entropy $H_\infty(Y|X)$ are respectively given by:*

$$H^{\text{low}}_\infty(Y|X) = -\log_2 \sum_{y \in \mathcal{Y}} \max_{x \in \mathcal{X}} P^{\text{post}}_{\max}[x, y], \ H^{\text{up}}_\infty(Y|X) = -\log_2 \sum_{y \in \mathcal{Y}} \max_{x \in \mathcal{X}} P^{\text{post}}_{\min}[x, y].$$

Next, we compute the confidence interval of the min-entropy $H_\infty(X)$. Given the observed frequencies $\hat{u}$, we construct expected frequencies $u_{\max}$ that give the largest vulnerability $\max_{x \in \mathcal{X}} p(x)$ such that $\chi^2_{(0.05, \#\mathcal{X}-1)} = \sum_{x \in \mathcal{X}} \frac{(\hat{u}(x) - u_{\max}(x))^2}{u_{\max}(x)}$. We calculate the empirical distribution $P^{\text{prior}}_{\max}[x] = \frac{u_{\max}(x)}{L}$. Similarly, we construct expected frequencies $u_{\min}$ giving the smallest vulnerability, and calculate the corresponding distribution $P^{\text{prior}}_{\min}$. Then we obtain the following:

Lemma 2. *The lower and upper bounds for the 95% confidence interval of the min-entropy $H_\infty(X)$ are respectively given by:*

$$H^{\text{low}}_\infty(X) = -\log_2 \max_{x \in \mathcal{X}} P^{\text{prior}}_{\max}[x], \quad H^{\text{up}}_\infty(X) = -\log_2 \max_{x \in \mathcal{X}} P^{\text{prior}}_{\min}[x].$$

Finally, we obtain a confidence interval for the min-entropy leakage:

Theorem 3. *The lower and upper bounds for a more than 95% confidence interval of the min-entropy leakage $\mathcal{L}(X; Y)$ are respectively given by:*

$$\mathcal{L}^{\text{low}}(X; Y) = H^{\text{low}}_\infty(X) - H^{\text{up}}_\infty(Y|X), \ \mathcal{L}^{\text{up}}(X; Y) = H^{\text{up}}_\infty(X) - H^{\text{low}}_\infty(Y|X).$$

Note that our estimation technique for min-entropy leakage requires a large number of trial runs (usually many more than that required to estimate mutual information) to ensure that no more than 20% of the non-zero expected frequencies are below 5, which is a prerequisite for χ^2 tests.

Fig. 1 shows an example of mutual information and min-entropy leakage estimation; the graph is generated with 1,000 estimates of leakage from the 4-diner DC-net described in depth in Section 6.1) in which the random bits are biased towards 0 with probability 0.75. The graph shows the true leakage result, the estimated results from 10,000 runs of LeakWatch, and the bounds for min-entropy leakage. Our mutual information result gives the exact distribution of the estimates and so LeakWatch calculates the exact 95% confidence interval.

In this case, we observe that the estimation of min-entropy leakage is slightly biased and that it demonstrates more variation in the range of results than mutual information, although other examples (especially examples with unique maximum probabilities) demonstrate more variation in the mutual information estimate.

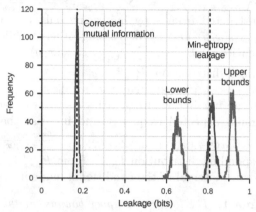

Fig. 1. The sampling distributions of mutual information and min-entropy leakage (and the lower/ upper bounds for min-entropy leakage's confidence interval)

In all cases, our bounds for the mutual information estimate are better than our bounds for min-entropy leakage; this is because we find the exact distribution of the estimates for mutual information and so can find a more accurate confidence interval.

4   The Design of LeakWatch

LeakWatch is a robust tool intended for testing general-purpose, real-world Java programs where the presence of information leakage vulnerabilities may be a concern. It repeatedly executes a target program, recording the secret and observable values it encounters, and then uses the estimation results described in Sections 2 and 3 to find bounds on the information leakage from the program.

We target Java because of its enterprise popularity and common usage in large software projects. LeakWatch requires minimal modifications to be made to the target program's source code: the analyst simply inserts calls to the LeakWatch API methods, `secret()` and `observe()` (indicating the occurrence of a secret and observable value respectively), identifies the name of the *main class* containing the target program's main method and instructs LeakWatch to estimate the leakage from that program. The repeated execution of the program in a manner that guarantees the correctness of the leakage estimation — including handling idiosyncrasies of the Java Virtual Machine (JVM), such as class-loading — and computation of the leakage estimation are then performed by LeakWatch. As the target program is repeatedly executed, LeakWatch automatically determines whether the amount of secret and observable information gathered is sufficient to produce a reliable leakage estimation; no further user interaction is required.

An important requirement of our statistical tests is that the sampled data is independent and identically distributed. This requirement is easily fulfilled if the target program does not rely on any external state (e.g., a value read from a file) that may change between executions. Programs that rely on some external state that does not have a statistically significant effect on the observable behaviour of the program can also be analysed without modification. It may be possible to modify programs that do rely on external state (e.g., by replacing a network read with a randomly generated value) and still obtain useful results.

4.1   Collecting Sufficient Program Execution Data

For our estimation results to be meaningful, we must collect enough samples to ensure that the estimated joint distribution of the secret and observable information that occurs in the program is a close approximation of the true distribution. Recall from Theorem 2 that the mean and variance of the distribution from which mutual information estimates are drawn are both defined as Taylor series. For efficiency reasons, LeakWatch only evaluates the first-order Taylor polynomial (e.g., $\hat{I}(X;Y) - (\#\mathcal{X} - 1)(\#\mathcal{Y} - 1)/2n$ for the point estimate of mutual information). Evaluating more terms in the Taylor series is computationally expensive because the joint distribution of X and Y must be enumerated differently for each term. For a small number of samples n, it is likely that the $O(n^{-2})$ and higher-order terms are too large for the first-order Taylor polynomial to be a good approximation of the sum of the series, and so $\hat{I}(X;Y) - (\#\mathcal{X} - 1)(\#\mathcal{Y} - 1)/2n$ will change as n increases. However, for a large enough number of samples, the higher-order terms quickly become small enough to have no meaningful effect on the result, and $\hat{I}(X;Y) - (\#\mathcal{X} - 1)(\#\mathcal{Y} - 1)/2n$ will no longer change as n increases.

Based on this observation, LeakWatch uses the following heuristic to automatically determine when a sufficient amount of trial run data has been collected to minimise the higher-order terms in the Taylor series and therefore provide an accurate mutual information estimate. It computes an estimate $\hat{I}(X;Y)$ after $\max(\#\mathcal{X} \times \#\mathcal{Y}, 100)$ samples have been collected, and stops collecting samples if all of the following conditions are met:
1) $\#\mathcal{X}, \#\mathcal{Y} > 1$ (otherwise a leakage measure cannot be computed from the joint probability distribution);
2) $\#\mathcal{X}$ and $\#\mathcal{Y}$ have remained constant since these conditions were last checked (otherwise the values in condition 4 cannot be compared meaningfully);
3) the minimum number of samples $(4 \times \#\mathcal{X} \times \#\mathcal{Y})$ has been collected;
4) the value $\hat{I}(X;Y) - (\#\mathcal{X} - 1)(\#\mathcal{Y} - 1)/2n$ has not changed beyond a certain amount, configurable by the analyst, since these conditions were last checked (otherwise the higher-order Taylor series terms are non-negligible).

If these conditions are not met, the process is repeated again when $\#\mathcal{X} \times \#\mathcal{Y}$ more samples have been collected.

This heuristic allows LeakWatch to produce accurate mutual information estimates and confidence intervals for target programs containing both small and large numbers of unique secret and observable values that occur with a non-negligible probability. The initial number of samples $\max(\#\mathcal{X} \times \#\mathcal{Y}, 100)$ prevents LeakWatch from terminating too early when analysing very small systems (e.g., those containing fewer than ten unique secret and observable values in total) due to the low value of $\#\mathcal{X} \times \#\mathcal{Y}$ in these systems.

To estimate min-entropy leakage, we need many more trial runs than we need to estimate mutual information. As mentioned in Section 3, we require that no more than 20% of the non-zero expected frequencies are below 5; LeakWatch therefore collects samples until this condition as well as the first three conditions in the above procedure for mutual information estimation are met.

5   Implementing LeakWatch

To test a program for information leakage, an analyst simply imports the LeakWatch API class into their Java program and tags the secret and publicly-observable data with the API's `secret()` and `observe()` methods. Execution and sandboxing of the target program are achieved using the core Java libraries, and leakage estimates are calculated by leakiEst [19,20], our information leakage estimation library for Java, which now implements our min-entropy leakage result from Section 3; this ensures that LeakWatch is not tethered to a particular version or implementation of the JVM specification.

We now discuss two implementation issues: ensuring the independence of target program executions, and automatically providing programs with simulated user input.

5.1   Ensuring the Independence of Target Program Executions

When a Java program is executed, a new JVM is created; this involves loading and uncompressing many megabytes of Java class files. To generate test data efficiently, LeakWatch uses the same JVM to execute each trial run of the program. However, ensuring that programs sharing the same JVM execute independently (a requirement for our statistical estimation method) is not trivial to guarantee.

Java programs consist of one or more classes that are loaded into memory on-demand; the task of locating the bytecode that defines a class, parsing the bytecode, and returning a reference to the new class to the caller is performed by a *classloader*, itself a Java class. A class with a given name may be loaded only once by a given classloader. The JVM contains three classloaders by default, arranged in a hierarchy: the *bootstrap classloader* loads the core Java classes (e.g., those whose names begin with `java.`), the *extensions classloader* loads the Java extension classes (e.g., those that perform cryptographic operations), and the *system classloader* loads other classes. This hierarchy is strictly enforced; e.g., the system classloader delegates the loading of `java.lang.String` to the extensions classloader, which in turn delegates it to the bootstrap classloader. By default, this means that both LeakWatch's classes and the target program's classes are loaded by the system classloader.

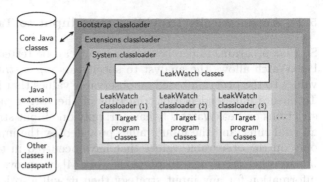

Fig. 2. The LeakWatch classloader hierarchy. Multiple copies of the target program can be executed simultaneously and in isolation using separate instances of the LeakWatch classloader.

LeakWatch runs the target program by invoking the main method in the target program's main class and waiting for it to return. Because a class may contain static member variables, having the system classloader load the target program's classes would be problematic: LeakWatch would not be able to "reset" the value of static member variables present in the target program's classes before invoking the main class's main method again, so some state may be preserved between executions of the target program. This potentially violates the independence of trial runs.

LeakWatch solves this problem by loading target program classes with its own classloader, positioned in the hierarchy between the system classloader and any classloaders used by the target program (see Fig. 2). Before each invocation of the main class's main method, a new LeakWatch classloader is initialised; it contains only the definition of the main class. As the main method executes, the LeakWatch classloader creates a new instance of any class required by the target program; subsequent requests for the class with that name will return this instance of the class, rather than the instance that would usually be returned by the system classloader. When the main method returns, LeakWatch destroys this classloader (and therefore any class loaded by it), ensuring that earlier invocations of the main method cannot interfere with future invocations. This guarantee even holds when multiple instances of the LeakWatch classloader exist concurrently, allowing LeakWatch to perform multiple isolated invocations of the main method at the same time using multithreading.

If a class is usually loaded by either the bootstrap or extensions classloaders, the LeakWatch classloader must delegate the request to them, so all executions of the target program "see" the same copies of the Java API classes. Although information could be shared between executions in this way, it is only possible with methods in a handful of classes (e.g., `java.lang.System`'s `setProperty()` method) and it is easy for the analyst to verify whether they are used.

5.2 Automatically Providing User Input to Target Programs

So that programs that rely on user input can be tested for information leakage, LeakWatch allows the analyst to specify an *input strategy* that provides input values to the program based on observable values that have previously occurred. To ensure independence of trial runs of the target program, we place two restrictions on LeakWatch's behaviour: only one input strategy may be defined for all trial runs, and the input values provided by the input strategy must depend only on the observable values that have occurred in the current trial run, and not in other trial runs. In previous work [4], we proved that if a program leaks information for any input strategy then it will also leak a non-zero amount of information for the input strategy that selects all possible inputs uniformly, so the uniform input strategy is a good default strategy.

Input can be provided to Java programs in many ways. We focus on input provided via the *standard input stream*, a universal method of supplying data to software; in Java, this stream is accessed with the static member variable `System.in` of type `java.io.InputStream`, whose `read()` method returns the next byte from the input buffer.

Operating systems provide a single standard input stream to a process; this means that all classes loaded by a particular JVM read from the same `System.in` stream. This is problematic because LeakWatch's classes and the target program's classes all execute within the same JVM; even though LeakWatch sandboxes each execution of the target program using its own classloader, all instances of the target program will share (and therefore read from) the same input stream. This is most noticeable when using multithreading to perform multiple isolated executions of the target program concurrently: two instances of a program reading 20 bytes of input from `System.in` will conflict, each using the `read()` method to read approximately 10 bytes from the same stream. This leaves both instances of the program with meaningless input, and violates the requirement that trial runs be independent and identically distributed.

We solve both problems by transforming every target class that reads from the standard input stream to instead read from an *input driver*, a mock object that mimics `System.in`. When using LeakWatch to analyse a program that reads from the standard input stream, the analyst must also write an appropriate input driver to supply input when it is required. The purpose of the input driver is to implement the input strategy described above: like `System.in`, it is a subclass of `java.io.InputStream`, but its `read()` method may consult the list of observable values that have been encountered so far during execution and return a stream of bytes comprising the selected input to the target program. When classes are loaded by LeakWatch's classloader, their bytecode is dynamically transformed (using the ASM [21] library) so that all references to `System.in` are replaced with references to the analyst's input driver. The loading of the input driver class is also performed by LeakWatch's classloader, so each execution of the target program believes it alone is reading from the standard input stream; this means that concurrent executions of a target program that reads from the standard input stream can progress without interfering with each other.

6   Practical Applications

We now present three examples demonstrating how LeakWatch can be applied to real-world situations to detect the presence of information leaks, quantify their size, and remove or mitigate them; they were benchmarked on a desktop computer with a quad-core CPU and 4GB of RAM. The source code for these examples is available for download from [13].

6.1   A Poorly-Implemented Multi-Party Computation Protocol

The *dining cryptographers problem* [22] investigates how anonymity can be guaranteed during secure multi-party computation. Informally: a group of cryptographers dine at a restaurant, and the waiter informs them that the bill is to be paid anonymously; it may be paid by any of the diners, or (e.g.) by the national security agent sitting at an adjacent table. After the bill has been paid, how do the diners collectively discover whether one of them paid the bill, while respecting their fellow diners' right to anonymity?

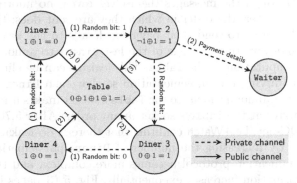

Fig. 3. An overview of the Java DC-net implementation. Diner 2 pays the bill; the final result is 1, indicating that one of the Diners paid.

The *DC-net* is a solution to the dining cryptographers problem; it provides unconditional sender and recipient untraceability. Briefly, each diner generates a random bit visible only to them and the diner to their left, giving each diner sight of two separate randomly-generated bits; each diner computes the XOR of these two bits and announces the result publicly to the rest of the table — except for the payer, who announces the inverse of their XOR computation. The XOR of the announcements themselves allow each diner to verify whether one of them paid: if this value is 1, one of the diners claimed to have paid; if it is 0, nobody claimed to have paid. This protocol preserves the anonymity of the payer; however, care must be taken when implementing the protocol to ensure that side-channels do not leak information about the payer's identity.

This example implements a multithreaded, object-oriented DC-net in Java (see Fig. 3). Four Diners are seated at a Table and — for the purposes of verifying whether the code contains an information leak — one of them is randomly selected to be the payer; the identity of the payer is marked as a secret with secret(). The Diners then concurrently execute the protocol described above: they privately exchange their randomly-generated bits with each other using the socket libraries in the Java API, and the payer sends their payment details to the Waiter over another private socket. The Diners then announce the results of their XOR computation to the rest of the `Table`; the messages sent to the `Table`'s socket are publicly visible, and are marked as observable with `observe()`. LeakWatch then answers the question "what does a passive attacker learn about the payer's identity by watching the messages sent to the `Table`?".

After 2,600 trial runs (taking 9 minutes to perform the required number of trial runs and 300ms to calculate the leakage estimate), LeakWatch estimates that there are ca. 1.15 of a possible 2 bits of mutual information between the identity of the payer and the messages the `Diners` broadcast to the `Table`. The min-entropy leakage is found to be 0.47 bits after 6,080 trial runs; 11 minutes were spent performing the trial runs, and 221ms were spent calculating the estimate. Although the messages themselves reveal no information about the identity of the payer, the order in which they are sent does: the additional time taken by the payer to send their payment details to the `Waiter` means that, more often than not, they are one of the last `Diners` to announce the result of their XOR computation to the `Table`. This leakage can be eliminated in several ways; e.g., modifying the implementation so that each `Diner` waits 100ms before sending their announcement to the `Table`'s socket makes it more likely that messages will arrive at the `Table`'s socket in any order. After 5,700 trial runs of this modified DC-net, LeakWatch confirms that there is no leakage of the payer's identity.

By increasing the number of `Diners` participating in the DC-net, the communication protocol becomes more complex, and the amount of observable information increases exponentially. Fig. 5 (3 pages below) shows the amount of time LeakWatch takes to estimate the leakage from a simplified DC-net, with all socket-based communication removed and a new leak caused by biased random bit generation inserted (a 0 is generated with probability 0.75, rather than 0.5). The graph shows that, as more `Diners` are added to this simplified DC-net, the amount of time LeakWatch takes to perform a number of trial runs that is sufficient to compute an accurate leakage estimate increases exponentially (ca. 2 hours when 17 `Diners` participate). The amount of time required to estimate the size of the leak also increases exponentially, but remains comparatively very small (ca. 12 seconds when 17 `Diners` participate), indicating that the vast majority of LeakWatch's time is spent collecting sufficient trial run data, and not computing leakage estimates.

6.2   Analysing the Design of Stream Ciphers

Crypto-1 is a stream cipher used to encrypt transmissions in commercial RFID tags. The design of this cipher was kept secret, but careful analysis (e.g., [23]) revealed that it is based on a 48-bit linear feedback shift register (LFSR). Each keystream bit is generated by applying two functions (f_a, f_b) to 20 bits of the state, and then applying a third function (f_c) to the outputs of these functions. In this example we use LeakWatch to show that the mutual information between the state bits and the keystream bits reveals much of this structure.

The initial state of the LFSR is derived from the key; to simplify the example, we assume that we can set the initial state directly. Information about the structure of Crypto-1 is revealed by loading different initial states into the LFSR and observing the output from the final Boolean function f_c. Using a Java implementation of Crypto-1, an LFSR is created with a randomly-generated initial state, and the first output bit from f_c is computed. The value of this bit is marked as observable with observe(). Another LFSR is created with the same initial state as before, but with the value of the bit at index i flipped with probability $\frac{1}{2}$ — the decision about whether or not to flip this bit is marked as secret information with secret(). The output from f_c in this second cipher is then computed, and its value is also marked as observable with observe(). The question being asked here is "what is the correlation between the LFSR bit at index i being flipped and the output of f_c changing?"; informally, this can be seen as the influence of the bit at index i on the cipher's keystream.

By running LeakWatch 48 times, each time using a different value of i between 0 and 47 (taking a total of 19 seconds to perform the trial runs and a total of 425ms to produce the 48 leakage estimates), LeakWatch reveals which indices of the LFSR are tapped and passed as input to the Boolean functions; each execution of LeakWatch performs approximately 220 trial runs to determine the influence that that particular bit has on the keystream. Fig. 4 graphs the influence of each LFSR bit on the output of the cipher; points that fall above the dashed line near the x axis indicate a statistically significant correlation between flipping the LFSR bit at the index on the x axis and the first bit of the keystream changing. By reading off these indices on the x axis, we see which bits are tapped to produce the keystream. Moreover, the relative vertical distances between the points for each group of four indices reveal two distinctive patterns: these are the Boolean functions f_a

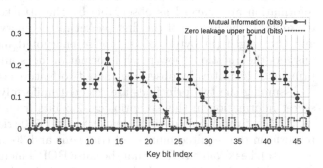

Fig. 4. The influence over the first bit of the keystream of each bit in a 48-bit secret initial state for Crypto-1

and f_b (i.e., the pattern for groups $\{9, 11, 13, 15\}$ and $\{33, 35, 37, 39\}$ represents f_a, and the pattern for groups $\{17, 19, 21, 23\}$, $\{25, 27, 29, 31\}$ and $\{41, 43, 45, 47\}$ represents f_b); it is therefore possible to "see" which indices are tapped by each of these functions, as indicated by the dashed lines between the points in each group. The slight variation in the groups' distances from the x axis is accounted for by the third Boolean function f_c, into which the output from the other Boolean functions is fed.

This analysis shows that the output of this popular but flawed cipher reveals a lot of information about its internal design; it is therefore unsurprising that the cipher's design was fully reverse-engineered. The same technique can also be used to analyse other LFSR-based stream ciphers, such as Hitag-2 [24].

6.3   Recipient Disclosure in OpenPGP Encrypted Messages

OpenPGP [25] is a data encryption standard. In a typical usage scenario, encrypted OpenPGP messages contain two *packets*: the first contains a randomly-generated symmetric session key encrypted with the recipient's public key, and the second contains the sender's message, encrypted under the session key. Although OpenPGP provides message confidentiality and integrity, it does not necessarily provide recipient confidentiality because the first packet contains the recipient's *key ID* — the low 64 bits of the SHA-1 hash of their public key — which may be used to corroborate the recipient's identity with a resource mapping public keys to identities, such as an OpenPGP key server.

To demonstrate this, we present an example where two principals attempt to communicate securely using OpenPGP while concealing their identities from a passive attacker with the ability to read messages sent over the communication medium; the OpenPGP API is provided by the BCPG Java library [26]. In the program, a sender is chosen randomly from a pool of six principals, and a recipient is chosen from the remaining five; their identities are both marked as secret (with secret()). The sender greets the recipient by name, encrypts the greeting with the recipient's public key, and sends the encrypted message over an insecure medium, where it is monitored by the attacker. Two pieces of information are marked as observable by the attacker using separate calls to observe(): the header of the first packet in the encrypted OpenPGP message, and the length (in bytes) of the entire encrypted message. Thus, LeakWatch answers the question "how much information does an attacker learn about the principals' identities by observing these two features of the encrypted traffic?".

Assuming the two principals are selected uniformly, there are ca. 4.9 bits of secret information in this scenario (ca. 2.6 bits from the sender's identity and ca. 2.3 bits from the recipient's identity). After 550 trial runs (taking 17 seconds to perform the required number of trial runs and 300ms to produce the leakage estimate), LeakWatch reveals that, because BCPG includes the recipient's key ID in the first packet, there is a leakage of ca. 2.52 bits about the secret information: there is complete leakage of the recipient's identity, and a further leakage of ca. 0.2 bits of the sender's identity, because the attacker also knows that the sender is not the recipient.

Some OpenPGP implementations mitigate this leakage of the recipient's identity; e.g., GnuPG features a -R option that replaces the key ID in the first packet with a string of null bytes. By patching BCPG to do the same, the leakage decreases to ca. 1.86 bits after 350 trial runs: the recipient's identity is no longer leaked completely via the first packet, but because the attacker knows the format of the unencrypted message being sent, the length of the second packet still reveals some information about the recipient's identity (because the sender's encrypted message will be longer when greeting a recipient with a longer name).

Fig. 5 shows how increasing the number of bits in the first packet that are observable by the attacker affects LeakWatch's execution time. It reveals a result similar to that in Section 6.1: as the number of bits in the observable output increases, the amount of time required for LeakWatch to perform the number of trial runs required to estimate leakage increases exponentially (ca. 6 hours when the observation size reaches 132 bits); this is because of the exponentially-increasing number of trial runs required to verify whether parts of the randomly-generated encrypted session key leak information about the principals' identities. The amount of time required to estimate the size of the information leak from the trial run data, however, remains comparatively very small (ca. 1.5 seconds when the observation size reaches 132 bits), as it does in Section 6.1.

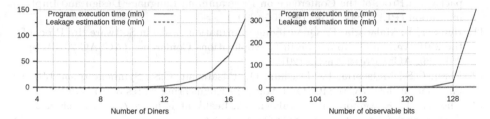

Fig. 5. The effect on LeakWatch's execution time of increasing the amount of secret or observable information in the examples in Sections 6.1 (the number of Diners, left) and 6.3 (the number of observable bits in the encrypted OpenPGP message, right).

7   Conclusion

We have presented new theoretical results and practical techniques for the statistical estimation of information leakage from real-world Java programs, based on trial runs. In particular, we have described a new method for estimating min-entropy leakage and its confidence interval, and a technique for ensuring the collection of a sufficient number of samples. We have also presented a mechanism that ensures the independence of trial runs of Java programs, and applied our information leakage model and estimation techniques to input-consuming Java programs. Using three examples, we have demonstrated that our robust information leakage analysis tool LeakWatch can uncover information leakage vulnerabilities in Java programs.

References

1. Shannon, C.E.: A Mathematical Theory of Communication. Bell System Technical Journal 27(3), 379–423 (1948)
2. Smith, G.: On the Foundations of Quantitative Information Flow. In: de Alfaro, L. (ed.) FOSSACS 2009. LNCS, vol. 5504, pp. 288–302. Springer, Heidelberg (2009)
3. Smith, G.: Quantifying Information Flow Using Min-Entropy. In: Proc. of the 8th Conference on Quantitative Evaluation of Systems (QEST 2011), pp. 159–167 (2011)
4. Chothia, T., Kawamoto, Y., Novakovic, C., Parker, D.: Probabilistic Point-to-Point Information Leakage. In: Proc. of the 26th IEEE Computer Security Foundations Symposium (CSF 2013), pp. 193–205. IEEE Computer Society (June 2013)
5. Moddemeijer, R.: On estimation of entropy and mutual information of continuous distributions. Signal Processing 16, 233–248 (1989)
6. Brillinger, D.R.: Some data analysis using mutual information. Brazilian Journal of Probability and Statistics 18(6), 163–183 (2004)

7. Boreale, M., Paolini, M.: On formally bounding information leakage by statistical estimation (2014) (Unpublished Manuscript)
8. Biondi, F., Legay, A., Traonouez, L.-M., Wąsowski, A.: QUAIL: A Quantitative Security Analyzer for Imperative Code. In: Sharygina, N., Veith, H. (eds.) CAV 2013. LNCS, vol. 8044, pp. 702–707. Springer, Heidelberg (2013)
9. Mu, C., Clark, D.: A tool: quantitative analyser for programs. In: Proc.of the 8th Conference on Quantitative Evaluation of Systems (QEST 2011), pp. 145–146 (2011)
10. McCamant, S., Ernst, M.D.: Quantitative Information Flow as Network Flow Capacity. In: Proc. of the Conference on Programming Language Design and Implementation (PLDI 2008), pp. 193–205 (2008)
11. Heusser, J., Malacaria, P.: Quantifying Information Leaks in Software. In: Proc. of the 2010 Annual Computer Security Applications Conference (ACSAC 2010), pp. 261–269. ACM Press, Austin (2010)
12. Phan, Q.S., Malacaria, P., Tkachuk, O., Păsăreanu, C.S.: Symbolic quantitative information flow. ACM SIGSOFT Software Engineering Notes 37(6), 1–5 (2012)
13. Chothia, T., Kawamoto, Y., Novakovic, C.: LeakWatch, http://www.cs.bham.ac.uk/research/projects/infotools/leakwatch/
14. Chatzikokolakis, K., Chothia, T., Guha, A.: Statistical Measurement of Information Leakage. In: Esparza, J., Majumdar, R. (eds.) TACAS 2010. LNCS, vol. 6015, pp. 390–404. Springer, Heidelberg (2010)
15. Denning, D.E.: Cryptography and Data Security. Addison-Wesley (May 1982)
16. Myers, A.C., Liskov, B.: Complete, Safe Information Flow with Decentralized Labels. In: Proc. of the 1998 IEEE Symposium on Security and Privacy, pp. 186–197. IEEE Computer Society, Oakland (1998)
17. Pearson, K.: X. on the criterion that a given system of deviations from the probable in the case of a correlated system of variables is such that it can be reasonably supposed to have arisen from random sampling. Philosophical Magazine Series 5 50(302), 157–175 (1900)
18. Diez, D.M., Barr, C.D., Cetinkaya-Rundel, M.: OpenIntro Statistics. CreateSpace (2012)
19. Chothia, T., Kawamoto, Y., Novakovic, C.: A Tool for Estimating Information Leakage. In: Sharygina, N., Veith, H. (eds.) CAV 2013. LNCS, vol. 8044, pp. 690–695. Springer, Heidelberg (2013)
20. Kawamoto, Y., Chatzikokolakis, K., Palamidessi, C.: Compositionality Results for Quantitative Information Flow. In: Proc. of the 11th International Conference on Quantitative Evaluation of Systems, QEST 2014 (to appear, September 2014)
21. OW2 Consortium: ASM, http://asm.ow2.org
22. Chaum, D.: The Dining Cryptographers Problem: Unconditional Sender and Recipient Untraceability. Journal of Cryptology, 65–75 (1988)
23. Garcia, F.D., van Rossum, P., Verdult, R., Schreur, R.W.: Wirelessly pickpocketing a Mifare Classic card. In: IEEE Symposium on Security and Privacy (S&P 2009), pp. 3–15. IEEE (2009)
24. Verdult, R., Garcia, F.D., Balasch, J.: Gone in 360 seconds: Hijacking with Hitag2. In: 21st USENIX Security Symposium (USENIX Security 2012), pp. 237–252. USENIX Association (2012)
25. Callas, J., Donnerhacke, L., Finney, H., Shaw, D., Thayer, R.: OpenPGP Message Format, http://tools.ietf.org/html/rfc4880
26. Legion of the Bouncy Castle Inc.: The Legion of the Bouncy Castle Java Cryptography APIs, https://www.bouncycastle.org/java.html

SIGPATH: A Memory Graph Based Approach for Program Data Introspection and Modification

David Urbina[1], Yufei Gu[1], Juan Caballero[2], and Zhiqiang Lin[1]

[1] UT Dallas
[2] IMDEA Software Institute
firstname.lastname@utdallas.edu, juan.caballero@imdea.org

Abstract. Examining and modifying data of interest in the memory of a target program is an important capability for security applications such as memory forensics, rootkit detection, game hacking, and virtual machine introspection. In this paper we present a novel memory graph based approach for program data introspection and modification, which does not require source code, debugging symbols, or any API in the target program. It takes as input a sequence of memory snapshots taken while the program executes, and produces a path signature, which can be used in different executions of the program to efficiently locate and traverse the in-memory data structures where the data of interest is stored. We have implemented our approach in a tool called SIGPATH. We have applied SIG-PATH to game hacking, building cheats for 10 popular real-time and turn-based games, and for memory forensics, recovering from snapshots the contacts a user has stored in four IM applications including Skype and Yahoo Messenger.

Keywords: program data introspection, memory graph, game hacking.

1 Introduction

Many security applications require examining, and possibly modifying, data structures in the memory of a target program. These data structures store private, often sensitive, *data of interest* such as running processes in an OS, unit and resource information in online games, and credentials and contact information in Instant Messengers (IM). Such capability is crucial for memory forensics [1–4], rootkit detection [5–7], game hacking [8], reverse engineering [9–11], and virtual machine introspection (VMI) [12].

We call the process of examining in-memory data structures of a target program from an external introspector *program data introspection* (PDI). The introspector can run concurrently with the target on the same OS, e.g., a user-level debugger or a kernel module, or out-of-VM for improved isolation and higher privilege. The introspection can be done online as the program runs or offline on a snapshot of the target's memory.

The main challenges in EDI are how to efficiently locate the in-memory data structures storing the data of interest and how to traverse them to examine their data. Prior memory analysis works reuse the target's binary code or APIs to dump the data of interest (e.g., the UNIX `ps` command to list processes) [13, 14], or leverage the target's source code and debugging symbols [5, 15, 16]. However, most application-level programs do not expose external APIs to examine the data of interest and commercial off-the-self (COTS) programs rarely have source code or debugging symbols available.

M. Kutyłowski and J. Vaidya (Eds.): ESORICS 2014, Part II, LNCS 8713, pp. 237–256, 2014.

In this paper we propose a novel memory-based approach for program data introspection and modification that does not require source code or debugging symbols for the target program, or the target to expose any APIs. Our lightweight approach takes as input memory snapshots taken while the program runs and generates *path signatures* that capture how to efficiently retrieve the data of interest in memory by traversing pointers starting from the program's global variables.

Prior techniques that reverse-engineer data structures from binary programs through static (TIE [10]) or dynamic (REWARDS [9] and Howard [11]) analysis have three limitations for PDI. First, even if they recover the data structures related to the data of interest they do not address how to locate those data structures in memory. Second, they aim to recover all data structures used by a program, thus requiring very high coverage of the application's code, even when only a few data structures may be related to the data of interest. Third, they do not address recursive data structures (e.g., lists, trees) where much data of interest is stored.

More similar to our approach are techniques that compare memory snapshots such as LAIKA [17] and KARTOGRAPH [8]. However, these techniques have two limitations. First, they do not allow to reuse their results, i.e., every time the program executes they need to redo their expensive analysis. In contrast, our path signatures are created once and can then be used in many program executions. Second, they compare memory snapshots at the page level, including large chunks of dead memory. In contrast, we propose a novel technique to build a *memory graph* from a memory snapshot, structuring the live memory of a process. To the best of our knowledge ours is the first technique that can build an accurate memory graph without tracking the execution of the target program from its start and without source code or symbols, simply by using introspection on a memory snapshot. The memory graph is at the core of two techniques used to locate the data of interest in memory: *structural memory diffing*, which compares memory snapshots based on their underlying graph structure; and *fuzzing*, which modifies memory and observes its effects.

We have implemented our memory graph based approach to PDI into SIGPATH, a tool that creates path signatures to efficiently locate *and* traverse the (potentially recursive) data structures storing the data of interest. SIGPATH also provides an introspection component that takes as input a path signature and can examine and modify the data of interest while the program runs (and also from a memory snapshot). We have applied SIGPATH to two important security applications: *game hacking* and *memory forensics*.

Game Hacking. The goal of game hacking is modifying the in-memory data structures of a game to cheat it into providing the player with an advantage, e.g., an immortal unit. SIGPATH's path signatures can be used to efficiently examine the game's data structures as it executes to locate the resource targeted by the cheat. Once located, it can modify its value. Our cheats need to be constructed only once and can then be used every time the game is played without further analysis. We have evaluated SIGPATH on 10 popular RTS and turn-based games, building a variety of cheats for them.

Memory Forensics. The path signatures produced by SIGPATH can be used to retrieve private data from a memory snapshot of a suspect's computer. We apply SIGPATH to recover the list of contacts from a variety of IM applications a suspect may have been running when the snapshot was taken. Such a snapshot can be obtained by connecting an external memory capture device to the Firewire interface of the suspect's laptop if left unattended, even if the laptop screen was locked. We have successfully applied SIGPATH to recover the user contacts from 4 popular IM applications including Skype and Yahoo Messenger.

In short, this paper makes the following contributions:

- We propose a novel technique to build a memory graph exclusively from a memory snapshot by introspecting the OS data structures. The memory graph is the foundation of structural memory diffing and fuzzing, two techniques for identifying the location of the data of interest in memory.
- We develop a novel memory-based path signature generation technique, which does not require source code, debugging symbols, or API information from the target program. The produced path signatures capture how to find a data structure in memory and how to traverse it (even if recursive) to examine its data.
- We implement SIGPATH, a tool that generates path signatures from memory snapshots and uses them to introspect live programs or snapshots. We evaluate SIGPATH for game hacking and memory forensics.

2 Overview and Problem Definition

SIGPATH generates path signatures that capture how to reach the data of interest by traversing pointers from the program's global variables. Our path signatures have 3 important properties: they have *high coverage*, are *efficient* and *stable*.

First, despite their name, our path signatures capture multiple paths in memory. This is fundamental because the data of interest may be stored in an array or in a recursive data structure, e.g., a list or a tree. Here, the introspection needs to examine *all* instances of the data of interest in those data structures, e.g., all entries in a list. Second, our path signatures are stable. They are created once per program and can then be applied to any execution of that program, i.e., the paths they capture occur across executions. Third, our path signatures are efficient; they can quickly locate the data of interest by traversing a few pointers. They do not need to scan the (potentially huge) address space of the application. This makes them suitable for online introspection while the target program runs, when efficiency is key, as the program may frequently modify the introspected data structures. Of course, they can also be used offline on a snapshot of memory taken while the program was running.

Running Example. To demonstrate our techniques throughout the paper we use a simplified instant messaging application (`im.exe`) that stores the contacts of the user in the data structures shown in Figure 1.

```
typedef struct _contacts {      typedef struct _node {
    unsigned int num_groups;        struct _node *next;
    node_t **groups;                char *email;
} contacts_t;                   } node_t;
contacts_t *mycontacts;
```

Fig. 1. Data structures used by our example IM application to store the user contacts

The application allows the user to store contacts in 16 groups (`groups` array in `contacts_t`). For each group array entry there is a linked list (`node_t`) that stores the email addresses of the users in the group. The application accesses the contact information from the `mycontacts` global variable. The data of interest is the email addresses of the user contacts.

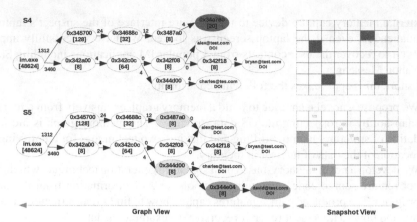

Fig. 2. On the left, simplified memory graph for two consecutive snapshots with the memory diffing results highlighted. On the right, the same memory at the page level.

2.1   The Memory Graph

The memory of a process has an inherent graph structure, which can be represented as a *memory graph*. A memory graph is a directed labeled graph $G = (V, E)$, where nodes (V) correspond to contiguous regions of *live memory*, often called buffers or objects. Nodes can represent modules loaded by the application or live heap allocations. Edges (E) represent pointers and capture the points-to relationships between live buffers when the snapshot was taken. The left side of Figure 2 shows the memory graphs for two snapshots in our running example. The path at the top of both memory graphs corresponds to data structures not shown in Figure 1.

A crucial characteristic of our approach is that it operates on a memory graph, which structures the otherwise chaotic memory of a process. The memory graph has 3 fundamental advantages over the page level representation of memory offered by a snapshot: (1) it captures only live memory; (2) it enables analyzing subgraphs of interest, e.g., only the memory reachable from the main module of the application; and (3) it captures *structural locality*, e.g., that two nodes belong to the same recursive data structure.

A snapshot of the memory of a process often comprises hundreds of MBs, of which large parts correspond to noise. This noise has two main components: dead memory and live memory largely independent of the application. Dead memory is very common in the heap. For example, LAIKA notes that only 45% of the heap is occupied by live objects, the rest being dead allocations and reserved memory not yet allocated [17]. The memory graph removes the noise introduced by dead memory. Furthermore, much live memory corresponds to external libraries, e.g., OS and graphics libraries, and the heap allocations used to store their internal data. The application requires these external libraries and their data to function but is largely independent of them. The memory graph enables further eliminating noise by removing memory only reachable by independent external libraries. The reduction in noise achieved by the memory graph is fundamental for finding the data of interest (i.e., a needle) in memory (i.e., the haystack). Our experimental results show that using the memory graph reduces the size of the memory of a process that needs to be analyzed by up to 73%.

In addition, the graph representation captures structural locality, i.e., nodes in the same data structure appear close, even if they have distant starting addresses. Structural locality enables identifying recursive data structures such as lists or trees. This is fundamental because the data of interest is often stored in recursive data structures, which need to be *traversed* to extract all data of interest instances (e.g., all users in a contact list). As illustrated in Figure 2, at the page level representation it is very difficult to identify recursive data structures, thus missing the multiple instances of data of interest they may store.

Clearly, the memory graph is a very effective representation of the memory of a process, but to the best of our knowledge there is currently no solution on how to build an accurate memory graph from a memory snapshot. The main challenge when building the memory graph is to identify where the nodes are located, i.e., their start address and size. Prior works that operate on memory snapshots such as LAIKA [17] and KARTO-GRAPH [8] do not offer a solution for this. In this work we propose a novel approach to build the memory graph that applies introspection on OS data structures to extract fine-grained information about the location and size of the loaded modules and the live heap allocations. We describe this process in §3.2.

2.2   Path Signatures

A path signature is a directed labeled graph $S = (V_S, E_S)$. Nodes correspond to memory buffers and can be of two types: root and normal ($V_S = V_{root} \cup V_{nor}$). Edges correspond to pointers and can be of three types: *normal, recursive,* and *array* ($E_S = E_{nor} \cup E_{rec} \cup E_{arr}$). A path signature has a single root node corresponding to the module (i.e., executable or DLL), where the path starts. A normal node represents a buffer in memory and is labeled with its size in bytes. Figure 3 shows the path signature for our running example where the root is the im.exe module and the Normal node corresponds to an instance of contacts_t.

A normal pointer corresponds to a concrete pointer in the path to the data of interest. It is a tuple (src, dst, o) where $src, dst \in V_S$ are the source and destination nodes ($src \neq dst$), and o is the offset in the src node where the pointer is stored. In Figure 3 there are 3 normal pointers (with offsets 3460,4,4) and the one with offset 3460 corresponds to the mycontacts global variable.

A recursive pointer is an abstraction representing that the path to the data of interest traverses a recursive data structure. During introspection SIG-PATH needs to extract all instances of the data of interest in the recursive data structure, so the recursive pointer needs

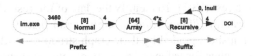

Fig. 3. Path signature for running example

to be unrolled multiple times. In our running example, traversing the next pointer of the linked list once leads to one email, traversing it twice to a different email, and so on. A recursive pointer is a tuple $(src, dst, o, cond)$ where src, dst, o are the same as in a normal pointer and *cond* is a boolean condition that captures when the end of the recursion has been reached, e.g., when the recursive pointer is null. We call the source node of a recursive pointer, a recursive node. In Figure 3 the `Recursive` node corresponds to an instance of `node_t` and its recursive pointer to `next`.

An array pointer is an abstraction representing that the path to the data of interest traverses an array of pointers (or an array of a data type that contains a pointer). Again, the introspection needs to extract all instances of the data of interest reachable from the array, so all pointers in the array need to be traversed. An array pointer is a tuple $(src, dst, o, step, size)$. Iterating from o in $step$ increments until $size$ returns all offsets of the src node where a pointer to be traversed is stored. If o is zero and $size$ corresponds to the size of src we omit them and call src an array node. In Figure 3 the `Array` node corresponds to the `groups` pointer array.

A path signature comprises two parts: the *prefix* and the *suffix*. The prefix is the initial part of the path signature before any recursive or array pointer. It captures a single path in memory leading from the root to the entry point of the data structure that stores all instances of the data of interest (an array of lists in our example). The suffix captures multiple paths inside that data structure that need to be traversed to examine all instances of the data of interest. The presence of recursive and array pointers is what makes the suffix capture multiple paths. Signatures that have no suffix indicate that the program stores a single instance of the data of interest.

2.3 Approach Overview

Using SIGPATH comprises three phases: *preparation*, *signature generation*, and *introspection*. The offline preparation and signature generation phases run once to produce a stable path signature to the data of interest. The introspection phase can run many times applying the path signature to examine, and possibly modify, the data of interest in different executions of the application. In some scenarios, preparation and signature generation could be run by one entity and introspection by another, e.g., when a company sells game cheats to end-users who apply them. Next, we introduce each phase.

Preparation. The first step in our approach is to gather a sequence of memory snapshots during the execution of the application (§3.1). All snapshots come from the same execution and between two consecutive snapshots an analyst takes an application-specific action related to the data of interest. For example, in our IM application the analyst inserts new contacts, taking a snapshot after each insertion. Next, SIGPATH builds a memory graph for each snapshot, which structures the application's live memory when the snapshot was taken (§3.2). Then, SIGPATH labels which nodes in each graph store the data of interest (§3.3). To identify the data of interest it uses a combination of three techniques: *memory diffing*, *value scanning*, and *fuzzing*. Memory diffing compares consecutive snapshots guided by their graph structure to identify their differences; value scanning searches for values of the data of interest using different encodings; and fuzzing modifies values in memory while monitoring the modification's effect. Preparation is the only phase where an analyst is involved, specifically for collecting the snapshots and during fuzzing (needed for only 12% of programs).

Path Signature Generation. The annotated memory graphs and the snapshots are passed to the automatic path signature generation process (§4). For each memory graph it first extracts all simple paths leading to the data of interest. Then, it identifies recursive pointers in each path and path prefixes that appear in all snapshots. Next, it locates arrays in those paths. Finally, it generalizes the paths by removing absolute addresses, and outputs stable path signatures.

Introspection. The generated path signatures can be used for examining and modifying the data of interest in different executions (or snapshots) of the application. To apply the signature, SIGPATH first identifies the base address of the root module and then traverses the signature pointers, unrolling recursive and array pointers as needed. For online introspection (and fuzzing) we have implemented two instrospectors: a user-level one that reads and modifies the target application's memory using the `ReadProcessMemory` and `WriteProcessMemory` functions, and a customized KVM monitor that introspects an application running in a VM (used for applications that check if they are monitored). For modifying the data of interest, if the data encoding is known (e.g., found through value scanning) SIGPATH can modify the data of interest to an arbitrary value. Otherwise, it can modify it to a previously observed value or fuzz it with arbitrary values until the desired effect is observed.

3 Preparation

3.1 Collecting the Snapshots

The first step in our approach is to take a number of memory snapshots while running the application. A snapshot is a dump of the content of all physical memory pages that are part of the application's address space at the time the snapshot is taken, the base virtual address of those pages, and additional metadata. SIGPATH supports two types of snapshots: Minidumps [18] produced by Microsoft's off-the-shelf tools running in parallel with the target on the same OS (e.g., WindDbg, Visual Studio, Windows Task Manager), and out-of-VM snapshots produced by the TEMU emulator [19]. The snapshots are collected at different times during the same execution. An analyst takes a snapshot before and after an action. There are positive and negative actions.

- A positive action forces the application to operate on the data of interest, leaking some information about its location in memory. For example, in our running IM example the analyst inserts a series of new contacts through the GUI taking a snapshot after each insertion. Each insertion forces the application to add the contact into its internal data structures. In a game hacking scenario where the goal is to create a unit that cannot be killed, the analyst orders one of her units to attack another of her units, forcing the game to reduce the life of the second unit.
- A negative action makes the program *not* to operate on the data of interest. The simplest negative action is to let time pass without doing anything, which helps identifying memory areas that change value independently of the data of interest.

The analyst selects one positive and one negative action for each application. It produces a sequence with an initial snapshot followed by a number of positive and negative snapshots (taken after the positive and the negative action, respectively). Obtaining both positive and negative snapshots is fundamental to structural memory diffing, detailed in §3.3. When possible, the analyst also annotates the snapshots with the value of the data of interest being inserted or modified, e.g., the contact's email address or the unit's life.

In some cases, value annotations cannot be added, e.g., when the game displays a unit's life using a bar rather than a value.

In our running example, the analyst inserts the email addresses of two contacts tagging each as group 1 and then another two tagged as group 2. It produces a sequence of 6 snapshots: one before any insertion, a positive snapshot after each insertion, and a negative snapshot a few seconds later without taking any action.

3.2 Building the Memory Graph

For each memory snapshot SIGPATH builds a memory graph $G = (V, E)$ using Algorithm 1. A node $v \in V$ corresponds to a live memory buffer and has three attributes: type, start address, and size. A node can be of 2 types: a module loaded into the application's address space (main executable or DLL) and a live heap buffer. An edge $p \in E$ is a tuple $(src, dst, o_{src}, o_{dst})$, where $src, dst \in V$ are the source and destination nodes, o_{src} is the offset in the src node where the pointer is stored, and o_{dst} is the offset into dst where the pointer points-to. For pointers to the head of the destination node we omit o_{dst}.

Algorithm 1: Memory Graph Creation

Input: A Memory Snapshot S
Output: A Memory Graph G

1 $H \leftarrow IntrospectHeap(S)$;
2 $M \leftarrow IntrospectModules(S)$;
3 $X \leftarrow IntrospectStack(S)$;
4 $V \leftarrow H \cup M \cup X$;
5 $G \leftarrow (V, \emptyset)$;
6 **for each** $v \in V$ **do**
7 $\quad b \leftarrow ReadNodeBlock(S, v)$;
8 $\quad P \leftarrow FindPointers(V, b)$;
9 $\quad$ **for each** $p \in P$ **do**
10 $\quad \quad \lfloor \quad G.AddEdge(p)$;

11 **return** G;

Nodes. SIGPATH extracts the node information using introspection on the OS data structures present in the memory snapshot. Introspection is very efficient, recovering all live objects (including their size) at once from the snapshot. The alternative would be to hook the heap allocation/deallocation and module load/unload functions during program execution. tracking the size and lifetime of those objects. We have used this approach in the past and found it problematic due to: (1) being expensive and cumbersome as it has to track execution from the start (including process creation and initialization), (2) need to identify and track hundreds of Windows allocation functions built atop the Heap Manager, (3) the targeted program may contain protections against tracing (e.g., games check for debuggers and Skype rejects PIN-based tracing). These problems justify our lightweight memory introspection approach.

The introspected data structures are OS-specific and we focus on the Windows platform because that is where most proprietary programs run. SIGPATH supports both Windows 7 and Windows XP. The data structures containing the module and heap information are stored in user-level memory and can be accessed following paths starting at the Process Environment Block (PEB), whose address is included in the snapshots.

The live heap allocations can be recovered from the Windows heap management data structures. In Windows, heaps are segments of pages controlled by the Heap Manager from which the application can allocate and release chunks using OS-provided functions. Each process has a default heap provided by the OS and can create additional heaps. Standard C/C++ functions such as `malloc` or `new` allocate memory from the CRT heap. As far as we know, no prior tool extracts the individual heap allocations of a process, so we have manually built a path signature (Fig. 4, top) to introspect the

Heap Manager's data structures (based on the information on the `ntdll.dll` PDB file and external sources, e.g., [20]). SIGPATH uses this signature to automatically recover the live heap allocations from a memory snapshot. The signature captures that a process has an array of heaps (_HEAP), each containing a linked list of segments (_HEAP_SEGMENT) where each segment points to a list of the individual heap entries (_HEAP_ENTRY). Each heap entry contains the start address and size of a live heap buffer. For each heap entry SIGPATH adds a node to the memory graph.

In contrast with the heap allocations there are off-the-shelf tools that can extract the loaded modules [21,22] but we have also built our own path signature (Fig. 4, bottom). The loaded modules can be recovered from the loader information in _PEB_LDR_DATA, which points to three lists with the loaded modules in different orderings (InLoadOrder, InMemoryOrder, and InInitializationOrder). Each list entry contains among others the module name, load address, and total module size. Note that for each loaded module there is a single node in the memory graph, representing the module's code and data. We could alternatively build a separate node for each module region (e.g., .data, .text) by parsing the PE header in memory. However, this is not needed as offsets from the module base are stable.

Pointers. To extract the pointers SIGPATH scans the ranges in the snapshot that correspond to live buffers. Each consecutive four bytes (8 for 64-bit) in a live buffer that forms an address pointing inside the range of a live buffer is considered a candidate pointer.

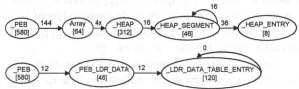

Fig. 4. Path signatures for examining the heaps and loaded modules of a process in Windows 7

This pointer detection technique is similar to the mark phase of a garbage collector and was also used by LAIKA. It can find spurious pointers (e.g., 1% of integers and 3% of strings point to the heap [17]). However, the advantage of using the memory graph is that only live memory is considered, so the probability of spurious pointers is significantly smaller. In addition, as will be shown in §4, the probability of an spurious pointer ending up in a path signature is negligible because a spurious pointer would have to appear at the same address in all snapshots and in the path to the data of interest to end up in a signature.

Reducing the Graph Size. Full memory graphs can contain hundreds of thousands of nodes. To reduce their size, SIGPATH includes only loaded modules shipped with the application, i.e., it excludes any libraries that are shipped with the OS. In addition, it removes any nodes not reachable from the remaining modules, e.g., those only reachable from the OS libraries. Again, as stated earlier, the memory graph we constructed can contain on average 27% of the memory in the corresponding snapshot.

3.3 Finding the Data of Interest

SIGPATH needs to identify which nodes store instances of the data of interest to extract paths leading to them. For this, it uses a combination of three techniques: *structural memory diffing*, *value scanning*, and *fuzzing*. The first two are new evolutions of previously proposed techniques for identifying data of interest in games, and our *fuzzing* is inspired by vulnerability discovery techniques.

In particular, *structural memory diffing* significantly evolves the snapshot diffing technique in KARTOGRAPH [8] and *value scanning* is used among others by the CHEAT-ENGINE [23]. Our *structural memory diffing* and *value scanning* techniques differ in that they operate on the memory graph rather than on the unstructured raw memory, which makes them substantially more accurate. For example, compared with the page level diffing in KARTOGRAPH [8], *structural memory diffing* greatly reduces the memory to diff as illustrated in Fig. 2, where the page level view (right) contains many more changes due to dead and unrelated memory. Our evaluation (§5) shows an average memory reduction of 82% on the memory graph after the application of structural memory diffing. In addition, *structural memory diffing* enables comparing the structure of the changes, which is fundamental to identify changes in the same recursive data structure.

Structural Memory Diffing. Given a sequence of memory graphs $G_1, \ldots, G_n$ and the corresponding snapshots $S_1, \ldots, S_n$ structural memory diffing compares each pair of consecutive memory graphs G_i, G_{i+1} extracting 3 sets: the nodes added into G_{i+1} and not present in G_i ($A_{i,i+1}$), the nodes removed from G_i and not present in G_{i+1} ($R_{i,i+1}$), and the modified nodes present in both ($M_{i,i+1}$). Fig. 2 highlights the nodes in these 3 sets after diffing the two memory graphs.

To obtain the set of changes across all snapshots, structural memory diffing computes the intersection of the sets of nodes (and byte ranges in them) modified across pairs of positive snapshots and then substracts the modifications in the negative snapshots (as they are unrelated to the data of interest):

$$M = \bigcap_{i=1}^{p-1} M_{i,i+1}^P \setminus \bigcup_{i=1}^{n-1} M_{i,i+1}^N$$

where $M_{i,i+1}^P$ and $M_{i,i+1}^N$ represent the nodes modified between snapshot i and positive or negative snapshot $i + 1$, respectively.

It also computes the union of all sets of nodes added across pairs of positive snapshots minus the removed ones, and then substracts the set of nodes removed in the negative snapshots:

$$A = \bigcup_{i=1}^{p-1} A_{i,i+1}^P \setminus \bigcup_{i=1}^{p-1} R_{i,i+1}^P \setminus \bigcup_{i=1}^{n-1} R_{i,i+1}^N$$

where $A_{i,i+1}^P$ represents the set of nodes added between snapshot i and positive snapshot $i + 1$, and $R_{i,i+1}^P$ and $R_{i,i+1}^N$ represent the set of nodes removed between snapshot i and positive or negative snapshot $i+1$, respectively. These two sets (M, A) are passed to the next technique as candidate locations storing data of interest.

Value Scanning. If the snapshots have a value annotation, SIGPATH linearly scans the buffers output by memory diffing for the annotated value using common encodings. In our running example the first 4 snapshots are annotated respectively with: *alex@test.com*, *bryan@test.com*, *charles@test.com*, and *david@test.com*. SIGPATH scans for the ASCII and Unicode versions of those email addresses. Similarly, for a unit's life it uses encodings such as short, integer, long, float, and double.

Note that we only use value scanning during preparation, as scanning memory at introspection while the program runs is too slow and precisely one of the reasons to generate path signatures. Also, value scanning is applied after structural memory diffing has significantly reduced the number of candidates. This is important because some values may not be discriminating enough and would match many locations otherwise. Value scanning is a simple yet surprisingly effective technique, and if it finds a value it also identifies its encoding. However, it does not work when the value is very common (e.g., zero); when the data uses non-standard encoding; is obfuscated or encrypted; or when the value to search is unknown.

Fuzzing. If multiple candidate nodes are still left the analyst uses fuzzing. In fuzzing, the analyst modifies the value of memory locations and monitors the effect of the modification. If the modification produces a visually observable result such as modifying the unit's life or changing the name of a contact on the screen, then the node stores the data of interest. Fuzzing is an online technique, similar to the process of modifying the data of interest in game hacking.

4   Path Signature Generation

The input to the signature generation is a sequence of pairs $\langle S_i, G_i \rangle$ where G_i is the memory graph for snapshot S_i, annotated with the nodes storing the data of interest. The output is a set of stable path signatures. Algorithm 2 describes the signature generation. For each memory graph G_i, SIG-PATH first extracts the set of simple paths rooted at one of the loaded modules and leading to any of the nodes

---

Algorithm 2: Path Signature Generation

Input: A sequence of pairs $\langle S_i, G_i \rangle$, and the data of interest d
Output: A set of stable path signatures $SIGS$ for d

1 $SIGS \leftarrow \emptyset$;
2 $NSP \leftarrow \emptyset$;
3 **for each** $G_i \in \langle S_i, G_i \rangle$ **do**
4 $\quad SP_i \leftarrow ExtractSimplePaths(G_i, d)$;
5 $\quad NSP \leftarrow NSP \cup FindRecursivePointers(SP_i)$;

6 $CP \leftarrow FindSetsOfPathsWithCommonPrefix(NSP)$;
7 **for each** $pathSet \in CP$ **do**
8 $\quad C \leftarrow ChunkPaths(pathSet)$;
9 $\quad$ **if** $EquivalentChunks(C)$ **then**
10 $\quad\quad A \leftarrow FindArrays(C)$;
11 $\quad\quad sig \leftarrow MergeChunks(C, A)$;
12 $\quad\quad SIGS \leftarrow SIGS \cup sig$;

13 $SIGS \leftarrow GeneralizePathSignatures(SIGS)$;
14 **return** $SIGS$;

---

labeled as data of interest (line 4). Simple paths do not contain repeating vertices (i.e., no loops) and for each data of interest node SIGPATH may extract multiple simple paths, possibly rooted at different nodes. Fig. 5 shows the 5 paths extracted from the 4 positive snapshots (S2–S5) in our running example.

Next, SIGPATH searches for recursive pointers in each of the paths (line 5). A recursive pointer is a pointer that points-to a node of the same type as the node holding the pointer. If a path contains two consecutive nodes of the same type, then the pointer linking them is recursive. As we do not know the type of each node, we approximate it using its size and internal structure. In particular, for each pair of consecutive nodes of the same size, we compare the offsets of all the pointers stored in each node, including those not in the path and taking special care of null pointers, as well as the offset of any ASCII or Unicode string they may store. If the offsets are identical, we consider the nodes to be of the same type and mark the pointer linking them as recursive.

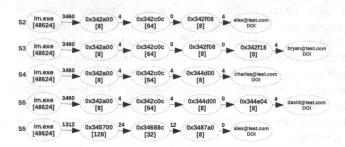

Fig. 5. Paths from 4 snapshots of running example

Then, SIGPATH searches for stable prefixes, which are path prefixes that appear in at least one path from each memory graph (line 6). Such prefixes capture structural proximity, i.e., data in the same data structure. To identify stable prefixes SIGPATH compares the paths node by node, considering two nodes from different paths equivalent if the source offset of the pointer leading to them, their address, and their size are identical. Shared prefixes stop at recursive pointers. Once the stable prefixes are identified, any paths that do not contain a stable prefix are removed as they cannot lead to a stable path signature. If no stable prefix is found, the process stops. However, this situation is unlikely and does not happen in our experiments. Fig. 6 shows the paths in our running example after identifying recursive pointers and stable prefixes.

Stable prefixes that reach the data of interest correspond already to stable path signatures and can proceed to generalization. For the remaining paths, SIGPATH splits them into chunks (line 8), ending a chunk at a recursive node (dashed vertical lines in Fig. 6). Then, it compares the shape of each chunk across the paths. If

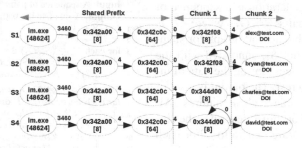

Fig. 6. Recursive pointers and stable prefix in paths from running example

the nodes in the chunk have the same address, are data of interest nodes, or have the same size and internal structure, they are considered equivalent. In Fig. 6 all four nodes in chunks 1 and 2 are equivalent. If the chunks are not equivalent, the shared prefix cannot generate a stable signature, so the paths containing them are removed (line 9).

For each chunk where the nodes are equivalent, SIGPATH looks for arrays (line 10). If the offset of the pointers leading to the chunk are different across snapshots there may be an array that is being exited through different array elements. This is the case with the last node in the shared prefix in Fig. 6, which leads to chunk 1 through offset 0 and 4 in different snapshots. Here, SIGPATH computes the greatest common denominator (gcd) of the offsets of the pointers leading to the chunk. If the gcd is larger or equal to the word size, the node is flagged as an array with $step = gcd$. The array size is determined by the largest offset leading to the chunk plus the $step$, accounting for NULL entries and being limited by the heap object size.

At this point, only stable paths that reach the data of interest in each of the snapshots remain and their chunks and arrays can be combined into a path signature (line 11). Finally, the path signatures are generalized by removing the nodes' memory addresses, since the same node on different executions will have different addresses (line 13). Fig. 3 shows the resulting stable path signature for our running example.

5 Evaluation

We have implemented the memory graph construction, finding the data of interest, and path signature generation components of SIGPATH using 3,400 lines of Python code (excluding external libraries). In addition, the user-level introspector comprises 1,500 lines of C++ and the KVM introspector with another 1,800 lines of C. In this section we present our evaluation results.

Experiment Setup. Table 1 presents the applications used to evaluate SIGPATH. For each application it details the different data of interest for which we use SIGPATH to produce a path signature. Applications are grouped into 3 categories: instant messengers (IM), real-time games (RTS), and board games (BG). The goal with IM applications is to retrieve from a given memory snapshot the user contacts the application stores (email address or contact identifier). In RTS games the goal is

Table 1. Applications used in our evaluation

Type	Application	Version	Data of Interest
IM	Yahoo Msg	11.5	Email
	Skype	6.6.0.106	Contact ID
	Pidgin	2.10.7	Email
	Miranda	0.10	Contact ID
RTS	SimCity 4	–	Money
	StarCraft	1.15	Mineral, Gas, CC life, SCV life
	Age of Empires II	0.14	Gold, Wood, Iron, Food
	WarCraft III	1.24	Gold, Wood
	Dune 2000	1.02	Money
	Emperor	1.04	Money
	Warlords Battlecry III	1.03	Gold, Hero experience
	C&C Generals	1.80	Money
BG	Spider Solitaire	5.10	Cards, Points
	Monopoly	1.00	Money

to modify the game's state at runtime to gain advantage, i.e., to cheat. The cheater plays against a variable number of adversaries controlled by remote players (or by the computer), and his goal is to (unfairly) beat them by obtaining an unlimited number of resources and units that heal themselves. Finally, in board games, the cheater plays against the computer and his goal is to set high scores to impress his friends.

All applications are 32-bit and run on both Windows 7 and Windows XP SP3 Virtual Machines. Experiments are performed on an host Intel Xeon with 16 cores 2.4GHz, with 48GB RAM, running Red Hat Enterprise 64-bit with kernel 2.6.32.

Collecting the Snapshots. For each application and data of interest we select a positive action and take snapshots after performing the action. For IM applications the positive action is inserting a new contact. For RTS games and resources (i.e., money, mineral, gas, gold, wood, iron, food) it is to put a unit to collect the resource, taking a snapshot when the resource counter increases. For StarCraft and the life of a unit (CC life, SCV life) it is to order one unit to attack the target unit (CC, SCV) taking a snapshot whenever the target's life decreases. For Warlords Battlecry III and the Hero experience it is to use the Hero unit to kill other units, taking a snapshot after each killing, which

Table 2. Evaluation results for the preparation and signature generation phases

Application	DOI	#Snaps.	Avg. Size (MB)	Avg. #Nodes	Avg. #Ptr	Avg. Size (MB)	Avg. Filtered Size (MB)	Avg. Ratio (%)	Memory Diffing (MB)	Value Scanning (bytes)	Fuzzing (bytes)	Encoding	#Nodes	#Paths	#Sig.
Yahoo Msg	Email	6	93	8,422	14,837	20	19	20	2	16	-	ASCII	2	6	1
Skype	Contact ID	6	102	3,761	12,618	70	63	61	8	20	-	ASCII	7	10	1
Pidgin	Email	6	52	6,305	41,981	5.6	5.5	10	1	32	-	ASCII	7	123	2
Miranda	Contact ID	6	34	671	5,790	6.2	6	17	2	16	-	ASCII	4	11	1
SimCity 4	Money	6	269	32,643	128,637	102	97	36	13	4	-	Integer	1	1	1
StarCraft	Minerals	10	45	1,069	1,672	5.5	5.2	12	1.1	4	-	Integer	1	1	1
	Gas	10	45	1,069	1,672	5.5	5.2	12	1.1	4	-	Integer	1	1	1
	CC life	10	45	1,069	1,672	5.5	5.2	12	1.1	2	-	Short	1	1	1
	SCV life	10	45	1,069	1,672	5.5	5.2	12	1.1	2	-	Short	1	1	1
Age of Empires II	Gold	6	157	488	1,709	85	79	50	5	4	-	Float	1	1	1
	Food	6	157	488	1,709	85	79	50	5	4	-	Float	1	1	1
	Wood	6	157	488	1,709	85	79	50	5	4	-	Float	1	1	1
	Iron	6	157	488	1,709	85	79	50	5	4	-	Float	1	1	1
WarCraft III	Gold	6	269	4,419	12,649	27	24	8	9	4	-	Integer	1	2	1
	Wood	6	269	4,419	12,649	27	24	8	9	4	-	Integer	1	2	1
Dune 2000	Money	6	40	842	1,575	10	10	4	2	4	-	Integer	1	1	1
Emperor	Money	10	114	37,129	10,232	70	65	57	7	102	4	Integer	1	4	1
Warlords Battlecry III	Gold	6	218	13,242	5,784	42	41	18	1	2	-	Short	1	1	1
	Hero XP	6	218	13,242	5,784	42	41	18	1	2	-	Short	1	1	1
C&C Generals	Money	10	339	2,537	140,157	68	56	17	10	4	-	Integer	1	2	1
Spider Solitaire	Cards	6	26	372	819	3	3	12	1	-	4	(Integer)	18	18	1
	Points	6	26	372	819	3	3	12	1	4	-	Integer	1	1	1
Monopoly	Money	6	114	4,628	55,389	24	19	17	8	2	-	Short	1	2	1

increases the Hero's experience. For Spider (both cards and points) it is to move a card from one stack of cards to another and for Monopoly to buy some new property, which reduces the player's money. By default we collect 6 snapshots for each application. We take an initial snapshot, then apply the positive action 4 times, and finally collect a final snapshot after 5 minutes of inactivity (negative action). When finding the data of interest, if SIGPATH cannot locate it (i.e., too many candidate locations are left), we redo this process doubling the number of positive actions.

The first part of Table 2 summarizes the snapshot collection. It presents the number of snapshots taken for each game and the average size in Megabytes of those snapshots. For all games except StarCraft, Emperor, and C&C Generals the first batch of 6 snapshots was enough to identify the data of interest. These three games exhibit a large number of memory changes between snapshots, which makes it more difficult to pinpoint the data of interest. Taking a second batch of snapshots was enough to locate the data of interest. The snapshots are in Windows Minidump format and contain all user-level memory pages (0–0x7fffffff). The largest snapshots correspond to RTS games and all applications increase their memory usage as time passes.

Generating the Memory Graphs. The next part of Table 2 shows the average number of nodes and pointers in the memory graphs generated from the snapshots. These numbers are obtained after removing all nodes unreachable from the modules shipped with the program's executable, i.e., those only reachable from Windows libraries. The numbers show that memory graphs can be large comprising up to tens of thousands of nodes and over a hundred thousand pointers. However, their total size is still a small fraction of the snapshot size, as an important fraction of the pages in the snapshot corresponds to dead memory and OS data structures. Additionally, we also present the average size of the graph before and after removing unreachable nodes. Finally, we show the ratio between the average graph size and the average snapshot size, representing the fraction of the original process memory that needs to be examined. The results show that using the memory graph translates in an average 73% reduction of the memory space.

Finding the Data of Interest. The following part of Table 2 captures the combination of techniques needed to identify the data of interest, its encoding, and the total number of nodes flagged storing data of interest. We depicted the average size of memory space where the data of interest must be searched for after the application of each technique. A dash sign represents that the technique was not needed.

In 22 of 23 cases the combination of structural memory diffing and value scanning located the data of interest. This combination is very powerful as structural memory diffing first reduces the set of candidate locations up to 82% on average of the memory graph, and then value scanning pinpoints the data of interest. Without memory diffing, value scanning flagged too many candidate locations. For the money in Emperor, we needed to apply fuzzing as two candidate nodes remained after memory diffing and value scanning. For the cards in Spider, value scanning does not apply because we move cards rather than inserting data. In this case, a combination of structural memory diffing and fuzzing identifies the data of interest.

Signature Generation. The last part of Table 2 shows the number of paths passed to the signature generation and the final number of path signatures produced. For cases where multiple paths are input to the signature generation, the common prefix extraction identifies which of those paths are stable and discards the rest. For all applications except Pidgin, there is only one stable path and thus have a single path signature. We find that Pidgin stores two different copies of the contact's email address. Both of them are stored in the same contacts data structure but their paths differ on the final steps. Both paths are stable producing two different signatures, both of which can be used to identify the contact emails during introspection.

For RTS games and Monopoly, the path signatures have a single node indicating that those games store resources, unit life, and unit experience in global variables, likely for performance reasons. One could naively think that such signatures do not contain important information, but this is hardly so. They capture at which offset and in which module the global variable is stored. This enables to quickly introspect the application without having to scan all modules for a value that is likely to appear many times. During preparation, our approach combines memory diffing, value scanning, and fuzzing

Table 3. Path signatures produced by SIGPATH

Application	DOI	Segment	Example Signature
Yahoo Msg	Email	Heap	yahoo.exe[2394323]→ A(32)[4]→ B(46)[*4][32]→ C(12)[4]→ D[0]"Email"
Skype	Contact ID	Heap	skype.exe[7930844]→ A(64)[60]→ B(2062)[136]→ C(686)[16]→ D(488)[244] → E(553)[360] → F(256)[8*x]→ G[0]"Contact ID"
Pidgin	Email	Heap	libpurple.dll[495776]→ A(12)[0]→ B(48)[16]→ C(56)[*8][48]→ D(64)[32] → E[0]"Email"
		Heap	libpurple.dll[495776]→ A(12)[0]→ B(48)[16]→ C(56)[*8][48]→ D(64)[56] → E(40)[32]→ F[0]"Email"
Miranda	Contacts ID	Heap	yahoo.dll[147340]→ A(12)→ B(92)[32]→ C(12)[*0][8]→ D(28)[4] → E[0]"Contact ID"
SimCity 4	Money	Global	SimCity 4.exe[25674647]"Money"
StarCraft	Mineral	Global	StarCraft.exe[1569012]"Mineral"
	Gas	Global	StarCraft.exe[1569060]"Gas"
	CC Life	Global	StarCraft.exe[2241505] "Command Center Life"
	SCV life	Global	StarCraft.exe[2241231]"SCV life"
Age of Empires II	Gold	Global	empires2.exe[4564562]"Gold"
	Wood	Global	empires2.exe[4564566]"Wood"
	Food	Global	empires2.exe[4564570]"Food"
	Iron	Global	empires2.exe[4564574]"Iron"
WarCraft III	Gold	Global	war.exe[3022425]"Gold"
	Wood	Global	war.exe[3022445]"Wood"
Dune 2000	Money	Global	dune2000.dat[3901300]"Money"
Emperor	Money	Global	game.dat[3530433]"Money"
Warlords Battlecry III	Gold	Global	Battlecry III.exe[3400232]"'Gold"
	Hero XP	Global	Battlecry III.exe[2374828]"Hero XP"
C&C Generals	Money	Global	game.dat[55456432]"Money"
Spider Solitaire	Card	Heap	spider.exe[73744]→ A(120)[4*x]→ B(4)[0]→ C(12)[*8]"Card"
	Points	Global	spider.exe[77664]"Points"
Monopoly	Money	Global	Monopoly.exe[3230202]"Money"

to accurately pinpoint the location of the data of interest, so that there is no need to check during online introspection which candidate is the right location. The root of the path signatures is not always the main module of the application, e.g., *libpurple.dll* in Pidgin. A special case happens with games where the main executable starts a separate process in charge of the game, such as in Emperor and C&C Generals. Table 3 shows the path signatures in a path-like representation.

Performance Evaluation. We have measured the execution time and memory usage of SIGPATH. On average it takes an analyst 25 minutes to collect the 6 snapshots, the largest being 45 minutes for Warcraft III. After that, SIGPATH takes on average 10 minutes to produce the path signatures. The slowest generation is 22 minutes for Pidgin due to the large number of candidate paths. Overall, it takes 35–60 minutes to create the signatures. Signature generation is memory consuming because it requires operating on large memory graphs and snapshots. The largest memory consumption was C&C Generals with close to 4GB. We plan to add optimizations to minimize the number of memory graphs and raw pages from snapshots to be simultaneously loaded in memory.

Application: Game Hacking. For each tested game in Table 2 and data of interest pair we create a cheat and use SIGPATH to identify the location of the data of interest in memory, modifying it with the cheat's value. During preparation we identified the encoding for each data of interest, so here we only need to select an appropriate value. For RTS games we select a large number corresponding to a ridiculously high amount of resources, unit life, or unit experience. For board games we select a very large score and make sure that the game stores it in its high score list. The cheats work flawlessly. As an example, one cheat for StarCraft increases the Command Center unit life to 9,999 points, even if the maximum life of that unit type is 1,500 points. After the cheat the game continues operating correctly and the unit's life is accepted to be 9,999. Setting the life to zero is even a better cheat as it makes the unit immortal.

Application: Memory Forensics. We evaluated whether our path signatures are able to recover all email contacts stored by the IM programs in Table 2, given a snapshot taken from a suspect's computer. We run each IM application and insert 3 new contacts (different from the ones inserted when collecting the snapshots during preparation) taking a single snapshot for each application after all insertions. Then, we use the introspection component of SIGPATH to apply the signature on the snapshot. SIGPATH successfully identifies and dumps the email addresses of all 3 contacts in all 4 IM applications. This demonstrates that the generated path signatures can examine all instances of the data of interest stored in a data structure. It also demonstrates that they can be used to examine a different execution from the one used to generate them.

6   Limitations and Future Work

Obfuscation. Our approach works with many common code protections such as those used by Skype [24]. For data obfuscation, if the data of interest is encrypted SIGPATH can still find it using structural memory diffing and fuzzing, and can modify it by replaying a previously seen (encrypted) value. Other obfuscation techniques such as data structure randomization (DSR) [25] target data analysis techniques. SIGPATH cannot handle DSR, but DSR requires expensive code refactoring to existing programs.

Correlating Actions and Effects. Our memory diffing technique requires positive actions chosen by the analyst to affect the data of interest. And, our fuzzing technique requires modifications of the data of interest to be observable by the analyst. Such direct relationships between analyst actions and effects on the data of interest was easy to find in our applications. However, other scenarios may prove more difficult.

Complex Code Idioms. Some complex code idioms are unsupported or only supported partially by SIGPATH. For example, while SIGPATH handles most unions, a subtle case is a union of two types, both with a pointer at the same offset and only one those pointers leading to the data-of-interest, which produces an unstable path. Another issue are tail-accumulator arrays; while our array detection technique identifies the array at the end of the node, full support would require handling variable-length nodes. Also problematic are data structures whose traversal requires computation, e.g., masking the bottom 7 bits of a pointer field used as a reference count. Finally, custom allocators hide the proper structure of memory, but can be identified by recent techniques [26].

3D Support. VirtualBox, QEMU, and XEN do not support 3D graphics, required by some recent games like StarCraft2. We are developing a VMWare introspector for these.

7 Related Work

Game Hacking. Hoglund and McGraw [27] describe common game cheating techniques such as memory editing, code injection, and network traffic forgery. CHEAT-ENGINE [23] is an open source engine that uses value scanning to identify the data of interest while the game runs. As acknowledged by the author, such approach does not work with highly dynamic online games. KARTOGRAPH [8] is a state-of-the-art tool for hacking games. It differs from SIGPATH in two key properties. First, SIGPATH produces path signatures, which can be reused to cheat the game in many runs without redoing the analysis. In addition, SIGPATH operates on memory graphs while KARTOGRAPH operates at the page level. The memory graph removes dead memory and unrelated data, and enables structural memory diffing, which improves accuracy over the page level diffing in KARTOGRAPH.

Data Structure Reverse Engineering. Prior works recover data structures using program analysis without source code or debugging symbols, e.g., REWARDS [9], HOWARD [11], and TIE [10]. In contrast, SIGPATH employs a lightweight memory-based approach that locates the data of interest and generates a path signature to it, avoiding the need to recover all data structures. Most similar is LAIKA [17], which applies machine learning to identify data structures in a memory snapshot, clusters those of the same type, and computes the similarity of two snapshots. SIGPATH differs in that it produces path signatures that identify the exact location of the data of interest in memory and that its structural memory diffing operates on a memory graph rather than at the page level.

Memory Forensics. Prior work identifies data structures in memory by traversing pointers starting from program (kernel) global variables and following the points-to relationships to reach instances of the data structure. KOP [5], MAS [16], FATKIT [1] and VOLATILITY [3] all use such technique. While SIGPATH also leverages this approach the substantial difference is that these works require access to the target's source code or its data structure definitions in symbol files. They also often involve sophisticated points-to analysis (e.g., for `void` pointers), whereas SIGPATH simply requires memory snapshots. Instead of object traversal, other works use data structure signatures to *scan* for instances of data structures in memory, such as PTFINDER [2], Robust-Signatures [6], and SIGGRAPH [7]. SIGPATH differs in that it produces path signatures that do not require to scan memory and also in that it does not require access to the type definitions in the source code.

Virtual Machine Introspection (VMI). LIVEWIRE [12] demonstrated the concept of VMI and there is a significant amount of works that improve VMI for better practicality, automation, and wider applications such as VMWATCHER [15], SBCFI [28], VIRTUOSO [13] and VMST [14]. The difference with SIGPATH is that these systems focus on kernel level introspection, whereas SIGPATH focuses on user level data introspection. Recently, TAPPAN ZEE BRIDGE [29] finds hooking points at which to interpose for active monitoring. Our work differs on being snapshot-based and producing path signatures.

8 Conclusion

In this paper we have presented a novel memory graph based approach for program data introspection and modification that generates path signatures directly from memory snapshots, without requiring source code, debugging symbols, or APIs in the target program. To this end, we have developed a number of new techniques include a technique for generating a memory graph directly from a snapshot without tracking the program execution; a structural memory diffing technique to compare the graph structure of two snapshots; and a signature generation technique that produces path signatures that capture how to efficiently locate and traverse the in-memory data structures where the data of interest is stored. We have implemented our techniques into a tool called SIGPATH and have evaluated SIGPATH for hacking popular games and for recovering contact information from IM applications.

Acknowledgements. The authors thank the anonymous reviewers for their feedback. This material is based upon work supported by The Air Force Office of Scientific Research under Award No. FA-9550-12-1-0077. This research was also partially supported by the Spanish Government through Grant TIN2012-39391-C04-01 and a Juan de la Cierva Fellowship for Juan Caballero. All opinions, findings and conclusions or recommendations expressed herein are those of the authors and do not necessarily reflect the views of the sponsors.

References

1. Petroni Jr., N.L., Walters, A., Fraser, T., Arbaugh, W.A.: Fatkit: A framework for the extraction and analysis of digital forensic data from volatile system memory. Digital Investigation 3(4), 197–210 (2006)
2. Schuster, A.: Searching for processes and threads in Microsoft Windows memory dumps. Digital Investigation 3(suppl.-1), 10–16 (2006)
3. Walters, A.: The volatility framework: Volatile memory artifact extraction utility framework, https://www.volatilesystems.com/default/volatility
4. Lin, Z., Rhee, J., Wu, C., Zhang, X., Xu, D.: Dimsum: Discovering semantic data of interest from un-mappable memory with confidence. In: Proceedings of Network and Distributed System Security Symposium, San Diego, CA (February 2012)
5. Carbone, M., Cui, W., Lu, L., Lee, W., Peinado, M., Jiang, X.: Mapping Kernel Objects to Enable Systematic Integrity Checking. In: Proceedings of the 16th ACM Conference on Computer and Communications Security, Chicago, IL (November 2009)
6. Dolan-Gavitt, B., Srivastava, A., Traynor, P., Giffin, J.: Robust Signatures for Kernel Data Structures. In: Proceedings of the 16th ACM Conference on Computer and Communications Security, Chicago, IL (November 2009)
7. Lin, Z., Rhee, J., Zhang, X., Xu, D., Jiang, X.: SigGraph: Brute Force Scanning of Kernel Data Structure Instances Using Graph-based Signatures. In: Proceedings of the 18th Annual Network and Distributed System Security Symposium, San Diego, CA (February 2011)
8. Bursztein, E., Hamburg, M., Lagarenn, J., Boneh, D.: OpenConflict: Preventing Real Time Map Hacks in Online Games. In: Proceedings of the IEEE Symposium on Security and Privacy, Oakland, CA (May 2011)
9. Lin, Z., Zhang, X., Xu, D.: Automatic Reverse Engineering of Data Structures from Binary Execution. In: Proceedings of the 17th Annual Network and Distributed System Security Symposium, San Diego, CA (February 2010)

10. Lee, J., Avgerinos, T., Brumley, D.: TIE: Principled Reverse Engineering of Types in Binary Programs. In: Proceedings of the 18th Annual Network and Distributed System Security Symposium, San Diego, CA (February 2011)
11. Slowinska, A., Stancescu, T., Bos, H.: Howard: A Dynamic Excavator for Reverse Engineering Data Structures. In: Proceedings of the 18th Annual Network and Distributed System Security Symposium, San Diego, CA (February 2011)
12. Garfinkel, T., Rosenblum, M.: A Virtual Machine Introspection Based Architecture for Intrusion Detection. In: Proceedings of the 10th Annual Network and Distributed Systems Security Symposium, San Diego, CA (February 2003)
13. Dolan-Gavitt, B., Leek, T., Zhivich, M., Giffin, J., Lee, W.: Virtuoso: Narrowing the Semantic Gap in Virtual Machine Introspection. In: Proceedings of the IEEE Symposium on Security and Privacy, Oakland, CA (May 2011)
14. Fu, Y., Lin, Z.: Space Traveling across VM: Automatically Bridging the Semantic-Gap in Virtual Machine Introspection via Online Kernel Data Redirection. In: Proceedings of the IEEE Symposium on Security and Privacy, San Francisco, CA (May 2012)
15. Jiang, X., Wang, X., Xu, D.: Stealthy Malware Detection Through VMM-Based Out-of-the-Box Semantic View Reconstruction. In: Proceedings of the 14th ACM Conference on Computer and Communications Security, Alexandria, VA (November 2007)
16. Cui, W., Peinado, M., Xu, Z., Chan, E.: Tracking Rootkit Footprints with a Practical Memory Analysis System. In: Proceedings of the USENIX Security Symposium (August 2012)
17. Cozzie, A., Stratton, F., Xue, H., King, S.T.: Digging for Data Structures. In: Proceedings of the 8th Symposium on Operating System Design and Implementation, San Diego, CA (December 2008)
18. Microsoft: Minidump definitions, http://msdn.microsoft.com/en-us/library/windows/desktop/ms680378.aspx
19. Yin, H., Song, D.: TEMU: Binary Code Analysis via Whole-System Layered Annotative Execution. Technical Report UCB/EECS-2010-3, EECS Department, University of California, Berkeley, CA (January 2010)
20. McDonald, J., Valasek, C.: Practical windows xp/2003 heap exploitation (2009)
21. Russinovich, M., Cogswell, B.: Vmmap, http://technet.microsoft.com/en-us/sysinternals/dd535533.asp
22. Russinovich, M.: Process explorer, http://technet.microsoft.com/en-us/sysinternals/bb896653
23. Team, C.E.: Cheat engine, http://www.cheatengine.org/
24. Biondi, P., Desclaux, F.: Silver Needle in the Skype. In: BlackHat Europe (March 2006)
25. Lin, Z., Riley, R.D., Xu, D.: Polymorphing Software by Randomizing Data Structure Layout. In: Proceedings of the 6th SIG SIDAR Conference on Detection of Intrusions and Malware and Vulnerability Assessment, Milan, Italy (July 2009)
26. Chen, X., Slowinska, A., Bos, H.: Who Allocated my Memory? Detecting Custom Memory Allocators in C Binaries. In: Working Conference on Reverse Engineering (October 2013)
27. Hoglund, G., McGraw, G.: Exploiting Online Games: Cheating Massively Distributed Systems, 1st edn. Addison-Wesley Professional (2007)
28. Petroni Jr., N.L., Hicks, M.: Automated Detection of Persistent Kernel Control-Flow Attacks. In: Proceedings of the 14th ACM Conference on Computer and Communications Security, Alexandria, VA (October 2007)
29. Dolan-Gavitt, B., Leek, T., Hodosh, J., Lee, W.: Tappan zee (north) bridge: Mining memory accesses for introspection. In: Proceedings of the 2013 ACM SIGSAC Conference on Computer & Communications Security (November 2013)

ID-Based Two-Server Password-Authenticated Key Exchange

Xun Yi[1], Feng Hao[2], and Elisa Bertino[3]

[1] School of CS and IT, RMIT University, Australia
[2] School of Computing Science, Newcastle University, UK
[3] Department of Computer Science, Purdue University, USA

Abstract. In two-server password-authenticated key exchange (PAKE) protocol, a client splits its password and stores two shares of its password in the two servers, respectively, and the two servers then cooperate to authenticate the client without knowing the password of the client. In case one server is compromised by an adversary, the password of the client is required to remain secure. In this paper, we present a compiler that transforms any two-party PAKE protocol to a two-server PAKE protocol. This compiler is mainly built on two-party PAKE and identity-based encryption (IBE), where the identities of the two servers are used as their public keys. By our compiler, we can construct a two-server PAKE protocol which achieves implicit authentication with only two communications between the client and the servers. As long as the underlying two-party PAKE protocol and IBE scheme have provable security without random oracles, the two-server PAKE protocol constructed by our compiler can be proven to be secure without random oracles.

Keywords: Password-authenticated key exchange, identity-based encryption, Diffie-Hellman key exchange, Decisional Diffie-Hellman problem.

1 Introduction

Bellovin and Merritt [4] were the first to introduce password-based authenticated key exchange (PAKE), where two parties, based only on their knowledge of a password, establish a cryptographic key by exchange of messages. A PAKE protocol has to be immune to on-line and off-line dictionary attacks. In an off-line dictionary attack, an adversary exhaustively tries all possible passwords in a dictionary in order to determine the password of the client on the basis of the exchanged messages. In on-line dictionary attack, an adversary simply attempts to login repeatedly, trying each possible password. By cryptographic means only, none of PAKE protocols can prevent on-line dictionary attacks. But on-line attacks can be stopped simply by setting a threshold to the number of login failures.

Since Bellovin and Merritt [4] introduced the idea of PAKE, numerous PAKE protocols have been proposed. In general, there exist two kinds of PAKE settings, one assumes that the password of the client is stored in a single server and another assumes that the password of the client is distributed in multiple servers.

M. Kutyłowski and J. Vaidya (Eds.): ESORICS 2014, Part II, LNCS 8713, pp. 257–276, 2014.

PAKE protocols in the single-server setting can be classified into three categories as follows.

- *Password-only PAKE*: Typical examples are the "encrypted key exchange" (EKE) protocols given by Bellovin and Merritt [4], where two parties, who share a password, exchange messages encrypted by the password, and establish a common secret key. The formal model of security for PAKE was firstly given in [3, 7]. Based on the security model, PAKE protocols [1, 2, 9, 10, 17, 21, 23] have been proposed and proved to be secure.
- *PKI-based PAKE*: PKI-based PAKE protocol was first given by Gong et al. [18], where the client stores the server's public key in addition to share a password with the server. Halevi and Krawczyk [19] were the first to provide formal definitions and rigorous proofs of security for PKI-based PAKE.
- *ID-based PAKE*: ID-based PAKE protocols were proposed by Yi et al. [33, 34], where the client needs to remember a password in addition to the identity of the server, whereas the server keeps the password in addition to a private key related to its identity. ID-based PAKE can be thought as a trade-off between password-only and PKI-based PAKE.

In the single-server setting, all the passwords necessary to authenticate clients are stored in a single server. If the server is compromised, due to, for example, hacking or even insider attacks, passwords stored in the server are all disclosed. To address this problem, the multi-server setting for PAKE was first suggested in [15, 20], where the password of the client is distributed in n servers.

PAKE protocols in the multi-server setting can be classified into two categories as follows.

- *Threshold PAKE*: The first PKI-based threshold PAKE protocol was given by Ford and Kaliski [15], where n severs, sharing the password of the client, cooperate to authenticate the client and establish independent session keys with the client. As long as $n - 1$ or fewer servers are compromised, their protocol remains secure. Jablon [20] gave a protocol with similar functionality in the password-only setting. MacKenzie et al. proposed a PKI-based threshold PAKE protocol which requires only t out of n servers to cooperate in order to authenticate the client. Their protocol remains secure as long as $t - 1$ or fewer servers are compromised. Di Raimondo and Gennaro [27] suggested a password-only threshold PAKE protocol which requires fewer than $1/3$ of the servers to be compromised.
- *Two-server PAKE*: Two-server PKI-based PAKE was first given by Brainard [8], where two servers cooperate to authenticate the client and the password remains secure if one server is compromised. A variant of the protocol was later proved to be secure in [28]. The first two-server password-only PAKE protocol was given by Katz et al. [24], in which two servers symmetrically contribute to the authentication of the client. The protocol in the server side can run in parallel. Efficient protocols [30–32, 22] were later proposed, where the front-end server authenticates the client with the help of the back-end server and only the front-end server establishes a session key with the

client. These protocols are asymmetric in the server side and have to run in sequence. Recently, Yi et al. gave a symmetric solution [35] which is even more efficient than asymmetric protocols [22, 30–32].

In this paper, we will consider the two-server setting for PAKE only. A typical example is the two-server PAKE protocol given by Katz et al. [24], which is built upon the two-party PAKE protocol (i.e., the KOY protocol [23]), where two parties, who share a password, exchange messages to establish a common secret key. Their basic two-server protocol is secure against a passive (i.e., "honest-but-curious") adversary who has access to one of the servers throughout the protocol execution, but cannot cause this server to deviate from its prescribed behavior. In [24], Katz et al. also showed how to modify their basic protocol so as to achieve security against an active adversary who may cause a corrupted server to deviate arbitrarily from the protocol. The core of their protocol is the KOY protocol. The client looks like running two KOY protocols with two servers in parallel. However, each server must perform a total of roughly 70 exponentiations (i.e., each server's work is increased by a factor of roughly 6 as compared to the basic protocol [24]). In general, this construction implies a compiler which transfers a two-party PAKE protocol to a two-server PAKE protocol. The compiler employs a two-party PAKE protocol between the client and the servers.

Our Contribution. In this paper, we propose a new compiler to construct a two-server PAKE protocol with any two-party PAKE protocol. Our compiler employs the two-party PAKE protocol between two servers when they authenticate the client.

To achieve the goal, our compiler needs an identity-based encryption (IBE) scheme to protect the messages (containing the password information) from the client to the two servers. The basic idea is: first of all, the client splits its password into two shares and each server keeps one share of the password in addition to a private key related to its identity. In key exchange, the client sends to each server one share of the password encrypted according to the identity of the server. From the client messages, both servers can derive the same one-time password, by which the two servers can run a two-party PAKE protocol to authenticate the client. Our compiler also needs a public key encryption scheme for the servers to protect the messages (containing the password information) from the servers to the client. The one-time public key is generated by the client and sent to the servers along with the password information in the first phase.

In an IBE scheme, the decryption key of a server is usually generated by a Private Key Generator (PKG). Therefore the PKG can decrypt any messages encrypted with the identity of the server. As mentioned in [5], using standard techniques from threshold cryptography, the PKG can be distributed so that the master-key is never available in a single location. In order to prevent a malicious PKG from decrypting the password information encrypted with the identity of a server, a strategy is to employ multiple PKGs which cooperate to generate the decryption key for the server. As long as one of the PKGs is honest to follow the protocol, the decryption key for the server is known only to the server. Since we can assume that the two servers in two-server PAKE never collude, we can also assume that at least one of the PKGs do not collude with other PKGs.

We define an ID-based security model for two-server PAKE. Unlike the ID-based security model for single-server PAKE defined in [33, 34], an adversary can compromise one of the two servers, each having one share of the password. Based on our security model, we provide a rigorous proof of security for our compiler. Our compiler does not rely on the random oracle model as long as the underlying primitives themselves do not rely on it. For example, by using the KOY protocol [23] and the Waters IBE scheme [29] and the Cramer-Shoup public key encryption scheme [12], our compiler can construct a two-server PAKE with provable security in the standard model.

We also compare our ID-based two-server PAKE protocol with the Katz et al.'s two-server PAKE protocol [24] with provable security in the standard model. The Katz et al.'s protocol is password-only, where the client needs to remember the password only and refer to common public parameters, and each server, having a public and private key pair, and keeps a share of the password. Our protocol is identity-based, where the client needs to remember the password in addition to the meaningful identities of the two servers, and refer to common public parameters, including the master public key, and each server, having a private key related to his identity, keeps a share of the password.

In terms of setting, the Katz et al.s protocol is superior to our protocol. However, in the Katz et al.'s protocol, each server performs approximately six times the amount of the work as the KOY protocol, whereas in our protocol, each server performs the same amount of work as the KOY protocol in addition to one IBE decryption and one public key encryption. In addition, the Katz et al.'s protocol needs three communications between the client and the servers to achieve implicit authentication, whereas our protocol achieves implicit authentication with only two communications between the client and the servers.

Organization. In Section 2, we introduce our security model for ID-based two-server PAKE. In Section 3, we present our ID-based two-server PAKE compiler. After that, in Section 4, a sketch of security proof for our protocol is provided. We conclude this paper in Section 5.

2   Definitions

A formal model of security for two-server PAKE was given by Katz et al. [24] (based on the MacKenzie et al.'s model for PKI-based PAKE [26]). Boneh and Franklin [5] defined chosen ciphertext security for IBE under chosen identity attack. Combining the two models, we give an ID-based model for two-server PAKE.

Participants, Initialization and Passwords. An ID-based PAKE protocol involves three kinds of protocol participants: (1) A set of clients (denoted as Client), each of which requests services from servers on the network; (2) A set of servers (denoted as Server), each of which provides services to clients on the network; (3) A group of Private Key Generators (PKGs), which generate public parameters and corresponding private keys for servers.

We assume that ClientServerTriple is the set of triples of the client and two servers, where the client is authorized to use services provided by the two servers, $\text{Client} \cap \text{Server} = \emptyset$, $\text{User} = \text{Client} \cup \text{Server}$, and any $\text{PKG} \notin \text{User}$. It is obvious that $\text{ClientServerTriple} \subseteq \text{Client} \times \text{Server} \times \text{Server}$.

Prior to any execution of the protocol, we assume that an initialization phase occurs. During initialization, the PKGs cooperate to generate public parameters for the protocol, which are available to all participants, and private keys for servers, which are given to the appropriate servers. The user may keep the public parameter in a personal device, such as a smart card or a USB flash drive. When the PKGs generate the private key for a server, each PKG generates and sends a private key component to the server via a secure channel. The server then derives its private key by combining all private key components from all PKGs. **We assume that at least one of PKGs is honest to follow the protocol.** Therefore, the private key of the server is known to the server only.

For any triple $(C, A, B) \in \text{ClientServerTriple}$, we assume that the client C chooses its password pw_C independently and uniformly at random from a "dictionary" $\mathcal{D} = \{\text{pw}_1, \text{pw}_2, \cdots, \text{pw}_N\}$ of size N, where $\mathcal{D} \subset \mathbb{Z}_p$, N is a fixed constant which is independent of any security parameter, and p is a large prime. The password is then split into two shares $\text{pw}_{C,A}$ and $\text{pw}_{C,B}$ and stored at the two servers A and B, respectively, for authentication. **We assume that the two servers never collude to determine the password of the client.** The client C needs to remember pw_C to log into the servers A and B.

For simplicity, we assume that each client C shares its password pw_C with exactly two servers A and B. In this case, we say that servers A and B are associated with C. A server may be associated with multiple clients.

Execution of the Protocol. In the real world, a protocol determines how users behave in response to input from their environments. In the formal model, these inputs are provided by the adversary. Each user is assumed to be able to execute the protocol multiple times (possibly concurrently) with different partners. This is modeled by allowing each user to have unlimited number of instances (please refer to [3]) with which to execute the protocol. We denote instance i of user U as U^i. A given instance may be used only once. The adversary is given oracle access to these different instances. Furthermore, each instance maintains (local) state which is updated during the course of the experiment. In particular, each instance U^i is associated with the following variables, initialized as NULL or FALSE (as appropriate) during the initialization phase.

- sid_U^i, pid_U^i and sk_U^i are variables containing the session identity, partner identity, and session key for an instance U^i, respectively. Computation of the session key is, of course, the ultimate goal of the protocol. The session identity is simply a way to keep track of the different executions of a particular user U. Without loss of generality, we simply let this be the (ordered) concatenation of all messages sent and received by instance U^i. The partner identity denotes the identity of the user with whom U^i believes it is interacting. For a client C, sk_C^i consists of a pair $(\text{sk}_{C,A}^i, \text{sk}_{C,B}^i)$, which are the two keys shared with servers A and B, respectively.

- acc_U^i and term_U^i are boolean variables denoting whether a given instance U^i has been accepted or terminated, respectively. Termination means that the given instance has done receiving and sending messages, acceptance indicates successful termination. In our case, acceptance means that the instance is sure that it has established a session key with its intended partner; thus, when an instance U^i has been accepted, sid_U^i, pid_U^i and sk_U^i are no longer NULL.
- state_U^i records any state necessary for execution of the protocol by U^i.
- used_U^i is a boolean variable denoting whether an instance U^i has begun executing the protocol. This is a formalism which will ensure each instance is used only once.

The adversary $\mathcal{A}$ is assumed to have complete control over all communications in the network (between the clients and servers, and between servers and servers) and the adversary's interaction with the users (more specifically, with various instances) is modelled via access to oracles. The state of an instance may be updated during an oracle call, and the oracle's output may depend upon the relevant instance. The oracle types include:

- $\text{Send}(C, i, A, B, M)$ – This sends message M to a client instance C^i, supposedly from two servers A and B. Assuming $\text{term}_C^i = \text{FALSE}$, this instance runs according to the protocol specification, updating state as appropriate. The output of C^i (i.e., the message sent by the instance) is given to the adversary, who receives the updated values of sid_C^i, pid_C^i, acc_C^i, and term_C^i. This oracle call models the active attack to a protocol. If M is empty, this query represents a prompt for C to initiate the protocol.
- $\text{Send}(S, i, U, M)$ – This sends message M to a server instance S^i, supposedly from a user U (either a client or a server). Assuming $\text{term}_S^i = \text{FALSE}$, this instance runs according to the protocol specification, updating state as appropriate. The output of S^i (i.e., the message sent by the instance) is given to the adversary, who receives the updated values of sid_S^i, pid_S^i, acc_S^i, and term_S^i. If S is corrupted, the adversary also receives the entire internal state of S. This oracle call also models the active attack to a protocol.
- $\text{Execute}(C, i, A, j, B, k)$ – If the client instance C^i and the server instances A^j and B^k have not yet been used (where $(C, A, B) \in \text{ClientServerTriple}$), this oracle executes the protocol between these instances and outputs the transcript of this execution. This oracle call represents passive eavesdropping of a protocol execution. In addition to the transcript, the adversary receives the values of sid, pid, acc, and term for client and server instances, at each step of protocol execution. In addition, if $S \in \{A, B\}$ is corrupted, the adversary is given the entire internal state of S.
- $\text{Corrupt}(S)$ – This sends the private key of the server S in addition to all password information stored in the server S to the adversary. This oracle models possible compromising of a server due to, for example, hacking into the server.
- $\text{Corrupt}(C)$ – This query allows the adversary to learn the password of the client C, which models the possibility of subverting a client by, for example,

witnessing a user typing in his password, or installing a "Trojan horse" on his machine.

- Reveal(U, U', i) – This outputs the current value of session key $\mathsf{sk}^i_{U,U'}$ held by instance U^i if $\mathsf{acc}^i_U = \mathsf{TRUE}$, where $U' \in \mathsf{pid}^i_U$. This oracle call models possible leakages of session keys due to, for example, improper erasure of session keys after use, compromise of a host computer, or cryptanalysis.
- Test(U, U', i) – This oracle does not model any real-world capability of the adversary, but is instead used to define security. Assume $U' \in \mathsf{pid}^i_U$, if $\mathsf{acc}^i_U = \mathsf{TRUE}$, a random bit b is generated. If $b = 0$, the adversary is given $\mathsf{sk}^i_{U,U'}$, and if $b = 1$ the adversary is given a random session key. The adversary is allowed only a single Test query, at any time during its execution.

Partnering. Let $(C, A, B) \in \mathsf{ClientServerTriple}$. For the client instance C^i, let $\mathsf{sid}^i_C = (\mathsf{sid}^i_{C,A}, \mathsf{sid}^i_{C,B})$, where $\mathsf{sid}^i_{C,A}$ (resp., $\mathsf{sid}^i_{C,B}$) denotes the ordered sequence of messages sent to / from the client C and the server A (resp., server B). For the server instance A^j, let $\mathsf{sid}^j_A = (\mathsf{sid}^j_{A,C}, \mathsf{sid}^j_{A,B})$, where $\mathsf{sid}^j_{A,C}$ denotes the ordered sequence of messages sent to / from the server A and the client C, and $\mathsf{sid}^j_{A,B}$ denote the ordered sequence of message sent to / from the server A and the server B. We say that instances C^i and A^j are partnered if (1) $\mathsf{sid}^i_{C,A} = \mathsf{sid}^j_{A,C} \neq \mathsf{NULL}$ and (2) $A \in \mathsf{pid}^i_C$ and $C \in \mathsf{pid}^j_A$. We say that instances A^j and B^k are partnered if (1) $\mathsf{sid}^j_{A,B} = \mathsf{sid}^k_{B,A} \neq \mathsf{NULL}$ and (2) $A \in \mathsf{pid}^k_B$ and $B \in \mathsf{pid}^j_A$.

Correctness. To be viable, a key exchange protocol must satisfy the following notion of correctness: If a client instance C^i and server instances A^j and B^k runs an honest execution of the protocol with no interference from the adversary, then $\mathsf{acc}^i_C = \mathsf{acc}^j_A = \mathsf{acc}^k_B = \mathsf{TRUE}$, and $\mathsf{sk}^i_{C,A} = \mathsf{sk}^j_{A,C}$, $\mathsf{sk}^i_{C,B} = \mathsf{sk}^k_{B,C}$ and $\mathsf{sk}^i_{C,A} \neq \mathsf{sk}^i_{C,B}$.

Freshness. To formally define the adversary's success we need to define a notion of freshness for a session key, where freshness of a key is meant to indicate that the adversary does not trivially know the value of the session key. We say a session key $\mathsf{sk}^i_{U,U'}$ is fresh if (1) both U and U' are not corrupted; (2) the adversary never queried Reveal(U, U', i); (3) the adversary never queried Reveal(U', U, j) where U^i and U'^j are partnered.

Advantage of the Adversary. Informally, the adversary succeeds if it can guess the bit b used by the Test oracle. We say an adversary $\mathcal{A}$ succeeds if it makes a single query Test(U, U', i) to a fresh instance U^i, with $\mathsf{acc}^i_U = \mathsf{TRUE}$ at the time of this query, and outputs a single bit b' with $b' = b$ (recall that b is the bit chosen by the Test oracle). We denote this event by Succ. The advantage of adversary $\mathcal{A}$ in attacking protocol P is then given by $\mathsf{Adv}^P_{\mathcal{A}}(k) = 2 \cdot \mathsf{Pr}[\mathsf{Succ}] - 1$, where the probability is taken over the random coins used by the adversary and the random coins used during the course of the experiment (including initialization phase).

An adversary can always succeed by trying all passwords one-by-one in an on-line impersonation attack. A protocol is secure if this is the best an adversary can do. The on-line attacks correspond to Send queries. Formally, each instance for which the adversary has made a Send query counts as one on-line attack. Instances with which the adversary interacts via Execute are not counted as on-line attacks. The number of on-line attacks represents a bound on the number of passwords the adversary could have tested in an on-line fashion.

Definition 1. Protocol P is a secure two-server protocol for PAKE if, for all dictionary size N and for all PPT adversaries $\mathcal{A}$ making at most $Q(k)$ on-line attacks, there exists a negligible function $\varepsilon(\cdot)$ such that $\mathsf{Adv}_{\mathcal{A}}^P(k) \leq Q(k)/N + \varepsilon(k)$.

3 Our Compiler for Two-Server PAKE Protocol

3.1 Description of Our Compiler

In this section, we present our compiler transforming any two-party PAKE protocol P to a two-server PAKE protocol P'. Besides P, we need an identity-based encryption scheme (IBE) as our cryptographic building block. If we remove authentication elements from our compiler, our key exchange protocol is essentially the Diffie-Hellman key exchange protocol [13]. A high-level description of our compiler is given in Figure 1, in which the client C and two servers A and B establish two authenticated keys, respectively.

We present the protocol by describing initialization and execution.

Initialization. Given a security parameter $k \in \mathbb{Z}^*$, the initialization includes:

Parameter Generation: On input k, (1) m PKGs cooperate to run Setup^P of the two-party PAKE protocol P to generate system parameters, denoted as params^P. (2) m PKGs cooperate to run Setup^E of the IBE scheme to generate public system parameters for the IBE scheme, denoted as params^E, and the secret $\mathsf{master\text{-}key}^E$. Assume that $\mathcal{G}$ is a generator of IBE plaintext group $\mathbb{E}$ with an order n. (3) m PKGs cooperate to choose a large cyclic group $\mathbb{G}$ with a prime order q and two generators g_1, g_2, and two hash functions, $H_1 : \{0,1\}^* \to Z_n^*$ and $H_2 : \{0,1\}^* \to Z_q^*$, from a collision-resistant hash family. The public system parameters for the protocol P' is $\mathsf{params} = \mathsf{params}^{P,E} \bigcup \{\mathbb{E}, \mathcal{G}, n, \mathbb{G}, q, g_1, g_2, H_1, H_2\}$ and the secret $\mathsf{master\text{-}key}^E$ is secretly shared by the PKGs in a manner that any coalition of PKGs cannot determine $\mathsf{master\text{-}key}^E$ as long as one of the PKGs is honest to follow the protocol.

Remark. Taking the Waters' IBE scheme [29] for example, m PKG agree on randomly chosen $\mathcal{G}, \mathcal{G}_2 \in \mathbb{G}$ and each PKG randomly chooses $\alpha_i \in \mathbb{Z}_p$ and broadcast $\mathcal{G}^{\alpha_i}$ with a zero-knowledge proof of knowing α_i and a signature. Then we can set $\mathcal{G}_1 = \mathcal{G}^{\sum_i \alpha_i}$ as the public master key and the secret $\mathsf{master\text{-}key}^E = \mathcal{G}_2^{\sum_i \alpha_i}$. The secret master key is privately shared among m PKGs and unknown to anyone even if $m-1$ PKGs maliciously collude.

Key Generation: On input the identity S of a server $S \in \mathsf{Server}$, params^E, and the secret sharing $\mathsf{master\text{-}key}^E$, PKGs cooperate to run $\mathsf{Extract}^E$ of the IBE scheme and generate a private (decryption) key for S, denoted as d_S, in a manner that any coalition of PKGs cannot determine d_S as long as one of the PKGs is honest to follow the protocol.

Public: $P, \mathsf{IBE}, \mathbb{E}, \mathcal{G}, n, q, \mathbb{G}, q, g_1, g_2, H_1, H_2$

Client C	**Server** A	**Server** B
pw_C	$(\mathcal{G}^{\mathsf{pw}_{C,A}}, g_2^{\mathsf{pw}_{C,A}^*}, d_A)$	$(\mathcal{G}^{\mathsf{pw}_{C,B}}, g_2^{\mathsf{pw}_{C,B}^*}, d_B)$

$(= \mathsf{pw}_{C,A} + \mathsf{pw}_{C,B} (mod\ n))$
$(= \mathsf{pw}_{C,A}^* + \mathsf{pw}_{C,B}^* (mod\ q))$

$\mathsf{pw}_1 \overset{R}{\leftarrow} \mathbb{Z}_n^*$
$\mathsf{pw}_2 = \mathsf{pw}_C - \mathsf{pw}_1 (mod\ n)$
$r_c, x_1, x_2, y_1, y_2, z \overset{R}{\leftarrow} \mathbb{Z}_q^*$
$W_c = g_1^{r_c}, X = g_1^{x_1} g_2^{x_2}, Y = g_1^{y_1} g_2^{y_2}, Z = g_1^z$
$h = H_1(C, W_c, X, Y, Z)$
$E_a = \mathsf{IBE}(\mathcal{G}^{\mathsf{pw}_1 h^{-1}}, A)$
$E_b = \mathsf{IBE}(\mathcal{G}^{\mathsf{pw}_2 h^{-1}}, B)$

$\xrightarrow{\quad \mathsf{msg}_2 = \langle C, W_c, X, Y, Z, E_b \rangle \quad}$

$\xleftarrow{\quad \mathsf{msg}_1 = \langle C, W_c, X, Y, Z, E_a \rangle \quad}$

	$h' = H_1(C, W_c, X, Y, Z)$	$h' = H_1(C, W_c, X, Y, Z)$
	$\omega_a = \mathsf{IBD}(E_a, d_A)^{h'}/\mathcal{G}^{\mathsf{pw}_{C,A}}$	$\omega_b = \mathcal{G}^{\mathsf{pw}_{C,B}}/\mathsf{IBD}(E_b, d_B)^{h'}$
	$= \mathcal{G}^{\mathsf{pw}_1 - \mathsf{pw}_{C,A}}$	$= \mathcal{G}^{\mathsf{pw}_{C,B} - \mathsf{pw}_2}$

$\xleftarrow{\quad P(\omega_a, \omega_b) \quad}$

if $\mathsf{acc}_A^P = \mathsf{TRUE}$	if $\mathsf{acc}_B^P = \mathsf{TRUE}$
$r_a, r_1 \overset{R}{\leftarrow} \mathbb{Z}_q^*, W_a = g_1^{r_a}$	$r_b, r_2 \overset{R}{\leftarrow} \mathbb{Z}_q^*, W_b = g_1^{r_b}$
$S_1 = g_1^{r_1}, T_1 = g_2^{r_1},$	$S_2 = g_1^{r_2}, T_2 = g_2^{r_2},$
$h_a = H_2(A, W_a, C, W_c)$	$h_b = H_2(B, W_b, C, W_c)$
$U_1 = g_2^{\mathsf{pw}_{C,A}^* h_a^{-1}} Z^{r_1}$	$U_2 = g_2^{\mathsf{pw}_{C,B}^* h_b^{-1}} Z^{r_2}$
$h_1 = H_2(S_1, T_1, U_1)$	$h_2 = H_2(S_2, T_2, U_2)$
$V_1 = X^{r_1} Y^{h_1 r_1}$	$V_2 = X^{r_2} Y^{h_2 r_2}$
$\mathsf{acc}_A = \mathsf{TRUE}, \mathsf{sk}_{A,C} = W_c^{r_a}$	$\mathsf{acc}_B = \mathsf{TRUE}, \mathsf{sk}_{B,C} = W_c^{r_b}$
else return $\perp$	else return $\perp$

$\xleftarrow{\quad \mathsf{msg}_A = \langle A, S_1, T_1, U_1, V_1, W_a \rangle \quad}$

$\xrightarrow{\quad \mathsf{msg}_B = \langle B, S_2, T_2, U_2, V_2, W_b \rangle \quad}$

$h_a' = H_2(A, W_a, C, W_c), h_1' = H_2(S_1, T_1, U_1)$
$h_b' = H_2(B, W_b, C, W_c), h_2' = H_2(S_2, T_2, U_2)$
if $\{S_1^{x_1 + h_1' y_1} T_1^{x_2 + h_1' y_2} = V_1\} \wedge \{S_2^{x_1 + h_2' y_1} T_2^{x_2 + h_2' y_2} = V_2\} \wedge \{(U_1/S_1^z)^{h_a'} (U_2/S_2^z)^{h_b'} = g_2^{\mathsf{pw}_C}\}$
$\mathsf{acc}_C = \mathsf{TRUE}, \mathsf{sk}_{C,A} = W_a^{r_c}, \mathsf{sk}_{C,B} = W_b^{r_c}$
else return $\perp$

Fig. 1. Two-Server PAKE Protocol P'

Remark. In the Waters' IBE scheme with m PKG , each PKG computes one component of the private key for a server S, i.e., $(\mathcal{G}_2^{\alpha_i} H(S)^{r_i}, \mathcal{G}^{r_i})$, where H is the Waters' hash function, and sends it to the server via a secure channel. Combining all components, the server can construct its private key $d_S = (\mathcal{G}_2^{\sum_i \alpha_i} H(S)^{\sum_i r_i}, \mathcal{G}^{\sum_i r_i})$, which is known to the server only even if $m-1$ PKGs maliciously collude. In addition, the identity of a server is public, meaningful, like an e-mail address, and easy to remember or keep. Anyone can write down the identity of a server on a note.

Password Generation: On input a triple $(C, A, B) \in$ Client ServerTriple, a string pw_C, the password, is uniformly drawn from the dictionary $\mathcal{D} = \{\mathsf{pw}_1, \mathsf{pw}_2, \cdots, \mathsf{pw}_N\}$ by the client C, and randomly split into $\mathsf{pw}_{C,A}$ and $\mathsf{pw}_{C,B}$ such that $\mathsf{pw}_{C,A} + \mathsf{pw}_{C,B} = \mathsf{pw}_C (mod\ n)$, and $\mathsf{pw}_{C,A}^*$ and $\mathsf{pw}_{C,B}^*$ such that $\mathsf{pw}_{C,A}^* + \mathsf{pw}_{C,B}^* = \mathsf{pw}_C(mod\ q)$, and stored in the servers A and B, respectively. We implicitly assume that $N < min(n, q)$, which will certainly be true in practice.

Protocol Execution. Given a triple $(C, A, B) \in$ Client ServerTriple, the client C (knowing its password pw_C) runs the protocol P' with the two servers A (knowing $\mathcal{G}^{\mathsf{pw}_{C,A}}$, $g_2^{\mathsf{pw}_{C,A}^*}$ and its private key d_A) and B (knowing $\mathcal{G}^{\mathsf{pw}_{C,B}}$, $g_2^{\mathsf{pw}_{C,B}^*}$ and its private key d_B) to establish two session keys, respectively, as shown in Figure 1.

At first, the client randomly chooses pw_1 from Z_n^* and computes $\mathsf{pw}_2 = \mathsf{pw}_C - \mathsf{pw}_1(mod\ n)$. Next the client C randomly chooses $r_c, x_1, x_2, y_1, y_2, z$ from Z_q^* and computes $W_c = g_1^{r_c}, X = g_1^{x_1} g_2^{x_2}, Y = g_1^{y_1} g_2^{y_2}, Z = g_1^z, h = H_1(C, W, X, Y, Z)$, where (X, Y, Z) is one-time public encryption key and (x_1, x_2, y_1, y_2, z) is one-time private decryption key of the Cramer-Shoup public key encryption scheme [12].

Next, according to the identities of the two servers A and B, the client C performs the identity-based encryptions $E_a = \mathsf{IBE}(\mathcal{G}^{\mathsf{pw}_1 h^{-1}}, A), E_b = \mathsf{IBE}(\mathcal{G}^{\mathsf{pw}_2 h^{-1}}, B)$.

Then, the client sends $\mathsf{msg}_1 = \langle C, W, X, Y, Z, E_a \rangle$ and $\mathsf{msg}_2 = \langle C, W, X, Y, Z, E_b \rangle$ to the two servers A and B, respectively.

After receiving $\mathsf{msg}_1 = \langle C, W, X, Y, Z, E_a \rangle$ from C, the server A computes $h' = H_1(C, W, X, Y, Z), \omega_a = \mathsf{IBD}(E_a, d_A)^{h'} / \mathcal{G}^{\mathsf{pw}_{C,A}} = \mathcal{G}^{\mathsf{pw}_1 - \mathsf{pw}_{C,A}}$, where IBD denotes identity-based decryption.

After receiving $\mathsf{msg}_2 = \langle C, W, X, Y, Z, E_b \rangle$ from C, the server B computes $\omega_b = \mathcal{G}^{\mathsf{pw}_{C,B}} / \mathsf{IBD}(E_a, d_B)^{h'} = \mathcal{G}^{\mathsf{pw}_{C,B} - \mathsf{pw}_2}$, where $h' = H_1(C, W, X, Y, Z)$.

Because $\mathsf{pw}_C = \mathsf{pw}_{C,A} + \mathsf{pw}_{C,B}(mod\ n)$ and $\mathsf{pw}_C = \mathsf{pw}_1 + \mathsf{pw}_2(mod\ n)$, we have $\mathsf{pw}_1 - \mathsf{pw}_{C,A} = \mathsf{pw}_{C,B} - \mathsf{pw}_2(mod\ n)$ and thus $\omega_a = \omega_b$.

Using ω_a and ω_b as one-time password, the servers A and B run a two-party PAKE protocol P to establish a session key. If the server A accepts the session key as an authenticated key according to P (i.e., $\mathsf{acc}_A^P = \mathsf{TRUE}$), it randomly chooses two integers r_a, r_1 from $\mathbb{Z}_q^*$ and computes $W_a = g_1^{r_a}, S_1 = g_1^{r_1}, T_1 = g_2^{r_1}, h_a = H_2(A, W_a, C, W_c), U_1 = g_2^{\mathsf{pw}_{C,A}^* h_a^{-1}} Z^{r_1}, h_1 = H_2(S_1, T_1, U_1), V_1 = X^{r_1} Y^{h_1 r_1}, \mathsf{sk}_{A,C} = W_c^{r_a}$, where $\mathsf{sk}_{A,C}$ is the session key between A and C and

(S_1, T_1, U_1, V_1) is the Cramer-Shoup encryption of $g_2^{\mathsf{pw}_{C,A}^* h_a^{-1}}$. Then the server A sets $\mathsf{acc}_A = \mathsf{TRUE}$ and replies to the client C with $\mathsf{msg}_A = \langle A, S_1, T_1, U_1, V_1, W_a \rangle$.

If the server B accepts the session key as an authenticated key according to P (i.e., $\mathsf{acc}_B^P = \mathsf{TRUE}$), it randomly chooses two integers r_b, r_2 from $\mathbb{Z}_q^*$ and computes $W_b = g_1^{r_b}, S_2 = g_1^{r_2}, T_2 = g_2^{r_2}, h_b = H_2(A, W_b, C, W_c), U_2 = g_2^{\mathsf{pw}_{C,B}^* h_b^{-1}} Z^{r_2}$, $h_2 = H_2(S_2, T_2, U_2), V_2 = X^{r_2} Y^{h_2 r_2}, \mathsf{sk}_{B,C} = W_c^{r_b}$, where $\mathsf{sk}_{B,C}$ is the session key between B and C and (S_2, T_2, U_2, V_2) is the Cramer-Shoup encryption of $g_2^{\mathsf{pw}_{C,B}^* h_b^{-1}}$. Then the server B sets $\mathsf{acc}_B = \mathsf{TRUE}$ and replies to the client C with $\mathsf{msg}_B = \langle B, S_2, T_2, U_2, V_2, W_b \rangle$.

Finally, after the client C receives msg_A and msg_B, it computes $h_a' = H_2(A, W_a, C, W_c), h_1' = H_2(A, S_1, T_1, U_1), h_b' = H_2(B, W_b, C, W_c), h_2' = H_2(B, S_2, T_2, U_2)$, and check if

$$S_1^{x_1 + h_1' y_1} T_1^{x_2 + h_1' y_2} = V_1, S_2^{x_1 + h_2' y_1} T_2^{x_2 + h_2' y_2} = V_2, (U_1/S_1^z)^{h_a'} (U_2/S_2^z)^{h_b'} = g_2^{\mathsf{pw}_C}.$$

If so, the client C sets $\mathsf{acc}_C = \mathsf{TRUE}$ and computes two session keys $\mathsf{sk}_{C,A} = W_a^{r_c}, \mathsf{sk}_{C,B} = W_b^{r_c}$.

3.2 Correctness, Explicit Authentication, and Efficiency

Correctness. Assume that a client instance C^i and server instances A^j and B^k runs an honest execution of the protocol P' with no interference from the adversary and the two-party PAKE P has the correctness property.

With reference to Figure 1, the server instances A^j and B^k are able to derive the same one-time password ω_a ($= \omega_b$). Because P has the correctness property, after running P based on ω_a and ω_b, the server instances A^j and B^k accept the established session key as an authenticated key. This indicates that the client C has provided a correct password pw_C. Next, the server instances A^j and B^k compute the session keys with the client C, i.e., $\mathsf{sk}_{A,C} = W_c^{r_a}$ and $\mathsf{sk}_{B,C} = W_c^{r_b}$, and let $\mathsf{acc}_A^j = \mathsf{TRUE}$ and $\mathsf{acc}_B^k = \mathsf{TRUE}$.

With reference to Figure 1, we have $h_a' = h_a, h_1' = h_1, h_b' = h_b, h_2' = h_2$, and

$$S_1^{x_1 + h_1' y_1} T_1^{x_2 + h_1' y_2} = g_1^{r_1(x_1 + h_1 y_1)} g_2^{r_1(x_2 + h_1 y_2)}$$
$$= (g_1^{x_1} g_2^{x_2})^{r_1} (g_1^{y_1} g_2^{y_2})^{r_1 h_1} = X^{r_1} Y^{h_1 r_1} = V_1,$$

$$U_1/S_1^z = g_2^{\mathsf{pw}_{C,A}^* h_a^{-1}} (g_1^z)^{r_1} / (g_1^{r_1})^z = g_2^{\mathsf{pw}_{C,A}^* h_a'^{-1}},$$

$$S_2^{x_1 + h_2' y_1} T_2^{x_2 + h_2' y_2} = g_1^{r_2(x_1 + h_2 y_1)} g_2^{r_2(x_2 + h_2 y_2)}$$
$$= (g_1^{x_1} g_2^{x_2})^{r_2} (g_1^{y_1} g_2^{y_2})^{r_2 h_2} = X^{r_2} Y^{h_2 r_2} = V_2,$$

$$U_2/S_2^z = g_2^{\mathsf{pw}_{C,B}^* h_b^{-1}} (g_1^z)^{r_2} / (g_1^{r_2})^z = g_2^{\mathsf{pw}_{C,B}^* h_b'^{-1}},$$

$$(U_1/S_1^z)^{h_a'}(U_2/S_2^z)^{h_b'} = g_2^{\mathsf{pw}_{C,A}^*} g_2^{\mathsf{pw}_{C,B}^*} = g_2^{\mathsf{pw}_C}.$$

If the three checks succeed, the client C computes two session keys, i.e., $\mathsf{sk}_{C,A} = W_a^{r_c}, \mathsf{sk}_{C,B} = W_b^{r_c}$, and lets $\mathsf{acc}_C^i = \mathrm{TRUE}$. Since $W_c = g_1^{r_c}, W_a = g_1^{r_a}, W_b = g_1^{r_b}$, we have $\mathsf{sk}_{C,A} = W_a^{r_c} = g_1^{r_a r_c} = W_c^{r_a} = \mathsf{sk}_{A,C}$ and $\mathsf{sk}_{C,B} = W_b^{r_c} = g_1^{r_b r_c} = W_c^{r_b} = \mathsf{sk}_{B,C}$. In addition, because r_a, r_b are chosen randomly, the probability of $\mathsf{sk}_{C,A} = \mathsf{sk}_{C,B}$ is negligible. Therefore, our protocol has the correctness property.

Explicit Authentication. By running the two-party PAKE protocol P based on w_a (derived by $\mathsf{pw}_{C,A}$) and w_b (derived by $\mathsf{pw}_{C,B}$), the two servers A and B can verify if the client C provides a password pw_C such that $\mathsf{pw}_C = \mathsf{pw}_{C,A} + \mathsf{pw}_{C,B}(mod\ n)$. In addition, by checking that $(U_1/S_1^z)^{h_a'}(U_2/S_2^z)^{h_b'} = g_2^{\mathsf{pw}_C}$ (involving pw_C), the client C can verify if the two servers provide two shares of the password, $\mathsf{pw}_{C,A}^*$ and $\mathsf{pw}_{C,B}^*$, such that $\mathsf{pw}_C = \mathsf{pw}_{C,A}^* + \mathsf{pw}_{C,B}^*(mod\ q)$. This shows that when $\mathsf{acc}_A^j = \mathrm{TRUE}$, the server A knows that its intended client C and server B are authentic, and when $\mathsf{acc}_C^i = \mathrm{TRUE}$, the client C knows that its intended servers A and B are authentic. Our protocol achieves the implicit authentication by only two communications between the client and the servers. Using standard techniques, however, it is easy to add explicit authentication to any protocol achieving implicit authentication.

Efficiency. The efficiency of our protocol depends on performance of the underlying two-party PAKE protocol and IBE scheme. Suppose that our compiler uses the KOY PAKE protocol [23] and the Waters IBE scheme [29] as cryptographic building blocks, the performance comparison of the Katz et al. two-server PAKE protocol [24] (secure against active adversary) and our protocol can be shown in Table 1.

In Table 1, Exp., Sign. and Pairing for computation (comp.) represent the computation complexities of a modular exponentiation, a signature generation and a pairing, respectively. Exp. and Sign. in communication (comm.) denote

Table 1. Performance Comparison of Katz et al. Protocol and Our Protocol

	Katz et al. Protocol [24]	Our Protocol
Public Keys	Client: None	Client: None
	Sever A: Public Key pk_A	Server A: A
	Sever B: Public Key pk_B	Server B: B
Private Keys	Client: pw_C	Client: pw_C
	Sever A: $\mathsf{pw}_{C,A}$, Private Key sk_A	Server A: $\mathsf{pw}_{C,A}, \mathsf{pw}_{C,A}^*, d_A$
	Sever B: $\mathsf{pw}_{C,B}$, Private Key sk_B	Server B: $\mathsf{pw}_{C,B}, \mathsf{pw}_{C,B}^*, d_B$
Computation Complexity	Client: 21(Exp.)+1(Sign)	Client: 23(Exp.)
	Server: about 6(KOY)	Server: about 1(KOY)+ 2(Pairing)+9(Exp.)
Communication Complexity	Client/Server: 27(Exp.)+1(Sign)	Client/Server: 24(Exp.)
	Server/Server: about 2(KOY)	Server/Server: about 1(KOY)

the size of the modulus and the size of the signature. KOY stands for the computation or communication complexity of the KOY protocol. From Table 1, we can see that the client has almost the same computation and communication complexities in both protocols, but the server in our protocol has about $1/3$ of the computation complexity, $1/2$ of the communication complexity of the Katz et al. two-server PAKE protocol if the computation of a pairing approximates to the computation of 4 exponentiations. Furthermore, our protocol achieves implicit authentication with only two communications between the client and the servers, whereas the Katz et al. two-server PAKE protocol needs three communications between the client and the servers to achieve implicit authentication.

The purpose of the users personal device is to keep public parameters. To efficiently compute 23 modular exponentiations, the client may load the public parameters from the personal device into a computing device.

4   Proof of Security

Based on the security model defined in Section 2, we have the following theorem:

Theorem 1. Assuming that (1) the identity-based encryption (IBE) scheme is secure against the chosen-ciphertext attack; (2) the Cramer-Shoup public key encryption scheme is secure against the chosen-ciphertext attack; (3) the decisional Diffie-Hellman problem is hard; (4) the protocol P is a secure two-party PAKE protocol with explicit authentication; (5) H_1, H_2 are collision-resistant hash functions, then the protocol P' illustrated in Figure 1 is a secure two-server PAKE protocol according to Definition 1.

Proof. Given an adversary $\mathcal{A}$ attacking the protocol, we imagine a simulator $\mathcal{S}$ that runs the protocol for $\mathcal{A}$.

First of all, the simulator $\mathcal{S}$ initializes the system by generating params $=$ params$^{P,E} \bigcup \{\mathbb{E}, \mathcal{G}, n, \mathbb{G}, q, g_1, g_2, H_1, H_2\}$ and the secret master-key^E. Next, Client, Server, and Client ServerTriple sets are determined. Passwords for clients are chosen at random and split, and then stored at corresponding servers. Private keys for servers are computed using master-key^E.

The public information is provided to the adversary. Considering $(C, A, B) \in$ ClinetServerTriple, we assume that the adversary $\mathcal{A}$ chooses the server B to corrupt and the simulator $\mathcal{S}$ gives the adversary $\mathcal{A}$ the information held by the corrupted server B, including the private key of the server B, i.e., d_B, and one share of the password of the client C, $\mathcal{G}^{\mathsf{pw}_{B,C}}$ and $g_2^{\mathsf{pw}_{B,C}^*}$. After computing the appropriate answer to any oracle query, the simulator $\mathcal{S}$ provides the adversary $\mathcal{A}$ with the internal state of the corrupted server B involved in the query.

We view the adversary's queries to its Send oracles as queries to four different oracles as follows:

- Send(C, i, A, B) represents a request for instance C^i of client C to initiate the protocol. The output of this query is msg$_1 = \langle C, W_c, X, Y, Z, E_a \rangle$ and msg$_2 = \langle C, W_c, X, Y, Z, E_b \rangle$.

- $\mathsf{Send}(A, j, \mathsf{msg}_1)$ represents sending message msg_1 to instance A^j of the server A. The output of this query is either $\mathsf{msg}_A = \langle A, S_1, T_1, U_1, V_1, W_a \rangle$ or $\perp$.
- $\mathsf{Send}(C, i, \mathsf{msg}_A | \mathsf{msg}_B)$ represents sending the message $\mathsf{msg}_A | \mathsf{msg}_B$ to instance C^i of the client C. The output of this query is either $\mathsf{acc}_C^i = \mathsf{TRUE}$ or $\perp$.
- $\mathsf{Send}^P(A, j, B, M)$ represents sending message M to instance A^j of the server A, supposedly by the server B, in the two-party PAKE protocol P. The input and output of this query depends on the protocol P.

When $\mathcal{A}$ queries the Test oracle, the simulator $\mathcal{S}$ chooses a random bit b. When the adversary completes its execution and output a bit b', the simulator can tell whether the adversary succeeds by checking if (1) a single Test query was made regarding some fresh session key $\mathsf{sk}_{U,U'}^i$, and (2) $b' = b$. Success of the adversary is denoted by event Succ. For any experiment P, we denote $\mathsf{Adv}_{\mathcal{A}}^P = 2 \cdot \Pr[\mathsf{Succ}] - 1$, where $\Pr[\cdot]$ denotes the probability of an event when the simulator interacts with the adversary in accordance with experiment P.

We will use some terminology throughout the proof. A given message is called oracle-generated if it was output by the simulator in response to some oracle query. The message is said to be adversarially-generated otherwise. **An adversarially-generated message must not be the same as any oracle-generated message**.

We refer to the real execution of the experiment, as described above, as P_0. We introduce a sequence of transformations to the experiment P_0 and bound the effect of each transformation on the adversary's advantage. We then bound the adversary's advantage in the final experiment. This immediately yields a bound on the adversary's advantage in the original experiment.

Experiment P_1: In this experiment, the simulator interacts with the adversary as P_0 except that the adversary does not succeed, and the experiment is aborted, if any of the following occurs:

1. At any point during the experiment, an oracle-generated message (e.g., msg_1, msg_2, msg_A, or msg_B) is repeated.
2. At any point during the experiment, a collision occurs in the hash function H_1 or H_2 (regardless of whether this is due to a direct action of the adversary, or whether this occurs during the course of the simulator's response to an oracle query).

It is immediate that events 1 occurs with only negligible probability, event 2 occurs with negligible probability assuming H_1, H_2 as collision-resistant hash functions. Put everything together, we are able to see that

Claim 1. If H_1 and H_2 are collision-resistant hash functions, $|\mathsf{Adv}_{\mathcal{A}}^{P_0}(k) - \mathsf{Adv}_{\mathcal{A}}^{P_1}(k)|$ is negligible.

Experiment P_2: In this experiment, the simulator interacts with the adversary $\mathcal{A}$ as in experiment P_1 except that the adversary's queries to Execute oracles are handled differently: in any $\mathsf{Execute}(C, i, A, j, B, k)$, where the adversary $\mathcal{A}$ has not queried corrupt(A), but may have queried corrupt(B), the plaintext $\mathcal{G}^{\mathsf{pw}_1 h^{-1}}$ in the ID-based encryption E_a is replaced with a random element in $\mathbb{E}$.

The difference between the current experiment and the previous one is bounded by the probability that an adversary breaks the semantic security of the identity-based encryption (IBE) scheme. More precisely, we have

Claim 2. If the identity-based encryption (IBE) scheme is semantically secure, $|\mathsf{Adv}_{\mathcal{A}}^{P_1}(k) - \mathsf{Adv}_{\mathcal{A}}^{P_2}(k)|$ is negligible.

Experiment P_3: In this experiment, the simulator interacts with the adversary $\mathcal{A}$ as in experiment P_2 except that: for any Execute(C, i, A, j, B, k) oracle, where the adversary $\mathcal{A}$ has not queried corrupt(A), but may have queried corrupt(B), the plaintext $g_2^{\mathsf{pw}_{C,A}^* h_a^{-1}}$ in the Cramer-Shoup encryption (S_1, T_1, U_1, V_1) is replaced by a random element in the group $\mathbb{G}$.

The difference between the current experiment and the previous one is bounded by the probability that an adversary breaks the semantic security of the Cramer-Shoup encryption scheme. More precisely, we have

Claim 3. If the Cramer-Shoup encryption scheme is semantically secure, $|\mathsf{Adv}_{\mathcal{A}}^{P_2}(k) - \mathsf{Adv}_{\mathcal{A}}^{P_3}(k)|$ is negligible.

Experiment P_4: In this experiment, the simulator interacts with the adversary $\mathcal{A}$ as in experiment P_3 except that: for any Execute(C, i, A, j, B, k) oracle, where the adversary $\mathcal{A}$ has not queried corrupt(A), but may have queried corrupt(B), the session keys $\mathsf{sk}_{C,A}$ and $\mathsf{sk}_{A,C}$ are replaced with a same random element in the group $\mathbb{G}$.

The difference between the current experiment and the previous one is bounded by the probability to solve the decisional Diffie-Hellman (DDH) problem over $(\mathbb{G}, g, q)$. More precisely, we have

Claim 4. If the decisional Diffie-Hellman (DDH) problem is hard over $(\mathbb{G}, q, g)$, $|\mathsf{Adv}_{\mathcal{A}}^{P_3}(k) - \mathsf{Adv}_{\mathcal{A}}^{P_4}(k)|$ is negligible.

If $|\mathsf{Adv}_{\mathcal{A}}^{P_3}(k) - \mathsf{Adv}_{\mathcal{A}}^{P_4}(k)|$ is non-negligible, we show that the simulator can use $\mathcal{A}$ as a subroutine to solve the DDH problem with non-negligible probability in a similar way as follows.

Given a DDH problem (g^α, g^β, Z), where α, β are randomly chosen from $\mathbb{Z}_q^*$ and Z is either $g^{\alpha\beta}$ or a random element z from $\mathbb{G}$, the simulator replaces W_c with g^α, and W_a with g^β, and the session keys $\mathsf{sk}_{C,A}$, $\mathsf{sk}_{A,C}$ with Z. When $Z = g^{\alpha\beta}$, the experiment is the same as the experiment P_3. When Z is a random element z in $\mathbb{G}$, the experiment is the same as the experiment P_4. If the adversary can distinguish the experiments P_3 and P_4 with non-negligible probability, the simulator can solve the DDH problem with non-negligible probability. Assuming that the DDH problem is hard, Claim 4 is true.

In experiment P_4, the adversary's probability of correctly guessing the bit b used by the Test oracle is exactly $1/2$ when the Test query is made to a fresh client instance C^i or a fresh server instance A^j invoked by an Execute(C, i, A, j, B, k) oracle, even if the adversary queried corrupt(B) (i.e., the adversary corrupted the server B). This is so because the session keys $\mathsf{sk}_{C,A}$ and $\mathsf{sk}_{A,C}$ for such instances in P_4 are chosen at random from $\mathbb{G}$, and hence there is no way to distinguish whether the Test oracle outputs a random session key or the "actual" session key (which is just a random element, anyway). Therefore, all passive adversaries cannot win the game, even if they can query Corrupt(B) oracles.

The rest of the proof concentrates on the instances invoked by Send oracles.

Experiment P_5: In this experiment, we modify the simulator's responses to $\mathsf{Send}(A, j, \mathsf{msg}_1)$ and $\mathsf{Send}(C, i, \mathsf{msg}_A|\mathsf{msg}_B)$ queries.

Before describing this change we introduce some terminology. For a query $\mathsf{Send}(A, j, \mathsf{msg}_1)$, where msg_1 is adversarially - generated, if $\mathsf{acc}_A^j = \mathsf{TRUE}$, then msg_1 is said to be valid. Otherwise, msg_1 is said to be invalid. Similarly, for a query $\mathsf{Send}(C, i, \mathsf{msg}_A|\mathsf{msg}_B)$, where $\mathsf{msg}_A|\mathsf{msg}_B$ is adversarially-generated, if $\mathsf{acc}_C^i = \mathsf{TRUE}$, then $\mathsf{msg}_A|\mathsf{msg}_B$ is said to be valid. Otherwise, it is said to be invalid. Informally, valid messages use correct passwords while invalid messages do not. Given this terminology, we continue with our description of experiment P_5. When the adversary makes oracle query $\mathsf{Send}(A, j, \mathsf{msg}_1)$, the simulator examines msg_1. If it is adversarially-generated and valid, the simulator halts and acc_A^j is assigned the special value ∇. In any other case, (i.e., msg_1 is oracle-generated, or adversarially-generated but invalid), the query is answered exactly as in experiment P_4. When the adversary makes oracle query $\mathsf{Send}(C, i, \mathsf{msg}_A|\mathsf{msg}_B)$, the simulator examines $\mathsf{msg}_A|\mathsf{msg}_B$. If the message is adversarially-generated and valid, the simulator halts and acc_C^i is assigned the special value ∇. In any other case, (i.e., $\mathsf{msg}_A|\mathsf{msg}_B$ is oracle-generated, or adversarially-generated but invalid), the query is answered exactly as in experiment P_4.

Now, we change the definition of the adversary's success in P_5. At first, we define that a server instance A^j is fresh if the adversary has not queried Corrupt(A) and a client instance C^i is fresh if the adversary has not queried Corrupt(C). If the adversary ever queries $\mathsf{Send}(A, j, \mathsf{msg}_1)$ oracle to a fresh server instance A^j with $\mathsf{acc}_A^j = \nabla$ or $\mathsf{Send}(C, i, \mathsf{msg}_A|\mathsf{msg}_B)$ oracle to a fresh client instance C^i with $\mathsf{acc}_C^i = \nabla$, the simulator halts and the adversary succeeds. Otherwise the adversary's success is determined as in experiment P_4.

The distribution on the adversary's view in experiments P_4 and P_5 are identical up to the point when the adversary queries $\mathsf{Send}(A, j, \mathsf{msg}_1)$ oracle to a fresh server instance with $\mathsf{acc}_A^j = \nabla$ or $\mathsf{Send}(C, i, \mathsf{msg}_A|\mathsf{msg}_B)$ oracle to a fresh client instance with $\mathsf{acc}_C^i = \nabla$. If such a query is never made, the distributions on the view are identical. Therefore, we have

Claim 5. $\mathsf{Adv}_{\mathcal{A}}^{P_4}(k) \leq \mathsf{Adv}_{\mathcal{A}}^{P_5}(k)$.

Experiment P_6: In this experiment, the simulator interacts with the adversary $\mathcal{A}$ as in experiment P_5 except that the adversary's queries to $\mathsf{Send}(C, i, A, B)$ and $\mathsf{Send}(A, j, \mathsf{msg}_1)$ oracles are handled differently: in any $\mathsf{Send}(C, i, A, B)$, where the adversary $\mathcal{A}$ has not queried corrupt(A), but may have queried corrupt(B), the plaintext $\mathcal{G}^{\mathsf{pw}_1 h^{-1}}$ in E_a is replaced with a random element in the group $\mathbb{E}$; in any $\mathsf{Send}(A, j, \mathsf{msg}_1)$, where the adversary $\mathcal{A}$ has not queried corrupt(A), but may have queried corrupt(B), the plaintext $g_2^{\mathsf{pw}_{C,A}^* h_a^{-1}}$ in the Cramer - Shoup encryption (S_1, T_1, U_1, V_1) (if any) is replaced with a random element in the group $\mathbb{G}$.

As we prove Claims 2 and 3, we can prove

Claim 6. If both the IBE scheme and the Cramer-Shoup scheme are semantically secure, $|\mathsf{Adv}_{\mathcal{A}}^{P_5}(k) - \mathsf{Adv}_{\mathcal{A}}^{P_6}(k)|$ is negligible.

In experiment P_6, msg_1 and msg_A from Execute and Send oracles become independent of the password pw_C used by the client C in the view of the adversary $\mathcal{A}$, even if $\mathcal{A}$ may require Corrupt(B). In addition, although the adversary who has corrupted the server B is able to obtain $\mathcal{G}^{\mathsf{pw}_2}$, $\mathcal{G}^{\mathsf{pw}_{C,B}}$ and $g_2^{\mathsf{pw}_{C,B}^*}$, they are independent of the password pw_C in the view of the adversary because the references msg_1 and msg_A are independent of the password in the view of the adversary. In view of this, any off-line dictionary attack cannot succeed.

The adversary $\mathcal{A}$ succeeds only if one of the following occurs: (1) the adversary queries Send(A, j, msg_1) oracle to a fresh server instance A^j for adversarially-generated and valid msg_1, that is, $\mathsf{acc}_A^j = \nabla$ (let Succ_1 denote this event); (2) the adversary queries Send$(C, i, \mathsf{msg}_A | \mathsf{msg}_B)$ oracle to a fresh client instance C^i for adversarially-generated and valid $\mathsf{msg}_A | \mathsf{msg}_B$, that is, $\mathsf{acc}_C^i = \nabla$ (let Succ_2 denote this event); (3) neither Succ_1 nor Succ_2 happens, the adversary wins the game by a Test query to a fresh instance C^i or a server instance A^j.

To evaluate $\Pr[\mathsf{Succ}_1]$ and $\Pr[\mathsf{Succ}_2]$, we assume that the adversary $\mathcal{A}$ has corrupted the server B and consider four cases as follows.

Case 1. The adversary $\mathcal{A}$ modifies $\mathsf{msg}_1 = \langle C, W_c, X, Y, Z, E_a \rangle$ from the client by changing W_c, X, Y, Z and then the plaintext $\mathcal{G}^{\mathsf{pw}_1} h^{-1}$ in E_a. Changing the plaintext in a ciphertext works with a public key cryptosystem with homomorphic property, such as the ElGamal scheme [14]. It does not work with the IBE scheme which is secure against the chosen-ciphertext attack. The best the adversary can do is choosing W_c', X', Y', Z' such that $H_1(C, W_c', X', Y', Z') = H_1(C, W_c, X, Y, Z)$. But H_1 is a collision-resistant hash function. Therefore, the probability of Succ_1 in this case is negligible.

Case 2. The adversary $\mathcal{A}$ forges $\mathsf{msg}_1' = \langle C, W_c', X', Y', Z'\ E_a' \rangle$ by choosing his own W_c', X', Y', Z', E_a'. In this case, the best the adversary can do is to choose $r_c', x_1', x_2', y_1', y_2'$ and computes $W_c' = g_1^{r_c'}$, $X' = g_1^{x_1'} g_2^{x_2'}$, $Y' = g_1^{y_1'} g_2^{y_2'}$, $Z' = g_1^{z'}$, $h^* = H_1(C, W_c', X', Y', Z')$ and performs identity-based encryption $E_a' = \mathsf{IBE}(\mathcal{G}^{-\mathsf{pw}_{C,B}} h^{*-1}, A)$, and sends msg_1' to the server A. Note that the adversary $\mathcal{A}$ has corrupted B and know $\mathcal{G}^{\mathsf{pw}_{C,B}}$. After receiving msg_1', the server A derives $\omega_a = \mathcal{G}^{-\mathsf{pw}_{C,B} - \mathsf{pw}_{C,A}} = \mathcal{G}^{-\mathsf{pw}_C}$ and then runs two-party PAKE protocol P with the server B (controlled by the adversary) on the basis of ω_a. Without knowing ω_a, the probability of Succ_1 depends on the protocol P. If P is a secure two-party PAKE protocol with explicit authentication, $\Pr[\mathsf{Succ}_1] \leq Q^P(k)/N + \varepsilon(k)$ for some negligible function $\varepsilon(\cdot)$, where $Q^P(k)$ denotes the number of on-line attacks in the protocol P.

Case 3. The adversary $\mathcal{A}$ modifies $\mathsf{msg}_A = \langle A, S_1, T_1, U_1, V_1, W_a \rangle$ from the server A. In msg_A, (S_1, T_1, U_1, V_1) is a Cramer-Shoup encryption of $g_2^{\mathsf{pw}_{C,A}^* h_a^{-1}}$, where $h_a = H_2(A, W_a, C, W_c)$. If the adversary $\mathcal{A}$ changes the plaintext in (S_1, T_1, U_1, V_1), the message becomes invalid because the Cramer-Shoup encryption scheme is secure against the chosen ciphertext attack. The best the the adversary can do is choosing his own W_a' such that $H_2(A, W_a', C, W_c) = H_2(A, W_a, C, W_c)$. But H_2 is a collision-resistant hash function. Therefore, the probability of Succ_2 in this case is negligible.

Case 4. The adversary $\mathcal{A}$ forges $\mathsf{msg}_A' = \langle A, S_1', T_1', U_1', V_1', W_a' \rangle$ by choosing a password pw_C' from the dictionary $\mathcal{D}$ and $r_a', r_1' \in \mathbb{Z}_q^*$ and computing $W_a' = g_1^{r_a'}, S_1' = g_1^{r_1'}, T_1' = g_2^{r_1'}, h_a^* = H_2(A, W_a', C, W_c), U_1 = g_2^{(\mathsf{pw}_C' - \mathsf{pw}_{C,B}^*)h_a^{*-1}} Z^{r_1'}, h_1^*$ $= H_2(S_1', T_1', U_1'), V_1 = X'^{r_1'} Y'^{h_1^* r_1'}$. Then $\mathcal{A}$ sends $\mathsf{msg}_A' | \mathsf{msg}_B$ to the client, suppose that msg_B is constructed as defined by the protocol. In this case, the event Succ_2 occurs if and only if $\mathsf{pw}_C' = \mathsf{pw}_C$. Therefore, $\Pr[\mathsf{Succ}_2] \leq Q^C(k)/N$, where $Q^C(k)$ denotes the number of on-line attacks to the client instance C^i.

The above discussion shows that

Claim 7. If (1) P is a secure two-party PAKE protocol with explicit authentication; (2) the IBE scheme and the Cramer-Shoup scheme are secure against the chosen-ciphertext attack; (4) H_1 and H_2 are collision-resistant hash functions, then $\Pr[\mathsf{Succ}_1 \vee \mathsf{Succ}_2] \leq Q(k)/N + \varepsilon(k)$, where $Q(k)$ denotes the number of on-line attacks and $\varepsilon(k)$ is a negligible function.

Remark. If a public key encryption scheme is secure against the chosen-ciphertext attack (CCA), it is secure against the chosen-plaintext attack (CPA) (i.e., it is semantically secure).

In experiment P_6, the adversary's probability of success when neither Succ_1 nor Succ_2 occurs is $1/2$. The preceding discussion implies that

$$Pr_{\mathcal{A}}^{P_6}[\mathsf{Succ}] \leq Q(k)/N + \varepsilon(k) + 1/2 \cdot (1 - Q(k)/N - \varepsilon(k))$$

and thus the adversary's advantage in experiment P_6

$$\begin{aligned}
\mathsf{Adv}_{\mathcal{A}}^{P_6}(k) &= 2Pr_{\mathcal{A}}^{P_6}[\mathsf{Succ}] - 1 \\
&\leq 2Q(k)/N + 2\varepsilon(k) + 1 - Q(k)/N - \varepsilon(k) - 1 \\
&= Q(k)/N + \varepsilon(k)
\end{aligned}$$

for some negligible function $\varepsilon(\cdot)$. The sequence of claims proved above show that

$$\mathsf{Adv}_{\mathcal{A}}^{P_0}(k) \leq \mathsf{Adv}_{\mathcal{A}}^{P_6}(k) + \varepsilon(k) \leq Q(k)/N + \varepsilon(k)$$

for some negligible function $\varepsilon(\cdot)$. This completes the proof of the theorem.

5   Conclusion

In this paper, we present an efficient compiler to transform any two-party PAKE protocol to a two-server PAKE protocol from identity-based encryption. In addition, we have provided a rigorous proof of security for our compiler without random oracle. Our compiler is in particular suitable for the applications of password-based authentication where an identity-based system has already established.

References

1. Abdalla, M., Fouque, P.A., Pointcheval, D.: Password-based authenticated key exchange in the three-party setting. In: Vaudenay, S. (ed.) PKC 2005. LNCS, vol. 3386, pp. 65–84. Springer, Heidelberg (2005)
2. Abdalla, M., Pointcheval, D.: Simple password-based encrypted key exchange protocols. In: Menezes, A. (ed.) CT-RSA 2005. LNCS, vol. 3376, pp. 191–208. Springer, Heidelberg (2005)
3. Bellare, M., Pointcheval, D., Rogaway, P.: Authenticated key exchange secure against dictionary attacks. In: Preneel, B. (ed.) EUROCRYPT 2000. LNCS, vol. 1807, pp. 139–155. Springer, Heidelberg (2000)
4. Bellovin, S.M., Merritt, M.: Encrypted key exchange: Password-based protocol secure against dictionary attack. In: Proc. 1992 IEEE Symposium on Research in Security and Privacy, pp. 72–84 (1992)
5. Boneh, D., Franklin, M.: Identity based encryption from the Weil pairing. In: Kilian, J. (ed.) CRYPTO 2001. LNCS, vol. 2139, pp. 213–229. Springer, Heidelberg (2001)
6. Boneh, D., Katz, J.: Improved efficiency for CCA-secure cryptosystems built using identity based encryption. In: Menezes, A. (ed.) CT-RSA 2005. LNCS, vol. 3376, pp. 87–103. Springer, Heidelberg (2005)
7. Boyko, V., MacKenzie, P.D., Patel, S.: Provably secure password-authenticated key exchange using Diffie-Hellman. In: Preneel, B. (ed.) EUROCRYPT 2000. LNCS, vol. 1807, pp. 156–171. Springer, Heidelberg (2000)
8. Brainard, J., Juels, A., Kaliski, B., Szydlo, M.: Nightingale: A new two-server approach for authentication with short secrets. In: Proc. 12th USENIX Security Symp., pp. 201–213 (2003)
9. Bresson, E., Chevassut, O., Pointcheval, D.: Security proofs for an efficient password-based key exchange. In: Proc. CCS 2003, pp. 241–250 (2003)
10. Bresson, E., Chevassut, O., Pointcheval, D.: New security results on encrypted key exchange. In: Bao, F., Deng, R., Zhou, J. (eds.) PKC 2004. LNCS, vol. 2947, pp. 145–158. Springer, Heidelberg (2004)
11. Canetti, R., Halevi, S., Katz, J.: Chosen-ciphertext security from identity-based encryption. In: Cachin, C., Camenisch, J.L. (eds.) EUROCRYPT 2004. LNCS, vol. 3027, pp. 207–222. Springer, Heidelberg (2004)
12. Cramer, R., Shoup, V.: A practical public key cryptosystem provably secure against adaptive chosen ciphertext attack. In: Krawczyk, H. (ed.) CRYPTO 1998. LNCS, vol. 1462, pp. 13–25. Springer, Heidelberg (1998)
13. Diffie, W., Hellman, M.: New directions in cryptography. IEEE Transactions on Information Theory 32(2), 644–654 (1976)
14. ElGamal, T.: A public-key cryptosystem and a signature scheme based on discrete logarithms. IEEE Transactions on Information Theory 31(4), 469–472 (1985)
15. Ford, W., Kaliski, B.S.: Server-assisted generation of a strong secret from a password. In: Proc. 5th IEEE Intl. Workshop on Enterprise Security (2000)
16. Gentry, C.: Practical identity-based encryption without random oracles. In: Vaudenay, S. (ed.) EUROCRYPT 2006. LNCS, vol. 4004, pp. 445–464. Springer, Heidelberg (2006)
17. Goldreich, O., Lindell, Y.: Session-key generation using human passwords only. In: Kilian, J. (ed.) CRYPTO 2001. LNCS, vol. 2139, pp. 408–432. Springer, Heidelberg (2001)

18. Gong, L., Lomas, T.M.A., Needham, R.M., Saltzer, J.H.: Protecting poorly-chosen secret from guessing attacks. IEEE J. on Selected Areas in Communications 11(5), 648–656 (1993)

19. Halevi, S., Krawczyk, H.: Public-key cryptography and password protocols. ACM Transactions on Information and System Security 2(3), 230–268 (1999)

20. Jablon, D.: Password authentication using multiple servers. In: Naccache, D. (ed.) CT-RSA 2001. LNCS, vol. 2020, pp. 344–360. Springer, Heidelberg (2001)

21. Jiang, S., Gong, G.: Password based key exchange with mutual authentication. In: Handschuh, H., Hasan, M.A. (eds.) SAC 2004. LNCS, vol. 3357, pp. 267–279. Springer, Heidelberg (2004)

22. Jin, H., Wong, D.S., Xu, Y.: An efficient password-only two-server authenticated key exchange system. In: Qing, S., Imai, H., Wang, G. (eds.) ICICS 2007. LNCS, vol. 4861, pp. 44–56. Springer, Heidelberg (2007)

23. Katz, J., Ostrovsky, R., Yung, M.: Efficient password-authenticated key exchange using human-memorable passwords. In: Pfitzmann, B. (ed.) EUROCRYPT 2001. LNCS, vol. 2045, pp. 475–494. Springer, Heidelberg (2001)

24. Katz, J., MacKenzie, P., Taban, G., Gligor, V.: Two-server password-only authenticated key exchange. In: Ioannidis, J., Keromytis, A.D., Yung, M. (eds.) ACNS 2005. LNCS, vol. 3531, pp. 1–16. Springer, Heidelberg (2005)

25. MacKenzie, P., Patel, S., Swaminathan, R.: Password-authenticated key exchange based on RSA. Intl. J. Information Security 9(6), 387–410 (2010)

26. MacKenzie, P., Shrimpton, T., Jakobsson, M.: Threshold password-authenticated key exchange. J. Cryptology 19(1), 27–66 (2006)

27. Di Raimondo, M., Gennaro, R.: Provably Secure Threshold Password-Authenticated Key Exchange. J. Computer and System Sciences 72(6), 978–1001 (2006)

28. Szydlo, M., Kaliski, B.: Proofs for two-server password authentication. In: Menezes, A. (ed.) CT-RSA 2005. LNCS, vol. 3376, pp. 227–244. Springer, Heidelberg (2005)

29. Waters, B.: Efficient identity-based encryption without random oracles. In: Cramer, R. (ed.) EUROCRYPT 2005. LNCS, vol. 3494, pp. 114–127. Springer, Heidelberg (2005)

30. Yang, Y., Bao, F., Deng, R.H.: A new architecture for authentication and key exchange using password for federated enterprise. In: Sasaki, R., Qing, S., Okamoto, E., Yoshiura, H. (eds.) SEC 2005. IFIP AICT, vol. 181, pp. 95–111. Springer, Heidelberg (2005)

31. Yang, Y., Deng, R.H., Bao, F.: A practical password-based two-server authentication and key exchange system. IEEE Trans. Dependable and Secure Computing 3(2), 105–114 (2006)

32. Yang, Y., Deng, R.H., Bao, F.: Fortifying password authentication in integrated healthcare delivery systems. In: Proc. ASIACCS 2006, pp. 255–265 (2006)

33. Yi, X., Tso, R., Okamoto, E.: ID-based group password-authenticated key exchange. In: Takagi, T., Mambo, M. (eds.) IWSEC 2009. LNCS, vol. 5824, pp. 192–211. Springer, Heidelberg (2009)

34. Yi, X., Tso, R., Okamoto, E.: Identity-based password-authenticated key exchange for client/server model. In: SECRYPT 2012, pp. 45–54 (2012)

35. Yi, X., Ling, S., Wang, H.: Efficient two-server password-only authenticated key exchange. IEEE Trans. Parallel Distrib. Syst. 24(9), 1773–1782 (2013)

Modelling Time for Authenticated Key Exchange Protocols

Jörg Schwenk

Horst Görtz Institute for IT-Security, Ruhr-University Bochum
joerg.schwenk@rub.de

Abstract. The notion of time plays an important role in many practically deployed cryptographic protocols, ranging from One-Time-Password (OTP) tokens to the Kerberos protocol. However, time is difficult to model in a Turing machine environment.

We propose the first such model, where time is modelled as a global counter $\mathcal{T}$. We argue that this model closely matches several implementations of time in computer environments. The usefulness of the model is shown by giving complexity-theoretic security proofs for OTP protocols and HMQV-like one-round AKE protocols.

Keywords: Authenticated key agreement, timestamps, provable security, OTP, Kerberos.

1 Introduction

The Notion of Time in Cryptography. In cryptography, time values are used for many different purposes: To limit the lifetime of public keys in X.509 certificates, to reduce the impact of breaking an authentication protocol to a certain time slot, and to guarantee the freshness of messages. For each of these purposes, a different model is necessary to formally define the security goals. Moreover, in real implementations either local or global clocks may be used. Again, this requires different computational models: based on interactive Turing Machines (the standard TM model for cryptographic protocols) for global (external) clocks, or (still to be defined) synchronized Turing Machines for local clocks.

In this paper, we try to start a discussion on the formal modelling of time. We concentrate on timestamps to guarantee freshness, and on global clocks. This allows us to use interactive Turing Machines in our computational model, and to stay as close as possible to the definition for secure authentication protocols given in [1]. *Our focus is on the model, not on the cryptographic techniques; thus our proofs are fairly straightforward.*

Authentication. Authentication is, besides key agreement, the most important security goal in cryptographic protocols. Loosely speaking, an authentication protocol is secure if the probability that an *active* adversary breaks the protocol is the same as for a *passive* adversary. For many cryptograhic protocols, authentication is of major importance: TLS is used to authenticate the server

M. Kutyłowski and J. Vaidya (Eds.): ESORICS 2014, Part II, LNCS 8713, pp. 277–294, 2014.

(e.g. through EV certificates), and One-Time-Password (OTP) schemes (e.g. SecureID) or Kerberos (and WWW variants like OpenID or SAML) have been designed as authentication protocols.

Authentication with nonces. Replay attacks are one major threat for authentication protocols, so the *freshness* of a message must be guaranteed. In practical implementations, this is achieved by securely including "new" values into some protocol messages: either nonces chosen by the other party, or timestamps.

Nonces can easily be modelled in a Turing machine based environment: They are either read from a random input tape, or they are randomly generated by a probabilistic Turing machine. The security analysis then only has to take into account the probability distribution of these values. However, for one-sided authentication, this implies at least two messages, and for mutual authentication at least three messages, since each authenticating party has to receive back the nonce chosen by itself, and returned by the authenticated party.

Authentication with Timestamps. Timestamps are more difficult to model, because time is not measurable for a Turing machine after it finished its computation, and waits for fresh input. (In practice, this is comparable to the problem of using time in smartcard computations: If the smart card is disconnected from power supply, it is no longer able to even increase a local clock.) However, timestamps enable us to design more efficient protocols, with less latency. *Thus timestamps can be seen as a replacement for nonces, but they are not identical: They allow us to design more efficient protocols.*

Reduction-based proofs in a Turing Machine model. A Turing Machine (TM) is a *mathematical* model of a (von Neumann) computer [2]. The famous Church-Turing thesis states that any computable algorithm can be implemented using a TM. Since a TM is a mathematical object, mathematical proof techniques can be applied, and these proofs form the basis of all theoretical computer science. On the other hand, subtle errors in the model may invalidate such proofs [3].

Definition 1 (Turing Machine [2]). *A Turing Machine $\mathcal{M}$ is a tuple $\mathcal{M} = (Q, \Gamma, b, \Sigma, \delta, q_0, F)$, where Q is a finite, non-empty set of states, Γ is the tape alphabet, $b \in \Gamma$ is the blank symbol, $\Sigma \subseteq \Gamma - \{b\}$ is the input alphabet, $q_0 \in Q$ is the initial state, $F \subseteq Q$ is the set of final or accepting states, and $\delta : (Q - F) \times \Gamma \rightarrow Q \times \Gamma \times \{L, R\}$ is a partial function called the transition function. A Turing machine is started by setting its internal state to q_0, writing the input string on the (infinite) tape, and positioning its read/write head on the first input symbol. As long as no accepting state is reached, $\delta(s, q) = (s', q', m)$ is evaluated, where s is the actual state of the TM, and q is the symbol read by the read/write head from the tape. As a result of this evaluation of δ, the internal state of $\mathcal{M}$ is set to s', the symbol q' is written on the tape by overwriting q, anf the read/write head either moves right ($m = R$) or left ($m = L$).*

In cryptography, complex systems are shown to be secure by giving a polynomial reduction to a well-studied assumption (e.g. factoring of large integers, or

$P \neq NP$). The basis for this research was the formalization of all computational processes as (probabilistic) Turing Machines (TM). Research on reduction-based proofs for cryptographic protocols started with the seminal paper of Bellare and Rogaway [1] in 1993. Up to the best of our knowledge, randomness played an important role in all subsequent papers, but time stamps were never investigated, except in informal models (Section 2).

Modelling Time. Time plays an important role in IT security: X.509 certificates and other security tokens have a validity period, some One-Time-Password (OTP) systems need loosely synchronized clocks between hardware token and server, GPS Spoofing may only be detected by comparing internal clock values with the time contained in GPS signals, and malware may protect itself by querying external time sources.

However, running an internal (independent) clock always means measuring some physical parameter: movements of a pendulum, oscillation rate of a crystal, or an electronic transition frequency. *Thus the main problem with time is that we simply cannot model "real" time in a Turing Machine based model. All formal models claiming to be able to model time must therefore be carefully checked if they satisfy all restrictions imposed by Definition 1 or one of its variants. If they deviate from this strict formalism, the results may become invalid.*

Instead, we have to find a suitable approximation for time, which preserves the most important security guarantees offered by "real" time.[1]

If we look at one implementation of time, we get a motivation for the choice of our model: The Network Time Protocol (NTP, [4]) delivers the actual time to an application *on request.* Thus in our model we have chosen to implement time as a global counter $\mathcal{T}$, which is accessible to all Turing machines in our computing environment. If a fresh message has to be sent, the sending TM request a timestamp $ts = (t, aux)$ from $\mathcal{T}$. Upon reception of such a request, $\mathcal{T}$ first increases its local counter $(t \leftarrow t + 1)$. Then the actual value t is returned, optionally with auxiliary data aux appended. This auxiliary data may e.g. be a digital signature, to prevent Denial-of-Service attacks by an adversary who would issue large values like $t + 2^k >> t$.

One can easily derive variants of this model, for example: Turing Machines may query $\mathcal{T}$ whenever they are activated, or even on each computation step they make. Each query may increase the counter, or a different pattern may be designed to increase it. The channel between $\mathcal{T}$ and the process oracles may be insecure, authentic, or even *untappable* [5], the latter guaranteeing that the adversary may never influence the communication with the time source. From all these variants, we have chosen what we believe to be the simplest model, which however offers similar security guarantees than the other variants.

The Notion of Time-Security. Our starting point is the definition of secure authentication protocols, given in the seminal paper by Bellare and Rogaway [1]. They motivated their definitions by introducing a *benign adversary*, who forwards all messages faithfully. They defined an authentication protocol to be

---

[1] Please note that other usecases of time may cause additional modeling problems.

secure if the winning probability of any adversary is (up to a negligible difference) equal to the winning probability of this benign adversary. They showed
that this condition is, for many protocols using random nonces, equivalent to
requiring that both parties only accept if they have *matching conversations* (cf.
Definition 3). Our main goal is to find a replacement for the concept of *matching conversations*, since in one- and two-message protocols, this concept is not
applicable: here the responder oracle *always* has a matching conversation to the
initiator oracle, but due to replay attacks active adversaries may influence the
system significantly: With a benign adversary, there is at most one responder
oracle that will accept on a single message; with an active adversary, there may
be arbitrary many.

In this paper we only consider cryptographic protocols consisting of one or two
messages.[2] (If we have three messages, we can use random nonces, and achieve
better security goals.) Thus there always is one oracle (responder) that has to
decide whether to accept or reject after receiving a single message, and before
(or without) sending a message. We will consider a protocol to be *time-secure*, if
for each initiator oracle that has sent a message there is at most one responder
oracle that accepts, and that this responder oracle will accept only if the message
was forwarded unmodified by the adversary. The second goal can be achieved
by using cryptographic primitives like message authentication codes or signature
schemes, but for the first goal we need *timestamps*.

For two-message protocols, we can additionally base the acceptance condition
for initiator oracles (which send and receive one message) on the classical notion
of matching conversations (if a nonce is used, which is however *not* the case in
all previously proposed two-message protocols), or we can also apply the notion
of time-security here.

Scope of our results. The results presented in this paper are directly applicable
to OTP schemes based on counters, e.g. all OTP schemes based on the HOTP
algorithm [6], which is the basis for many commercially deployed OTP schemes.
HOTP uses an 8 Byte counter, a shared key between initiator and responder,
and HMAC-SHA-1 as the MAC algorithm. The counter value at the initiator is
incremented with every OTP generation, whereas the counter at the server is
only incremented after a successful authentication, to the counter value used in
the OTP. This exactly mirrors our time model. However, usability considerations
have lead to the introduction of a truncation function, which reduces the entropy
of the OTP significantly, and thus a throttling scheme must be used to prevent
exhaustive MAC searches. These usability enhancements are out-of-scope here.

OTP schemes using loosely synchronized clocks (e.g. RSA SecureID or TOTP
[7]) are based on clock counters, the main difference to HOTP being that the
responder counter is increased independantly. We could modify the acceptance
condition and the communication with $\mathcal{T}$ at the responder to include this in our
model (see Appendix); however, in oder to get similar security properties, we

---

[2] Please note that we need a different security definition for each protocol type, but
our definition of time remains unchanged.

would also have to add a second counter at the responder, in order to prevent replay attacks of OTPs within one given time step (default value is 30 seconds).

For two-message protocols, our results can be used to devise new protocols which may achieve explicit authentication for both initiator and responder, in addition to authenticated key exchange. With respect to the latter property, the model presented here is "weak" in the sense that it does not consider queries like *RevealDHExponent* or *RevealState* [8]; again, this is in order to keep the model (and the proofs) simple.

One important motivation for considering a hybrid definition of explicit authentication (using nonces and timestamps) was the fact that the two-party two-message building blocks of the Kerberos protocol. In the full paper [9] we give a security proof for a modified version of the basic Kerberos building block.

Contribution. The contributions of this paper are as follows:

- We propose the first theoretically consistent model for timestamps in cryptograhic protocols, which covers all Turing Machine-based implementations.
- We give a security definition for explicit authentication extending [1], applicable to a wide range of protocols.
- We show the usefulness of our definition by giving examples of secure one and two message protocols, together with formal security proofs.

2   Related Work

Timestamps. An overview on usage and security problems of timestamps can be found in [10]. (See [11] for an updated version.) Moran et al. [12] use a different model for timestamping documents: they assume that a unique random string is broadcasted in each time period. An actual overview on hash-then-publish timestamping can be found in [13]. [14] shows that if malleable encryption (e.g. a streamcipher) is used, timestamp based authentication protocols may fail. [15] covers one-time passwords, but in the different context of password-based authenticated key exchange (PAKE). Please note that *Lamport timestamps*, which play an inportant role in distributed systems, are a completely different concept.

Authenticated Key Exchange. Reasearch on formal security models for two-party authentication and authenticated key exchange (AKE) protocols started with the seminal paper of Bellare and Rogaway [1]. In [16], 3-party session key distribution protocols were investigated, but authentication was omitted. In the following years, research on cryptographic protocols focused either on authenticated group key exchange [17], or the higly efficient two-message protocols (see below). Explicit authentication was difficult to achieve in these protocols, thus variants of the AKE model introduced by Canetti and Krawczyk [18] were used.

Authenticated Key Exchange with Timestamps. In a paper whose goals are closest to our work, Barbosa and Farshin [19] introduce two different models (one based on Canetti-Krawczyk and one following Bellare-Rogaway) to model AKE with timestamps, and a total of 6 theorems. In [19], time is modeled as a local clock LocalTime, which is incremented by sending TICK requests. In comparison to our work (we use a global clock), [19] has a couple of drawbacks, the most important being that there is no mathematically sound definition of the local clock as part of a Turing machine.

Two-message protocols. In 1986, Matsumoto et al. [20] first studied implicitly authenticated Diffie-Hellman protocols, which results in a line of research generated many protocols. Research on this topic was re-initiated by the introduction of the MQV [21,22], KEA1 [23] and HMQV [24] protocols. The latter is formally proven secure in a modified CK [18] model, where no explicit authentication is defined (only authenticated key exchange). A short overview on the employed models is given in [25].

3   Formal Model

In this section, we describe the *execution environment*, where we try to model normal protocol execution, the *adversarial capabilities*, which describe against which type of adversary our protocol should be secure, and the *security model* which describes security games where the winning events correspond to a security breach of the protocol. In this and the following sections, we use standard notations and for cryptographich primitives (cf. [9]).

3.1   Execution Environment

Parties and process oracles We distinguish between *parties* $\{P_1, \ldots, P_n\}$ and process oracles π_i^s, $i \in \{1, \ldots, l\}$, run by party P_i. These process oracles and the party itself are modelled as Turing machines. Oracles can be initialized, can send and receive messages according to the protocol specification, and terminate either in finished, accept or reject state[3]. The complete set of states for oracles is $\Lambda = \{\texttt{not\_initialized}, \texttt{wait}, \texttt{finished}, \texttt{accept}, \texttt{reject}\}$. In addition, we have two special parties $\mathcal{T}$ and $\mathcal{A}$.

Each party P_i has two local variables: A local time counter T_i, and a long-lived key k_i. This long-lived key is either a public key pair, or a list of $n - 1$ symmetric keys shared with the other parties.

Long-lived keys of party P_i can be accessed for cryptographic operations, and the counter values t_i of P_i can be increased, by all process oracles (or oracles, for short) $\pi_i^1, \ldots, \pi_i^l$ of this party. Computed nonces, intermediate state values, and session keys are only known to a single oracle. If a session key is computed by an oracle π_i^s, the value k is stored in a variable K when the oracle enters accept or finished state. The current state of each oracle is stored in variable

---

[3] We need an additional final finished state for one-message protocols because initiator oracles always have to reach a final state, but this can be no winning event for the adversary.

Λ, and the transcript of all messages sent and received (in chronological order) in variable $T^{i,s}$.

There is one special party $\mathcal{T}$, which has a local counter T with actual state t; on request, this party increases the value of t by 1 and returns the actual value of t as a message $ts = (t, aux)$ over the network.

The adversary $\mathcal{A}$ is another special party which implements, as a Turing machine, a strategy to break the cryptographic protocol. The event(s) which define a protocol break are modelled as winning events in different games defined below.

Initiator and responder oracles. Our security definition is focused on protocols with one and two messages; for protocols with three and more messages nonces can be used instead of timestamps, and the classical definitions and results from the Bellare-Rogaway and Canetti-Krawczyk models apply. For our security definitions, we need to distinguish between *initiator* and *responder* oracles.

Definition 2. *An oracle who sends the first message in a protocol is called* initiator, *and an oracle who receives the first message is called* responder.

Increase local time on message reception. Each party P_i has a local timer T_i with actual state t_i. Each time a message with a valid timestamp $ts = (t, aux)$ is received by some oracle π_i^s, the value t is compared to the actual state t_i. If $t \leq t_i$, the message is rejected. If $t > t_i$, the message is validated further, and t_i is replaced by the (greater) value t: $t_i \leftarrow t$. (This is how many smartcards handle time.) Only after this update of the local timer T_i, π_i^s may accept or send a message (if required by the protocol specification).

Retrieve actual time when sending a message. When trying to send a message to P_j, π_i^s has no knowledge about the local time t_j. Therefore the oracle requests an (authenticated) new timestamp $ts = (t, aux)$ from $\mathcal{T}$, and compares it with T_i. If $t > T_i$, this value is securely included in the protocol message.

Remark: Without any interference from an active adversary, t is guaranteed to be strictly greater than all local time values. However, an active adversary controlling the network may replay old time values.

Non-authenticated Time. In practice, timestamps may be signed, or they may be sent unauthenticated. For our model, we have chosen that timestamps are *not* authenticated. The reason for this is simple: The only attack that signed timestamps would prevent is a Denial-of-Service (DoS) attack, where the adversary would intercept the time request of an oracle, and return a large time value $t^* = t + 2^k$. All parties receiving a valid message containing this time value will be blocked for 2^k time periods.

However, our model uses an active adversary with complete control on the network. Thus he can always perform DoS attacks, e.g. disconnect some party for 2^k time periods from the network. Thus the power of our adversary is not increased by omitting signatures.

In a weaker adversarial model however, e.g. where the adversary controls only well-defined parts of a communication network, authenticated timestamps may make sense.

Local states of oracles. An initiator oracle π_i^s will, after being initiated, retrieve the actual time value t, prepare and send a message of the form[4] $(P_i, P_j, t, n_i^s, m, \sigma)$ where P_j denotes the identity of the intended receiving party, n_i^s a nonce chosen randomly by π_i^s, m the actual message, and σ the cryptographic protection of the message.

In a one-message protocol, π_i^s will immediately switch to finished state, and can no longer be activated; here the nonce may be omitted. A responder oracle π_j^t will be activated by a protocol message, which will be checked according to the protocol specification. If the check succeeds, π_j^t will switch to accept state.

In a two-message protocol, after sending the first message, an initiator oracle π_i^s will switch to a wait state to wait for a response message, and can also no longer be activated to send messages. A responder oracle π_j^t will be activated by a message, which will be checked according to the protocol specification. If the check succeeds, π_j^t will prepare a response message which includes the nonce from the received message, send this message, and switch to accept mode. Upon reception of a message from some responder, an initiator oracle will check if this message contains the nonce from the first message, and if the message is valid according to the protocol specification. If both criteria are fulfilled, it will switch to accept mode.

Matching Conversations. Bellare and Rogaway [1] have introduced the notion of *matching conversations* in order to define correctness and security of an AKE protocol precisely. We adapt this notion and use it accordingly to define secure authentication for all following protocol types.

Recall, that $\mathsf{T}^{i,s}$ consists of all messages sent and received by π_i^s in chronological order (not including the initialization-symbol $\top$). We also say that $\mathsf{T}^{i,s}$ is the *transcript* of π_i^s. For two transcripts $\mathsf{T}^{i,s}$ and $\mathsf{T}^{j,t}$, we say that $\mathsf{T}^{i,s}$ is a *prefix* of $\mathsf{T}^{j,t}$, if $\mathsf{T}^{i,s}$ contains at least one message, and the messages in $\mathsf{T}^{i,s}$ are identical to and in the same order as the first $|\mathsf{T}^{i,s}|$ messages of $\mathsf{T}^{j,t}$.

Definition 3 (Matching conversations). *We say that π_i^s has a* matching conversation *to π_j^t, if*

- $\mathsf{T}^{j,t}$ *is a prefix of $\mathsf{T}^{i,s}$ and π_i^s has sent the last message(s), or*
- $\mathsf{T}^{i,s} = \mathsf{T}^{j,t}$ *and π_j^t has sent the last message(s).*

We say that two processes π_i^s and π_j^t have matching conversations *if π_i^s has a matching conversation to process π_j^t, and vice versa.*

3.2 Adversarial Capabilities

We assume that the adversary completely controls the network, including access to the time oracle $\mathcal{T}$. He may learn session keys, and he may learn some long-

---

[4] The exact structure of the message is specified for each protocol separately.

lived keys. All this is modelled through queries. The Send query models that the adversary completely controls the network: All messages are sent to $\mathcal{A}$, who may then decide to drop the message, to store and replay it, or to alter and forward it. Thus messages received through a Send query are handled by the process oracles exactly like real protocol messages: They may be rejected, they may be answered, or they may start or terminate a protocol session. The Send message enables the adversary to initiate and run an arbitrary number of protocol instances, sequential or in parallel.

The Reveal and Corrupt queries model real world attacks: Brute force key searches or malware attacks on PC systems in case of the Reveal query, and e.g. sidechannel of fault attacks on smartcards in the case of the Corrupt query. Finally the Test query is one important building block in defining security of a protocol (more precisely: key indistinguishability). Formally stated:

- Send(π_i^s, m): The adversary can use this query to send any message m of his own choice to oracle π_i^s. The oracle will respond according to the protocol specification, depending on its internal state. If $m = \top$ consists of a special symbol $\top$, then π_i^s will respond with the first protocol message.
- Reveal(π_i^s): Oracle π_i^s responds to a Reveal-query with the contents of variable K. Note that we have $k \neq \emptyset$ only if $\Lambda \in \{\texttt{accept}, \texttt{finished}\}$.
- Corrupt(P_i): This query is used in a public key setting. Oracle π_i^1 responds with the private key sk_i from the long-term key pair $k_i = (pk_i, sk_i)$ of party P_i. Then the party and all its oracles are marked as corrupted.
- Corrupt(P_i, j): This query is used in symmetric key settings. Oracle π_i^1 responds with the long-term secret key $k_{i,j}$ shared between party P_i and party P_j. Then this key is marked as corrupted.
- Test(π_i^s): This query may only be asked once throughout the game. Oracle π_i^s handles this query as follows: If the oracle has state $K = \emptyset$, then it returns some failure symbol $\perp$. Otherwise it flips a fair coin b, samples a random elem'ent $k_0 \xleftarrow{\$} \mathcal{K}$, sets $k_1 = k$ to the 'real' session key, and returns k_b.

Definition 4. *An oracle is called* corrupted *if it is marked as corrupted (public key case), or if it uses a corrupted long-term key in its computations (symmetric case).*

3.3 Security Model 1: One-Message Protocols

One-message protocols like OTP are used for explicitly authenticating a party. Thus we have to find a definition for secure authentication taking into account the ideas from [1], and the pecularities of our definition of time.

A *benign* adversary $\mathcal{A}$ is an adversary that forwards messages without modifying them. We would like to define a secure authentication protocol as a protocol where the winning probability of any adversary equals, up to a negligible difference, the winning probability of a benign adversary.

Freshness vs. validity time periods. One major difference to [1], due to our definition of time, is the fact that even with a benign adversary there are situations where the responder oracle may not accept: Assume there are two different initiator oracles $\pi_{A_1}^{s_1}$ and $\pi_{A_2}^{s_2}$, who both intend to send a message to party B. They retrieve two time values t_1, t_2 from T, with $t_2 = t_1 + 1$. Now if $\pi_{A_2}^{s_2}$ is the first oracle who actually sends a message to B, then some responder oracle π_B^t will accept this message, and increase $T_B := t_2$. If now $\pi_{A_1}^{s_1}$ sends its message, it will be rejected due to the fact that $t_1 < T_B$. Please note that this may happen even if a benign adersary also forwards all messages in the same order as received.

Real-world protocols avoid this problem by defining validity time periods: A message will be accepted if it is not older than, say, 5 minutes, or if it was received at a time that is within the timeframe explicitly mentioned in the message. However, including validity time periods in the model poses different problems: either replay attacks will become possible during the validity time frame and we must change our security definitions, or we have to introduce an additional counter at each party for each other party to exclude these replay attacks (see Appendix).

Thus, for the sake of clarity, we decided to keep the model of time simple, and to accept the consequence that even with benign adversaries, responder oracles may not accept.

Replay attacks. The main class of attack we want to protect against is *replay attacks*. In a replay attack, A may intercept a message sent by a sending oracle, and forward it to two or more receiving oracles. We would like to call a protocol secure if at most one of these receiving oracles accepts, because this is exactly what we can expect from a benign adversary. To achive this goal across several parties, we have to include the identity of the receiving party in the first message.

Security Game G_{A-1}. In this game, the challenger C sets up a protocol environment with n parties $P_1, ..., P_n$, and prepares l protocol oracles $\pi_i^1, ..., \pi_i^l$ for each party. If initiated by the adversary by a special start message, these oracles act as initiator oracles, and if initiated with a normal protocol message, they act as responder oracles. C generates long-lived keys (or long-lived key pairs, resp.) for each party (for each pair of parties, resp.), and simulates the time oracle T. T and all counters $T_i, i \in \{1, ..., n\}$ are initialized to 0.

A may now ask up to q Send and Corrupt queries. A wins the game if there are at least two responder oracles that accept the same message, or if there is a responder oracle that accepts a message from an uncorrupted expected sender which has not been issued by any sender oracle.

Definition 5. *A protocol Π is a (τ, q, ϵ) time-secure authentication protocol, if for each adversary A that runs in time τ and asks at most q queries, with probability at least $1 - \epsilon$ we have that*

1. *for each responder oracle that accepts, there is exactly one uncorrupted finished initiator oracle, and*
2. *for each finished initiator oracle, there is at most one responder oracle that accepts.*

Authenticated Key Exchange. We will now extend the definition to key exchange. Here each session key should be indistinguishable from a randomly chosen key, for any adversary.

Security Game G_{AKE-1}. The setup of this game is the same as in G_{A-1}. In addition, the adversary is allowed to ask upt to $q - 1$ Reveal queries, and one Test query to an oracle π_i^s, subject to the following conditions:

- If π_i^s is an initiator, then no Reveal query may be asked to any responder oracle receiving the message from π_i^s.
- If π_i^s is an responder, then no Reveal query may be asked to the unique initiator oracle that has sent the message, and the party of this initiator oracle ust be uncorrupted.

At the end of the game, $\mathcal{A}$ issues a bit b' and wins the game if $b = b'$, where b is the bit chosen by π_i^s in answering the Test query.

Definition 6. *A one-message protocol Π is a (τ, q, ϵ) time-secure authenticated key exchange protocol, if Π is a (τ, q, ϵ) time-secure authentication protocol in the sense of Definition 5, and if for each adversary $\mathcal{A}$ that runs in time τ and asks at most q queries, in Game G_{AKE-1} we have that that*

$$Adv_\mathcal{A} = |Pr(b = b') - 1/2| \leq \epsilon$$

3.4 Security Model 2: Two-Message Protocols

With the publication of HMQV [26] research on one-round key agreement protocols intensified. However, since the responder is always subject to replay attacks, the notion of *authentication protocol* developed in [1] was given up, and was replaced by a new definition for *authenticated key exchange* proposed by Canetti and Krawczyk [18].

In this section, we try to give a new definition of a secure authentication protocol, by combining timestamps and nonces. We use this hybrid approach since this is a building block of the Kerberos protocol, where several two-message protocols of this kind are combined.[5]

Remark: Please note that this definition does not apply to two-message protocols currently discussed in the literature, because most of them neither use timestamps nor nonces.

Security Game G_{A-2}. In this game, the setup is identical to Game G_{A-1}. $\mathcal{A}$ may now ask up to q Send and Corrupt queries. $\mathcal{A}$ wins the game if there are at least two responder oracles that accept the same message, if there is a responder oracle that accepts a message from an uncorrupted expected sender which has not been issued by any sender oracle, or if there is a initiator oracle that accepts without having a matching conversation with a responder.

---

[5] It should be clear that we also can achive mutual authentication by simply applying the one-message protocol of Section 4 in both directions, using the model for authentication proposed there.

Definition 7. *A two-message protocol Π is a (τ, q, ϵ) time-nonce-secure authentication protocol, if for each adversary $\mathcal{A}$ that runs in time τ and asks at most q queries, with probability at least $1 - \epsilon$ we have that*

1. *for each responder oracle that accepts, there is exactly one uncorrupted finished initiator oracle,*
2. *for each finished initiator oracle, there is at most one responder oracle that accepts, and*
3. *for each initiator oracle that accepts, there is exactly one responder oracle that has a matching conversation.*

Authenticated Key Exchange We will again extend the definition to key exchange. Here each session key should be indistinguishable from a randomly chosen key, for any adversary.

Security Game G_{AKE-2}. The setup of this game is the same as in G_{A-1}. In addition, the adversary is allowed to ask up to $q - 1$ Reveal queries, and one Test query to an uncorrupted oracle π_i^s, subject to the following conditions:

- If π_i^s is an initiator, then no Reveal query may be asked to any responder oracle receiving the message from π_i^s, and all responder oracles must be uncorrupted.
- If π_i^s is an responder, then no Reveal query may be asked to the unique initiator oracle that has sent the message, and the party of this initiator oracle must be uncorrupted.

At the end of the game, $\mathcal{A}$ issues a bit b' and wins the game if $b = b'$, where b is the bit chosen by π_i^s in answering the Test query.

Definition 8. *A two-message protocol Π is a (τ, q, ϵ) time-nonce-secure authenticated key exchange protocol, if Π is a (τ, q, ϵ) time-nonce-secure authentication protocol in the sense of Definition 7, and if for each adversary $\mathcal{A}$ that runs in time τ and asks at most q queries, we have that*

$$Adv_{\mathcal{A}} = |Pr(b = b') - 1/2| \leq \epsilon$$

in Game G_{AKE-2}.

4   One-Time-Passwords

In a One-Time-Password (OTP) protocol, an initiator (party A) wants to authenticate against a responder (party B). To achieve this goal, A requests a timestamp from $\mathcal{T}$, and appends a cryptographic checksum to the message consisting of the identifiers of A and B, and the timestamp t. Typically, symmetric cryptography is used in OTP protocols. Thus in our example, we assume that a message authentication code MAC is used for this purpose. The OTP protocol is defined in Figure 1.

A: $(k_{AB}, \ldots), t_A$ B: $(k_{AB}, \ldots), t_B$
π_A^s π_B^t

request t from $\mathcal{T}$; $t_A := t$;
$mac_A^s := \mathsf{MAC}(k_{AB}, A|B|t)$
$$otp = (A, B, t, mac_A^s)$$
$\xrightarrow{\hspace{3cm}}$

If $mac_A^s \neq \mathsf{MAC}(k_{AB}, A|B|t)$
reject; If $t \leq t_B$ reject;
$t_B := t$; accept

Fig. 1. The One-message Authentication protocol Π_{OTP}

Theorem 1. *If* MAC *is a* $(\tau_{MAC}, \epsilon_{MAC}, q_{MAC})$ *secure message authentication code, then* Π_{OTP} *is a* (τ, q, ϵ) *time-secure authentication protocol with* $\tau_{MAC} \approx \tau$, $q_{MAC} \approx q$, *and*

$$\epsilon \leq n^2 \cdot \epsilon_{MAC}.$$

5   One-Round Authentication Protocols

We first give an example of a two-message mutual authentication protocol without key exchange, to exemplify the use of our model. In the second part of this section, we will extend this to authenticated key exchange, where the session key is chosen by the responder. This special choice is made to closely match the building blocks of Kerberos, and can easily be extended to other key exchange methods.

5.1   Authentication

Theorem 2. *If* MAC *is a* $(\tau_{MAC}, \epsilon_{MAC}, q_{MAC})$ *secure message authentication code, then the* Π_{H2A} *protocol defined in Figure 2 is a* (τ, q, ϵ) *time-nonce-secure authentication protocol with respect to Definition 7 with* $\tau \approx \tau_{MAC}$, $q \approx q_{MAC}$, *and*

$$\epsilon \leq n^2 \cdot \epsilon_{MAC} + n^2 l \cdot \left(\frac{(nl)^2}{2^\lambda} + \epsilon_{MAC} \right).$$

5.2   Authenticated Key Exchange

The novel authenticated key exchange protocol presented in Figure 3 is modelled after the building blocks of the Kerberos protocol: authentication and session key encryption are based on symmetric cryptography, and the session key is chosen by the responder (the Kerberos server). Variants of this protocol are used three times sequentially in Kerberos, with the same initiator (the Kerberos client), but different responders (Ticket Granting Ticket Server, Ticket Server, Server).

$$A: (k_{AB}, \dots), t_A \qquad\qquad\qquad\qquad B: (k_{AB}, \dots), t_B$$
$$\pi_A^s \qquad\qquad\qquad\qquad\qquad\qquad \pi_B^t$$

request t from $\mathcal{T}$; $t_A := t$;
    choose n_A;
$mac_A^s := \mathsf{MAC}(k_{AB}, A|B|t|n_A)$

$$\xrightarrow{\quad A, B, t, n_A, mac_A^s \quad}$$

reject if
$mac_A^s \neq \mathsf{MAC}(k_{AB}, A|B|t|n_A)$;
If $t \leq t_B$ reject; $t_B := t$;
$mac_B^t := \mathsf{MAC}(k_{AB}, B|A|n_A)$;
accept

$$\xleftarrow{\quad B, A, n_A, mac_B^t \quad}$$

If $mac_B^t \neq \mathsf{MAC}(k_{AB}, B|A|n_A)$
    reject;
If n_A is not correct reject;
    accept

Fig. 2. The Two-message Authentication protocol Π_{H2A}

$$A \qquad\qquad\qquad\qquad\qquad\qquad B$$
$$(k_{AB} = (k_{AB}^e, k_{AB}^m), \dots), t_A \qquad\qquad (k_{AB} = (k_{AB}^e, k_{AB}^m), \dots), t_B$$
$$\pi_A^s \qquad\qquad\qquad\qquad\qquad\qquad \pi_B^t$$

request t from $\mathcal{T}$; $t_A := t$;
    choose n_A;
$mac_A^s := \mathsf{MAC}(k_{AB}^m, A|B|t|n_A)$

$$\xrightarrow{\quad A, B, t, n_A, mac_A^s \quad}$$

reject if
$mac_A^s \neq \mathsf{MAC}(k_{AB}^m, A|B|t|n_A)$;
If $t \leq t_B$ reject; $t_B := t$;
    choose k;
$c_B^t := \mathsf{SE.Enc}(k_{AB}^e, k)$;
$mac_B^t :=$
$\mathsf{MAC}(k_{AB}^m, B|A|n_A|c_B^t)$; accept

$$\xleftarrow{\quad B, A, n_A, c_B^t, mac_B^t \quad}$$

If $mac_B^t \neq$
$\mathsf{MAC}(k_{AB}^m, B|A|n_A|c_B^t)$ reject
If n_A is not correct reject
$k := \mathsf{SE.Dec}(k_{AB}^e, c_B^t)$; accept

Fig. 3. The One-Round Authenticated Key Exchange ($\mathcal{ORAKE}1$) protocol

Theorem 3. *If* MAC*is a* $(\tau, \epsilon_{MAC}, q_{MAC})$ *secure message authentication code, and* SE *is a* $(\tau, \epsilon_{SE}, q_{SE})$ *secure symmetric encryption scheme, then the* Π_{ORAKEl} *protocol defined in Figure 3 is a* (τ, q, ϵ) *time-secure authented key exchange protocol with respect to Definition 8 with*

$$\epsilon \leq n^2 \cdot \epsilon_{MAC} + ln^2(\frac{(nl)^2}{2^\lambda} + \epsilon_{MAC}) + n^2 \cdot \epsilon_{SE}.$$

6 Conclusion and Future Work

In this paper we have presented a first simple formal model to prove the security of timestamp-based authentication protocols, with reduction-based proofs, in a Turing Machine environment. We tried to formalize the security goal that replay attacks are prevented by timestamps.

This model can be extended in various directions: (1) Most time-based security infrastructures or protocols use validity time frames, which can be modelled by allowing the responder to query the time oracle $\mathcal{T}$ on reception of a message. However, precautions must be taken to disallow replay attacks. (2) If time is involved, the power of an active adversary should be restricted to get more realistic security models: currently, DoS attacks by the adversary cannot be prevented.

References

1. Bellare, M., Rogaway, P.: Entity authentication and key distribution. In: Stinson, D.R. (ed.) CRYPTO 1993. LNCS, vol. 773, pp. 232–249. Springer, Heidelberg (1994)
2. Hopcroft, J.E., Motwani, R., Ullman, J.D.: Introduction to Automata Theory, Languages, and Computation. 3rd edn. Addison-Wesley (2006)
3. Hofheinz, D., Shoup, V.: Gnuc: A new universal composability framework. Cryptology ePrint Archive, Report 2011/303 (2011), http://eprint.iacr.org/
4. Mills, D., Martin, J., Burbank, J., Kasch, W.: Network Time Protocol Version 4: Protocol and Algorithms Specification. RFC 5905 (Proposed Standard) (June 2010)
5. Magkos, E., Burmester, M., Chrissikopoulos, V.: Receipt-freeness in large-scale elections without untappable channels. In: Schmid, B., Stanoevska-Slabeva, K., Tschammer, V. (eds.) Towards the E-Society. IFIP, vol. 202, pp. 683–694. Springer, Boston (2001)
6. M'Raihi, D., Bellare, M., Hoornaert, F., Naccache, D., Ranen, O.: HOTP: An HMAC-Based One-Time Password Algorithm. RFC 4226 (Informational) (December 2005)
7. M'Raihi, D., Machani, S., Pei, M., Rydell, J.: TOTP: Time-Based One-Time Password Algorithm. RFC 6238 (Informational) (May 2011)
8. Cremers, C.J.F.: Session-state reveal is stronger than ephemeral key reveal: Attacking the naxos authenticated key exchange protocol. In: Abdalla, M., Pointcheval, D., Fouque, P.-A., Vergnaud, D. (eds.) ACNS 2009. LNCS, vol. 5536, pp. 20–33. Springer, Heidelberg (2009)

9. Schwenk, J.: Modelling time, or a step towards reduction-based security proofs for otp and kerberos. IACR Cryptology ePrint Archive 2013, 604 (2013)
10. Massias, H., Avila, X.S., Quisquater, J.J.: Timestamps: Main issues on their use and implementation. In: WETICE, pp. 178–183. IEEE Computer Society (1999)
11. Haber, S., Massias, H.: Time-stamping. In: van Tilborg, H.C.A., Jajodia, S. (eds.) Encyclopedia of Cryptography and Security, 2nd edn., pp. 1299–1303. Springer (2011)
12. Moran, T., Shaltiel, R., Ta-Shma, A.: Non-interactive timestamping in the bounded-storage model. J. Cryptology 22(2), 189–226 (2009)
13. Buldas, A., Niitsoo, M.: Optimally tight security proofs for hash-then-publish time-stamping. In: [27], pp. 318–335
14. Liu, Z., Lu, M.: Authentication protocols with time stamps: – encryption algorithm dependent. In: Arabnia, H.R. (ed.) International Conference on Internet Computing, pp. 81–86. CSREA Press (2006)
15. Paterson, K.G., Stebila, D.: One-time-password-authenticated key exchange. In: [27], pp. 264–281
16. Bellare, M., Rogaway, P.: Provably secure session key distribution: The three party case, pp. 57–66 (1995)
17. Manulis, M.: Provably secure group key exchange (2007)
18. Canetti, R., Krawczyk, H.: Analysis of key-exchange protocols and their use for building secure channels. In: Pfitzmann, B. (ed.) EUROCRYPT 2001. LNCS, vol. 2045, pp. 453–474. Springer, Heidelberg (2001)
19. Barbosa, M., Farshim, P.: Security analysis of standard authentication and key agreement protocols utilising timestamps. In: Preneel, B. (ed.) AFRICACRYPT 2009. LNCS, vol. 5580, pp. 235–253. Springer, Heidelberg (2009)
20. Matsumoto, T., Takashima, Y., Imai, H.: On seeking smart public-key-distribution systems. IEICE Transactions E69-E(2), 99–106 (1986)
21. Menezes, A., Qu, M., Vanstone, S.A.: Some new key agreement protocols providing mutual implicit authentication. In: Second Workshop on Selected Areas in Cryptography, SAC 1995 (1995)
22. Law, L., Menezes, A., Qu, M., Solinas, J.A., Vanstone, S.A.: An efficient protocol for authenticated key agreement. Des. Codes Cryptography 28(2), 119–134 (2003)
23. Bellare, M., Palacio, A.: The knowledge-of-exponent assumptions and 3-round zero-knowledge protocols. In: Franklin, M. (ed.) CRYPTO 2004. LNCS, vol. 3152, pp. 273–289. Springer, Heidelberg (2004)
24. Krawczyk, H.: HMQV: A high-performance secure diffie-hellman protocol. In: Shoup, V. (ed.) CRYPTO 2005. LNCS, vol. 3621, pp. 546–566. Springer, Heidelberg (2005)
25. Choo, K.K.R., Boyd, C., Hitchcock, Y.: Examining indistinguishability-based proof models for key establishment protocols. In: Roy, B. (ed.) ASIACRYPT 2005. LNCS, vol. 3788, pp. 585–604. Springer, Heidelberg (2005)
26. Krawczyk, H.: HMQV: A high-performance secure Diffie-Hellman protocol. In: Shoup, V. (ed.) CRYPTO 2005. LNCS, vol. 3621, pp. 546–566. Springer, Heidelberg (2005)
27. Steinfeld, R., Hawkes, P. (eds.): ACISP 2010. LNCS, vol. 6168. Springer, Heidelberg (2010)

A   Proofs of Theorems 1, 2 and 3

Proof of Theorem 1. Game G_0 is the original game, where our adversary tries to force an oracle to accept with $otp*$ which is either faked, or has already been accepted by a different oracle. Thus we have $\epsilon_0 = \epsilon$.

In G_1, we guess the initiator party A, and the receiver party B. They share a common symmetric key k_{AB}. Our guess is that the adversary will succeed in making one receiver oracle π_B^t accept either a fake OTP $otp*$, or that two oracles π_B^t and $\pi_B^{t'}$ will accept the same OTP otp. If our guess is wrong, we abort the game, and the adversary looses. Thus his winning probability is reduced by a factor n^2. $n^2 \cdot \epsilon_1 = \epsilon_0$.

In G_2, we abort the game if the adversary $\mathcal{A}$ forges a valid message authentication code MAC for key k_{AB}. This may happen only with probability ϵ_{MAC}: The simulator replaces all MAC computations involving the key k_{AB} with calls to a MAC challenger $\mathcal{C}_{MAC}$ which uses a randomly chosen MAC key k; if $\mathcal{A}$ forges a valid message authentication code *mac* for a fresh otp message which has not been queried from the MAC challenger, then we have broken the MAC challenge. Thus we have $\epsilon_1 \leq \epsilon_2 + \epsilon_{MAC}$.

Since we have excluded MAC forgeries in this game, we are left with OTPs $otp = (C, S, ts, \mathsf{MAC}(k_{CS}, C.S.ts))$ which were generated by non-corrupted oracles, where only the value ts may be influenced by the adversary. Thus condition 1 of Definition 5 is always true (i.e. holds with probability 1), and we are left with condition 2.

If $\mathcal{A}$ tries to send otp to any oracle of a party $T \neq S$, T will not accept because the target identity is different. If $\mathcal{A}$ tries to send otp to oracle π_C^s, but otp has already been accepted by π_C^t, π_C^s will not accept because $ts \leq t_C$. Thus also condition 2 is always fulfilled (i.e. holds with probability 1) we have $\epsilon_2 = 0$.   □

Proof of Theorem 2. Adversary $\mathcal{A}$ can win the game by either making an initiator oracle accept, or a responder oracle, or both. Thus we have $\epsilon \leq \epsilon_I + \epsilon_R$.

Since we can apply the proof of Theorem 1 to the responder oracle, we have $\epsilon_R \leq n^2 \cdot \epsilon_{MAC}$.

Thus we are left with the proof for the initiator oracle. The proof is modelled as a short sequence of games. Game G_0 is the original game, but the adversary only wins this game if an initiator oracle to accepts. Thus we have $\epsilon_0 = \epsilon_I$.

In G_1, we guess the initiator oracle π_A^s that will accept, and the responder party B. They share a common symmetric key k_{AB}. If our guess is wrong, we abort the game, and the adversary looses. Thus his winning probability is reduced by a factor $l \cdot n^2$. $l \cdot n^2 \cdot \epsilon_1 = \epsilon_0$.

In G_2, the simulator replaces all computations with the key k_{AB} with a MAC oracle. We abort the game if the adversary $\mathcal{A}$ forges a valid message authentication code MAC for this oracle. Thus we have $\epsilon_1 \leq \epsilon_2 + \epsilon_{MAC}$.

In G_3, we abort the game if two oracles choose the same nonce. The probability for this is bounded above by $\frac{(nl)^2}{2^\lambda}$. Thus we have $\epsilon_2 \leq \epsilon_3 + \frac{(nl)^2}{2^\lambda}$.

Since we have excluded MAC forgeries and nonce collisions, $\mathcal{A}$ can only make an initiator oracle accept if he forwards a message from one of the (possibly many) responder oracles that have received the message from the initator oracle containing the chosen nonce. Thus there is a matching conversation, and we have $\epsilon_3 = 0$. ☐

Proof of Theorem 3. Adversary $\mathcal{A}$ can win the game by either breaking the acceptance condition, or key indistinguishability, or both. Thus we have $\epsilon \leq \epsilon_A + \epsilon_{KE}$.

Since we can apply the proof of Theorem 2 to the responder oracle, we have
$$\epsilon_A \leq n^2 \cdot \epsilon_{MAC} + ln^2\left(\frac{(nl)^2}{2^\lambda} + \epsilon_{MAC}\right).$$

Thus we are left with the proof for key indisinguishability. In Game G_1, we first have to guess the symmetric key k^e_{AB} that will be used to encrypt the session key for the test oracle. If we guessed wrong, the adversary loses the game. Thus we loose a factor n^2 in this game.

In Game G_2, we replace all computations involving the key k^e_{AB} with our SE-challenger. Since $\mathcal{A}$ is not allowed to corrupt the key used in the test session, we can still simulate all protocol messages. Now if $\mathcal{A}$ is able to distinguish real from random keys, our SE-challenger is able to break the CCA-security of the symmetric encryption scheme. ☐

B   Modeling Validity Time Intervals

To be able to model validity time intervals, the model can be modified as follows.

Retrieve actual time when sending a message. When trying to send a message to P_j, π_i^s requests a new timestamp $ts = (t, aux)$ from $\mathcal{T}$, and compares it with T_i. If $t > t_i$, the oracle calculates another value $t_{exp} := t + n_{exp}$. Both t and t_{exp} are securely included in the protocol message.

Increase local time on message reception. Each party P_i has a local timer T_i with actual state t_i. Each time a message with a timestamp t_j is received from some oracle π_j^t, the oracle π_i^s receiving this message compares the value t_j to the actual state t_i of T_i. If $t_j \leq t_i$, the message is rejected. If $t_j > t_i$, t_i is replaced by the (greater) value t_j: $t_i \leftarrow t_j$, and the message is validated further. Now π_i^s requests a new timestamp $ts = (t, aux)$ from $\mathcal{T}$, and compares it with t_{exp} from the message. If $t_{exp} \leq t$, the message is rejected, else $t_i \leftarrow t$ and the message is validated further.

Zero-Knowledge Password Policy Checks and Verifier-Based PAKE

Franziskus Kiefer and Mark Manulis

Surrey Centre for Cyber Security,
Department of Computing, University of Surrey, UK
mail@franziskuskiefer.de, mark@manulis.eu

Abstract. Zero-Knowledge Password Policy Checks (ZKPPC), introduced in this work, enable blind registration of client passwords at remote servers, i.e., client passwords are never transmitted to the servers. This eliminates the need for trusting servers to securely process and store client passwords. A ZKPPC protocol, executed as part of the registration procedure, allows clients to further prove compliance of chosen passwords with respect to password policies defined by the servers.

The main benefit of ZKPPC-based password registration is that it guarantees that registered passwords never appear in clear on the server side. At the end of the registration phase the server only receives and stores some verification information that can later be used for authentication in a suitable Verifier-based Password Authenticated Key Exchange (VPAKE) protocol.

We give general and concrete constructions of ZKPPC protocols and suitable VPAKE protocols for ASCII-based passwords and policies that are commonly used on the web. To this end we introduce a reversible mapping of ASCII characters to integers that can be used to preserve the structure of the password string and a new randomized password hashing scheme for ASCII-based passwords.

Keywords: Password policies, password registration, authentication, verification, password hashing, ASCII passwords, verifier-based PAKE.

1 Introduction

Password policies set by organizations aim at enforcing a higher level of security on used passwords by specifying various requirements that apply during their selection process and the actual usage. Especially, when passwords are selected and used by users in a remote way strong, password policies can help not only to protect data behind individual user accounts but also to prevent malicious activities from compromised accounts that could further harm the organization due to liability issues or even lead to a compromise of the entire system or service. It is known that in the absence of any password policy users tend to choose "weak" passwords that are easily guessable and have higher risk of being compromised through dictionary attacks [1]. It is worth noting that coming up

M. Kutyłowski and J. Vaidya (Eds.): ESORICS 2014, Part II, LNCS 8713, pp. 295–312, 2014.
© Springer International Publishing Switzerland 2014

with a good password policy is still considered a difficult task since policies must also remain usable in practice [2].

In this work we focus on widely used password policies that specify the requirements on the selection of passwords such as the minimum password length, define sets of admissible password characters, and may contain further restrictions on the number of characters from each set. These requirements are typically enforced during the initial password registration process and aim at preventing users from choosing "weak" passwords. These policies are often extended with additional restrictions on the usage of passwords by requiring users to change their passwords within a certain period of time.

When users select passwords for remote access to systems or services on their own, the password policy enforcement mechanism must be able to verify that selected passwords comply with the existing policy. This compliance check can be performed either on the client side or on the server side. For instance, when a commodity web browser is used to register for some web service the policy can be checked within the browser using scripts embedded into the registration website, or on the server side upon the initial transmission of the password (e.g. over a TLS channel). Both approaches, however, have security risks as discussed in the following. If policy enforcement is performed solely on the client side, the server must trust the client to obey the policy and execute the check correctly. This is not a threat if the compliance check is assumed to be in the interest of an honest user. Nonetheless, malicious users or users who are lazy to remember complicated passwords can easily circumvent such script-based verification and register passwords that are not compliant with the policy. The corresponding service provider might want to exclude this threat. In this case the compliance check must be performed on the server side. In order to perform policy check with available technologies the client's password must be transmitted to the server, possibly over a secure channel. This ultimately requires the client to trust the server to process and store the received password in a secure way. While many servers adopt the current state-of-the-art approach for storing passwords in a hashed form, e.g. using PBKDF2 [3,4] or bcrypt [5], with a random salt to protect against server compromise or re-use attacks, there have been many known cases, e.g. [6,7,8,9], where passwords have been stored in clear and compromised subsequently. The ultimate goal, therefore, is to avoid trusting servers with secure processing and storage of user passwords.

This goal imposes two main challenges: (1) in the registration phase users must be able to choose passwords and prove their policy compliance to a remote server without actually transmitting their passwords, and (2) after the registration phase users must be able to authenticate themselves to the server using their passwords without transmitting them. Interestingly, authentication protocol addressing the second challenge already exist in form of Password-Authenticated Key Exchange (PAKE) protocols, e.g. [10,11,12,13]. PAKE protocols offer authentication and computation of secure session keys in a password-only setting in a way that makes it hard for an active adversary to recover passwords via off-line dictionary attacks. Traditional PAKE protocols, however, assume that the password is used in clear on the server sides. To alleviate the threat that passwords are revealed immediately when server's database is compromised, the so-called Verifier-based PAKE (VPAKE) protocols [14,15,16] assume that instead of plain password servers are using some verification information that is derived from the password such that if an attacker breaks into the server and compromises its database it must still execute an expensive offline dictionary attack to recover the plain password. For this reason VPAKE protocols offer a better protection than PAKE. The aforementioned trust assumption on the server to securely process and store passwords becomes irrelevant if the password setup only transmits password verification information to the server, which can later be used in VPAKE protocols. In combination with password policy enforcement this approach would however require a solution to the first challenge; namely the client must be able to prove that the verification information for VPAKE has been derived from a password that complies with the server's password policy.

Zero-Knowledge Password Policy Checks (ZKPPC). Our first contribution, in Section 5, is the concept of Zero-Knowledge Password Policy Checks (ZKPPC), a new class of protocols that allows servers to perform policy checks on client passwords without ever receiving them in clear. ZKPPC protocols can be used for blind registration of policy-conform passwords and thus solve the aforementioned challenge of password setup where only password verification information is supposed to be stored at the server and where the server cannot be trusted to process passwords securely. We present a security model for ZKPPC, a general ZKPPC framework, and a concrete ZKPPC protocol based on Pedersen commitments. In the construction of ZKPPC protocols we make use of the new randomized password hashing scheme, introduced in Section 4 and the reversible structure-preserving mapping of ASCII-based password strings to integers, introduced in Section 3.

ZKPPC-compliant VPAKE. Our second contribution are one-round VPAKE protocols, in Section 6, that can be used with verification information obtained from our blind password registration protocols based on ZKPPC. We design VPAKE protocols based on the framework from [16]. We propose a general VPAKE protocol that can be used in combination with our general ZKPPC framework for ASCII-based passwords and policies and a concrete VPAKE construction that suits particularly well with our ZKPPC-based blind password registration protocol that is based on Pedersen commitments and our randomized password hashing scheme.

2   Concept Overview and Building Blocks

Our concept entails performing a zero-knowledge password policy check during the client registration phase, which results in password verification information being passed on to the server, and later use of this verification information on the server side as input to a suitable VPAKE protocol for the purpose of authentication. A client wishing to register its user id and password at a remote server that maintains a password policy will initially pick a password and execute the ZKPPC protocol with the server. The ZKPPC protocol ensures that client's password complies with server's password policy and is linked to the verification information communicated at the end of the registration phase. This verification information is computed through a randomised password hashing scheme and includes (partial) randomness that was used by the client in the ZKPPC protocol. Plain password is never transmitted to the server and the only way for the server to reveal it is to execute an expensive offline dictionary attack. That is, an honest-but-curios server would have to perform about the same amount of computation to recover plain passwords as an attacker who breaks into that server at any time. The server will be able to recognise and reject any cheating attempt of the client to set up a non-policy conform password, still without learning the latter. In the realization of this concept we apply the following building blocks.

Zero-Knowledge Proofs. A *proof of knowledge* PoK between prover P and verifier V for a (public) binary relation $R = \{(C, w)\}$ is denoted $\mathsf{PoK}\{(w) : (C, w) \in R\}$ where w is a secret witness for C. PoK is a *zero-knowledge proof of knowledge* ZKPoK if V is convinced that $(C, w) \in R$ without learning any information about w known by P. More formally, an interactive PoK for $R = \{(C, w)\}$ between P and V is a ZKPoK if the following holds:

- Completeness: For any $(C, w) \in R$, honest verifier $V(C)$ accepts in the interaction with an honest prover $P(C, w)$.
- Soundness: If an honest $V(C)$ accepts in the interaction with a malicious prover $P^*(C)$ then there exists an efficient *knowledge extractor* Ext that extracts a witness w for C from the interaction with $P^*(C)$.
- Zero-Knowledge: For any $(C, w) \in R$ there exists an efficient *simulator* Sim such that the views of a malicious verifier $V(C)$ in interactions with $\mathsf{Sim}(C)$ and an honest prover $P(C, w)$ remain indistinguishable.

Commitments. A *commitment scheme* $\mathsf{C} = (\mathsf{CSetup}, \mathsf{Com}, \mathsf{Open})$ contains three polynomial time algorithms and satisfies the following properties:

- Completeness: For all $p_C \leftarrow \mathsf{CSetup}(\lambda)$, $x \in \mathbb{X}$, $r \in \mathbb{S}$: $x \leftarrow \mathsf{Open}(p_C, C, d)$ for all $(C, d) \leftarrow \mathsf{Com}(p_C, x; r))$.
- Binding: For all PPT algorithms A that on input $p_C \leftarrow \mathsf{CSetup}(\lambda)$ output (C, d, d') there exists a negligible function $\varepsilon(\cdot)$ such that

$$\Pr[x \neq x' \wedge x \leftarrow \mathsf{Open}(p_C, C, d) \wedge x' \leftarrow \mathsf{Open}(p_C, C, d')] \leq \varepsilon(\lambda)$$

- Hiding: For all PPT algorithms $A = (A_1, A_2)$ where A_1 on input $p_C \leftarrow \mathsf{CSetup}(\lambda)$ outputs x_0 and x_1 of the same length and where A_2 on input $(C, d) \leftarrow \mathsf{Com}(p_C, x_b; r)$ for a random bit $b \in \{0, 1\}$, $r \in \mathbb{S}$ outputs bit b' there exists a negligible function $\varepsilon(\cdot)$ such that $|\Pr[b = b'] - 1/2| \leq \varepsilon(\lambda)$.

A commitment scheme is said to be *(additively) homomorphic* if for all $p_C \leftarrow$ CSetup(λ), $(C_i, d_i) \leftarrow$ Com$(p_C, x_i; r_i)$ with $x_i \in \mathbb{X}$ and $r_i \in \mathbb{S}$ for $i \in 0, \ldots, m$ it holds that $\prod_{i=0}^m C_i = $ Com$(p_C, \sum_{i=0}^m x_i; \psi_{i=0}^m r_i)$ for some function ψ. We will omit p_C and d from the notation and write $C \leftarrow$ Com$(x; r)$ to denote the commitment of x using randomness r.

Pedersen commitments [17]. The commitment scheme from [17] is perfectly hiding and additively homomorphic. Its CSetup(λ) algorithm outputs (g, h, p, λ), where g and h are generators of a cyclic group G of prime order p of length λ and the discrete logarithm of h with respect to g is unknown. Com$(x; r)$ for $x, r \in \mathbb{Z}_p^*$ outputs $C = g^x h^r$ and $d = (x, r)$. Open(C, d) returns x iff $C = g^x h^r$.

Set Membership Proofs on Committed Values. These zero-knowledge proofs can be used to prove that a committed value x is an element of a specific set Ω. Let $C \leftarrow$ Com$(x; r)$ be some commitment of x with randomness r. The corresponding proof for $x \in \Omega$ is defined as ZKPoK$\{(\xi, \rho) : C \leftarrow$ Com$(\xi; \rho) \wedge \xi \in \Omega\}$. We will use SMP$(\xi, \rho, \Omega)$ as a shorter notation for this proof.

Labeled Public Key Encryption. A *labeled encryption scheme* E = (KGen, Enc, Dec) is IND-CCA2 secure for all PPT algorithms $A = (A_1, A_2)$ where A_1 on input pk for $(pk, sk) \leftarrow$ KGen(λ) and access to the decryption oracle Dec$(sk, \cdot)$ outputs two messages m_0 and m_1 of equal length and a label ℓ and where A_2 on input $c \leftarrow$ Enc$^\ell(pk, m_b; r)$ for a random bit $b \in_R \{0, 1\}$ with access to the decryption oracle outputs bit b' without querying Dec$(sk, (\ell, c))$ there exists a negligible function $\varepsilon(\cdot)$ such that $|\Pr[b' = b] - \frac{1}{2}| \leq \varepsilon(\lambda)$.

Labeled Cramer-Shoup Encryption [18]. The labeled CS encryption scheme from [18] is IND-CCA2 secure. Its key generation algorithm KGen(λ) outputs $sk = (x_1, x_2, y_1, y_2, z)$ and $pk = (p, g_1, g_2, h, c, d, H_k)$ with $c = g_1^{x_1} g_2^{x_2}, d = g_1^{y_1} g_2^{y_2}, h = g_1^z$, where g_1 and g_2 are generators of a cyclic group G of prime order p of length λ and $H_k : \{0, 1\}^* \mapsto \mathbb{Z}_p^*$ is a hash function. The encryption algorithm Enc$^\ell(pk, m; r)$ outputs $C = (u_1, u_2, e, v)$ where $u_1 = g_1^r$, $u_2 = g_2^r$, $e = mh^r$ and $v = (cd^\xi)^r$ with $\xi = H_k(\ell, u_1, u_2, e)$. The decryption algorithm Dec$^\ell(sk, C)$ outputs $m = e/u_1^z$ if $u_1^{x_1 + y_1 \cdot \xi'} u_2^{x_2 + y_2 \cdot \xi'} = v$ with $\xi' = H_k(\ell, u_1, u_2, e)$.

Smooth Projective Hashing (SPHF). Let $L = \{C\}$ denote a language with $L \subset X$ such that $C \in L$ if there exists a witness w for C. A SPHF for $L \subset X$, as defined in [19], consists of the following algorithms:

- HKGen(L) generates a hashing key hk for L.
- PKGen(hk, L, C) derives the projection key hp, possibly depending on C.
- Hash(hk, L, C) outputs the hash value h, for any $C \in X$.
- PHash(hp, L, C, w) outputs the hash value h, for any $C \in L$ with witness w.

A SPHF is correct if for all $C \in L$ with witness w: Hash$(hk, L, C) =$ PHash(hp, L, C, w). A SPHF is smooth if for all $C \notin L$, the hash value h is indistinguishable from a random element in G.

SPHF for Labeled CS Ciphertexts [19]. Let $L_m = \{(\ell, C) | \exists r, C \leftarrow \texttt{Enc}^\ell(pk, m; r)\}$, where $pk = (p, g_1, g_2, h, c, d, H_k)$. Note that $C = (u_1, u_2, e, v)$, where $u_1 = g_1^r$, $u_2 = g_2^r$, $e = mh^r$, and $v = (cd^\xi)^r$ with $\xi = H_k(\ell, u_1, u_2, e)$. A perfectly smooth SPHF from [19] for L_m is defined as follows:

- $\texttt{HKGen}(L_m)$ generates a hashing key $\texttt{hk} = (\eta_1, \eta_2, \theta, \mu, \nu) \in_R \mathbb{Z}_p^{1 \times 5}$.
- $\texttt{PKGen}(\texttt{hk}, L_m)$ derives the projection key $\texttt{hp} = (\texttt{hp}_1, \texttt{hp}_2) = (g_1^{\eta_1} g_2^\theta h^\mu c^\nu, g_1^{\eta_2} d^\nu)$.
- $\texttt{Hash}(\texttt{hk}, L_m, C)$ outputs the hash value $h = u_1^{\eta_1 + \xi \eta_2} u_2^\theta (e/m)^\mu v^\nu$.
- $\texttt{ProjHash}(\texttt{hp}, L_m, C, r)$ outputs the hash value $h = (\texttt{hp}_1 \texttt{hp}_2^\xi)^r$.

3 Modeling Passwords and Policies

In the following we model passwords and their dictionaries. Note that password strings are typically mapped to integers before they are processed in cryptographic operations. For our purposes such integer mapping must be able to preserve password structures. In particular, the way a password string is composed from single characters must remain visible from the resulting integer value. As part of password modeling we describe an appropriate encoding scheme that maps password strings defined over the alphabet of printable ASCII characters to integers while preserving their structures. We further model and define password policies as regular expressions over different ASCII character sets.

3.1 Password Strings and Dictionaries

We consider *password strings* pw over the *ASCII alphabet* Σ containing all 94 *printable* ASCII characters.[1] We split $\Sigma = d \cup u \cup l \cup s$ into four subsets:

- set of **digits** $d = [0 - 9]$ (or ASCII codes $[48 - 57]$),
- set of **upper case letters** $u = [A - Z]$ (or ASCII codes $[65 - 90]$)
- set of **lower case letters** $l = [a - z]$ (or ASCII codes $[97 - 122]$)
- set of **symbols** $s = [!"\#\$\%\&'()*+,-./ :;<=>?@ [\backslash]^\_\` \{|\}\sim]$ (or ASCII codes $[33 - 47, 58 - 64, 91 - 96, 123 - 126]$)

By $\mathcal{D}$ we denote a *general dictionary* containing all strings that can be formed from printable ASCII characters, i.e. all power sets of Σ. A *password string* $pw = (c_0, \ldots, c_{n-1}) \in \Sigma^n \subset \mathcal{D}$ of length n is an ordered set of characters $c_i \in \Sigma$.

3.2 Structure-Preserving Mapping of Password Strings to Integers

Mapping of Password Characters to Integers. In order to preserve the character structure of a password string pw upon its mapping to an integer we first define a *character mapping* function $\texttt{CHRtoINT} : \Sigma \mapsto \mathbb{Z}_{95}$ for any printable

---

[1] Although we do not consider password strings consisting of other characters, our approach is easily adaptable to UTF-8 and other character sets.

ASCII character $c \in \Sigma$ that internally uses its decimal ASCII code $\mathtt{ASCII}(c)$ to output an integer in $\mathbb{Z}_{95}$:

$$\mathtt{CHRtoINT}(c) = \begin{cases} \bot & \text{if } \mathtt{ASCII}(c) < 32 \\ \mathtt{ASCII}(c) - 32 & \text{if } 33 \leq \mathtt{ASCII}(c) \leq 126 \\ \bot & \text{if } 126 < \mathtt{ASCII}(c) \end{cases}$$

Position-Dependent Mapping of Password Characters to Integers. A printable ASCII character $c \in \Sigma$ may appear at any position $i \in [0, n-1]$ in a password string $pw \in \Sigma^n$. For every position i we require a different integer to which $c_i \in pw$ can be mapped to. Assuming a reasonable upper bound $n_{\max}$ on the password length n, i.e. $n \leq n_{\max}$, we define four integer sets Ω_x, $x \in \Sigma' = \{d, u, l, s\}$, where d, u, l, s are the identifiers of the four ASCII character subsets that were used to define Σ as follows:

- $\Omega_d = \{95^i \mathtt{CHRtoINT}(c)\}$ for all digits $c \in d$ and $i = 0, \ldots, n_{\max} - 1$. Note that $|\Omega_d| = 10 n_{\max}$.
- $\Omega_u = \{95^i \mathtt{CHRtoINT}(c)\}$ for all upper case letters $c \in u$ and $i = 0, \ldots, n_{\max} - 1$. Note that $|\Omega_u| = 26 n_{\max}$.
- $\Omega_l = \{95^i \mathtt{CHRtoINT}(c)\}$ for all lower case letters $l \in u$ and $i = 0, \ldots, n_{\max} - 1$. Note that $|\Omega_l| = 26 n_{\max}$.
- $\Omega_s = \{95^i \mathtt{CHRtoINT}(c)\}$ for all symbols $c \in s$ and $i = 0, \ldots, n_{\max} - 1$. Note that $|\Omega_s| = 32 n_{\max}$.

Any password character $c_i \in pw$, $i \in [0, n_{\max} - 1]$ can therefore be mapped to one of the four sets Ω_x, $x \in \Sigma'$ with the *position-dependent character mapping* function $\mathtt{CHRtoINT_i} : \Sigma \mapsto \Omega_x$, defined as

$$\mathtt{CHRtoINT_i}(c, i) = 95^i \mathtt{CHRtoINT}(c)$$

We write $\pi_i \leftarrow \mathtt{CHRtoINT_i}(c, i)$ for the integer value of the ith character $c_i \in pw$.

Mapping of Password Strings to Integers. A *password mapping* function $\mathtt{PWDtoINT} : \Sigma^n \mapsto \mathbb{Z}_{95^{n_{\max}}}$ that maps any password string $pw = (c_0, \ldots, c_{n-1}) \in \Sigma^n$ to an integer in a larger set $\mathbb{Z}_{95^{n_{\max}}}$ in a way that preserves the ith position of each character c_i is defined as follows:

$$\mathtt{PWDtoINT}(pw) = \sum_{i=0}^{n-1} 95^i \mathtt{CHRtoINT}(c_i) = \sum_{i=0}^{n-1} \mathtt{CHRtoINT_i}(c_i, i) \text{ for } c_i \in pw$$

We will use pw to denote a password string and $\pi \leftarrow \mathtt{PWDtoINT}(pw)$ for its integer value. Note that $\pi = \sum_{i=0}^{n-1} \pi_i$.

The mapping computed through $\mathtt{PWDtoINT}$ is injective and reversible. For example, $\pi = 797353$ is the integer value of password string $pw = (2, \mathrm{A}, \mathrm{x})$. The string can be recovered by concatenation of $797353 \mod 95 = 18 \cong 2$ at position 0, $(797353 \mod 95^2) - (797353 \mod 95) = 3135 = 33 \cdot 95^1 \cong \mathrm{A}$ at position 1 and $797353 - (797353 \mod 95^2) = 794200 = 88 \cdot 95^2 \cong \mathrm{x}$ at position 2.

3.3 Password Policies

A *password policy* $f = (R, n_{\min}, n_{\max})$ is modeled using a *regular expression* R over $\Sigma' = \{d, u, l, s\}$, a *minimum length* $n_{\min}$ and a *maximum length* $n_{\max}$ that a password string pw must fulfill.[2] We write $f(pw) = \texttt{true}$ to indicate that the policy is satisfied by the password string pw. For example,

- $f = (\texttt{ds}, 6, 10)$ means that pw must have between 6 and 10 characters with at least one digit and one symbol.
- $f = (\texttt{uss}, 8, 12)$ means that pw must have between 8 and 12 characters with at least one upper-case letter and two symbols.
- $f = (\texttt{duls}, 8, 16)$ means that pw must have between 8 and 16 characters with at least one character of each type.

Remark 1. Note that in practice password policies do not specify $n_{\max}$. We leave it for the server administrator to decide whether $n_{\max}$ should be mentioned explicitly in f or fixed in the system to allow for all reasonable password lengths.

4 Randomized Password Hashing

A *password hashing* scheme Π that is used to compute password verification information for later use in VPAKE protocols from [16] is defined as follows:

- $\texttt{PSetup}(\lambda)$ generates password hashing parameters $\texttt{p}_\texttt{P}$. These parameters contain implicit descriptions of random salt spaces $\mathbb{S}_P$ and $\mathbb{S}_H$.
- $\texttt{PPHSalt}(\texttt{p}_\texttt{P})$ generates a random pre-hash salt $s_P \in_R \mathbb{S}_P$.
- $\texttt{PPreHash}(\texttt{p}_\texttt{P}, pw, s_P)$ outputs the pre-hash value P.
- $\texttt{PHSalt}(\texttt{p}_\texttt{P})$ generates a random hash salt $s_H \in_R \mathbb{S}_H$.
- $\texttt{PHash}(\texttt{p}_\texttt{P}, P, s_P, s_H)$ outputs the hash value H.

In the above syntax the algorithm $\texttt{PPreHash}$ is *randomized* with a pre-hash salt s_P, which extends the syntax from [16], where $\texttt{PPreHash}$ is deterministic (and realized in constructions as a random oracle output $\mathcal{H}(pw)$). In contrast we are interested in algebraic constructions of both $\texttt{PPreHash}$ and $\texttt{PHash}$ to allow for efficient proofs of knowledge involving pre-hash values P. The randomization of $\texttt{PPreHash}$ further increases the complexity of an offline dictionary attack that recovers pw from P since it removes the ability of an attacker to pre-compute pairs (P, pw) and use them directly to recover pw (see also Section 5.4). We write $H \leftarrow \texttt{Hash}_\texttt{P}(pw, r)$ to denote $H \leftarrow \texttt{PHash}(\texttt{p}_\texttt{P}, P, s_P, s_H)$ with $P \leftarrow \texttt{PPreHash}(\texttt{p}_\texttt{P}, pw, s_P)$, where $r = (s_P, s_H)$ combines the randomness used in $\texttt{PHash}$ and $\texttt{PPreHash}$. A secure Π must satisfy the following security properties. Note that password-hiding is a new property that is used in ZKPPC to ensure that password hashes H do not leak any information about pw. The remaining four properties are from [16], updated where necessary to account for the randomized $\texttt{PPreHash}$:

---

[2] The way password policies are modeled in this work is suitable for policies that put restrictions on the password length and the nature of password characters. Other types of policies, e.g. search for natural words in a password (cf. dropbox password-meter) are currently not supported by our framework and thus left for future work.

- Password hiding: For all PPT algorithms $A = (A_1, A_2)$ where A_1 on input $p_P \leftarrow \text{PSetup}(\lambda)$ outputs two equal-length password strings pw_0 and pw_1 and where A_2 on input $H \leftarrow \text{PHash}(p_P, P, s_P, s_H)$, where $s_H \leftarrow \text{PHSalt}(p_P)$, $s_P \leftarrow \text{PPHSalt}(p_P)$, and $P \leftarrow \text{PPreHash}(p_P, pw_b, s_P)$ for a random bit $b \in_R \{0,1\}$ outputs bit b' there exists a negligible function $\varepsilon(\cdot)$ such that $|\Pr[b' = b] - \frac{1}{2}| \leq \varepsilon(\lambda)$.
- Pre-image resistance (called tight one-wayness in [16]): For all PPT algorithms A running in time at most t, there exists a negligible function $\varepsilon(\cdot)$ such that

$$\Pr[(i, P) \leftarrow A^{Hash_P(\cdot)}(p_P); \text{Finalise}(i, P) = 1] \leq \frac{\alpha t}{2^\beta t_{\text{PPreHash}}} + \varepsilon(\lambda),$$

  for small α and t_{PPreHash} being the running time of PPreHash, where $p_P \leftarrow \text{PSetup}(\lambda)$ and each ith invocation of $Hash_P(\cdot)$ returns (H, s_H) with $H \leftarrow \text{PHash}(p_P, P, s_P, s_H)$ and stores $T[i] \leftarrow \text{PPreHash}(p_P, pw, s_P)$, where $s_H \leftarrow \text{PHSalt}(p_P)$, $s_P \leftarrow \text{PPHSalt}(p_P)$, and $pw \in_R \mathcal{D}$. $\text{Finalise}(i, P) = 1$ if $T[i] = P$. (Note that $Hash_P(\cdot)$ does not return s_P.)
- Second pre-image resistance: For all PPT algorithms A there exists a negligible function $\varepsilon(\cdot)$ such that for $P' \leftarrow A(p_P, P, s_H)$

$$\Pr[P' \neq P \wedge \text{PHash}(p_P, P, s_H) = \text{PHash}(p_P, P', s_H)] \leq \varepsilon(\lambda),$$

  with $p_P \leftarrow \text{PSetup}(\lambda), s_P \leftarrow \text{PPHSalt}(p_P), s_H \leftarrow \text{PHSalt}(p_P)$ and $P \leftarrow \text{PPreHash}(p_P, pw, s_P)$ for any $pw \in \mathcal{D}$.
- Pre-hash entropy preservation: For all polynomial time samplable dictionaries $\mathcal{D}$ with min-entropy β, and any PPT algorithm A, there exists a negligible function $\varepsilon(\lambda)$ such that for $(P, s_P) \leftarrow A(p_P)$ with $p_P \leftarrow \text{PSetup}(\lambda)$ and random password $pw \in_R \mathcal{D}$:

$$\Pr[s_P \in \mathbb{S}_P \wedge P = \text{PPreHash}(p_P, pw, s_P)] \leq 2^{-\beta} + \varepsilon(\lambda).$$

- Entropy preservation: For all polynomial time samplable dictionaries $\mathcal{D}$ with min-entropy β, and any PPT algorithm A, there exists a negligible function $\varepsilon(\lambda)$ such that for $(H, s_P, s_H) \leftarrow A(p_P)$

$$\Pr[s_P \in \mathbb{S}_P \wedge s_H \in \mathbb{S}_H \wedge H = \text{Hash}_P(p_P, pw, s_P, s_H)] \leq 2^{-\beta} + \varepsilon(\lambda),$$

  where $p_P \leftarrow \text{PSetup}(\lambda)$ and $pw \in_R \mathcal{D}$.

4.1 Randomized Password Hashing from Pedersen Commitments

We introduce a randomized password hashing scheme $\Pi = (\text{PSetup}, \text{PPHSalt}, \text{PPreHash}, \text{PHSalt}, \text{PHash})$ for ASCII-based passwords using Pedersen commitments. We assume that $\pi \leftarrow \text{PWDtoINT}(pw)$ and construct Π as follows:

- $\text{PSetup}(\lambda)$ generates $p_P = (p, g, h, \lambda)$ where g, h are independent generators of a cyclic group G of prime order p of length λ.

- PPHSalt(p_P) generates a pre-hash salt $s_P \in_R \mathbb{Z}_p^*$.
- PPreHash(p_P, π, s_P) outputs the pre-hash value $P = g^{s_P \pi}$.
- PHSalt(p_P) generates a hash salt $s_H \in_R \mathbb{Z}_p^*$.
- PHash(p_P, P, s_P, s_H) outputs hash value $H = (H_1, H_2) = (g^{s_P}, P h^{s_H})$.

Observe that $H_2 = H_1^\pi h^{s_H}$, i.e., H_1 can be seen as a fresh generator that is used to compute the Pedersen commitment H_2. The security properties of our password hashing scheme Π follow from the properties of the underlying cyclic group G and from the security of Pedersen commitments. We argue informally:

- The *password hiding* property of the scheme, assuming that pw_0 and pw_1 are mapped to corresponding integers π_0 and π_1 in $\mathbb{Z}_{95^n}$, is perfect and holds based on the perfect hiding property of the Pedersen commitment scheme. Note that the adversary receives the corresponding hash value $H = (H_1, H_2) = (g^{s_P}, P h^{s_H})$, where $H_2 = g^{s_P \pi} h^{s_H}$ is a Pedersen commitment on π with respect to two independent bases g^{s_P} and h. The ability of A to distinguish between π_0 and π_1 can thus be turned into the attack on the hiding property of the commitment scheme.
- The *pre-image resistance* holds since s_P and s_H are randomly chosen on every invocation of $Hash_P(\cdot)$ with a negligible probability for a collision and H_2 is a perfectly hiding commitment with bases g^{s_P} and h. Therefore, for any given output $(H = (H_1, H_2), s_H)$ of $Hash_P(\cdot)$, A must perform 2^β exponentiations $H_1^{\pi^*}$, one for each candidate π^*, in order to find $P = H_2 h^{-s_H}$. This roughly corresponds to 2^β invocations of PPreHash.
- The *second pre-image resistance* holds since H_1 is uniform in G and H_2 is a computationally binding commitment with bases g^{s_P} and h. Note that for any P' generated by A, $H_1^\pi h^{s_H} = P' h^{s_H}$ is true only if $P' = H_1^\pi$.
- The *pre-hash entropy* and *hash entropy* preservation hold since H_1 is a generator of G such that for every (P, s_P) chosen by the pre-hash entropy adversary, $\Pr[P = H_1^\pi] \leq 2^{-\beta} + \varepsilon(\lambda)$, and for every (H, s_H) chosen by the hash entropy adversary, $\Pr[H_2 = H_1^\pi h^{s_H}] \leq 2^{-\beta} + \varepsilon(\lambda)$ for a random $pw \in_R \mathcal{D}$.

5   ZKPPC and Password Registration

We first define the ZKPPC concept enabling a client to prove compliance of its chosen passwords pw with respect to a server's password policy f without disclosing pw. We propose a general framework for building ZKPPC protocols for ASCII-based passwords and a concrete ZKPPC instantiation. We further explain how to build registration protocols that use ZKPPC as a building block.

5.1   Zero-Knowledge Password Policy Checks

A Password Policy Check (PPC) is an interactive protocol between a client C and a server S where server's password policy f and the public parameters of a password hashing scheme Π are used as a common input. At the end of the PPC execution S accepts $H \leftarrow Hash_P(pw, r)$ for any password $pw \in \mathcal{D}$ of client's choice if and only if $f(pw) = \texttt{true}$. A PPC protocol is a proof of knowledge for pw and r such that $H \leftarrow \texttt{Hash}_P(pw, r)$ and $f(pw) = \texttt{true}$. It thus includes the requirements on completeness and soundness. In addition, a ZKPPC protocol is a PPC protocol with zero-knowledge property to ensure that no information about pw is leaked to S. More formally,

Definition 1 (ZKPPC). *Let* $\Pi = (\texttt{PSetup}, \texttt{PPHSalt}, \texttt{PPreHash}, \texttt{PHSalt}, \texttt{PHash})$ *be a password hashing scheme and* f *be a password policy. A ZKPPC protocol is a zero-knowledge proof of knowledge protocol between a prover* C *(client) and a verifier* S *(server), defined as*

$$\mathsf{ZKPoK}\{(pw, r) : \ f(pw) = \texttt{true} \wedge H = \texttt{Hash}_P(pw, r)\}.$$

5.2 A General ZKPPC Framework for ASCII-Based Passwords

We present a general ZKPPC construction for password strings pw composed of printable ASCII characters using a commitment scheme $\mathsf{C} = (\texttt{CSetup}, \texttt{Com}, \texttt{Open})$, a password hashing scheme $\Pi = (\texttt{PSetup}, \texttt{PPHSalt}, \texttt{PPreHash}, \texttt{PHSalt}, \texttt{PHash})$ and appropriate set membership proofs SMP. We assume that the common input of C and S includes $\mathsf{p}_P \leftarrow \texttt{PSetup}(\lambda)$, $\mathsf{p}_C \leftarrow \texttt{CSetup}(\lambda)$, and the server's password policy $f = (R, n_{\min}, n_{\max})$ that is communicated to C beforehand.

The ZKPPC protocol proceeds as follows (see also Figure 1 for an overview). Let R_j be the jth character of R. R_j uniquely identifies one of the four ASCII subsets of $\Sigma = d \cup u \cup l \cup s$ and one of the four integer sets Ω_x, $x \in \Sigma' - \{d, u, l, s\}$. Let $\Omega_\Sigma = \bigcup_{x \in \Sigma'} \Omega_x$ be a joint integer set of these four sets. The client picks an ASCII string $pw = (c_0, \dots, c_{n-1})$ such that $f(pw) = \texttt{true}$, computes integer values $\pi_i \leftarrow \texttt{CHRtoINT}_i(c, i)$ for all $i = 0, \dots, n - 1$ and $\pi \leftarrow \texttt{PWDtoINT}(pw) = \sum_{i=0}^{n-1} \pi_i$, and the password hash $H \leftarrow \texttt{Hash}_P(\pi, (s_P, s_H))$ using salt $s_P \leftarrow \texttt{PPHSalt}(\lambda)$ and $s_H \leftarrow \texttt{PHSalt}(\lambda)$. For each position $i = 0, \dots, n - 1$ the client computes commitment $C_i \leftarrow \texttt{Com}(\pi_i, r_i)$ and sends its password hash H with the set of commitments $\{C_i\}$ to S that by checking $|\{C_i\}| \in [n_{\min}, n_{\max}]$ will be able to check the password length requirement from f. Since $f(pw) = \texttt{true}$, for each R_j in R the client can determine the first character $c_j \in pw$ that fulfils R_j and mark it as *significant*. Let $\{c_{i_1}, \dots c_{i_{|R|}}\}$ denote the set of significant characters from pw that is sufficient to fulfill R. For each significant $c_{i_j} \in pw$, $j = 1, \dots, |R|$ client C as prover and server S as verifier execute a set membership proof $\mathsf{SMP}(\pi_{i_j}, r_{i_j}, \Omega_x)$, i.e. proving that position-dependent integer value π_{i_j} committed to in C_{i_j} is in Ω_x for one of the four ASCII subsets in Σ identified by R_j. These SMPs ensure that characters fulfill R. For every other character $c_i \in pw$, $i \neq i_j$, $j = 1, \dots, |R|$ client C as prover and server S as verifier execute $\mathsf{SMP}(\pi_i, r_i, \Omega_\Sigma)$ proving that position-dependent integer value π_i committed to in C_i is in the joint integer set Ω_Σ. This proves that each remaining c_i is a printable ASCII character without disclosing its type and thus ensures that S doesn't learn types of (remaining) password characters that are not necessary for R. Note that in the notation $\mathsf{SMP}(\pi_i, r_i, \Omega')$ used in Figure 1, set Ω' is either one of Ω_x, $x \in \Sigma'$ if π_i represents a significant character or Ω_Σ for all remaining characters.

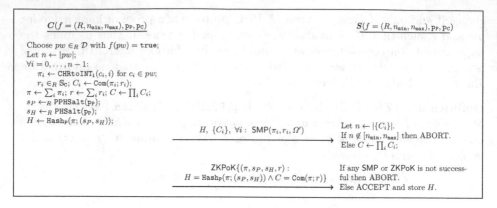

Fig. 1. General ZKPPC Framework for ASCII-based Passwords

If all SMPs are successful then S is convinced that commitments $\{C_i\}$ contain some integer values π_i representing characters c_i that fulfill R and that $n \in [n_{\min}, n_{\max}]$. This doesn't complete the proof yet since two issues remain: (1) committed π_i are not yet linked to the integer value π that represents pw, and (2) the client hasn't proved yet that this π was used to compute the hash value H. In order to address (1) and (2) our ZKPPC framework first uses the homomorphic property of the commitment scheme. Both C and S independently compute $C \leftarrow \prod_{i=0}^{n-1} C_i = \text{Com}(\sum_{i=0}^{n-1} \pi_i, r) = \text{Com}(\pi, r)$, where $r = \sum_{i=0}^{n-1} r_i$, whereas C additionally uses the knowledge of all r_i to compute r. As a last step of the ZKPPC protocol client C as prover and server S as verifier execute a ZKPoK proof that C knows π and random salts (s_P, s_H) that were used to compute H and that π is an integer contained in the (combined) commitment C for which the client knows the (combined) randomness r. If this final ZKPoK is successful then S accepts the hash value H.

In reference to Definition 1, our ZKPPC framework in Figure 1 tailors the general statement $f(pw) = \text{true}$ to ASCII-based policies $f = (R, n_{\min}, n_{\max})$ and corresponding password hashing schemes Π so that the resulting ZKPPC proof is of the following form:

$$\text{ZKPoK}\{(\pi, r, \{\pi_i\}, \{r_i\} \text{ for } i = 0, \ldots, n-1):$$
$$C_i = \text{Com}(\pi_i, r_i) \wedge \prod_i C_i = \text{Com}(\pi, \sum_i r_i) \wedge \pi_i \in \Omega' \wedge H = \text{Hash}_\text{p}(\pi, r)\}.$$

Theorem 1. *If* $\text{C} = (\text{CSetup}, \text{Com}, \text{Open})$ *is an (additively) homomorphic commitment scheme,* $\Pi = (\text{PSetup}, \text{PPHSalt}, \text{PPreHash}, \text{PHSalt}, \text{PHash})$ *a secure randomized password hashing scheme,* SMP *a zero-knowledge set membership proof and* ZKPoK *a zero-knowledge proof of knowledge, then the protocol from Figure 1 is a ZKPPC protocol according to Definition 1.*

Proof. Protocol *completeness* follows by inspection. To prove *soundness* we assume that the server accepts H from a malicious client that was not computed as $\mathsf{Hash_P}(\pi, r)$ for integer π that represents a policy-conform password string pw. By construction of the protocol the client must have either (1) cheated in one of the $\mathsf{SMP}(\pi_i, r_i, \Omega')$ proofs or the final ZKPoK proof which contradicts the soundness properties of those proofs, or (2) was is able to compute H in two different ways, as $\mathsf{Hash_P}(\pi, r)$ using π that corresponds to a policy-conform $pw \in \mathcal{D}$ and as $\mathsf{Hash_P}(\pi^*, r^*)$ using π^* for some $pw^* \in \mathcal{D}$ that is not policy-conform, which contradicts to the second pre-image resistance of Π, or (3) was is able to compute at least one C_i in two different ways, as $\mathsf{Com}(\pi_i, r_i)$ using π_i that corresponds to a character c_i that is significant for the regular expression R and as $\mathsf{Com}(\pi_i^*, r_i^*)$ using π_i^* that doesn't fulfill any character R_j from R, which contradicts to the binding property of C.

To prove the *zero-knowledge* property we need to build a simulator Sim to simulate the view of the server. Sim internally uses the simulators for SMP proofs and the ZKPoK proofs to simulate server's view, thereby relying on the password hiding property of Π and the hiding property of C in the simulation of H and every C_i, respectively. $\qquad\square$

Remark 2. Depending on the maximal password length $n_{\max}$ and complexity of $f = (R, n_{\min}, n_{\max})$ using range proofs instead of set membership proofs, may be more efficient. Although ZKPPC complexity is currently dominated by set membership proofs, passwords in practice are rather short and policies not too complex, so that set membership proofs will be sufficiently efficient in most cases. Further notice that leakage of password length n to the server is not considered as an attack against the ZKPPC protocol. For policies those regular expression R implicitly defines $n_{\min}$ the length n can be hidden using the homomorphic property the commitment scheme C, i.e., by combining commitments C_i for π_i representing (remaining) password characters that are not needed to satisfy R.

5.3   A Concrete ZKPPC Protocol for ASCII-Based Passwords

We show feasibility of our approach by giving a concrete ZKPPC protocol construction for ASCII-based passwords in a cyclic group G of prime order p. The protocol is built from the Pedersen commitment scheme $\mathsf{C} = (\mathsf{CSetup}, \mathsf{Com}, \mathsf{Open})$ from Section 2 and the randomized password hashing scheme $\Pi = (\mathsf{PSetup}, \mathsf{PPHSalt}, \mathsf{PPreHash}, \mathsf{PHSalt}, \mathsf{PHash})$ from Section 4.1 that share the same group G. In particular, public parameters used by C and S in the ZKPPC protocol are defined as (p, g, h, λ) where g and h are independent generators of G. For set membership proofs $\mathsf{SMP}(\pi_i, r_i, \Omega')$ we adopt a three-move honest-verifier proof $\mathsf{ZKPoK}\{(\pi_i, r_i) : C_i = g^{\pi_i} h^{r_i} \wedge (\pi_i = \omega_0 \vee \cdots \vee \pi_i = \omega_{|\Omega'|})\}$ for $\omega_j \in \Omega'$, whose length is proportional to $|\Omega'|$. Assuming that for each $\omega_j \in \Omega'$ the corresponding value $g^{\omega_j} \in G$ is pre-computed this proof can be realized as $\mathsf{ZKPoK}\{(\pi_i, r_i) : C_i = g^{\pi_i} h^{r_i} \wedge (C_i = g^{\omega_0} h^{r_i} \vee \cdots \vee C_i = g^{\omega_{|\Omega'|}} h^{r_i})\}$.[3]

---

[3] More efficient SMPs, e.g. [20], can possibly be used with a different commitment and password hashing scheme. In this case care must be taken when it comes to the instantiation of VPAKE that must be able to handle password hashes generated in ZKPPC (cf. Section 6).

The final ZKPoK proof is instantiated as a three-move honest-verifier proof $\mathsf{ZKPoK}\{(\pi, s_P, s_H, r) : H_1 = g^{s_P} \wedge H_2 = H_1^\pi h^{s_H} \wedge C = g^\pi h^r\}$ that proceeds in the following classical way. C picks random $k_\pi, k_{s_P}, k_{s_H}, k_r \in \mathbb{Z}_p$, computes $t_1 = g^{k_{s_P}}$, $t_2 = H_1^{k_\pi} h^{k_{s_H}}$, and $t_3 = g^{k_\pi} h^{k_r}$, and sends (t_1, t_2, t_3) to S that replies with a random challenge $c \in \mathbb{Z}_p$. C computes $a_1 = k_{s_P} + cs_P \bmod p$, $a_2 = k_\pi + c\pi \bmod p$, $a_3 = k_{s_H} + cs_H \bmod p$ and $a_4 = k_r + cr \bmod p$, and sends (a_1, a_2, a_3, a_4) to S that accepts the proof if $g^{a_1} = t_1 H_1^c$, $H_1^{a_2} h^{a_3} = t_2 H_2^c$, and $g^{a_2} h^{a_4} = t_3 C^c$ holds.

Remark 3. The honest-verifier ZK property of the adopted three-move SMP and ZKPoK protocols is sufficient since ZKPPC will be executed as part of the registration protocol over a server-authenticated secure channel (cf. Section 5.4) where the server is assumed to be honest-but-curios. If ZKPPC protocol is executed outside of such secure channel then common techniques from [21] can be applied to obtain ZK property in presence of malicious verifiers. We also observe that all SMP and ZKPoK protocols can be made non-interactive (in the random oracle model) using the techniques from [22].

5.4   Blind Registration of Passwords Based on ZKPPC

Blind registration of passwords based on our generic ZKPPC construction from Section 5.2 proceeds in *three* main stages and requires server-authenticated secure channel (e.g. TLS) between C and S: (1) S sends its password policy f to C; (2) C picks its user login credentials, containing id (e.g. its email address) which C wants to use for later logins at S, and initiates the execution of the ZKPPC protocol. If the ZKPPC protocol is successful then C has a policy-conform password pw and S receives id and the password hash $H = \mathsf{Hash_P}(\pi, r)$; (3) C sends used random salt r to S and S stores a tuple (id, H, r) in its password database.

The use of server-authenticated secure channel guarantees that no active adversary A can impersonate honest S and obtain (id, H, r) nor can A mount an attack based on modification of server's policy f, e.g. by replacing it with a weaker one. Especially, r needs protection since knowledge of (H, r) enables an offline attack that recovers pw. Assuming an efficiently samplable dictionary $\mathcal{D}$ with min-entropy β a brute force attack would require at most 2^β executions of $\mathsf{Hash_P}(\pi^*, r)$, where $\pi^* \leftarrow \mathsf{PWDtoINT}(pw^*)$, $pw^* \in \mathcal{D}$.

The execution of the ZKPPC protocol in the second stage doesn't require a secure channel due to the assumed ZK property. However, if secure channel is in place then we can work with the *honest-verifier* ZK property, which may lead to more efficient ZKPPC constructions. Note that S is not assumed to be fully malicious but rather honest-but-curios since it cannot be trusted to process plain passwords in a secure way. By modeling S as a malicious party in the ZKPPC protocol we can offer strong guarantees that no information about pw is leaked to S in the second stage and so the only way for S to recover pw at the end is to mount an offline dictionary attack using r from the third stage.

The resulting password registration protocol guarantees that no server S can do better in recovering client's pw than any attacker A who compromises S

during or after the registration phase. This is an ideal security requirement for the registration of passwords that will be used in authentication protocols with password verifiers on the server side. Note that security of such verifier-based authentication protocols implies that any A who breaks into S cannot recover pw better than by mounting an offline dictionary attack. Our approach thus extends this requirement to password registration protocols.

For our concrete ZKPPC construction from Section 5.3 we can modify the third stage of the registration protocol such that instead of $r = (s_P, s_H)$ server S receives only s_H and stores (id, H, s_H), where $H = (H_1, H_2)$, $H_2 = H_1^\pi h^{s_H}$. This trick helps to significantly increase the complexity of an offline dictionary attack. Note that pre-image resistance of Π guarantees that an offline password test based on equality $H_1^\pi = H_2 h^{-s_H}$ would require 2^β exponentiations $H_1^{\pi^*}$ until $\pi^* = \pi$ is found. Note that if s_P is disclosed then the above equality can be re-written to $g^\pi = (H_2 h^{-s_H})^{1/s_P}$ and a pre-computed table $T = (\pi^*, g^{\pi^*})$ would immediately reveal $\pi^* = \pi$. The computation of T requires 2^β exponentiations g^{π^*} but T would need to be computed only once. This also explains why we use Π with randomized PPreHash.

6   VPAKE Protocols for ZKPPC-Registered Passwords

We now focus on suitable VPAKE protocols where the server S using (id, H, r) stored from the ZKPPC-based registration protocol can authenticate the client C that uses only its pw. Such protocols can be constructed with a general VPAKE framework introduced by Benhamouda and Pointcheval [16]. Their framework constructs one-round VPAKE protocols with C and S sending one message each, independently, using a generic password hashing scheme $\Pi =$ (PSetup, PPHSalt, PPreHash, PHSalt, PHash) with deterministic PPreHash, labeled public key encryption scheme $E = $ (KGen, Enc, Dec), and secure SPHFs (HKGen, PKGen, Hash, ProjHash) for two languages $L_H = \{(\ell, C) \mid \exists r : C = \mathrm{Enc}^\ell(pk, H; r)\}$ and $L_{s,H} = \{(\ell, C) | \exists P, \exists r : C = \mathrm{Enc}^\ell(pk, H; r) \wedge H = \mathrm{PHash}(p_P, P, s)\}$. Their approach can directly be used for our generic scheme Π with randomized PPreHash if we assume that $L_{s,H}$ is defined using $s = (s_P, s_H)$. This readily gives us a generic VPAKE protocol that is suitable for our general ZKPPC construction for ASCII-based passwords in Figure 1 and those security follows from the analysis of the framework in [16].

For the concrete VPAKE construction based on our scheme Π from Section 4.1 we can use labeled CS encryption scheme for E from Section 2. The common input of C and S contains the CS public key $pk = (p, g_1, g_2, h, c, d, H_k)$, where generators $g_1 = g$ and h must be the same as in the ZKPPC protocol from Section 5.3. Since $H = (H_1, H_2)$ we need to slightly update the language $L_H = \{(\ell, C) | \exists r : C = \mathrm{Enc}^\ell(pk, H_2; r)\}$ by using H_2 as an encrypted message. We can still use the SPHF for CS ciphertexts from Section 4.1 to handle this L_H. Since the pre-hash salt s_P is not transmitted in the registration phase, i.e. S stores (id, H, s_H) where $H = (H_1, H_2)$ with $H_1 = g_1^{s_P}$ and $H_2 = H_1^\pi h^{s_H}$, we replace $L_{s,H}$ with the following language $L_{s_H, H} = \{(\ell, C) | \exists \pi, \exists r : C = \mathrm{Enc}^\ell(pk, g_1^\pi; r) \wedge H_2 = H_1^\pi h^{s_H}\}$ and construct a suitable SPHF for $L_{s_H, H}$ as follows:

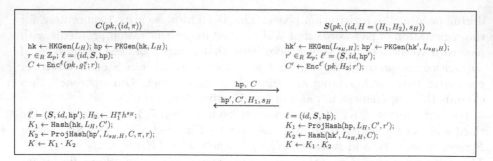

Fig. 2. A VPAKE Protocol for Blindly Registered ASCII-based Passwords

- $\texttt{HKGen}(L_{s_H,H})$ generates $\texttt{hk} = (\eta_1, \eta_2, \theta, \mu, \nu) \in_R \mathbb{Z}_p^{1 \times 5}$.
- $\texttt{PKGen}(\texttt{hk}, L_{s_H,H})$ derives $\texttt{hp} = (\texttt{hp}_1, \texttt{hp}_2, \texttt{hp}_3) = (g_1^{\eta_1} g_2^{\theta} h^{\mu} c^{\nu}, g_1^{\eta_2} d^{\nu}, g_1^{\mu} H_1^{-\mu})$.
- $\texttt{Hash}(\texttt{hk}, L_{s_H,H}, C)$ outputs hash value $h = u_1^{\eta_1 + \xi \eta_2} u_2^{\theta} [e/(H_2 h^{-s_H})]^{\mu} v^{\nu}$.
- $\texttt{ProjHash}(\texttt{hp}, L_{s_H,H}, C, \pi, r)$ outputs hash value

$$h = (\texttt{hp}_1 \texttt{hp}_2^{\xi})^r \texttt{hp}_3^{\pi} = g_1^{\eta_1 r} g_2^{\theta r} h^{\mu r} c^{\nu r} g_1^{\eta_2 \xi r} d^{\nu \xi r} (g_1^{\mu} H_1^{-\mu})^{\pi}.$$

Note that projection key $\texttt{hp}$ depends on $H_1 \in G$, which can be seen as a parameter in the definition of $L_{s_H,H}$, but $\texttt{hp}$ does not depend on C. The resulting VPAKE protocol can thus still proceed in one round. The smoothness of our SPHF construction for $L_{s_H,H}$ can be proven as follows. Let $\pi \leftarrow \texttt{PWDtoINT}(pw)$, $H_2 = H_1^{\pi} h^{s_H}$, with $H_1 = g_1^{s_P}$ for some unknown s_P, and $(\ell, C = (u_1, u_2, e, v)) \notin L_{s_H,H}$, i.e. $C \leftarrow \texttt{Enc}^{\ell}(pk, g_1^{\pi^*}; r)$ for some $\pi^* \neq \pi$. Assuming the second pre-image resistance of Π it follows that $(u_1, u_1^{\xi}, u_2, e/(H_2 h^{-s_H}), v) \neq (g_1^r, g_1^{r\xi}, g_2^r, g_1^{\pi - s_P \pi} h^r, (cd^{\xi})^r)$ with overwhelming probability for all $(r, r\xi) \in \mathbb{Z}_p^2$. Since $(\texttt{hp}_1, \texttt{hp}_2, \texttt{hp}_3)$ are linearly independent the resulting hash value $h = u_1^{\eta_1} u_1^{\xi \eta_2} u_2^{\theta} [e/(H_2 h^{-s_H})]^{\mu} v^{\nu}$ is uniformly distributed in G.

Our concrete VPAKE construction is illustrated in Figure 2. We assume that C uses $\pi \leftarrow \texttt{PWDtoINT}(pw)$ as its input and has already sent its login name id to S who picked the corresponding tuple (id, H, s_H) from its password database. Note that C can also act as initiator and send its id as part of its message, in which case S must act as a responder. Which SPHF algorithms $\texttt{HKGen}$, $\texttt{PKGen}$, $\texttt{Hash}$, $\texttt{ProjHash}$ are used by C and S is visible from the input language, either L_H or $L_{s_H,H}$. By inspection one can see that if both C and S follow the protocol and H used on the server side is a password hash of π used on the client side then both parties compute the same (secret) group element $K = K_1 \cdot K_2$. Note that C derives K_1 using its own hashing key $\texttt{hk}$ and received server's CS ciphertext C' that encrypts H_2, whereas S derives K_1 using client's projection key $\texttt{hp}$, its own C' and r'. Similarly, S derives K_2 using its own hashing key $\texttt{hk}'$ and received client's CS ciphertext C that encrypts g_1^{π}, whereas C derives K_2 using server's projection key $\texttt{hp}'$, its own C and r. Security of this VPAKE protocol follows from the security of the generic scheme.

7   Conclusion

The proposed ZKPPC framework with additional password registration and VPAKE protocols presented in this work can be used to securely register passwords chosen by clients at remote servers while simultaneously achieving the following properties: (1) registered passwords are never disclosed to the server and the only way for the server or any attacker who compromises the server to recover passwords is by mounting an expensive offline dictionary attack; (2) each registered password provably satisfies server's password policy, which is ensured through the use of homomorphic commitments and appropriate set membership proofs; (3) servers can authenticate clients those passwords were registered using the ZKPPC framework by means of efficient VPAKE protocols. We believe that the concept underlying the ZKPPC framework and its current realization for ASCII-based passwords and policies can solve problems related to the inappropriate handling of user passwords that frequently occurs in the real world.

Future work may include extension of the ZKPPC concept towards Two-Server PAKE (2PAKE) protocols, e.g. [23], where the client password is secretly shared amongst two servers from which at most one is assumed to be compromisable. Under this security assumption 2PAKE servers fully eliminate threats from offline dictionary attacks. However, blind registration of policy-conform passwords for 2PAKE protocols under this security assumption is a challenge.

Acknowledgements. This research was supported by the German Science Foundation (DFG) through the project PRIMAKE (MA 4957).

References

1. Ur, B., Kelley, P.G., Komanduri, S., Lee, J., Maass, M., Mazurek, M.L., Passaro, T., Shay, R., Vidas, T., Bauer, L., Christin, N., Cranor, L.F.: How Does Your Password Measure Up? The Effect of Strength Meters on Password Creation. In: USENIX Security 2012, p. 5. USENIX Association (2012)
2. Inglesant, P., Sasse, M.A.: The true cost of unusable password policies: password use in the wild. In: CHI, pp. 383–392. ACM (2010)
3. Kaliski, B.: PKCS #5: Password-Based Cryptography Specification Version 2.0. RFC 2898 (Informational) (September 2000)
4. Turan, M.S., Barker, E., Burr, W., Chen, L.: Recommendation for password-based key derivation, pp. 800–132. NIST Special Publication (2010)
5. Provos, N., Mazières, D.: A Future-Adaptable Password Scheme. In: USENIX Annual Technical Conference, FREENIX Track, pp. 81–91 (1999)
6. Reuters: Trove of Adobe user data found on Web after breach: security firm (2014), http://www.reuters.com/article/2013/11/07/us-adobe-cyber attack-idUSBRE9A61D220131107 (accessed: April 01, 2014)
7. Cubrilovic, N.: RockYou Hack: From Bad To Worse (2014), http://techcrunch.com/2009/12/14/rockyou-hack-security-myspace-facebook-passwords/ (accessed: April 01, 2014)
8. Reuters, T.: Microsoft India store down after hackers take user data (2014), http://ca.reuters.com/article/technologyNews/idCATRE81C0E120120213 (accessed: April 01, 2014)

9. Goodin, D.: Hack of Cupid Media dating website exposes 42 million plaintext passwords (2014), http://arstechnica.com/security/2013/11/hack-of-cupid-media-dating-website-exposes-42-million-plaintext-passwords/ (accessed: April 01, 2014)
10. Bellovin, S.M., Merritt, M.: Encrypted Key Exchange: Password-Based Protocols Secure Against Dictionary Attacks. In: IEEE S&P 1992, pp. 72–84. IEEE CS (1992)
11. Bellare, M., Pointcheval, D., Rogaway, P.: Authenticated key exchange secure against dictionary attacks. In: Preneel, B. (ed.) EUROCRYPT 2000. LNCS, vol. 1807, pp. 139–155. Springer, Heidelberg (2000)
12. Canetti, R., Halevi, S., Katz, J., Lindell, Y., MacKenzie, P.: Universally Composable Password-Based Key Exchange. In: Cramer, R. (ed.) EUROCRYPT 2005. LNCS, vol. 3494, pp. 404–421. Springer, Heidelberg (2005)
13. Pointcheval, D.: Password-Based Authenticated Key Exchange. In: Fischlin, M., Buchmann, J., Manulis, M. (eds.) PKC 2012. LNCS, vol. 7293, pp. 390–397. Springer, Heidelberg (2012)
14. Bellovin, S.M., Merritt, M.: Augmented Encrypted Key Exchange: A Password-Based Protocol Secure against Dictionary Attacks and Password File Compromise. In: ACM CCS 1993, pp. 244–250. ACM (1993)
15. Gentry, C., MacKenzie, P.D., Ramzan, Z.: A Method for Making Password-Based Key Exchange Resilient to Server Compromise. In: Dwork, C. (ed.) CRYPTO 2006. LNCS, vol. 4117, pp. 142–159. Springer, Heidelberg (2006)
16. Benhamouda, F., Pointcheval, D.: Verifier-Based Password-Authenticated Key Exchange: New Models and Constructions. IACR Cryptology ePrint Archive 2013, 833 (2013)
17. Pedersen, T.P.: Non-Interactive and Information-Theoretic Secure Verifiable Secret Sharing. In: Feigenbaum, J. (ed.) Advances in Cryptology - CRYPTO 1991. LNCS, vol. 576, pp. 129–140. Springer, Heidelberg (1992)
18. Cramer, R., Shoup, V.: A Practical Public Key Cryptosystem Provably Secure Against Adaptive Chosen Ciphertext Attack. In: Krawczyk, H. (ed.) CRYPTO 1998. LNCS, vol. 1462, pp. 13–25. Springer, Heidelberg (1998)
19. Benhamouda, F., Blazy, O., Chevalier, C., Pointcheval, D., Vergnaud, D.: New smooth projective hash functions and one-round authenticated key exchange. Cryptology ePrint Archive, Report 2013/034 (2013), http://eprint.iacr.org/
20. Camenisch, J., Chaabouni, R., Shelat, A.: Efficient Protocols for Set Membership and Range Proofs. In: Pieprzyk, J. (ed.) ASIACRYPT 2008. LNCS, vol. 5350, pp. 234–252. Springer, Heidelberg (2008)
21. Cramer, R., Damgård, I., MacKenzie, P.D.: Efficient Zero-Knowledge Proofs of Knowledge Without Intractability Assumptions. In: Imai, H., Zheng, Y. (eds.) PKC 2000. LNCS, vol. 1751, pp. 354–373. Springer, Heidelberg (2000)
22. Fiat, A., Shamir, A.: How to Prove Yourself: Practical Solutions to Identification and Signature Problems. In: Odlyzko, A.M. (ed.) Advances in Cryptology - CRYPTO 1986. LNCS, vol. 263, pp. 186–194. Springer, Heidelberg (1987)
23. Kiefer, F., Manulis, M.: Distributed Smooth Projective Hashing and Its Application to Two-Server Password Authenticated Key Exchange. In: Boureanu, I., Owesarski, P., Vaudenay, S. (eds.) ACNS 2014. LNCS, vol. 8479, pp. 199–216. Springer, Heidelberg (2014)

Bitcoin Transaction Malleability and MtGox

Christian Decker and Roger Wattenhofer

ETH Zurich, Switzerland
cdecker@tik.ee.ethz.ch, wattenhofer@ethz.ch

Abstract. In Bitcoin, transaction malleability describes the fact that the signatures that prove the ownership of bitcoins being transferred in a transaction do not provide any integrity guarantee for the signatures themselves. This allows an attacker to mount a malleability attack in which it intercepts, modifies, and rebroadcasts a transaction, causing the transaction issuer to believe that the original transaction was not confirmed. In February 2014 MtGox, once the largest Bitcoin exchange, closed and filed for bankruptcy claiming that attackers used malleability attacks to drain its accounts. In this work we use traces of the Bitcoin network for over a year preceding the filing to show that, while the problem is real, there was no widespread use of malleability attacks before the closure of MtGox.

Keywords: Bitcoin, Transaction, Signature, Malleability, MtGox, Theft.

1 Introduction

In recent years Bitcoin [1] has gone from a little experiment by tech enthusiasts to a global phenomenon. The cryptocurrency is seeing a rapid increase in adoption as well as in value. Bitcoin is inching closer to the stated goal of creating a truly decentralized global currency that facilitates international trade.

A major contribution of the success that Bitcoin is having today has to be attributed to the emergence of Bitcoin exchanges. A Bitcoin exchange is a platform that facilitates buying and selling bitcoins for fiat money like US dollars. This enables a larger public to come in contact with bitcoins, increasing their value as a means to pay for goods and services. Exchanges also provide the ground truth for the value of bitcoins by publishing their trade book and allowing market dynamics to find a price for the traded bitcoins. Finally, much of the media attention focuses on the rapid gain in value that these services have enabled.

However, centralized exchanges are also potential points of failure, in a system that is otherwise completely decentralized. Several high value thefts from these services have made the headlines, never failing to predict the impending doom of Bitcoin as a whole. Additionally a small and mostly sentiment driven market, combined with a quick and easy way to buy and sell bitcoins, facilitates flash crashes and rapid rallies for no apparent reason.

The first, and for a long time largest, Bitcoin exchange was MtGox. Founded in 2010 it was a first stop for many early adopters. With the creation of other

M. Kutyłowski and J. Vaidya (Eds.): ESORICS 2014, Part II, LNCS 8713, pp. 313–326, 2014.

exchanges its monopoly slowly faded, but in February 2014 it still accounted for close to 70% of all bitcoins ever traded. In February 2014 MtGox had to file for bankruptcy and suspend operations following the loss of over 500 million USD worth of bitcoins owned by its customers.

As the principal cause for the loss, MtGox cited a problem in the Bitcoin protocol: *transaction malleability*. A user could request a withdrawal from MtGox to a Bitcoin address. The exchange would then create a corresponding transaction and publish it to the Bitcoin network. Due to the way MtGox tracked confirmation of these transactions it could be tricked, exploiting transaction malleability, into believing the transaction to have failed even though it was later confirmed by the network. MtGox would then credit the amount back to the user's account. Effectively the user would have doubled the withdrawn bitcoins, once from the withdrawal and once on its account on MtGox.

In this work we investigate two fundamental questions: Is transaction malleability being exploited? And is the claim that it has been used to bring down MtGox plausible?

2 Transaction Malleability

The Bitcoin network is a distributed network of computer nodes controlled by a multitude of owners. They collectively implement a replicated ledger that tracks the address balances of all users. Each user may create an arbitrary number of addresses that can be used to send and receive bitcoins. An address is derived from an ECDSA key pair that is later used to prove ownership of the bitcoins associated with that address.

The only operation allowed to modify address balances are *transactions*. A transaction is a signed data structure that on the one hand claims some bitcoins associated with a sending address and on the other hand reassigns them to receiving addresses. Transactions are identified by the SHA256 hash of their serialized representation. A transaction consists of one or more *inputs* and an ordered list of one or more *outputs*. An input is used to specify which bitcoins will be transferred, while an output specifies the address that should be credited with the bitcoins being transferred. Formally, an output is a tuple comprising the value that is to be transferred and a *claiming condition*, expressed in a simple scripting language. An input includes the hash of a previous transaction, an index, and a *claiming script*. The hash and index form a reference that uniquely identifies the output to be claimed and the claiming script proves that the user creating the transaction is indeed the owner of the bitcoins being claimed.

2.1 Bitcoin Scripts

The scripting language is a, purposefully non-Turing complete, stack-based language that uses single byte opcodes. The use of the scripting language to set up both the claiming conditions and the claiming scripts allows the creation of complex scenarios for the transfer of bitcoins. For example, it is possible to create multi-signature addresses that require m-of-n signatures to spend the associated bitcoins for arbitration purposes. However, the vast majority of transactions use standard scripts that set up a claiming condition requiring the claiming script to provide a public key matching the address and a valid signature of the current transaction matching the public key. For this reason the standard claiming script is generally referred to as *scriptSig* (a script encoding a signature), whereas the standard claiming condition is referred to as *scriptPubKey* (a script requiring a public key and a signature). Figure 1 shows the structure of the standard claiming condition (scriptPubKey) as well as the standard claiming script (scriptSig).

Of particular interest in this work are the OP_PUSHDATA operations which specify a number of following bytes to be pushed as a string on the stack. Depending on the length of the string one of several possible flavors may be used. The simplest is a single byte with value between $0x00$ and $0x4b$, also called OP_0 which simply encodes the length of the string in itself. Additionally, three other operations allow pushing data on the stack, namely OP_PUSHDATA1, OP_PUSHDATA2 and OP_PUSHDATA4, each followed by 1, 2 or 4 bytes, respectively, encoding a little endian number of bytes to be read and pushed on the stack.

In order to verify the validity of a transaction t_1 claiming an output of a previous transaction t_0 the scriptSig of t_1 and the scriptPubKey specified in t_0 are executed back to back, without clearing the stack in between. The scriptSig of t_1 pushes the signature and the public key on the stack. The scriptPubKey of t_0 then duplicates the public key (OP_DUP) and replaces the first copy with its RIPEMD160 hash (OP_HASH160), this 20 byte derivative of the public key is also encoded in the address. The address from the scriptPubKey is then pushed on the stack and the two top elements are then tested for equality (OP_EQUALVERIFY). If the hash of the public key and the expected hash match, the script continues, otherwise execution is aborted. Finally, the two elements remaining on the stack, i.e., the signature and the public key, are used to verify that the signature signs t_1 (OP_CHECKSIG).

Listing 1.1. scriptPubKey

```
OP_DUP
OP_HASH160
OP_PUSHDATA*
<pubKeyHash>
OP_EQUALVERIFY
OP_CHECKSIG
```

Listing 1.2. scriptSig

```
OP_PUSHDATA*
<sig>
OP_PUSHDATA*
<pubKey>
```

Fig. 1. The standard claiming condition and claiming script as used by simple transactions transferring bitcoins to an address backed by a single public key

Notice that, although the scriptSigs are attached to the inputs of the transaction, they are not yet known at the time the signature is created. In fact a signature may not sign any data structure containing itself as this would create a circular dependency. For this reason all the claiming scripts are set to a script consisting only of a single OP_0 that pushes an empty string on the stack. The user signing the transaction then iterates through the inputs, temporarily replaces the scriptSig field with the corresponding scriptPubKey[1] from the referenced output, and creates a signature for the resulting serialized transaction. The signatures are then collected and inserted at their respective positions before broadcasting the transaction to the network.

The fact that the integrity of the scriptSig cannot be verified by the signature is the source for transaction malleability: the claiming script may be encoded in several different ways that do not directly invalidate the signature itself. A simple example replaces the OP_0 that pushes the public key on the stack with OP_PUSHDATA2 followed by the original length. The claiming script is changed from 0x48<sig>41<pubKey> to 0x4D4800<sig>4D4100<pubKey>. The encoded signature is valid in both cases but the hash identifying the transaction is different.

Besides these changes in the way pushes are encoded, there are numerous sources of malleability in the claiming script. A Bitcoin Improvement Proposal (BIP) by Wuille [2] identifies the following possible ways to modify the signature and therefore exploit malleability:

1. ECDSA signature malleability: signatures describe points on an elliptic curve. Starting from a signature it is trivial to mathematically derive a second set of parameters encoding the same point on the elliptic curve;
2. Non-DER encoded ECDSA signatures: the cryptographic library used by the Bitcoin Core client, OpenSSL, accepts a multitude of formats besides the standardized DER (Distinguished Encoding Rules) encoding;
3. Extra data pushes: a scriptPubKey may push additional data at the beginning of the script. These are not consumed by the corresponding claiming condition and are left on the stack after script termination;
4. The signature and public key may result from a more complex script that does not directly push them on the stack, but calculates them on the fly, e.g., concatenating two halves of a public key that have been pushed individually;
5. Non-minimal encoding of push operations: as mentioned before there are several options to specify identical pushes of data on the stack;
6. Zero-padded number pushes: excessive padding of strings that are interpreted as numbers;
7. Data ignored by scripts: if data pushed on the stack is ignored by the scriptPubKey, e.g., if the scriptPubKey contains an OP_DROP, the corresponding push in the scriptSig is ignored;
8. Sighash flags can be used to ignore certain parts of a script when signing;
9. Any user with access to the private key may generate an arbitrary number of valid signatures as the ECDSA signing process uses a random number generator to create signatures;

---

[1] The use of the scriptPubKey in the signed data as placeholder for the scriptSig is likely to avoid collisions.

2.2 Malleability Attacks

One of the problems that Bitcoin sets out to solve is the problem of *double spending*. If an output is claimed by two or more transactions, these transactions are said to *conflict*, since only one of them may be valid. A *double spending attack* is the intentional creation of two conflicting transactions that attempt to spend the same funds in order to defraud a third party.

Research so far has concentrated on a classical version of the double spending attack. An attacker would create two transactions: (1) a transaction that transfers some of its funds once to a vendor accepting bitcoins and (2) a transaction that transfers those same funds back to itself. The goal would then be to convince the vendor that it received the funds, triggering a transfer of goods or services from the vendor to the attacker, and ensuring that the transaction returning the funds to the attacker is later confirmed. This would defraud the vendor as the transfer to the vendor would not be confirmed, yet the attacker received the goods or services.

A *malleability attack*, while a variant of the double spending attack, is different from the above. The attacker no longer is the party issuing the transaction, instead it is the receiving party. The attacker would cause the victim to create a transaction that transfers some funds to an address controlled by the attacker. The attacker then waits for the transaction to be broadcast in the network. Once the attacker has received a copy of the transaction, the transaction is then modified using one of the above ways to alter the signature without invalidating it. The modification results in a different transaction identification hash. The modified transaction is then also broadcast in the network. Either of the two transactions may later be confirmed.

A malleability attack is said to be successful if the modified version of the transaction is later confirmed. The mechanics of how transactions are confirmed are complex and are out of scope for this work. For our purposes it suffices to say that the probability of a malleability attack to be successful depends on the distribution of nodes in the Bitcoin network first seeing either of the transactions (cf. [3–5]). So far the attack has not caused any damage to the victim. To be exploitable the victim also has to rely solely on the transaction identity hash to track and verify its account balance. Should a malleability attack be successful the victim will only see that the transaction it issued has not been confirmed, crediting the amount to the attacker or attempting to send another transaction at a later time. The attacker would have effectively doubled the bitcoins the victim sent it.

It is worth noting that the reference client (Bitcoin Core) is not susceptible to this attack as it tracks the unspent transaction output set by applying all confirmed transactions to it, rather than inferring only from transactions it issued.

3   MtGox Incident Timeline

In this section we briefly describe the timeline of the incident that eventually led to the filing for bankruptcy of MtGox. The timeline is reconstructed from a series of press release by MtGox as well as the official filings and legal documents following the closure.

Following several months of problems with Bitcoin withdrawals from users, MtGox announced [6] on February 7 that it would suspend bitcoin withdrawals altogether. The main problem with withdrawals was that the associated Bitcoin transactions would not be confirmed. After this press release it was still possible to trade bitcoins on MtGox, but it was not possible to withdraw any bitcoins from the exchange. Specifically [6] does not mention transaction malleability.

In order to trade on MtGox, users had transferred bitcoins and US dollars to accounts owned by MtGox. Each user would have a virtual account that is credited with the transferred amounts at MtGox. The withdrawal stop therefore denied users access to their own bitcoins. While fiat currency was still withdrawable, such a withdrawal involved a long process that would sometimes fail altogether.

The first press release was followed by a second press release [7] on February 10, 2014. This press release claims that the problem for the non-confirming withdrawal transactions has been identified and names transaction malleability as the sole cause:

> "Addressing Transaction Malleability: MtGox has detected unusual activity on its Bitcoin wallets and performed investigations during the past weeks. This confirmed the presence of transactions which need to be examined more closely.
> Non-technical Explanation: A bug in the bitcoin software makes it possible for someone to use the Bitcoin network to alter transaction details to make it seem like a sending of bitcoins to a bitcoin wallet did not occur when in fact it did occur. Since the transaction appears as if it has not proceeded correctly, the bitcoins may be resent. MtGox is working with the Bitcoin core development team and others to mitigate this issue."

Allegedly a user of MtGox would request a withdrawal and listen for the resulting transaction. The transaction would then be intercepted and replaced by a modified version that would then race with the original transaction to be confirmed. Should the original transaction be confirmed, the user would receive its balance only once, but not lose any bitcoins by doing so. Should the modified transaction be confirmed, then the user would receive the bitcoins twice: once via the modified withdrawal transaction and a second time when MtGox realized that the original withdrawal transaction would not confirm and credit the users account. Implicitly in this press release MtGox admits to using a custom client that tracks transaction validity only via its hash, hence being vulnerable to the transaction malleability attack.

Two more press releases followed on February 17 and February 20, both claiming that the withdrawals would resume shortly and that a solution had been found that would eliminate the vulnerability to malleability attacks. On February 23 the website of MtGox returned only a blank page, without any further explanation, resulting in a trading halt and the complete disappearance of Mt-Gox. Finally on February 28 MtGox announced during a press conference that it would be filing for bankruptcy in Japan and in the USA [8, 9].

4   Measurements

Due to the nature of double spending attacks, they may only be detected while participating in the network. As soon as one of the two conflicting transactions is considered to be confirmed the nodes will drop all other conflicting transactions, losing all information about the double spending attack. Malleability attacks being a subset of double spending attacks suffer from the same limitation.

We created specialized nodes that would trace and dump all transactions and blocks from the Bitcoin network. These include all double spending attacks that have been forwarded to any of the peers our nodes connected to. Our collection of transactions started in January 2013. As such we are unable to reproduce any attacks before January 2013. The following observations therefore do not consider attacks that may have happened before our collection started.

Our nodes were instructed to keep connection pools of 1,000 connections open to peers in the Bitcoin network. On average we connected to 992 peers, which at the time of writing is approximately 20% of the reachable nodes. According to Bamert et al. [3] the probability of detecting a double spending attack quickly converges to 1 as the number of sampled peers increases. We therefore feel justified in assuming that the transactions collected during the measurements faithfully reflect the double spending attacks in the network during the same period.

4.1   Global Analysis

Given the set of all transactions, the first task is to extract all potential double spend attacks. In general double spending attacks can be identified by associating a transaction with each output that it claims. Should there be more than one transaction associated with the same output the transactions conflict. The malleability attack being a specialized case of the double spend attack could also be identified by this generic procedure, however we opted for a simpler process. Removing the signature script from a transaction results in the signed part of the transaction, forcing all malleability attacks to produce the same unique key. The unique key is then used to group transactions together into *conflict sets*.

During the measurement period a total of 35,202 conflict sets were identified, each evidence of a malleability attack. Out of these conflict sets 29,139 contained a transaction that would later be confirmed by a block. The remaining 6,063 transactions were either invalid because they claimed non-existing outputs, had incorrect signatures, or they were part of a further double spending.

The *conflict set value* is defined as the number of bitcoins transferred by any one transaction in the conflict set. The outputs of the transactions in a conflict set are identical, since any change to them would require a new signature. In particular the value of outputs may not be changed. Each transaction in a conflict set therefore transfers an identical amount of bitcoins. Summing the value of all conflict sets results in a total of 302,700 bitcoins that were involved in malleability attacks.

As mentioned in Section 2.1, there are a multitude of ways to use the malleability in the signature encoding to mount a malleability attack. The most prominent type of modification was replacing the single byte OP_0 with OP_PUSHDATA2 which then encodes the length of the data to push on the stack with 2 bytes. The resulting signature script would be 4 bytes longer, because two strings are usually pushed on the stack, but would still encode the same DER encoded signature and the same public key, hence still be valid. A total of 28,595 out of the 29,139 confirmed attacks had this type of modifications. For the remaining 544 conflict sets we were unable to identify the original transactions. All transactions in these conflict sets had genuine signatures with the correct opcodes and did not encode the same signature. We therefore believe these transactions to be the result of users signing raw transactions multiple times, e.g., for development purposes.

In order for a malleability attack to be exploitable two conditions have to be fulfilled: (a) the modified transaction has to be later confirmed and (b) the system issuing the transaction must rely solely on the transaction's original hash to track its confirmation. The first condition can be easily reconstructed from the network trace and the Bitcoin blockchain since only one of the transactions will be included in the blockchain. The second condition is not detectable in our traces since it depends on the implementation of the issuing system. In particular, it is not possible to determine whether two payments with the same value to the same address were intended as two separate payments or whether an automated system issued the second one believing the first to be invalid.

We call a malleability attack successful if it resulted in the modified transaction to be later confirmed in a block, i.e., when condition (a) holds. From the data derived from the attack classification we can measure the rate of successful malleability attacks. Out of the 28,595 malleability attacks that used an OP_PUSHDATA2 instead of the default OP_0 only 5,670 were successful, i.e., 19.46% of modified transactions were later confirmed. Considering the value in malleable transactions the success rate is comparable with 21.36%. This reduces the total profit of the successful attacks from 302,700 to 64,564. The strong bias towards the original transaction is explained by the fact that the probability of being confirmed depends on the distribution of the transaction in the network [3]. During a malleability attack the attacker listens for an incoming transaction that match its address, modifies it and redistributes it. In the meantime however the original transaction has been further forwarded in the network and the modified transaction is not forwarded by nodes seeing the original transaction. The attacker must connect to a large sample of nodes in the network for two reasons: (a) intercept the original transaction as soon as possible and (b)

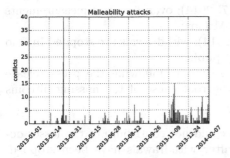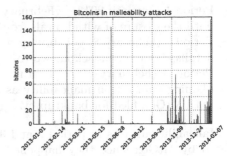

Fig. 2. Malleability attacks during period 1, before the press release blaming transaction malleability as the sole cause of losses

compensate the head start that the original transaction has compared to the modified transaction.

So far we assumed that the conflict sets were a direct result of a targeted attack by an attacker against a service. There are however other causes for this kind of conflict that should not go unmentioned. An automated system may inadvertently create, sign a transaction and broadcast a transaction multiple times. Due to a random parameter in the signing process the system would produce a different signature each time, causing the conflict that we detected. This appears to be the case with transactions having conflict set cardinality larger than 2, that would often not be confirmed.

4.2 The MtGox Incident

Returning to the specific case of the MtGox incident of February 2014, that eventually lead to the closure and the bankruptcy filing later that same month. In the press release of February 10, the transaction malleability bug was explicitly named as the root cause of the loss. The loss is later detailed as amounting to over 850,000 bitcoins, of which 750,000 bitcoins were customer owned bitcoins that were managed by MtGox. At the time of the first press release bitcoins were trading at 827 US Dollars per bitcoin,[2] resulting in a total value of lost bitcoins of 620 million US Dollars.

Assuming malleability attacks have indeed been used to defraud MtGox, then we should be able to verify the claim by finding the transactions used for the attack in our dataset. The above mentioned total amount of 302,700 bitcoins involved in malleability attacks already disproves the existence of such a large scale attack. However, it could well be that malleability attacks contributed considerably in the declared losses.

Reconstructing the timeline of the attacks from the announcements made by MtGox we identify 3 time periods:

---

[2] Exchange rate taken as the open value on MtGox of February 7, 2014.

- Period 1 (January 2013 — February 7, 2014): over a year of measurements until the closure of withdrawals from MtGox;
- Period 2 (February 8 — February 9, 2014): withdrawals are stopped but no details about the attack known to the public;
- Period 3 (February 10 — February 28): time following the press release blaming transaction malleability as the root cause of the missing bitcoins until MtGox filed for bankruptcy.

Malleability attacks in period 2 and 3 could not contribute to the losses declared by MtGox since they happened after withdrawals have been stopped. Figure 2 visualizes both the number of bitcoins involved in malleability attacks as well as the number of attacks during period 1. During this period a total of 421 conflict sets were identified for a total value of 1,811.58 bitcoins involved in these attacks. In combination with the above mentioned success rate of malleability attacks we conclude that overall malleability attacks did not have any substantial influence in the loss of bitcoins incurred by MtGox.

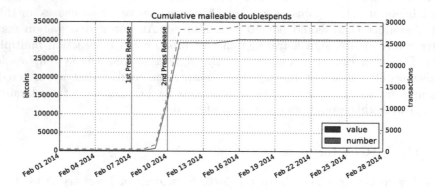

Fig. 3. Cumulative graph of the number and value of malleability attacks during the time of the press releases

During period 2, we gathered 1,062 conflict sets, totalling 5,470 bitcoins. A noticeable increase of attacks at 17:00 UTC on February 9, from 0.15 attacks per hour to 132 attacks per hour. While we do not have any information about the time the second press release has been published, the measured increase in attacks at 17:00 UTC and the date on the press release, hints at a time between 0:00 and 2:00 JST. The sudden increase suggests that immediately following the press release other attackers started imitating the attack, attempting to exploit the same weakness that had allegedly been used against MtGox.

After the second press release, in period 3, there is a sudden spike in activity. Between February 10 and 11 we identified 25,752 individual attacks totalling 286,076 bitcoins, two orders of magnitude larger than all attacks from period 1 combined. A second, smaller, wave of attacks starts after February 15, with a total of 9,193 bitcoins. The attacks have since calmed, returning to levels comparable to those observed in period 1, before the press releases. Figure 3 summarizes the situation plotting the cumulative value and number of malleability attacks in February 2014, i.e., from the end of period 1 to period 3.

The strong correlation between the press releases and the ensuing attacks attempting to exploit the same weakness is a strong indicator that the attacks were indeed triggered by the press releases.

Assuming MtGox had disabled withdrawals like they stated in the first press release, these attacks can not have been aimed at MtGox. The attacks therefore where either attempts to investigate transaction malleability or they were aimed at other businesses attempting to imitate the purveyed attack for personal gain. The sheer amount of bitcoins involved in malleability attacks would suggest that the latter motive was prevalent.

It remains questionable whether other services have been informed by MtGox in time to brace for the sudden increase in malleability attacks. Should this not be the case then the press release may have harmed other businesses by triggering imitators to attack them.

4.3 Beyond Our Data

In the previous subsections we presented an analysis of malleability attacks based on data we collected for over a year preceding the bankruptcy filing by MtGox. We have limited the analysis to the timespan we have first hand data, starting January 2013. Clearly attacks may have happened even before our measurements started. However, in our opinion, it is unlikely that transaction malleability was exploited on a large scale before our measurements, and not during our measurements. After all, why would an attacker, having found such a lucrative attack before 2013, suddenly stop exploiting it? It seems more likely that an attacker would use this risk-free and successful attack more often and with larger amounts of bitcoins!

While it is not possible to detect all malleability attacks without participating in the network at the time they occur, we can estimate the number of attacks preceding our measurements, just by reading the blockchain. By far the most common modification during our measurements was the use of non-minimal push opcodes, over 98% out of all attacks use this modification. Successful attacks, i.e., those that were eventually confirmed, can be found by searching for this modification in the set of all confirmed transactions. Given the success rate and the number of successful attacks we can extrapolate the number of attacks that were attempted before our measurements began.

By inspecting all confirmed transactions for signature scripts that do not use minimal push opcodes we found a total of 48 transactions, involving a total of 33.92 bitcoins, before our measurements started, i.e., in the period 2009 – 2012. Assuming that the success rate of 21.34% did not change significantly, we can extrapolate a total of less than 160 bitcoins involved in a few hundreds of attempted malleability attacks preceding our measurements. This is equivalent to less than 10% of the attacks identified during our measurements.

Besides the temporal restriction of our study, we also restricted ourselves to one specific attack, made possible by transaction malleability. Malleability attacks as defined in Section 2.2 require that both the original and the modified transaction are broadcast in the Bitcoin network. This reflects the description of the attack in the MtGox press release of February 10, 2014 [7].

In addition to broadcasting the transactions in the network, MtGox also published withdrawal transactions on their website. This may have resulted in a different attack, only partially covered by this work. MtGox sometimes created invalid transactions with non-canonical signatures which would not be forwarded by newer Bitcoin clients. An attacker could retrieve the invalid transactions, correct the signatures and release the corrected transactions into the network.

We were able to collect these invalid transactions until October 2013, but not after that. The collected invalid transactions were considered when creating the conflict sets and figures in the analysis. It is however possible that some transactions did not even reach the Bitcoin network, and that some different type of attack might have played a role in MtGox' loss. We would like to stress that this paper does focus on malleability attacks only, as defined by MtGox and in this paper. Other types of attacks are outside the scope of this paper.

Finally, it is worth noting that the attacks described in this work could have been countered by adhering to basic best practices. Failed transactions should not be automatically retried, since a failure to confirm is indicative of other errors, as would have been the case with non-canonical signatures or malleability attacks. Should automatic retrial be desired, then the transaction issuer must ensure that the same inputs are reused. By doing so the issuer ensures that the funds are transferred at most once, even if an attacker may arbitrarily delay the transaction or exploit transaction malleability to render the original transaction unrecognizable.

5   Related Work

Transaction malleability has been known about since at least 2010, when it was first documented. It has however received very little attention so far as it was categorized as a low priority issue.

Andrychowicz et al. [10, 11] mention transaction malleability as a potential problem in contracts and two party computations based on Bitcoin transactions. These schemes can be used for example to implement a fair coin toss [12], auctions or decentralized voting. Their method to eliminate transaction malleability in their protocols resembles our construction of conflict sets, i.e., eliminating malleable parts of the transaction in the hash calculation. However, they limit their observations to advanced schemes for encoding contracts and two party computations.

A related class of doublespending attacks, which we shall refer to as classical doublespending, has received far more attention. In this class of attacks the transaction issuer creates two transactions to defraud the receiving party. Karame et al. [5] first studied the problem of arising from fast transactions, i.e., accepting non-confirmed transactions. Rosenfeld [13] showed that the success probability of a doublespending attack can be further increased if coupled with computational resources. Bamert et al. [3] later improved the security of accepting fast payments by observing how transactions are propagated in the network.

To the best of our knowledge this paper is the first publication describing transaction malleability and the resulting malleability attack in detail.

6   Conclusion

The transaction malleability problem is real and should be considered when implementing Bitcoin clients. However, while MtGox claimed to have lost 850,000 bitcoins due to malleability attacks, we merely observed a total of 302,000 bitcoins ever being involved in malleability attacks. Of these, only 1,811 bitcoins were in attacks before MtGox stopped users from withdrawing bitcoins. Even more, 78.64% of these attacks were ineffective. As such, barely 386 bitcoins could have been stolen using malleability attacks from MtGox or from other businesses. Even if all of these attacks were targeted against MtGox, MtGox needs to explain the whereabouts of 849,600 bitcoins.

References

1. Nakamoto, S.: Bitcoin: A peer-to-peer electronic cash system,
   https://bitcoin.org/bitcoin.pdf (Online; accessed March 26, 2014)
2. Wuille, P.: BIP 0062: Dealing with Malleability (2014),
   https://github.com/bitcoin/bips (Online; accessed March 10, 2014)
3. Bamert, T., Decker, C., Elsen, L., Welten, S., Wattenhofer, R.: Have a snack, pay with bitcoin. In: IEEE Internation Conference on Peer-to-Peer Computing (P2P), Trento, Italy (2013)
4. Decker, C., Wattenhofer, R.: Information propagation in the bitcoin network. In: IEEE International Conference on Peer-to-Peer Computing (P2P), Trento, Italy (September 2013)
5. Karame, G., Androulaki, E., Capkun, S.: Two Bitcoins at the Price of One? Double-Spending Attacks on Fast Payments in Bitcoin. In: Proc. of Conference on Computer and Communication Security (2012)
6. MtGox: Mtgox press release announcing the stop of withdrawals (2014),
   https://www.mtgox.com/press_release_20140210.html
   (Online; accessed February 10, 2014)
7. MtGox: Mtgox press release about transaction malleability (2014), https://www.mtgox.com/press_release_20140210.html (Online; accessed February 10, 2014)
8. MtGox: Announcement regarding an application for commencement of a prodedure of civil rehabilitation, https://www.mtgox.com/img/pdf/20140228-announcement_eng.pdf (Online; accessed March 19)
9. MtGox: Announcement regarding the applicability of us bankruptcy code chapter 15, https://www.mtgox.com/img/pdf/20140314-announcement_chapter15.pdf (Online; accessed March 19)

10. Andrychowicz, M., Dziembowski, S., Malinowski, D., Mazurek, Ł.: Fair two-party computations via the bitcoin deposits. Technical report, Cryptology ePrint Archive (2013)
11. Andrychowicz, M., Dziembowski, S., Malinowski, D., Mazurek, Ł.: How to deal with malleability of bitcoin transactions. arXiv preprint arXiv:1312.3230 (2013)
12. Back, A., Bentov, I.: Note on fair coin toss via bitcoin. arXiv preprint arXiv:1402.3698 (2014)
13. Rosenfeld, M.: Analysis of hashrate-based double spending (2012), https://bitcoil.co.il/Doublespend.pdf (Online; accessed February 17, 2014)

Election Verifiability for Helios under Weaker Trust Assumptions*

Véronique Cortier[1], David Galindo[1], Stéphane Glondu[2], and Malika Izabachène[1,3]

[1] LORIA - CNRS, France
[2] INRIA Nancy Grand Est, France
[3] École Polytechnique Féminine, France

Abstract. Most electronic voting schemes aim at providing verifiability: voters should trust the result without having to rely on some authorities. Actually, even a prominent voting system like Helios cannot fully achieve verifiability since a dishonest bulletin board may add ballots. This problem is called *ballot stuffing*.

In this paper we give a definition of verifiability in the computational model to account for a malicious bulletin board that may add ballots. Next, we provide a generic construction that transforms a voting scheme that is verifiable against an honest bulletin board and an honest registration authority (*weak verifiability*) into a verifiable voting scheme under the weaker trust assumption that the registration authority and the bulletin board are *not simultaneously* dishonest (*strong verifiability*). This construction simply adds a registration authority that sends private credentials to the voters, and publishes the corresponding public credentials.

We further provide simple and natural criteria that imply weak verifiability. As an application of these criteria, we formally prove the latest variant of Helios by Bernhard, Pereira and Warinschi weakly verifiable. By applying our generic construction we obtain a Helios-like scheme that has ballot privacy and strong verifiability (and thus prevents ballot stuffing). The resulting voting scheme, Helios-C, retains the simplicity of Helios and has been implemented and tested.

Keywords: voting protocols, individual verifiability, universal verifiability, ballot stuffing, ballot privacy, Helios.

1 Introduction

Ideally, a voting system should be both private and verifiable. Privacy ensures that no one knows that a certain voter has voted in a particular way. Verifiability ensures that voters should be able to check that, even in the presence of dishonest tallying authorities, their ballots contribute to the outcome (individual verifiability) and that the the published result corresponds to the intended votes of the voters (universal verifiability). One leading voting system designed to achieve both privacy and verifiability is Helios [1], based on a classical voting system proposed by Cramer, Gennaro and Schoenmakers [2] with variants proposed by Benaloh [3]. Helios is an open-source voting system that has

---

* The research leading to these results has received funding from the European Research Council under the European Union's Seventh Framework Programme (FP7/2007-2013) / ERC grant agreement n° 258865.

M. Kutyłowski and J. Vaidya (Eds.): ESORICS 2014, Part II, LNCS 8713, pp. 327–344, 2014.

been used several times to run real-world elections, including the election of the president of the University of Louvain-La-Neuve and the election of the 2010, 2011, and 2012 new board directors of the International Association for Cryptographic Research (IACR) [4]. Helios has been shown to ensure ballot privacy for successively stronger notions of privacy and more accurate implementations [5–7].

The remaining question is whether the result of an election run through Helios does correspond to the votes cast by the voters. Put in other words, is Helios verifiable? According to Juels, Catalano and Jakobsson (JCJ) definition [8], Helios is individually and universally verifiable[1], although we are not aware of any proof of verifiability in a computational model. In fact, Bernhard, Pereira and Warinschi (BPW) [7] showed recently that existing Helios versions [9] are not verifiable due to the use of a weak version of the Fiat-Shamir transformation in the non-interactive zero-knowledge proofs of ballot well-formedness. They showed that when the standard version of Fiat-Shamir is used, then Helios has ballot privacy but they do not prove verifiability. The forthcoming Helios version 4.0 is planned to incorporate these changes [9].

Still, JCJ's definition assumes the bulletin board to be honest: an attacker may cast dishonest ballots on the behalf of dishonest voters but no extra ballots may be added nor deleted. This means for example that the result of the election of the 2012 board of the IACR can be trusted only under the assumption that the election server was neither dishonest nor attacked, during the whole duration of the election. This is a rather unsatisfactory assumption, since adding a few extra ballots may easily change the outcome of an election. In the case of Helios, this is mitigated by the fact that voters' identities are public. If the bulletin board adds ballots, it has to tell which voters are supposed to have cast these ballots. Thus hopefully, these voters should notice that the server wrongly cast ballots on their names and would complain. Such complaints are however not guaranteed since absentees typically do not care much about the election. Things may be even worse. In some countries (like France), whether someone voted or not is a private information (that can be accessed only by voters of the same precinct, through a rather heavy procedure). It is therefore forbidden to publicly reveal the identities of the voters who cast a vote. Moreover, publishing voters identities compromises privacy in the future: once the public key of the election will be broken (say in 20 years), everyone will learn the vote of each voter. A simple alternative consists in removing the disclosure of voters' identities. This variant of Helios remains perfectly practical and of course still preserves ballot privacy. But it then becomes completely straightforward for a corrupted bulletin board to add as many ballots as needed to change the legitimate election result.

Election Verifiability under Weaker Trust Assumptions. We first provide an extension of the definition of individual and universal verifiability by Juels, Catalano and Jakobsson [8], that accounts for ballot stuffing. Throughout the paper we will sometimes use *verifiability* to refer to *individual and universal verifiability*. Intuitively, a voting scheme is *verifiable* if the result corresponds to the votes of

---

[1] JCJ uses the terms *correctness* and *verifiability*, which we rename as *individual and universal verifiability* and *tally uniqueness* respectively, as we think the latter terminology matches better the e-voting literature and it is also more accurate.

- all honest voters that have checked that their vote was cast correctly (in Helios, this amounts into checking that the encrypted vote appears on the bulletin board);
- at most n valid votes where n is the number of corrupted voters (i.e. the attacker may only use the corrupted voters to cast valid votes);
- a subset of the votes cast by honest voters that did not check their vote was cast correctly (in practice, many voters do not perform any check).

As in [8], this definition requires the tally function to admit *partial tallying* (that is, it is possible to compute the tally by blocks and then retrieve the final result). This is satisfied by most election systems, notably those consisting on counting the number of votes that every candidate from a given list received, and those whose outcome is the multiset of cast votes.

Our first main contribution is a generic construction that transforms any verifiable voting scheme that assumes both the registration authority and the bulletin board honest, into a verifiable voting scheme under the weaker trust assumption that the registration authority and the bulletin board are not *simultaneously* dishonest. We show that our transformation also turns ballot privacy and tally uniqueness (as defined in Section 3.3) w.r.t. honest bulletin board and registration authority, into ballot privacy and tally uniqueness w.r.t. non simultaneously dishonest bulletin board and registration authority. Throughout the paper we will sometimes use *strong verifiability* to refer to *individual and universal verifiability against non simultaneously dishonest bulletin board and registration authority*.

We stress that verifiability cannot come without trust assumptions: the key issue relies on the fact that some mechanism is necessary to *authenticate* voters, that is, to make sure that Bob is not voting in the name of Alice. In Helios-like protocols, the bulletin board is the only authority that controls the right to vote. It may therefore easily stuff itself, that is, it may easily add ballots. To control the bulletin board, it is necessary to consider an additional authority. In our solution, a so-called *registrar* authority, provides each voter with a private credential (actually a signing key) that has a public part (the verification key). The set of all public credentials is public and, in particular, known to the bulletin board. Then each voter simply signs his ballot with his private credential. Note that the association between a public credential and the corresponding voter's identity does not need to be known and actually, should not be disclosed to satisfy e.g. the French requirements regarding voting systems. It is also possible to have the registration authority to generate the credentials off-line and to distribute them using a non-digital channel, e.g. snail mail. This minimizes the risk of Internet-based attacks against the registration authority. We have designed our solution having in mind the guidelines set for the e-voting setup used for the expatriates at the 2012 French legislative elections [10].

The advantage of our approach relies on its simplicity: the additional authority is only responsible for generating and distributing the credentials of the voters. Once it is done, it can erase these records. It consists on one offline layer added on top of the existing voting protocol; therefore it needs not to be changed and its infrastructure is kept. In particular, our solution does not require any additional server.

We have also considered the possibility of using anonymous credentials [11]. Our preliminary conclusion discards a direct application in our transformation. This is due to the fact that anonymous credentials allow its owners to unlinkably "show" the same credential multiple times. In our case this property potentially allows a voter to vote several times without being detected, and then verifiability cannot be achieved.

Criteria for Universal Verifiability. Since proving verifiability against cheating tallying authorities, even assuming honest bulletin board and registration authority, may not be easy, we provide a simple and natural criteria that implies verifiability. We show that any *correct* and *accurate* voting protocol with *tally uniqueness* is universally verifiable (w.r.t. an honest bulletin board). Correctness accounts for the natural property that the tally of just honestly cast ballots should always yield the expected result (typically the sum of the votes). Accuracy ensures that any ballot (possibly dishonest) that passes the verification check (e.g. valid proof, well-formedness of the ballots) corresponds to a valid vote. Tally uniqueness ensures that two different results cannot be announced for a single election. Our criteria are satisfied in particular by Helios and we expect it to be satisfied by many existing voting protocols. As a result we provide the *first proof* of verifiability for the Helios-BPW voting scheme [7] in a computational model.

A Verifiable Helios-Like Scheme That Prevents Ballot Stuffing. By applying our generic construction to Helios-BPW we obtain a voting scheme, that we name as Helios with Credentials (Helios-C), which is verifiable against cheating tallying authorities under the weak assumption that the bulletin board and the registration authority are not simultaneously dishonest. Helios-C is ballot private if the tallying authority behaves honestly. We have implemented Helios-C and used it in a mock election.

Related Work. To the best of our knowledge, the only proofs of verifiability for Helios have been conducted in abstract models. Delaune, Kremer and Ryan [12] define individual and universal verifiability in a symbolic model and prove that Helios satisfy both. Like for all symbolic models, the cryptographic primitives are abstracted by terms and are not analyzed. Küsters *et al.* have put forward quantitative measurements of verifiability and accountability in [13–15] that take into account ballot stuffing. In particular, [15] gives accountability measures on several abstractions of Helios. In contrast to [15], our verifiability framework is less expressive, but on the contrary we prove verifiability in the computational model. Verifiability proofs like those of [12] and [13–15] can typically not detect flaws that on the cryptographic primitives, like those found by Bernhard, Pereira and Warinschi [7]. Groth [16] studies a generalized version of Helios in the Universal Composability framework, but it does not address universal verifiability.

2   Syntax of a Voting System

Election systems typically involve several entities. For the sake of simplicity we consider each entity to consist of only one individual but all of them could be thresholdized.

1. *Election Administrator*: Denoted by $\mathcal{E}$, is responsible for setting up the election. It publishes the identities id of eligible voters, the list of candidates and the result function ρ of the election (typically counting the number of votes every candidate received).
2. *Registrar*: Denoted by $\mathcal{R}$, is responsible for distributing secret credentials to voters and registering the corresponding public credentials.

3. *Trustee:* Denoted by $\mathcal{T}$, is in charge of tallying and publishing a final result.
4. *Voters*: The eligible voters $id_1, \ldots, id_\tau$ are participating in the election.
5. *Bulletin board manager*: Denoted by $\mathcal{B}$, is responsible for processing ballots and storing valid ballots in the bulletin board BB.

2.1 Voting Algorithms

We continue by describing the syntax for an electronic voting protocol that we will be using thorough the paper. The syntax below considers *single-pass* schemes, namely systems where voters only have to post a single message in the board. A voting protocol is always relative to a family of result functions $\mathcal{R} = \{\rho_\tau\}_{\tau \geq 1}$ for $\tau \in \mathbb{N}$, where $\rho_\tau : \mathbb{V}^\tau \to \mathbf{R}$, $\mathbf{R}$ is the result space and $\mathbb{V}$ is the set of admissible votes. A voting protocol $\mathcal{V} = $ (Setup, Credential, Vote, Validate, Box, VerifyVote, Tally, Verify) consists of eight algorithms whose syntax is as follows:

Setup(1^λ) on input a security parameter 1^λ, outputs an election public/secret pair $(\mathbf{pk}, \mathbf{sk})$, where $\mathbf{pk}$ typically contains the public key of the election and/or a list of credentials L. We assume $\mathbf{pk}$ to be an implicit input of the remaining algorithms.

Credential($1^\lambda, id$) on inputs a security parameter 1^λ and an identifier id, outputs the secret part of the credential usk_{id} and its public credential upk_{id}, where upk_{id} is added to the list $L = \{\mathsf{upk}_{id}\}$.

Vote($id, \mathsf{upk}, \mathsf{usk}, v$) is used by voter id to cast his choice $v \in \mathbb{V}$. It outputs a ballot b, which may/may not include the identifier id or the public credential upk. The ballot b is sent to the bulletin board through an authenticated channel. At some point, the voter may reach a state where he/she considers his/her vote has been counted, typically after having run the algorithm VerifyVote defined below. The voter then set CheckedVoter(id, v, b) to true.

Validate(b) on input a ballot b returns 1 for well-formed ballots and 0 otherwise.

Box(BB, b) takes as inputs the bulletin board BB and a ballot b and outputs an updated BB. Typically, this algorithm performs some checks on b with respect to the contents of BB and, possibly, a local state st. Depending on these checks, BB and st are updated; in any case BB remains unchanged if Validate(b) rejects (that is returns 0). We say that BB is well-formed if Validate(b) $= 1$ for every $b \in$ BB.

VerifyVote(BB, $id, \mathsf{upk}, \mathsf{usk}, b$) is a typically light algorithm intended to the voters, for checking that their ballots will be included in the tally. On inputs the board BB, a ballot b, and the voter's identity and credentials id, usk, upk, returns 1 or 0.

Tally(BB, $\mathbf{sk}$) takes as input the bulletin board BB and the secret key $\mathbf{sk}$. After some checks, it outputs the tally ρ, together with a proof of correct tabulation Π. Possibly, $\rho = \perp$, meaning the election has been declared invalid.

Verify(BB, ρ, Π) on inputs the bulletin board BB, and a pair (ρ, Π), checks whether Π is a valid proof of correct tallying for ρ. It returns 1 if so; otherwise it returns 0.

The exact implementation of the algorithms of course depends on the voting protocol under consideration. In Helios, the authenticated channel is instantiated by a login and a password and we have $\mathsf{upk}_{id} \in \{\emptyset, id, pid\}$ depending on the variants. $\mathsf{upk}_{id} = id$ corresponds to the standard case where the identity of the voter is appended to the ballot and displayed on the bulletin board. $\mathsf{upk}_{id} = pid$, where pid is a pseudonym on identity id, corresponds to the case where only pseudonyms are displayed, to provide more privacy to the voters. Finally, $\mathsf{upk}_{id} = \emptyset$ corresponds to the case where only the raw ballot is displayed on the bulletin board. We provide in Section 5 a complete description of the Helios protocol and our variant of it.

2.2 Correctness

Next we define the minimal requirement, called *correctness*, that any voting protocol must satisfy. It simply requires that honest executions yield the expected outcome, that is, honestly cast ballots are accepted to the BB (and pass the verification checks) and that, in an honest setting, the tally procedure always yields the expected outcome (that is, the result function). Let $\mathsf{BB} := \{\emptyset\}$. A voting scheme is *correct* if: (1) For $i \in \{1, \ldots, \tau\}$, it holds that $\mathsf{Validate}(b_i) = 1$, $\mathsf{VerifyVote}\big(\mathsf{Box}(\mathsf{BB}, b_i), id_i, \mathsf{upk}_i, \mathsf{usk}_i, b_i\big) = 1$, and $\mathsf{Box}(\mathsf{BB}, b_i) = \mathsf{BB} \cup \{b_i\}$, where $b_i \leftarrow \mathsf{Vote}(id_i, \mathsf{upk}_i, \mathsf{usk}_i, v_i)$ for some $v_i \in \mathbb{V}$; (2) $\mathsf{Tally}(\{b_1, \ldots, b_\tau\}, \mathsf{sk})$ outputs $(\rho(v_1, \ldots, v_\tau), \Pi)$; and (3) $\mathsf{Verify}(\{b_1, \ldots, b_\tau\}, \rho(v_1, \ldots, v_\tau), \Pi) = 1$. The above properties can be relaxed to hold only with overwhelming probability.

3   Verifiability Definitions

In this section we give individual and universal verifiability definitions in which the election administrator is honest, but trustee and voters are assumed to be dishonest. As emphasized in Introduction, verifiability partly relies on the authentication of the voters. There are various ways to authenticate voters, but in each case, it requires some trust assumptions. Our minimal trust assumption is that the registrar and the bulletin board are *not simultaneously* dishonest. We further define a property, that we call *tally uniqueness*, where no party is assumed be honest (except for the election administrator).

Partial Tallying. We focus on voting protocols that admit *partial tallying*. This property is specified by two natural requirements usually satisfied in most election scenarios. Firstly, the result function $\rho : \mathbb{V}^\tau \to \mathbf{R}$ for $\mathcal{V}$ must admit *partial counting*, namely $\rho(S_1 \cup S_2) = \rho(S_1) \star_{\mathbf{R}} \rho(S_2)$ for any two lists S_1, S_2 containing sequences of elements $v \in \mathbb{V}$ and where $\star_{\mathbf{R}} : \mathbf{R} \times \mathbf{R} \to \mathbf{R}$ is a commutative operation. For example, the standard result function that counts the number of votes per candidate admits partial counting. Secondly, the algorithm Tally must admit *partial tallying*, i.e. let $(\rho_1, \Pi_1) \leftarrow \mathsf{Tally}(\mathsf{BB}_1, \mathsf{sk})$ and $(\rho_2, \Pi_2) \leftarrow \mathsf{Tally}(\mathsf{BB}_2, \mathsf{sk})$. Let $(\rho, \Pi) \leftarrow \mathsf{Tally}(\mathsf{BB}_1 \cup \mathsf{BB}_2, \mathsf{sk})$ with ρ different from invalid and BB_1 and BB_2 disjoint. Then, $\rho = \rho_1 \star_{\mathbf{R}} \rho_2$, with overwhelming probability.

3.1   Strong Verifiability

We say that a voting scheme achieves *strong verifiability* if it has individual and universal verifiability under the sole trust assumption that the registrar and the bulletin board are *not simultaneously* dishonest. More formally, a voting scheme has strong verifiability if it has *verifiability against a dishonest bulletin board* and *verifiability against a dishonest registrar*. These are defined below.

Election Verifiability against a Dishonest Bulletin Board. This is an extension of security property already addressed in [8, 17]. Our novelty is that we assume the bulletin board to be possibly dishonest, and in particular it may stuff ballots in the name of voters who did never cast a vote. Of course, a verifiable protocol should forbid or at least detect such a malicious behavior.

We consider an adversary against individual and universal verifiability that is allowed to corrupt trustee, users and bulletin board. Only the registration authority is *honest*. More precisely, for the bulletin board, we let the adversary replace or delete any ballot. The adversary only looses control on the bulletin board once the voting phase ends and before the tallying starts. Indeed, at this point it is assumed that everyone has the same view of the public BB.

Let L denote the set of public credentials, $\mathcal{U}$ the set of public/secret credentials pairs, and $\mathcal{CU}$ the set of corrupted users. The adversary can query oracles $\mathcal{O}$reg, $\mathcal{O}$corrupt and $\mathcal{O}$vote. Let HVote contain triples (id, v, b) that have been output by $\mathcal{O}$vote (if voter id voted multiple times, only the last ballot is retained); while the list Checked consists of all pairs $(id, v, b) \in$ HVote such that CheckedVoter$(id, v, b) = 1$, that is, Checked corresponds to voters that have checked that their ballots will be counted (typically running VerifyVote).

- $\mathcal{O}$reg(id): invokes algorithm Credential(λ, id), it returns upk$_{id}$ and keeps usk$_{id}$ secret. It also updates the lists $L = L \cup \{$upk$_{id}\}$ and $\mathcal{U} = \mathcal{U} \cup \{(id, upk_{id}, usk_{id})\}$.
- $\mathcal{O}$corrupt(id): firstly, checks if an entry $(id, *, *)$ appears in $\mathcal{U}$; if not, stops. Else, outputs (upk$_{id}$, usk$_{id}$) and updates $\mathcal{CU} = \mathcal{CU} \cup \{(id, upk_{id})\}$.
- $\mathcal{O}$vote(id, v): if $(id, *, *) \notin \mathcal{U}$ or $(id, *) \in \mathcal{CU}$ or $v \notin \mathbb{V}$, aborts; else returns $b = $ Vote$(id, upk_{id}, usk_{id}, v)$ and replaces any previous entry $(id, *, *)$ in HVote with (id, v, b).

Any voting scheme should guarantee that the result output by Tally(BB, **sk**) counts the actual votes cast by honest voters. In particular an adversary controlling a subset of eligible voters, the trustee and the bulletin board, should not be able to alter the output of

> Experiment $\mathsf{Exp}^{\mathsf{verb}}_{\mathcal{A}, \mathcal{V}}(\lambda)$
>
> (1) $(\mathbf{pk}, \mathbf{sk}) \leftarrow$ Setup(λ)
>
> (2) $(\mathsf{BB}, \rho, \Pi) \leftarrow \mathcal{A}^{\mathcal{O}\mathsf{reg}, \mathcal{O}\mathsf{corrupt}, \mathcal{O}\mathsf{vote}}$
>
> (3) if Verify$(\mathsf{BB}, \rho, \Pi) = 0$ return 0
>
> (4) if $\rho = \perp$ return 0
>
> (5) if $\exists (id_1^A, v_1^A, *), \ldots, (id_{n_A}^A, v_{n_A}^A, *) \in$ HVote$\backslash$Checked
>
> $\qquad \exists v_1^B, \ldots, v_{n_B}^B \in \mathbb{V}$ s.t. $0 \leq n_B \leq |\mathcal{CU}|$
>
> $\qquad$ s.t. $\rho = \rho\left(\{v_i^E\}_{i=1}^{n_E}\right) \star_{\mathbf{R}} \rho\left(\{v_i^A\}_{i=1}^{n_A}\right) \star_{\mathbf{R}} \rho\left(\{v_i^B\}_{i=1}^{n_B}\right)$
>
> return 0 else return 1
>
> where Checked $= \{(id_1^E, v_1^E, b_1^E), \ldots, (id_{n_E}^E, v_{n_E}^E, b_{n_E}^E)\}$

Fig. 1. Verifiability against a malicious bulletin board

the tally so that honest votes are not counted in ρ. More precisely, verifiability against a dishonest board shall guarantee that ρ as output by the algorithm Tally actually counts:

1. votes cast by honest voters who *checked* that their ballot appeared in the bulletin board (corresponds to $\{v_i^E\}_{i=1}^{n_E}$ in Figure 1);
2. a subset of the votes cast by honest voters who *did not check* this. Indeed it can not be ensured that ρ counted their votes but it might still be the case that some of their ballots were not deleted by the adversary (corresponds to $\{v_i^A\}_{i=1}^{n_A}$ in Figure 1).
3. For corrupted voters, it is only guaranteed that the adversary cannot cast more ballots than users were corrupted, and that ballots produced by corrupted voters contribute to ρ only with admissible votes $v \in \mathbb{V}$ (corresponds to $\{v_i^B\}_{i=1}^{n_B}$).

The verifiability against a malicious board game is formally given by experiment $\mathsf{Exp}_{\mathcal{A}}^{\mathsf{verb}}$ in Figure 1. We say that a voting protocol $\mathcal{V}$ is *verifiable against a dishonest board* if there exists a negligible function $\nu(\lambda)$ such that, for any PPT adversary $\mathcal{A}$, $\mathsf{Succ}_{\mathcal{V}}^{\mathsf{verb}}(\mathcal{A}) = \Pr\left[\mathsf{Exp}_{\mathcal{A},\mathcal{V}}^{\mathsf{verb}}(\lambda) = 1\right] < \nu(\lambda)$.

Election Verifiability against a Dishonest Registration Authority. The corresponding experiment $\mathsf{Exp}_{\mathcal{A},\mathcal{V}}^{\mathsf{verg}}$ defining verifiability against a malicious registration authority and malicious trustee and voters, but honest bulletin board, is very similar to the experiment in Figure 1. The adversary has access to oracles $\mathcal{O}\mathsf{vote}(id, v)$ and $\mathcal{O}\mathsf{corrupt}(id)$ as before, and is additionally given access to an oracle $\mathcal{O}\mathsf{cast}(id, b)$, which runs $\mathsf{Box}(\mathsf{BB}, b)$. This models the fact that the adversary cannot delete nor add ballots anymore since the bulletin box is now honest. However, the adversary is not given in this experiment access to the $\mathcal{O}\mathsf{reg}$ oracle, since it controls the registrar and thus can register users arbitrarily, even with malicious credentials. The adversary uses $\mathcal{O}\mathsf{corrupt}(id)$ to define voter id as a corrupted user, i.e. voter id's actions are under the control of the adversary.

In $\mathsf{Exp}_{\mathcal{A},\mathcal{V}}^{\mathsf{verg}}$, the adversary does not output BB, since the bulletin board is honest. Note that a dishonest registration authority may prevent some voters from voting by providing wrong credentials. Depending on the protocol, voters may not notice it, therefore some honestly cast ballots may be discarded.

We say that $\mathcal{V}$ is *verifiable against a dishonest registration authority* if there exists a negligible function $\nu(\lambda)$ such that, $\mathsf{Succ}_{\mathcal{V}}^{\mathsf{verg}}(\mathcal{A}) = \Pr\left[\mathsf{Exp}_{\mathcal{A},\mathcal{V}}^{\mathsf{verg}}(\lambda) = 1\right] < \nu(\lambda)$, for any PPT adversary $\mathcal{A}$.

3.2 Weak Verifiability

We say that a voting scheme has *weak verifiability* if it has individual and universal verifiability assuming that the bulletin board and the registration authority are *both* honest. That is, an adversary in the weak verifiability game can only corrupt a subset of voters and the trustee.

The experiment $\mathsf{Exp}_{\mathcal{A},\mathcal{V}}^{\mathsf{verw}}$ defining *weak verifiability*, is a variation of the experiment $\mathsf{Exp}_{\mathcal{A},\mathcal{V}}^{\mathsf{verg}}$. In this case, the adversary can only add ballots to the box via $\mathcal{O}\mathsf{cast}$ (so it cannot stuff the ballot box nor delete ballots). The adversary is only allowed to register voters through $\mathcal{O}$reg, and can only access voters' secret credentials by calling the $\mathcal{O}$corrupt oracle. We say that a voting protocol $\mathcal{V}$ is *weakly verifiable* if there exists a negligible function $\nu(\lambda)$ such that, $\mathsf{Succ}_{\mathcal{V}}^{\mathsf{verw}}(\mathcal{A}) = \Pr\left[\mathsf{Exp}_{\mathcal{A},\mathcal{V}}^{\mathsf{verw}}(\lambda) = 1\right] < \nu(\lambda)$, for any PPT adversary $\mathcal{A}$.

3.3 Tally Uniqueness

In addition to verifiability, Juels, Catalano and Jakobsson [8], as well as Delaune, Kremer and Ryan [12], put forward the notion of *tally uniqueness*. Tally uniqueness of a voting protocol ensures that the tally of an election is unique. In other words, two different tallies $\rho \neq \rho'$ can not be accepted by the verification algorithm, even if all the players in the system are malicious.

More formally, the goal of the adversary against tally uniqueness is to output a public key $\mathbf{pk}$, that contains a list of public credentials, a bulletin board BB, and two tallies $\rho \neq \rho'$, and corresponding proofs of valid tabulation Π and Π', such that both pass verification, i.e. $\mathsf{Verify}(\mathsf{BB}, \rho, \Pi) = \mathsf{Verify}(\mathsf{BB}, \rho', \Pi') = 1$. A voting protocol $\mathcal{V}$ has *tally uniqueness* if every PPT adversary $\mathcal{A}$ has a negligible advantage in this game.

Intuitively, verifiability ensures that the tally corresponds to a plausible instantiations of the players (onto property) while tally uniqueness ensures that, given a tally, there is at most one plausible instantiation (one-to-one property).

4 Sufficient Conditions for Verifiability

In this section we identify sufficient conditions for (individual and universal) verifiability in single-pass voting protocols. In the first place, Section 4.1, we define a property for voting protocols, that we call *accuracy*, and we show that it implies weak verifiability. As explained in the introduction, weak verifiability is not a completely satisfactory property, but it is the highest verifiability level that can be achieved in remote voting systems where the only the bulletin board authenticates voters and therefore it can easily stuff itself. This is notably the case for Helios [9]. Nevertheless, we give in Section 4.3 a generic construction that transforms a voting protocol that has weak verifiability, into a voting protocol that has strong verifiability, namely it is verifiable under the weaker trust assumption that the registrar and the board are *not simultaneously* dishonest.

4.1 Accuracy

We introduce a property for voting protocols that is called *accuracy*. We say that a voting protocol $\mathcal{V}$ has *accuracy* (equivalently it is accurate) if for any ballot b it holds with overwhelming probability that

1. ($\mathsf{Validate}(b) = 1 \;\wedge\; \mathsf{Verify}(\{b\}, \rho_b, \Pi_b) = 1$) $\implies \rho_b = \rho(v_b)$ for some $v_b \in \mathbb{V}$
2. $\mathsf{Verify}\left(\mathsf{BB}, \mathsf{Tally}(\mathsf{BB}, \mathbf{sk})\right) = 1$ for any bulletin board BB

Condition 1 reflects the natural requirement that even a dishonest ballot that passes the validity test corresponds to an admissible vote. In Helios-like protocols, this is typically ensured by requiring the voter to produce a proof that the encrypted vote belongs to $\mathbb{V}$. Condition 2 guarantees that the proof produced by a faithful run of the tally procedure passes the verification test. In practice, this property usually holds by design.

4.2 A Sufficient Condition for Weak Verifiability

We show that correctness (Section 2.2), accuracy (Section 4.1) and tally uniqueness (Section 3.3) suffice to ensure weak verifiability against a dishonest tallying authority. Since these properties are simple and easy to check, this result may often ease the proof of verifiability. We illustrate this fact by using these criteria to give in Section 5 a simple proof that Helios-BPW is weakly verifiable.

Theorem 1. *Let $\mathcal{V}$ be a correct, accurate and tally unique voting protocol that admits partial tallying. Then $\mathcal{V}$ satisfies weak verifiability.*

The proof is given in the full version [18].

Signature Schemes with Verification Uniqueness. We aim at designing a generic construction that provides strong verifiability. Our construction relies on an existentially-unforgeable (EUF-CMA) signature scheme as a building block, whose syntax and properties are given next.

Definition 1 (Signature scheme). *A signature scheme consists of three algorithms $\mathcal{S} =$ (SKey, Sign, SVerify), such that*

- SKey(1^λ) *outputs a pair of verification/signing keys* (upk, usk).
- Sign(usk, m) *on inputs a signing key* usk *and a message m outputs a signature σ.*
- SVerify(upk, m, σ) *on inputs a verification key* upk, *a message m and a string σ, outputs 0/1, meaning invalid/valid signature.*

A signature scheme must satisfy correctness, *namely* SVerify(upk, m, Sign(usk, m)) $=$ 1 *with overwhelming probability, where* (upk, usk) $\leftarrow$ SKey(1^λ).

We further need to control the behaviour of the signature scheme when keys are (dishonestly) chosen outside the expected range. More precisely, we need to ensure that the output of SVerify(upk, m, σ) is deterministic, even for inputs outside the corresponding domains. We call this *verification uniqueness*.

4.3 A Sufficient Condition for Strong Verifiability

We provide a generic construction that protects any voting scheme that has weak verifiability, that is assuming that the bulletin board and registrar are *both* honest, into a voting scheme that has string verifiability, that is under the weaker assumption that board and registrar are *not simultaneously* dishonest.

Let $\mathcal{V} = (\mathsf{Setup'}, \mathsf{Credential'}, \mathsf{Vote'}, \mathsf{VerifyVote'}, \mathsf{Validate'}, \mathsf{Box'}, \mathsf{Tally'}, \mathsf{Verify'})$ be a voting protocol, possibly without credentials, like Helios. Our generic construction transforms $\mathcal{V}$ into $\mathcal{V}^{\mathsf{cred}}$ as follows. We first require the registration authority to create a public/secret credential pair $(\mathsf{upk}, \mathsf{usk})$ for each voter. Each key pair corresponds to a *credential* needed to cast a vote. The association between credentials and voters does not need to be publicly known and only the unordered list of verification keys (the public credentials) is published. In the resulting voting scheme $\mathcal{V}^{\mathsf{cred}}$, every player acts as in $\mathcal{V}$ except that now, each voter further signs his/her ballot with his/her signing key usk. Moreover, the bulletin board, upon receiving a ballot, performs the usual checks and further verifies the signature (that should correspond to one of the official verification keys). The board also needs to maintain an internal state st that links successful voters' authentications with successful signature verifications, i.e. it keeps links (id, upk_{id}). This is needed to prevent a dishonest voter id', who has gained knowledge of several secret credentials $\mathsf{usk}_1, \ldots, \mathsf{usk}_t$, from stuffing/overriding the board with ballots containing the corresponding public credentials $\mathsf{upk}_1, \ldots, \mathsf{upk}_t$. We call this a *multiple impersonation attack*. Our generic transformation is summarized in Figure 2.

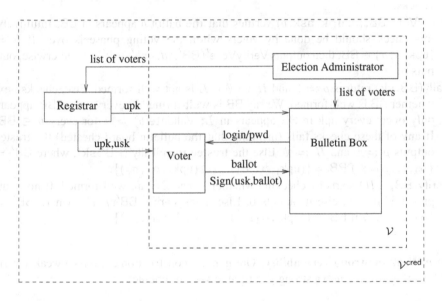

Fig. 2. Generic construction for strong verifiability

Formally, let $\mathcal{S} = (\mathsf{SKey}, \mathsf{Sign}, \mathsf{SVerify})$ be a signature scheme. Let us consider $\mathcal{V}^{\mathsf{cred}} = (\mathsf{Setup}, \mathsf{Credential}, \mathsf{Vote}, \mathsf{Validate}, \mathsf{Box}, \mathsf{VerifyVote}, \mathsf{Tally}, \mathsf{Verify})$ the voting protocol with credentials obtained from $\mathcal{V}$ and $\mathcal{S}$ as follows:

$\mathsf{Setup}(1^\lambda)$ runs $(\mathbf{pk'}, \mathbf{sk'}) \leftarrow \mathsf{Setup'}(1^\lambda)$ and sets $\mathbf{pk} \leftarrow (\mathbf{pk'}, L), \mathbf{sk} \leftarrow \mathbf{sk'}$, where L is a list initialized to empty that is defined below. Let us recall that $\mathbf{pk'}$ potentially contains a list L' of public credentials inherited from $\mathcal{V'}$. Returns $(\mathbf{pk}, \mathbf{sk})$. We say that L is *ill-formed* if $|L| > \tau$, (i.e. there are more public credentials than eligible voters) or if L has repeated elements.

Credential$(1^\lambda, id)$ is run by the registrar and computes $(\text{upk}, \text{usk}) \leftarrow \text{SKey}(1^\lambda)$; the bulletin board computes $(\text{upk}', \text{usk}') \leftarrow \text{Credential}'(1^\lambda, id)$. The list L is updated as $L \leftarrow L \cup \{\text{upk}\}$. Next, $\mathbf{upk} \leftarrow (\text{upk}, \text{upk}')$ and $\mathbf{usk} \leftarrow (\text{usk}, \text{usk}')$ are returned.

Vote$(id, \mathbf{upk}, \mathbf{usk}, v)$ runs $\alpha \leftarrow \text{Vote}'(id, \text{upk}', \text{usk}', v)$, $\sigma \leftarrow \text{Sign}(\text{usk}, \alpha)$ and returns a ballot $b \leftarrow (\text{upk}, \alpha, \sigma)$, which is sent to the bulletin board through an authenticated channel[2].

Validate(b) parses $b = (\text{upk}, \alpha, \sigma)$. If $\text{SVerify}(\text{upk}, \alpha, \sigma) \neq 1$ outputs 0. Else, outputs Validate'(α).

Box(BB, b) parses $b = (\text{upk}, \alpha, \sigma)$ after a successful authentication, by voter id with credentials $(\text{upk}', \text{usk}')$, to the bulletin board. BB is let unchanged if $\text{upk} \notin L$, or if Validate(b) rejects. Next (1) if an entry of the form $(id, *)$ or $(*, \text{upk})$ exists in its local state st, then: (1.a) if $(id, \text{upk}) \in st$ and $\alpha \in \text{Box}'(\text{BB}', \alpha)$ (BB' is updated with α), then removes any ballot in BB containing upk, updates $\text{BB} \leftarrow \text{BB} \cup \{b\}$, and returns BB; (1.b) else, returns BB. Otherwise, (2) adds (id, upk) to st, and (2.a) if $\alpha \in \text{Box}'(\text{BB}', \alpha)$, adds b to BB, and returns BB; else (2.b) returns BB. The checks in Steps (1) and (2) are performed to prevent multiple impersonation attacks.

VerifyVote$(\text{BB}, id, \mathbf{upk}, \mathbf{usk}, b)$ verifies that the ballot b appears in BB. Intuitively, this check should be done by voters when the voting phase is over. If $b = (\text{upk}, \alpha, \sigma) \in \text{BB}$, then outputs VerifyVote'$(\text{BB}', id, \text{upk}', \text{usk}', \alpha)$. Otherwise, outputs 0.

Tally$(\text{BB}, \mathbf{sk})$ returns $\rho := \perp$ and $\Pi := \emptyset$ if L is not well-formed. Else, checks next whether BB is well-formed. We say BB is well-formed if: every upk in BB appears only once; every upk in BB appears in L; Validate$(b) = 1$ for every $b \in \text{BB}$. If any of these checks fails (meaning that the bulletin board cheated) the trustee outputs $\rho := \perp$ and $\Pi := \emptyset$. Else the trustee runs Tally'$(\text{BB}', \mathbf{sk})$, where $\text{BB}' = \{\alpha_1, \ldots, \alpha_\tau\}$ if $\text{BB} = \{(\text{upk}_1, \alpha_1, \sigma_1), \ldots, (\text{upk}_\tau, \alpha_\tau, \sigma_\tau)\}$.

Verify(BB, ρ, Π) starts by checking whether L and BB are well-formed. If not, outputs 1 if $\rho = \perp$; else it outputs 0. Else, runs Verify'(BB', ρ, Π), where $\text{BB}' = \{\alpha_1, \ldots, \alpha_\tau\}$ if $\text{BB} = \{(\text{upk}_1, \alpha_1, \sigma_1), \ldots, (\text{upk}_\tau, \alpha_\tau, \sigma_\tau)\}$.

From Weak to Strong Verifiability. Our generic construction converts a weakly verifiable voting scheme into a strongly verifiable voting scheme.

Theorem 2. *Let $\mathcal{V}$ be a voting protocol that satisfies weak verifiability, admits partial tallying and satisfies tally uniqueness. Let $\mathcal{S}$ be an existentially unforgeable signature scheme. Then $\mathcal{V}^{\text{cred}}$ satisfies strong verifiability.*

Proof. It is a consequence of Lemma 1 and Lemma 2 below.

Lemma 1. *Let $\mathcal{V}$ satisfy weak verifiability and tally uniqueness. Let $\mathcal{S}$ be an existentially unforgeable signature scheme. Then $\mathcal{V}^{\text{cred}}$ has verifiability against a dishonest bulletin board.*

---

[2] This channel is built around the credential information $(id, \text{upk}', \text{usk}')$.

This lemma is proven by showing that any adversary against the verifiability of $\mathcal{V}^{cred}$, controlling the bulletin board, is "as powerful" as any adversary against the weak verifiability of $\mathcal{V}$, unless it can break the existential unforgeability of the signature scheme $\mathcal{S}$. The proof is given in the full version [18].

Lemma 2. *Let $\mathcal{V}$ be weakly verifiable and tally unique. Then $\mathcal{V}^{cred}$ has verifiability against a dishonest registrar.*

Note that Lemma 2 relies on the weak verifiability of the voting scheme. Indeed, if the registrar is dishonest, it has all the credentials. Therefore only the bulletin board may prevent him from stuffing the box. Typically, weakly verifiable schemes assume an authenticated channel between the voters and the box, e.g. using some password-based authentication mechanism. This simple proof is given in the full version [18].

Theorem 3. *If $\mathcal{V}$ satisfies tally uniqueness and $\mathcal{S}$ satisfies verification uniqueness, then $\mathcal{V}^{cred}$ preserves tally uniqueness.*

Our transformation also preserves ballot privacy. Intuitively, this is due to the fact that our transformation of the original protocol does not significantly change the behaviour of the underlying voting scheme. In particular, every valid ballot produced by our transformed voting scheme corresponds to a valid ballot in the original voting scheme, and viceversa. In the full version of this work we give a proof of ballot privacy using the game-based game definition from [7]. The reduction is straightforward and there are no technical difficulties involved.

Theorem 4. *If $\mathcal{V}$ satisfies privacy then $\mathcal{V}^{cred}$ satisfies privacy.*

5   Helios-C : Helios with Credentials

In this section we modify the design of Helios 4.0 voting system [9]. Actually, the current version does not ensure ballot privacy due to the fact that dishonest voters may duplicate ballots [5]. We therefore consider a slight modification of Helios 4.0 that includes weeding of duplicate ballots and that has been proved secure w.r.t. ballot privacy [7]. We aim at achieving (individual and universal) verifiability under a weaker trust assumption. Our modification consists in adding (verifiable) credentials to prevent ballot stuffing. We name it Helios-C, as a shortening for Helios with Credentials. For readability, we describe Helios for a single choice election (voters may simply vote 0 or 1). It can be easily generalized to elections with several candidates. We assume an authenticated channel between each voter and the bulletin board. This is typically realized in Helios through password-based authentication.

We use the ElGamal [19] IND-CPA cryptosystem $\mathcal{D} = (\mathsf{KeyGen}, \mathsf{Enc}, \mathsf{Dec})$ in a given group $\mathbb{G}$ where the Decisional Diffie-Hellman assumption holds; the Schnorr signature scheme $\mathcal{S} = (\mathsf{SKeyGen}, \mathsf{Sign}, \mathsf{SVerify})$ [20] over the group $\mathbb{G}$; the NIZK proof system [21, 22] $\mathsf{DisjProof}_H(g, \mathsf{pk}, R, S)$ to prove in zero-knowledge that (R, S) encrypts g^0 or g^1 (with proof builder $\mathsf{DisjProve}$ and proof verifier $\mathsf{DisjVerify}$); and the NIZK proof system [21] $\mathsf{EqDl}_G(g, R, \mathsf{vk}, c)$ to prove in zero-knowledge that $\log_g \mathsf{vk} =$

$\log_R c$ for $g, R, \mathsf{vk}, c \in \mathbb{G}$ (with proof builder PrEq and proof verifier VerifyEq). H and G are hash functions mapping to $\mathbb{Z}_q$.

Formally, Helios-C consists of eight algorithms $\mathcal{V}^{\mathsf{heliosc}} = (\mathsf{Setup}, \mathsf{Credential}, \mathsf{Vote}, \mathsf{Validate}, \mathsf{VerifyVote}, \mathsf{Box}, \mathsf{Tally}, \mathsf{Verify})$ defined below:

$\mathsf{Setup}(1^\lambda)$ chooses $\mathbb{G}$ a cyclic group of order q and $g \in \mathbb{G}$ a generator. It randomly chooses $\mathsf{sk} \xleftarrow{R} \mathbb{Z}_q$ and sets $\mathsf{pk} = g^{\mathsf{sk}}$. Hash functions $G, H : \{0,1\}^* \to \mathbb{Z}_q$ are chosen. It outputs $\mathbf{pk} \leftarrow (\mathbb{G}, q, \mathsf{pk}, L, G, H, \mathbb{V} = \{0,1\})$, the public key of the election and $\mathbf{sk} = (\mathbf{pk}, \mathsf{sk})$, with L initialized as the empty set.

$\mathsf{Credential}(1^\lambda, id, L)$ generates a signing key pair for each voter. It runs $(\mathsf{upk}, \mathsf{usk}) \leftarrow \mathsf{SKeyGen}(1^\lambda)$. It adds upk to L and outputs $(\mathsf{upk}, \mathsf{usk})$.

$\mathsf{Vote}\,(id, \mathsf{upk}, \mathsf{usk}, v)$ it is used by a voter of identity id with credentials $(\mathsf{upk}, \mathsf{usk})$ to create a ballot b corresponding to vote v as follows:
  (1) Encrypts $v \in \{0,1\}$ as $C = \mathsf{Enc}(\mathsf{pk}, g^v) = (R, S)$. Computes a proof $\pi = \mathsf{DisjProve}_H(g, \mathsf{pk}, R, S, r)$ showing that the encrypted vote is 0 or 1.
  (2) Computes $\sigma \leftarrow \mathsf{Sign}(\mathsf{usk}, (C, \pi))$, namely a signature on the ciphertext and its proof. The ballot is defined as $b = (\mathsf{upk}, (C, \pi), \sigma)$.
  (3) The voter submits the ballot b by authenticating itself to the bulletin board.

$\mathsf{Validate}(b)$ checks that the ballot is *valid*, that is, that all proofs are correct. Formally, it parses the ballot b as $(\mathsf{upk}, (C, \pi), \sigma)$. It then checks whether: (1) $\mathsf{upk} \in L$; (2) $\mathsf{DisjVerify}_H(g, \mathsf{pk}, C, \pi) = 1$; (4) $\mathsf{SVerify}(\mathsf{upk}, \sigma, (C, \pi))$ accepts. If any step fails, it returns 0; else it returns 1.

$\mathsf{VerifyVote}(id, \mathsf{upk}, \mathsf{usk}, b)$ returns the value of the test $b \in \mathsf{BB}$.

$\mathsf{Box}(\mathsf{BB}, b)$ parses $b = (\mathsf{upk}, (C, \pi), \sigma)$ after a successful authentication from a voter id. BB is let unchanged if $\mathsf{upk} \notin L$, or $\mathsf{Validate}(b)$ rejects or C appears previously in BB. Next, (1) if an entry of the form $(id, *)$ or $(*, \mathsf{upk})$ exists in its local state st, then: (1.a) if $(id, \mathsf{upk}) \in st$, removes any previous ballot in BB containing upk, updates $\mathsf{BB} \leftarrow \mathsf{BB} \cup \{b\}$ and returns BB; (1.b) else, returns BB. Otherwise, (2) adds (id, upk) to st, updates $\mathsf{BB} \leftarrow \mathsf{BB} \cup \{b\}$ and returns BB.

$\mathsf{Tally}(\mathsf{BB}, \mathbf{sk})$ consists of the following steps:
  (1) Runs $\mathsf{Validate}(b)$ for every $b \in \mathsf{BB}$. Outputs $\rho = \bot$ and $\Pi = \emptyset$ if any such b is rejected.
  (2) Parses each ballot $b \in \mathsf{BB}$ as $(\mathsf{upk}_b, (C_b, \pi_b), \sigma_b)$.
  (3) Checks whether upk_b appears in a previous entry in BB or whether $\mathsf{upk}_b \notin L$. If so, outputs $\rho = \bot$ and $\Pi = \emptyset$. Else,
  (4) Computes the result ciphertext $C_\Sigma = (R_\Sigma, S_\Sigma) = (\prod_{b \in \mathsf{BB}} R_b, \prod_{b \in \mathsf{BB}} S_b)$, where $C_b = (R_b, S_b)$. This of course relies on the homomorphic property of the El Gamal encryption scheme.
  (5) Computes $g^\rho \leftarrow S_\Sigma \cdot (R_\Sigma)^{-\mathsf{sk}}$. Then ρ to be published is obtained from g^ρ in time $\sqrt{\tau}$ for ρ lying in the interval $[0, \tau]$ and τ equals the number of legitimate voters.
  (6) Finally $\Pi := \mathsf{PrEq}_G\left(g, \mathsf{pk}, R_\Sigma, S_\Sigma \cdot (g^\rho)^{-1}, \mathsf{sk}\right)$.

$\mathsf{Verify}(\mathsf{BB}, \rho, \Pi)$

(1) Performs the checks (1-3) done in Tally. If any of the checks fails, then returns 0 unless the result is itself $\perp$, in which case outputs 1. Else,

(2) Computes the result ciphertext $(R_\Sigma, S_\Sigma) = \left(\prod_{b \in \mathsf{BB}} R_b, \prod_{b \in \mathsf{BB}} S_b \right)$.

(3) Returns the output of $\mathsf{VerifyEq}_G \left(g, \mathsf{pk}, R_\Sigma, S_\Sigma \cdot (g^\rho)^{-1}, \Pi \right)$.

Theorem 5. *Helios-C has tally uniqueness, strong verifiability and ballot privacy under the Decisional Diffie-Hellman assumption in the Random Oracle Model.*

Since Helios-C = Helios-BPW^{cred} and the Schnorr signature scheme is EUF-CMA in the Random Oracle Model under the Discrete Logarithm assumption in $\mathbb{G}$, Theorem 2 (Section 4.3) allows to deduce the strong verifiability of Helios-C from the weak verifiability of Helios-BPW. Finally, since Helios-BPW has ballot privacy under the DDH assumption in the Random Oracle Model (Theorem 3 in [7]), then Helios-C has ballot privacy under the same assumptions.

Theorem 6. *Helios-BPW is weakly verifiable under the Discrete Logarithm assumption in the Random Oracle Model.*

Proof. We need to show that Helios-BPW is correct, accurate and has tally uniqueness thanks to Theorem 1. We omit the proof of correctness for Helios-BPW since it easily follows from the correctness of the involved primitives, i.e. the ElGamal cryptosystem, Schnorr signature and NIZKs.

Let us show that Helios-BPW has tally uniqueness, where Helios-BPW = (Setup', Vote', Validate', VerifyVote', Box', Tally,' Verify'). The output of Verify' is determined by the outputs of the verification tests of the NIZK systems DisjProof$_H$ and EqDl$_G$, which constitute proof of memberships to the corresponding languages with negligible error probability, and hence the output of Verify' is unique on his inputs.

With respect to the accuracy of Helios-BPW, we need to show that for any ballot b it holds that if Validate'$(b) = 1$ and Verify'$(\{b\}, \rho_b, \Pi_b) = 1$, then $\rho_b = \rho(v_b)$ for some $v_b \in \mathbb{V}$. Let $\alpha = (C, \pi)$ be such that DisjVerify$(g, \mathsf{pk}, C, \pi) = 1$. Since DisjProof$_H$ is a NIZK obtained by applying Fiat-Shamir to a Σ-protocol [23], then DisjProof$_H$ is a proof that $(g, \mathsf{pk}, R_b, S_b) \in \mathcal{L}_{\mathsf{EqDl}}$ or $(g, \mathsf{pk}, R_b, S_b \cdot g^{-1}) \in \mathcal{L}_{\mathsf{EqDl}}$ with soundness error $1/q$. In other words, if Validate'$(b) = 1$ and Verify'$(\{b\}, \rho_b, \Pi_b) = 1$, then $v_b \in \{0, 1\}$ with overwhelming probability. This proves accuracy of Helios-BPW. $\square$

6 Implementation

We have implemented a proof of concept of Helios-C, openly accessible at [24], and tested it in a mock election in our lab.

In Helios-C credentials are generated by a third-party provider and sent to the voters by snail mail. Clearly, it would be cumbersome for voters to copy their signature key by typing it. We used a trick that consists in sending only the random seed used for generating the key, which can be encoded in about 12-15 alphanumeric characters depending on the desired entropy. It is expected that this seed is used by the provider to add the generated public key to L, then sent (as a password) to its rightful recipient and immediately destroyed.

candidates	2	5	10	20	30	50
enc+proofs	600	1197	2138	4059	6061	9617
sign	196	215	248	301	358	484
sig verif	< 10	< 10	< 10	< 10	< 10	< 10
ballot verif	110	210	390	720	1070	1730

Fig. 3. Overhead in miliseconds induced by adding credentials to Helios

Our variant of Helios requires voters to additionally sign their ballots. Table 3 shows the overhead induced by the signature, for various numbers of candidates (from 2 to 50). The two first lines are timings on the client side: the first one indicates the time needed by the voter's browser to form the ballot (without signature) while the second line indicates the computation time for signing. The third and fourth lines indicate the computation time on the server side for performing the verification tests (well-formedness of the ballot, validity of the proofs of knowledge and validity of the signature). Since the ballot includes the public key of the voter, the server simply needs to verify one signature for each ballot and to verify that the public keys indeed belongs to the set of authorized keys, which can be done in logarithmic time. We use a 256-bit multiplicative subgroup of a 2048-bit prime field for ElGamal and Schnorr operations. The figures have been obtained on a computer with an Intel(R) Core(TM) i7-2600 CPU @ 3.40GHz, running Firefox 18. Unsurprisingly, the overhead of the signature is small compared to the computation time of the whole ballot.

We have tested our implementation in a mock election in June 2013, among approximately 30 voters. The result of the election and in particular all its public data (including ballots) can be found at [24].

In practice, it is also needed to provide a password/credential recovery procedure in case voters lose their credentials. In case revoting is authorized, we further assume that the registrar keeps the link between users and public credentials during the election so that the old (lost) credential can be erased from the authorized list.

7   Conclusion

We have presented a generic construction that enforces strong verifiability. Applied to Helios, the resulting system Helios-C prevents ballot stuffing, still retaining the simplicity of Helios, as demonstrated by our test election, under the trust assumption that registrar and bulletin board are *not simultaneously* dishonest. For simplicity, we have presented our framework for a single vote (yes/no vote) and for a single trustee. All our results can be easily extended to multiple candidates elections and multiple trustees, possibly with threshold decryption as described in [25].

We would like to point out a more appealing variant of our transformation from a theoretical point of view. In this variant, voters generate their individual credentials (i.e. a signing key pair) by themselves. Thus a malicious registrar cannot sign on behalf of honest users, as it would only be responsible of registering credentials for eligible voters. We think, however, that letting the registrar generate credentials on behalf of voters, as we do in Helios-C, is a more practical choice: most voters will not have the required knowledge to perform the critical procedure of generating credentials with a minimum of security guarantees.

Even if most ballot counting functions admit partial tallying, especially for practical counting functions, some functions do not admit partial tallying, like the majority function. As future work, we plan to investigate whether we can devise a definition of verifiability for schemes that do not admit partial tallying.

Strong verifiability of Helios-C assumes that either the registration authority or the ballot box is honest. We could further thresholdize the registration authority, by distributing each credential among several registrars. We plan to explore the possibility to go further and design a (practical) voting scheme that offers verifiability without any trust assumption (like vote by hand-rising), and ballot privacy under some trust assumptions, like the fact that some of the authorities are honest.

References

1. Adida, B., de Marneffe, O., Pereira, O., Quisquater, J.J.: Electing a university president using open-audit voting: Analysis of real-world use of Helios. In: Proceedings of the 2009 Conference on Electronic Voting Technology/Workshop on Trustworthy Elections (2009)
2. Cramer, R., Gennaro, R., Schoenmakers, B.: A secure and optimally efficient multi-authority election scheme. In: Fumy, W. (ed.) Advances in Cryptology - EUROCRYPT 1997. LNCS, vol. 1233, pp. 103–118. Springer, Heidelberg (1997)
3. Benaloh, J.: Ballot casting assurance via voter-initiated poll station auditing. In: Proceedings of the Second Usenix/ACCURATE Electronic Voting Technology Workshop (2007)
4. International association for cryptologic research, Elections page at http://www.iacr.org/elections/
5. Cortier, V., Smyth, B.: Attacking and fixing Helios: An analysis of ballot secrecy. In: CSF, pp. 297–311. IEEE Computer Society (2011)
6. Bernhard, D., Cortier, V., Pereira, O., Smyth, B., Warinschi, B.: Adapting Helios for provable ballot secrecy. In: Atluri, V., Diaz, C. (eds.) ESORICS 2011. LNCS, vol. 6879, pp. 335–354. Springer, Heidelberg (2011)
7. Bernhard, D., Pereira, O., Warinschi, B.: How not to prove yourself: Pitfalls of the Fiat-Shamir heuristic and applications to Helios. In: Wang, X., Sako, K. (eds.) ASIACRYPT 2012. LNCS, vol. 7658, pp. 626–643. Springer, Heidelberg (2012)
8. Juels, A., Catalano, D., Jakobsson, M.: Coercion-resistant electronic elections. In: Chaum, D., Jakobsson, M., Rivest, R.L., Ryan, P.Y.A., Benaloh, J., Kutylowski, M., Adida, B. (eds.) Towards Trustworthy Elections. LNCS, vol. 6000, pp. 37–63. Springer, Heidelberg (2010)
9. Adida, B., de Marneffe, O., Pereira, O.: Helios voting system, http://www.heliosvoting.org
10. Pinault, T., Courtade, P.: E-voting at expatriates' MPs elections in France. In: Kripp, M.J., Volkamer, M., Grimm, R. (eds.) Electronic Voting. LNI, vol. 205, pp. 189–195. GI (2012)
11. Camenisch, J., Lysyanskaya, A.: An efficient system for non-transferable anonymous credentials with optional anonymity revocation. In: Pfitzmann, B. (ed.) EUROCRYPT 2001. LNCS, vol. 2045, pp. 93–118. Springer, Heidelberg (2001)
12. Delaune, S., Kremer, S., Ryan, M.D., Steel, G.: A formal analysis of authentication in the TPM. In: Degano, P., Etalle, S., Guttman, J. (eds.) FAST 2010. LNCS, vol. 6561, pp. 111–125. Springer, Heidelberg (2011)
13. Küsters, R., Truderung, T., Vogt, A.: Accountability: definition and relationship to verifiability. In: Al-Shaer, E., Keromytis, A.D., Shmatikov, V. (eds.) ACM Conference on Computer and Communications Security, pp. 526–535. ACM (2010)

14. Küsters, R., Truderung, T., Vogt, A.: Verifiability, privacy, and coercion-resistance: New insights from a case study. In: IEEE Symposium on Security and Privacy, pp. 538–553. IEEE Computer Society (2011)
15. Küsters, R., Truderung, T., Vogt, A.: Clash attacks on the verifiability of e-voting systems. In: IEEE Symposium on Security and Privacy, pp. 395–409. IEEE Computer Society (2012)
16. Groth, J.: Evaluating security of voting schemes in the universal composability framework. In: Jakobsson, M., Yung, M., Zhou, J. (eds.) ACNS 2004. LNCS, vol. 3089, pp. 46–60. Springer, Heidelberg (2004)
17. Juels, A., Catalano, D., Jakobsson, M.: Coercion-resistant electronic elections. In: Atluri, V., di Vimercati, S.D.C., Dingledine, R. (eds.) WPES, pp. 61–70. ACM (2005)
18. Cortier, V., Galindo, D., Glondu, S., Izabachène, M.: Election verifiability for Helios under weaker trust assumptions. HAL - INRIA Archive Ouverte/Open Archive, Research Report RR-8855 (2014), http://hal.inria.fr/hal-01011294
19. Gamal, T.E.: A public key cryptosystem and a signature scheme based on discrete logarithms. IEEE Transactions on Information Theory 31(4), 469–472 (1985)
20. Schnorr, C.P.: Efficient signature generation by smart cards. J. Cryptology 4(3), 161–174 (1991)
21. Chaum, D., Pedersen, T.P.: Wallet databases with observers. In: Brickell, E.F. (ed.) Advances in Cryptology - CRYPTO 1992. LNCS, vol. 740, pp. 89–105. Springer, Heidelberg (1993)
22. Cramer, R., Damgård, I.B., Schoenmakers, B.: Proofs of partial knowledge and simplified design of witness hiding protocols. In: Desmedt, Y.G. (ed.) Advances in Cryptology - CRYPTO 1994. LNCS, vol. 839, pp. 174–187. Springer, Heidelberg (1994)
23. Hazay, C., Lindell, Y.: Efficient Secure Two-Party Protocols - Techniques and Constructions. Information Security and Cryptography. Springer (2010)
24. Glondu, S.: Helios with Credentials: Proof of concept and mock election results, http://stephane.glondu.net/helios/
25. Cortier, V., Galindo, D., Glondu, S., Izabachène, M.: Distributed ElGamal à la Pedersen: Application to Helios. In: Sadeghi, A.R., Foresti, S. (eds.) WPES, pp. 131–142. ACM (2013)

CoinShuffle: Practical Decentralized Coin Mixing for Bitcoin

Tim Ruffing, Pedro Moreno-Sanchez, and Aniket Kate

MMCI, Saarland University
{tim.ruffing,pedro,aniket}@mmci.uni-saarland.de

Abstract. The decentralized currency network Bitcoin is emerging as a potential new way of performing financial transactions across the globe. Its use of pseudonyms towards protecting users' privacy has been an attractive feature to many of its adopters. Nevertheless, due to the inherent public nature of the Bitcoin transaction ledger, users' privacy is severely restricted to *linkable anonymity*, and a few transaction deanonymization attacks have been reported thus far.

In this paper we propose CoinShuffle, a completely decentralized Bitcoin mixing protocol that allows users to utilize Bitcoin in a truly anonymous manner. CoinShuffle is inspired by the accountable anonymous group communication protocol Dissent and enjoys several advantages over its predecessor Bitcoin mixing protocols. It does not require any (trusted, accountable or untrusted) third party and it is perfectly compatible with the current Bitcoin system. CoinShuffle introduces only a small communication overhead for its users, while completely avoiding additional anonymization fees and minimalizing the computation and communication overhead for the rest of the Bitcoin system.

Keywords: Bitcoin, decentralized crypto-currencies, coin mixing, anonymity, transaction linkability, mix networks.

1 Introduction

Bitcoin [1] is a fully decentralized digital crypto-currency network that does not require any central bank or monetary authority. Over the last few years we have observed an unprecedented and rather surprising growth of Bitcoin and its competitor currency networks [2, 3, 4]. Despite a few major hiccups, their market capitalizations are increasing tremendously [5]. Many now believe that the concept of decentralized crypto-currencies is here to stay.

Nevertheless, these decentralized currency systems are far from perfect. Traditional payment systems rely on a trusted third party (such as a bank) to ensure that money cannot be spent twice. Decentralized currencies such as Bitcoin employ a global replicated append-only transaction log and proof-of-work (POW) instead to rule out double-spending. This requires managing a public ledger such that every transaction is considered valid only after it appears in the ledger. However, given that the Bitcoin transactions of a user (in particular, of

M. Kutyłowski and J. Vaidya (Eds.): ESORICS 2014, Part II, LNCS 8713, pp. 345–364, 2014.

her pseudonyms, called *Bitcoin addresses*) are linkable, the public transaction ledger constitutes a significant privacy concern: Bitcoin's reliance on the use of pseudonyms to provide anonymity is severely restricted.

Several studies analyzing the privacy implications of Bitcoin indicate that Bitcoin's built-in privacy guarantees are not satisfactory. Barber et al. [6] observe that Bitcoin exposes its users to the possible linking of their Bitcoin addresses, which subsequently leads to a weak form of anonymity. Meiklejohn et al. [7] demonstrate how to employ a few basic heuristics to classify Bitcoin addresses that are likely to belong to the same user; this is further refined by Spagnuolo, Maggi, and Zanero [8]. Koshy, Koshy, and McDaniel [9] show that it is possible to identify ownership relationships between Bitcoin addresses and IP addresses.

Recently, some efforts have been made towards overcoming the above attacks and providing stronger privacy to the Bitcoin users by *mixing* multiple transactions to make input and output addresses of transactions unlinkable to each other. In this direction, some third-party mixing services [10, 11, 12] were first to emerge, but they have been prone to thefts [7]. Mixcoin [13] allows to hold these mixing services accountable in a reactive manner; however, the mixing services still remain single points of failure and typically require additional mixing fees. Zerocoin [14] and its successors [15, 16, 17] provide strong anonymity without any third party, but lack compatibility with the current Bitcoin system.

Maxwell proposes CoinJoin [18] to perform mixing in a manner that is perfectly compatible with Bitcoin, while ensuring that even a malicious mixing server cannot steal coins. CoinJoin is actively used in practice [19] but suffers from a substantial drawback: The mixing server still needs to be trusted to ensure anonymity, because it learns the relation between input and output addresses. To tackle this problem, Maxwell mentions the possibility to use secure multi-party computation (SMPC) with CoinJoin to perform the mixing obliviously without a trusted server. Yang [20] proposes a concrete scheme based on SMPC sorting. However, against a fully malicious attacker, generic SMPC as well as state-of-the-art SMPC sorting [21, 22] is not yet practical for any reasonable number of parties required in mixing to ensure a good level of anonymity. Furthermore, it is not clear how to ensure robustness against denial-of-service (DoS) attacks in these approaches, because a single user can easily disrupt the whole protocol while possibly remaining unidentified. As a result, defining a practical and secure mixing scheme is considered an open problem by the Bitcoin community [23, 24, 25].

Our Contribution. We present CoinShuffle, a completely decentralized protocol that allows users to mix their coins with those of other interested users. CoinShuffle is inspired by CoinJoin [18] to ensure security against theft and by the accountable anonymous group communication protocol Dissent [26] to ensure anonymity as well as robustness against DoS attacks. The key idea is similar to decryption mix networks, and the protocol requires only standard cryptographic primitives such as signatures and public-key encryption. CoinShuffle is a practical solution for the Bitcoin mixing problem and its distinguishing features are as follows:

No Third Party. CoinShuffle preserves Bitcoin's decentralized trust ideology: it is executed exclusively by the Bitcoin users interested in unlinkability for their Bitcoin transactions, and it does not require any trusted, accountable, or untrusted third party. The unlinkability of transactions is protected as long as at least any two participants in a run of the protocol are honest.

Compatibility. CoinShuffle is fully compatible with the existing Bitcoin network. Unlike other decentralized solutions, it works immediately on top of the Bitcoin network without requiring any change to the Bitcoin rules or scripts.

No Mixing Fee. In absence of a third party that acts as a service provider, CoinShuffle does not charge its users any additional mixing fees. It also performs well in terms of Bitcoin transaction fees, because the participants are only charged the fee for a single mixing transaction.

Small Overhead. Our performance analysis demonstrates that CoinShuffle introduces only a small communication overhead for a participant (less than a minute for an execution with 20 participants), while the computation overhead remains close to negligible. Finally, CoinShuffle introduces only minimal additional overhead for the rest of the Bitcoin network.

Outline. In Section 2, we explain the basics of the Bitcoin protocol and Bitcoin mixing. We define the problem of secure mixing in detail in Section 3. In Sections 4 and 5, we outline and specify the CoinShuffle protocol. We analyze its properties in Section 6 and evaluate its performance in Section 7. We discuss related work in Section 8 and conclude in Section 9.

2   Background

We start by presenting the basics of Bitcoin as well as Bitcoin mixing, the most prevalent approach to strengthening users' anonymity in the system. We explain only the aspects of the Bitcoin protocol that are relevant for mixing and refer the reader to the original Bitcoin paper [1] and the developer documentation [27] for further details.

2.1   Bitcoin

Bitcoin (symbol: ฿) is a digital currency run by a decentralized network. The Bitcoin network maintains a public ledger (called *blockchain*) whose purpose is to reach consensus on the set of transactions that have been validated so far in the network. As long as the majority of computation power in the system is honest, transactions accepted by the system cannot be changed or invalidated, thus preventing double-spending of money.

User accounts in the Bitcoin system are identified using pseudonymous addresses. Technically, an address is the hash of a public key of a digital signature scheme. To simplify presentation, we do not differentiate between the public key and its hash in the remainder of the paper. Every user can create an arbitrary number of addresses by creating fresh key pairs.

The owner of an address uses the corresponding private key to spend coins stored at this address by signing *transactions*. In the simplest form, a transaction

Input Addresses	Output Addresses
A: ฿2	X: ฿3
	Y: ฿2
B: ฿7	Z: ฿4
σ_A	
σ_B	

Fig. 1. A valid Bitcoin transaction with multiple input addresses and multiple output addresses. This transaction is signed using both the private key for input address A and the private key for input address B; the corresponding signatures are denoted by σ_A and σ_B, respectively.

transfers a certain amount of coins from one address (the *input address*) to another address (the *output address*). While multiple sets of coins may be stored at one address, we assume in the remainder of the paper that only one set of coins is stored at an address; these coins can only be spent together. This simplification is purely for the sake of readability.

As depicted in Fig. 1, transactions can include multiple input addresses as well as multiple output addresses. Three conditions must be fulfilled for a transaction to be valid: First, the coins spent by the transaction must not have been already spent by another transaction in the blockchain. Second, the sum of the input coins must equal the sum of the output coins.[1] Third, the transaction must be signed with the private keys corresponding to all input addresses.

2.2 Bitcoin Mixing

The most prevalent approach to improve anonymity for Bitcoin users is the idea of hiding in a group by *Bitcoin mixing*: the users in the group exchange their coins with each other to hide the relations between users and coins from an external observer. Assume that in a group of several users, every user owns exactly one Bitcoin (฿1). In the simplest form, mixing is done with the help of a trusted third-party mixing server, the *mix*: every user sends a fresh address in encrypted form to the mix and transfers her coin to the mix. Then, the mix decrypts and randomly shuffles the fresh addresses and sends ฿1 back to each of them. While such public mixes are deployed in practice [28, 10, 11, 12], they suffer from two severe drawbacks: First, the mix might just steal the money and never return it to the users. Second, the mix learns which output address belongs to a certain input address. Thereby, users' anonymity relies on the assumption that the mix does not log or reveal the relation between input and output addresses.

2.3 Bitcoin Mixing with a Single Transaction

Assume a group of users would like to mix their coins with the help of a third-party mix. To solve the problem that the mix can steal the money, Maxwell proposes CoinJoin [18]: The mix generates one single *mixing transaction* containing the users' current addresses as inputs and the shuffled fresh addresses as

---

[1] In practice, a small transaction fee is typically required. In that case, the sum of the input coins must exceed the sum of the output coins by the amount of the fee.

outputs. Recall that a transaction with several input addresses is only valid if it has been signed with all keys belonging to those input addresses. Thus each user can verify whether the generated mixing transaction sends the correct amount of money to her fresh output address; if this is not true the user just refuses to sign the transaction and the protocol aborts without transferring any coins.

Several implementations of CoinJoin are already actively being used [19, 29, 30], and the Bitcoin developers consider adding CoinJoin to the official Bitcoin client [31]. Still, the problem that the mix learns the relation between input and output addresses persists, and no fully anonymous and efficient solution has been proposed to the best of our knowledge.

3   Problem Definition

In this section, we define the properties that a Bitcoin mixing protocol should satisfy. Furthermore, we present the threat model under which we would like to achieve these properties.

3.1   Design Goals

A Bitcoin mixing protocol must achieve the following security and privacy goals.

Unlinkability. After a successful Bitcoin mixing transaction, honest participants' input and output addresses must be unlinkable.

Verifiability. An attacker must not be able to steal or destroy honest participants' coins.

Robustness. The protocol should eventually succeed even in the presence of malicious participants as long as the communication links remain reliable.

Besides ensuring security and privacy, a Bitcoin mixing protocol must additionally overcome the following system-level challenges:

Compatibility. The protocol must operate on top of the Bitcoin network, and should not require any change to the existing system.

No Mixing Fees. The protocol should not introduce additional fees specifically required for mixing. As every mixing transaction necessarily requires a Bitcoin transaction fee, the protocol must ensure that this transaction fee remains as low as possible.

Efficiency. Even users with very restricted computational capacities should be able to run the mixing protocol. In addition, the users should not be required to wait for a transaction to be confirmed by the Bitcoin network during a run of the protocol, because this inherently takes several minutes.[2]

Small Impact on Bitcoin. The protocol should not put a large burden on the efficiency of the Bitcoin network. In particular, the size of the executed transactions should not be prohibitively large because all transactions have to be stored in the blockchain and verified by all nodes in the network.

---

[2] Several confirmations are recommended, each taking 10 minutes on average. As mixing inherently requires at least one transaction, it is adequate to wait for confirmations at the end of a run, provided the run fails gracefully if the transaction is not confirmed.

3.2 Non-goals

Bitcoin users who wish to participate in a mixing protocol need a bootstrapping mechanism to find each other, e.g., through a public bulletin board acting as facilitator or through a peer-to-peer protocol specifically crafted for this purpose. A malicious facilitator may try to undermine unlinkability by forcing an honest participant to run the protocol only with malicious participants. Thus, in general, the bootstrapping mechanism should resist attempts to exclude honest users from the protocol. Since the Bitcoin network does not allow nodes to send arbitrary messages, the participants must additionally agree on a channel for further communication during bootstrapping. We consider bootstrapping to be orthogonal to our work and assume that it is available to all Bitcoin users.

The main goal of a Bitcoin mixing protocol is the unlinkability between input and output addresses in a mixing transaction. If *after* the mixing, a user would like to spend the mixed coins associated with the output address while maintaining her anonymity, she has to ensure that network metadata, e.g., her IP address, does not reveal her identity or make the spending transaction linkable to a run of the mixing protocol. This problem is not in the scope of the Bitcoin mixing protocol and can be addressed, e.g., by connecting to the Bitcoin network via an anonymous communication protocol such as Tor [32].

3.3 Threat Model

For unlinkability and verifiability, we assume an active network attacker. (Robustness cannot be ensured in the presence of an active network attacker, because such an attacker can always stop the communication between the honest participants.)

We do *not require any trust assumption on a particular party*: for verifiability and robustness, we assume that an honest participant can be faced with an arbitrary number of malicious participants. For unlinkability, we require that there are at least two honest participants in the protocol. Otherwise the attacker can trivially determine the mapping between input and output addresses and meaningful mixing is not possible.

4 Solution Overview

Our main contribution is *CoinShuffle*, a Bitcoin mixing protocol that achieves the aforementioned goals. In this section, we give an overview of our solution.

4.1 Main Idea

To ensure verifiability, our protocol follows the CoinJoin paradigm (Section 2.3): A group of users jointly create a single mixing transaction and each of them can individually verify that she will not lose money by performing the transaction. In case of a fraud attempt, the defrauded user can just refuse to sign the transaction.

Unlinkability and robustness, however, are the most challenging problems: To create a mixing transaction while assuring that input addresses are not linkable to fresh output addresses, the participants shuffle their output addresses in an oblivious manner, similar to a decryption mix network [33]. This shuffling is inspired from one phase of the accountable anonymous group messaging protocol Dissent [26, 34], which builds on an anonymous data collection protocol due to Brickell and Shmatikov [35]. We are able to simplify and optimize ideas from Dissent. For instance, the number of encryption operations is reduced by a factor of four. Even though the special nature of the problem that we would like to solve enables most of these optimizations, we conjecture that one of them is not particular to our setting and can be applied to Dissent. We refer readers that are familiar with Dissent to Appendix A for details and a high-level comparison.

The shuffling provides robustness in the sense that attacks that aim to disrupt the protocol can be detected by honest users and at least one misbehaving participant can be identified and excluded.[3] The other participants can then run the protocol again without the misbehaving participant.

4.2 Protocol Overview

The main part of the CoinShuffle protocol can roughly be split into three phases as depicted in Fig. 2. (As elaborated later, the complete instantiation contains more phases.) If the protocol does not run successfully, an additional blame phase will be reached. In the following we give an overview of every phase. Assume that every participant holds the same amount of coins at some Bitcoin address. This address will be one of the input addresses in the mixing transaction, and every protocol message from this participant is supposed to be signed with the private signing key that belongs to this address.

Announcement. Every participant generates a fresh ephemeral encryption-decryption key pair, and broadcasts the resulting public encryption key.

Shuffling. Every participant creates a fresh Bitcoin address, designated to be her output address in the mixing transaction. Then the participants shuffle the freshly generated output addresses in an oblivious manner, similar to a decryption mix network [33].

In more detail, every participant (say participant i in a predefined shuffling order) uses the encryption keys of all participants $j > i$ to create a layered encryption of her output address. Then, the participants perform a sequential shuffling, starting with participant 1: Each participant i expects to receive $i - 1$ ciphertexts from participant $i - 1$. Upon reception, every participant strips one layer of encryption from the ciphertexts, adds her own ciphertext and randomly shuffles the resulting set. The participant sends the shuffled set of ciphertexts to the next participant $i + 1$. If everybody acts according to the protocol, the decryption performed by the last participant results in a shuffled list of output addresses. The last participant broadcasts this list.

---

[3] This property is called *accountability* in Dissent. We use a different term to avoid confusion with the concept of accountable Bitcoin mixing services in Mixcoin [13].

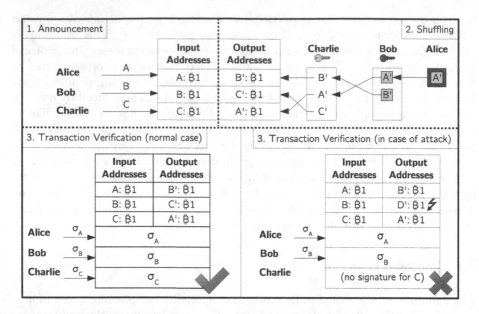

Fig. 2. Overview of CoinShuffle: First, the participants announce their input addresses. Second, they shuffle their fresh output addresses obliviously. (Colored boxes represent ciphertexts encrypted with the respective encryption key.) Third, the participants check if all their output addresses are contained in the final list of output addresses. In this case (left-hand side), the transaction is signed by the participants and submitted to the Bitcoin network. If, on the contrary, an output address is missing (e.g., C' has been replaced by D', right-hand side), the transaction does not become valid and the participants enter the blame phase to find out which participant deviated from the protocol specification. Even though not explicit in the figure, all messages are signed.

Transaction Verification. Each participant can individually verify if her output address is indeed in the list. If this is true, every participant deterministically creates a (not yet signed) mixing transaction that spends coins from all input addresses and sends them to the shuffled list of output addresses. Every participant signs the transaction with her Bitcoin signing key and broadcasts the signature.

Upon receiving signatures from all other participants, every participant is able to create a fully-signed version of the mixing transaction. The transaction is thus valid and can be submitted to the Bitcoin network.

Blame. In every step of the previous phases, every participant checks that all other participants follow the protocol. If some participant deviates from the protocol, an honest participant would report the deviation and the protocol enters the blame phase, which is then performed to identify the misbehaving participant. The misbehaving participant can then be excluded from a subsequent run of the protocol. There are three cases in which participants enter the blame phase. First, the blame phase is entered if some participant does not have enough coins at her input address to perform the mixing transaction, or if she just spends the money at the input address before the mixing protocol is completed. In both situations, the Bitcoin network provides evidence for the misbehavior. Second, the blame phase is entered if the shuffling has not been performed correctly. In that case, the participants can broadcast their ephemeral decryption keys, along with the messages they have received. This information allows every participant to replay the computations of the rest of participants and expose the misbehaving one. Third, participants could equivocate in the broadcasts of the protocol, e.g., by sending different public keys to different participants in the announcement phase. All participants exchange messages before creating the mixing transaction to ensure that nobody has equivocated. In case of equivocation, the blame phase is entered. Since all protocol messages are signed, the equivocating participant can be identified; two signed messages that are different but belong to the same sender and the same broadcast step provide evidence of the misbehavior.

5   The CoinShuffle Protocol

This section details the CoinShuffle protocol, first by covering its cryptographic building blocks and later by formally describing the protocol.

5.1   Cryptographic Primitives

To connect CoinShuffle to Bitcoin, the participants use the Elliptic Curve Digital Signature Algorithm (ECDSA) already deployed in Bitcoin. Formally, we require the signature scheme in CoinShuffle to be (weakly) unforgeable under chosen-message attacks (UF-CMA). Given a message m and a signing key sk, we denote by $\mathsf{Sig}(sk, m)$ the signature of m using sk. The verification algorithm $\mathsf{Verify}(vk, \sigma)$ outputs 1 if σ is a valid signature for m under the verification key vk.

CoinShuffle requires an IND-CCA secure public-key encryption scheme. We denote by $\mathsf{Enc}(ek, m)$ the ciphertext that encrypts the message m with the encryption key ek. For all possible outputs (ek, dk) of the key generation algorithm, we have that if c is a valid ciphertext encrypted with encryption key ek, then the decryption algorithm $\mathsf{Dec}(dk, c)$ outputs the message m contained in c, or $\bot$ otherwise. The encryption scheme must adhere to several additional conditions: First, it must be possible to check if a pair of bitstrings (ek, dk) is a valid key pair, i.e., a possible output of the key generation algorithm. This can be achieved, e.g., as described in [26, Appendix]. Second, we require the encryption algorithm Enc to be length-regular, i.e., for all encryption keys ek and messages m and m' with $|m| = |m'|$, we have $|\mathsf{Enc}(ek, m)| = |\mathsf{Enc}(ek, m')|$ with probability 1. We denote the layered encryption of m with multiple keys by $\overline{\mathsf{Enc}}((ek_1, \ldots, ek_n), m) := \mathsf{Enc}(ek_1, \mathsf{Enc}(ek_2, \ldots \mathsf{Enc}(ek_n, m) \ldots))$. Finally, we require a collision-resistant hash function H.

5.2   Core Protocol Description

We assume that every participant $i \in \{1, \ldots, N\}$ already possesses a Bitcoin address, i.e., a public verification key vk_i and the corresponding signing key sk_i.

The address vk_i will be one of the *input addresses* of the mixing transaction. The order of the participants is publicly known, e.g., the lexicographical order of the verification keys. We further assume that every participant already knows the verification keys of all other participants. All participants have already agreed upon a fresh session identifier τ and an amount $Ƀ\nu$ of coins that they would like to mix. Since the participants use their private Bitcoin keys to sign protocol messages, we require an encoding that ensures that protocol messages are distinct from Bitcoin transactions. This guarantees that participants cannot be tricked into signing transactions unknowingly. During the whole protocol, parties ignore incorrectly signed messages and unexpected messages.

To simplify presentation, we assume implicitly that signed messages can be extracted from their signatures. We write $\sigma_{a,b}$ for the signature produced by participant a in phase b.

Phase 1: Announcement. Every participant $i \in \{2, \ldots, N\}$ randomly chooses a fresh ephemeral encryption-decryption key pair (ek_i, dk_i) and broadcasts $\sigma_{i,1} = \mathsf{Sig}(sk_i, (ek_i, 1, \tau))$. After participant i receives a correctly signed message $\sigma_{j,1}$ from each participant j, she checks that the address vk_j holds at least $Ƀ\nu$ to ensure that enough money is available to carry out the mixing transaction. Otherwise, participant i enters the blame phase.

Phase 2: Shuffling. Every participant chooses a fresh Bitcoin address, i.e., the verification key vk_i' of a fresh verification-signing key pair (vk_i', sk_i'). The signing key sk_i' is kept secret and can be used to spend the mixed coins that will be associated with the *output address* vk_i' after a successful run of the protocol.

Participant 1 creates a layered encryption $c_1 = \overline{\mathsf{Enc}}((ek_2, \ldots, ek_N), vk_i')$ of her output address vk_i' and sends $\sigma_{1,2} = \mathsf{Sig}(sk_1, (C_1, 2, \tau))$ to participant 2, where $C_1 = (c_1)$ is the unary vector with the component c_1. Upon receiving a vector C_{i-1}, participant $i \in \{2, \ldots, N-1\}$ decrypts each message in the vector. Afterwards, she encrypts her Bitcoin output address vk_i' with the public keys of the remaining $(N-i)$ participants, obtaining $c_i = \overline{\mathsf{Enc}}((ek_{i+1}, \ldots, ek_N), vk_i')$. Then participant i adds c_i to the vector of decrypted messages and shuffles the extended vector randomly, obtaining a new vector C_i. If a decryption fails or if two decryption operations lead to the same output, participant i enters the blame phase. Otherwise, participant i sends $\sigma_{i,2} = \mathsf{Sig}(sk_i, (C_i, 2, \tau))$ to participant $i + 1$.

Phase 3: Broadcast of the Output. Upon receiving $\sigma_{N-1,2}$, participant N strips the last layer of encryption of every ciphertext in the vector C_{N-1}. Then participant N shuffles the resulting vector of output addresses after extending it by her own output address vk_N', obtaining the final vector T_{out}. Finally, participant N broadcasts $\sigma_{N,3} = \mathsf{Sig}(sk_N, (T_{out}, 3, \tau))$ to the rest of the participants. If the protocol has been correctly carried out by all participants, every participant has received a copy of the shuffled vector T_{out} of output addresses at this point. Every participant i checks if her output address vk_i' is contained in T_{out}, and otherwise enters the blame phase.

Phase 4: Equivocation Check. To ensure that nobody has equivocated during a broadcast, every participant i computes $h_i = \mathsf{H}((ek_2, \ldots, ek_N), T_{out})$ and broadcasts $\sigma_{i,4} = \mathsf{Sig}(sk_i, (h_i, 4, \tau))$. After having received a correctly signed message from each participant j, participant i checks if there are two participants a and b with $h_a \neq h_b$. In this case, participant i enters the blame phase.

Phase 5: Transaction Verification and Submission. Every participant deterministically creates a (not yet signed) mixing transaction tx that spends ฿ν from each of the input addresses in $T_{in} = (vk_1, \ldots, vk_N)$ and sends ฿ν to each of the output addresses in T_{out}. Participant i signs the transaction tx according to the specification of the Bitcoin protocol and broadcasts the signature $\sigma_{i,5} = \mathsf{Sig}(sk_i, tx)$. Upon receiving a valid signature $\sigma_{j,5}$ from each participant j, participant i adds all signatures to tx and submits the resulting valid transaction to the Bitcoin network. Participant i checks if any of the other participants has spent her money reserved for mixing in the meantime. If this is the case, participant i enters the blame phase. Otherwise the protocol is finished.

Phase 6: Blame. This phase is only reached when any of the checks described above fails. When a participant i enters the blame phase, it broadcasts a signed message explaining the reason for entering the blame phase. Depending on the failed check, additional information may be included as follows:

1. If the Bitcoin network reports that the value of the coins at an input address is below ฿ν, or that the coins at an input address vk_j have already been spent, participant i broadcasts the transaction that sent the insufficient coins to the input address or the transaction that spent the coins, respectively.

2. If there are participants i and j with $h_i \neq h_j$: Participants i and j publish all signed messages that have been received in phase 1 and phase 3. Note that these messages contain all encryption keys $(ek_2, \ldots, ek_N)$ and the final vector T_{out}. Every participant recomputes h_i and h_j and checks if they have been correctly reported. If not, this exposes participant i or j. If both h_i and h_j have been reported correctly, there are two cases: First, a participant has equivocated in phase 1 by sending different encryption keys to i and j. Second, participant N has equivocated in phase 3 by sending different vectors of output addresses to i and j. In either case, the published messages expose the misbehaving participant.

3. If in phase 2, a decryption fails, a duplicate ciphertext is detected, or if after phase 2 an output address is missing in the final vector, the participants perform the skipped equivocation check in phase 4, but only for the encryption keys: Every participant i computes $h'_i = \mathsf{H}((ek_2, \ldots, ek_N))$ and broadcasts $\mathsf{Sig}(sk_i, (h'_i, 4, \tau))$. After having received a correctly signed message from each participant j, participant i checks that there are no two participants a and b with $h'_a \neq h'_b$. Otherwise, the protocol continues as in the case above. If the equivocation check succeeds, every participant i signs and broadcasts her decryption key dk_i together with all messages that have been received in phases 2 and 3. The participants verify that all key pairs (ek_i, dk_i) are valid and blame the participant with an invalid key pair otherwise. If all key pairs are valid, the participants have enough information to replay phases 2 and 3 on their own and identify at least one misbehaving participant.

At the end of the blame phase, at least one misbehaving participant is identified and excluded from the protocol. The remaining participants can start a new run of the protocol without the misbehaving participant, using a fresh session identifier.

It is worth noting that, whenever the blame phase is reached, the participants do not construct a transaction that is accepted by the Bitcoin network.

5.3   Practical Considerations

Transaction Fees. In practice, the Bitcoin network charges a small fee for mixing transactions[4] to prevent DoS attacks that flood the network with a large number of transactions [36]. Transaction fees can easily be dealt with in Coin-Shuffle. Before creating the transaction, the N participants calculate the required fee μ and reduce the size of each output by μ/N, splitting the fee equally among all participants. This ensures that the transaction will be accepted by the Bitcoin network. If a participants tries to cheat by deviating from this policy, e.g., to pay a lower fee, the mixing transaction will not become valid as only the correct transaction will be signed by the honest participants.

Change Addresses. A user that would like to spend exactly ₿ x typically does not hold an input address with exactly this balance, but rather an address with a higher balance ₿ $(x + y)$. In order to perform the payment, the user will create a transaction with one input ₿ $(x + y)$ and two outputs: ₿ x go to the address of the payee and ₿ y go to a *change address* belonging to the original user.

The use of change addresses is supported in CoinShuffle: Participants can announce additional change addresses in phase 1, if they do not have an address holding exactly the mixing amount ₿ ν. In phase 5, every participant adds all the change addresses as outputs of the mixing transaction tx before it is signed. CoinShuffle still preserves the unlinkability between the input addresses and the (regular) output addresses of the honest participants.

Communication and Liveness. In practice, broadcasts can be implemented by sending all messages to a randomly chosen *leader* that relays the messages to all participants. Furthermore, instead of misbehaving actively, participants might passively disrupt a protocol run by simply going offline at any time, either maliciously or due to a network failure or asymmetric connectivity. This problem is not particular to CoinShuffle and can be handled using the same techniques as in Dissent [26], which in turn borrows ideas from PeerReview [37]. We only present the idea and refer the reader to the original papers for details. When the protocol states that a participant i must receive a properly signed message from participant j, but participant j does not send such a message within a predefined timeout period, i suspects j. In this case, i asks another participant k (or several participants) to request the desired message from j and relay it to i. If k does not receive the message either, also k suspects j and can in turn ask other members. In case nobody receives the message from j, i.e., everybody suspects j eventually, the participants can start a new run of the protocol without j.

---

[4] At the time of writing, a fee of ₿ 0.0001 ($\approx$ \$ 0.06) per 1000 bytes of transaction size is mandatory for transactions of at least 1000 bytes. Due to their nature, mixing transactions contain several addresses and are typically larger than 1000 bytes. A mixing transaction with 25 participants has an approximate size of 5000 bytes.

6   Analysis

We discuss why CoinShuffle achieves the design goals described in Section 3.1.

6.1   Security Analysis

Recall that we aim for three security and privacy properties, namely unlinkability, verifiability and robustness. We explain why CoinShuffle achieves all of these.

Unlinkability. A Bitcoin mixing protocol provides unlinkability if given a single output address vk' from a successful mixing transaction, the scenario that vk' belongs to some honest user a is indistinguishable from the scenario that vk' belongs to a different honest user $b \neq a$.

First, observe that we do not have to consider failed runs of the protocol. Indeed, if the blame phase is reached, the attacker might be able to link an output address to an input address, e.g., if the participants publish decryption keys. However, if the blame phase is reached, the mixing transaction and in particular the generated output addresses are discarded and the protocol will be restarted with fresh output addresses.

Now consider a successful run of the protocol, i.e., assume that the blame phase has not been reached. Observe that phase 4 of the protocol ensures that no participant has equivocated while announcing her ephemeral encryption key in phase 1. Let i be the highest index of an honest participant in the shuffling order and let $U_{<i}$ be the set of honest participants with index smaller than i. Participant i has received a vector C_{i-1} of $i-1$ ciphertexts. All messages that have been sent so far in the shuffling phase have been encrypted with ek_i (and other keys). These messages do not reveal the link between input and output addresses, because the attacker does not know dk_i and thus cannot observe which output address is contained in which layered ciphertext.

We continue by arguing that the output of participant i does not reveal the link between input and output addresses either. Since the shuffling has been performed successfully and the blame phase has not been reached, the ciphertexts in vector C_{i-1} that belong to the users in $U_{<i}$ have not been tampered with. Furthermore, because we have excluded equivocation, these ciphertexts share the same structure, i.e., they are all of the form $\overline{\mathsf{Enc}}((ek_i, \ldots, ek_N), vk'_j)$ for $j \in U_{<i}$ and uniquely defined encryption keys $ek_i, \ldots, ek_N$. Participant i strips one layer of encryption from the ciphertexts in C_{i-1}, adds her own ciphertext and shuffles the resulting vector C_i. Consequently, participant i outputs a randomly shuffled vector C_i that contains at least $|U_{<i}| + 1$ honestly generated ciphertexts of the form $\overline{\mathsf{Enc}}((ek_{i+1}, \ldots, ek_N), vk'_j)$ for $j \in U_{<i} \cup \{i\}$, where all output addresses vk'_j have the same fixed length, because they are Bitcoin addresses. Let D_i be the a vector that is obtained by keeping only those honestly generated ciphertexts and removing the others from C_i. D_i is implicitly associated with a permutation π of the output addresses of the honest participants in $U_{<i} \cup \{i\}$.

Since i is honest and does not collude with malicious participants, the IND-CCA property of the encryption scheme ensures that all pairs of possible output vectors D_i^0 and D_i^1 (resulting from potentially different permutations π_0 and π_1 of the output addresses) are indistinguishable.[5] Note that at least two different permutations $\pi_0 \neq \pi_1$ exist, because by assumption, there are at least two honest participants whose ciphertexts can be shuffled, which implies $|U_{<i}| \geq 1$.

Verifiability. A Bitcoin mixing protocol ensures verifiability if no attacker can steal or destroy honest participants' coins. This is immediate from the description of CoinShuffle: a honest participant i signs the final mixing transaction only if she has verified that (i) her own output address vk_i' is included in the list of output addresses, and (ii) the amount sent to the output address is the amount of coins taken from her input address (possibly reduced by a transaction fee).

Robustness. A Bitcoin mixing protocol ensures robustness if it finishes even in the presence of malicious participants. Since CoinShuffle enters the blame phase if a run does not successfully create a transaction, we have to argue why at least one misbehaving participant can be identified in the blame phase. We distinguish the same cases as in the blame phase of the protocol description:

1. In this case, the signed announcement message together with the evidence from the Bitcoin network proves that the participant in question misbehaved.

2. Recall that participants i and j publish all signed messages that have been received in phases 1 and 3. If h_i or h_j have been computed incorrectly, this is evidence that i or j, respectively, has misbehaved. If both h_i and h_j have been reported correctly, the published messages expose the equivocating participant.

3. If a participant detects an invalid key pair, the signed announcement message (containing the purported encryption key) and the signed message in the blame phase containing the purported decryption key provide evidence of misbehavior. Otherwise, the participants have enough information to replay the steps of each participant in phases 2 and 3 and identify the misbehaving participant. The signed messages of phases 1 to 3 prove the misbehavior.

Double-Spending. Note that due the nature of the Bitcoin network, a malicious participant might disrupt the protocol by a double-spending attempt: Shortly before all participants submit the mixing transaction to the network, the malicious participant submits a transaction that spends her input coins that have actually been designated for mixing. The Bitcoin network will eventually reach consensus which of the two transactions becomes valid and discard the other one to ensure that coins cannot be double-spent. If the malicious transaction is accepted, honest parties do not lose their coins, but the mixing will have failed. Then, it might be the case that a restart of the protocol is not possible because the participants have already gone offline, in the belief that the protocol has been successful.

We consider protection against double-spending in Bitcoin to be orthogonal to our work [38]. Typically, the attacker's goal in double-spending is to make a recipient of a transaction believe that she has received some coins. As a result

---

[5] Note that the length-regularity of Enc implies that not only the output addresses but also the inner layers of encryptions (at the same depth) have the same length. This is necessary, because otherwise the IND-CCA property does not guarantee indistinguishability for the encryptions of these inner ciphertexts.

the recipient will, e.g., hand over a valuable good to the attacker, even though the transaction will be invalidated and replaced by a different one that sends the coins back to attacker. However, this attack is not possible in mixing, because sender and recipient are the same party. Instead, invalidating a mixing transaction is only an attack against robustness. If protection against a double-spending attack becomes necessary to ensure robustness, the participants will have to wait for the transaction to be confirmed by the Bitcoin network before they go offline.

6.2   System Analysis

We discuss why CoinShuffle achieves the desired system-level goals.

Compatibility. CoinShuffle does not require any change to the Bitcoin protocol or to the transaction format, because a successful run of CoinShuffle results in a transaction that is valid according to the current rules of Bitcoin. Thus the protocol is immediately deployable.

No Mixing Fees. Systems in which a trusted third party performs the mixing typically charge users two fees: a transaction fee as defined in Bitcoin and a mixing fee required by the trusted third party [10, 11, 12]. In CoinShuffle, however, no mixing fee is required. Users who jointly execute CoinShuffle are only charged the transaction fee as defined in the currently deployed Bitcoin protocol.

Efficiency. As signatures and hash functions are already used in Bitcoin, public-key encryption is the only cryptographic primitive added by CoinShuffle. This allows to run the protocol even on computationally restricted hardware. The performance evaluation (Section 7) shows the practical feasibility of CoinShuffle.

Small Impact on Bitcoin. Upon successful protocol execution, the participants jointly create only a single Bitcoin transaction that must be stored in the public blockchain and has to be verified by all nodes in the network. Thus, the execution of CoinShuffle introduces only a minimal overhead in terms of storage and computation for nodes in the Bitcoin network.

7   Performance Evaluation

We have developed a proof-of-concept implementation [39] of CoinShuffle leveraging an existing implementation of the Dissent protocol. In particular, we have implemented phases 1 to 5 of the protocol (Section 5.2), which suffice to measure the performance of a single successful run without disruption.

The implementation is written in Python and uses OpenSSL to sign and encrypt messages. As required by the Bitcoin network, signatures have been implemented using ECDSA on the `secp256k1` elliptic curve [40] at a security level of 128 bits. We use the Elliptic Curve Integrated Encryption Scheme (ECIES) [40] on the same curve together with standard AES in CBC mode for encryption. The communication among the participants has been implemented using TCP. When a message is broadcast, it is first sent to the first participant in the shuffling order, who in turn sends a copy to every participant.

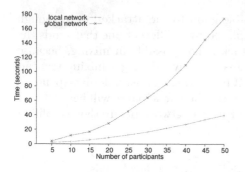

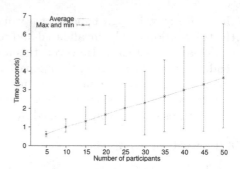

Fig. 3. Overall execution time   **Fig. 4.** Processing time per node

We tested our implementation in Emulab [41], a testbed for distributed systems, in which network parameters such as topology or bandwidth of links can be easily configured. In this setting, we have run several experiments under controlled network conditions. We consider two scenarios: a local network and a global network. In the former, we connected all the participants to a LAN with 100 Mbit/s bandwidth without delays. In the latter, we split the participants in two LANs of 100 Mbit/s bandwidth each. Both LANs were connected through a router with a bandwidth of 20 Mbit/s and a delay of 50 ms. In the global network scenario we considered the worst case for the shuffling phase: participants with an odd index in the shuffling order were placed in one LAN while participants with an even index were placed in the other LAN. Thus every message in the shuffling phase had to traverse the whole network.

We have run the protocol with different numbers of participants, ranging from 5 to 50. Figure 3 shows the overall time needed to create a Bitcoin transaction in a run without misbehaving participants. In the local network, 50 participants need approximately 40 seconds to run CoinShuffle, while in the global network, slightly less than 3 minutes are necessary to complete the protocol.

Figure 4 shows the overhead of the computation carried out by every participant on average. As expected, the average processing time increases linearly with the number of participants, because every participant must shuffle a vector of ciphertexts containing one ciphertext more than the previous participant. Furthermore, the computation overhead constitutes only a small fraction of the overall time. In the case of 50 participants, the average computation time is slightly larger than 3 seconds, which constitutes approximately 2% of the overall time in the local network scenario and less than 1% in the global network setting.

In summary, the experimental results demonstrate the feasibility of the Coin-Shuffle protocol even in scenarios with a large number of participants.

8   Related Work

Zerocoin [14], an extension to Bitcoin, was among the first proposals to provide unlinkability between individual Bitcoin transactions without introducing a trusted party. It employs a cryptographic accumulator of minted *zerocoins* and a zero-knowledge proof of inclusion of a certain zerocoin within the accumulator. Zerocoin introduces a significant computation and communication overhead: the size of the proof that has to be stored in the blockchain for each transaction is prohibitively large (i.e., approximately 25 KB) and far exceeds the size of the Bitcoin transaction itself.

Recently, there have been some proposals to reduce the Zerocoin proof size. Garman et al. [16] propose a set of extensions to Zerocoin that reduces the proof size by modeling the cost of forging a coin and picking cryptographic parameters to make such forgery uneconomical. Both Pinocchio Coin [15] and Zerocash [17] are promising improvements of Zerocoin that significantly reduce the proof size (to less than 1 KB) and the computational costs. Nevertheless, this line of research is severely restricted in terms of adaptability. Zerocoin and all of the above extensions require substantial modifications to the Bitcoin system. Thus, Zerocoin and its variants cannot be directly deployed in Bitcoin. Instead, they would need an incremental deployment that requires acceptance by the majority of the Bitcoin nodes (measured in computational resources). So far, it looks unlikely for the Bitcoin network to employ the Zerocoin strategy [42]. In contrast, while requiring more communication, CoinShuffle is immediately adaptable and works on top of the existing Bitcoin network.

The Mixcoin [13] protocol facilitates anonymous Bitcoin payments without making any modifications to the Bitcoin protocol. Here, Bitcoin users send their coins to a central accountable mix which in turn replies with a guarantee of returning the funds to the user. Afterwards, the mix sends the coins back to the user ensuring unlinkability between the user input and output addresses. Although the mix can be held accountable for thefts, the system still has several drawbacks. First, the use of a central mix introduces a single point of failure, where the mix becomes a suitable target for DoS attacks from competing mixes as well as governmental agencies. Second, the provided accountability is reactive in nature, and the mix can still steal users' coins before going out of business. Third, a payment in Mixcoin requires two Bitcoin transactions and additionally a fee charged by the mix. Finally, unlinkability is only guaranteed against external observers, because mix learns which address belongs to which user. In comparison to Mixcoin, CoinShuffle relies on the interaction between the users in the mixing to achieve unlinkability, verifiability, robustness, and cost effectiveness without a trusted third party.

Maxwell [43] sketches a modification to the CoinJoin protocol using blind signatures to avoid the problem of a centralized mix learning the relation between input and output addresses. This protocol employs the anonymous communication network Tor [32] as a building block to provide unlinkability. In contrast, CoinShuffle provides full resistance against traffic correlation attacks by using a decentralized high-latency mix network run only by the participants.

9   Conclusion

The linkable pseudonymity provided by the Bitcoin system leads to significant privacy concerns for its users. A few solutions that aim at mixing transactions of a group of users have been proposed in the last two years to address this concern; however, none of them has been found to be satisfy all requirements of a practical and compatible solution. In this paper, we have presented the Bitcoin mixing protocol CoinShuffle, which is secure, robust, and perfectly compatible with the existing Bitcoin system. Adhering to the Bitcoin ideology, CoinShuffle is completely decentralized, and it neither requires any third party nor introduces any additional anonymization fees for the users.

We implemented CoinShuffle and tested it in a local as well as in a global network scenario in the Emulab environment. Our experiments demonstrate that CoinShuffle introduces only a small (suitable for Bitcoin) computation and communication overhead to a participant, even when the number of CoinShuffle participants is large (≈ 50). Moreover, CoinShuffle leads only to a minimal overhead for the Bitcoin blockchain and thus for the rest of the Bitcoin network.

Finally, although we have focused on the crypto-currency Bitcoin in the paper, we stress that our protocol is compatible with all competing currencies derived from Bitcoin, e.g., Litecoin [2], Mastercoin [4], and others.

Acknowledgments. We thank Bryan Ford for his insightful comments on an earlier draft and Henry Corrigan-Gibbs for helping us with running the proof-of-concept implementation on Emulab. We further thank the anonymous reviewers for their helpful comments. This work was supported by the German Universities Excellence Initiative.

References

[1] Nakamoto, S.: Bitcoin: A peer-to-peer electronic cash system. Technical report (2008), https://bitcoin.org/bitcoin.pdf

[2] Litecoin, https://litecoin.org

[3] Ripple, https://ripple.com

[4] Mastercoin, http://www.mastercoin.org

[5] BitInfoCharts, http://bitinfocharts.com/comparison/transactions-marketcap-btc-ltc.html (accessed on March 28, 2014)

[6] Barber, S., Boyen, X., Shi, E., Uzun, E.: Bitter to better — how to make Bitcoin a better currency. In: Keromytis, A.D. (ed.) FC 2012. LNCS, vol. 7397, pp. 399–414. Springer, Heidelberg (2012)

[7] Meiklejohn, S., Pomarole, M., Jordan, G., Levchenko, K., McCoy, D., Voelker, G.M., Savage, S.: A fistful of bitcoins: Characterizing payments among men with no names. In: IMC 2013, pp. 127–140. ACM (2013)

[8] Spagnuolo, M., Maggi, F., Zanero, S.: BitIodine: Extracting intelligence from the Bitcoin network. In: FC 2014. Springer (2014)

[9] Koshy, P., Koshy, D., McDaniel, P.: An analysis of anonymity in Bitcoin using P2P network traffic. In: FC 2014. Springer (2014)

[10] Bitcoin Fog, http://www.bitcoinfog.com

[11] BitLaundry, http://app.bitlaundry.com

[12] BitLaunder, https://bitlaunder.com

[13] Bonneau, J., Narayanan, A., Miller, A., Clark, J., Kroll, J.A., Felten, E.W.: Mixcoin: Anonymity for Bitcoin with accountable mixes. In: FC 2014. Springer (2014)

[14] Miers, I., Garman, C., Green, M., Rubin, A.D.: Zerocoin: Anonymous distributed e-cash from Bitcoin. In: S&P 2013, pp. 397–411. IEEE Press (2013)

[15] Danezis, G., Fournet, C., Kohlweiss, M., Parno, B.: Pinocchio Coin: Building Zerocoin from a succinct pairing-based proof system. In: PETShop 2013, pp. 27–30. ACM (2013)

[16] Garman, C., Green, M., Miers, I., Rubin, A.D.: Rational Zero: Economic security for Zerocoin with everlasting anonymity. In: 1st Workshop on Bitcoin Research (2014), https://fc14.ifca.ai/bitcoin/papers/bitcoin14_submission_12.pdf

[17] Ben-Sasson, E., Chiesa, A., Garman, C., Green, M., Miers, I., Tromer, E., Virza, M.: Zerocash: Decentralized anonymous payments from Bitcoin. In: S&P 2014. IEEE Press (2014)

[18] Maxwell, G.: CoinJoin: Bitcoin privacy for the real world. Post on Bitcoin Forum (August 2013), https://bitcointalk.org/index.php?topic=279249

[19] Qkos Services Ltd.: Shared Coin, https://sharedcoin.com

[20] Yang, E.Z.: Secure multiparty Bitcoin anonymization. Blog posting (2012), http://blog.ezyang.com/2012/07/secure-multiparty-bitcoin-anonymization/

[21] Jónsson, K.V., Kreitz, G., Uddin, M.: Secure multi-party sorting and applications. IACR ePrint Cryptology Archive 2011/122, https://eprint.iacr.org/2011/122

[22] Hamada, K., Kikuchi, R., Ikarashi, D., Chida, K., Takahashi, K.: Practically efficient multi-party sorting protocols from comparison sort algorithms. In: Kwon, T., Lee, M.-K., Kwon, D. (eds.) ICISC 2012. LNCS, vol. 7839, pp. 202–216. Springer, Heidelberg (2013)

[23] Rosenfeld, M.: Using mixing transactions to improve anonymity. Post on Bitcoin Forum (December 2011), https://bitcointalk.org/index.php?topic=54266

[24] Murphant (pseudonym). Post on Bitcoin Forum (August 2013), https://bitcointalk.org/index.php?topic=279249.msg3057216#msg3057216

[25] Maxwell, G.: Post on Bitcoin Forum (September 2013), https://bitcointalk.org/index.php?topic=279249.msg3013970#msg3013970

[26] Corrigan-Gibbs, H., Ford, B.: Dissent: Accountable anonymous group messaging. In: CCS 2010, pp. 340–350. ACM (2010)

[27] Bitcoin project: Bitcoin developer documentation, https://bitcoin.org/en/developer-documentation

[28] Möser, M., Böhme, R., Breuker, D.: An inquiry into money laundering tools in the Bitcoin ecosystem. In: ECRIME 2013. IEEE Press (2013)

[29] Duffield, E., Hagan, K.: Darkcoin: Peer-to-peer crypto currency with anonymous blockchain transactions and an improved proof-of-work system. Technical report (March 2014), http://www.darkcoin.io/downloads/DarkcoinWhitepaper.pdf

[30] Buterin, V., Malahov, J., Wilson, C., Hintjens, P., Taaki, A., et al.: Dark Wallet, https://darkwallet.unsystem.net

[31] van der Laan, W.J.: Implement coinjoin in wallet. GitHub Issue #3226 of official Bitcoin repository, https://github.com/bitcoin/bitcoin/issues/3226

[32] Dingledine, R., Mathewson, N., Syverson, P.: Tor: The second-generation onion router. In: USENIX Security 2004, pp. 21–37. USENIX Assoc. (2004)

[33] Chaum, D.L.: Untraceable electronic mail, return addresses, and digital pseudonyms. Communications of the ACM 24(2), 84–90 (1981)

[34] Syta, E., Johnson, A., Corrigan-Gibbs, H., Weng, S.C., Wolinsky, D., Ford, B.: Security analysis of accountable anonymous group communication in Dissent. ACM Transactions on Information and System Security (TISSEC) (to appear)

[35] Brickell, J., Shmatikov, V.: Efficient anonymity-preserving data collection. In: SIGKDD 2006, pp. 76–85. ACM (2006)

[36] Transaction fees. Bitcoin Wiki, https://en.bitcoin.it/w/index.php?title= Transaction_fees&oldid=45501 (revision as of March 28, 2014)
[37] Haeberlen, A., Kouznetsov, P., Druschel, P.: PeerReview: Practical accountability for distributed systems. In: SOSP 2007, pp. 175–188. ACM (2007)
[38] Karame, G.O., Androulaki, E., Capkun, S.: Double-spending fast payments in Bitcoin. In: CCS 2012, pp. 906–917. ACM (2012)
[39] Ruffing, T., Moreno-Sanchez, P., Kate, A.: CoinShuffle: Practical decentralized coin mixing for Bitcoin. Full version of this paper and prototype implementation, http://crypsys.mmci.uni-saarland.de/projects/CoinShuffle
[40] Certicom Research: Sec 1: Elliptic curve cryptography, http://www.secg.org/download/aid-780/sec1-v2.pdf
[41] White, B., Lepreau, J., Stoller, L., Ricci, R., Guruprasad, S., Newbold, M., Hibler, M., Barb, C., Joglekar, A.: An integrated experimental environment for distributed systems and networks. In: OSDI 2002, pp. 255–270. USENIX (December 2002)
[42] Thread on Bitcoin Forum, https://bitcointalk.org/index.php?topic=175156
[43] Maxwell, G.: Post on Bitcoin Forum (2013), https://bitcointalk.org/index.php?topic=279249.msg2984051#msg2984051

A   High-Level Comparison with Dissent

CoinShuffle has been inspired by the shuffling phase of the Dissent protocol [26, 34], which adds robustness to a data collection protocol due to Brickell and Shmatikov [35]. The fact that CoinShuffle is crafted specially to be used on top of the Bitcoin protocol allows us to apply several optimizations. In the following we describe the two most important improvements as compared to Dissent. We assume the reader to be familiar with the Dissent protocol [26, 34].

First, observe that in Dissent, the shuffling phase must hide participants' inputs even in case of failure, i.e., even if the blame phase is reached. For that, Dissent needs N additional inner layers of encryption, because each message is additionally encrypted with the encryption keys of all participants. This makes it possible to introduce an additional step after the shuffling: Participants check first if the shuffling was performed correctly, and they reveal their inner decryption keys only if the check succeeds. In contrast, hiding the plaintexts is not necessary in a failed run of CoinShuffle, because the plaintexts are only fresh Bitcoin addresses that are discarded when the protocol fails; it is not a problem to create new addresses in the subsequent run of the protocol. As a result, the additional inner layers of encryption are not necessary in CoinShuffle.

Second, the description of the shuffling phase of Dissent specifies that every participant sends and receives a vector of N ciphertexts. In CoinShuffle, every participant i receives a vector of only $i-1$ ciphertexts and sends only i ciphertexts to the next participant. The communication overhead is thereby further reduced, and fewer encryption and decryption operations are necessary as compared to Dissent. We conjecture that this improvement is also applicable to the shuffling phase of Dissent, but we leave a formal treatment for future work.

LESS Is More: Host-Agent Based Simulator for Large-Scale Evaluation of Security Systems

John Sonchack[1] and Adam J. Aviv[2]

[1] University of Pennsylvania, Philadelphia, PA 19104, USA
[2] United States Naval Academy, Annapolis, MD 21402, USA

Abstract. Recently proposed network security systems have demonstrated the benefits of *scale* for achieving many security goals, including the detection of worm outbreaks, botnets, and denial of service attacks. However, scale is also a barrier to further advancement of such systems: obtaining and working with appropriately large data sets is difficult, and existing simulation techniques are ill suited for this domain. To overcome these challenges, we propose a host behavior simulator, LESS, designed for evaluating large scale network security systems. LESS build and automatically configures the behaviors of host agents using background traffic samples and malicious traffic models. In turn, host agents communicate with each other throughout a simulation, generating traffic records. We demonstrate the applicability and benefits of LESS by tuning it with publicly available traces, and then using generated records to *reproduce* results from several recently proposed systems. We also used LESS to *extend* the evaluations of these systems, highlighting dimensions of large scale security system performance that would be difficult to study without simulation.

Keywords: Data Challenges, Large Scale Security, Simulation, Agent Based, Stochastic.

1 Introduction

Many recently proposed network security systems leverage *scale* [1, 2, 3, 4, 5]. By analyzing diverse data sets gathered from many vantage points, a network security system can identify macroscopic host behavior patterns that cannot be observed at the local network level. Although beneficial, the scale of such proposed techniques also results in a high bar for advancement and investigation from the general research community [6, 7]. Internet- or ISP- scale data sets appropriate for studying large-scale security systems are difficult to acquire and share. Furthermore, data sets of sufficient scale that are publicly available often lack context that is important for meaningful evaluation, such as ground truth about which traffic is malicious. These data limitations affect the ability of researchers to reproduce existing results, and limit the dimensions in which they can analyze their systems.

In this paper, we argue that novel simulation techniques specifically designed to analyze large scale security systems can directly address these challenges. In

M. Kutyłowski and J. Vaidya (Eds.): ESORICS 2014, Part II, LNCS 8713, pp. 365–382, 2014.

other areas of network research, simulation has proven an effective tool to overcome similar data-related challenges. However, available simulation tools do not model the usage and behavior patterns in a way well suited for evaluating large scale security systems. We propose an alternate simulation strategy that is agent based: the **L**arge-scale **E**valuation for **S**ecurity **S**imulation (LESS). LESS generates host agents that communicate and generate traffic based on behavior defined by tunable stochastic processes. LESS automatically tunes these processes using small samples of real traffic and user provided models of well defined network security threats.

We implemented the LESS simulator, and assessed its effectiveness by using it to re-evaluate four large scale network security systems. These systems were originally evaluated on real traffic traces, inaccessible to the public. However, using publically available network traffic samples, intuitive malicious traffic models, and previously published traffic parameters, LESS generated traces that *reproduced* results from the original evaluations, *confirming prior results with access to just public data*. Furthermore, LESS allowed us to *extend* the original evaluations, *studying prior systems in new dimension that could not be achieved with the original data*. These results suggest that domain-specific simulation, and LESS in particular, is a vital tool in studying large scale collaborative security techniques.

In summary, our contributions are:

- The design and implementation of LESS: an agent based simulator for evaluating large scale network security systems.
- A tunable, stochastic host-behavior process that allows hosts-agents to generate background traffic based on parameters from real traffic samples, and malicious traffic based on parameters from intuitive threat models.
- Simulation based *reproductions* and *extensions* of results from four large scale security system evaluations.

In the remainder of this paper, we examine the intersection of large scale security systems and simulation based analysis. First, in Section 2, we discuss related simulation techniques. Next, in Section 3, we summarize four recently proposed large scale security systems, and their evaluations. We discuss the implementation of LESS in Section 4. Then, in Section 5, we use LESS, along with publicly accessible data sets, to reproduce and extend the evaluations of the surveyed security systems. Finally, we discuss limitations and future work in Section 6, and conclude in Section 7.

2   Related Work

Simulation offers many benefits for computer network related research [8]. Discrete event simulators [9], and virtual networks [10] provide frameworks for simulating many network connected devices on a single machine, and are useful for evaluating distributed systems. However, these tools require users to completely specify the actions of each simulated device, making them ill-suited for evaluating large scale security systems, which are designed to detect or prevent specific types of malicious activity based on usage patterns. Our work is complementary: LESS models inter-host communication patterns and behaviors, but *not* the networks that connect hosts.

Traffic generators, such as [11] generate synthetic packets to be carried on real or virtual networks. These systems model packet and payload level features, and are used to evaluate techniques that are sensitive to these features, such as congestion control [12]. However, large scale network security systems are sensitive to higher level features, such as traffic dispersion or host communication patterns. LESS is orthogonal to synthetic traffic generators, in that it models these higher level network-flow properties and is better suited for evaluating large scale security systems.

User behavior modeling has been proposed to generate specific classes of non-malicious Internet traffic, such as HTTP traffic [13]. LESS differs in two important ways from these systems: first, it models behavior patterns at the *host* level; second, it allows users to augment hosts with *malicious* behaviors that model large scale security threats such as worm outbreaks [14], correlated attackers [4], and bot communication networks [15]. Thus, LESS applies similar behavior modeling techniques, but in a way better suited for evaluating large scale security systems.

Simulation techniques tailored for specific classes of security systems have been proposed; Sommers et al. [16] craft flow payloads to evaluate and tune intrusion detection systems, and Chen et al. [17] propose a simulator for evaluating worm outbreaks in a peer-to-peer network. These techniques are complementary to LESS in scope and scale, but motivated by the common observation that other network simulation techniques are ill-suited for security research.

Testbed systems, such as Lariat [18], are platforms that use real or virtualized networks along with complex models of host behaviors to evaluate security systems of varying scale. Testbeds require careful tuning: the authors of Lariat, for example, estimated that configuring their system to test a new intrusion detection system takes approximately four months [18]. In contrast, LESS uses more general models that can be automatically fit to and validated against real traffic traces. Simpler models also lead to quicker run times: each simulation that we ran to generate experimental results for Section 5 executed in one hour or less. LESS and security testbeds could be used complementary: for example, the preliminary evaluation of a new technique could be done using LESS, followed by a testbed evaluation of the system in a specific scenario.

LESS applies two general classes of simulation techniques to large scale security system experimentation. First, *agent based simulation* [19], in which complex systems are modeled as a set of agents that interact with each other based on individual decision processes. Second, *stochastic simulation* [20], in which systems are analyzed with inputs drawn from statistical distributions of real observations. More specifically, LESS models usage in a large scale network from the perspective of a collection of *host agents* that interact with each other in a client-server model to generate both *background* and *malicious* traffic. The actions and behaviors of these host agents are defined by processes that are *configured stochastically*, with distributions derived from real sample traces.

3   Large Scale and Collaborative Security Systems

In this section, we summarize four systems that demonstrate both the potential of large scale security and the data related challenges of experimentation in this domain.

3.1   Entropy Based Anomaly Detection

Wagner et al. [1] observed that large scale security threats, such as worm outbreaks and high volume DDoS attacks, skew the distribution of flow level traffic features such as source and destination IP addresses. Based on these observations, they proposed a technique to detect such events by measuring the entropy of traffic features.

Wagner et al. evaluated their technique using large scale traces from the outbreaks of two real worms. Such traces are difficult to acquire, and do not allow researchers to analyze how worm behavior properties (*e.g.* inter-scan time) affect system performance. LESS allows researchers to work around these issues by generating background traffic based on parameters measured from publicly accessible samples, and malicious traffic based on parameters selected by tunable threat models.

3.2   Highly Predictive Blacklisting

The Highly Predictive Blacklisting System [3] generates blacklists customized for individual networks by analyzing the attack patterns of malicious hosts across multiple collaborating networks. The proposed approach is based on the observation that many attackers target small, stable sets of networks [4].

The authors evaluated this system on a set of over 700 million Intrusion Detection System log entries submitted to DShield [21] by over 1500 networks over a two month period of time. This data set cannot be used to measure false alert rates, as IDS log entries alone do not provide sufficient context to determine the true maliciousness of the hosts causing alerts. LESS can provide perspective on how false alerts affect a system, by using well defined malicious traffic models and record sets where malicious traffic is clearly marked.

3.3   Peer-to-peer Botnet Detection

Coskun et al.. [5] proposed a technique to detect peer-to-peer bots by correlating host communication patterns, based on the observation that the bot-hosts in a network are more likely to communicate with common external hosts.

The authors evaluate their approach by mixing a 24 hour trace collected at the boarder of a university network containing approximately 2000 hosts, and

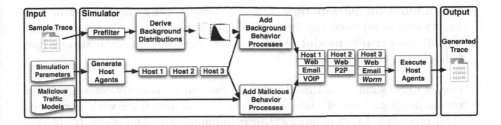

Fig. 1. An overview of LESS

communication records from approximately 900 bots from the Nugache botnet. A data set from one botnet does not allow researchers to measure how the topology of the peer-to-peer botnet affects their systems. With LESS, however, users can estimate the effects of this factor with a tunable botnet traffic model. Further, this data set is from a single network, which makes it difficult to analyze how a security system will perform at other networks that carry different types of traffic. LESS can generate data sets based on samples of traffic from other networks, which in turn can be used to estimate how robust a security system is to diverse network conditions.

3.4 Collaborative Anomaly Detection

Boggs et al. [2] proposed a technique to significantly reduce the false positive rate of anomaly detectors, by correlating the alerts generated by detectors deployed at multiple networks. Their system is based on the observation that if multiple unrelated hosts or networks observe similar anomalies, they are more likely to be due to a common attack.

Boggs et al. evaluated the proposed technique on eight weeks of traffic collected at two university web servers. Their evaluation demonstrates how challenging it is to collect sufficiently detailed data from multiple administrative domains. LESS is beneficial in this scenario because it allows users to simulate many networks based on parameters drawn from a single, more accessible traces.

4   Simulation for Large Scale Network Security

LESS, illustrated in Figure 1, generates traces for evaluating large scale security systems by generating host agents, assigning them stochastic processes that define their behavior, and then recording their activities in a simulation where the host agents execute their behavior processes. A behavior process models a single host's communication pattern using a single class of network applications (*e.g.* web, email, VOIP, worm). LESS accepts the following inputs:

- a **sample trace** containing representative background traffic, which LESS measures statistics from to configure non-malicious host behavior;

- two **simulation parameters** N and T, that specify the number of host agents to generate and the duration of the simulation;
- a **malicious traffic model** M, which LESS uses to configure malicious host behavior processes.

When a LESS simulation runs, the host agents autonomously determine *when* to communicate and *which other host agents* to communicate with using their behavior processes. LESS monitors their communications and generates records consisting of timestamps, source and destination host IDs, and source and destination ports.

4.1   Preprocessing

LESS configures the background behavior processes of its host agents with measurements derived from a user provided sample trace. The sample trace can be anonymized and without payloads. In our LESS based security system re-evaluations, discussed in Section 5, we used short, publicly available traces collected by CAIDA from single Internet backbone links [22], and found that they were more than sufficient.

The preprocessing stage of LESS has three steps. First, it converts the trace into flow level records using Argus [23]. Next, it classifies the flow records based on their application type. In our current iteration, LESS classifies based on destination port; however, there are many more advanced techniques for traffic classification, such as [24]. Finally, LESS determines the client / server roles of each pair of communicating hosts. In our current version, we identify servers by port (*i.e.* the server is the host using a well known port below 1024). There are also more advanced techniques for identifying clients and servers that can be integrated into LESS [25]. LESS currently discards all flows in which neither port is well known.

4.2   Assigning Applications to Host Agents

After preprocessing the input trace, LESS generates N host agents and determines which applications types each host agent will model, based on three statistic samples measured from the input trace:

- **client application count sample**, or the number of application types each host from the input trace uses as a client;
- **server application count sample**, or the number of application types each host from the input trace uses as a server;
- **application host percent sample**, or the percentage of hosts from the input trace that use each application.

LESS then assigns a set of client and server applications to each host agent h with the following procedure:

1. draw a client count c from the client application count sample and a server count s from the server count sample;
2. select c applications observed in the input trace randomly without repetition, weighted by the application host percent sample, and assign them to h's client application set;
3. select s applications observed in the input trace randomly without repetition, weighted by the application host percent sample, and assign them to h's server application set;

4.3 Configuring Background Traffic Generation Processes

Next, LESS configures a behavior process for each client application type assigned to each host agent. A background behavior process accepts the following parameters:

- **connection inter-generation distribution:**, a distribution that defines how long the host agent waits before generating a new connection using the modeled application;
- **server count**: a parameter that defines the maximum number of servers the host agent should connect to with the modeled application;
- **server weight distribution**: a distribution that defines the preference of the host agent for connecting to each host agent that serves the modeled application;
- **community ID**: a parameter that specifies which community the host agent belongs to for the modeled application;
- **inter-community ratio**: a parameter that specifies the host agent's preference for connecting to servers belonging to its own community.

A background behavior process consists of the following two steps, that repeat until the end of the simulation:

1. **Connection Generation:** determine when to generate the next connection by drawing a sample from the *connection inter-generation distribution*, and adding it to the current timestamp.
2. **Destination Selection:** when the timestamp computed in 1 arrives, determine what host agent to initiate a connection with using a decision process that narrows the range of possible destinations by first determining whether to connect with a previously contacted host or a new host (based on whether this process has reached its *server count*), and then determining whether to connect with a host agent inside or outside of its community (based on the process's *inter-community ratio*) After removing the host agents that do not satisfy the criteria selected above, LESS selects one of the remaining host agents randomly, weighted by the *server weight distribution*.

LESS selects inputs for a background behavior process p that models the use of application a by a single host agent with measurements from the input trace, as follows:

1. LESS measures the connection inter-generation distributions and server counts of all hosts that use application a in the input trace, and randomly selects one inter-generation distribution and one server count for p;
2. LESS measures the server weight distribution for application a, and assigns it to all processes that model a, including p.
3. LESS groups all the hosts from the input trace that use application a into communities using the algorithm described in [26], and then selects a community ID for each process that models application a by selecting a community at random, weighted by the size of the community in the input trace;
4. Finally, LESS selects an inter-community ratio for process p at random from the inter-community ratios of all hosts that belong to the corresponding community from the input trace.

4.4   Configuring Malicious Traffic Generation Processes

LESS also adds malicious behavior processes to host agents, based on user provided models of malicious network behavior. Below, we define the three models that we apply in Section 5 to re-evaluate large scale security systems. These models are straightforward, and based on previously published observations about malicious host behavior.

The models are also tunable, with parameters specified by the user. All of the models accept the following three parameters:

- N: the number of host agents that model the malicious behavior;
- I: an inter-event timing distribution for the malicious behavior processes;
- T: the start time of the malicious behavior processes.

Random Worm Outbreak Model The random worm outbreak model, based on observations from [14], simulates the propagation of a randomly spreading worm. This model accepts inputs N, I, and T, as defined above.

To augment the hosts with this malicious behavior, LESS first selects N host agents and marks them as vulnerable to the worm. At time T, a randomly selected vulnerable host initiates the following *propagation algorithm*, which repeats indefinitely:

1. Select a target host, uniformly at random.
2. Send a probe to the host. If the host is marked as vulnerable, mark the host as infected and start the propagation algorithm on that host.
3. Select an inter-probe time from I. At time *currenttime + selectedtime*, repeat from step 1.

Targeted Attacker Model The targeted attacker model simulates attackers that persistently target a small number of networks. This phenomenon has previously been observed in large scale alert repositories [4], and is similar in nature to Advanced Persistent Threats [27].

In addition to N, I, and T, this model also accepts an input C: a distribution measuring the number of networks targeted by each attacker.

To augment hosts with this malicious behavior, LESS first groups all hosts into networks of size between 2 and 128, chosen uniformly at random. It then selects N host agents uniformly at random, and marks them as targeted attackers. For each attacker, LESS draws a value c from C, and then randomly selects c networks for the attacker to target. Finally, at time T, the host agents marked as targeted attackers begin running the follow traffic generation algorithm:

1. Select a target network from the list of targeted networks assigned to this host agent.
2. Select a host in that network uniformly at random.
3. Initiate a connection to the selected host agent.
4. Select an inter-attack time from I. At time *currenttime + selectedtime*, repeat from step 1.

P2P Botnet Communication Model The last model simulates a network of infected hosts communicating in a peer-to-peer overlay network, which increases botnet resilience [15].

In addition to N, I, and T, this model also accepts an input G: a graph generation algorithm.

To augment hosts with this malicious behavior, LESS selects N host agents uniformly at random to mark as bots. Next, the simulator uses G to generate an overlay graph O, connecting all of the bots. Finally, at time T, the host agents marked as bots begin running the following traffic generation algorithm:

1. Select a bot to communicate with by choosing one uniformly at random from the host agents that the given bot shares an edge with in O.
2. Initiate a connection with the selected host.
3. Select an inter-communication time from I. At time *currenttime + selectedtime*, repeat from 1.

4.5 Executing the Simulation

After generating the host agents and augmenting them with background and malicious behavior processes, LESS signals the host agents to begin their behavior processes. Host agents log their activities: the timestamp, destination, and application used in each connection; and these logs are collected after the simulation finishes. LESS is currently a single threaded application written in Python, and maintains event ordering using a queue. We have found this sufficiently fast (*i.e.* each of our trials finishes in under an hour on an Intel i7 laptop); however, since host agents make decisions autonomously, LESS is well suited to scaling, as we discuss in Section 6.

5   Evaluation

In this section, we analyze the four previously discussed large scale network security systems using LESS. We present two types of results, *reproduced* results that

Table 1. LESS setting for our re-evaluations of entropy-based anomaly detection [1], Highly Predictive Blacklisting [3], peer-to-peer botnet detection [5], and cross domain anomaly detection [2]

Param.	Description	[1]	[3]	[5]	[2]
H	*Number of Hosts*	100, 000	100, 000	100, 000	100, 000
S	*Simulation Duration*	100	100	100	100
M	*Malicious Model*	Worm Outbreak	Targeted Attacker	P2P Botnet	Worm Outbreak
N	*Malicious Host Count*	1250 − 5000	5000	904	5000
T	*Attack Start Time*	0	0	0	0
I	*Inter-attack Distribution*	$\mathcal{N}$ (.1, .001),	From [4]	$\mathcal{N}$ (.1, .001)	$\mathcal{N}$ (.1, .001)
C	*Target Count Distribution*	-	From [4]	-	-
D	*Number of Peers*	-	-	5 − 30	-

validate parts of the original evaluations of these systems, and *extended* results that apply simulation to go beyond the original evaluations. These results serve multiple purposes. First, they demonstrate that the generalized models used by LESS are capable of evoking realistic performance from large scale security systems. Second, they validate and extend the evaluations of the studied systems. Finally, they demonstrate use cases for LESS, and how it complements existing analysis methods.

5.1   Experimental Setup

Table 1 lists the parameters we tuned LESS with, unless otherwise noted. LESS derives configurations for background traffic generation from 60 seconds of CAIDA's anonymized 2012 Internet survey [22], a trace containing approximately 800000 hosts with payloads stripped and prefix preserving host and destination IP anonymization. We also apply the three malicious traffic models described in Section 4 with varying parameters that we describe in a per experiment basis. For the purpose of these evaluations, we also re-implemented each of these systems in Python based on the original published algorithms.

To compare results from LESS based simulations with original results, we converted graphs from the original evaluations into numeric data with the Plot Digitizer tool [28]. All plots in this section labeled *Original* are based off of this digitized data.

5.2   Entropy Based Detector

Wagner et al. tested their entropy based method for detecting large scale security threats on a trace collected during the Code Red [29] worm outbreak. We were able to produce similar results using LESS and the random worm outbreak model with the following parameters: $N = 5000$, $I = \mathcal{N}$ (.1, .001), $T = 0$. Figure 2 illustrates both the original results, and our results from our simulation based re-evaluation.

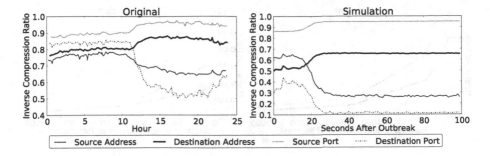

Fig. 2. Original entropy detection results from [1], and entropy detection results in a LESS simulation

There are several quantitative differences between the results. First, the simulated outbreak reached the maximum entropy more quickly, due to the shorter time scale of the simulation. Second, the baseline entropy values differ significantly. We validated that the baseline entropy values in the simulated experiment corresponded to the average entropy values from our source CAIDA trace [1]. Despite the differences between the baseline entropies, these results are *qualitatively* similar: the entropy of each feature either increased in both experiments or decreased in both experiments.

The quantitative differences illustrate a benefit of LESS: by deriving the traffic model from a recent CAIDA trace, we are able to investigate how a system proposed when background network conditions were significantly different would perform in a present-day scenario. Another important benefit of simulation in this domain is the ability to evaluate large scale security techniques under different threat conditions. Figure 3 shows the results of a set of experiments where we used LESS to compare the destination IP address entropy rate during the outbreaks of worms with different average scan per

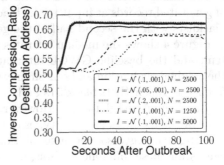

Fig. 3. Extending the results of [1] with LESS, by measuring the technique's sensitivity to different worm outbreak behaviors

second rates (I) and vulnerable population sizes (N). Scan rate and vulnerable population size both increase the entropy rate and make the change more sudden. However, according to our simulation there is an upper bound on both the maximum entropy rate and how rapidly the change can occur.

---

[1] average source IP entropy: 0.6133, average destination IP entropy: 0.5618, average source port entropy: 0.9289, average destination port entropy: 0.3518

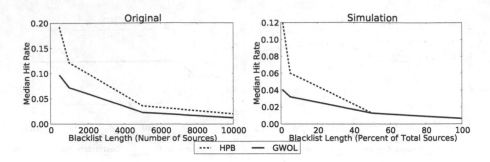

Fig. 4. Predictive (HPB) and Global(GWOL) blacklist hit rates as blacklist length increases, from the original HPB evaluation [3], and simulation experiments with LESS.

5.3 Highly Predictive Blacklisting

Zhang et al. compared the performance of blacklists generated using their system to blacklists generate using a baseline system by measuring blacklist *hit rates*, or the number of IP addresses blocked / the length of the blacklist. They used data from the Dshield repositories for their experiments, so to re-evaluate their system we configured LESS using statistics about Dshield repository logs measured in [4]. We selected values for C, the target count distribution, and I, the inter attack timing distribution, based on their measurements. We used the first half of generated records as input to the blacklist generators, and tested the resulting blacklists with the second half of the generated records.

Figure 4 shows the median hit rates for blacklists generated by the HPB system, and the baseline GWOL alternative, as blacklist length varies, for both the original evaluation and our simulation based re-evaluation. The relative difference between HPB blacklists and GWOL blacklists were similar in both the real and simulated data sets. However, there were quantitative differences: the scale of the hit rates for both types of blacklists were different, and the blacklist hit rates converged sooner in simulation. We believe that there are two primary causes for these differences. First, our simulation likely differed with respect to the number of attackers, as we were unable to determine how many attackers the original data set contained. Blacklist hit rate is very sensitive to this parameter, as it directly affects the number of attacks a network is likely to observe. Additionally, our parameters were derived from measurements of the DShield repository taken approximately 3 years before the HPB system was proposed; the threat landscape, and likely DShield itself, has changed significantly in that time.

Despite these differences, our simulation based analysis reaches the same conclusion as that done on a real, large scale data set: HPB generated blacklists achieve higher hit rates than GWOL generated blacklists, especially when they are short. This demonstrates that LESS allows researchers to reach the same qualitative conclusions, but using significantly higher level and easier to obtain data. Statistical summaries, like those we used as input for this experiment, reveal much less sensitive information and are significantly smaller than large scale traces or IDS log sets.

We also extended the evaluation by studying the *detection rate* (*i.e.* percentage of attackers detected by a blacklist) and *false alert rate*(*i.e.* percentage of non-attacker hosts that the blacklist generates alerts for) of generated blacklists. Figure 5 illustrates an experiment where we varied the number of non-malicious records provided to the HPB and GWOL generators, and measured the true and false positive rates of the resulting blacklists. As more false alerts were submitted to the blacklist generation systems, the detection rates of the generated blacklists decreased while their false alert rates increased. In all cases, the HPB blacklists performed better than the GWOL blacklists. However, the benefit of HPB blacklists

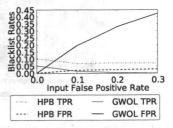

Fig. 5. Extending [3] with LESS: the true and false positive rates (TPR & FPR) of blacklists as the false positive rates of input IDSes varies

increased with the number of false alerts, revealing that not only does HPB achieve higher hit rates, but that it is also *more robust to inaccurate input*.

Although this experiment was straightforward to perform with LESS, it was impossible using the original data set, which is composed of IDS alert logs that lack sufficient information to determine the true maliciousness of the hosts that caused alerts.

5.4 Peer-to-Peer Bot Detector

Coskun et al. evaluated their peer-to-peer botnet detector with traffic from approximately 900 Nugache bots grafted into a 24 hour trace collected at the border of a university network containing approximately 2000 active hosts.

To evaluate this system with LESS, we used the peer-to-peer malicious traffic model to augment 904 host agents with malicious behavior. We set the malicious timing distribution $I = \mathcal{N}\ (.1, .001)$, and generated an overlay network for the bot hosts using the NetworkX [30] library to generate a random regular graph [31]. The regular graph generation algorithm requires one parameter: D, the desired degree of each node in the generated graph.

We then replicated the original experimental procedures with the generated data set, selecting M of the 904 agents augmented with the bot behavior at random, to act as the bot nodes in the simulated evaluation network, and $2000 - M$ non-malicious host agents at random, to act as the innocuous hosts in the simulated evaluation network.

Figure 6 shows measurements taken in both the original re-evaluation, and our re-evaluation with LESS (using $D = 21$), of the number of bot and non-bot hosts detected by the system as M, the number of bots grafted into the trace, varied. Despite our background traffic being modeled after data collected from a different network, our results were very similar to the original results, suggesting that their approach would generalize well to other networks.

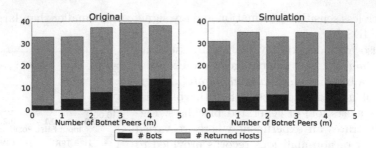

Fig. 6. Number of bots and non-bots detected by the system proposed in [5], in the original evaluation and our LESS based re-evaluation

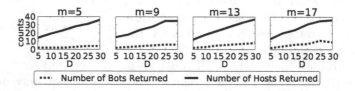

Fig. 7. Extending [5]: evaluating the performance of the botnet detector as bot structure, parameterized by (D), varied in LESS simulations

We also extended the results from the original evaluation, by analyzing the technique's performance as D changed. Figure 7 shows how the number of bots detected and number of hosts returned change, for different M values, as D varied between 1 and 21. This result demonstrates that the density of the botnet communication overlay graph has a large effect on the effectiveness of the system: as the density decreased, so did the accuracy of the detection technique, particularly for larger M values.

Also, this result demonstrates that LESS allows researchers to work backwards from a published result to determine properties that the underlying data set is likely to have. As an example, in our preliminary research with the bot detection technique, we first generated botnet communication graphs using preferential attachment [32] and Erdos-Renyi [33] models, based on previous results that suggested these models fit peer-to-peer overlay networks. However, we found that these models led to less accurate reproduction of the original results, leading us to conclude that the random regular graph generation algorithm is a better fit for the communication network of the Nugache bots used in the original evaluation.

5.5   Collaborative Anomaly Detection

Boggs et al. tested their proposed cross-domain anomaly detection technique on a small deployment involving 3 HTTP servers located at different administrative domains. Using LESS, we examined the potential for larger scale deployment of a similar correlation technique. We implemented a simple threshold based anomaly detector, that monitors all the hosts in a network and generates an alert whenever an external host initiates more than T connections with hosts inside the network in a 1 second period of time. Each network determines T independently, by measuring the distribution of external to internal connections per second in a training data set, and then setting T to the 75th percentile value.

For this experiment, we ran LESS with the worm outbreak model and parameters set to $N = 5000$, $I = \mathcal{N}\,(.1, .001)$, and $T = 0$, and divided the $100,000$ host agents into networks of uniformly at random selected sizes between 2 and 128. We submitted the first half of generated traffic to the training process for each network, and then ran the anomaly detector on the traffic received by each network during the second half of the simulation. We then compared the false positive rates of two different strategies for raising alerts, depicted in Figure 8: first, an *autonomous* strategy, in which each network raises an alert for each anomalous IP address detected; second, a *collaborative* strategy, in which each network raises an alert for an anomalous IP address only if the IP address has generated an alert at another collaborating network.

The benefits of collaboration increase very rapidly, with orders of magnitude fewer false alerts when under 20 networks participate in the collaborative system, suggesting that even a small deployment would have large benefits. There are many other questions about collaborative defense which we do not address here due to space constraints (*e.g.* who should collaborate? what kind of information should collaborators share? how does scale affect detection rate). Such questions are relevant to all the systems we have studied. LESS allows researchers to explore these issues, without facing the often impossible challenge of acquiring a large scale data set, or data sets from many different administrative domains.

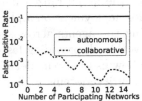

Fig. 8. Extending [2]: evaluating the benefit of cross-domain collaborative anomaly detection when used at scale, in a LESS simulation

6   Discussion

Section 5 demonstrates that LESS simulations can evoke realistic performance from large scale and collaborative network security systems, and has many use cases. In this section, we discuss current limitations and potential expansions to our simulator, as well as integration with other systems and techniques.

Long Term Temporal Dynamics and System Evolution: LESS, the security systems we evaluated, and the threats they were designed to defend against, all only take short term temporal properties, such as inter-arrival time, into account. However, the Internet is a dynamic, evolving network: new hosts connect to it and network applications are launched; hosts change IP addresses and networks; and user behaviors follow diurnal patterns [8]. These, and other long term dynamics, could potentially affect the performance of security systems. By integrating evolutionary network models [34] and parameters that describe longer term dynamics into host agent models, our simulator could be used to evaluate their effects.

Flow Payloads and Packets Due to the volume of traffic that large scale network security systems analyze, most are prohibited from analyzing traffic at the payload or packet level. LESS generates traffic records that do not contain these details. However, LESS hosts' traffic generation processes could be augmented with payload and packet generation techniques such as [11]. This would allow our simulator to evaluate a broader class of security systems, and provide a platform to investigate the benefits of large scale collaboration and data sharing for security systems that monitor lower level data.

Scalability and Testbed Integration Our current implementation of LESS is single threaded. However, each host agent behaves autonomously, deciding, on its own, when to generate traffic and which other host agents to communicate with. Due to the decentralized nature of this process, LESS's architecture is well suited for deployment on a physical or virtual testbed [10, 9].The benefits of distributing the agents across such a testbed are twofold: first, it would distribute the workload, providing faster simulations; second, and more importantly, it would allow us to also model and evaluate the effects of network topology on large scale security systems.

7   Conclusion

Large scale and collaborative security systems have demonstrated great potential. However, scale also presents data related research challenges. Although simulation is an effective tool for overcoming these data challenges in non-security domains, existing simulation tools are not well suited to evaluating large scale security systems. We propose a simulator designed specifically for the large-scale security system domain, LESS, which generates host agents, configures them with stochastic behavior processes, and monitors their activities throughout simulations to collect experimentation data sets. LESS configures non-malicious host behaviors with measurements from real traces, and malicious host behaviors with user defined threat models. We used LESS to validate and extend the evaluations of four recently proposed large scale security systems, demonstrating not only that LESS generates realistic and usable data sets, but also that LESS can compliment existing analysis techniques and real data by allowing researchers to evaluate systems in different dimensions. LESS, and future specially designed simulation tools, can help researchers analyze more complex issues and advance the promising field of large scale and collaborative security.

Acknowledgements. We wish to thank the anonymous reviewers for their feedback. This research was partially supported by ONR grants N001614WX30023 and N00014-12-1-0757, and DoD grant contract number H98230-14-C-0137.

References

[1] Wagner, A., Plattner, B.: Entropy based worm and anomaly detection in fast ip networks. In: WETICE (2005)

[2] Boggs, N., Hiremagalore, S., Stavrou, A., Stolfo, S.J.: Cross-domain collaborative anomaly detection: so far yet so close. In: Sommer, R., Balzarotti, D., Maier, G. (eds.) RAID 2011. LNCS, vol. 6961, pp. 142–160. Springer, Heidelberg (2011)

[3] Zhang, J., Porras, P., Ullrich, J.: Highly predictive blacklisting. In: USENIX Security, vol. 8, pp. 107–122 (2008)

[4] Katti, S., Krishnamurthy, B., Katabi, D.: Collaborating against common enemies. In: ACM IMC (2005)

[5] Coskun, B., Dietrich, S., Memon, N.: Friends of an enemy: identifying local members of peer-to-peer botnets using mutual contacts. In: Proceedings of the 26th Annual Computer Security Applications Conference (2010)

[6] Sonchack, J., Aviv, A., Smith, J.M.: Bridging the data gap: Data related challenges in evaluating large scale collaborative security systems. In: 6th Workshop on Cyber Security Experitmentation and Testing (2013)

[7] Aviv, A.J., Haeberlen, A.: Challenges in experimenting with botnet detection systems. In: USENIX 4th CSET Workshop (2011)

[8] Floyd, S., Paxson, V.: Difficulties in simulating the internet. IEEE/ACM Transactions on Networking (TON) 9(4), 392–403 (2001)

[9] Riley, G.F.: The georgia tech network simulator. In: Proceedings of the ACM SIGCOMM MoMeTools Workshop, pp. 5–12. ACM (2003)

[10] Lantz, B., Heller, B., McKeown, N.: A network in a laptop: rapid prototyping for software-defined networks. In: Proceedings of the 9th ACM SIGCOMM Workshop on Hot Topics in Networks, p. 19. ACM (2010)

[11] Weigle, M.C., Adurthi, P., Hernández-Campos, F., Jeffay, K., Smith, F.D.: Tmix: a tool for generating realistic tcp application workloads in ns-2. ACM SIGCOMM Computer Communication Review 36(3), 65–76 (2006)

[12] Konda, V., Kaur, J.: Rapid: Shrinking the congestion-control timescale. In: IEEE INFOCOM 2009, pp. 1–9. IEEE (2009)

[13] Cao, J., Cleveland, W.S., Gao, Y., Jeffay, K., Smith, F.D., Weigle, M.: Stochastic models for generating synthetic http source traffic. In: INFOCOM 2004, vol. 3, pp. 1546–1557. IEEE (2004)

[14] Moore, D., Shannon, C., Voelker, G.M., Savage, S.: Internet quarantine: Requirements for containing self-propagating code. In: IEEE INFOCOM 2003, pp. 1901–1910. IEEE (2003)

[15] Grizzard, J.B., Sharma, V., Nunnery, C., Kang, B.B., Dagon, D.: Peer-to-peer botnets: Overview and case study. In: HOTBOTS, pp. 1–8 (2007)

[16] Sommers, J., Yegneswaran, V., Barford, P.: Recent advances in network intrusion detection system tuning. In: IEEE 40th Annual CISS, pp. 1490–1495 (2006)

[17] Chen, G., Gray, R.S.: Simulating non-scanning worms on peer-to-peer networks. In: ACM INFOSCALE, p. 29 (2006)

[18] Rossey, L.M., Cunningham, R.K., Fried, D.J., Rabek, J.C., Lippmann, R.P., Haines, J.W., Zissman, M.A.: Lariat: Lincoln adaptable real-time information assurance testbed. In: IEEE Aerospace Conference Proceedings 2002, vol. 6, pp. 6–2671. IEEE (2002)

[19] Bonabeau, E.: Agent-based modeling: Methods and techniques for simulating human systems. PNAS 99(suppl. 3), 7280–7287 (2002)

[20] Ripley, B.D.: Stochastic simulation, vol. 316. Wiley. com (1987)

[21] Dshield.org, `http://www.dshield.org/`

[22] Caida data overview, `http://www.caida.org/data/overview/`

[23] Argus: Audit records generation and utilization system, `http://qosient.com/argus/`

[24] Xie, G., Iliofotou, M., Keralapura, R., Faloutsos, M., Nucci, A.: Subflow: Towards practical flow-level traffic classification. In: IEEE INFOCOM, 2012 Proceedings, pp. 2541–2545. IEEE (2012)

[25] Tan, G., Poletto, M., Guttag, J.V., Kaashoek, M.F.: Role classification of hosts within enterprise networks based on connection patterns. In: USENIX Annual Technical Conference, General Track, pp. 15–28 (2003)

[26] Blondel, V.D., Guillaume, J.L., Lambiotte, R., Lefebvre, E.: Fast unfolding of communities in large networks. Journal of Statistical Mechanics: Theory and Experiment 2008(10), P10008 (2008)

[27] Hutchins, E.M., Cloppert, M.J., Amin, R.M.: Intelligence-driven computer network defense informed by analysis of adversary campaigns and intrusion kill chains. Leading Issues in Information Warfare & Security Research 1, 80 (2011)

[28] Plot digitizer, `http://plotdigitizer.sourceforge.net/`

[29] Moore, D., Shannon, C., et al.: Code-red: a case study on the spread and victims of an internet worm. In: Proceedings of the 2nd ACM SIGCOMM Workshop on Internet Measurment, pp. 273–284. ACM (2002)

[30] Hagberg, A., Swart, P., Schult, D.: Exploring network structure, dynamics, and function using networkx. Technical report, Los Alamos National Laboratory, LANL (2008)

[31] Steger, A., Wormald, N.C.: Generating random regular graphs quickly. Combinatorics Probability and Computing 8(4), 377–396 (1999)

[32] Barabási, A.L., Albert, R.: Emergence of scaling in random networks. Science 286(5439), 509–512 (1999)

[33] Erdos, P., Renyi, A.: On random graphs i. Publ. Math. Debrecen 6, 290–297 (1959)

[34] Dorogovtsev, S.N., Mendes, J.F.: Evolution of networks. Advances in Physics 51(4), 1079–1187 (2002)

Detecting Insider Information Theft Using Features from File Access Logs

Christopher Gates[1], Ninghui Li[1], Zenglin Xu[1],
Suresh N. Chari[2], Ian Molloy[2], and Youngja Park[2]

[1] Purdue University
[2] IBM Research
{gates2,ninghui,xu218}@cs.purdue.edu,
{schari,molloyim,young_park}@us.ibm.com

Abstract. Access control is a necessary, but often insufficient, mechanism for protecting sensitive resources. In some scenarios, the cost of anticipating information needs and specifying precise access control policies is prohibitive. For this reason, many organizations provide employees with excessive access to some resources, such as file or source code repositories. This allows the organization to maximize the benefit employees get from access to troves of information, but exposes the organization to excessive risk. In this work we investigate how to build profiles of normal user activity on file repositories for uses in anomaly detection, insider threats, and risk mitigation. We illustrate how information derived from other users' activity and the structure of the filesystem hierarchy can be used to detect abnormal access patterns. We evaluate our methods on real access logs from a commercial source code repository on tasks of user identification and users seeking to leak resources by accessing more than they have a need for.

Keywords: file, access, insider threat.

1 Introduction

Theft of critical information by malicious insiders is a major threat. Companies may suffer critical damages when disgruntled employees steal intellectual property. There are ample evidences where organizations have suffered significantly due to leakage of large amount of sensitive information accessed by insiders who have legitimate access control privileges to access such information. Insider threats can be caused either by malicious employees or negligent employees who either have their credentials stolen or their devices compromised by malware.

Current access control paradigms, such as role-based access control [1], multi-level security [2], or originator access control [3], are insufficient to deal with this threat of malicious insiders [4]. It is often difficult to a priori predict future needs and configure access control to enforce least privilege in highly dynamic environments. For example, many organizations provide employees access to large data and source code repositories that make it easier to learn and build upon past success without having to reinvent the wheel; in healthcare environments, emergencies often dictate needs. In these cases it

M. Kutyłowski and J. Vaidya (Eds.): ESORICS 2014, Part II, LNCS 8713, pp. 383–400, 2014.

is thus desirable to allow broader access to resources and monitor for potential abuse later. Such systems expose themselves to risk from malicious insiders who can abuse their authorizations by making many access requests, building up aggregate risk.

In this paper we investigate the approach of using filesystem-derived features to detect such insider threats. We evaluate our techniques on a real dataset derived from a commercial source-code repository from a large organization to detect malicious insiders stealing sensitive information. The techniques developed are applicable to any large file repository or web-based information system, such as a wiki.

Most existing solutions for anomaly detection [5–8] only consider an individual resource or command, or aggregate statistics about file-related operations [9]. These systems often yield high false positive rates, especially for new users or resources. Building profiles based on past history or other resources accessed [10] often results in a blowup in the number of probability point estimates.

One existing approach is to adopt a risk-based access control model [4]. For example, in FuzzyMLS [11], one quantifies the risk entailed by the access to each file, and sums up such risk. The risk is independent of a user's access history—and the access history of other users—and depends on a risk-model on known user- and file-attributes. Such a model is not flexible in dynamic environments and has a high cost to deploy.

Our key insight is that the file system hierarchy, in addition to the behavior of other users, provides meaningful information regarding the relevance of a resource. For example, the location of a new file often indicates the project, component, revision, owner, or type of the file. We discuss how to extract and leverage this information for anomaly / normality testing. Our key idea is to detect abnormal accesses based on comparing a user's current accesses with the history. The hypothesis is that there is significant self-similarity in most user's accesses. That is, each user's accesses during the current time period will be similar to what the user has accessed in the past.

We approach the problem in two steps. In the first step, we define a scoring function that computes the score for the pair of a history (which we abstract as a set of files accessed during the history) and a file that is currently accessed. This scoring function can take into consideration extra information, such as file hierarchy and the histories of other users.

In the second step, we explore how to use such a scoring function to detect malicious insider behaviors. We propose and evaluate several models for scoring and aggregation, and evaluate how well each performs at identifying anomalous behavior. We evaluate our methods on real dataset of access logs, and find that filesystem hierarchy derived features are promising in the field of risk scoring and anomaly detection.

The rest of this paper is organized as follows. In Section 2, we present related work. In Section 3 we define the problem and provide an adversarial model for the scenarios we consider in this work. Details of our proposed approach are presented in Sections 4. We provide a description of the test system and experimental results in Section 5, and conclude in Section 6.

2 Related Work

Most related work is in the area of anomaly or intrusion detection. Denning [7] presented the first host-based intrusion detection system leveraging statistics (frequency, inter-arrival time, etc.) of events for alerting. Javitz and Valdes [12] later implemented the concept as IDES. These works focus on building statistical profiles of past behavior and issuing alerts when new events exceed significant thresholds, such as a set number of standard deviations.

There has been an abundance of work on network-based intrusion detection [13–16], typically measuring anomalies in the rate or volume of the traffic [13], abnormal numbers of distinct hosts or ports [17], or similarity to known malicious behavior [18], such as blacklists[1] and signatures [19]. Salem et al. [5] present a survey of research on insider attacks for host and network intrusions.

There is relatively little work specifically looking at filesystem events for anomaly detection. Stolfo et al. [10] use filesystem features—primarily filename, working directory, and parent directory—to detect rootkits and other malicious activity. No features are derived from the relationship between two files in the filesystem, and each resource is treated as an opaque identifier. Deviations from first and second order density estimators [8] are used to score events. The system estimates the probability of a previously unseen event.

Huang and Wong [20] discuss the use of a Fuse virtual filesystem to monitor for filesystem anomalies. It uses a "baseline" library of profiles, but provides no details on how this library is generated or how filesystem requests are scored against the library. The TripWire File Integrity system[2] detects anomalies in filesystems by testing for unexpected changes in files using a file digest, similar to how ZFS detects file corruption [21], and cannot be used to detect violations of confidentiality.

Senator et al. [9] use statistical anomalies in file events, specifically the fraction of file events on removable media, to detect injected malicious activity into activity logs obtained from workstations at Raytheon.

Bowen et al. [22] suggest using decoy files to detect malicious insiders. Decoys are files that contain tainted information whose use can be tracked, e.g., credentials or account information. Their system relies on traceable or booby trapped resources rather to detect malicious insiders rather than by analyzing resources users typically require. It is more difficult to perform such attacks in software code repositories where use of the software is more difficult to detect.

Chen and Malin [6] propose an anomaly detection method that clusters weighted graphs of users' access to resources. Their clustering approach is similar to a hybrid of k-nearest neighbor and spectral analysis. If a user does not access similar resources to other users, or changes the cluster of similar users over time, they are considered an anomaly. This work is the most similar to ours in that it considers the resources other users access, but it does not consider the relationships between resources implicit in the filesystem or file names.

3   Problem Definition

At a high level, the problem we want to answer is how to detect malicious insiders who try to steal files they have the privilege or clearance to access. In this section, we

---

[1] https://developers.google.com/safe-browsing/
[2] http://www.tripwire.com/it-security-software/scm/
file-integrity-monitoring/

introduce a concrete formulation of this problem. Note that while we are using the term "files" here, our approach is applicable to other types of resources where similarity can be measured.

We assume the following inputs. Let $\mathcal{F}$ denote the set of all files with associated information, e.g., the file hierarchy, the type of the files, etc. We are given A_j^t for $1 \leq t \leq T$ and $1 \leq j \leq N$, where N denotes the number of users, j ranges over all users, T is the index of the current time period, t ranges over all time periods, and each $A_j^t \subseteq \mathcal{F}$ denotes the set of files accessed by user j during the t'th time period. We use $A_j^{t_1:t_2}$ to denote $A_j^{t_1} \cup A_j^{t_1+1} \cup \cdots \cup A_j^{t_2}$. We use $\mathbf{A}$ to denote the matrix consisting of all A_j^t's.

For the output, we want to identify the users that are malicious in time period T. More specifically, we want a mechanism M that outputs a non-negative real number when given $\mathbf{A}, \mathcal{F}, j$, where an output of 0 denotes completely normal behavior, and the larger the value, the more suspicious the j'th user activity during the t'th time period. Then the j indices with the highest values are considered abnormal.

3.1 Adversary Model

We try to detect malicious insiders whose objective is to steal (i.e., download/check out) files. We assume that the attacker needs to steal a substantial number of files, and is aware of the mechanism that is being deployed. We consider two kinds of attackers.

- An *impetuous* attacker is one who turns malicious only at time T. An employee who turns malicious after learning that he will be fired soon belongs to this kind.
- A *patient* attacker is one who is malicious at a time earlier than T. Such an attacker can alter his normal access pattern over time to make the attacking activities in time T look benign.

3.2 Challenges and Evaluation Criteria

An important challenge is how to evaluate such a mechanism. While our formulation is close to classification problems in machine learning, one challenge is that we have very little labeled data, and the few labels we have are of limited reliability, containing both false negatives and false positives. To deal with this challenge of limited or missing labels, we treat this as an unsupervised learning problem, and build models using only the access data. We assume this data is *mostly* benign when training and testing. For data representing malicious activity, we inject file accesses representing attempts to steal files. Such data are not used in training, and are used only for testing the effectiveness of our approaches at detecting users with such injected accesses. We vary the number of file accesses injected into one user's access from around 500 to around 12,000, and evaluate the robustness of different approaches.

A second challenge is to be resilient to patient adversary who knows about the deployed mechanism, and may carry out evasion attacks. To evaluate effectiveness against such adversaries, we evaluate how the adversarial strategy of accessing a few files among the files one plan to steal (i.e., among the files to be injected) impacts the effectiveness of different methods.

4 Proposed Approaches

Some currently deployed systems use the number of files that are accessed as a feature for detecting. This approach, however, is unlikely to be sharp enough to achieve the needed tradeoff between false positives and false negatives. Our intuition is that it should be possible to exploit more information between the files that are accessed in the current period, A_j^T, against the files that have been accessed during the history, $A_j^{T-\ell:T-1}$, which we use A_j^H as a short hand. We drop the subscript j when it is not important. First, if all files that one user currently accesses have been accessed in the recent past by the user, then this is unlikely to be a malicious theft. Second, even if many of the currently-accessed files have not accessed, if they are similar to the files that have been accessed, then this is less likely to be malicious theft. Many ways to measure similarity exist. One possibility is based on the hierarchical structure of the file. Files under the same directory may be viewed as more similar than files that are far apart in the hierarchy. Files that are accessed by essentially the same set of users may be viewed as more similar than files that are accessed by mostly disjoint sets of users. Files that have similar meta-data attribute values, such as file types (e.g., C source code files versus HTML files) may be viewed as more similar. In summary, we want to measure both the "amount" of accesses and the "similarity" of accesses.

At the center of our approach is a function that assigns a score for each file f when given an access history A^H, we use the notation score$[f|A^H]$ to represent the scoring of f when given A^H. Intuitively, this function measures how "unexpected" a file f is, when given A^H as access history. We desire the following algebraic properties for such a score function:

1. score$[f|A^H]$ is low when $f \subseteq A^H$. The intuition is that a file already accessed is considered quite normal.
2. score$[f|A_1^H] \leq$ score$[f|A_2^H]$ when $A_1^H \supseteq A_2^H$, and as a corollary, score$[f|\emptyset]$ should be high.

We construct score$[f|A^H]$ by using a composition of two functions, a similarity measure between two files, and an aggregation function. For each new access f the scoring function is mapped against f and each file in the user's history. The aggregation function reduces the result into a final score. The general function is:

$$\text{score}[f|A^H] = \text{agg}_{g \in A^H} \text{score}(f, g)$$

To instantiate this, we need to define both the aggregation function and a scoring function. The score(f, g) function dictates how two files relate to each other while the agg expresses how a single file f relates to the entire history A^H. In the remainder of this section we present several possible instantiations, and methods to use the scoring function.

4.1   The Scoring Function: score(f, g)

The scoring function for two individual files defines how files relate to each other within the system. We will explore several different techniques to classify their relationships.

Binary Equality. The most basic method is to define a score to test for equality between two files:

$$\text{score}(f, g) = \begin{cases} 0 & \text{when } f = g \\ 1 & \text{when } f \neq g \end{cases}$$

This method works well when users consistently access the same set of files, but cannot adequately handle new resources, such as new files in the same directory as previous requests.

Full Distance. This approach measure the distance between two files if one were to walk the hierarchy to the least common ancestor, lca, which is normalized by the worst case scenario where the lca is the root of the filesystem.

$$\text{score}(f, g) = \frac{\text{length}(f, \text{lca}(f, g)) + \text{length}(g, \text{lca}(f, g))}{\text{length}(f, \text{root}) + \text{length}(g, \text{root})}$$

Lowest Common Ancestor (LCA). Another approach is to look at the lowest common ancestor between the two files. This gives a distance to the branch point, but does not consider how far away the other file is from that branch point. The full distance between two files can sometimes lead to longer than expected paths if there is a deeply nested structure where most of the accesses are occurring at the leafs. This approach evaluates the distance based on the branch of the filesystem being accessed as opposed to the exact files being accessed, and under some types of systems and hierarchies may be a more appropriate scoring technique.

$$\text{score}(f, g) = \frac{\text{length}(f, \text{lca}(f, g))}{\text{length}(f, \text{root})}$$

Note that this is not symmetric, that is $\text{score}(f, g) \equiv \text{score}(g, f)$ is not necessarily true.

Log LCA. The previous method penalizes files near the root more than files deep within the hierarchy. The penalty incurred for being near the root may be too harsh, and so different ways of scaling the score may be applied. One way to scale the score is to take the log of the distances values, which adjusts the scores so files that are very shallow are not penalized as much as the previous technique.

$$\text{score}(f, g) = \frac{log(\text{length}(f, \text{lca}(f, g)) + 1)}{log(\text{length}(f, \text{root}) + 1)}$$

Different scaling techniques also affect how the score of non-exact matches relate to the score of exact matches. In the case of this technique, exact matches still have a score of 0, while matches within the same directory or close directories will have a higher score relative to the non-scaled score.

Access Similarity. Given user sets U_f and U_g which contain the users who access files f and g in the history, we use the Jaccard Distance to define the score function between f and g.

$$\text{score}(f, g) = 1 - \frac{|U_f \cap U_g|}{|U_f \cup U_g|}$$

The underlying hypothesis for this scoring method is that files dissimilar in the hierarchy may be similar for other reasons, and this association is elevated by user access patterns. For example, the specification and implementation files in a source code repository and their corresponding documentation. This is closely related to collaborative filtering, where new resources are suggested based on previous requests.

Discussion. The above techniques are the primary score functions that we examine in this work, but is not meant to be an exhaustive list of filesystem derived features. Future work will consider the order and frequency of file accesses, as well as other file metadata, such as the type. We also note that it is highly unlikely any single scoring function will be sufficient in all possible use cases or for all file requests. We will investigate how well each scoring function performs at discriminating abnormal activity in Section 5.

4.2 The Aggregation Function: $\text{agg}_{g \in A^H}$

A single file $f \in A^T$ generates $|A^H|$ different scores, one for each $g \in A^H$. The agg function defines the way that the system aggregates the $|A^H|$ scores to create a single score for the specific f.

Min Score. One approach is to take min, i.e., $\text{agg}_{g \in A^H} \text{score}(f, g) = \min_{g \in A^H} \text{score}(f, g)$. The advantage of this approach is that it is simple, and in many cases captures the distance effectively. Even a single access in a certain area may be useful to predict where the next accesses are going to occur. The downside of this is that it is susceptible to seeding attacks by "patient adversaries" who may perform a single access in an area that they plan to later access much more broadly. That single access can hide many later accesses and undermine certain scoring functions.

Average. To mitigate the patient adversary attack described above, one can calculate the aggregate score as the average of all similarity score values. This increases the effort for an adversary to seed their history with files similar to the intended target, but may increase the aggregate risk scores for diverse users.

K-Nearest Scores. An alternative that balances the tradeoffs of the minimum and average aggregate functions is to compute the average of the k files in A^H that have the lowest score. This is also vulnerable to "patient adversaries", who can seed the past with a few files in different locations, however it takes more of an effort and some knowledge of k to be effective.

4.3 Feature Generation

The previous techniques produce a way to determine the score for any specific file, in this section we focus on how to use those scores to generate a feature set for a specific user. We look at how to use these scores for inner (to self) and outer (to others) approaches to feature generation.

4.3.1   Cumulative Score

Individual $score(f, A^H)$ results taken as a single value are not able to provide any meaningful context as to possibly malicious behavior. Rather, the scores for all $f \in A^T$ taken together provide more information. We focus on two primary ways of accumulating the risk into a single feature, summing and averaging the scores.

Since we are primarily concerned with a user stealing information, the method of summing the scores together is one obvious choice since it will generate a higher value when more files are accessed, we define this as

$$sumScore = \sum_{k=1}^{M} score[f_k | A_j^H]$$

where $f_k \in A_j^T$ and $M = |A_j^T|$ is the number of unique files accessed in the current period. A user who exceeds a risk budget could be flagged and their behavior reviewed. However, summing the scores will result in very unstable values, for instance in one period a user may perform 10x or 100x more accesses then they did in the previous or next period. Any technique which builds a model of the user's expected behavior would need to normalize the information or handle these drastically different cases accordingly.

Averaging the user's scores against the total number of unique accesses they performed is one natural way to normalize the data, $aveScore = \frac{sumScore}{M}$. In this way, activity between periods can be compared more naturally since all values will be in $[0,1]$, and the overall score will be effected by the portion of files that receive a high or low score.

One way to use both the sum or average is to create a single score for each user as they relate to their own history. That is, for a set of users U, and $j \in U$, we calculate the $sumScore$ or $aveScore$ given A_j^T and A_j^H. However, this does not use all the information that is available.

4.3.2   Self Score vs. Relative Scores

Instead of taking a single score for user j, we can generate a matrix of scores $\mathbf{x}$ where $x_{i,j} = aveScore_{i,j}$ using A_i^T and A_j^H. Each row in the matrix represents a single user's current set of accesses A_i^T, and each column indicates how that user relates to the history of the j'th user, A_j^H. The advantage here is that instead of requiring a single score to be fixed above some threshold, we can instead evaluate how all the scores change in the same period. It may be that a user's behavior deviates from their own A^H by a relatively high degree, however if that user's behavior stays consistent to most of the other A^Hs, then this can be an indication that the new behavior reflects a user legitimately accessing new files. Conversely, if a user stays consistent to their own behavior, but deviates highly from all the other A^Hs then this can indicate other types of abnormal behavior.

The novelty here is that in most cases either a global model of user behavior is trained and used to detect abnormal behavior, or a specific profile given one user's history is trained. While the global model is capable of incorporating some of the more complex relationships within the data, it can be difficult to do on such high dimensional and sparse data.

4.4 Using the Features

Given the scores and features constructed in the previous subsection, we now turn to how to use this information.

4.4.1 Self Score Evaluation

The most basic way in which to use the similarity score is to look directly at the $sumScore$ or $aveScore$ for the user's own profile. There are two ways we may want to use this information during an evaluation, anomaly detection and profile identification.

Profile Identification This is also an effective way to associate an unknown $A_?^T$ to the actual user it belongs to. In this process we generate $score[A_?^T|A_j^H]$ for all $j \in U$, and the A_i^H with the lowest scores generally help to identify the user that actually generated the accesses.

Anomaly Detection If the score for a particular set of accesses is above some threshold, then it is marked as abnormal.

We will see in our evaluation that even this simple metric on the scores can be effective. This is the only technique that we use which only looks at a user own score, the rest of this section discusses techniques that look at the all of the scores as a larger set of features, comparing a single access pattern back to all users' histories.

4.4.2 Mean Vector

This technique is similar to centroid based clustering techniques with known user labels for all points. Given the full features $\mathbf{x}$ where $x_{i,j} = score[A_i^T|A_j^H]$ over many time periods, we find a mean vector to represent each user, which is essentially the center point for a cluster that will represent a specific user's expected behavior. The advantage of this technique is that each user's accesses will relate to other users in specific ways based on similar access patterns and job responsibilities so it adds more information into the system. Once we know the mean vectors for all users, we can compare any new feature vector to determine how close that vector is to the mean of each specific user. Cosine Similarity is used to measure the distance between the centroids and new feature vectors. This handles outliers in the training period well by smoothing the expectation out over all the training points. However this does not account well for cases where a user may be performing several different job functions over different periods but works well in general.

5   Experimental Results

The techniques presented can be applied to any system that manages sensitive resources, such as document repositories, online wikis, and source code repositories. While we extensively leverage the filesystem hierarchy, the presented techniques are general enough to be adapted to other domains. For example, the Wikipedia ontology or the shortest path between two URLs can be used as a substitute.

In our experiments we focus on a commercial source code repository for a large organization. Source code is an attractive target for malicious insiders and has an extremely high value, such as the theft of Goldman Sachs source code by Sergey Aleynikov [23], and negative impact to the organization, for example the RSA SecureID[3] or Adobe breaches[4]. Source code is often organized into hierarchies, and access is often limited by job function and expertise. Source code has many of the characteristics of other file repositories that make anomaly detection difficult. Files are not consistently accessed, and become stable over time, e.g., libraries, while new files are constantly being added or removed. Further, many users require different levels of access. Those responsible for building code require broad read-only access, while many developers need narrow read-write access. Debugging may often require an employee to investigate how other components function to narrow down root causes. This all makes finding stable and consistent access patterns challenging.

The source code management system we use in our study is Configuration Management Version Control (CMVC). Each file in CMVC is associate with a filename and a location in a hierarchy, and files can be grouped into components orthogonal to the filesystem hierarchy. For example, not all files in a directory need to be in the same components, and a component can contain files from any directory. The components may be further nested, and users are granted access to check in and check out files by authorizing them to components. CMVC also includes extensive reporting, task and defect management, and release levels to make administration of large projects easier.

Lines from the log consist of a timestamp, userID, action performed on a resource, and the name of the resource. The logs contain additional lines which relate to other information such as reporting and defects, however we limit our view of the logs to the file activity. For our task, we consider only accesses that result in file reading. CMVC does not log which component a request pertains to, and we do not have access to the access control lists, historical or current.

For our task we analyze one year of log data consisting of approximately two-thousand users. There are $\sim$512k unique files and $\sim$133k unique directories in the filesystem. Since there must be some history for all of our techniques to be useful, there is a single period of learning the initial history. Then there are 10 meaningful periods of training data, and a final period used for testing.

5.1   Portion of Files Accessible

One way to measure the effectiveness of each scoring technique is to measure how well it scores files that the user does access compared to files that the user does not access in a given time period. We generate a set of uniformly sampled files to represent the 'All Possible Access' group, while using each user's actual accesses for the other group.

Figure 1 plots t at every increment of .05 between 0 and 1, the x and y values are generated by the following formulas :

---

[3] http://www.darkreading.com/attacks-and-breaches/
rsa-securid-breach-cost-$66-million/d/d-id/1099232?

[4] http://arstechnica.com/security/2013/10/adobe-source-code-and-
customer-data-stolen-in-sustained-network-hack/

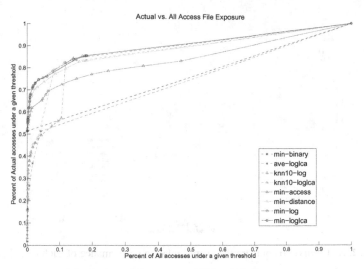

Fig. 1. Actual Access vs. All Possible Accesses

$$x(t) = \frac{1}{N} \sum_{i=1}^{N} \frac{\text{\# files in hierarchy for user i under score t}}{\text{\# files in hierarchy}}$$

$$y(t) = \frac{1}{N} \sum_{i=1}^{N} \frac{\text{\# files access by user i under score t}}{\text{\# of files accessed by user i}}$$

The x value represents, averaged across all users, how many files in the complete hierarchy have a score under threshold t. The y value represents, averaged across all users, the number of actual accessed files in a given period that have a score under threshold t.

In an ideal scenario, with knowledge of the future, all legitimate accesses made in a given period would receive a score less than all of the files from the group the user did not access. This would create a line from the upper left, $(0,1)$, to the upper right, $(1,1)$, of the graph. Given unpredictable human behavior and shifting responsibilities, this is of course impossible, and so we desire a scoring function which gets closer to the upper left but also allows for changing behavior.

All techniques which use min as the aggregation function start their curve at ~52% since on average a user accessed around half of their files in a previous time period, and exact matches get a score of 0 for all min techniques. The min-loglca and min-log stand out as performing the best among the techniques across all thresholds. The knn10-lca and knn10-loglca show a marked difference between the lca vs loglca techniques.

Averaging the distance between all files in the history to the current file does not perform well overall in this task. Originally this seemed like one possibly useful technique since it naturally weights branches of the hierarchy with more accesses, however, this potential advantage seems to be overwhelmed by other properties of the access behavior and file hierarchy.

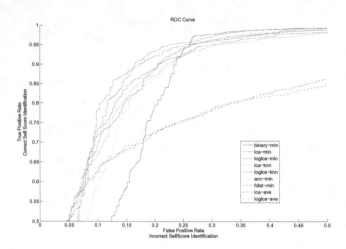

Fig. 2. ROC curve to compare the overall relative performance of each technique

The binary score function in Figure 1 is represented by two points and creates the line from (0,.52) to (1,1). The binary technique is useful given the nature of our target system, a source code repository where roughly half of accesses have already been performed in the past. However, under different conditions where most accesses are new and unique, such as classified documents or medical records, then repeat accesses to the same data across multiple time periods could be less common and this signal would become weaker.

5.2 Profile Identification

Another task we explore is how effective each technique is at identifying which user generated a specific set of access. That is, given a random A^T, how well can we predict which user generated that set of accesses. For this task we compute $\mathbf{x}$ where $x_{i,j} = aveScore_{i,j}$ as specified in Section 4.3.2. We denote the cases where $i = j$ as the "SelfScore", and the cases where $i \neq j$ as "OtherScore". The percent of self scores and other scores that are assigned a score in a specific range for a subset of techniques are presented in the Appendix in Figure 5 and the ROC curves for all techniques are presented in Figure 2 in this section. This gives an indication of how well each technique performs in identifying a user's own behavior. One thing to note here is that user accesses can be highly correlated, and so it is not necessarily abnormal for some "OtherScores" to have low values.

The generic scaling for depth, taking the log of the lowest common ancestor and log of the distance to root, has a slight performance impact for our data, seen in the difference between Figures 5(a) and 5(b) and in Figure 2.

Given the outcome from Figure 1 and 2 we focus the remaining experiments on the min-loglca technique to generate features. The min-binary technique is used as a baseline that only counts unique accesses in the current period given all previous periods. This is different from counting the unique accesses in the current period, which we also use as another baseline since this is the most commonly used statistic in related work.

5.3   Attacker

The primary goal for the attacker we model is on data exfiltration of varying degrees. While there are other potential attacks, such as targeted insertion or deletion, for this evaluation we only focus on the general problem of stealing information. Due to the nature of the target application domain there are several assumptions that we make about the data and the attacker.

Arbitrarily Self Control. An attacker using account u_i can arbitrarily control file accesses in A_i^T and A_i^H.

Restricted Overall Control. An attacker is not able to control another user's activity on the system.

Targeted Knowledge. The attacker has knowledge of the files or directories they are targeting, and does not have to perform a read all on the root of the repository.

Location Stability. For the purposes of this evaluation, we assume that files are stable in their location in the hierarchy. It is possible that files can be moved, but given the log data, this is very infrequent. Additionally, if an attacker wants to directly move a file, then the action is captured in the logs and will count as both a read from the source and write to the destination, which would translate to the same general information as just reading or writing a file directly.

With this in mind we discuss two attack types that we test against, impetuous and patient attackers.

5.3.1   Impetuous Attacker

An impetuous attacker is a user who does not have the time or ability to create a crafted attack. It represents an employee who is suddenly laid off or leaving the company, a naive user who is unaware of the protections in place, or an attacker who is afraid of being detected and so they grab as much data as quickly as possible.

To model an impetuous attacker, we generate injections that consist of randomly selected directories that contain file counts in various ranges, we then inject all files under that directory into the accesses in A^T to simulate that the user accessed all information under a specific directory. We generate data for 3 ranges to capture the effect that different access counts have on detection: 500-1000 accesses contains 10 unique attacks, 1000-2500 accesses contains 12 unique attacks and 5000+ accesses contains 2 unique attacks. We compare the detection rates for all injections in a given range against the actual accesses to determine the true positive and false positive rate for various techniques.

Figure 3 demonstrates detection when a user has abnormal access activity. SumScore and AveScore for each user, as defined in Section 4.3.1, are generated with the logIcamin technique. NewUnique is equivalent to taking the SumScore of binary-min for a user's own profile.

Unique accesses in the current period and NewUnique access are a baseline, AveScore and SumScore are calculated against the user's own profile. The MeanDistance is calculated as discussed in Section 4.4.2, using the historic **x** vectors from the previous periods as training data to learn an expected profile for each user. Multiplying the MeanDistance by the NewUnique gives a higher score to abnormal behavior that

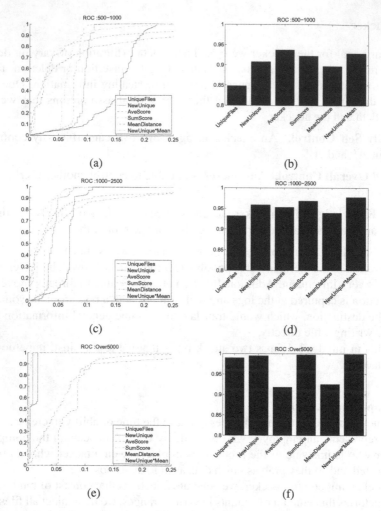

Fig. 3. Demonstrates the performance of detecting various quantities of injected files into otherwise normal behavior

also accesses many files compared to abnormal behavior that only accesses a few files, and is similar to the difference between AveScore and SumScore.

The NewUnique value generally performs well in our tests, however this is in part due to the nature of our dataset where many accesses are not unique in the actual data. On average, users access ∼600 unique files in the test period, and ∼300 of those are new files the user has not previously accessed.

The AveScore performs best in the lowest range, since it is able to differentiate between expected and unexpected behavior, while the SumScore performs better as the injected file counts increase since this more strongly penalizes larger sets of unique accesses. The MeanDistance alone does not perform best overall, but scaled by the number of NewUnique accesses performs well in the 500-1000 range, and best in the 1000-2500 and 5000+ ranges.

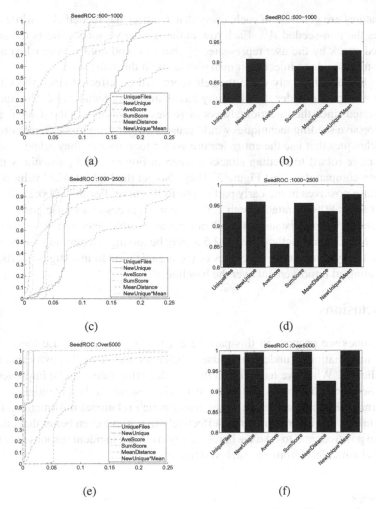

Fig. 4. Demonstrates the performance of detecting various quantities of injected files when the attacker also seeds an attack ahead of time.

5.3.2 Patient Attacker

Our attack model assumes that the attacker is capable of injecting accesses into their own training periods, we model this as a patient attacker who has both the time and knowledge to craft a more meaningful attack in order to manipulate the detection techniques. Under this model, an attacker has arbitrary control over their own score, but less control over their relation to other profiles.

We use the same set of injections as the impetuous attack evaluation. To model the patient attacker we seed file accesses from the injection into the A^H, and then generate the features vectors $\mathbf{x}$ from A^T based off of the seeded A^H. We injected seeds for various access counts, but find that a single seed access is nearly as effective as most strategies, and so we present only single access seed results in Figure 4.

The features are generate in such a way that $x_{i,i}$ uses the seeded A^H, while $x_{i,j}$ for $i \neq j$ uses the non-seeded A^H. Each row in the feature vector $\mathbf{x}$ reflects the outcome of a seeded attack by the user represented by that row, and not the case when all users spontaneously decide to inject their own profiles with the same seed.

Any techniques that only use a the self score will be affected since the self score is easy to manipulate under the hierarchy based similarity techniques. The SumScore is less affected since the injection always increases the score over the normal activity. More aggressive seeding techniques would cause a bigger drop in the SumScore AUC.

The techniques that use the entire feature vector for a user as they relate to all other users are more robust to seeding attacks as seen in Figure 4 and particularly they are stable when compared against Figure 3. They also get the highest AUC value and lead to fewer false positives in the early part of the ROC curve. For the 1000:2500 case we can detect about 80% of attacks with 2.5% of normal accesses as false positives using the NewUnique*MeanDistance method, compared to 80% detection at just below 5% FP for the NewUnique method. While 2.5% may be too high depending on the number of users in the system and the resources of the organization to investigate alerts, this is still a meaningful improvement over the baseline.

6   Conclusions

The techniques we propose in this paper are a first step to better use hierarchy and similarity information to understand a user's behavior and detect behavior that is most likely malicious. While we have shown that the detection rates can be improved using our proposed methods, this is just a first step. There seems to be potential in collaborative learning on this complex data that contains rich relational information. The end goal is to utilize this information more effectively to achieve even better detection with fewer false positives and to take the burden away from the incident response teams who have to deal with alerts from any such system.

References

1. Sandhu, R.S., Coyne, E.J., Feinstein, H.L., Youman, C.E.: Role-based access control models. IEEE Computer 29(2), 38–47 (1996)
2. Bell, D.E., LaPadula, L.J.: Secure computer systems: Unified exposition and Multics interpretation. Technical Report ESD-TR-75-306, Mitre Corporation (March 1976)
3. Park, J., Sandhu, R.: Originator control in usage control. In: Proceedings of the Third International Workshop on Policies for Distributed Systems and Networks 2002 (2002)
4. Horizontal integration: Broader access models for realizing information dominance, JASON Report JSR-04-132 (2004)
5. Salem, M., Hershkop, S., Stolfo, S.: A Survey of Insider Attack Detection Research. In: Insider Attack and Cyber Security, pp. 69–90 (2008)
6. Chen, Y., Malin, B.: Detection of anomalous insiders in collaborative environments via relational analysis of access logs. CODASPY 2011: Proceedings of the First ACM Conference on Data and Application Security and Privacy (February 2011)
7. Denning, D.E.: An Intrusion-Detection Model. IEEE Transactions on Software Engineering SE-13(2), 222–232 (1987)

8. Apap, F., Honig, A., Hershkop, S., Eskin, E., Stolfo, S.J.: Detecting malicious software by monitoring anomalous windows registry accesses. In: Wespi, A., Vigna, G., Deri, L. (eds.) RAID 2002. LNCS, vol. 2516, p. 36. Springer, Heidelberg (2002)

9. Senator, T.E., Goldberg, H.G., Memory, A., Young, W.T., Rees, B., Pierce, R., Huang, D., Reardon, M., Bader, D.A., Chow, E., Essa, I., Jones, J., Bettadapura, V., Chau, D.H., Green, O., Kaya, O., Zakrzewska, A., Briscoe, E., Mappus, R.I.L., McColl, R., Weiss, L., Dietterich, T.G., Fern, A., Wong, W.K., Das, S., Emmott, A., Irvine, J., Lee, J.Y., Koutra, D., Faloutsos, C., Corkill, D., Friedland, L., Gentzel, A., Jensen, D.: Detecting insider threats in a real corporate database of computer usage activity. In: KDD 2013: Proceedings of the 19th ACM SIGKDD International Conference on Knowledge Discovery and Data Mining, ACM Request Permissions (August 2013)

10. Stolfo, S.J., Hershkop, S., Bui, L.H., Ferster, R., Wang, K.: Anomaly detection in computer security and an application to file system accesses. In: Hacid, M.-S., Murray, N.V., Raś, Z.W., Tsumoto, S. (eds.) ISMIS 2005. LNCS (LNAI), vol. 3488, pp. 14–28. Springer, Heidelberg (2005)

11. Cheng, P.C., Rohatgi, P., Keser, C., Karger, P.A., Wagner, G.M., Reninger, A.S.: Fuzzy MLS: An Experiment on Quantified Risk-Adaptive Access Control. In: IEEE Symposium on Security and Privacy (2007)

12. Javitz, H.S., Valdes, A.: The SRI IDES Statistical Anomaly Detector. Research in Security and Privacy (1991)

13. Paxson, V.: Bro: A System for Detecting Network Intruders in Real-Time. Computer Networks 31(23-24), 2435–2463 (1999)

14. Sommer, R., Paxson, V.: Outside the closed world: On using machine learning for network intrusion detection. In: 2010 IEEE Symposium on Security and Privacy (SP), pp. 305–316 (2010)

15. Mahoney, M.V., Chan, P.K.: Learning nonstationary models of normal network traffic for detecting novel attacks. In: KDD 2002: Proceedings of the Eighth ACM SIGKDD International Conference on Knowledge Discovery and Data Mining. ACM Request Permissions (July 2002)

16. Lee, W., Xiang, D.: Information-theoretic measures for anomaly detection. In: Proceedings of the 2001 IEEE Symposium on Security and Privacy, S&P 2001, pp. 130–143 (2001)

17. Lakhina, A., Crovella, M., Diot, C., Lakhina, A., Crovella, M., Diot, C.: Mining anomalies using traffic feature distributions, vol. 35. ACM (October 2005)

18. Mathur, S., Coskun, B., Balakrishnan, S.: Detecting hidden enemy lines in IP address space. In: NSPW 2013: Proceedings of the 2013 Workshop on New Security Paradigms Workshop (December 2013)

19. Jamshed, M.A., Lee, J., Moon, S., Yun, I., Kim, D., Lee, S., Yi, Y., Park, K.: Kargus: a highly-scalable software-based intrusion detection system. In: CCS 2012: Proceedings of the 2012 ACM Conference on Computer and Communications Security. ACM Request Permissions (October 2012)

20. Huang, L., Wong, K.: Anomaly Detection by Monitoring Filesystem Activities. In: 2011 IEEE 19th International Conference on Program Comprehension (ICPC), pp. 221–222. IEEE (January 2011)

21. Bonwick, J.: Zfs end-to-end data integrity (December 2005)

22. Bowen, B.M., Hershkop, S., Keromytis, A.D., Stolfo, S.J.: Baiting inside attackers using decoy documents. In: Chen, Y., Dimitriou, T.D., Zhou, J. (eds.) SecureComm 2009. LNICST, vol. 19, pp. 51–70. Springer, Heidelberg (2009)

23. Glovin, D., Harper, C.: Goldman trading-code investment put at risk by theft (2009)

A   Appendix

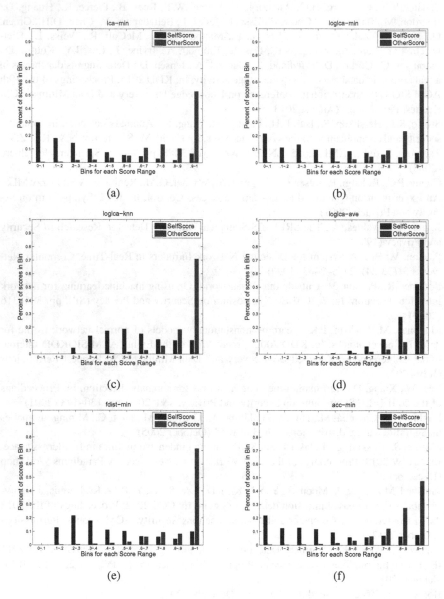

Fig. 5. The percent of Self Scores vs Other Scores in each score range for various techniques using the aveScore output

SRID: State Relation Based Intrusion Detection for False Data Injection Attacks in SCADA

Yong Wang[1,2], Zhaoyan Xu[1], Jialong Zhang[1], Lei Xu[1],
Haopei Wang[1], and Guofei Gu[1]

[1] SUCCESS Lab, Texas A&M University, College Station, Texas, USA
[2] Department of Information Security, Shanghai University of Electric Power,
Shanghai, China
wybaidu@gmail.com, {z0x0427,jialong,xray2012,haopei,guofei}@cse.tamu.edu

Abstract. Advanced false data injection attack in targeted malware intrusion is becoming an emerging severe threat to the Supervisory Control And Data Acquisition (SCADA) system. Several intrusion detection schemes have been proposed previously [1, 2]. However, designing an effective real-time detection system for a resource-constraint device is still an open problem for the research community. In this paper, we propose a new relation-graph-based detection scheme to defeat false data injection attacks at the SCADA system, even when injected data may seemly fall within a valid/normal range. To balance effectiveness and efficiency, we design a novel detection model, *alternation vectors with state relation graph*. Furthermore, we propose a new inference algorithm to infer the injection point(s), i.e., the attack origin, in the system. We evaluate SRID with a real-world power plant simulator. The experiment results show that SRID can detect various false data injection attacks with a low false positive rate at 0.0125%. Meanwhile, SRID can dramatically reduce the search space of attack origins and accurately locate most of attack origins.

Keywords: Intrusion Detection System, Cyber Security in SCADA, False Data Injection Attack.

1 Introduction

In recent years, we have witnessed that the great technical innovation has intrinsically changed our definition about the data acquisition and control system. Nowadays, when current Supervisory Control And Data Acquisition (SCADA) system starts to connect a great number of sensors to highly-flexible distributed networks, it is no longer *closed* and *single-functional*, but instead *open*, and *complex*. Across the waves of such innovation, cyber security of SCADA systems attracts a lot of research attention. Especially after the Stuxnet[3] worm spread across Iran nuclear infrastructure and occupied the headline of news and media, we naturally ask the question: is our SCADA system ready for the challenges brought by such malware intrusion?

M. Kutyłowski and J. Vaidya (Eds.): ESORICS 2014, Part II, LNCS 8713, pp. 401–418, 2014.

Unfortunately, we may not be confident enough to declare a secure SCADA system: Our existing system is still connected to vulnerable networks which integrate multiple communication protocols and lack proper data validation and authentication [4–7]. It implies that attackers can easily infiltrate the network and compromise the whole control system. Besides that, the potential vulnerability of industrial control system software may also become the Achilles' heel and open a back-door for those malicious attackers. As stated in a vulnerability trends report from Symantec [8], the number of vulnerabilities targeting at SCADA systems has undergone an *exponential* uptrend since 2011. For example, there were over 800% more vulnerabilities discovered in 2012 than the number discovered in 2010.

Therefore, deploying intrusion detection onto SCADA systems becomes a pressing task for security practitioners. Multiple schemes, such as behavior-based scheme [9] and bloom-filter-based scheme [1], have been proposed. However, when we review the recent intrusion incidents conducted by targeted malware, such as the infamous Stuxnet malware, we find these IDS schemes are neither complete nor accurate. In particular, there are two problems causing current IDS systems vulnerable to targeted malware's intrusion:

First, the current design of many IDS systems follows a hierarchical and distributed structure, in an attempt to secure all sensors and devices in the system [10]. However, with too high-level view and always limited resources, this may be ineffective and inefficient to handle some attacks deeply targeting at some specific critical control component. In reality, it has been evidenced that malware shows special interest in some key component, e.g., Stuxnet only infects Siemens S7-3000 devices which control the centrifuge and pumps. Therefore, an IDS scheme that can automatically find and protect the critical control component(s) is a more effective solution to detect targeted malware's intrusion.

Second, many IDS systems follow the idea of traditional intrusion detection schemes, which detect abnormal communication flow(s) between devices. However, in the context of SCADA, our first priority is to ensure the validity of system status. Therefore, we think our detection target should be invalid system *states*. As an illustration, we examine the Stuxnet worm again: when the control device has been compromised, the Stuxnet periodically modifies the frequency to 1410 Hz and then to 2 Hz and then to 1064 Hz, and thus affects the operation of the connected motors by changing their rotational speed. Typically, such behaviors cannot be detected by existing IDS because each of its operation is under the valid threshold of IDS's detection rules. However, the system states, or the relations between continuous states, violate the normal disciplines, and such inconsistency is a clear evidence when intrusion happens in the SCADA system.

In this paper, we propose a novel relation-graph-based intrusion detection scheme, SRID, which aims to detect false data injection attacks in SCADA systems. In particular, given a SCADA system, SRID automatically analyzes the system and extracts independent *components* (each component is a logically independent control system, more details defined in Section 2.3). Then, for each component, SRID extracts the internal relations among different system variables and derives a graph model to describe valid system states. To achieve a balance between effectiveness and efficiency, we propose *alternation vector* and *state relation graph* as our detection model. To further figure out the origins of attacks, i.e, which device (among all possible data sources) has been compromised, we propose an inference algorithm to deduce what is the possible compromised device causing the inconsistency.

To evaluate the effectiveness and efficiency of SRID, we test it with a real-world power plant simulator with 142 system variables. We then inject malformed data into the simulator with both single-point and multi-point injection schemes. As shown in the result, almost all the injected data and origins can be accurately detected and inferred.

In summary, our paper makes the following contributions:

- We introduce a graph-based scheme for SCADA systems to detect advanced false data injection attacks, even when injected data fall within the valid/normal range of signal specification. SRID is a systematic approach to monitor system states, detect *inconsistent states* and infer the *compromised origins*.
- We propose multiple novel intrusion detection models for SCADA, such as *alternation vectors* and *state relation graphs*, to achieve real-time detection on resource-constrained devices.
- We evaluate our system with a real-world power plant simulator and SRID performs with a 95.83% detection rate and a 0.0125% false positive rate. Meanwhile, our inference module can also achieve a high accuracy in locating injected data origins.

2   Background and Problem Statement

2.1   Background

SCADA(supervisory control and data acquisition) is an advanced control system which collects the data from *system variables* in real-time, operates with encoded signals over communication channels, and provides control of local/remote equipment. These years, as SCADA systems have been widely applied in Smart Grid systems for data monitoring and state estimation [11], cyber security on SCADA has attracted more and more public attention as an emerging, cross-disciplinary research topic. Among those attacks, false data injection attack is of particular interest since it directly affects the reliability and robustness of systems. As defined in related work [11], false data injection is a generalized attack which injects any type of malformed data into the data acquisition system. Such malformed data can be in any form, such as the measurement data from sensors [12], or even the control commands from programmable logic circuits [13].

To detect such injected data, there are two lines of research work. In the first direction, researchers treat the injected data as an injected signal and detect it using bad-data (e.g., data out of normal ranges) processing schemes. As a common detection strategy, existing studies, such as [14, 15], introduce artificial redundancy to mitigate the effect of injected data. These approaches have been proved to be effective for securing the integrity of small numbers of system variables. The common assumption of these work is that the attacker has only *limited* access to system resources, i.e, altering a small amount of measurement data of sensors or meters. However, when well-crafted malware has been involved in the arm race, such assumption may no longer be held because malware has strong abilities to propagate itself among similar devices and manipulate multiple data signals at the same time.

To defeat malware's intrusion, another line of research concentrates on deploying existing intrusion detection techniques onto SCADA systems. Multiple different detection models, such as statistic-based [16], behavior-based [9] and bloom-filter-based [1], have been proposed. However, as a highly complicated control system, deploying similar or identical rules on different control components is not an ideal choice. For example, the centrifuge control component may require different policies from the gas pump control component. In addition, most existing IDS systems only enforce detection rules on each communication flow, they lack a global view of relationship among different variables to determine whether the whole system is under attack or not.

2.2 Assumption and Approach Overview

In this paper, we focus on detecting false data injection attacks on SCADA systems. To be concrete, we assume the following strong attack model:

- An attacker has the ability to inject single or multiple data at any time.
- The injected data can fall into the valid range of signal specification, which can cause a difficult time for many existing anomaly-based detection schemes.

In this paper, we provide a relation-graph-based intrusion detection scheme for SCADA systems. Our proposal is trying to achieve two tasks complementing the existing intrusion detection schemes:

- **Component-based Policy**: Our scheme automatically analyzes the internal relations among system variables. Then we extract components for each independent control sub-system. Based on each component, we provide different detection rules. Through such component-based policy, we can not only reduce the redundant overhead but also provide more accurate results.
- **Correlation Model**: Our detection model is based on the internal relations among different system variables and states. Hence, we design correlation graphs (for system variables) and state relation graphs (for system states) to describe the valid behavior patterns of our target SCADA system. Therefore, SRID is designed to protect the system from entering invalid running status.

Next, we provide our definition of *component* and *correlation model*.

2.3   Terminology

Definition of Component: In our definition, we define a component as an sub-system which controls an independent set of system variables. As an illustration, we show an example of the controlling component of a power plant boiler in Figure 1. In this system, coal is automatically transported into boiler based on the temperature meter. If the temperature is high, few coal will be transported into the system. Otherwise, more coal is needed. The pressure is proportional to the temperature, which is collected by the temperature meter. Thus, higher temperature generates higher pressure. Since all these system variables affect the control of the boiler, we treat them as a component.

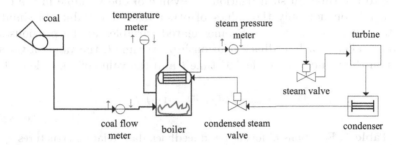

Fig. 1. An Example of False Data Injection

In this example, we find a component:{t(temperature), p(pressure), c(coal)}. The component is normally a subset of the whole control system. In our design, we allow users to customize the system variable subset. Also, we provide another automatic way to extract independent components from a SCADA system.

Definition of Correlation Model: In the above example, suppose that the attacker can compromise the temperature meter to inject fake data into the system. In order to evade bad-data based detection, she keeps changing the value of temperature meter to a valid low value. While the temperature keeps lower, the coal will continuously be transported. Finally, the boiler could blast.

Note that there is no detectable bad data. Hence, bad-data processing scheme will be less effective in this case. However, if we further examine the relation among different meters, we can find the inconsistency: while the attacker can modify the temperature meter to a lower value, the value from the pressure meter is unchanged, which undoubtedly violates the proportional relation between two meters. Our definition of State-Correlation is based on such insight.

Formally, we define the Correlation Model as the correlation between different variables x_i under different time states t_i.

$$c(x_{i,t_i}) = f(x_1, x_2, x_3, ..., x_n) \tag{1}$$

More specifically, we consider two types of variable correlation models in our definition:

Forward Correlation: The forward correlation is a static structure, in which all system variables will not be affected by the time. Thus, the value of one variable in the current state only depends on the values of other related variables in the simultaneous state. Given the power system variables $\mathbf{x} = (x_1, x_2, ..., x_n)^T$, Equation 2 reflects such forward relation. At any time t, the value of variable i depends on the values of other variables such as variable j, variable k at time t.

$$x_{i,t} = f(x_{j,t}, x_{k,t}...) \tag{2}$$

Since the values of system variables do not depend on time t in the forward correlation structure, Equation 3 can be further simplified as:

$$x_i = f(x_j, x_k...) \tag{3}$$

Feedback Correlation: The feedback correlation is a dynamic structure corresponding to the time. In such relation, the value of one variable in the current state depends on not only the values of other related variables in simultaneous states but also the values of some related variables in the previous state. Equation 4 reflects such feedback relationship. At time t, the value of variable i depends on the value of variable j at time t and the value of variable k at time $t-1$.

$$x_{i,t} = f(x_{j,t}, x_{k,t-1}...) \tag{4}$$

Table 1. Functions of forward and feedback data relation structures

structure \ variable	x_0	x_1	x_2	x_3	x_4	x_5	x_6
forward	x_0	$x_0 * x_0$	$x_1 - x_0$	x_2/x_1	$x_2 - x_3$	$\sin(x_4)$	$\cos(x_5)$
feedback	$x_{0,t}$	$x_{0,t} \times x_{0,t}$	$x_{1,t} - x_{t,0}$	$(x_{2,t}/x_{t,1}) + x_{5,t-1}$	$x_{2,t} - x_{3,t}$	$\sin(x_{4,t})$	$\cos(x_{5,t})$

We illustrate another example to describe the correlation model as shown in Table 1. Given system variables $\mathbf{x} = (x_0, x_1, x_2, x_3, x_4, x_5, x_6)^T$, Table 1 shows the relationship of different variables in different types of models. For example, variable x_1 in the forward data relation structure equals the squares of x_0 and variable x_3 equals x_2/x_1; Variable x_3 in the feedback data relation structure equals $x_{2,t}/x_{1,t} + x_{5,t-1}$.

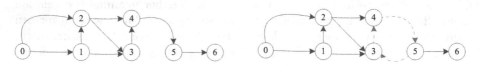

(a) forward relation graph of variables   (b) feedback relation graph of variables

Fig. 2. Forward and Feedback Correlation Model

Based on the table description, we further generate a *correlation graph*, which is shown in Figure 2. In the figure, the dash line shows the feedback correlation, in which the value of x_3 depends on the value of x_1 and x_2 from the current state and the value of x_5 from the previous state.

3   System Design

In this section, we present the detailed design of SRID. As seen in Figure 3, there are three basic steps of SRID: *Component Analysis, Detection Model Generation* and *Origins Inference*. In the first step, SRID automatically analyzes the internal relations between different variables in the SCADA system. In the second step, we propose a graph-based detection model, *alternation vectors with state relation graphs*, for efficient online intrusion detection. Finally, our inference model traces back the intrusion and infers the possible compromised origins.

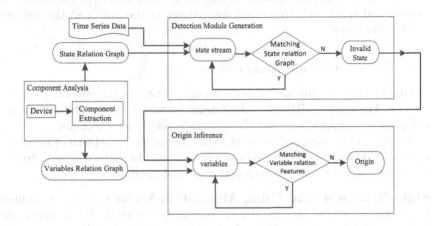

Fig. 3. Architecture of SRID

3.1   Component Analysis

In the first step, our target is to find the internal relations among system variables inside each independent component. As we discussed, the component can be expressed as a set of system variables, such as $x_1, x_2, ...x_n$. The goal of component analysis is to derive the forward and backward correlations, which can be expressed as correlation graphs, illustrated in Figure 2.

To build such relations, the most straightforward and easiest solution is to allow the system designer to specify in advance. With the involvement of human assistance, we can obtain an accurate model which specifies the mathematical relations of each variable. However, since such human effort is tedious and sometimes not available, we can propose another approach for automatic extraction.

The idea is to apply classic control variate method which alters one variable's value at a time. When we alter one variable, we record whether any of other variables has been changed or not. If some variable changes, we build a directed edge from the control variable to the alternated variable in the graph. Then we reset the system, and change another variable in the second round. The process iteratively continues till we find all the relations between variables.

The control variate method can describe the forward correlation between variables. For the feedback correlation, we apply program analysis on the device's firmware. The idea is to conduct data flow analysis on each variable and determine whether the previous states may affect its current value or not. To achieve that, we collect a set of execution traces for the firmware from t_0 to time window limit t_m. Then we apply the data flow analysis across different traces and find whether the previous variable affects the following states. If so, we draw a feedback line (as seen in Figure 2) in our graph.

One sample output of this step is the correlation graph illustrated in Figure 2. Based on the graph, we can extract all connected components. As we mentioned, we allow users to specify the analyzed component in advance. However, if the user does not specify any component beforehand, we can analyze the whole SCADA system and treat each connected component in the graph as the subject(s) of our further steps.

3.2 Detection Model Generation

In the second step, we study the *changing* pattern of the variables for the component. The task of SRID is to determine, at time t_i, given the current states of component variables, whether the system is under attack or not?

To answer the question, we need to first describe the pattern of normal system operation. In our design, we propose a novel way, *alternation vectors*, to represent real-time states of a component under normal operation.

State Representation Using Alternation Vectors. Suppose a component has n variables $(x_1, x_2, ..., x_n)^T$. At each time t, a state can be represented by a vector of different variable such as $(x_{1,t}, x_{2,t}, ..., x_{n,t})^T$. For that, we have to store the concrete value for each variable and such scheme may consume large amount of memory space when the vector is high dimensional. In our scheme, we apply alternation vector, which only records the alternation relations between two continuous states. It can be expressed with Equation 5:

$$f_1(x_{i,t}) = \begin{cases} 1 & x_{i,t} - x_{i,t-1} > 0 \\ 0 & x_{i,t} - x_{i,t-1} = 0 \quad or \quad t = t_0 \\ -1 & x_{i,t} - x_{i,t-1} < 0 \end{cases} \quad, i \in 1, 2, \cdots, n \qquad (5)$$

For the initialization state, t_0, we define $f(x_{i,t0}) = 0$. If the value of variable i increases from the last value, we use 1 to indicate the increase. Also if the value of variable i decreases from the last state, we use -1 to indicate the decrease. If the value keeps the same, we denote it as 0.

Using alteration vectors, we can model a constantly changing component by a series of alternation vectors in a time window from t_0 to t_m. The advantage of alternation vectors is to save memory for each state. Since we only store 2 bits for each variable's state, our scheme is efficient for resource-constraint devices.

Based on the alternation vectors, we discuss our detection scheme using state relation graphs.

State Relation Graph. Our intrusion detection model is based on *state relation graphs*. The state relation graph is a directed graph $G(V, E)$, which describes the normal states of the component. To construct the relation graph, we need to run SRID and collect all the information about those normal states in a training stage.

Suppose that we run SRID to train the model from a time window t_0 to t_m, and we have n different variables in the analyzed component. At each time slot t_i, we compute the alternation vector based on its previous state at t_{i-1} and current state. For each alternation vector, we create one node in the graph. If we find the node has been created before, we directly use the existing node. Then we create one edge which points from the t_{i-1} state's node to t_i state's node. Each edge is marked with a time stamp t_i. This process continues until we enumerate all the states in the time window.

The state relation graph for our illustration example(in Section 2.3) is shown in Figure 4(a). In theory, there are at most 3^n different alternation vectors in the graph. However, for a practical system, the space is normally limited. For the illustrated example, we have 7 variables and only 37 different state nodes in the graph.

Using the graph, we can build our detection model. The idea for our intrusion detection model is to assure that the variables satisfy the normal changing rule. Intuitively, the malicious injected data, such as Stuxnet's malformed frequency data, can be easily detected since it clearly violates the normal changing rules.

Reduced State Relation Graph. There are two possible problems directly using the state relation graph for detection: First, since we have to maintain the time information for each edge, we have to consume considerable memory to store the trained model. It may complicate the matching process and overburden the resource-constrained device. Secondly, strictly following the transition edges may cause some false positives if some states are not stable.

Therefore, we optimize our state relation graph and remove the time stamp information for each edge. After removing time stamps, there are many duplicated edges existed in the graph. Hence, in the second step, we traverse the whole graph and remove all duplicated edges. The example's reduced state relation graph is shown in Figure 4(b). As we can see, the graph is greatly simplified and, if we apply linked list structure, it only consumes less than 360 bytes to store the whole graph in memory.

Based on the reduced state graph, we summarize the detection steps:

- *Step I:* In detection phase, if we find the new alternation vector is not a node in the graph, we directly generate an alert for *Invalid State*. Since we can store all the nodes in a hashtable, it takes $O(1)$ to fulfill the check.
- *Step II:* If it is a valid state in the graph, we have to check whether it is reachable from the previous state or not. If it is not reachable from the previous state, we generate an alert for *Invalid Transition*. It takes $O(1)$ space to maintain the last transition state and $O(1)$ time to detect the invalid transition (use a hashtable for each node's edge).

In all, SRID can find possible intrusion/false data in $O(1)$ time which is particularly attractive for real-time detection. Meanwhile, with limited number of

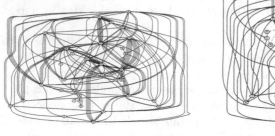

(a)Original State Relation Graph   (b)Reduced State Relation Graph

Fig. 4. Time-series State Relation Graph Reduction

possible states, it also saves the memory consumption and achieves a better balance between effectiveness and efficiency.

3.3   Attack Origins Inference

The goal of the origins inference model is to infer the possible injection point. Our inference is based on the correlation graph which is generated in Component Analysis. As we introduced befor, the correlation graph describes the internal relations of variables in the component. Therefore, when we detect the violated state, we can trace back the dependence of violated variable(s) and find the possible origin(s).

Next, we analyze our inference algorithms in several possible scenarios.

Scenario I: Known Mathematics Correlation

As we discussed in Section 3.1, we allow users to provide the mathematical relations for the correlation graph. In this case, we have pre-knowledge about the variable relation. We believe it is a valid assumption because existing bad-data processing schemes [14, 15, 17] hold the similar assumption.

With knowing the mathematical correlation, our inference algorithms can precisely locate all possible injection points, no matter whether it is a single-point injection or multiple-point injection. To illustrate that, we go through an

Table 2. Example of Origin Inference

Infer Variable	x_0	x_1	x_2	x_3	x_4	x_5	x_6
math correlation	x_0	$x_0 * x_0$	$x_1 - x_0$	x_2/x_1	$x_2 - x_3$	$\sin(x_4)$	$\cos(x_5)$
Original value	4	16	12	0.75	11.25	-0.9678	0.5671
Injection value				3.5			
Invalid state	4	16	12	3.5	8.5	-0.7985	0.6978
Inference result	0	0	0	1	0	0	0

inference example in Table 2. We first reconstruct the time series data of the whole component. As shown in Table 2, a false data 3.5 is injected to x_3. Such injection will also change the value of variables x_3, x_4, x_5, x_6. To infer the origins of false data injection, we check the inner relation among the variables based on their values in invalid states. For example, the value of x_3 should be $x_2/x_1 = 0.75$, however, the value of x_3 in the invalid state is 3.5. Such inconsistency indicates that the variable x_3 is the attack origin. For variable x_4, $x_4 = x_2 - x_3 = 8.5$, which is the same as the value of x_4 in invalid state, thus x_4 is not the attack origin. In the same way, x_1, x_2, x_4, x_5, x_6 are not the origins of the false data injection attack.

Scenario II: Single Point Injection

When the attacker has only limited access to the system, our inference model can also deduce its source even without the knowledge of mathematical correlation in advance. In the single point injection case, the attacker can only inject one data in the system. The inference algorithm is based on the backward dependence traversal which starts from the violated node in the correlation graph. We backward check whether the previous variable deviates from the normal value or not. If the deviation is above our pre-defined deviation threshold δ, we mark it as a possible compromised variable. We iteratively continue till we find the first valid variable. Since we only have one injection point, the last compromised variable, with its corresponding device, is considered as the injection point.

Scenario III: Multiple Points Injection

When there are multiple injection points, our correlation graph may not locate the precise points, but it can still generate a set of possible compromised variables. It is also computed by the backward dependence traversal till we reach the root node of the dependence chain. We believe our infer algorithm can save a great amount of work in the investigation.

Finally, our overall inference algorithm is presented in Algorithm 1.

4   Evaluation

To evaluate the performance of SRID, we test it with a boiler simulator of a real power plant.

4.1   Data Collection

The boiler system is the core part of a power plant generator, which makes it a popular target for malware. Thus we test our SRID with a common boiler system simulator in a coal power plant. To find the mathematical relationship among different variables, we reverse engineering the boiler simulator system. 142 variables are extracted from the boiler system. Figure 5 shows the relation graph of variables and the dash line represents the feedback structures.

4.2   Overhead Analysis

To evaluate the overhead of SRID, we check how many states generated/maintained by SRID. Since there are 142 variables in the boiler system,

---

Algorithm 1. SRID: STATE RELATION BASED INTRUSION DETECTION
FOR FALSE DATA INJECTION ATTACK

Input: A sequence of power system state $\langle state(1, t), state(2, t) \dots, state(n, t)\rangle$
Output: When dose the false data $state(k, i)$ injection attack happen? , where is the original injected data $variable(j)$?

1 △   **injectionDetectModel**
2 $time \leftarrow t_0$
3 $stateFeatureGraph[N, N] \leftarrow normalStateFeatures$
4 **while** $time < timeEnd$ **do**
5 | $state[n, time] \leftarrow input(dataFlow)$
6 | $index \leftarrow 0$
7 | **while** $index < N$ **do**
8 | | **if** $state[index, time] < min(state[index])$ **or** $> max(state[index])$ **then**
9 | | | **return** out of normal range
10 | | **else if** $state[index, time] \in stateFeatureGraph$ **then**
11 | | | $index \leftarrow index + 1$
12 | | | continue;
13 | | **else**
14 | | | $i \leftarrow time$
15 | | | $k \leftarrow index$
16 | | | **return** $state(k, i)$
17 | $time \leftarrow time + 1$

18 △   **originsInferModel**
19 $index \leftarrow 0$
20 $M \leftarrow variableNumber$
21 $variable[M] \leftarrow input(state(k,i))$
22 $variableRelationFeature[M, M] \leftarrow normalVariableRelationFeatures$
23 **while** $index < M$ **do**
24 | $variable[index] \leftarrow input(variableDataFlow)$
25 | **if** $varialbe[index] \in variableRelationFeature$ **then**
26 | | $index \leftarrow index + 1$
27 | | continue;
28 | **else**
29 | | $j \leftarrow index$
30 | | **return** $variable(j)$

31 **return** $state(k, i), variable(j)$

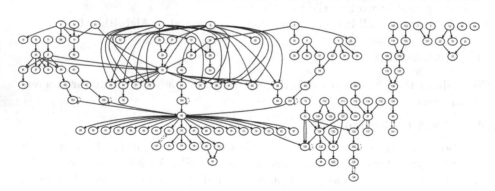

Fig. 5. Variable Relation Graph of the Boiler System in a Power Plant

theoretically there will be 3^{142} states. We train our system with different duration t. Figure 6 shows the number of generated states along with different training duration.

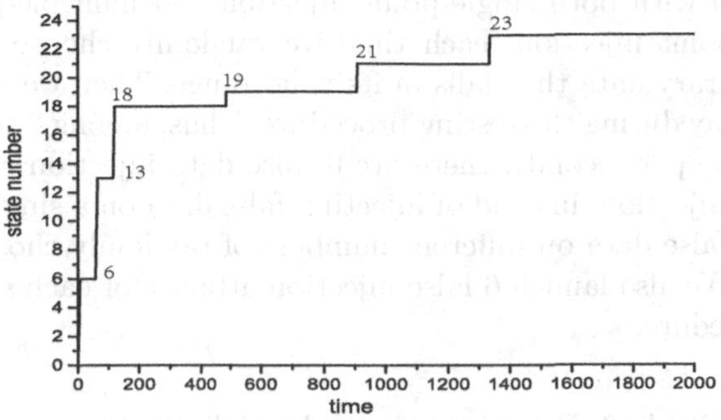

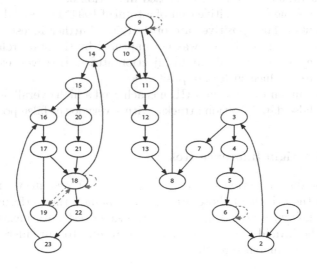

Fig. 6. States Number Distribution

We can see that after 1,366s, there is no more new states generated and the total number of states is only 23, which is much smaller than 3^{142}. Thus such state graph can be stored in memory for realtime analysis.

4.3   Attack Detection Results

To evaluate the detection results, we first run the boiler system for 2,000s (0-2,000s, the values of variables recorded every second, a time granularity used for this evaluation but could be adjusted based on practical need/constraint) to generate the corresponding state relation graph as shown in Figure 7. Then we continue running the boiler system for another 2,000s (2,000-4,000s) to detect when the data injection attacks happen.

Fig. 7. State Relation Graph of the Boiler

We test SRID with both single-point injection and multiple-point injection. For the single-point injection, each time we randomly choose a variable and inject with arbitrary data that falls in its valid range. Then we randomly inject 6 times in this way during the testing procedure. Thus, among 2,000 total testing data records (one per second), there are 6 false data injection attacks. For the multiple-points injection, instead of injecting false data on a single variable each time, we inject false data on different numbers of randomly chosen variables at the same time. We also launch 6 false injection attacks for each situation during the testing procedure.

Table 3. Detection on false data injection attacks

Types	False data injection		SRID detection	
	Injected variables	Injection attacks	Detected attacks	False positives
Single injection	1	6	6	0
Multi-injection1	2	6	6	0
Multi-injection2	3	6	6	0
Multi-injection3	4	6	5	1

Table 3 shows the detection results. SRID can detect all the single injection attacks without false positives. For multiple-points injection, SRID can still detect all attacks with 2 and 3 variables injection without any false positives and false negatives. However, it failed to detect one multiple-points injection attack with 4 variables. This leads to an overall detection rate of 95.83% (23 out of 24 attacks). Further analysis shows that this missed attack is because two continuous injections on two related states happen to satisfy the learned (normal) alternation relationship. While it is possible, we believe that this is difficult be exploited by attackers, as further discussed in Section 5.

SRID also has one false positive (out of a total of 1994*4 normal data records), which represents a false positive rate of 0.0125%. Further investigation shows that it is because a normal state was not captured by the state relation graph. Thus, SRID reports it as a false data injection attack. However, extending the training time can reduce such false positives.

In summary, in our evaluation SRID has achieved a high overall detection rate of 95.83% for false data injection attacks, with a very lower false positive rate of 0.0125%.

4.4 Attack Origin Inference Results

Once the false data injection is detected in the boiler system, we need to find out what are the origins of those attacks. To evaluate the performance of our attack origin inference algorithm, we use the same test data mentioned above and submit the invalid states from detection results to our inference scheme. Table 4 shows the inference results.

Table 4. Origin inference on data injection attacks (TP means inferred true attack origins, and FP means inferred false positive origins. For Multi-injection3, we only test the attack origin inference on the 5 successfully detected true attacks.)

Types	False data injection		SRID Inference		
	Injected variables	Injection attacks	Total affected variables	Total TP	Total FP
Single injection	1	6	40	6/6	0
Multi-injection1	2	6	94	12/12	0
Multi-injection2	3	6	62	18/18	0
Multi-injection3	4	5	421 (avg. 84 per attack)	13/20	260

SRID accurately infers all the true attack origins without any false positive in the case of single injection, multi-injection1, and multi-injection2. For example, for the single-point injection case, totally 6 variables (1 in each attack) are injected with the false data, which lead to totally 40 affected variables that change their values, and SRID can successfully infer the 6 exact attack origins without false positives. In the case of multi-injection3, SRID does not infer all attack origins (inferred 13/20) and due to the large number of variables affected by the attacks (each randomly injected attack affected 84 variables on average, causing trouble for the inference), SRID unavoidably involves considerable false positives (on average 52 in each multi-injection3 attack inference result). However, we argue that SRID still significantly reduces the search space of affected variables (reducing from 421 to 273) and locates most of true attack origins, which is still useful in practice.

Further analysis shows that if the false data is injected on source variables (i.e., source vertex in the variable relation graph), all the children variables of source variables will change their values according to their relations. Thus, there will not exist any inconsistency among those variables. In this case, SRID can not accurately locate the attack origins.

In summary, SRID can dramatically reduces the search space of attack origins and even accurately locate most of true attack origins.

5   Discussion

In this section, we discuss possible problems and evasions of SRID.

Limitation of Component Analysis: One of our design challenges of SRID is how to handle the case when the system is a blackbox to defenders. To solve that, we present our component analysis to handle the challenge. However, there exists some limitation for the scheme. First, the classic control variate method may not be precise if the relation between variables is not instantly reactive. Second, we apply dynamic program analysis to handle feedback relations. However, if we cannot find the data-flow between different execution traces, we cannot find the accurate model. As a result, it may cause some false positives in the final detection result.

To solve these issues, one possible solution is mentioned in Section 3.3, i.e., applying manual effort to describe the mathematical correlation model. Since it is a common assumption for many existing bad-data detection schemes [14], we believe it is still feasible in many real-world circumstances.

Possible Evasions: To evade our SRID, attackers can modify the initial state at t_0, and introduce the inconsistency at the beginning of the time series. Such attack cannot be detected by SRID. Hence, we assume we can ensure the integrity at the starting point t_0. We think it is a reasonable assumption because the initial integrity check is required by most of the devices.

Another possible way to evade our system is to inject the data that affects all other related states at the same time. It means the attacker has the *full* control of the component, which, we believe, is not realistic in the practical scenario. In this case, our system cannot detect the data injection attack. However, if the injection data violates the threshold of some variable, which introduces new states in our graph, SRID can still detect it.

Also, it is possible to overburden SRID using Denial of Service (DoS) attacks. It can be achieved by injecting a large amount of false data continuously. Even though such situation rarely happens in practice, we believe that our system can still outperform existing schemes because SRID applies different policies for different components and each component cannot be easily separated for distributed detection.

Complement to Existing Schemes: Last but not least, we need to emphasize that our scheme is not trying to replace existing intrusion detection systems in the field. Our scheme is complementary to existing schemes and especially useful when we try to protect the critical component in the system. However, some anomaly-based [18] and behavior-based [9] schemes provide a consistent protection for the entire SCADA system, which is not the focus of SRID.

6   Related Work

Existing intrusion detection solutions in SCADA can be classified into two categories.

In the first category, existing approaches [1, 5, 12, 13, 19, 20] monitor the abnormal behaviors using predefined rules to detect attacks. SmartAnalyzer [9, 10, 12, 13] detects possible attacks on advanced metering infrastructure (AMI). It applies a verification engine to determine whether the sensor behaviors obey with the predefined threat constraints, such as reachability constraint, security pairing constraint, report schedule constraint, resource constraint, cyber bandwidth constraint, priority delivery constraint and quality of delivery constraint. Another behavior-rule based intrusion detection system, BRIDS [9], is proposed to secure the SCADA system in a distributed way. In [1], an idea of using bloomer-filter to detect intrusion in resource-constrained devices is proposed.

In the second category, researchers applied state estimation to mitigate bad data in the data acquisition sensor [15, 17, 21–26]. This kind of approach is widely used to detect and identify bad data in power systems, such as power flow analysis [26] and topology errors detection [25]. The detection methods include primary detection for residual detection [21] and inflection point detection [23]. However, the application domains of these approaches are very limited, since they only target at detecting data injection attacks with minor data alternation [11].

Our work is different from all previous work with a stronger attack model, in which we assume powerful attackers can even evade rule-based detection schemes by understanding each variable's threshold in advance. Meanwhile, the state estimation solution also has the limitation of handling arbitrary data injection.

7   Conclusion

In this paper, we propose a novel intrusion detection system, named SRID, to detect intrusion in SCADA systems. Our main defense focus is the false data injection attack and SRID can not only detect such attack but also deduce the possible attack origins in an effective and efficient way. In addition, we propose a new graph-based detection model which combines the state alternation vectors and state relation graph. From the evaluation results, we can see our new design can effectively detect various data injection attacks and infer attack origins.

References

1. Parthasarathy, S., Kundur, D.: Bloom filter based intrusion detection for smart grid scada. In: Proc. of the 25th IEEE Canadian Conference on Electrical & Computer Engineering (CCECE 2012), pp. 1–6 (April 2012)
2. Amin, S., Litrico, X., Sastry, S., Bayen, A.: Cyber security of water scada systems (i) analysis and experimentation of stealthy deception attacks. IEEE Transactions on Control Systems Technology 21(5), 1963–1970 (2013)
3. Stuxnet, http://en.wikipedia.org/wiki/Stuxnet
4. Cardenas, A.A., Amin, S., Lin, Z.S., Huang, Y.L., Huang, C.Y., Sastry, S.: Attacks against process control systems: Risk assessment, detection, and response. In: Proc. of the 6th ACM Symposium on Information, Computer and Communications Security, ASIACCS 2011 (March 2011)
5. Valenzuela, J., Wang, J., Bissinger, N.: Real-time intrusion detection in power system operations. IEEE Transactions on Power Systems 28(2), 1052–1062 (2013)
6. Stouffer, K., Falco, J., Scarfone, K.: Guide to industrial control systems (ics) security. In: NIST Special Publication (2013)
7. Sridhar, S., Hahn, A., Govindarasu, M.: Cyber physical system security for the electric power grid. IEEE Transactions on Power Systems 100(1), 210–224 (2012)
8. Scada vulnerabilities
9. Mitchell, R., Chen, I.: Behavior-rule based intrusion detection systems for safety critical smart grid applications. IEEE Transcations on Smart Grid 4(3), 1254–1263 (2013)
10. Berthier, R., Sanders, W., Khurana, H.: Intrusion detection for advanced metering infrastructures: Requirements and architectural directions. In: Proc. of First IEEE International Conference on Smart Grid Communications (SmartGridComm 2010), pp. 350–355 (October 2010)

11. Liu, Y., Ning, P., Reiter, M.K.: False data injection attacks against state estimation in electric power grids. ACM Transactions on Information and System Security 14(1), 21–32 (2011)

12. Rahman, M., AL-Shaer, E., Bera, P.: A noninvasive threat analyzer for advanced metering infrastructure in smart grid. IEEE Transcations on Smart Grid 4(1), 273–287 (2013)

13. Rahman, M., Bera, P., Al-Shaer, E.: Smartanalyzer: A noninvasive security threat analyzer for ami smart grid. In: Proc. of the 31st IEEE International Conference on Computer Communications (INFOCOM 2012), pp. 2255–2263 (March 2012)

14. Esmalifalak, M., Shi, G., Han, Z., Song, L.: Bad data injection attack and defense in electricity market using game theory study. IEEE Transactions on Smart Grid 4(1), 160–169 (2013)

15. Hagh, M., Mahaei, S., Zare, K.: Improving bad data detection in state estimation of power systems. International Journal of Electrical and Computer Engineering (IJECE 2011) 1(2), 85–92 (2011)

16. Ning, P., Jajodia, S.: Intrusion detection techniques (2003)

17. Xu, W., Wang, M., Tang, A.: On state estimation with bad data detection. In: Proceedings of 50th IEEE Conference on Decision and Control and European Control Conference (CDC-ECC 2011), pp. 5989–5994 (December 2011)

18. Reeves, J., Ramaswamy, A., Locasto, M., Bratus, S., Smith, S.: Intrusion detection for resource-constrained embedded control systems in the power grid. International Journal of Critical Infrastructure Protection 5(2), 74–83 (2012)

19. McDonald, M.J., Conrad, G.N., Service, T.C., Cassidy, R.H.: A retrofit network intrusion detection system for modbus rtu and ascii industrial control systems. In: Proc. of the 45th Hawaii International Conference on System Science (HICSS 2012), pp. 2338–2345 (January 2012)

20. Diaz, J.: Using snort for intrusion detection in modbus tcp/ip communications (2011)

21. Bi, S., Zhang, Y.: Defending mechanisms against false-data injection attacks in the power system state estimation. In: Proc. of the 2011 IEEE International Workshop on Smart Grid Communications and Networks (GC Wkshps 2011), pp. 1162–1167 (December 2011)

22. Xie, L., Mo, Y., Sinopoli, B.: False data injection attacks in electricity markets. In: Smart Grid Communications, pp. 226–231 (October 2010)

23. Feng, Y., Foglietta, C., Baiocco, A., Panzieri, S., Wolthusen, S.D.: Malicious false data injection in hierarchical electric power grid state estimation systems. In: Proc. of the 4th International Conference on Future Energy Systems (e-Energy 2013), pp. 183–192 (May 2013)

24. Tan, R., Krishna, V.B., Yau, D.K., Kalbarczyk, Z.: Impact of integrity attacks on real-time pricing in smart grids. In: Proc. of the 2013 ACM SIGSAC Conference on Computer & Communications Security (CCS 2013), pp. 439–450 (November 2013)

25. Pajic, S.: Power System State Estimation and Contingency Constrained Optimal Power Flow-A Numerically Robust Implementation. PhD thesis, Worcester Polytechnic Institute (2007)

26. Lin, J., Yu, W., Yang, X., Xu, G., Zhao, W.: On false data injection attacks against distributed energy routing in smart grid. In: 2012 IEEE/ACM Third International Conference on Cyber-Physical Systems (ICCPS 2012), pp. 183–192 (April 2012)

Click Fraud Detection on the Advertiser Side

Haitao Xu[1], Daiping Liu[1], Aaron Koehl[1],
Haining Wang[1], and Angelos Stavrou[2]

[1] College of William and Mary, Williamsburg, VA 23187, USA
{hxu,liudptl,amkoeh,hnw}@cs.wm.edu
[2] George Mason University, Fairfax, VA 22030, USA
astavrou@gmu.edu

Abstract. Click fraud—malicious clicks at the expense of pay-per-click advertisers—is posing a serious threat to the Internet economy. Although click fraud has attracted much attention from the security community, as the direct victims of click fraud, advertisers still lack effective defense to detect click fraud independently. In this paper, we propose a novel approach for advertisers to detect click frauds and evaluate the return on investment (ROI) of their ad campaigns without the helps from ad networks or publishers. Our key idea is to proactively test if visiting clients are full-fledged modern browsers and passively scrutinize user engagement. In particular, we introduce a new functionality test and develop an extensive characterization of user engagement. Our detection can significantly raise the bar for committing click fraud and is transparent to users. Moreover, our approach requires little effort to be deployed at the advertiser side. To validate the effectiveness of our approach, we implement a prototype and deploy it on a large production website; and then we run 10-day ad campaigns for the website on a major ad network. The experimental results show that our proposed defense is effective in identifying both clickbots and human clickers, while incurring negligible overhead at both the server and client sides.

Keywords: Click Fraud, Online Advertising, Feature Detection.

1 Introduction

In an online advertising market, advertisers pay ad networks for each click on their ads, and ad networks in turn pay publishers a share of the revenue. As online advertising has evolved into a multi-billion dollar business [1], click fraud has become a serious and pervasive problem. For example, the botnet "Chameleon" infected over 120,000 host machines in the U.S. and siphoned $6 million per month from advertisers [2].

Click fraud occurs when miscreants make HTTP requests for destination URLs found in deployed ads [3]. Such HTTP requests issued with malicious intent are called fraudulent clicks. The incentive for fraudsters is to increase their own profits at the expense of other parties. Typically a fraudster is a publisher or an advertiser. Publishers may put excessive ad banners on their pages

M. Kutyłowski and J. Vaidya (Eds.): ESORICS 2014, Part II, LNCS 8713, pp. 419–438, 2014.
© Springer International Publishing Switzerland 2014

and then forge clicks on ads to receive more revenue. Unscrupulous advertisers make extensive clicks on a competitor's ads with the intention of depleting the victim's advertising budget. Click fraud is mainly conducted by leveraging clickbots, hiring human clickers, or tricking users into clicking ads [4].

In an act of click fraud, both an ad network and a publisher are beneficiaries while an advertiser is the only victim, under the pay-per-click model. Although the ad network pays out to the publisher for those undetected click fraud activities, it charges the advertiser more fees. Thus, the ad network still benefits from click fraud. Only the advertiser is victimized by paying for those fraudulent clicks. Therefore, advertisers have the strongest incentive to counteract click fraud. In this paper, we focus on click fraud detection from the perspective of advertisers.

Click fraud detection is not trivial. Click fraud schemes have been continuously evolving in recent years [3–7]. Existing detection solutions attempt to identify click fraud activities from different perspectives, but each has its own limitations. The solutions proposed in [8–10] perform traffic analysis on an ad network's traffic logs to detect publisher inflation fraud. However, an advanced clickbot can conduct a low-noise attack, which makes those abnormal-behavior-based detection mechanisms less effective. Haddadi [11] proposed exploiting bait ads to blacklist malicious publishers based on a predefined threshold. Motivated by [11], Dave et al. [4] proposed an approach for advertisers to measure click-spam ratios on their ads by creating bait ads. However, running bait ads increases advertisers' budget on advertisements.

In this paper, we propose a novel approach for an advertiser to independently detect click fraud attacks conducted by clickbots and human clickers. Our approach enables advertisers to evaluate the return on investment (ROI) of their ad campaigns by classifying each incoming click traffic as fraudulent, casual, or valid. The rationale behind our design lies in two observed invariants of legitimate clicks. The first invariant is that a legitimate click should be initiated by a real human user on a real browser. That is, a client should be a real full-fledged browser rather than a bot, and hence it should support JavaScript, DOM, CSS, and other web standards that are widely followed by modern browsers. The second invariant is that a legitimate ad clicker interested in advertised products must have some level of user engagement in browsing the advertised website.

Based on the design principles above, we develop a click fraud detection system mainly composed of two components: (1) a proactive functionality test and (2) a passive examination of browsing behavior. The functionality test actually challenges a client for its authenticity (a browser or a bot) with the assumption that most clickbots have limited functionality compared to modern browsers and thus would fail this test. Specifically, a client's functionality is validated against web standards widely supported by modern browsers. Failing the test would induce all clicks generated by the client to be labelled as fraudulent. The second component passively examines each user's browsing behaviors on the advertised website. Its objective is to identify human clickers and those more advanced clickbots that may pass the functionality test. If a client passes the functionality test and also shows enough browsing engagement on the advertised website, the corresponding click is labelled as valid. Otherwise, a click is labelled as casual if the corresponding client passes the functionality test but shows insufficient browsing behaviors. A casual click could be generated by a human clicker or by an unintentional user. We have no attempt to distinguish these two since neither of them is a potential customer from the standpoint of advertisers.

To evaluate the effectiveness of the proposed detection system, we build a prototype and deploy it on a large production web server. Then we run ad campaigns at one major ad network for 10 days. The experimental results show that our approach can detect much more fraudulent clicks than the ad network's in-house detection system and achieve low false positive and negative rates. We also measure the performance overhead of our detection system on the client and server sides.

Note that our detection mechanism can significantly raise the bar for committing click fraud and is potentially effective in the long run after public disclosure. To evade our detection mechanism, clickbots must implement all the main web standards widely supported by modern browsers. And a heavy-weight clickbot will risk itself of being readily noticeable by its host. Likewise, human clickers must behave like real interested users by spending more time, browsing more pages, and clicking more links on the advertised sites, which contradicts their original intentions of earning more money by clicking on ads as quickly as possible. At each point, the net effect is a disincentive to commit click fraud.

The remainder of the paper is organized as follows. We provide background knowledge in Section 2. Then, we detail our approach in Section 3 and validate its efficacy using real-world data in Section 4. We discuss the limitations of our work in Section 5 and survey related work in Section 6. Finally, we conclude the paper in Section 7.

2   Background

Based on our understanding of the current state of the art in click fraud, we first characterize clickbots and human clickers, the two main actors leveraged to commit click fraud. We then discuss the advertiser's role in inhibiting click fraud. Finally, we describe the web standards widely supported by modern browsers, as well as feature detection techniques.

2.1   Clickbots

A clickbot behaves like a browser but usually has relatively limited functionality compared to the latter. For instance, a clickbot may not be able to parse all elements of HTML web pages or execute JavaScript and CSS scripts. Thus, at the present time, a clickbot is instantiated as malware implanted in a victim's computer. Even assuming a sophisticated clickbot equipped with capabilities close to a real browser, its actual browsing behavior when connected to the advertised website would still be different from that of a real user. This is because

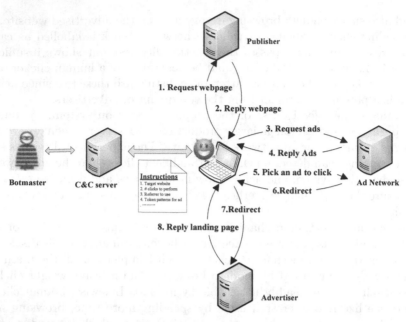

Fig. 1. How a clickbot works

clickbots are automated programs and are not sophisticated enough to see and think as human users, and as of yet, do not behave as human users.

A typical clickbot performs some common functions including initiating HTTP requests to a web server, following redirections, and retrieving contents from a web server. However, it does not have the ability to commit click fraud itself but instead acts as a relay based on instructions from a remote bot master to complete click fraud. A bot master can orchestrate millions of clickbots to perform automatic and large-scale click fraud attacks.

Figure 1 illustrates how a victim host conducts click fraud under the command of a botmaster. First, the botmaster distributes malware to the victim host by exploiting the host's security vulnerabilities, by luring the victim into a drive-by download or running a Trojan horse program. Once compromised, the victim host becomes a bot and receives instructions from a command-and-control (C&C) server controlled by the botmaster. Such instructions may specify the target website, the number of clicks to perform on the website, the referrer to be used in the fabricated HTTP requests, what kind of ads to click on, and when or how often to click [3].

After receiving instructions, the clickbot begins traversing the designated publisher website. It issues an HTTP request to the website (**step 1**). The website returns the requested page as well as all embedded ad tags on the page (**step 2**). An ad tag is a snippet of HTML or JavaScript code representing an ad, usually in an iframe. For each ad tag, the clickbot generates an HTTP request to the ad network to retrieve ad contents just like a real browser (**step 3**). The ad network returns ads to the clickbot (**step 4**). From all of the returned ads, the clickbot selects an ad matching the specified search pattern and simulates a click on the ad, which triggers another HTTP request to the ad network (**step 5**). The ad network logs the click traffic for the purpose of billing the advertiser and paying the publisher a share, and then returns an HTTP 302 redirect response (**step 6**). The clickbot follows the redirection path (possibly involving multiple parties) and finally loads the advertised website (**step 7**). The advertiser returns back the landing page[1] to the clickbot (**step 8**). At this point, the clickbot completes a single act of click fraud. Every time an ad is "clicked" by a clickbot, the advertiser pays the ad network and the involved publisher receives remuneration from the ad network. Note that a clickbot often works in the background to avoid raising suspicion, thus all HTTP requests in Figure 1 are generated without the victim's awareness.

2.2 Human Clickers

Human clickers are the people who are hired to click on the designated ads and get paid in return. Human clickers have financial incentives to click on ads as quickly as possible, which distinguishes them from real users who are truly interested in the advertised products. For instance, a real user tends to read, consider, think, and surf the website in order to learn more about a product before purchase. A paid clicker has few such interests, and hence tends to get bored quickly and spends little time on the site [12].

2.3 Advertisers

Advertisers are in a vantage point to observe and further detect all fraudulent activities committed by clickbots and human clickers. To complete click fraud, all fraudulent HTTP requests must be finally redirected to the advertised website, no matter how many intermediate redirections and parties are involved along the way. This fact indicates that both clickbots and human clickers must finally communicate with the victim advertiser. Thus, advertisers have the advantage of detecting clickbots and human clickers in the course of communication. In addition, as the revenue source of online advertising, advertisers have the strongest motivation to counteract click fraud.

2.4 Web Standards and Feature Detection Techniques

The main functionality of a browser is to retrieve remote resources (HTML, style, and media) from web servers and present those resources back to a user [13]. To correctly parse and render the retrieved HTML document, a browser should be compliant with HTML, CSS, DOM, and JavaScript standards which are represented by scriptable objects. Each object is attached with features including properties, methods, and events. For instance, the features attached to the DOM object include createAttribute, getElementsByTagName, title, domain, url, and

---

[1] Landing page is a single web page that appears in response to clicking on an ad.

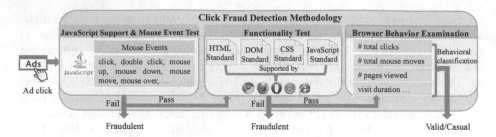

Fig. 2. Outline of click fraud detection mechanism

many others. Every modern browser supports those features. However, different browser vendors (and different versions) vary in support levels for those web standards, or they implement proprietary extensions all their own. To ensure that websites are displayed properly in all mainstream browsers, web developers usually use a common technique called feature detection to help produce JavaScript code with cross-browser compatibility.

Feature detection is a technique that identifies whether a feature or capability is supported by a browser's particular environment. One of the common techniques used is reflection. If the browser does not support a particular feature, JavaScript engines return null when referencing the feature; otherwise, JavaScript returns a non-null string. For instance, if the JavaScript statement "document.createElement" returns null in a specific browser, it indicates that the browser does not support the method createElement attached to the document object. Likewise, by testing a browser against a large number of fundamental features specified in web standards for modern browsers, we can estimate the browser's support level for those web standards, which helps validate the authenticity of the execution environment as a real browser.

Feature detection techniques have three primary advantages. First, feature detection can be an effective mechanism to detect clickbots. A clickbot cannot "pass" the feature detection unless it has implemented the main functionality of a real browser. Second, feature detection stresses the client's functionality thoroughly, and even a large pool of features can be used for feature detection in a fast and efficient manner. Lastly, the methods used for feature detection are designed to work across different browsers and will continue to work over time as new browsers appear, because new browsers fundamentally support reflection— even before implementing other features—and should also extend, rather than replace, existing web standards.

3   Methodology

Our approach mainly challenges a visiting client and its user engagement on the advertised site to determine whether the corresponding ad click is valid or not. To maximize detection accuracy, we also check the legitimacy of the origin (client's IP address) and the intermediate path (i.e., the publisher) of a click.

Figure 2 provides an outline of our approach. Our detection system consists of three components: (1) JavaScript support and mouse event test, (2) browser functionality test, and (3) browsing behavior examination.

For each incoming user, on the landing page, we test if the client supports JavaScript and if any mouse events are triggered. No JavaScript support or no mouse event indicates that the client may not be a real browser but a click-bot. Otherwise, we further challenge the client's functionality against the web standards widely supported by mainstream browsers. The client failed the functionality test is labelled as a clickbot. Otherwise, we further examine the client's browsing behavior on the advertiser's website and train a behavior-based classifier to distinguish a really interested user from a casual one.

3.1   JavaScript Support and Mouse Event Test

One simple way to detect clickbots is to test whether a client supports JavaScript or not. This is due to the fact that at least 98% of web browsers have JavaScript enabled [14] and online advertising services usually count on JavaScript support.

Monitoring mouse events is another effective way to detect clickbots. In general, a human user with a non-mobile platform (laptop/desktop) must generate at least one mouse event when browsing a website. A lack of mouse events flags the visiting client as a clickbot. However, this may not be true for users from mobile platforms (smartphones/pads). Thus, we only apply the mouse event test to users from non-mobile platforms.

Table 1. Tested browsers, versions and release dates

Chrome(10)	1.0.154	2.0.173	4.0.223	5.0.307.1	8.0.552.215
	4/24/2009	6/23/2009	10/24/2009	1/30/2010	12/2/2010
	12.0.742.100	16.0.912.63	20.0.1132.47	24.0.1312.57	27.0.1453.94
	6/14/2011	12/7/2011	6/28/2012	1/30/2013	5/24/2013
Firefox(10)	2.0	3.0	3.5	3.6	4.0
	10/24/2006	6/17/2008	6/30/2009	1/21/2010	3/22/2011
	7.0	11.0	15.0	19.0.2	20.0.1
	9/27/2011	3/13/2012	8/28/2012	3/7/2013	4/11/2013
IE(5)	6.0	7.0	8.0	9.0	10.0
	8/27/2001	10/18/2006	3/19/2009	3/14/2011	10/26/2012
Safari(10)	3.1	3.2	3.2.2	4.0	4.0.5
	3/18/2008	11/14/2008	2/15/2009	6/18/2009	3/11/2010
	5.0.1	5.0.3	5.1	5.1.2	5.1.7
	7/28/2010	11/18/2010	7/20/2011	11/30/2011	5/9/2012
Opera(10)	8.50	9.10	9.20	9.50	10.00
	9/20/2005	12/18/2006	4/11/2007	6/12/2008	9/1/2009
	10.50	11.00	11.50	12.00	12.15
	3/2/2010	12/16/2010	6/28/2011	6/14/2012	4/4/2013

3.2   Functionality Test

A client passing the JavaScript and mouse event test is required to further undergo a feature-detection based functionality test.

Table 2. Authentic feature set widely supported by modern browsers

Objects	Features
Browser Window (51)	closed, defaultStatus, document, frames, history, alert, blur, clearInterval, clearTimeout, close, confirm, focus, moveBy, moveTo, open, print, prompt, resizeBy, resizeTo, scroll, scrollBy, scrollTo, setInterval, setTimeout, appCodeName, appName, appVersion, cookieEnabled, platform, userAgent, javaEnabled, availHeight, vailWidth, colorDepth, height, width, length, back, forward, go, hash, host, hostname, href, pathname, port, protocol, search, assign, reload, replace
DOM(26)	doctype, implementation, documentElement, createElement, createDocumentFragment, createTextNode, createComment, createAttribute, getElementsByTagName, title, referrer, domain, URL, body, images, applets, links, forms, anchors, cookie, open, close, write, writeln, getElementById, getElementsByName
CSS(76)	backgroundAttachment, backgroundColor, backgroundImage, backgroundRepeat, border, borderStyle, borderTop, borderRight, borderBottom, borderLeft, borderTopWidth, borderRightWidth, borderBottomWidth, borderLeftWidth, borderWidth, clear, color, display, font, fontFamily, fontSize, fontStyle, fontVariant, fontWeight, height, letterSpacing, lineHeight, listStyle, listStyleImage, listStylePosition, listStyleType, margin, marginTop, marginRight, marginBottom, marginLeft, padding, paddingTop, paddingRight, paddingBottom, paddingLeft, textAlign, textDecoration, textIndent, textTransform, verticalAlign, whiteSpace, width, wordSpacing, backgroundPosition, borderCollapse, borderTopColor, borderRightColor, borderBottomColor, borderLeftColor, borderTopStyle, borderRightStyle, borderBottomStyle, borderLeftStyle, bottom, clear, clip, cursor, direction, left, minHeight, overflow, pageBreakAfter, pageBreakBefore, position, right, tableLayout, top, unicodeBidi, visibility, zIndex

To avoid false positives and ensure that each modern browser can pass the functionality test, we perform an extensive feature support measurement on the top 5 mainstream browsers [15]: Chrome, Firefox, IE, Safari, and Opera. To discern the consistently supported features, we uniformly select 10 versions for each browser vendor with the exception of 5 versions for IE. Table 1 lists the browsers we tested. As a result, we obtain a set of 153 features associated with web standards, including browser window, DOM, and CSS (see Table 2). All those features are supported by both desktop browsers and their mobile versions. These features are commonly and consistently supported by the 45 versions of browsers in the past ten years. We call this set the authentic-feature set. We also create a bogus-feature set, which has the same size as the authentic-feature set but is obtained by appending "123" to each feature in the authentic-feature set. Thus, every feature in the bogus-feature set should not be supported by any real browser. Note that we just use the string "123" as an example. When implementing our detection, the advertiser should periodically change the string to make the bogus-feature set hard to evade.

How to Perform the Functionality Test. Figure 3 illustrates how the functionality test is performed. For the first HTTP request issued by a client, the advertiser's web server challenges the client by responding as usual, but along with a mixed set of authentic and bogus features. While the size of the mixed set is fixed (e.g.,100), the proportion of authentic features in the set is randomly decided. Then, those individual authentic and forged features in the set are randomly selected from the authentic and bogus feature sets, respectively. The client is expected to test each feature in its environment and then report to the web server how many authentic features are in the mixed set as the response to the challenge.

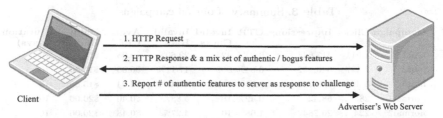

Fig. 3. How the functionality test is performed by advertiser's web server

A real browser should be able to report the correct number of authentic features to the web server after executing the challenge code, and thus passes the functionality test. However, a clickbot would fail the test because it is unable to test the features contained in the set and return the correct number. Considering some untested browsers may not support some authentic features, we set up a narrow range $[x - N, x]$ to handle this, where x is the expected number and N is a small non-negative integer. A client is believed to pass the test as long as its reported number falls within $[x - N, x]$. Here we set N to 4 based on our measurement results.

Evasion Analysis. Assume that a client receives a mixed set of 150 features from a web server and the set consists of 29 randomly selected authentic features and 121 randomly selected bogus features. Thus, the expected number should fall into the range [25,29]. Consider a crafty clickbot who knows about our detection mechanism in advance. The clickbot does not need to test the features, but just guesses a number from the possible range [0,150], and returns it to the server. In this case, the probability for the guessed number to successfully fall into [25,29] is only 3%. Thus, the clickbot has little chance (3%) to bypass the functionality test.

3.3 Browsing Behavior Examination

Passing the functionality test cannot guarantee that a click is valid. An advanced clickbot may function like a real browser and thus can circumvent the functionality test. A human clicker with a real browser can also pass the test.

However, clickbots and human clickers usually show quite different browsing behaviors on the advertised website from those of real users. Click fraud activities conducted by clickbots usually end up with loading the advertiser's landing page and do not show human behaviors on the site. For human clickers, their only purpose is to make more money by clicking on ads as quickly as possible. They tend to browse an advertised site quickly and then navigate away for the next click task. Instead, real interested users tend to learn more about a product and spend more time on the advertised site. They usually scroll up and down a page, click on their interested links, browses multiple pages, and sometimes make a purchase.

Therefore, we leverage users' browsing behaviors on the advertised site to detect human clickers and advanced clickbots. Specifically, we extract extensive

Table 3. Summary of our ad campaigns

Set	Campaign	Clicks	Impressions	CTR	Invalid Clicks	Invalid Rate	Avg. CPC	Daily Budget	Duration (days)
1	bait1	1,011	417,644	0.24%	425	29.60%	$0.08	$15.00	10
2	bait2	4,127	646,152	0.64%	852	17.11%	$0.03	$15.00	10
3	bait3	5,324	933,790	0.57%	1,455	21.46%	$0.04	$15.00	10
4	normal1	288	68,425	0.42%	18	5.88%	$0.40	$20.00	10
5	normal2	224	20,784	1.08%	10	4.27%	$0.48	$20.00	10
Total	NA	10,974	2,086,795	0.53%	2,760	25.15%	$0.06	$85.00	10

features from passively collected browsing traffic on the advertised website, and train a classifier for detection.

4 Experimental Results

In order to evaluate our approach, we run ad campaigns to collect real-world click traffic, and then analyze the collected data to discern its primary characteristics, resulting in a technique to classify click traffic as either fraudulent, casual, or valid.

4.1 Running Ad Campaigns

To obtain real-world click traffic, we signed up with a major ad network and ran ad campaigns for a high-traffic woodworking forum website. Motivated by the bait ad technique proposed in [11], we created three bait ads for the site and made the same assumption as the previous works [4,11,16], that very few people would intentionally click on the bait ads and those ads are generally clicked by clickbots and fraudulent human clickers. Bait ads are textual ads with nonsense content, as illustrated in Figure 4. Note that our bait ads were generated in English. In addition, we created two normal ads, for which the ad texts describe the advertised site exactly. Our goal of running ad campaigns is to acquire both malicious and authentic click traffic for validating our click fraud detection system. To this end, we set the bait ads to be displayed on partner websites of any language across the world but display normal ads only on search result pages in English to avoid publisher fraud cases from biasing the clicks on the latter normal ads. We expect that most, if not all, clicks on bait ads and normal ads are fraudulent and authentic, respectively.

We ran our ad campaigns for 10 days. Table 3 provides a summary of our ad campaigns. Our ads had 2 million impressions[2], received nearly 11 thousand clicks and had a click-through rate (CTR) of 0.53% on average. Among these, 2.7 thousand clicks were considered by the ad network as illegitimate and were not charged. The invalid click rate was 25.15%. The average cost per click (CPC) was $0.06. Note that the two normal ads only received 512 clicks accounting for 4.67% of the total. The reason is that although we provided quite high bids for

---

[2] An ad being displayed once is counted as one impression.

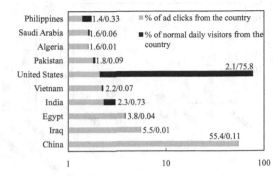

Anchor Groundhog Estate
www.sawmillcreek.org
Variance Flock Accurate Chandelier
Cradle Naphtha Librettist Headwind

Fig. 4. A bait ad with the ad text of randomly selected English words

Fig. 5. Distribution of click traffic vs. that of normal traffic by country

normal ads, our normal ads still cannot compete with those of other advertisers for top positions and thus received fewer clicks.

4.2   Characterizing the Click Traffic

We characterize the received click traffic by analyzing users' geographic distribution, browser type, IP address reputation, and referrer websites' reputations. Our goal, through statistical analysis, is to have a better understanding of both the users who clicked on our ads and the referrer websites where our ads were clicked. Although the ad network reported that our ads attracted close to 11 thousand clicks, we only caught on the advertised site 9.9 thousand clicks, which serve as data objects for both closer examination and validation of our approach.

Geographic Distribution. We obtain users' geographic information using an IP geolocation lookup service [17]. Our 9.9 thousand clicks originate from 156 countries. Figure 5 shows the distribution of ad clicks by the top 10 countries which generate the most clicks. The distribution of normal daily visitors to the advertised site by country is also given in Figure 5. Note that the data form 'X/Y' means that $X\%$ of ad clicks and $Y\%$ of normal daily visitors are from that specific country. The top 10 countries contribute 77.7% of overall clicks. China alone contributes over 55% of the clicks, while the United States contributes 2.1%. This is quite unusual because the normal daily visitors from China only account for 0.11% while the normal visitors from the United States close to 76%. Like China, Egypt, Iraq, and other generally non-English countries also contribute much higher shares of ad click traffic than their normal daily traffic to the site. The publisher websites from these countries are suspected to be using bots to click on our ads. Even worse, one strategy of our ad network partner may aggravate the fraudulent activities. The strategy says that when an ad has a high click through ratio on a publisher website, the ad network will deliver the ad to that publisher website more frequently. To guarantee that our ads attract as

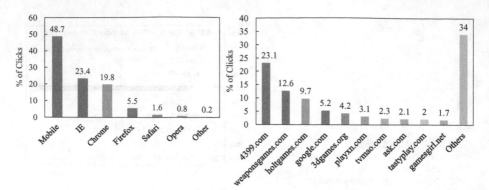

Fig. 6. Distribution of click traffic by browser **Fig. 7.** Distribution of click traffic by publisher

many clicks as possible within a daily budget, the ad network may deliver our ads to those non-English websites more often.

Browser Type. Next we examine the distribution of the browsers to see which browser vendors are mostly used by users to view and click on our ads. We extracted the browser information from the User-Agent strings of the HTTP requests to our advertised website.

Figure 6 shows the distribution of the browsers used by our ad clickers. IE, Chrome, Firefox, Safari, and Opera are the top 5 desktop and laptop browsers, which is consistent with the web browser popularity statistics from StatCounter [15]. Notably, mobile browsers alone contribute to nearly 50% of overall traffic, much larger than the estimated usage share of mobile browsers (about 18% [18]). Close scrutinization reveals that 40% of the traffic with mobile browsers originates from China. China generated over 50 percent of overall traffic, which skews the browser distribution.

Blacklists. A fraction of our data could be generated by clickbots and compromised hosts. Those malicious clients could also be utilized by fraudsters to conduct other undesirable activities, and are thus blacklisted. By looking up users' IP addresses in public IP blacklists [19], we found that 29% of the total hosts have ever been blacklisted.

Referrers. Another interesting question would be which websites host our ads and if their contents are really related to the keywords of our ads. According to the contextual targeting policy of the ad network, an ad should be delivered to the ad network's partner websites whose contents match the selected keywords for the ad.

We used the Referer field in the HTTP request header to locate the publishers that displayed our ads and then directed users to our advertised website. However, we can only identify publishers for only 37.2% of the traffic (3,685 clicks) because the remaining traffic either has a blank Referer field or has the domain of the ad network as the referer field. For example, the Referer field for more than 40% of traffic has the form of doubleclick.net. We then examined, among those detected publishers, which websites contribute to the most clicks. Note that publishers could be websites or mobile apps. We identified 499 unique websites and 5 apps in total. Those apps are all iPhone apps and only generate 28 clicks all together. The remaining 3,657 clicks are from the 499 unique websites. Figure 7 shows the distribution of the click traffic by those 504 publishers. The top 3 websites with the most clicks on our ads are all small game websites, which contribute to over 45% of publisher-detectable clicks. Actually, the top 7 websites are all small game websites. Small game websites often attract many visitors, and thus the ads on those websites are more likely to be clicked on. However, our keywords are all woodworking-related and evidently, the contents of those game websites do not match our keywords. According to the above mentioned contextual targeting policy, the ad network should have not delivered our ads to such websites. One possible reason is that from the perspective of the ad network, attracting clicks takes precedence over matching the ads with host websites.

4.3   Validating Detection Approach

As described before, our approach is composed of three main components: a JavaScript support and mouse event test, a functionality test, and a browsing behavior examination. Here we individually validate their effectiveness.

JavaScript Support and Mouse Event Test. Among the 9.9 thousand ad clicks logged by the advertised site, 75.2% of users do not support JavaScript. We labelled those users as clickbots. Note that this percentage may be slightly over-estimated considering that some users (at most 2% [14]) may have JavaScript disabled. In addition, those visits without support for JavaScript do not correlate with visits from mobile browsers. We have checked that nearly all mobile browsers provide support for JavaScript despite limited computing power. We then focused on the top 10 publisher websites with the most clicks to identify potentially malicious publishers. Figure 8 depicts the percentage of clicks without script support from those top 10 publishers. Among them, the two non-entertainment websites google.com and ask.com have low ratios, 9.4% and 15.2%, respectively. In contrast, the other 8 entertainment websites have quite high click ratios without script support. There are 86 visits from tvmao.com and none of them support JavaScript. We believe that all 86 clicks are fraudulent and generated by bots. Similarly, 99.1% of clicks from weaponsgames.com, 96.1% of clicks from 3dgames.org, and 95.3% from gamesgirl.net are without JavaScript support either. Such high ratios indicate that the invalid click rate in the real-world ad campaigns is much larger than the average invalid rate of 25.15% alleged by the ad network for our ad campaigns, as shown in Table 3.

We observed 506 ad clicks (with JavaScript support) that result in zero mouse events when arriving at our target site. Of those, 96 are initiated from mobile platforms including iPad, iPhone, Android, and Windows Phone. The remaining

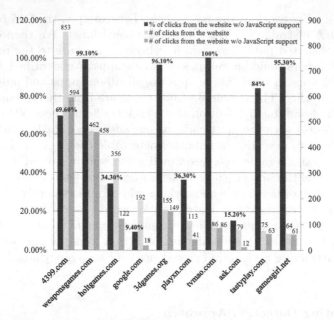

Fig. 8. Percentage of clicks without JavaScript support for the top 10 publisher websites contributing the most clicks

410 clicks are generated from desktop or laptop platforms. Those 410 ad clicks also have few other kinds of user engagement: no mouse clicks, no page scrolls, and short dwelling time. We labelled them as clickbots.

We further investigated the click traffic from 4399.com due to the fact that this website generated the most clicks on our ads among all identified publishers. The following several pieces of data indicate the existence of publisher fraud. First, all 853 clicks from 4399.com were generated within one day. Notably, up to 95 clicks were generated within one hour. Second, several IPs were found to click on our ads multiple times within one minute using the same User-Agent, and one User-Agent was linked to almost 15 clicks on average. Third, close to 70% of clients did not support JavaScript. Hence we suspect that the website owner used automated scripts to generate fraudulent clicks on our ads. However, the scripts are likely incapable of executing the JavaScript code attached to our ads. In addition, they probably spoofed IP address and User-Agent fields in the HTTP requests to avoid detection.

Functionality Test. The clickbots that cannot work as full-fledged modern browsers are expected to fail our functionality test. Among the logged 9.9 thousand clicks, 7,448 clicks without JavaScript support did not trigger the functionality test, and 35 of the remaining clicks with JavaScript support were observed to fail the functionality test and were subsequently labelled as clickbots. So far, 75.6% of clicks (7,483 clicks) had been identified by our detection mechanism to originate from clickbots. Among them, 99.5% (7,448 clicks) were simple click-

Table 4. Features extracted for each ad click

Feature Category	Feature Description
Mouse clicks	# of total clicks made on the advertised site # of clicks made only on the pages excluding the landing page # of clicks exclusively made on hyperlinks
Mouse scrolls	# of scroll events in total # of scroll events made on the pages excluding the landing page
Mouse moves	# of mousemove events in total # of mousemove events made only on the pages excluding the landing page
Pages views	# of pages viewed by a user
Visit duration	How long a user stays on the site
Execution efficiency	Client's execution time of JavaScript code for challenge
Legitimacy of origin	If the source IP is in any blacklist
Publisher's reputation	If the click originates from an disreputable website

bots without JavaScript support; and the rest 0.5% (35 clicks) were relatively advanced clickbots with JavaScript support yet failed the functionality test.

Browsing Behavior Examination. After completing the two steps above and discarding incomplete click data, 1,479 ad clicks (14.9 %) are left to be labelled. Among them, 1,127 ad clicks are on bait ads while the other 352 clicks are on normal ads. Here we further classify the click traffic into three categories—fraudulent, casual, and valid—based on user engagement, client IP, and publisher reputation information.

Features. We believe that three kinds of features are effective to differentiate advanced clickbots and human clickers from real users. (1) How users behave at the advertised site, i.e., users' browsing behavior information. (2) Who clicks on our ads, and a host with a bad IP is more likely to issue fraudulent clicks. (3) Where a user clicks on ads, and a click originating from a disreputable website tends to be fraudulent. Table 4 enumerates all the features we extracted from each ad click traffic to characterize users' browsing behaviors on the advertised site.

Ground truth. Previous works [4, 11, 16] all assume that very few people would intentionally click on bait ads and only clickbots and human clickers would click on such ads. That is, a click on a bait ad is thought to be fraudulent. However, this assumption is too absolute. Consider the following situation. A real user clicks on a bait ad unintentionally or just out of curiosity, without malicious intention. Then, the user happens to like the advertised products and begins browsing the advertised site. In this case, the ad click generated by this user should not be labelled as fraudulent. Thus, to minimize false positives, we partly accept the above common assumption, scrutinize those bait ad clicks which have shown rich human behaviors on the advertised site, and correct a-priori labels based on the following heuristics. Specifically, for a bait ad click, if the host IP address is not in any blacklist and the referrer website has a good reputation, this ad click is relabelled as valid when one of the following conditions holds: (1) 30 seconds of dwelling time, 15 mouse events, and 1 click; (2) 30 seconds of dwelling time, 10 mouse events, 1 scroll event, and 1 click; and (3) 30 seconds of dwelling time, 10 mouse events, and 2 page views. We believe the above conditions are strict enough to avoid mislabelling the ad clicks generated by bots and human clickers as valid clicks.

Note that our normal ads are only displayed on the search engine result pages with the expectation that most, if not all, clicks on normal ads are valid. The ad campaign report provided by the ad network in Table 3 confirms this, showing that the invalid click rate for normal ads is only 5.08% on average. Based on our design and the ad campaign report, we basically assume that the clicks on normal ads are valid. However, after further manually checking the normal ad clicks, we found that some of them do not demonstrate sufficient human behaviors, and these normal ad clicks will be relabelled as casual when one of the following two conditions holds: (1) less than 5 seconds of dwelling time; (2) less than 10 seconds of dwelling time and less than 5 mouse events. The casual click traffic could be issued by human users who unintentionally click on ads and then immediately navigate away from the advertised site. From the advertisers' perspective, such a click traffic does not provide any value when evaluating the ROI of their ad campaigns on a specific ad network, and therefore should be classified as casual.

Actually, if there is no financial transaction involved, only a user's intention matters whether the corresponding ad click is fraudulent or not. That is, only users themselves know the exact ground truth for fraudulent/valid/casual clicks. For those clicks without triggering any financial transactions, we utilize the above reasonable assumptions and straightforward heuristics to form the ground truth for fraudulent/valid/casual clicks.

Evaluation metrics. We evaluated our detection against two metrics—false positive rate and false negative rate. A false positive is when a valid click is wrongly labelled as fraudulent, and a false negative is when a fraudulent click is incorrectly labelled as valid.

Classification results. Using Weka [20], we chose a C4.5 pruned decision tree [21] with default parameter values (i.e., 0.25 for confidence factor and 2 for minimum number of instances per leaf) as the classification algorithm, and ran a 10-fold cross-validation. The false positive rate and false negative rate were 6.1% and 5.6%, respectively. Note that these are the classification results on those 1,479 unlabelled clicks. As a whole, our approach showed a high detection accuracy on the total 9.9 thousand clicks, with a false positive rate of 0.79% and a false negative rate of 5.6%, and the overall detection accuracy is 99.1%.

Overhead. We assessed the overhead induced by our detection on the client and server sides, in terms of time delay, CPU, memory and storage usages.

The only extra work required of the client is the execution of a JavaScript challenge script and to report the functionality test results to the server as an AJAX POST request. We measured the overhead on the client side using two metrics: source lines of code (SLOC) and the execution time of JavaScript code. The JavaScript code is only about 150 SLOC and we observed negligible impact on the client. We also estimated the client's execution time of JavaScript from the server side to avoid the possibility that the client could report a bogus execution time. Note that the execution time measured by the server contains a round trip time, which makes the estimated execution time larger than the actual execution time. Figure 9 depicts the 9.9 thousand clients' execution time of the JavaScript challenge code. About 80% of clients finished execution within

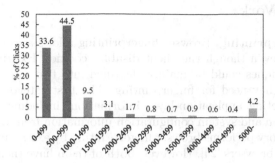

Fig. 9. Clients' execution time of JavaScript challenge code in milliseconds

one second. Assuming that the round trip time (RTT) is 200 milliseconds, the actual computation overhead incurred at the client side is merely several hundred milliseconds.

We used the SAR (System Activity Report) [22] to analyze server performance and measure the overhead on the server side. We observed no spike in server load. This is because most of work involved in our detection happens on the client side, and the induced click-related traffic is insignificant in comparison with server's normal traffic.

5 Discussion and Limitations

In this paper, we assume that a clickbot typically does not include its own JavaScript engine or access the full software stack of a legitimate web browser residing on the infected host. A sophisticated clickbot implementing a full browser agent itself would greatly increase its presence and the likelihood of being detected. A clickbot might also utilize a legitimate web browser to generate activities, and can thus pass our browser functionality test. To identify such clickbots, we could further detect whether our ads and the advertised websites are really visible to users by utilizing a new feature provided by some ad networks. The new feature allows advertisers to instrument their ads with JavaScript code for a better understanding of what is happening to their ads on the client side. With this feature, we could detect if our ad iframe is visible at the client's front-end screen rather than in the background, and if it is really focused and clicked on.

In addition, compared to our user-visit related features (dwelling time, mouse events, scroll events, clicks and etc.), user-conversation related features[3] are expected to have better discriminating power between clickbots, human clickers, and real users in browsing behaviors. However, our advertised site is a professional forum rather than an online retailer. If a user registers (creates an account) on the forum, it is analogous to a purchase at an online retailer. However, such conversion from guest to member is an event too rare to rely upon to enhance our classifier.

---

[3] Purchasing a product, abandoning an online cart, proactive online chat, etc.

6   Related Work

Browser Fingerprinting. Browser fingerprinting allows a website to identify a client browser even though the client disables cookies. Existing browser fingerprinting techniques could be mainly classified into two categories, based on the information they need for fingerprinting. The first category fingerprints a browser by collecting application-layer information, including HTTP request header information and system configuration information from the browser [23]. The second category performs browser fingerprinting by examining coarse traffic generated by the browsers [24]. However, both of them have their limitations in detecting clickbots. Nearly all the application-layer information can be spoofed by sophisticated clickbots, and browser fingerprints may change quite rapidly over time [23]. In addition, an advertiser often cannot collect enough traffic information for fingerprinting the client from just one visit to the advertiser. Compared to the existing browser fingerprinting techniques, our feature detection technique has three main advantages. First, clickbots cannot easily pass the functionality test unless they have implemented the main functionality present in modern browsers. Second, the client's functionality could be tested thoroughly at the advertiser's side even though the client visits the advertiser's landing page only once. Lastly, our technique works over time as new browsers appear because new browsers should also conform to the those web standards currently supported by modern browsers.

Revealed Click Fraud. Several previous studies investigate known click fraud activities, and clickbots have been found to be continuously evolving and become more sophisticated. As the first study to analyze the functionality of a clickbot, Daswani et al. [3] dissected Clickbot.A and found that the clickbot could carry out a low-noise click fraud attack to avoid detection. Miller et al. [5] examined two other families of clickbots. They found that these two clickbots were more advanced than Clickbot.A in evading click fraud detection. One clickbot introduces indirection between bots and ad networks, while the other simulates human web browsing behaviors. Some other characteristics of clickbots are described in [4]. Clickbots generate fraudulent clicks periodically and only issue one fraudulent click in the background when a legitimate user clicks on a link, which makes fraudulent traffic hardly distinguishable from legitimate click traffic. Normal browsers may also be exploited to generate fraudulent click traffic. The traffic generated by a normal browser could be hijacked by currently visited malicious publishers and be further converted to fraudulent clicks [7]. Ghost click botnet [6] leverages DNS changer malware to convert a victim's local DNS resolver into a malicious one and then launches ad replacement and click hijacking attacks. Our detection can identify each of these clickbots by actively performing a functionality test and can detect all other kinds of click fraud by examining their browsing behavior traffic on the server side.

Click Fraud Detection. Metwally et al. conducted an analysis on ad networks' traffic logs to detect publishers' non-coalition hit inflation fraud [8], coalition fraud [9], and duplicate clicks [10]. The main limitation of these works lies in that ad networks' traffic logs are usually not available to advertisers. Haddadi in [11] and Dave et al. in [4] suggested that advertisers use bait ads to detect fraudulent clicks on their ads. While bait ads have been proven effective in detection, advertisers have to spend extra money on those bait ads. Dave et al. [16] presented an approach to detecting fraudulent clicks from an ad network's perspective rather than an advertiser's perspective. Li et al. [7] introduced the ad delivery path related features to detect malicious publishers and ad networks. However, monitoring and reconstructing the ad delivery path is time-consuming and difficult to detect click frauds in real time. Schulte et al. [25] detected client-side malware using so-called program interactive challenge (PIC) mechanism. However, an intermediate proxy has to be introduced to examine all HTTP traffic between a client and a server, which would inevitably incur significant delay. Like [4, 11], our defense works at the server side but does not cause any extra cost for advertisers. Our work is the first to detect clickbots by testing their functionalities against the specifications widely conformed to by modern browsers. Most clickbots can be detected at this step, because they have either no such functionalities or limited functionalities compared to modern browsers. For the advanced clickbots and human clickers, we scrutinize their browsing behaviors on the advertised site, extract effective features, and train a classifier to identify them.

7   Conclusion

In this paper, we have proposed a new approach for advertisers to independently detect click fraud activities issued by clickbots and human clickers. Our proposed detection system performs two main tasks of proactive functionality testing and passive browsing behavior examination. The purpose of the first task is to detect clickbots. It requires a client to actively prove its authenticity of a full-fledged browser by executing a piece of JavaScript code. For more sophisticated clickbots and human clickers, we fulfill the second task by observing what a user does on the advertised site. Moreover, we scrutinize who initiates the click and which publisher website leads the user to the advertiser's site, by checking the legitimacy of the clients' IP addresses (source) and the reputation of the referring site (intermediate), respectively. We have implemented a prototype and deployed it on a large production website for performance evaluation. We have then run a real ad campaign for the website on a major ad network, during which we characterized the real click traffic from the ad campaign and provided advertisers a better understanding of ad click traffic, in terms of geographical distribution and publisher website distribution. Using the real ad campaign data, we have demonstrated that our detection system is effective in the detection of click fraud.

References

1. https://en.wikipedia.org/wiki/Online_advertising
2. http://www.spider.io/blog/2013/03/chameleon-botnet/

3. Daswani, N., Stoppelman, M.: The anatomy of clickbot.a. In: Proceedings of the Workshop on Hot Topics in Understanding Botnets (2007)
4. Dave, V., Guha, S., Zhang, Y.: Measuring and fingerprinting click-spam in ad networks. In: Proceedings of the Annual Conference of the ACM Special Interest Group on Data Communication (2012)
5. Miller, B., Pearce, P., Grier, C., Kreibich, C., Paxson, V.: What's clicking what? techniques and innovations of today's clickbots. In: Holz, T., Bos, H. (eds.) DIMVA 2011. LNCS, vol. 6739, pp. 164–183. Springer, Heidelberg (2011)
6. Alrwais, S.A., Dun, C.W., Gupta, M., Gerber, A., Spatscheck, O., Osterweil, E.: Dissecting ghost clicks: Ad fraud via misdirected human clicks. In: Proceedings of the Annual Computer Security Applications Conference (2012)
7. Li, Z., Zhang, K., Xie, Y., Yu, F., Wang, X.: Knowing your enemy: Understanding and detecting malicious web advertising. In: Proceedings of the ACM Conference on Computer and Communications Security (2012)
8. Metwally, A.: Sleuth: Single-publisher attack detection using correlation hunting. In: Proceedings of the International Conference on Very Large Data Bases (2008)
9. Metwally, A.: Detectives: Detecting coalition hit inflation attacks in advertising networks streams. In: Proceedings of the International Conference on World Wide Web (2007)
10. Metwally, A., Agrawal, D., Abbadi, A.E.: Duplicate detection in click streams. In: Proceedings of the International Conference on World Wide Web (2005)
11. Haddadi, H.: Fighting online click-fraud using bluff ads. In: ACM SIGCOMM Computer Communication Review (2010)
12. Daswani, N., Mysen, C., Rao, V., Weis, S., Gharachorloo, K., Ghosemajumder, S.: Online advertising fraud. In: Crimeware: Understanding New Attacks and Defenses. Addison-Wesley Professional (2008)
13. http://taligarsiel.com/Projects/howbrowserswork1.htm
14. https://developer.yahoo.com/blogs/ydnfourblog/many-users-javascript-disabled-14121.html
15. http://gs.statcounter.com/
16. Dave, V., Guha, S., Zhang, Y.: Viceroi: Catching click-spam in search ad networks. In: Proceedings of ACM Conference on Computer and Communications Security (2013)
17. http://www.maxmind.com/en/web_services
18. http://en.wikipedia.org/wiki/Usage_share_of_web_browsers
19. http://www.blacklistalert.org/
20. http://www.cs.waikato.ac.nz/ml/weka/
21. Quinlan, J.: C4.5: Programs for machine learning. Morgan Kaufmann Publishers (1993)
22. http://en.wikipedia.org/wiki/Sar_Unix
23. Eckersley, P.: How unique is your web browser? In: Proceedings of the Privacy Enhancing Technologies Symposium (2010)
24. Yen, T.-F., Huang, X., Monrose, F., Reiter, M.K.: Browser fingerprinting from coarse traffic summaries: Techniques and implications. In: Flegel, U., Bruschi, D. (eds.) DIMVA 2009. LNCS, vol. 5587, pp. 157–175. Springer, Heidelberg (2009)
25. Schulte, B., Andrianakis, H., Sun, K., Stavrou, A.: Netgator: Malware detection using program interactive challenges. In: Flegel, U., Markatos, E., Robertson, W. (eds.) DIMVA 2012. LNCS, vol. 7591, pp. 164–183. Springer, Heidelberg (2013)

Botyacc: Unified P2P Botnet Detection Using Behavioural Analysis and Graph Analysis

Shishir Nagaraja

School of Computer Science,
University of Birmingham, UK
s.nagaraja@cs.bham.ac.uk

Abstract. The detection and isolation of peer-to-peer botnets is an ongoing problem. We propose a novel technique for detecting P2P botnets. Detection is based on unifying behavioural analysis with structured graph analysis. First, our inference technique exploits a fundamental property of botnet design. Modern botnets use peer-to-peer communication topologies which are fundamental to botnet resilience. Second, our technique extends conventional graph-based detection by incorporating behavioural analysis into structured graph analysis, thus unifying graph-theoretic detection with behavioural detection under a single algorithmic framework. We carried out evaluation over real-world P2P botnet traffic and show that the resulting algorithm can localise the majority of bots with low false-positive rate.

Keywords: Traffic analysis, botnet detection, behavioural analysis, graph theory.

1 Introduction

The detection and isolation of peer-to-peer (P2P) botnets is an ongoing problem. P2P architectures are attractive as they offer low end-to-end routing delays and provide robustness against botnet response mechanisms by decentralising importance throughout the network.

In response to the proliferation of P2P botnets, many researchers have proposed the use of machine learning techniques. Essentially, these are partitioning tools which convert a dataset into clusters of similar data points under some definition of similarity. However, the context of statistical botnet detection fundamentally differs from non-security applications: the context is adversarial and the attacker controls the data of interest.

Partitioning algorithms leveraging traffic similarity require special statistical properties. First, cluster boundaries must be *precise* — approximate boundaries are not sufficient. Otherwise, botnets can exploit this weakness to "blend-in" with legitimate traffic clusters. We also require that the cluster definition is *robust* — the property that resists the addition of botnet points to non-botnet clusters. Current botnet detection techniques do not offer these properties.

To enable *precise and robust* characterisation of the legitimate data subspace (clusters), one approach is to leverage a fundamental design characteristic of modern botnets: its P2P communication architecture — P2P botnets use structured communication networks which are highly resistant to churn and adversarial takedown. However,

M. Kutyłowski and J. Vaidya (Eds.): ESORICS 2014, Part II, LNCS 8713, pp. 439–456, 2014.

anonymous proxies and NATs can hide P2P topologies from network monitors and thereby adversely affect detection based on the structural differences in the communication graphs of the embedded botnets vis a vis the background Internet graph.

Our approach is to unify two well understood principles of botnet detection (P2P connectivity and traffic similarity) into a single algorithm underlying out detection technique. This results in high detection accuracy as well as evasion resistance properties. At the core of our technique is a novel Markovian diffusion process defined over input traffic traces, that leverages patterns in connectivity as well as flow statistics. Evading detection against our approach may be hard. First, detection is based on a fundamental property of botnet operation; structured P2P topologies are a pre-requisite for botnet robustness. Second, we exploit the attacker's lack of knowledge of the precise form and structure of legitimate traffic. To be clear, we are not proposing heuristics. This paper realises the following contributions

- A link between network behavioural analysis and graph-theoretic approaches to botnet detection.
- An algorithm that takes non-linearity of network traffic into account.
- A systematic approach to selection of network traffic features for capturing behavioural information.
- A single algorithm that works at different levels of scale, in both enterprise and ISP settings.

2 Architecture

The need to perform efficient accounting, traffic engineering and load balancing, detection of malicious and disallowed activity, and other factors has led network operators to pursue infrastructures to monitor traffic across multiple vantage points. Internally, enterprises run intrusion detection systems to collect more fine-grained information about protocols and bit patterns occurring in packets while ISPs run monitoring infrastructures to collect information about flow-level traffic volumes.

Our architecture consists of the following parts.

Monitor: First, *traffic monitors* are responsible for observing and sampling traffic information from the data-plane, and building a compact representation that is used for analysis and detection. These monitors may run at end-hosts, or on routers within the network using monitoring techniques such as Cisco IOS's NetFlow [9] or sFlow, the Openflow standard. By default, NetFlow and sFlow *sample* traffic by processing one out of every 200 to 500 packets. However, advances in counter architectures [20] enable efficient tracking of the entire traffic flows in ISP networks without need for sampling. For enterprises, several products under the name of Security and Information Event Management (SIEM) systems now seek to store full traffic trace information. The constant threat of attacks suffered by modern networks has led operators to pursue infrastructures to monitor for anomalous behaviour across multiple vantage points.

Aggregator: Second, an *aggregator* component periodically receives observed communication traces from individual monitors, and merges them together to compute a *network-wide* communication trace dataset. This dataset contains the overlay topology corresponding to all pairs of intercommunicating hosts observable across the set of monitors. It runs an algorithm that analyses the communication traces. It then attempts to separate the dataset into two (possibly overlapping) subsets: the botnet trace, and the non-botnet communication traces. Bots (hosts that form the botnet communication graph) are then output as a set of *suspect* hosts. This list may then be sent to the set of clients that are *subscribers* to the service. The list may be used to install blacklists into routers, to configure intrusion detection, firewall systems, and traffic shapers; or as "hints" to human operators regarding which hosts should be investigated as being bots. The aggregator may optionally append a likelihood that each suspect IP address has engaged in a certain activity, so that clients can individually determine at what threshold to block traffic. Aggregators may be combined in a hierarchical fashion to further reduce control overhead. In other words, low-level aggregators can collect information from a subset of networks and hosts, and then in turn send their results to a higher-level aggregator.

Honeynet: Third, the network defender obtains botnet communication traces from a honeynet. Such traces are available from third-party sources or by building a small malware testbed. The honeynet is seeded with malware relevant to the defender. For instance, an oil and gas company, they might be particularly interested in targeted malware attacks. Once the relevant malware is seeded into the malware, it is allowed to connect to its control servers. The resulting traffic including C&C traffic is recorded and forms the seed input to the inference algorithm. IP communication headers and summary information for each traffic flow is recorded and used by the detection algorithm.

Inference Mechanism: Fourth, traffic traces from the aggregator and the honeynet is piped to our inference technique. The algorithms underlying our technique are able to partition the traffic into multiple botnet and non-botnet flow partitions.

3 The Problem

Our goal is to separate botnet C&C communication from legitimate network traffic. Consider a *communication graph* $G = (V, E)$ with V representing the set of hosts observed in traffic traces, and an edge $e \in E$ representing a *traffic flow*. Each edge e is a k-dimensional vector where k is a system parameter. Consider one or more *botnet graphs* $G_b = (H, M)$ embedded within the communication graph, where $H \subseteq V$ is the set of bots (infected hosts) and $M \subseteq H \times H \subseteq E$ are the corresponding edges (botnet flows). The objective of the inference algorithm is to detect subgraphs G_b whilst minimising false-negative rate and false-positive rate.

Graph techniques such as community detection algorithms, sybil detection algorithms, and other graph partitioning methods leverage the presence of a bottle-neck cut separating a subgraph of interest from the rest of the graph. This scenario is not applicable to botnets where there is no bottle-neck cut separating botnet edges and legitimate edges. From a graph-theoretic perspective, botnet detection is an edge-partitioning problem, an open research problem. Whereas conventional graph partitioning algorithms (community and sybil detection) are designed for vertex partitioning.

4 Inference Technique

4.1 The Methodology

Botnets create unique patterns in network traffic. These patterns manifest themselves in a number of ways which can be traced to the botnet's design. The use of structured P2P communication topologies increases resilience to bot-takedown, as well as the anonymity of messages on the botnet C&C channel when messages are routed via other bots.

A second source of patterns is statistical similarity of traffic patterns. Bots tend to have similar lifecycles of reconnaissance and initial compromise, followed by the establishment of a C&C (command and control) channel, which is in turn followed by attacks such as data-exfiltration or service denial attacks.

Botnet detection via the use of structured peer-to-peer topologies, similarity of traffic flow patterns, and collaboration involving a large number of infected hosts, have thus far been studied individually. In this paper, we propose a detection methodology that unifies these approaches. The intuition behind unifying graph-theoretic and statistical behavioural analysis, rather than their independent application, is to leverage feedback loops across these approaches.

The feedback loop is designed as a stochastic diffusion process over 'similar' traffic flows. It is based on a new type of random walk on graphs. Random walks allow us to reason about graph topology and have been heavily used in the development of graph partitioning techniques. To incorporate the notion of edge 'similarity', we apply theoretical tools from euclidean geometry. Each traffic flow is a vector whose scalar elements specify the Cartesian coordinates of a point with respect to a set of axes — one axis per element. The ensemble of points resulting from considering traffic flows constitutes a multi-dimensional geometric surface with a lot of structural information embedded within it.

Our inference algorithm constructs geometric surfaces whose structure depends on the communication graph as well as traffic-flow information. Our inference algorithm is a stochastic diffusion process over 'similar' edges. We start by representing traffic traces into a communication graph. We define a special random walk over this graph. The novelty of the walk is that state transition (choice of outgoing edge) depends on the incoming edge of a random walk step. This is done to incorporate the notion of edge 'similarity' — the walk has a bias towards similar flows. Flow similarity is defined using Euclidean distance in a high dimensional setting where each traffic flow is a vector whose scalar elements specify the Cartesian coordinates of a point with respect to a set of axes – one axis per element. The ensemble of points resulting from considering traffic flows constitutes a multi-dimensional geometric surface with a lot of structural information embedded within it.

4.2 Step1: Constructing the Dual Graph

From captured traffic traces, we construct a communication graph G where each edge $e \in E(G)$ is a traffic flow represented by a k-dimensional vector and whose nodes represent computers. This graph only contains topology information. We then construct a new graph that which is influenced by communication topology and the geometry of traffic-flow vectors. We achieve this by creating a dual graph.

To find the dual of the communication graph, we convert edges (traffic flows) into nodes. We then connect pairs of nodes (traffic flows) whose which are *locally similar*: flows must transition adjacent IP addresses (share a common node in G) and demonstrate flow-similarity (flow vectors must be less than a threshold distance apart). The intuition behind this step is that random walks on the dual graph will achieve the equivalent of entering and exiting nodes over closely related flows in the original communication graph. Note that this would not be normally possible because random walks are memoryless. Whereas we wish to study diffusion effects of walks over similar (traffic) edges rather than different edges in the original communication graph — this is one of the primary design features that will reduce the false-positive rate problem we discussed in the motivation sub-section above.

The dual of G is a weighted graph $\mathcal{D}(G)$. Each edge in G is a node in $\mathcal{D}(G)$ therefore $|V(\mathcal{D}(G))| = |E(G)|$. An edge between two nodes in $\mathcal{D}(G)$ is constructed as follows:

- *edge-adjacency:* For a edge e_{st} between nodes s, t in G, the set of adjacent edges is the set of all edges connecting s and x, or, t and y: $S_{e_{st}} = \{e_{st}, e_{xs}, e_{ty}\}$.
- *geometrical distance:* Each edge e in G is represented by a k-dimensional vector $(w_1, \ldots, w_k)$. The geometrical distance between a pair of edges e_i and e_j is given by:

$$W_{ij} = \begin{cases} e^{-\frac{||e_i - e_j||}{t}} & \text{if} ||e_i - e_j||^2 \leq \varepsilon \\ 0 & \text{otherwise} \end{cases} \tag{1}$$

, where the norm is the Euclidean norm in $\mathcal{R}^k$.
- Each edge e in G is a node e in the dual of G, namely $\mathcal{D}(G)$. We place an edge with weight W_{ij} between two nodes e_i and e_j in $\mathcal{D}(G)$, if they satisfy the edge-adjacency property above and are geometrically close enough ($W_{ij} \neq 0$).

4.3   Step2: Partitioning

Now that we have a graph-geometric representation ($\mathcal{D}(G)$) of the traffic, our next task is to separate subgraphs corresponding to different traffic characteristics. The geometric space within which traffic points reside is represented as the graph, and we explore the local and global properties of surfaces using random walks (as explained earlier).

Constructing the dual allows us to partition a communication into subgraphs with similar traffic flow behaviour and subgraphs that have a different expansion properties than the background graph they are embedded within. Consider the toy example of edge-partitioning a graph consisting of a set of nodes connected using one set of edges within a ring structure and using a second set of edges as a star structure as shown in Fig. 1(a). Without taking geometry into account (flow-similarity), computing the dual graph gives us Fig. 1(b), where star-edges have been converted into a clique subgraph that is weakly connected to a subgraph containing nodes that were edges constituting a ring in the original graph. Now, using random walks over the dual-graph, we can

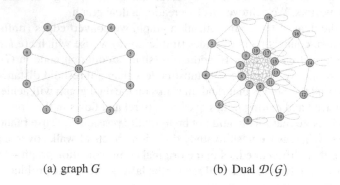

(a) graph G (b) Dual $\mathcal{D}(G)$

Fig. 1. A sample graph and its dual; vertex ids are reset in the dual

partition the ring-edges and the star-edges using the relative expansion properties of these two subgraphs in the dual.

Traffic data is represented as a graph with individual geometric surfaces represented as subgraph communities within a single connected component. A surface corresponds to a subset of $V(\mathcal{D}_C(G))$ that is richly intra-connected but sparsely connected with the rest of the graph. To partition traffic by similarity, we consider the algebraic connectivity properties of the graph. of each surface and locate **gaps** between dense surfaces.

Partitioning Technique. To find gaps that naturally partition the data, we find the Laplacian over the graph dual. Laplacian operator is efficient at finding gaps between geometric clusters.

The standard technique for detecting gaps using the Laplacian operator consists of considering the adjacency matrix A and the graph edges, with weights $w_1, w_2, \ldots, w_n$ on the edges, the Laplacian matrix is defined as $L = AI_w A^T$. Here I_w is a diagonal matrix with the weights placed along the diagonal i.e. $I_{ii} = w_i = d_i$, where d_i is the degree of node i. We then find the eigenvalues of the Laplacian matrix. There are standard techniques for computing eigenvalues, for instance the well known Lanczos algorithm which scales as $O(n \log n)$.

A partition for graph $G = (V, E)$ is defined as a partition of V into legitimate and botnet subgraphs L, and M, such that the number of edges across the gap $gap(L, M)/(|L||M|)$ is minimised. In such a scenario, the second smallest eigenvalue (λ_2) of L, yields a lower bound on the optimal cost of the gap is $(1 - \lambda_2)$. The eigenvector (v_2) corresponding to the second eigenvalue, bisects the graph into only two clusters based on the sign of the corresponding vector entry. Division into a larger number of clusters is achieved by repeated bisection. To prevent repetitive bisection from using trivial gaps we use the well known conductance metric.

Quality Metric. The quality of a partition is measured by its conductance, *the ratio of the number of its external connections to the number of its total connections.*

We let $d(i)$ denote the degree of vertex i. For $S \subset V(\mathcal{D}_C(G))$, we define $\delta(S) = \sum_{i \in S} d(i)$ as the volume of S. So,

$$\delta(V(\mathcal{D}_C(G))) = 2|E(\mathcal{D}_C(G))|$$

. Let $EE(S, V(\mathcal{D}_C(G)) \setminus S)$ be the set of edges connecting a vertex in S with a vertex in $V(\mathcal{D}_C(G)) \setminus S$. We define the conductance of a set of vertices S, written $\phi(S)$ as

$$phi(S) = \frac{EE(S, V(\mathcal{D}_C(G)) \setminus S)}{\min(\delta(S), \delta(V(\mathcal{D}_C(G)) \setminus S))}$$

The conductance of $\mathcal{D}_C(G)$ is then given by:

$$\min_{S \in V(\mathcal{D}_C(G))} \phi(S)$$

. To avoid obtaining trivial partitions, the conductance of a subgraph is normalised by the size of the partition.

Generalising the Approach. The Laplacian operator is applicable for linear contexts. However, since the botnet context is adversarial the attacker can architect bot traffic to behave in a non-linear manner. For instance, the attacker can engineer bot traffic to follow a non-linear geometric shape such as a sphere or a curved line. In such a case, a linear operator would make errroneous judgements. Since the adversary controls botnet traffic data, an assumption of linearity would be incorrect. The geometric interpretation of this assumption is that traffic feature vectors are points on a planar surface. However, a non-linear operator, being generic, (discards and) resists attacks based on exploiting this assumption. For instance, as a way of increasing the false-positive rate of detection, the botnet operator can alter botnet traffic vectors so they are a short euclidean distance from legitimate traffic vectors. In this case, a linear operator would be successfully misguided into accepting the botnet traffic as legitimate given their close proximity. However, a non-linear operator would be able to leverage the actual geometric structure of legitimate traffic (instead of assuming it is a planar surface) to resist botnet points being accepted into the legitimate cluster. Thus, we use the laplace-beltrami operator which allows valid distance measurements when the geometrical subspace is non-linear.

Let X denotes the set of functions defined on the vertices of $\mathcal{D}(G)$. The application of laplace-beltrami operator on a function results in another function in X, i.e $Lf \in X \forall f \in X$ since L is a function of functions: from X to X. An *eigenfunction* of the laplace-beltrami operator is a function f such that $Lf = \lambda f$ where λ is the eigenvalue of L and represents the scaling of f. By computing the eigenfunctions we obtain a compressed list of features that is expressed as a linear combination of the (larger number of) input features. This approach of using eigenfunctions for feature reduction prior to inference is well known within the machine learning community. We leverage this as a building block in our algorithm.

- To apply the laplace-beltrami operator, we compute $L = D - W$, where D is the diagonal matrix corresponding to W. L is a symmetric and positive matrix.

- Compute the eigenvectors and eigenvalues of $Lf = \lambda f$ ordered in the increasing order of the eigenvalues $\lambda_0 \leq \lambda_1 \leq \lambda_2 \ldots \lambda_{k-1}$.
- Ignore the first eigenvector $f_0 = (1, \ldots, 1)$ with eigenvalue $\lambda_0 = 0$.
- Each vertex i of $\mathcal{D}(G)$ is now expressed in terms of the m new features. The modified graph is referred to as $\mathcal{D}^C(G)$. Vertices of the modified graph are now available as $V(\mathcal{D}(G))_i = (f_1(i), \ldots, f_m(i))$.
- Each edge between a pair of vertices in $\mathcal{D}^C(G)$ is refreshed with an edge weight that corresponds to the new set of features. Each edge between vertices i and j is refreshed as follows:

$$
W'_{ij} = \begin{cases} e^{-\frac{||v_i - v_j||}{t}} & \text{if} ||v_i - v_j||^2 \leq \varepsilon \\ 0 & \text{otherwise} \end{cases} \tag{2}
$$

, where the norm is the Euclidean norm in $\mathcal{R}^m$.

5   Noise Tolerance

Our detection method leverages the attackers limited knowledge about the location and structure of the legitimate surface to bound statistical noise injected by an adaptive botmaster. Vectors corresponding to three categories – legitimate traffic, noise traffic introduced by the botmaster, and genuine botnet traffic – are represented in the dual graph. As described earlier, each traffic vector constitutes a vertex. An undirected edge exists between two vertices if they are within a ε threshold distance of each other.

An edge may exist between a noise vector and a legitimate vector if they are within close proximity. Such a *noise edge* allows "leakage" of walks between the legitimate and botnet surfaces contributing to false positives. Each noise edge connects a noise pack to vertices within a legitimate traffic surface.

To successfully evade detection, the attacker must succeed in placing a large number of noise points (*noise pack*) in close proximity of another surface, all points within the noise pack must be in close proximity of legitimate points rather than just a few. This requires knowledge of the location of a majority of the points in that surface. Our design leverages three important facts to limit the number and size of noise packs: *a*) legitimate surface graphs tend to have high *algebraic connectivity* (the smallest positive eigenvalue of its Laplacian matrix). *b*) large amounts of noise (compared to the number of noise edges) decreases algebraic connectivity.

Capping the number of noise edges: The evasion resistance property of our detection algorithm relies on limiting the number of noise edges (m). There are primarily two scenarios in which botnet malware might attempt to increase m:

- **No knowledge of legitimate subspace:** Botnet sprays noise randomly in the data space in the hope that some of these points will be near the legitimate surface. Spraying is achieved by the botnet altering behaviour by modifying traffic feature values. This is quite difficult to perform because the data space is large (theoretically infinite) whereas the legitimate surface is located on a relatively smaller geometric subspace.

- **Partial knowledge of legitimate subspace:** A second possibility is that the botnet has some awareness of legitimate surface points. For instance, this information may be gained by analysing legitimate traffic on the infected machine. It can add noise in the proximity of known legitimate points to create edges between the botnet surface and the legitimate surface. However, in doing so, the algebraic connectivity characteristics are disturbed by the small set of noise edges. The noise based on partial knowledge introduces a gap between the legitimate and botnet surface. This is true, unless the noise surface is in the proximity of a significant majority of points within the legitimate surface. This is very hard to accomplish unless the attacker has full knowledge of the legitimate traffic; high-level trends or summary information do not give information regarding structure and location of the legitimate surface, full traffic traces would be required.

6   Results

We evaluated our algorithm in two different experimental settings. We apply our algorithm on real botnet traces within an enterprise setting and measure its effectiveness.

Malware testbed: In order to obtain botnet traffic flows we created a testbed of 25 servers within a test network connected to the Internet. The computers was then seeded with samples from three peer-to-peer versions from well known botnet families: Zeus, Miner, and Spyeye. All three botnets have moved from centralised C&C servers to entirely P2P communication. Zeus and Spyeye are designed for stealing banking information while Miner steals Bitcoin credentials.

On each testbed computer, we instantiated 70 copies of a malware sample (at a time) within a hypervisor, i.e 1750 instances from each family, or a total of 5250 malware instances. The testbed allows the bot to connect with other bots in the wild which enables us to closely observe the actions of the bot and its interactions with other bots. The result is a lot of network traffic which will be *attack traffic by definition*. We exercised due diligence to prevent our testbed from being used as an attack platform. In particular, all probing, scanning, spam was blocked while DDOS attacks were rate-limited at the very least. However, command and control (C&C) incoming and outgoing traffic was allowed as this was essential for our study.

We set up traffic monitors on the backbone router at a university campus network using an electrical signal duplicator unit that works at up to 20Gbps. As opposed to port-mirroring, this approach allows us to capture packets at the line rate without inducing the effects of packet sampling. The traffic rate is typically 2.5–8Gbps.

We developed an efficient network flow capture tool that processes packet traces and generates flows. A flow is record of communication between a pair of hosts and is represented by a tuple containing a number of fields as given below. We consider UDP and TCP traffic. In the case of UDP traffic, the TCP fields listed are zeroed out as are optional TCP fields.

Each flow record is a tuple structure containing two parts; inter-flow values that are common to all flow records occurring within a ten-minute time period, and flow specific fields. The entire set of fields comprising a flow record are given below:

- Inter-flow statistics (fields) computed across the flows: *traffic volume, duration, distribution of packets per flow, distribution of flows per period, distribution of packets per flow, throughput distribution, distribution of inter-flow arrival times averaged distribution of inter-packet arrival times. Distributions are computed over a time interval of ten minutes.*
- Flow fields: *tcp/udp.source-port, tcp/udp.destination port, IP version, IP header length, ip.tos — precedence, ip.tos — delay, ip.tos — throughput, ip.tos — reliability, ip.tos — reserved, ip.tos — total length, ip.flags,*
  ip.fragmentoffset, ip.ttl , ip.protocol, Entropy of ip.id# distribution, Entropy of tcp.seq# distribution, Entropy of tcp.ack# distribution, tcp.offset, tcp.reserved, tcp.flags,
  tcp.maximum-segment-size, tcp.echotimedata

In the above list, each sample distribution is represented by the corresponding histogram. The first bin corresponds to $P(X < x) \leq 5\%$, the second bin corresponds to $P(X < x) \leq 15\%$ and so on.

Algorithm Application. We now consider the application of our algorithm on a real-world dataset. To access live traffic, we captured network traffic at a university gateway for a period of one month between March and April 2012. This dataset has 113,576 unique source IP addresses and 11,643,993 traffic flows. This includes 432,257 embedded botnet flows from seeded malware. This corresponds to a communication graph G_E containing both malware and non-malware edges.

The first step of our algorithm is to create the dual of G_E, namely $D(G_E)$. At this stage each edge (flow) becomes a node and nodes become edges, therefore flow-vectors are now associated with each node. An edge is constructed between two nodes if the Euclidean distance between the corresponding flow-vectors is less than a certain threshold ε. We used $\varepsilon = .0025$. This value controls the runtime of the generation of the dual. Our inference algorithm is not sensitive to high values of ε (leading to a denser graph), since the diffusion effects of the subsequent random walk process is controlled by the non-linear kernel function: $e^{-\frac{\|e_i - e_j\|}{t}}$ see Eqn. 1. We chose $t = 1$, but higher values will produce a sharper decay. Our choice of ε leads to $O(logE(D(G_E)))$ edges per node in the dual. This step leads to the to embedding of information from the communication graph topology and the geometry of network traffic, within the dual graph. Figure 4(a) shows a rendering of the dual with vertices represented by blue points and edges represented by the distance between vertices; the number of edges is too high to be represented graphically. Figures 4(b) through 4(f) show the dual graphs corresponding to the other five weeks of enterprise traffic with embedded botnet traffic.

The second step of our algorithm is dimensionality reduction. This step prevents the botnet from altering traffic patterns over time in order to "throw-off" the detection system. Thus the compressed feature set selected by the algorithm can vary from across time. Feature selection is carried out in an unsupervised manner. The compressed feature list is given by the ordered eigenvalues of the laplacian of the dual graph computed at the end of the previous step. The first eigenvalue is zero by definition and this is ignored. The eigenvectors corresponding to the eigenvalues represent the new mapping

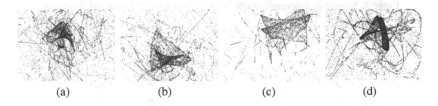

(a)   (b)   (c)   (d)

Fig. 2. Visual representation (top three dimensions) of network traffic after dimensionality reduction, at the end of Step 2 of our algorithm

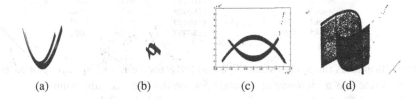

(a)   (b)   (c)   (d)

Fig. 3. Visual representation of the results of our inference algorithm showing isolated botnet traffic

of traffic data points as a function of the compressed feature list. The embedding of the various geometrical surfaces within this compressed space is shown in figure 3.

Thus far, our algorithm has only partitioned traffic into different surfaces. The botnet flows are partitioned into respective surfaces. After three iterations of the partitioning algorithm, we obtain a subgraph (surface) of size 432,256 nodes, containing 423,906 nodes corresponding to botnet flows, and 8,350 nodes corresponding to non-botflows. At this stage, our validation metric indicates that the sub-graph has a graph conductance of about 0.9 (In all other scenarios, the graph conductance is less than 0.5, so we can safely set our threshold of the graph conductance test to be 0.5).

Table 1. Zeus in enterprise traffic – detection and error rates of inference

	#Malicious flows	#gateway-flows	Detection%	% FP
Week1	3368	1211736	99.98	0.019
Week2	8836	1392755	99.93	0.037
Week3	3231	1109264	97.95	0.082
Week4	8349	1312952	98.09	0.041
Week5	8217	1130120	98.21	0.030

We evaluated the performance of detection on a weekly basis through our dataset. Each week, we collected gateway traces and combined it with that week's botnet traces. The previous week's data was discarded from the graph and dual generation. The honeynet seed traces were also fresh, thus corresponding traces from each week were input to our detection algorithm.

To evaluate performance, we are concerned with the *false positive rate* (the fraction of non-bot nodes that are detected as bots) and the *false negative rate* (the fraction of bot nodes that are not detected). The results of botnet detection for Zeus, Spyeye, and Miner are shown in Table 1, Table 2, and Table 3 respectively.

Table 2. Spyeye in enterprise traffic – detection and error rates of inference

	#Malicious flows	#gateway-flows	Detection%	% FP
Week1	8021	1346235	98.11	0.041
Week2	6295	1327479	98.77	0.064
Week3	4213	1180134	99.86	0.074
Week4	3538	1396174	97.86	0.047
Week5	5388	1186480	98.70	0.023

Table 3. Miner in enterprise traffic — detection and error rates of inference

	#Malicious flows	#gateway-flows	Detection%	% FP
Week1	1050	1590306	97.50	0.018
Week2	2735	1186212	96.64	0.064
Week3	5341	1560028	94.89	0.048
Week4	3099	1186929	95.52	0.062
Week5	4566	1154067	97.76	0.072

Detection rates ranged between 97% and 99% for Zeus and Spyeye. For Miner, the detection rate was a bit lower at around 95% on the average. Importantly, for all three peer-to-peer botnets, the false-positive rate was well below 0.1%.

6.1 Effects of Botnet Topology and Size

In the next set of experiments, we seek to understand the effectiveness of deploying our algorithm in a setting where a majority of the botnet communication graph is embedded within the network traffic captured from our vantage points. This is the case of multiple ISPs cooperatively running our inference algorithm.

To study this, we constructed a dataset where traffic flows from the Zeus botnet were embedded it within ISP traffic using various peer-to-peer structures. To improve realism, we build the background traffic communication graph by using real packet-level traces collected by CAIDA on OC192 Internet backbone links [2]. Since packet level information is not available, we only used flow-level features for our experiments with ISP data.

Another aspect we need to consider is the different sizes of botnets. An inference algorithm must be able to effectively detect small botnets as well as large botnets. This is important in order to be able to track the evolution of the botnet throughout its life-cycle right from the early stages of deployment to large-scale botnets which may pose significant threat due to the possible scale of geographical spread as well as size. We perform this experiment by keeping the size of the background traffic graph constant, and generating synthetic botnet topologies of varying sizes (between 100 and 100,000 bots).

Finally, we must also consider the effects of partial visibility. Clearly, obtaining access to the Internet traffic of all ISPs is a fairly difficult proposition. However, it is certainly likely that a fraction of ISPs can be incentivised to cooperate via a combination of legal and economic incentives. We also understand from previous work that a subset of ISPs typically have access to a significant fraction of botnet traffic. A study [1] of 4,000 IP addresses belonging to the Storm botnet found that 60% of inter-bot paths traverse top six ISPs, and 89% of the inter-bot paths traversed top ten ISPs. More recently, reports from anti-virus companies indicates that India has the second highest number of spam bots. Interestingly, the whole country is served by two major ISPs. To incorporate the effects of partial visibility, we construct the botnet graph, by selecting a random subset of nodes in the background communication graph (CAIDA) to be botnet nodes, and synthetically add bot flows between them corresponding to a particular structured overlay topology. We then simulate the effects of partial visibility by retaining only 55% of the total traffic flows in the combined graph and discarding 45% of the flows chosen uniformly at random.

We then pass the combined graph as input to our inference algorithm. By keeping track of which nodes are bots (this information is not passed to our algorithm), we can acquire "ground truth" to measure performance. To investigate sensitivity of our techniques to the particular overlay structure, we consider several alternative structured overlays, including (a) Chord [19], (b) de Bruijn [13], (c) Kademlia [14], and (d) the "robust ring" topology described in [11]. The remainder of this section contains results from running our algorithms over the joined botnet and Internet communication graphs, and measuring the ability to separate out the two from each other.

Table 4. CAIDA – results if only Tier-1 ISPs contribute views

Topology	$|V_B|$	% Detected	% FP
de Bruijn	1000	99.97	0.0011
	10000	99.98	0.0020
	100000	99.98	0.0170
Kademlia	1000	99.97	0.0040
	10000	99.97	0.0104
	100000	99.96	0.0350
Chord	1000	99.98	0.0017
	10000	99.97	0.0024
	100000	99.87	0.0202
LEET-Chord	1000	99.96	0.0040
	10000	99.65	0.0139
	100000	98.91	0.0613

Overall, we find performance to be fairly stable across multiple kinds of botnet topologies and sizes with detection rates higher than 98%. In addition, our algorithm is able to achieve a false positive rate of less than 0.06% on the harder-to-detect LEET-Chord topology. We find that as the size of the bot graph increases, performance degrades, but only by a small amount. For example, in Table 4, with the fully visible deBruijn topology, for 100 nodes the false positive rate is zero, while for 10,000 nodes the rate becomes 0.002%.

The high detection and low false-positive rates are better than state-of-the-art algorithms. It shows that the combination of traffic-flow features and graph-structure information holds good potential in designing reliable algorithms for botnet detection.

While our approach is not perfectly accurate, we envision it may be of use when coupled with other detection strategies (e.g., previous work on botnet detection [10,8], or if used to signal "hints" to network operators regarding which hosts may be infected.

7 Discussion

As we have demonstrated, starting with a certain definition of botnet behaviour — **traffic produced from the malware testbed,** graph theoretic analysis can help in identifying botnets in enterprise traffic. We now discuss the significance of our results and related insights.

The evaluation results indicates the usefulness of our approach. The main insight of our work is that both both legitimate and botnet traffic have specific geometry, i.e, traffic vectors lie on a low-dimensional geometric surface. The inference technique partitions the dataset into multiple botnet and legitimate surfaces.

The graph underpinning the partitioning process is constructed using both communication topology information and communication flow information. Since P2P topologies are a fundamental design requirement in order to maintain the botnet's resilience, the botmaster cannot evade detection without giving up resilience properties. Without P2P topologies underlying botnet communication, the C2 channel would not be robust enough to withstand take down attempts, thus forcing the attacker to choose between survivability and stealth.

At the same time, techniques to isolate the structured communication graphs induced by botnets depend on the integrity of communication links within traffic traces recorded by network monitoring systems. This can be a challenge when we consider the widespread use of NATs and other traffic aggregators. Aggregators hide the presence of communicating endpoints and appear as a few large nodes communicating with a large number of endpoints. This induces error into the inference process. If substantial parts of a P2P embedded botnet appear as leaf nodes connected to a few hubs, then the basis for isolating botnets from the background traffic by leveraging communication topology characteristics is substantially weakened.

Unifying both behavioural and structured graph approaches presents a credible approach to addressing the errors induced by traffic aggregators. When communication topology information is hidden using anonymous relays, or is otherwise incomplete, or mutilated in the dataset, the inference algorithm can recover from the errors. The construction of the dual graph driven by the statistical similarity of traffic flows still proceeds undisturbed. However the construction of the dual graph now involves a higher number of vector comparisons to dismantle the virtual high-degree node induced by the aggregator — instead of $O((log\ n)^2)$ vector comparisons in the normal case, we are required to carry out a significantly larger number of vector comparisons which is $O(n^2)$ in the worst case; when all the traffic is lumped into a single node. In practice, the computational effort to manage errors in topology is at least a large constant times $O((log\ n)^2)$.

Dynamic Feature Selection: Our inference algorithm incorporates dynamic feature selection instead of using a static heuristic-driven definition of which features are indicative of botnet traffic. The relevant feature set is derived as part of the dimensionality reduction step. This means that unlike static heuristics where the feature set has to be constantly updated by the network defender, we derive the feature set directly from the traffic traces. On the otherhand, this approach requires us to capture a large number of features beforehand which can increase the load on traffic monitoring. While the evaluation results are fairly positive, we have been unable to evaluate how dynamic feature selection behaves under botnet evolution. Dimensionality reduction simply selects a combination of features that capture most of the information contained in the dataset.

Scale: Our experiments show that the inference technique can scale to large traffic volumes, and in the presence of partial observations. This solves an number of practical problems concerning the use of different types of algorithms for enterprise detection and ISP-level detection. Thus engineering and training efforts can be concentrated on developing and operating a single functional piece of equipment, as opposed to having different solutions each for ISPs and enterprises.

8 Related Work

Bots are unique amongst networked malware in that they collectively maintain communication structures across nodes to resiliently distribute commands from a *command and control* node. The ability to coordinate and upload new commands to bots gives the botnet owner vast power when performing criminal activities, including the ability to orchestrate surveillance attacks, perform DDoS extortion, sending spam for pay, and phishing. This problem has worsened to a point where modern botnets control hundreds of thousands of hosts and generate revenue of millions of dollars per year for their owners [4].

8.1 Non-signature Based Methods

We now describe related work in non-signature based detection methods. None of the techniques we discuss in this section, have any evasion resistance properties.

BotMiner [5] detects infected hosts without previous knowledge of botnets. In this system, bots are identified by clustering hosts that exhibit similar communication and (possible) malicious activities. The clustering allows hosts to be groups according to the botnet that they belong to as hosts within the same botnet will have similar communication patterns, and will usually perform the same activities at the same time (such as a DDoS attack).

There are also schemes that combine network- and host-based approaches. The work of Stinson et al. [18] attempts to discriminate between locally-initiated versus remotely-initiated actions by tracking data arriving over the network being used as system call arguments using taint tracking methods. Following a similar approach, Gummadi et al. [6] whitelist application traffic by identifying and attesting human-generated traffic from a host which allows an application server to selectively respond to service requests. Finally, John et al. [12] present a technique to defend against spam botnets by automating the generation of spam feeds by directing an incoming spam feed into a Honeynet, then downloading bots spreading through those messages and then using the outbound spam generated to create a better feed.

Server Detection: DNS. Several works provide a detection mechanism to identify domains associated with malware at using centralised C&C channels.

Paxson et al [16] attempt to provide a detection mechanism that leverages the amount of information transmitted over a DNS channel in order to detect suspicious flows. The system allows for a upper bound to be set, any DNS flow that exceeds this barrier is flagged for inspection. The upper bound can be circumvented by limiting flows, but this has an impact the amount of data exfiltration/command issuing that can occur. The system looks primarily at data included within domain names, but also looks at inter-query timings and DNS packet field values, both of which can provide low capacity channels.

Perdisci et al [17] apply clustering to domains so they are grouped according to overlap in the returned IP addresses. By then comparing the clusters to previously labelled data, they can then be classified as flux or non-flux, revealing domains that make use of the same network.

8.2 Graph-Based Approaches

Several works [3,8,7,21,10] have previously applied graph analysis to detect botnets. The technique of Collins and Reiter [3] detects anomalies induced in a graph of protocol specific flows by a botnet control traffic. They suggest that a botnet can be detected based on the observation that an attacker will increase the number of connected graph components due to a sudden growth of edges between unlikely neighbouring nodes. While it depends on being able to accurately model valid network growth, this is a powerful approach because it avoids depending on protocol semantics or packet statistics. However this work only makes minimal use of spatial relationship information. Additionally, the need for historical record keeping makes it challenging in scenarios where the victim network is already infected when it seeks help and hasn't stored past traffic data, while our scheme can be used to detect pre-existing botnets as well. Illiofotou et al. [8,7] also exploit dynamicity of traffic graphs to classify network flows in order to detect P2P networks. It uses static (spatial) and dynamic (temporal) metrics centered on node and edge level metrics in addition to the largest-connected-component-size as a graph level metric.

More recently, Botgrep [15] presented a scheme that searches for expander graphs to discover P2P graphs within ISP traffic. The theoretical component of the algorithm presented is our work is much more stronger. Botgrep does not consider traffic flow categorisation and therefore would end up with high false-positive rates when its core assumption is broken — high-degree nodes should not be infected and have incoming or outgoing botnet traffic flows. In the operational context of a NAT (Network Address Translator), the traffic of hundreds of computers would be aggregated into a single IP address. Such NAT installations are getting rather popular: mobile broadband ISPs use carrier-NATs where thousands of mobile consumers are behind a NAT run by the ISP, and each user is on a separate port. Our inference algorithm, will be able to operate in such deployment contexts very well since it combines flow clustering with structured graph analysis; even if graph structure is obscured by the NAT the inference algorithm can still leverage non-linear subspace analysis over traffic flow data to isolate botnet traffic.

Further, as compared with other graph-based and behaviour-analysis schemes, we have shown (see Fig. 3) that there is more to application traffic than mere clustering: there are intricate geometrical surfaces corresponding to application traffic characteristics. Indeed our algorithm is quite generic and we hope that our results will encourage other researchers to apply our technique to other traffic classification problems.

9 Conclusion

The ability to localise bot-infected hosts at Internet scales represents both a very challenging problem. In this work, we have approached the problem of botnet detection with a security-by-design approach: detection evasion is based on the attacker's detailed knowledge of legitimate traffic traces. Thus detection is based on the fundamental properties of botnets which enables evasion resistant detection. In future work, we will provide formal bounds for evasion resistance.

In this work we have tried to build a link between graph-theoretic botnet detection approaches with network behavioural analysis approaches. Our approach works by leveraging patterns within the communication graph as well as within network traffic between Internet hosts from a set of traffic-monitoring vantage points, and then exploiting the intrinsic non-linear geometry of traffic in order to distinguish traffic flows that are part of the botnet. Behavioural analysis approaches (involving machine learning) are commonly criticised in the security community for assuming a static traffic profile of the botnet in the form of a feature list. As a first step towards being able to operate in an environment where the botnet evolves in response to the detection mechanism, we adopt the notion of dynamic feature selection.

Compared with results from previous work using graph-theoretic or behavioural analysis approaches, our techniques accomplish better results. This is not surprising since they exploit intuitions from both. However, our techniques do not achieve perfect accuracy, but they achieve a low enough false positive rate to be of substantial use, especially when combined with other complementary techniques. Finally, we do not attempt to address the challenging problem of botnet *response*. Future work may leverage our inferred botnet topologies by dropping crucial links to partition the botnet, based on the structure of the botnet graph.

References

1. Botlab: A real-time botnet monitoring platform, botlab.cs.washington.edu.
2. The Cooperative Association for Internet Data Analysis, http://www.caida.org/
3. Collins, M.P., Reiter, M.K.: Hit-list worm detection and bot identification in large networks using protocol graphs. In: Kruegel, C., Lippmann, R., Clark, A. (eds.) RAID 2007. LNCS, vol. 4637, pp. 276–295. Springer, Heidelberg (2007)
4. Franklin, J., Paxson, V., Perrig, A., Savage, S.: An inquiry into the nature and causes of the wealth of internet miscreants. In: ACM Conference on Computer and Communications Security, pp. 375–388. ACM, New York (2007)
5. Gu, G., Perdisci, R., Zhang, J., Lee, W.: BotMiner: Clustering Analysis of Network Traffic for Protocol- and Structure-Independent Botnet Detection. In: Proc. of the USENIX Security Symposium (2008)
6. Gummadi, R., Balakrishnan, H., Maniatis, P., Ratnasamy, S.: Not-a-Bot (NAB): Improving Service Availability in the Face of Botnet Attacks. In: NSDI 2009, Boston, MA (April 2009)
7. Iliofotou, M., Faloutsos, M., Mitzenmacher, M.: Exploiting dynamicity in graph-based traffic analysis: Techniques and applications. In: ACM CoNext (2009)
8. Iliofotou, M., Pappu, P., Faloutsos, M., Mitzenmacher, M., Varghese, G., Kim, H.: Graption: Automated detection of P2P applications using traffic dispersion graphs (TDGs). UC Riverside Technical Report, CS-2008-06080 (2008)
9. C. S. Inc. Cisco IOS Netflow, http://www.cisco.com/en/US/products/ps6601/products_ios_protocol_group_home.html
10. Jelasity, M., Bilicki, V.: Towards automated detection of peer-to-peer botnets: On the limits of local approaches. In: USENIX Workshop on Large-Scale Exploits and Emergent Threats, LEET (2009)
11. Jelasity, M., Billicki, V.: Towards automated detection of peer-to-peer botnets: On the limits of local approaches. In: USENIX Workshop on Large-Scale Exploits and Emergent Threats (LEET) (2009)
12. John, J.P., Moshchuk, A., Gribble, S.D., Krishnamurthy, A.: Studying spamming botnets using botlab. In: NSDI 2009: Proceedings of the 6th USENIX Symposium on Networked Systems Design and Implementation, pp. 291–306. USENIX Association, Berkeley (2009)
13. Kaashoek, M., Karger, D.: Koorde: A simple degree-optimal distributed hash table. In: Kaashoek, M.F., Stoica, I. (eds.) IPTPS 2003. LNCS, vol. 2735, pp. 98–107. Springer, Heidelberg (2003)

14. Maymounkov, P., Mazières, D.: Kademlia: A peer-to-peer information system based on the xor metric. In: Druschel, P., Kaashoek, M.F., Rowstron, A. (eds.) IPTPS 2002. LNCS, vol. 2429, pp. 53–65. Springer, Heidelberg (2002)

15. Nagaraja, S., Mittal, P., Hong, C.-Y., Caesar, M., Borisov, N.: BotGrep: Finding P2P bots with structured graph analysis. In: USENIX Security Symposium, pp. 95–110 (2010)

16. Paxson, V., Christodorescu, M., Javed, M., Rao, J., Sailer, R., Schales, D., Stoecklin, M.P., Thomas, K., Venema, W., Weaver, N.: Practical comprehensive bounds on surreptitious communication over dns. In: Proceedings of the 22Nd USENIX Conference on Security (2013)

17. Perdisci, R., Lee, W., Feamster, N.: Behavioral Clustering of HTTP-Based Malware and Signature Generation Using Malicious Network Traces. In: Proc. of the USENIX Symposium on Networked Systems Design & Implementation (2010)

18. Stinson, E., Mitchell, J.C.: Characterizing bots' remote control behavior. In: Lee, W., Wang, C., Dagon, D. (eds.) Botnet Detection. Advances in Information Security, vol. 36, pp. 45–64. Springer (2008)

19. Stoica, I., Morris, R., Karger, D., Kaashoek, M.F., Balakrishnan, H.: Chord: A scalable peer-to-peer lookup service for Internet applications. In: Proceedings of ACM SIGCOMM (August 2001)

20. Zhao, Q., Xu, J., Liu, Z.: Design of a novel statistics counter architecture with optimal space and time efficiency. In: ACM SIGMETRICS (June 2006)

21. Zhao, Y., Xie, Y., Yu, F., Ke, Q., Yu, Y., Chen, Y., Gillum, E.: Botgraph: Large scale spamming botnet detection. In: NSDI (2009)

A   Appendix

In the following figure, we show a two-dimensional visual of botnet traffic. The long lines are an artifact of DNS fast-flux.

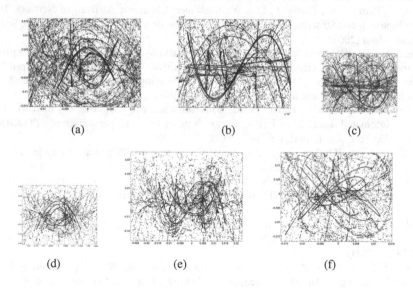

(a)   (b)   (c)

(d)   (e)   (f)

Fig. 4. Two dimensional representation of network traffic with embedded Zeus traffic, before feature selection. This figure shows the dual-graph $\mathcal{D}(\mathcal{G})$ of the traffic dataset.

Feature-Distributed Malware Attack: Risk and Defence

Byungho Min and Vijay Varadharajan

Advanced Cyber Security Research Centre
Department of Computing, Macquarie University, Sydney, Australia
{byungho.min,vijay.varadharajan}@mq.edu.au

Abstract. Modern computing platforms have progressed to more secure environments with various defensive techniques such as application-based permission and application whitelisting. In addition, anti-virus solutions are improving their detection techniques, especially based on behavioural properties. To overcome these hurdles, the adversary has been developing malware techniques including the use of legitimate digital certificates; hence it is important to explore possible offensive techniques in a security-improved environment.

In this paper, first we propose the new technique of *feature-distributed* malware that dynamically distributes its features to multiple software components in order to bypass various security mechanisms such as application whitelisting and anti-virus' behavioural detection. To evaluate our approach, we have implemented a tool that automatically generates such malware instances, and have performed a series of experiments showing the risks of such advanced malware. We also suggest an effective defence mechanism. It prevents loading of malicious components by utilising digital certificates of software components. We have implemented a Windows service that provides our defence mechanism, and evaluated it against the proposed malware. Another useful characteristic of our defence is that it is capable of blocking general abuse of legitimate digital certificates with dynamic software component loading.

Keywords: Security, Feature-Distribution Malware, Software Component.

1 Introduction

Modern computing platforms have progressed to more secure environments with various defensive techniques. For example, all the mainstream platforms such as Windows 8, Mac OS X 10.9, iOS and Android deploy an application-based permission model that determines which application is allowed to access which system services such as network activity, disk access, other hardware access and location service. Furthermore, on Mac OS X and iOS, each permission decision is made by the user at run time right after each permission is requested by the application, making them more secure than Android, where the list of all the

M. Kutyłowski and J. Vaidya (Eds.): ESORICS 2014, Part II, LNCS 8713, pp. 457–474, 2014.
© Springer International Publishing Switzerland 2014

requested permissions of an application is presented at installation time, and allowed at once when a user decides to install the application.[1] As a result of this progress, malware or compromised user applications on the modern platforms may not be able to achieve their goals. However, attackers have always developed new ways to overcome security hurdles. In recent years, there are at least two outstanding trends in malicious software. First, most malware instances, even mobile ones, have become modular [1, 2]. For instance, an initial module is responsible for installation, a networking module is in charge of command and control (C&C) communications, and a rootkit module starts other modules on every system boot so that they can perform respective functionalities. This strategy lowers the possibility of detection as well as minimises exposure of the malware and the attack operation in case of detection. Another trend in malicious software is the use of legitimate certificates [3–6] so malware is allowed to run and access system services, and not blocked or detected by security solutions like anti-virus. Therefore, new malware that bypasses the security restrictions imposed by the application-based permission model can emerge in the foreseeable future, and it is important to measure the risks of such malware attack and develop effective defence measures.

In this paper, first we present *feature-distributed* malware that can bypass not only the application-based security model, but also other security schemes such as application whitelisting and Egress filtering. Although many real world malware samples use various malicious component loading techniques [3–7], we take a different perspective on malicious dynamic component loading. Since no matter what technique is used, the most important objective for malware is to remain undetected and perform its malicious activities. And commodity PCs typically have several applications installed on them from web browser to media player, and many such applications use diverse (open or closed source) software components. We have categorised popular applications, such as Firefox and iTunes, and the libraries loaded by them, and then split malware functionalities to several components. Similar to other malicious component loading attacks [8], various attacks including remote ones are possible with our approach as described in Section 2. In addition, a more capable form of modular malware has been achieved due to the *dynamic feature distribution*. To evaluate the risks of our technique, we have implemented a tool that automatically generates feature-distributed malware using three malicious component types, and showed that wide range of malicious activities is possible, even under the application-based permission model and with the protection of security tools such as anti-virus, application whitelisting and Egress filtering.

Exploring the risks of the feature-distributed malware enabled us to devise *a novel defensive mechanism*. In essence, a host process (i.e. original main executable file of an application that loads other components) checks the signer information of components to be loaded when it verifies the validity of their digital signatures to prevent the feature-distributed malware. This mechanism

---

[1] This has made Android malware that requires several permissions to use social engineering techniques to acquire the permissions.

turned out to be effective in blocking most real world malware attacks that use stolen legitimate certificates. We have implemented this mechanism as a Windows service so that any application can integrate our APIs during component loading.

The remainder of this paper is structured as follows. Section 2 describes the background on malware features and the design of feature-distributed malware with its attack vectors. Implementation details of the malware are discussed in Section 3. Section 4 presents the evaluation of our offensive technique, including characteristics and risks of the malware attack. In Section 5, we present our general defensive technique to prevent the feature-distributed malware attack, and evaluate its effectiveness and performance impact. We conclude the paper with a discussion of future work in Section 6.

2 Feature-Distributed Malware

This section describes major features of modern malware, design of our feature-distributed malware, remote attack examples applied from other malicious component loading studies [8], and the feature distribution strategy.

2.1 Malware Features and Application-Based Permission

Extraction of modern malware characteristics should be conducted ahead of distributing features. For this purpose, we have surveyed technical reports on recent malware instances including Stuxnet, Duqu, Flame, Gauss, Shamoon, Red October and Careto [3–7, 9] and analysed several samples of them. Common features of them is summarised below, and full details of the analysis are available in our technical report [2]:

1. Local activity
   (a) Data collection: file list, files, OS account credentials, Bluetooth sniffing, microphone recording, hardware and software information, web credentials and browser cookies (via malicious browser plugin), instant messaging (IM, e.g. Skype) recording, keylogging, emails, screenshots, network shares, connected device list, information from connected devices (e.g. SMS and contacts), saved passwords from web browsers and FTP clients cyber assets (e.g. intellectual property)
   (b) Propagation: USB infection
   (c) Backdoor: Windows service installation or modification, account creation
   (d) Supporting: payload generation (e.g. autorun.inf for USB infection), initialisation (e.g. module listing and loading), filename generation (only these interesting files are collected), malware activity logging, security tool monitoring, uninstallation
2. Remote activity
   (a) Data collection: External IP address, network scanning

    (b) Propagation: account login attempt (using created or stolen credentials), serving man-in-the-middle attack, serving remote exploits such as MS08-067

    (c) Networking: several commands including update, run, and uninstall, data exfiltration, heart beating

As modern platforms such as iOS, Android and Mac OS X 10.9 are incorporating application-based permission model, some of the above activities cannot be performed by standalone malware or infected software. For example, microphone recording and Bluetooth sniffing require access to respective hardware access, and contact information collection requires access to Contacts application, which has to be explicitly approved by the user. Considering that most of recent malware consists of multiple modules (at application, service, or driver level) and their data collection and networking modules are usually running at user-level[2], this is a new hurdle for attackers to overcome.

2.2 Feature-Distributed Malware: Concept

Although the application-based permission model is strong enough to prevent current malware threats, it is still possible to bypass it if malware is properly implemented because there are still user-approved applications that have access to hardware and software resources. In particular, malware can perform its functionalities by dynamically distributing them to user-approved or system-approved applications. For example, a networking module that has migrated into an email application may not be able to dump OS password hashes, while a local data collection module that has migrated into an anti-virus service running under SYSTEM account can. On the other hand, the data collection module may not be allowed to communicate with its C&C server due to Egress filtering, whereas the networking module can perform the data exfiltration. This is the concept of our *"feature-distributed"* malware; malware modules cooperate in order to overcome application-based permission model and other security mechanisms such as application whitelisting and Egress filtering. In addition, the following advantages are achieved with the feature-distributed malware:

1. *More Adaptive*: when a victim installs a new application, the feature-distributed malware can further distribute its feature set to the new application without any attacker intervention. In addition, it performs self-recovery as long as there is at least one active malicious component as explained in Section 3, even when an application is updated (and so are its components).
2. *More Stealthy*: trusted and approved application hosts malicious modules. No new process for Windows services or applications are installed and executed; on the contrary, modern malware usually installs its modules as Windows services or drivers. Furthermore, malware that is detected by anti-virus becomes undetectable by distributing malicious features to multiple

---

[2] Kernel-level rootkit drivers are normally backdoors for persistent compromise.

applications (i.e. processes) as shown in Section 4. This is because anti-virus solutions determine maliciousness of a file or a process based on its static and dynamic characteristics; analysing all the interactions of multiple processes and components is yet to come since it can result in a serious performance issue and raise false positive rate.

3. *More Capable*: bypassing security mechanisms such as application whitelisting and Egress filtering is achieved.

2.3 Remote Attacks – Examples

Although any malware attack from drive-by download to USB infection is possible with the feature-distributed malware, we describe the attack vectors that are closely related to the concept of our proposed malware attack. These vectors assume that the malware has been delivered to a victim by an initial attack such as client-side attack or spear phishing, which is also assumed by most related work [10–18]. In addition, many real world malware attack operations including Careto, Red October, Gauss and Flame started as spear phishing.

Archive with component attack. The adversary can make an archive file that contains a normal document file and a malicious component file with an absolute path and overwrite option. Once the victim opens the archive, not only the files the victim expects to see, but also the malware components are extracted and placed in the designated path. For example, malicious `sqlite3.dll` can be extracted to the Apple iTunes' installation path. Next time iTunes starts up, the malware module is loaded by iTunes and performs its activities from feature distribution to malicious functionalities.

Carpet Bomb-based attack. The Carpet Bomb attack [19] can lead to remote code execution in connection with the feature-distributed malware. This attack happens, for instance, when Safari web browser accesses a malicious web page, and arbitrary files that can be the feature-distributed malware file are downloaded to the victim system without user consent. In particular, when the location of downloaded file corresponds to the malware's target software component, the malware will be loaded by its target application after the Carpet Bomb attack.

2.4 Feature Distribution Strategy

Since each application has different permission and privilege depending on its required functionalities, malware features discussed in Section 2.1 should be properly distributed. We categorise application types and discuss the pros and cons of each type as a malware module. An application can be included in more than one category. For example, Google Drive is a startup as well as a networking application. We have tested several of the below application types with the proposed malware concept, and have evaluated them in Section 4.

Startup (persistent). Most startup applications are automatically executed on every boot and they keep running. Examples include cloud storage like Google Drive and Dropbox, IM such as Skype, and anti-virus software. This type of applications runs all the time while the system is up (unless the user explicitly terminates it). However, they usually have user privilege (neither administrative nor SYSTEM), and may not be allowed for networking.

- *Appropriate Module*: initialisation (self-recovery and feature re-distribution that are explained in Section 3)

Startup (update checker). Some startup applications are executed on every system boot, but terminated after they finish required tasks. Examples are update checker of various applications such as Java and Flash plugins. They can connect to the Internet, and may have administrative privilege so that they can update the relevant software. But they run for a limited time, typically several seconds.

- *Appropriate Module*: heart beating module that reports a successful compromise and access maintenance.

Networking. Web browsers, email, IM, (S)FTP and other network clients, online games, and cloud storage applications are allowed for network activity. But they normally have user privilege, and run for a limited time (longer than update checker).

- *Appropriate Module (web browsers)*: "worm" (propagation) module since C&C communication pattern that is used for worm detection is randomised by the user; only when the user surfs the Internet, worm module performs its communication, and each individual person has different Internet use pattern.

- *Appropriate Module (the others)*: data exfiltration because (1) IM and email clients tend to run all the time, and (2) network clients can transfer a large amount of data compared to other networking software.

Security Solutions. Security tools such as anti-virus usually have the highest privilege (i.e. SYSTEM on Windows), and cannot be killed by the user and user level applications. However, it is much harder to load a malicious module in the context of these applications as they protect themselves from malware so that even the user cannot modify their components or configurations. In addition, some executables like local file scanner may not be allowed for networking.

- *Appropriate Module*: local data collection, logging malware activities, and rootkit module that maintains access, updates modules, and uninstalls all the modules when required.

Productivity. Productivity applications are varied from office suites to personal information manager such as password manger 1Password. Even though these applications are executed under user privilege, and do not run all the time, they are guaranteed to have access to relevant information including office documents to password database.

- *Appropriate Module*: local data collection module specialised for each application.

Media Management and Playback. Similar to productivity applications, this type of applications can access to their contents, which include personal photos, videos and voice memos.

- *Appropriate Module*: local data collection module specialised for each application.

Table 1. Open Source Libraries Tested with Feature-Distributed Malware

Library Name	Example of Applications
SQLite	AVG, iTunes, Adobe Reader, Google Drive
OpenSSL	Open Office, Mobogenie, Mumble
Network Security Services (NSS)	Chrome, AIM, Pidgin, Firefox, Thunderbird

Device management. iTunes and Mobogenie are two device management applications respectively for iOS and Android device. These applications have access to device information and contents such as contacts and photos.

- *Appropriate module*: data collection module specialised for each application.

3   Implementation

To realise our proposed feature-distributed malware, we have developed an automatic malware generator on Windows, which is based on our implementations of (1) three malicious component types and (2) malware features such as malware initialisation, feature distribution, and common malicious activities. In this section, we discuss implementation details and considerations of the generator and other techniques.

3.1   Three Malicious Component Types

As discussed in Section 2, a feature-distributed malware file (i.e. a software component or an archive) is placed at a certain path after it is delivered to a victim (e.g. via email attachment or network share) and opened. Then the file is loaded by target applications such as Firefox, which means that the newly placed malicious component has to provide all the functionalities of the original software component. On Windows, exported functions of DLL are the functionalities the malware has to provide. We have implemented three types of file-based malicious component that satisfies this requirement.

Source code modified component. One of the best ways of providing an entire functionality of a software component is to build them from source code. Many popular applications use open source libraries as given in Table 1, and this makes it feasible to implement malicious components using open source libraries. Open source libraries are also an attractive target for feature-distributed malware because (1) there is no need for trampolines (described below), thus no additional file is produced, (2) several popular open source libraries are used by many common applications in various application types, and (3) building a multi-platform malicious component is possible for many open source libraries. For example, Careto [3] is a multi-platform malware that uses an open source software for Mac OS X backdoor module. However, building an entire library can increase the size of malware, and it takes longer than making a dummy trampoline-style component. We have tested the proposed malware attack with three widely used libraries: SQLite, Network Security Services (NSS), and OpenSSL. They are being adopted by a huge number of applications, and a few representative examples are shown in Table 1. We edited the source code of these libraries so that they can be passed to the malware generator as an input and be merged with our malware feature implementation (Figure 1).

Trampoline-style Component. Software vendors or individual developers may get an open source library, and then edit some of its exported functions. Also, there are still various popular closed source libraries such as Microsoft C Runtime (CRT) library and Microsoft Foundation Class (MFC). In these cases, we have taken two approaches, and trampoline-style dummy library is one of them. Trampoline is a dummy function that finds its original export using its ordinal value, and jumps to it when it is invoked. Such trampolines must be implemented for all the exports of a target library so that the hosting application starts and functions correctly. We have implemented trampolines mainly in assembly code, and tested this approach with CRT and MFC libraries.

Even though the size of trampoline-style component is smaller than that of open source-based one, it cannot replace the original library, since it does not provide any actual functionality. In the current implementation, the feature-distributed malware searches for CRT libraries, and if required, renames (not replaces) them and copies the trampoline-style dummy library in the place of the original one. As a result, there comes an additional file introduced to the victim system when this type of component is used. Also, it cannot be used as an initial component because renaming can happen only when at least one malicious component is active.

Binary modified component. Another way of developing a malware component based on source-modified or closed source libraries is to manipulate them at the binary level. We have implemented an on the fly binary modification routine in our malware feature set that performs the following:

1. Add a new Portable Executable (PE) section.
2. Write binary shellcode that is built from our assembly and C code.
3. Modify Entry Point (EP) so that our shellcode is executed when the library is loaded.

When the modified component is loaded by an application, and the shellcode is executed, it loads its modifier library then jumps back to the original entry point (OEP) so that it can function as intended. For instance, if SQLite of iTunes modifies the CRT of Firefox, this CRT's shellcode loads the SQLite library of iTunes for malware functionalities. Because the newly loaded SQLite is loaded by a component of Firefox, it has the context of Firefox, not of iTunes. This enables the implementation of our shellcode to be concise and reliable, with the size of 408 bytes. We verified this approach with the two libraries tested for trampoline-style. Its limitation as a malicious component is similar to trampoline-style; it cannot be used as an initial module since it is an implemented feature and used in the malware, which should be used by an active malicious component. However, no additional file is introduced in the victim system since this approach modifies binaries on the fly.

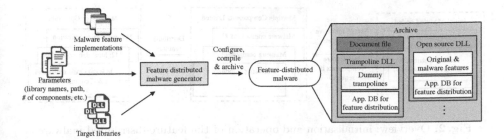

Fig. 1. Feature-distributed malware generator for archive with component attack

Anti-virus (AVG's case). As discussed in Section 2, major anti-virus solutions protect themselves, and AVG is not an exception. AVG anti-virus provides "AVG Self protection" that is composed of two filter drivers. When a user or a process (even with the highest privilege) tries to delete or modify those files, then the two drivers block such I/O requests. Similarly, new files cannot be added to the AVG folder. Therefore, it is much harder to replace or modify AVG's files [20]. After analysing AVG anti-virus, however, we found out that AVG fails to protect the self-protection filter drivers, even though it must block any unauthorised attempt to unload or detach them. As a result, AVG's two filter drivers can be detached by the user or malware using Filter Manager Control. After the detachment, arbitrary files belonging to AVG can be replaced or modified, which can be used in the feature-distributed malware.

3.2 Automatic Malware Generation

The final form of the feature-distributed malware is one single archive or software component that will be placed at a target path and then loaded by user applications. We have implemented a malware generator that automates the process of configuring, packaging and making the final component or archive file as depicted in Figure 1. The generator takes three inputs. First, user specifies several parameters such as libraries to be included, application database, final form to be generated (either an archive or a DLL file), absolute paths where the generated component is to be placed, and other malware parameters given in Table 3. Second, implemented malware features such as local password hash dump, C&C communication and the live binary modification routine are passed. These are embedded to the specified open source libraries at source code level. Lastly, source code of open source target libraries such as SQLite and OpenSSL are passed so that the generator can merge the malware features with the libraries. When merging them, the generator adds the malware features as a separate thread created in `DllMain()` so that it can run as long as the library is loaded in memory. When a trampoline-style library such as CRT is specified in the user input, relevant dummy trampoline DLL is generated and added to the final archive file with a path to Windows Temporary folder. The final archive is constructed with proper absolute paths and overwrite option using RAR or

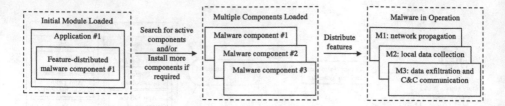

Fig. 2. Overview: initialisation and operation of the feature-distributed malware

TAR format according to the user parameter. This is possible because files of applications are usually not protected by the system, unlike files of security tools or critical system files that are protected by operating system feature such as Windows Resource Protection (WRP).

Among the input parameters, application database contains information about target applications including their categories, allowed permissions and privileges. This information is embedded in the malware so that it can initialise and dynamically distribute its features based on this information. Real world attackers behind advanced threat persistent operations usually profile their target systems, and then carefully install persistent malware for cyber espionage. Therefore, the adversary can customise application database based on initial profiling.

3.3   Malware Operation: Initialisation and Feature Distribution

Once a feature-distributed malware (i.e. a software component) is loaded by an attack vector described in Section 2, the initialisation process is started as shown in Figure 2. The component searches for other active components; remote procedure call (RPC) is used for inter-component communications. Depending on the number of active components and the configuration specified by the attacker, the first component searches for additional target libraries and replaces them with itself. For instance, a malicious `sqlite3.dll` loaded by iTunes searches for other instances of SQLite library. Preferences on libraries are specified in the malware parameter. When other instances of SQLite used by Open Office and AVG are found, the malware replaces the newly found components with itself so that they become a part of the feature-distributed malware. In the case of binary modification, target library is modified on the fly. After sufficient numbers of components become active, they dynamically distribute malware features based on their hosting process and the application database. In this example, Thunderbird component takes the networking role, Open Office module collects documents and other data, and AVG records keystrokes and logs malware activities. From this point on, the malware components perform their respective features.

When replacing a file that is currently open, the malware first renames the target, and then copies itself to the path because renaming is allowed for locked files on Windows. The renamed original file is deleted when the malicious DLL is

Table 2. Applications installed on the evaluation system

Application Name	Application Type	Component Name
Thunderbird	Networking (email client)	`mozsqlite3.dll`
Firefox	Networking (web browser)	`msvcr100.dll` (CRT)
Adobe Reader	Productivity	`sqlite3.dll`
Open Office	Productivity	`ssleay32.dll` (OpenSSL)
iTunes	Media player, iOS device manager	`sqlite3.dll`
Mobogenie	Startup, Android device manager	`ssleay32.dll` (OpenSSL)
AVG Free Anti-virus	Startup, Security	`avgntsqlitex.dll` (SQLite)

loaded. In the case of anti-virus software, nullification of self-protection feature is preceded the file replacement as explained in this section. In addition, if there are multiple candidates found after the initial search, the malware selects target components according to the following rule:

1. Search for open source libraries (no additional file resulted).
2. Search for trampoline-style target components if the number of malware components is less than user-specified value, rename the original files and copies the dummy trampoline file to the target paths located at Windows Temporary folder (additional file resulted).
3. Search for binary modification targets and modify them if the number of components is still less than three (live DLL modification performed, no additional file resulted).

Collected information is stored in the temporary folder and sent back to the attacker by the networking module such as Thunderbird's SQLite. Lastly, supporting features (Section 2.1) such as basic C&C and uninstallation function have also been implemented.

4   Evaluation

In this section, we first describe how the feature-distributed malware performs its activities, thus fulfilling usual malware requirements. Then we show how the malware can bypass security mechanisms such as application whitelisting, Egress filtering and anti-virus' behavioural detection. In the evaluations, Windows 7 Ultimate edition was used as the target system, and the applications shown in Table 2 were installed on the system.[3] These selected applications use at least one open source libraries including SQLite, NSS and OpenSSL. And the malware instances evaluated in this section were generated by our tool with the parameter values shown in Table 3.

---

[3] Some applications use more than one target libraries, even though only actual target library is specified. For example, Thunderbird loads NSS in addition to SQLite as shown in Figure 3.

Table 3. Common parameters for feature-distributed malware generation

Parameter	Value
	SQLite (Section 4.1)
Libraries used	SQLite, OpenSSL (Section 4.1)
	SQLite, OpenSSL, CRT (Section 4.4)
Library priority	SQLite > OpenSSL > NSS
Final format	RAR archive
Bait file	Annual report.docx
Path #1 (SQLite)	iTunes folder
Path #2 (OpenSSL)	Open Office folder
Path #3 (CRT)	Windows Temporary folder
Min. # of components	3 (varied from 1 to 4 in Section 4.4)
Dummy trampoline	Yes
Live binary modification	No
Attack AVG (when possible)	No (Yes/No in Section 4.4)
Application database	Application category, privilege, etc.

4.1 Malware Operation

This section describes two attacks that show fundamental operations of the proposed feature-distributed malware. Both attacks are archived with component attacks described in Section 2.3.

Attack with SQLite library. A RAR self-extracting (SFX) file delivered to a victim contains a normal document and a malicious SQLite library. When the victim opens the file, SQLite is extracted to iTunes folder and overwrites the existing one as specified in the RAR. Next time iTunes is launched, the replaced SQLite is loaded and the initialisation process begins as follows:

1. Collect basic system information (OS version, installed applications, etc.), and send when possible. iTunes uses network from time to time, so the iTunes component informs the attacker about this first compromise. However, other network activities such as file transfer are performed by networking component described below.
2. Start RPC and search for other active components.
3. After a predefined time (1 minute in the current implementation), check the number of active components. As the number is less than configured one (3), the SQLite component starts searching for other instances of SQLite.
4. When SQLite files of Thunderbird and AVG are found, and identified as not-infected, iTunes component replaces those instances with itself. In the case of AVG, disarming AVG is preceded as explained in Section 3.1. If the SQLite files found and are identified as infected, then the iTunes component waits until they become active, i.e. their hosting applications are launched.

After the three components become active, they split malware features according to their hosting applications (i.e. iTunes, Thunderbird, and AVG), and start performing their respective activities as follows:

1. iTunes: local data collection to Windows Temporary folder (files on the system including voice memos imported from iOS devices)
2. Thunderbird: network activity for C&C communication (e.g. archive and send collected data to the attacker)
3. AVG: local data collection to Windows Temporary folder (keystrokes & screenshots)

Attack with Multiple Libraries. This attack evaluates the feature-distributed malware in a more complex form. SQLite and OpenSSL are included in a RAR SFX archive with the normal document file, and extracted to relevant paths as specified in the parameter.[4] Initialisation process is similar to the above case, except that now there are two libraries and so preference comparison is performed when the two components become active. Because SQLite has a higher priority, iTunes component searches for an additional instance, and replaces Thunderbird's SQLite. If it cannot find any SQLite instance, OpenSSL of Open Office looks throughout the system for other instances of OpenSSL. Malware activities are logged and transferred back to the adversary so that it can adjust malware parameters. For instance, if the initial component(s) could not find enough number of target components, then the attacker can reduce this parameter value based on the collected system information.

4.2 Bypassing Application Whitelisting

Application whitelisting is more and more deployed, especially on specific-purpose systems such as SCADA and POS that do not need to be general purpose machines. In particular, ENISA recommends the use of whitelisting solutions, which restrict the execution of non-approved software and code [21].

We used AppLocker for application whitelisting. It is a security tool built in Windows 7 that allows only the configured applications to run on the system. Because (1) the feature-distributed malware consists of software components (not applications), and (2) all of its hosting applications (iTunes, Thunderbird, and Open Office in this example) are allowed in the configuration of AppLocker, we could verify each component performed respective roles without being blocked. This may look trivial since the malware compromised whitelisted applications from the start, but it apparently shows its importance, considering most modern malware instances including most advanced ones such as Stuxnet, Gauss and Careto have their own processes, which are blocked by application whitelisting mechanisms.

From this evaluation, we can infer how the feature-distributed malware can bypass application-based permission model as well. Application whitelisting can be thought as a more strict form of application-based permission model, which

---

[4] We have experimented another way of building the initial component such as SQLite so it contains other libraries such as OpenSSL and NSS in its PE sections. This reduces the number of files included in the archive file, but it increases the size of the initial component.

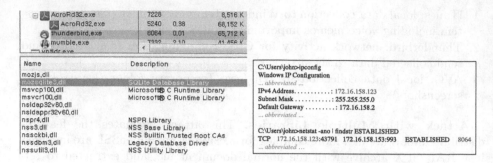

Fig. 3. Process ID (8064) of Thunderbird loading the malicious SQLite (left) and successful network connection by SQLite component under the Egress filtering environment (right)

allows only whitelisted applications to run on the system. Therefore, bypassing application-based permission policy can be done in a similar way.

4.3   Bypassing Egress Filtering

Egress filtering is increasingly being used and/or needed to block malware communications. It is required for compliance with Payment Card Industry Data Security Standard (PCI-DSS), Section 1.2.1 and 1.3.5 of version 2.0 [22]. Also, Egress filtering is recommended by US-CERT as a malware mitigation mechanism [23]. However, even under this network activity restriction, this evaluation shows that the feature-distributed malware bypasses Egress filtering rules, and connects back to the attacker.

Thunderbird is an email client, and hence it must be allowed in outgoing traffic rules. In this example, it tries a connection to the attacker since it is responsible for networking. We verified that the malicious SQLite component of Thunderbird bypassed Egress filtering firewall rules forced by Comodo Firewall as shown in Figure 3. Thunderbird (`thunderbird.exe`, process ID: 8064) is loading the malware component (`mozsqlite3.dll`) in Figure 3 (lefthand-side). And its process (8064) is making a network connection from the victim system (172.16.158.123) to the attacker (172.16.158.153) via the IMAP email protocol port (993) (righthand-side of Figure 3).

4.4   Bypassing Anti-virus

In the anti-virus bypassing evaluations discussed below, what we have tested is bypassing *behavioural* detection, not signature-based detection, because (1) our evaluation goal is to show the advantage of feature distribution, and (2) making a binary that passes signature-based detection is relatively easier to achieve using various code obfuscation tools.

Feature distribution and detectability. In this first evaluation, we first built a single component malware that passes AVG's signature-based detec-

Table 4. Anti-virus detection test

Detection	Application compromised (# of comp.)	Library used
Yes	iTunes (1)	SQLite
No	iTunes, AVG (2)	SQLite
No	iTunes, Firefox (2)	SQLite, CRT
No	iTunes, AVG, Adobe Reader (3)	SQLite
No	iTunes, AVG, Firefox (3)	SQLite, CRT
No	iTunes, AVG, Thunderbird (3)	SQLite
No	iTunes, Thunderbird, Open Office (3)	SQLite, OpenSSL
No	iTunes, Adobe Reader, Firefox (3)	SQLite, CRT
No	iTunes, Firefox, Mobogenie (3)	SQLite, OpenSSL, CRT
No	iTunes, AVG, Adobe Reader, Thunderbird (4)	SQLite
No	iTunes, AVG, Adobe Reader, Firefox (4)	SQLite, CRT
No	iTunes, Adobe Reader, Firefox, Thunderbird (4)	SQLite, CRT
No	iTunes, Adobe Reader, Open Office, Mobogenie (4)	SQLite, OpenSSL
No	iTunes, Firefox, Open Office, Thunderbird (4)	SQLite, OpenSSL, CRT

Table 5. Anti-virus (2014 versions) bypassed by the feature-distributed malware

Anti-virus name
AVAST Free, Pro, Internet Security
Avira Free, Commercial, Internet Security
Bitdefender Internet Security, Antivirus Plus
Kaspersky Anti-Virus, Internet Security
McAfee Antivirus Plus, Internet Security, Total Protection
NOD32 (ESET) Antivirus, Smart Security
Norton (Symantec) 360, Internet Security, AntiVirus

tion, but is detected by AVG's behavioural engine as a "Threat: General behavioural detection" when it starts its operation. Then we tested multiple malware instances that are functionally identical but have multiple components. As summarised in Table 4, none of the feature-distributed malware instances was detected during their operation once features are distributed. This is because anti-virus solutions determine behavioural maliciousness of a process based on the behaviours of this particular process, and each process hosting the feature-distributed malware performs only a portion of malware features.

Other anti-virus solutions. We have tested the feature-distributed malware's operation against several anti-virus solutions. The malware instance used for this experiment has four components, namely iTunes, Firefox, Open Office and Thunderbird (the last one in Table 4). Eighteen (18) solutions of seven antivirus vendors have been tested (AVG is excluded as it has been already discussed above), and Table 5 shows our feature-distributed malware performed its malicious activities without being detected by behavioural and signature-based engines of the tested anti-virus solutions.

4.5 Limitations

C&C communication of the current implementation is based on sbd that is a Netcat-clone, designed to be portable and offer strong encryption. Therefore, by-passing Egress filtering can be impossible if deep packet inspection is deployed on the host or the target network infrastructure. However, it can be easily overcome by serious attackers, since it is well-known that encapsulating any communication protocol inside another one such as actual HTTP or IMAP.

The implementation can be detected by file integrity monitoring solution. However, the probability is lower than most modern malware instances like Careto and Stuxnet. This security solution's major purpose is monitoring system's critical files and configurations or confidential folders [24]. In other words, application binaries are not major objects of monitoring. Moreover, some applications are frequently updated (e.g. three times in six weeks in the case of Firefox), thus not adequate for real-time integrity monitoring. As a result, these folders or files are often excluded from such integrity monitoring [25]. On the contrary, many of real world malware instances change critical system configurations for persistent compromise (e.g. installing a new service or driver with additional files or modifying existing service's configuration).

5 Defence against Feature Distributed Malware

This section proposes a new mechanism to prevent the feature-distributed malware attacks. We have implemented it as a Windows service with public APIs so that any application can use it. Thunderbird was used for the evaluation of its effectiveness and performance.

5.1 Proposed Defence Mechanism

Our suggestion is that an application should check the validity of the digital signature and *signer* information of a library before loading and using it, which is very easy to adopt from vendors' perspective. Typically, such verification can be performed prior to calling LoadLibrary() API that loads a library in the context of an application. Then, even though the malicious component has the full functionality of the original library, it cannot be loaded because it fails to pass the origin verification. Similarly, verifying both the digital signature and the signer can help most modern malware attacks that use stolen legitimate certificates. Nowadays, they are bypassing many security tools' detection and restriction because they have a *valid* digital signature. However, if software vendors develop their application according to our suggestion, malware instances signed with a stolen key cannot be loaded since the signer is different from the vendor's. In order to demonstrate our concept, we have implemented a Windows service rather than implementing it into individual applications. On the application side, it calls our service API before any invoke of LoadLibrary(). Then, the service extracts signer information from the digital signatures of the application binary and the library file to be loaded, and compares it. Only when the digital signature of the library is valid and *it is signed by the same entity as the application*, the service returns true. Although we have not added error handling code to each application, several recovery processes from simply excluding the modified library (if the application can still work with limited functionalities) to updating the modified component with a clean one are possible.

5.2   Evaluation of the Proposed Defence

Among the applications targeted in the attack evaluation (Section 4), we have selected Thunderbird for the evaluation of our defence mechanism. Code that uses the service API was added to both applications. Then the same attack scenario was launched on the victim system. The SQLite library file was successfully replaced by the archive file, but it was never loaded by Thunderbird since the replaced SQLite library is not signed by Mozilla Corporation who signed the Thunderbird executable file.

We have also conducted performance evaluations using Thunderbird. Even though Thunderbird loads more than 20 libraries, the application startup time delay was under $20ms$ on a Windows 7 machine with Intel Core i7 2.4 GHz CPU and 1GB of RAM. This result shows that our defence mechanism is practical and can be effectively applied to real world applications such as Thunderbird.

6   Concluding Remarks

In this paper, we have proposed a new advanced malware that distributes its features to multiple software components in order to bypass various security policies such as application whitelisting and security tools like anti-virus. A tool that automatically generates such malware has been developed, and malware instances generated by this tool have been evaluated, showing the risks of the proposed malware. We have also suggested an effective defence mechanism that utilises digital signatures of component files to prevent loading of malicious components. To evaluate the proposed solution, a Windows service has been implemented and tested.

Although we have focused on the development and evaluation of feature-distributed malware on Windows, the underlying principle is general and can also be applied to other client platforms including Mac OS X and Android because component-based software engineering is widely used on these platforms. We are especially interested in exploring the application of our feature-distributed malware on mobile platforms. The number of mobile malware has been surging [1], and application-based permission model is already prevalent on modern mobile platforms such as Android, where it is important to prepare appropriate defences against the emerging threat.

References

1. Zhou, Y., Jiang, X.: Dissecting android malware: Characterization and evolution. In: IEEE S&P, San Francisco, CA, USA (2012)
2. Min, B., Varadharajan, V.: Deep analysis on recent malware incidents. Technical report (2012)

3. Kaspersky Lab: Unveiling "Careto" - The Masked APT. Technical report (February 2014)
4. Kaspersky Lab: Gauss: Abnormal Distribution. Technical report (August 2012)
5. Anity Labs: Analysis Report on Flame Worm Samples. Technical report (July 2012)
6. Falliere, N., Murchu, L.O., Chien, E.: W32.Stuxnet dossier. Technical report (2011)
7. Chien, E., Murchu, L.O., Falliere, N.: W32.Duqu The precursor to the next Stuxnet. Technical report (November 2011)
8. Kwon, T., Su, Z.: Automatic detection of unsafe component loadings. In: ISSTA, Trento, Italy (2010)
9. Tarakanov, D.: Shamoon the Wiper in details (August 2012), `http://www.securelist.com/en/blog/208193795/Shamoon_the_Wiper_in_details`
10. Murad, K., Shirazi, S.N.-u.-H., Zikria, Y.B., Ikram, N.: Evading Virus Detection Using Code Obfuscation. In: Kim, T.-h., Lee, Y.-h., Kang, B.-H., Ślęzak, D. (eds.) FGIT 2010. LNCS, vol. 6485, pp. 394–401. Springer, Heidelberg (2010)
11. O'Kane, P., Sezer, S., McLaughlin, K.: Obfuscation: The Hidden Malware. IEEE Security & Privacy 9(5), 41–47 (2011)
12. Rad, B.B., Masrom, M., Ibrahim, S.: Camouflage in Malware: from Encryption to Metamorphism. International Journal of Computer Science and Network Security 12(8), 74–83 (2012)
13. Oberheide, J., Bailey, M., Jahanian, F.: PolyPack: an automated online packing service for optimal antivirus evasion. In: Proceedings of the 3rd USENIX Workshop on offensive technologies, Montreal, Canada (2009)
14. Alvarez, S., Zoller, T.: The Death of AV Defense in Depth? - revisiting Anti-Virus Software. In: CanSecWest, Vancouver, B.C., Canada (2008)
15. Alvarez, S.: Antivirus (In) Security. In: CCC (Chaos Communication Camp), Finowfurt, Germany (2007)
16. Jana, S., Shmatikov, V.: Abusing File Processing in Malware Detectors for Fun and Profit. In: IEEE Symposium on Security and Privacy (S&P) 2012, San Francisco, CA, USA, pp. 80–94 (2012)
17. Porst, S.: How to really obfuscate your PDF malware. In: ReCon, Montreal, Canada (July 2010)
18. Bilge, L., Dumitras, T.: Before we knew it: an empirical study of zero-day attacks in the real world. In: CCS 2012, Raleigh, NC, USA (October 2012)
19. Apple: About the security content of Safari 3.1.2 for Windows (April 2012), `http://support.apple.com/kb/HT2092`
20. Min, B., Varadharajan, V., Tupakula, U.K., Hitchens, M.: Antivirus security: naked during updates. Software: Practice and Experience (April 2013) (accepted)
21. ENISA: Appropriate security measures for smart grids. Technical report (December 2012)
22. PCI Security Standards Council: Payment Card Industry (PCI) Data Security Standard. Technical report (October 2010)
23. US-CERT: Malware Threats and Mitigation Strategies. Technical report (May 2005)
24. Tripwire: Assure system integrity, best of breed file integrity monitoring (2014), `http://www.tripwire.com/it-security-software/scm/file-integrity-monitoring`
25. Arnold, M.: Tripwire Policy (May 2010), `http://www.razorsedge.org/~mike/docs/tripwire.html`

RootkitDet: Practical End-to-End Defense against Kernel Rootkits in a Cloud Environment

Lingchen Zhang[1,2,4], Sachin Shetty[2], Peng Liu[3], and Jiwu Jing[1]

[1] State Key Laboratory of Information Security,
Institute of Information Engineering, Chinese Academy of Sciences
[2] College of Engineering, Tennessee State University
[3] College of IST, Penn State University
[4] University of Chinese Academy of Sciences

Abstract. In cloud environments, kernel-level rootkits still pose serious security threats to guest OSes. Existing defenses against kernel-level rootkit have limitations when applied to cloud environments. In this paper, we propose RootkitDet, an end-to-end defense system capable of detecting and diagnosing rootkits in guest OSes with the intent to recover the system modifications caused by the rootkits in cloud environments. RootkitDet detects rootkits by identifying suspicious code region in the kernel space of guest OSes through the underneath hypervisor, performs diagnosis on the code of the detected rootkit to categorize it and identify modifications, and reverses the modifications if possible to eliminate the effect of rootkits. Our evaluation results show that the RootkitDet is effective on detection of kernel-level rootkits and recovery modifications with less than 1% performance overhead to the guest OSes and the computation and network overhead is linear with the quantity of the VM instances being monitored.

Keywords: Hypervisor, VM, Kernel-level rootkit, Defense, Cloud.

1 Introduction

A kernel rootkit is a form of malware that may subvert the kernel to achieve various goals, especially hiding certain malicious processes from security monitoring, anti-virus software, intrusion detection, and VMI (virtual machine introspection). A typical way for a kernel rootkit to achieve its goals is to modify certain kernel data structures. During the past 10 years, kernel-level rootkits have been emerging as a major security threat. For example, MacAfee Avert Labs [1] reported that during the three-year period from 2004-2006, the number of rootkits had increased 600 percent. Rootkits have been leveraged by criminals to conduct bank fraud [2].

In this paper, we focus on defending against kernel rootkits in a cloud environment. In such cloud environments as Infrastructure as a Service (IaaS), Platform as a Service (PaaS), and Software as a Service (SaaS), kernel rootkits should be as useful to criminals/attackers as in non-cloud environments. Taking IaaS as an example, kernel rootkits may enable the criminal to keep a backdoor in a VM (virtual machine) for the attacker to gain whole control of the guest

M. Kutyłowski and J. Vaidya (Eds.): ESORICS 2014, Part II, LNCS 8713, pp. 475–493, 2014.

operating system. They may also hide some other malware which may inflict serious damage or launch stealthy attacks. Due to the hiding, this malware can become difficult to detect or eliminate by the administrator.

In a cloud environment, cloud providers are responsible for countering kernel rootkits in tenant VMs as they can fully leverage the security features of the underneath hypervisors. We focus on cloud environments since besides standard requirements such as effectiveness and efficiency, cloud environments have several unique requirements regarding how kernel rootkits should be countered. (R1) End-to-end defense is highly desired. Besides detecting a rootkit, cloud administrators also need to quickly reverse the malicious modifications made by the rootkit to its target VM. If the admin has to manually diagnose and reverse the malicious modifications, the availability and business continuity loss could be too much to be accepted by the tenant. (R2) Scalable defense. The total defense cost should be linear (if not sublinear) in the number of VMs being simultaneously protected. The defense should also facilitate dynamic addition and deletion of VMs. (R3) Adoptable defense. The defense should be compatible with existing commercial (and open source) cloud platforms.

Although many research works have been done to tackle kernel rootkits, existing defenses are limited in meeting the requirements cloud environments have. To see how existing defenses are limited, let us break down the existing kernel rootkit defenses into 4 classes which we will review shortly in Section 6: (1A) Detecting modified control or non-control data or violations of invariants [3] [4] [5] [6]. (1B) Preventing installation of kernel rootkits by performing analysis on the code being loaded into the kernel space [7] [8] [9]. (1C) Defending kernel rootkits by cooperating with anti-malware software [10] [11]. (1D) Protecting the kernel by restoring infected kernels to healthy state [12]. We may briefly summarize the limitations of these defenses in terms of the requirements as follows. (a) Defenses in Class 1A and 1C are not end-to-end or focus only on control data. (b) Defenses in Class 1B and 1D might be defeated by the rootkits leveraging novel techniques or kernel vulnerabilities [13] and some of them are not very easy to be adopted because they are designed based on special hypervisors. (c) Defenses in Class 1C are not very scalable because they have to create multiple instances of anti-malware sofware to monitor multiple VMs.

To overcome the above limitations, in this paper we propose RootkitDet, an end-to-end defense against kernel rootkits in a cloud environment. RootkitDet works as follows. First, it detects the kernel rootkits by looking for suspicious code in the kernel space of the guest OSes. Second, once a rootkit is detected, it will do diagnosis to precisely identify kernel data structures that were maliciously modified by the rootkit. Third, it attempts to reverse the modifications. Due to the following insight, RootkitDet employs a simple detection idea. *Insight*: A registration procedure can be leveraged to enable separation between legitimate code and rootkit code in the kernel space. After a rootkit is detected in guest OSes, RootkitDet attempts to eliminate the effect of the rootkit. RootkitDet first performs static analysis on the suspicious code to collect certain characteristic information of the rootkit. Then, it tries to categorize the rootkit heuristically according to the collected characteristic information. If the rootkit can be categorized, RootkitDet would be able to identify the kernel data structures that were malicious modified by the rootkit. Finally, RootkitDet reverses the modifications as follows: it restores the modified control data with pre-known values, and recovers the broken links between the modified non-control data and other data structures.

We have designed and implemented a RootkitDet system prototype atop KVM [14] (`qemu-kvm-1.2.0`).Our evaluation results show that RootkitDet can meet the requirements cloud environments have on kernel rootkits defense. In sum, our main contributions are as follows.

- RootkitDet offers end-to-end defense against kernel rootkits in a cloud environment: from detection to diagnosis to recovery. To the best of our knowledge, RootkitDet is the first work that focuses on end-to-end defense in cloud environments.
- RootkitDet is an effective defense. The evaluation results show that RootkitDet can detect a kernel rootkit as long as the rootkit inserts code into the kernel space of a guest OS. RootkitDet can do recovery (i.e., reverse the modifications by the rootkit) if the rootkit is categorized successfully.
- RootkitDet is a practical defense against kernel rootkits in cloud environments. The evaluation results show that the average performance overhead introduced in guest OSes is less than 1% when the max detection cycle is 16 seconds, and the total defense cost (CPU, network bandwidth) is linear in the number of the VMs being protected.

2   Threat Model and Assumptions

In this section, we present the threat model and assumptions for the kernel-level rootkits detection system.

2.1   Threat Model

A cloud user allocates several virtual machines to provide some services, web-based service most popular, to customers. We consider an attacker who intends to install a rootkit into the kernel of VMs to keep the control of the system and hide himself. Upon successful installation of a kernel-level rootkit, the attacker will control the entire VMs and do whatever attacks he wants to except system crash or DoS. Following are examples of attacks after a successful kernel-level rootkit installation: collection of confidential data, arbitrary modification of all memory contents, abuse of the computing capacity and network bandwidth.

To install the rootkit into the VMs, the attacker may take advantages of zero-day vulnerabilities in the kernel and application software running in the VMs to gain privilege of arbitrary code execution step by step. Due to the various objectives, the attackers have to craft specific code and insert them into the kernel space of the VMs. Return-oriented kernel-level rootkits are out of our scope because they can be used to install a rootkit but not run as long-term rootkits and are not reentrant for different processes. Due to similar reasons, DKOM(Direct Kernel Object Manipulation), ret-to-user and rootkits that are erased immediately after executed are also out of our scope.

2.2 Assumptions

We assume that modern CPUs of X86 architecture provide NX (non-executalbe) feature as part of page-based memory protection. For the sake of simplicity, we assume that the kernel of guest OSes supports loadable kernel modules(LKMs) and a LKM may be dynamically loaded into the kernel either explicitly by the administrator of the guest OS or implicitly by an application running in the guest OS. Moreover, we assume that kernel and modules may be vulnerable, but not malicious. Rootkits can be installed into the running kernel space but not exist in the kernel or modules when the kernel is built.

3 Overview of RootkitDet System

The goal of RootkitDet system is to provide an end-to-end defense against kernel-level rootkits in cloud environments. To achieve its goal, RootkitDet system takes three steps: detection, diagnosis and recovery. In this section, we describe the overview of RootkitDet system and its architecture.

3.1 Overview

The first step of RootkitDet system is to detect the kernel-level rootkits installed into the guest OSes. RootkitDet system identifies suspicious code, which is taken as the code of rootkits, in the kernel space of guest OSes. By "suspicious", we mean a memory region that is not supposed to hold any code or a region that holds illegitimate code. Legitimate code in the kernel space of a guest OS which is not infected by rootkits comprises kernel code and the code of benign LKMs. To separate the code of rootkits from legitimate code, we introduce a simple, practical and effective *registration procedure*.

Registration procedure is a requirement of RootkitDet system that the administrator of a guest OS registers the kernel and potential LKMs of the guest OS in advance. *Registration of the kernel* provides enough information to bridge semantic gap [11] in our system. To register a kernel that will run in a guest OS, the administrator should provide the source code, configuration file, *system.map* as well as the binary file of the kernel. The kernel of a guest OS should be registered prior to the execution of the virtual machine which the guest OS runs on. *Registration of LKMs* is critical to separating legitimate code and the rootkits. To register a LKM that is probable to be loaded during the lifetime of the guest OS, the administrator should provide the module's name and object file. A module should be registered before it is loaded into the kernel, even if the guest OS is running. We suppose that registration procedure is performed through a secure channel, which is unknown to the attacker.

To detect suspicious code in the kernel space of a guest OS, RootkitDet system reconstructs the page directory of the kernel space of the guest OS, identifies all executable regions and compares them with expected executable regions which hold legitimate code. RootkitDet system works as follows: First, it detects

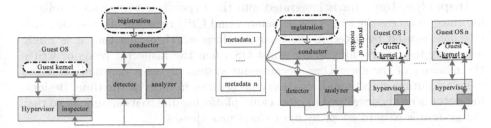

Fig. 1. Basic architecture (left) and scalable architecture (right) of RootkitDet

whether extra executable regions exist in the kernel space. Extra regions are different from that holds legitimate code. Second, it detects whether some code resides in unused space of modules. Finally, it detects malicious modifications to the legitimate code by computing SHA-1 checksums of the legitimate code and comparing them with expected values. Any mismatch means that legitimate code is modified by the rootkits.

The second step of RootkitDet system is to diagnose the detected rootkit. RootkitDet system attempts to categorize the detected rootkits and precisely identify the objects and data structures that are modified by the rootkit. To help categorization of a rootkit, we generate *profiles* of known typical rootkits in advance. RootkitDet system performs static analysis on the code of the detected rootkit to collect characteristic information, which is used to categorize the rootkit by matching with the profiles of known typical rootkits.

The profile of a typical rootkit includes: a) The tactic adopted by the rootkit to achieve its intention. We describe the tactic by a set of semantic actions, including external function calls, access to global variables and dynamic allocated data structures. b) The data structures that we should recover according to its tactic. In general, these data structures are dynamically allocated but we can find its location tracking down from a global variable with fixed location.

The final step of RootkitDet system is to recover the objects and data structures that were modified by the rootkit. The rootkit may make modifications to control data and non-control data. Control data are usually function pointers existing in kinds of data structures. Therefore, the expected values of control data are already known and it is easy to recover such modifications. By contrast, modifications to non-control data are various and usually there are no expected values for them. However, some modifications to non-control data break the links to other objects or violate some invariant that keeps in uninfected kernel. We can figure out how to recover such modifications in the kernel's context.

3.2 Architecture

As shown in Fig. 1, the basic system of RootkitDet comprises several components: registration, conductor, detector, analyzer and inspector. In our system, all components except inspector are independent of the hypervisor, and thus can run in a different OS running on a virtual machine or a physical machine.

Inspector. Inspector is integrated into the hypervisor to provide a reliable interface to access the kernel space memory and CPU registers of guest OS. This interface is used by detector and analyzer. It is worth noting that it is rarely necessary to stop running of the guest OS when the inspector reads or writes the memory of the guest OSes because our system accesses unusually changed memory during detection and recovery procedures in most of the time. Besides, inspector is easily developed in most cloud platforms due to its simplicity so that our system is easy to adopt by most cloud providers.

Detector. Detector performs three detection procedures to find out whether kernel-level rootkits exists in guest OS according to the commands coming from the conductor. In detection procedure 1, detector reconstructs the list of loaded modules and generates the list of executable regions in the kernel space, then compares them to find out whether extra executable regions exist besides the regions of the kernel code and registered modules. In detection procedure 2, detector checks whether some code resides in the unused space of each module. In detection procedure 3, detector calculates checksums for the code of the kernel and modules, and compares them with original ones, which are provided by the conductor, to check integrity of the legitimate code in the kernel space.

Detection procedure 1 and 2 might be bypassed because detector depends on the memory of guest OSes, which might be under the control of rootkits. For instance, a rootkit may tamper with the information of a module and change the module's code size to a bigger value, and put its code right behind the module's code, pretending itself as part of the module to escape from detection. We leave this problem to the conductor and the conductor resolves it when generating the original hash values for all of the modules.

Conductor. Conductor is the heart of our system. It periodically sends commands to detector to start detection procedures when the guest OS is running. Once rootkits are detected, it receives the detection report from detector, then raises an alert to the administrator and activates analyzer. Conductor also helps detector during detection procedure 3 by generating original checksums of the loaded modules of the guest OS as well as descriptions of each module, which are used to detect smart rootkits that escape from procedure 1 and 2.

Registration. Registration component stores information of the guest OSes provided by the administrator in registration procedure. It provides information of the kernel to bridge semantic gap in the three steps of RootkitDet system. Besides, it provides the necessary information of the kernel and legitimate modules to help RootkitDet system separate rootkits.

Analyzer. Analyzer diagnoses the code of the detected rootkit by performing static analysis to collect related characteristic information and attempts to categorize the detected rootkit heuristically. If the analyzer succeeds in categorizing the rootkit by matching the characteristic information with the profiles of known rootkits, it can finally perform recovery of the guest OSes.

The analyzer performs static analysis instead of dynamic analysis due to the following reasons. First, dynamic analysis is not applicable in practice due to its heavy overhead to guest OSes. Second, dynamic analysis requires the execution of the code of rootkits to analyze its behavior while static analysis does not. Finally, the characteristic information collected through static analysis is enough in most cases although it is sketchy and rough.

In order to monitor multiple guest OSes simultaneously, we expands our system into a scalable architecture as shown in Fig. 1. For each guest OS, we generate related meta-data of the kernel in advance, which includes: (1) *system.map* which contains names and locations of the kernel symbols, (2) checksum of the kernel code which is used to detect modifications to the running kernel code, (3) definitions of important data structures that might be referred to by the rootkits or during recovery, (4) type information of important global variables and dynamically allocated objects and their relationship in the kernel. Our system takes advantages of the kernel's meta-data to detect kernel-level rootkits and perform recovery. Besides, only one kernel's meta-data is necessary if all of the guest OSes are using the same kernel. Furthermore, several guest OSes can also runs on the same hypervisor if the hypervisor supports multiple guest OSes.

4 Design and Implementation of RootkitDet

In this section, we describe the system design and the implementation of the prototype of RootkitDet system.

4.1 Detection

Registration procedure. As mentioned above, registration procedure comprises registration of the kernel and registration of the legitimate modules. When the kernel of a guest OS is registered, we generate the meta-data of the kernel. *System.map* is provided by the administrator of the guest OS. We compute the original checksum of the kernel code by analyzing the binary file of the kernel. Definitions of important data structures and type information of important global variables and dynamic allocated objects are excerpts of the source code of the kernel. By "important", we mean the data structures and objects that might be accessed directly or indirectly by known rootkits and that might be accessed to recover modifications caused by known rootkits.

A module can be loaded either automatically by applications or manually by the administrator. A module loaded into the kernel is identified by its name, which is obtained from the filename of its original object file. To guarantee that a legitimate module is not taken as a rootkit by our system, the module must be registered before it is loaded into the kernel. When a module is registered, we store its original object file with its original filename, and analyze it to extract information of its exported symbols, which are useful when calculating original checksums of modules that depend on it.

For the sake of efficiency and other purposes, self-modifying code might be used in the kernel and modules to leverage advanced features of CPU, which we need to take into account during the calculation of checksums. As self-modifying code runs only in initialization stage of the kernel, we can compute all possible checksums of the kernel code by creating temporary VM instances with registered kernel and obtaining the kernel code after initialization stage. We generate the checksum of a module by simulating the relocation process of the module, and thus we replace customized instructions according to the state of the kernel to generate the proper original checksum of this module.

Detection procedures. To detect rootkits that insert code into the kernel space, our system performs three detection procedures as mentioned above. However, our system may raise false alarms in several situations. We discuss these problems and present solutions as follows.

Under some particular conditions, inconsistency between the executable regions and loaded modules may occur in the kernel of guest OSes, which causes a false positive in detection procedure 1. *Case 1:* When a module is loading, the kernel allocates another executable region for its initialization code, which is released immediately after the initialization code is executed. The temporary existence of initialization code of a module may cause a false positive. We confirm the detection of rootkits only when the detector continuously reports rootkits 3 times. *Case 2:* When a module is unloaded, the kernel doesn't release related regions until the total size reaches a threshold. The lazy clean-up may also cause false positive. We require a subtle modification to the kernel source code to release all free regions once a module is unloaded. This modification doesn't affect the efficiency of the kernel because unloading modules happens rarely in general.

Unused space usually exists below the code of a module because of the page-aligned allocation of memory. As far as we know, the kernel doesn't clear the memory regions allocated for modules before loading modules into them. As a result, the unused space may contain nonzero data, which cause a false positive in detection procedure 2. To eliminate this kind of false positive, we require a subtle modification to the kernel source code to clear the last page of memory regions allocated for modules.

The code of a module varies with the relocation address of the module when it is loaded into the kernel. We can't leverage previous work [9] to compute checksums of modules in detection procedure 3 because the original object files of modules are not required when the detector computes checksums in our system. To reduce the work of the detector, the original checksums of modules are provided by the conductor. The detector computes current checksums of legitimate code respectively, and compares them with original checksums. Any mismatch means modifications to the legitimate code.

Detection procedures are performed periodically instead of being triggered like Patagonix [15] due to the following reasons. First of all, the rootkits that are erased immediately after executed are out the scope of this paper, so periodic detection works properly in our system. Secondly, Patagonix also periodically performs a *refresh* to set all pages non-executable. Thirdly, our system focuses only on the kernel space instead of the space of all processes. The overhead of periodical detection is small. Fourth, unused space of modules should be checked although the pages are already legitimate to be executed. Finally, our system is more flexible to adjust periods of detection procedures.

```
static struct dentry* adore_proc_lookup(        ...                                ...
        struct inode *i,                        mov  %fs:0xc1416454, %eax          c1416454    r--  current
        struct dentry* d,                       incb 0x330(%eax)                  d0c0d4d4    r--  c10e6a08
        struct namedata* nd)                    mov 0x8(%esp), %eax               c10e6a08    --x  proc_root_lookup
{                                               mov %ebp, %ecx                     ...
        ...                                     mov %edi, %edx
        task_unlock(current);                   call *0xd0c0d4d4
        return orig_proc_lookup(i, d, nd);      ...
}
```

Fig. 2. The example binary code snippet(middle), with its associated C snippet(left) and associated output of static analysis

4.2 Diagnosis

To categorize the detected rootkit, we investigate well known typical rootkits according to the intentions that rootkits achieve and the tactics that rootkits adopt. For each typical rootkit, we generate a profile to describe its tactic to achieve its intention as well as modified data structures and objects that we should recover.

Generating the profiles. In our implementation, we generate profiles of typical rootkits manually due to the following reasons. First, rootkits may achieve different intentions together, and understanding the intentions and related tactics of rootkits requires manual effort. Second, data structures and objects that are accessed in the same tactic might subtly vary with the kernel version. Third, rootkits may implement the same tactic in different ways.

Using the profiles. To apply the profiles of known rootkits during diagnosis, we translate the profiles into ones that coordinate with the kernel running in the guest OS monitored by our system. Then the profiles of known rootkits are ready to categorize the detected rootkit. Categorization is done by matching certain characteristic information (collected from the detected rootkit) against the set of pre-generated profiles.

RootkitDet system performs static analysis on the code of rootkit to collect characteristic information. The characteristic information is divided into two groups. One group is the control flow information. Usually, a rootkit calls to some kernel functions to achieve its intentions, which we name *external function calls*. The other group is the global variables and dynamically allocated data structures accessed by the rootkit. In general, to access special data structure maintained by the kernel, the rootkit has to find it starting from a global variable and tracking down according to the relationship among different data structures. A global variable is actually a kernel symbol and usually accessed by its address which is constant. The characteristic information collected through static analysis is binary. RootkitDet system translates the characteristic information according to the meta-data of the kernel. Translated information is then used to categorize the detected rootkit.

We extract the instructions of the rootkit's code as discussed in Appendix 9.1, and suppose that we have figured out the code of the rootkit. Next, we address how we collect characteristic information of the rootkit through static analysis. We focus on external function calls and memory access during static analysis instead of the control flow of the code [7] [16]. Basically, what we need to do is to determine the values of CPU registers during static analysis. We create a static machine with a special CPU and stack to execute the code of rootkit statically. First, we use a pair <val, flags> to represent the value of a register, in which *val* represents the value while *flags* indicates validation of each byte of *val*. We update the pair instead of the value of registers when we execute instructions. So are the values on the stack. Therefore, we specially tackle instructions accessing the stack. Second, when an instruction involves read of memory other than the stack, we update *val* by the value of the memory and set *flags* by a value indicating *val* totally valid. Finally, some instructions load hard-coded immediate values into registers. In that case, we also update the *flags* of the target register according to the size of immediate value and the instruction type. In consequence, the values of registers that we can determine during static analysis are independent of execution environments. In most cases, we can determine the external function calls and accesses to global variables of the kernel, which we can use to infer the behavior of the suspicious code. Fig. 2 presents an example.

4.3   Recovery

If RootkitDet system successfully categorize the detected rootkit, it attempts to recover the infected kernel according to the profile of the rootkit. Data structures and objects that are modified by the rootkit are described in the profile of the rootkit. Combined with the meta-data of the kernel, *recovery-driven profile* is derived from the profile of the rootkit. Recovery-driven profile describes how to locate the modified data structures and objects and how to recover them.

As mentioned above, we usually know the expected values of the control data, which are the locations of kernel functions. Therefore, the key to recover control data is how to locate it. Data structures and objects maintained by the kernel can always be found tracking down from some global variable. Moreover, the address of global variables are constant and can be found in the meta-data of the kernel. As a result, the recovery-driven profile for control data describes the tracking path from the global variable to the object containing the control data. For example, a rootkit may overwrite the pointers of functions registered with the virtual file system layer by the pseudo random number generator (PRNG) to disable the PRNG [17]. The pointers of functions registered by the PRNG are stored in structures *random_fops* and *urandom_fops*, which are located in the object *devlist*, a list of memory devices that is a global variable. Therefore, the recovery-driven profile for the functions registered by PRNG contains the address of *devlist*, offsets of *random_fops* and *urandom_fops* in *devlist* as well as the real addresses of the functions registered by the PRNG.

Non-control data is different because the original values are either lost forever or not easy to calculate. Moreover, non-control data is different in the way to locate the related data structures or objects. For example, a rootkit hides a process by removing related item from the *pid_hash* table. Then we can't find the process tracking down from the *pid_hash* table. The only way to find the process is tracking down from *init_task* and checking each process whether it is not linked into the *pid_hash* table. As a result, the recovery-driven profile for non-control data describes how to restore the broken links or resolve violations of invariants as well as the tracking path from the global variable to the object containing the non-control data. If the original value of a non-control data are lost forever, we can not recover it. For example, we can not recover the entropy pool of PRNG if it is zeroed by a rootkit [17].

4.4 Implementation

In our implementation, we use *qemu-kvm-1.2.0* for creating instances of the guest OS, and compile *linux-2.6.32.60* for the guest kernel. Fig. 3 shows the internal components of the prototype of RootkitDet system.

Detector. We integrated the detector into qemu-kvm because the guest OSes are running as user processes on the host OS and the integration reduces inter-process communications. Moreover, we implement the inspector as part of the detector.

The detector consists of five components: inspector, data container, hash component, control component and communication component. Inspector is responsible for reading the registers and memory of the VM. Data container component constructs the necessary semantic data structures from the raw data of the VM's memory given by inspector according to the profile, and also stores data coming from the conductor through communication and control components. Hash components is used for calculating the current hash values for the kernel and modules'

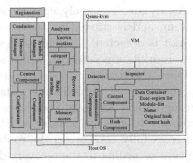

Fig. 3. Internal Components of RootkitDet

code. The communication component takes care of all of the communication with the conductor. The control component receives commands through the communication component from the conductor, then executes the commands and sends the response back to the conductor.

For the sake of flexibility, we implement the detector as a command-driven object, which is an I/O handler of qemu-kvm. It doesn't do anything until it receives a command from the conductor, and it goes back to the initial state as soon as it finishes that command. If the conductor doesn't send any commands to the detector, the VM runs the same as if there is no detector. Therefore, it is convenient for us to turn off/on this security feature of the VM when necessary.

Conductor. The conductor is a daemon process that periodically schedules detectors for monitored guest OSes and starts up the analyzer when rootkits are detected. It is also responsible for generation of original checksums of registered modules when requested.

To generate the original checksums of kernel modules, the conductor performs the same relocation work as the guest kernel does. The correct relocation work of a module depends on the following information: the original object file, the relocation address, the addresses of the used kernel symbols and the addresses of the used symbols of other modules. The conductor acquires the original object file of a module from the registration component and obtains its relocation address from the detector. The conductor can figure out the address of a kernel symbol by referring to the meta-data of the kernel. We create a database storing the relative addresses of symbols exported by registered modules. The conductor can calculate the absolute address of a symbol exported by a module by looking it up in the database and adding it up to the relocation address of the module. To resolve the potential dependency among modules during the relocation work, the conductor calculates original checksums after collecting the relocation addresses of all loaded modules from the detector. Consequently, the conductor can generate original checksums for all of the loaded modules and send them back to the detector.

We generate the original checksum of the kernel code in advance because the kernel code is constant and never changes after it starts up. We take the original checksum of the kernel code as part of the meta-data of the kernel.

Analyzer. The analyzer is actually an independent program in our prototype system, and is started up by the conductor when the detector reports that a rootkit is detected. Therefore, we save the resources consumed by the analyzer if no rootkits are detected, which is tenable in most times.

Once the detector reports that a rootkit is detected, the conductor starts up the analyzer immediately. Analyzer collects the characteristic information through static analysis, translates combining the meta-data of the kernel, and attempts to categorize the rootkit according to profiles of known rootkits. If it successfully categorizes the rootkit, it recovers modified data structures and objects according to the recovery-driven profile of the rootkit.

5   Evaluation of RootkitDet System

In this section, we present the evaluation results of our RootkitDet prototype. Our evaluation has two goals. The first goal is to evaluate RootkitDet's effectiveness for detecting kernel-level rootkits that compromise the code integrity of the OS kernel and recovering modified data to eliminate the effect of rootkits. The second goal is to measure the overhead introduced to guest OSes and extra resources consumed by RootkitDet.

All experiments are conducted on Dell PowerEdge M610 Server with a 2.40GHz Intel Xeon E5645 and 6GB memory. The hypervisor is qemu-kvm-1.2.0. The host OS is Ubuntu-12.04. We used Debian-squeeze with kernel version 2.6.32 as our guest OS. The detector is integrated into qemu-kvm, and thus runs with the guest OS. The conductor ran on another computer as a user process. They communicated with each other through TCP connections.

5.1   Effectiveness

To evaluate the effectiveness of RootkitDet system for detecting kernel-level rootkits, we install four representative rootkits in the guest OS monitored by our system. As shown in Table 1, different detection procedures detect the rootkits that hide the code in different regions.

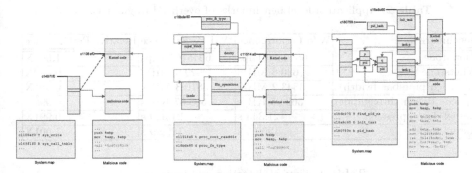

Fig. 4. hksc: hooking sys_write

Fig. 5. hkproc: hooking proc filesystem

Fig. 6. hidepc: manipulating pid hash table

Adore-ng [18] is implemented as kernel module and an extra executable region appears when it is installed. Therefore, it is detected by procedure 1. **Enyelkm** [19] is also implemented as a kernel module and thus detected by procedure 1. In addition, it also hijacks the control flow of the kernel by modifying the system call dispatch routine to intercept several system calls, and thus it is also detected by procedure 3. Despite of the probability that a rootkit's code resides in dynamically allocated executable regions or unused space of modules, we don't find one in wild. We implement **Icmp-cmd** and **Icmp-cmd_v2**, which execute commands specified by crafted ICMP packets, to evaluate the RootkitDet's effectiveness in detecting such rootkits. The code of them resides in a dynamically allocated executable region and unused space of a module, and thus they are detected by procedure 1 and 2 respectively.

To evaluate the effectiveness of RootkitDet system for eliminating the effect of rootkits, we develop 3 rootkits, hksc, hkproc and hidepc, which adopt different tactics to hide a specific user process from the guest system administrators, and install them in the guest OS monitored by our

Table 1. Rootkit detection

Rootkit	Method to insert code	DP
adore-ng	module	1
enyelkm	module and substitution	1, 3
icmp-cmd	executable region	1
icmp-cmd_v2	unused space	2

system. After detection of them, our system successfully categorizes them and performs recovery to reveal the hidden process.

Fig. 4 shows a rootkit hijacking *sys_write* system call to hide a specific process by tampering with what is displayed to the administrators of guest OSes. We recover the modified system call table to eliminate the effect of this rootkit. Fig. 5 shows a rootkit hooking the function pointer *proc_root_readdir* to hide a specific process by removing related *pid* entry in the *proc* file system. We find the hooked function pointer by tracking down from *proc_fs_type*, which is a global variable, and correct it with the real location of kernel function *proc_root_readdir*. Fig. 6 shows a rootkit hiding a specific process by removing related entry in the pid

Table 2. Application-level benchmarks of overhead to guest OSes

Benchmark	W/o Performance	W/i Performance	Relative Performance
Dhrystone	6040580.1 lps	6045164.7 lps	1.001X
Whetstone	630.6 MIPS	629.9 MIPS	0.999X
Lmbench(pipe bandwidth)	3843.2 MB/s	3810.3 MB/s	0.991X
Apache Bench(throughput)	569.95 KB/s	568.67 KB/s	0.998X
Kernel decompression	21.343 s	21.529 s	0.991X
Kernel build	1300.4 s	1292.9 s	1.001X

Table 3. Time of detection and recovery

Rootkit	Code size(byte)	detection time(ms)	analysis time(ms)	recovery time(ms)
hksc	407	< 1	14.6	3.7
hkproc	978	< 1	44.6	7.7
hidepc	565	< 1	29.1	204.8

hash table. We first find the *task_struct* of the hidden process by tracking down from *init_task*, and then relink it into the pid hash table to reveal the hidden process.

5.2   Overhead to the Guest OSes

To measure the performance cost introduced by our system to the guest OS, we run a set of application benchmarks to compare the performance of a guest OS that enables the detector with the one that does not. The application benchmarks and their configuration are presented as follows: 1) Dhrystone 2 of the UnixBench suite using register variables. 2) Double-precision whetstone of the UnixBench. 3) Pipe bandwidth of Lmbench measuring the performance of IPC interface provided by the kernel. 4) Apache Bench configured to issue 10,000 http requests (177B HTML file) through 1 client. 5) Kernel source code decompression using command `tar xjf` to extract the compressed tarball file of Linux 2.6.32 kernel. 6) Building a Linux 2.6.32 kernel.

We run detection procedure 1 in each second, procedure 2 in 4 seconds, procedure 3 in 16 seconds because of different complexity of them. Table 2 presents the results of these application level benchmarks. The second column shows the performance of the guest OS which doesn't enable the detector, while the third column shows the performance of the guest OS that enables the detector. The last column presents the relative performance. To reduce the effect of random factors, we run each benchmarks 10 times, and present the average results in the table. From table 2, we can see that the relative performance of the guest OS that enables the detector is above 0.99X, on both CPU intensive jobs and I/O intensive jobs. In other words, the performance cost is tolerable to most tasks.

Besides application level benchmarks, we also perform a micro-benchmark test on the detector. In the experiment result, detection procedure 1 costs the least time, which is 189 μs; detection procedure 2 costs more time, which is $713\mu s$; detection procedure 3 costs the most time, which is 47139 μs.

5.3   Performance

To measure the scalability of our system, we run multiple VM instances that enable the detector at the same time and measure the network bandwidth and CPU resources consumed by our system, i.e. the conductor. Fig. 7 shows the peak and average network bandwidths (input and output) consumed by the conductor are linear to the quantity of the VM instances. In addition, our system consumes 3% CPU cycles for every 10 guest OSes. As a result, our is scalable and efficient in the cloud environment.

To measure the efficiency of our system, we measure the time of detection and recovery against the 3 rootkits that hide a specific user process in the guest OS. Table 3 shows the evaluation result. The time of detection is less than 1 ms because the rootkits are implemented as modules which are detected by detection procedure 1. The time of analysis depends on the code size and pages of memory accessed by the code. The time of recovery mainly depends on the complexity of recovery.

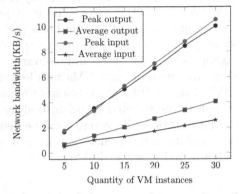

Fig. 7. Network bandwidth consumed by Conductor

6   Related Work

Kernel-level rootkits have been distributed in the underground hacker community for a long time [20]. In order to relieve the threat of kernel-level rootkits, many techniques or architectures are proposed. Most recently techniques or architectures leverages the security benefit of the hypervisor. They can be divided into 4 classes: (1) Detecting data modifications or violations of invariants in the kernel; (2) Preventing the installation of the rootkits by performing analysis on the code being loaded into the kernel space; (3) Defending kernel rootkits by cooperating with anti-malware software; (4) Protecting the kernel by restoring infected kernels to healthy state.

In class 1, SBCFI [5] detects persistent kernel control-flow attacks by identifying function pointers in kernel data structures to the kernel and modules' code. HookSafe [6] protects thousands of kernel hooks in a guest OS from being hijacked. Gibraltar *et al* [3] detects kernel rootkits by identifying data invariants in the kernel. The work of Petroni Jr *et al* [4] focuses on semantic integrity violations in kernel dynamic data. While these works focus on control/non-control data in the kernel, our system focuses on the code inserted into kernel space and attempts to perform recovery.

In class 2, the work of C. Kruegel *et al* [7] performs static analysis on the module that is being loaded and prevents it if it resembles the behavior of rootkits. Liveware [21] protects the guest OS kernel code and critical data structures from being modified. Our system improves by detecting the code added into the kernel space that is not in the form of a module. SecVisor [8], a tiny hypervisor that enforces page-level protection of the memory used by the code of the kernel and modules, prevents the installation of the kernel rootkits by ensuring the code integrity of guest OS kernel. NICKLE [9] protects the code integrity in the guest OS kernel by transparently routing guest kernel instruction fetches to shadow memory which contains authenticated code and is protected from write-access. However, they are not easy to be adopted in the cloud platforms based on different hypervisors because they require special features of the hypervisor.

VMWatcher [11] detects malware by providing semantic view of the guest OS to anti-malware software, and Lares [10] presents an architecture that gives the security tools the ability to do active monitoring. While they are cooperated with external security tools or anti-malware software, our system can defend rootkits alone and monitor more VMs with less effort.

VICI Agent [12], which belongs to class 4, applies different repair techniques to restore the infected kernel to healthy state after detecting kernel-modifying rootkit infections. However, it can be defeated by novel rootkits that insert new control-data in the kernel space instead of modifying existing control-data, such as Icmp-cmd mentioned in Section 5.

7   Discussions and Limitations

RootkitDet system is not perfect because of the following reasons. First, it cannot detect rootkits that are erased immediately after executed or that have no specific code in the kernel space, like return-oriented rootkits [22]. Second, it may not detect all of the code of a rootkit if the rootkit hides part of its code by switching NX-bit of the corresponding pages, therefore our system may lose some characteristic information of the rootkit during analysis. Third, it cannot prevent the installation of the kernel-level rootkits although it detects rootkits and recovers the kernel if possible. Fourth, it cannot certainly recover all modifications made by the rootkits, especially when categorization of the rootkits fails. Finally, the generation of instinct information of rootkits are not automatic. However, RootkitDet system are still useful and flexible in practice. In addition, it can perform quickly detection of kernel-level rootkits by only issuing detection procedure 1 and 2 because almost all of kernel-level rootkits in the wild introduce extra code into the kernel space and fewer and fewer of them modify the code of the kernel or modules. RootkitDet system provides the characteristic information of unknown rootkits to assist further investigation.

In future work, we can focus on the analysis and recovery of novel and unknown rootkits and automatic generation of rootkits' instinct information.

8 Conclusions

In this paper, we present the design, implementation and evaluation of the RootkitDet system, an end-to-end defense against kernel-level rootkit, which is efficient and practical in the cloud environment. RootkitDet system detects rootkits that insert code into kernel space of guest OSes, diagnoses the detected rootkit to precisely locate modifications caused by the rootkit, and attempts to recover the modifications. Our evaluation experiments show that the Rootkit-Det system can effectively detect kernel-level rootkits and reverse modifications if the rootkits are categorized successfully. In addition, the performance cost introduced to the guest OSes by our system is less than 1%, and the complexity of our system is linear with the quantity of the VM instances being monitored, which is acceptable in the cloud environment.

Acknowledgments. We thank the anonymous reviewers and our shepherd, Stefano Paraboschi for their constructive feedback to improve the paper. Lingchen Zhang was supported by ARO grant W911NF-12-1-0055. Sachin Shetty was supported by ARO grant W911NF-12-1-0055, NSF grant HRD-1137466, DHS grants 2011-ST-062-0000046 and 2010-ST-062-0000041. Peng Liu was supported by AFOSR W911NF1210055, ARO W911NF-09-1-0525, NSF CNS-1223710, and ARO W911NF-13-1-0421. Jiwu Jing was partially supported by the National 973 Program of China under award No.2014CB340603 and the National 863 Program of China under award No.2013AA01A214.

References

1. McAfee: Rootkits, Part 1 of 3: A Growing Threat. white paper (April 2006)
2. McAfee: 2010 Threat Predictions. white paper, McAfee AVERT Labs (December 2009)
3. Baliga, A., Ganapathy, V., Iftode, L.: Detecting kernel-level rootkits using data structure invariants. IEEE Transactions on Dependable and Secure Computing 8(5), 670–684 (2011)
4. Petroni Jr., N.L., Fraser, T., Walters, A., Arbaugh, W.A.: An architecture for specification-based detection of semantic integrity violations in kernel dynamic data. In: Proceedings of the 15th USENIX Security Symposium, pp. 289–304 (2006)
5. Petroni Jr., N.L., Hicks, M.: Automated detection of persistent kernel control-flow attacks. In: Proceedings of the 14th ACM Conference on Computer and Communications Security, pp. 103–115. ACM (2007)
6. Wang, Z., Jiang, X., Cui, W., Ning, P.: Countering kernel rootkits with lightweight hook protection. In: Proceedings of the 16th ACM Conference on Computer and Communications Security, pp. 545–554. ACM (2009)
7. Kruegel, C., Robertson, W., Vigna, G.: Detecting kernel-level rootkits through binary analysis. In: 20th Annual Computer Security Applications Conference 2004, pp. 91–100. IEEE (2004)
8. Seshadri, A., Luk, M., Qu, N., Perrig, A.: Secvisor: a tiny hypervisor to provide lifetime kernel code integrity for commodity oses. In: ACM SIGOPS Operating Systems Review, vol. 41, pp. 335–350. ACM (2007)

9. Riley, R., Jiang, X., Xu, D.: Guest-transparent prevention of kernel rootkits with vmm-based memory shadowing. In: Lippmann, R., Kirda, E., Trachtenberg, A. (eds.) RAID 2008. LNCS, vol. 5230, pp. 1–20. Springer, Heidelberg (2008)

10. Payne, B.D., Carbone, M., Sharif, M., Lee, W.: Lares: An architecture for secure active monitoring using virtualization. In: IEEE Symposium on Security and Privacy, SP 2008, pp. 233–247. IEEE (2008)

11. Jiang, X., Wang, X., Xu, D.: Stealthy malware detection through vmm-based out-of-the-box semantic view reconstruction. In: Proceedings of the 14th ACM Conference on Computer and Communications Security, pp. 128–138. ACM (2007)

12. Fraser, T., Evenson, M.R., Arbaugh, W.A.: Vici-virtual machine introspection for cognitive immunity. In: Annual Computer Security Applications Conference, ACSAC 2008, pp. 87–96. IEEE (2008)

13. Kemerlis, V.P., Portokalidis, G., Keromytis, A.D.: kguard: lightweight kernel protection against return-to-user attacks. In: USENIX Security Symposium (2012)

14. Linux-KVM: Linux-KVM, http://www.linux-kvm.org/page/Main_Page

15. Litty, L., Lagar-Cavilla, H.A., Lie, D.: Hypervisor support for identifying covertly executing binaries. In: Proceedings of the 17th Conference on Security Symposium, pp. 243–258 (2008)

16. Wagner, D., Dean, D.: Intrusion detection via static analysis. In: Proceedings of the 2001 IEEE Symposium on Security and Privacy, S&P 2001, pp. 156–168. IEEE (2001)

17. Baliga, A., Kamat, P., Iftode, L.: Lurking in the shadows: Identifying systemic threats to kernel data. In: IEEE Symposium on Security and Privacy, SP 2007, pp. 246–251. IEEE (2007)

18. Stealth: Announcing full functional adore-ng rootkit for 2.6 kernel, http://lwn.net/Articles/75991/

19. eNYe Sec: eNYeLKM v1.1, http://www.enye-sec.org/en/tags/enye-lkm/

20. Halflife: Abuse of the Linux-kernel for Fun and Profit. Phrack Magazine 5(50) (April 1997)

21. Garfinkel, T., Rosenblum, M.: A virtual machine introspection based architecture for intrusion detection. In: Proc. Network and Distributed Systems Security Symposium (2003)

22. Hund, R., Holz, T., Freiling, F.C.: Return-oriented rootkits: Bypassing kernel code integrity protection mechanisms. In: Proceedings of the 18th USENIX Security Symposium, pp. 383–398 (2009)

9   Appendix

9.1   Extracting Instructions

When a rootkit is detected by our system, we get a suspicious executable region where the code of the rootkit locates. To analyze the rootkit's code, we need extract instructions of the rootkit's code from the executable region first. The executable region is page-aligned and we don't know the exact location of the rootkit's code. Moreover, it is non-trivial task to distinguish code from data on X86 platforms. Therefore, it is difficult to find out the rootkit's code in the detected executable regions.

We notice that the code of rootkits usually comprises a set of functions and the instructions are continuous unless a jump instruction occurs. Several successive instructions of a function compose an instruction block ending with a branch, jump, call or return instruction. If an instruction block ends with a return instruction, no more blocks follows it in logic. If a block ends with a call instruction, the next block starts right behind the call instruction. If a block ends with a jump instruction, the address of the following block can be calculated from the address of the jump instruction and its content. If a block ends with a branch instruction, two blocks follow it in logic: one is just behind it and the starting address of the other can be calculated from the address of the branch instruction and its content.

Consequently, we can figure out all of the instruction blocks of a function as long as we find the first block. That is to say, we should find the first instruction of a function. We search the first instruction from the first byte of the executable region which starts at the lowest address if multiple regions exist. If the first instruction starts here, we can figure out the whole function. Otherwise, we should encounter an illegal instruction in all probability during the process of extracting instruction blocks. If it is not the first instruction, we march on by one byte. We repeat this step until we figure out the first instruction.

Modeling Network Diversity for Evaluating the Robustness of Networks against Zero-Day Attacks

Lingyu Wang[1], Mengyuan Zhang[1], Sushil Jajodia[2], Anoop Singhal[3], and Massimiliano Albanese[2]

[1] Concordia Institute for Information Systems Engineering, Concordia University
{wang,mengy_zh}@ciise.concordia.ca
[2] Center for Secure Information Systems, George Mason University
{jajodia,malbanes}@gmu.edu
[3] Computer Security Division, National Institute of Standards and Technology
anoop.singhal@nist.gov

Abstract. The interest in diversity as a security mechanism has recently been revived in various applications, such as Moving Target Defense (MTD), resisting worms in sensor networks, and improving the robustness of network routing. However, most existing efforts on formally modeling diversity have focused on a single system running diverse software replicas or variants. At a higher abstraction level, as a global property of the entire network, diversity and its impact on security have received limited attention. In this paper, we take the first step towards formally modeling network diversity as a security metric for evaluating the robustness of networks against potential zero day attacks. Specifically, we first devise a biodiversity-inspired metric based on the effective number of distinct resources. We then propose two complementary diversity metrics, based on the least and the average attacking efforts, respectively. Finally, we evaluate our algorithm and metrics through simulation.

Keywords: Security Metrics, Diversity, Network Security, Zero Day Attack, Network Robustness.

1 Introduction

Computer networks are playing the role of nerve systems in many critical infrastructures, governmental and military organizations, and enterprises. Protecting such mission critical networks means more than just patching known vulnerabilities and deploying firewalls or IDSs. Evaluating the network's robustness against potential zero day attacks (i.e., attacks exploiting previously unknown vulnerabilities) is equally important. The fact that Stuxnet employs four different zero day vulnerabilities [1] has clearly demonstrated the real-world significance of defending networks against zero day attacks. On the other hand, dealing with unknown vulnerabilities is clearly a challenging task.

In a slightly different context, software diversity has previously been regarded as a security mechanism for improving the robustness of a software system [2] (a more detailed review of related work will be given later in Section 6). By comparing outputs [3] or behaviors [4] of multiple software replicas or variants with diverse implementation

M. Kutyłowski and J. Vaidya (Eds.): ESORICS 2014, Part II, LNCS 8713, pp. 494–511, 2014.

details, security attacks may be detected and tolerated as Byzantine faults [5]. Although the earlier diversity-by-design approaches are usually regarded as impractical due to the implied development and deployment cost, recent works show more promising results on employing either opportunistic diversity already existing among different software systems [6], or automatically generated diversity, e.g., through randomization of address space [7,8], instruction set [9], or data space [10]. More recently, diversity has found new applications in Moving Target Defense (MTD) [11], resisting sensor worms [12], and improving the robustness of network routing [13].

However, at a higher abstraction level, as a global property of the entire network, the concept of *network diversity* and its impact on security has received less attention. In this paper, we take the first step towards formally modeling network diversity as a security metric, for the purpose of evaluating a network's robustness with respect to zero day attacks. More specifically, following the discussion of several use cases, we propose a series of network diversity metrics as follows.

- First, we propose a network diversity metric function by adapting well known mathematical models of biodiversity in ecology. The metric is based on the number of distinct resources in a network, while considering the uneven distribution of resources and similarity between different resources. This first metric is more suitable for evaluating the scale of potential infection by a malware, and it is also a building block of the other two metrics. The main limitation is that it ignores potential causal relationships between resources in a network.
- Second, we design a network diversity metric based on the least attacking effort required for compromising critical assets, while taking into account the causal relationships between resources. We also study the complexity and design heuristic algorithms for computing the metric efficiently. This second metric is suitable for measuring a network's capability of resisting intrusions or malware that employ multiple related zero day attacks. The main limitation is that, by focusing on the least attacking effort, it only provides a partial picture about the threat and cannot reflect the average attacking effort.
- Third, we devise a Bayesian network-based model to define network diversity as a conditional probability based on the effect of diversity on the average attack likelihood. This probabilistic metric provides a complementary measure to the above metric by depicting the average attacking effort required by attackers. We show how this metric can be instantiated from existing standard vulnerability databases.
- Finally, we evaluate the proposed heuristic algorithm and metrics through simulation results, and we discuss practical limitations of our approach.

The main contribution of this paper is twofold. First, to the best of our knowledge, this is the first effort on formally modeling network diversity as a security metric for defending networks against zero day attacks. Second, the modeling effort not only improves understanding of the network diversity concept, but may lead to better, quantitative approaches to employing diversity for improving network security.

The rest of this paper is organized as follows. Section 2 describes use cases and defines a biodiversity-inspired metric. Section 3 then presents the least attacking effort-based metric. Section 4 presents the probabilistic diversity metric. Section 5 presents simulation results. Section 6 reviews related work, and finally Section 7 discusses main limitations of this work and concludes the paper.

2 Preliminaries

This section motivates the study through several use cases and defines a biodiversity-inspired network diversity metric.

2.1 Use Cases

Use Case 1: Stuxnet and SCADA Security. Stuxnet is one of the first malware that employ multiple (four) different zero day attacks [1], which clearly indicates, in a mission critical system, such as supervisory control and data acquisition (SCADA) in this case, the risk of zero day attacks and multiple unknown vulnerabilities is very real. Therefore, it is important to provide network administrators a systematic way for evaluating such a risk. On the other hand, this is clearly a challenging task due to the lack of prior knowledge about vulnerabilities or attacking methods.

We next take a closer look at Stuxnet's attack strategies to illustrate how a network diversity metric may help here. Stuxnet targets the programmable logic controllers (PLCs) on control systems of gas pipelines or power plants [1]. Such PLCs are mostly programmed using Windows machines not connected to the network. Therefore, Stuxnet adopts a multi-stage approach, by first infecting Windows machines owned by third parties (e.g., a contractor or insider), next spreading to the organization's Windows machines through the LAN, and finally covering the last hop to targeted machines, which are disconnected from the LAN, through removable flash drives [1].

Clearly, a sufficient presence of vulnerable Windows machines inside the organization is a necessary condition for Stuxnet to propagate and eventually infect the targeted PLCs. On the other hand, the degree of software diversity along potential attack paths leading from the network perimeter to the PLCs can be regarded as a critical metric of the network's capability of resisting a threat like Stuxnet. Our objective in this paper is to provide a rigorous study of such diversity metrics.

Use Case 2: Worm Propagation. To make our discussion more concrete, we will refer to the running example shown in Figure 1 from now on. Suppose our main concern is the potential propagation of worms or bots inside a network. A common belief is that the more diversified the network is, the higher degree of robustness it will have against a worm propagation. In other words, we can just count the number (percentage) of different resources inside the network, and use that count as a diversity metric. Although such a definition of diversity is natural and intuitive, it clearly has limitations.

For example, in Figure 1, suppose host 1, 2 and 3 are all Web servers running IIS, and host 4 a storage server. Clearly, the above count-based diversity metric will indicate a lack of diversity among the three Web servers and suggest replacing IIS with other software, such that a worm will unlikely infect all three. However, assuming all three Web servers would read from a network share on the storage server (host 4), then eventually a worm can still propagate to all four hosts through the network share, even if it cannot infect all three Web servers directly.

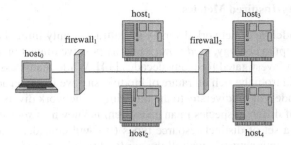

Fig. 1. The Running Example

The lesson here is, a naive approach, such as counting the number of resources in a network, may produce misleading results because it ignores the causal relationships between resources. Therefore, after we discuss the count-based metric in Section 2.2, we will address this limitation with a *goal oriented* approach in Section 3.

Use Case 3: Targeted Attack. Suppose now we are more concerned with a targeted attack on the storage server, host 4, launched by human attackers. Following above discussions, an intuitive solution is to diversify resources along any *path* leading to the critical asset (host 4), for example, between hosts 1 (or 2, 3) and host 4. Although this is a valid observation, realizing it will demand a rigorous study of the causal relationships between different resources, because host 4 is only as secure as the weakest path (representing the least attacking effort) leading to it. We will propose a formal metric and corresponding algorithm based on such an intuition in Section 3.

On the other hand, the least attacking effort by itself is not sufficient. Suppose now host 1 and 2 are diversified to run IIS and Apache, respectively, and firewall 2 will only allow host 1 and 2 to reach host 4. Although the least attacking effort has not changed, this diversification effort has provided attackers more opportunities to reach host 4 (by exploiting either IIS or Apache). That is, misplaced diversity may hurt security, which will be captured by a probabilistic metric we will introduce in Section 4.

Use Case 4: MTD through Combinations of Web, Application, and Database Servers. In this case, suppose host 1 and 2 are Web servers, host 3 an application server, and host 4 a database server. A Moving Target Defense (MTD) approach attempts to achieve better security by varying in time the software components at those three tiers [11]. A common misconception here is that the combination of different components at the three tiers will increase diversity, and the degree of diversity is equal to the product of diversity at those three tiers. However, this is usually not the case. For example, a single flaw in the application server (host 3) may result in a SQL injection that compromises the database server (host 4) and consequently leaks the root user's password. In addition, diversity over time may actually provide attackers more opportunities to find flaws. The lesson here is again that, an intuitive observation may be misleading, and formally modeling network diversity is necessary.

2.2 Biodiversity-Inspired Metrics

Although the modeling of network diversity has attracted only limited attention, a corresponding concept in ecology, *biodiversity*, and its positive impact on the ecosystem's stability has been investigated for many decades [14]. While many lessons may potentially be borrowed from the rich literature of biodiversity, we focus on adapting existing mathematical models of biodiversity to the modeling of network diversity in this paper.

The number of different species in an ecosystem is known as *species richness* [15]. Similarly, given a set of distinct resource types (we will consider similarity between resources later) R in a network, we call the cardinality $| R |$ the *richness* of resources in the network. An obvious limitation of this richness metric is that it ignores the relative abundance of each resource type. For example, the two sets $\{r_1, r_1, r_2, r_2\}$ and $\{r_1, r_2, r_2, r_2\}$ have the same richness of 2 but clearly different levels of diversity.

To address this limitation, the Shannon-Wiener index, which is essentially the Shannon entropy using natural logarithm, is used as a *diversity index* to group all systems with the same level of diversity, and the exponential of the diversity index is regarded as the *effective number* metric [16]. The effective number basically allows measuring diversity in terms of the number of equally-common species, even if in reality all species are not equally common. In the following, we borrow this concept to define the effective resource richness and our first diversity metric.

Definition 1 (Effective Richness and d_1-Diversity). *In a network G composed of a set of hosts $H = \{h_1, h_2, \ldots, h_n\}$, a set of resource types $R = \{r_1, r_2, \ldots, r_m\}$, and the resource mapping $res(.) : H \rightarrow 2^R$, let $t = \sum_{i=1}^{n} | res(h_i) |$ (total number of resource instances), and let $p_j = \frac{|\{h_i : r_j \in res(h_i)\}|}{t}$ ($1 \leq i \leq n, 1 \leq j \leq m$) (relative frequency of each resource). We define the network's diversity as $d_1 = \frac{r(G)}{t}$, where $r(G)$ is the the network's effective richness of resources, defined as*

$$r(G) = \frac{1}{\prod_1^n p_i^{p_i}}$$

One limitation of the effective number-based metric is that similarity between different resource types is not taken into account and all resource types are assumed to be entirely different, which is not realistic (e.g., the same application can be configured to fulfill totally different roles, such as NGinx as a reverse proxy or a web server, respectively, in which case these should be regarded as different resources with high similarity). To remove this limitation, we borrow the similarity-sensitive biodiversity metric recently introduced in [17] to re-define resource richness. With this new definition, the above diversity metric d_1 can now handle similarity between resources.

Definition 2 (Similarity-Sensitive Richness). *In Definition 1, suppose a similarity function is given as $z(.) : [1, m] \times [1, m] \rightarrow [0, 1]$ (a larger value denoting higher similarity and $z(i, i) = 1$ for all $1 \leq i \leq m$), let $zp_i = \sum_{j=1}^{m} z(i, j) p_j$. We define the network's effective richness of resources, considering the similarity function, as*

$$r(G) = \frac{1}{\prod_1^n zp_i^{p_i}}$$

Note that we will simply use "the number of distinct resources" to refer to the richness of resources from now on. It is to be understood that such a term can always be replaced with the effective richness concepts given in Definition 1 and 2 to handle the uneven distribution of different resource types and the similarity between resources; in other words, these are not limitations of our models.

3   Network Diversity Based on Least Attacking Effort

This section models network diversity based on the least attacking effort. Section 3.1 defines the metric, and Section 3.2 discusses the complexity and algorithm.

3.1   The Model

In order to model diversity based on the least attacking effort while considering causal relationships between different resources, we first need a model of such relationships and possible zero day attacks. Our model is similar to the *attack graph* model [18,19], although our model focuses on remotely accessible resources (e.g., services or applications that are reachable from other hosts in the network), which will be regarded as placeholders for potential zero day vulnerabilities, instead of known vulnerabilities (we will discuss how to integrate known vulnerabilities into our model in Section 4). To build intuitions, we revisit Figure 1 by making following assumptions:

- Accesses from outside firewall 1 are allowed to host 1 but blocked to host 2;
- Accesses from host 1 or 2 are allowed to host 3 but blocked to host 4 by firewall 2;
- Hosts 1 and 2 provide *http* service;
- Host 3 provides *ssh* service;
- Host 4 provides both *http* service and *rsh* service;

Figure 2 depicts a corresponding *resource graph* model, which is syntactically equivalent to an attack graph, but models zero day attacks rather than known vulnerabilities. Each pair in plaintext is a self-explanatory security-related condition (e.g., connectivity $\langle source, destination \rangle$ or privilege $\langle privilege, host \rangle$), and each triple inside a box is a potential exploit of resource $\langle resource, source\ host, destination\ host \rangle$; the edges point from the pre-conditions to a zero day exploit (e.g., from $\langle 0, 1 \rangle$ and $\langle user, 0 \rangle$ to $\langle http, 0, 1 \rangle$), and from that exploit to its post-conditions (e.g., from $\langle http, 0, 1 \rangle$ to $\langle user, 1 \rangle$). Note we have omitted exploits or conditions involving firewall 2 for simplicity. We simply regard resources of different types as entirely different (their similarity can be handled using the effective resource richness given in Definition 2). Also, we take the conservative approach of considering all resources (services and firewalls) to be potentially vulnerable to zero day attacks. Definition 3 formally introduces the concept of resource graph.

Definition 3 (Resource Graph). *Given a network composed of a set of hosts H, a set of resources R with the resource mapping $res(.) : H \to 2^R$, a set of zero day exploits $E = \{\langle r, h_s, h_d \rangle \mid h_s \in H, h_d \in H, r \in res(h_d)\}$ and the collection of their pre- and post-conditions C, a resource graph is a directed graph $G(E \cup C, R_r \cup R_i)$ where $R_r \subseteq C \times E$ and $R_i \subseteq E \times C$ are the pre- and post-condition relations, respectively.*

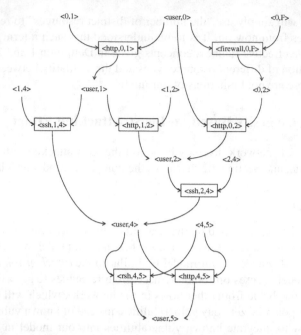

Fig. 2. An Example Resource Graph

Next we consider how attackers may potentially attack a critical network asset, modeled as a goal condition, with the least effort. In Figure 2, we follow the simple rule that
any zero day exploit may be executed if all its pre-conditions are satisfied, and executing the exploit will cause all its post-conditions to be satisfied. We may then observe six
attack paths as shown in Table 1 (the second and third columns can be ignored for now
and will be explained shortly). Intuitively, each attack path is a sequence of exploits
whose pre-conditions are all satisfied, either initially, or as post-conditions of preceding
exploits in the same path. Definition 4 formally introduces the concept of attack path.

Table 1. Attack Paths

Attack Path	# of Steps	# of Resources
1. $\langle http, 0, 1 \rangle \rightarrow \langle ssh, 1, 4 \rangle \rightarrow \langle rsh, 4, 5 \rangle$	3	3
2. $\langle http, 0, 1 \rangle \rightarrow \langle ssh, 1, 4 \rangle \rightarrow \langle http, 4, 5 \rangle$	3	2
3. $\langle http, 0, 1 \rangle \rightarrow \langle http, 1, 2 \rangle \rightarrow \langle ssh, 2, 4 \rangle \rightarrow \langle rsh, 4, 5 \rangle$	4	3
4. $\langle http, 0, 1 \rangle \rightarrow \langle http, 1, 2 \rangle \rightarrow \langle ssh, 2, 4 \rangle \rightarrow \langle http, 4, 5 \rangle$	4	2
5. $\langle firewall, 0, F \rangle \rightarrow \langle http, 0, 2 \rangle \rightarrow \langle ssh, 2, 4 \rangle \rightarrow \langle rsh, 4, 5 \rangle$	4	4
6. $\langle firewall, 0, F \rangle \rightarrow \langle http, 0, 2 \rangle \rightarrow \langle ssh, 2, 4 \rangle \rightarrow \langle http, 4, 5 \rangle$	4	3

Definition 4 (Attack Path). *Given a resource graph $G(E \cup C, R_r \cup R_i)$, we call $C_I = \{c : c \in C, (\nexists e \in E)(\langle e, c \rangle \in R_i)\}$ the set of initial conditions. Any sequence of zero day exploits $e_1, e_2, \ldots, e_n$ is called an attack path in G, if $(\forall i \in [1, n])(\langle c, e_i \rangle \in R_r \rightarrow (c \in C_i \vee (\exists j \in [1, i-1])(\langle e_j, c \rangle \in R_i)))$, and for any $c \in C$, we use $seq(c)$ for the set of attack paths $\{e_1, e_2, \ldots, e_n : \langle e_n, c \rangle \in R_i\}$.*

We are now ready to consider how diversity should be defined based on the least attacking effort, which intuitively corresponds to the shortest path. However, there are actually several possible ways for choosing such shortest paths and for defining the metric, as we will illustrate through our running example in the following.

- First, as shown in the second column of Table 1, path 1 and 2 are the shortest in terms of the *steps* (i.e., the number of zero day exploits). Clearly, the shortest path in terms of steps does not reflect the least attacking effort, since path 4 may actually take less effort than path 1, as attackers may reuse their exploit code, tools, and skills while exploiting the same *http* service on three different hosts.
- Next, as shown in the third column, path 2 and 4 are the shortest in terms of the number of distinct resources [1]. This option is more reasonable than the above one, since it takes into consideration the saved effort in reusing the same exploits. However, although both path 2 and 4 have the same number of distinct resources (2), they clearly do not reflect the same diversity.
- Another attractive option is to base on the minimum ratio $\frac{\# \, of \, resources}{\# \, of \, steps}$ (which is given by path 4 in this example), since such a ratio reflects the potential improvements in terms of diversity (e.g., the ratio $\frac{2}{4}$ of path 4 indicates there is 50% potential improvement in diversity). However, although not shown in this example, we can easily imagine a very long attack path minimizing such a ratio (e.g., an attack path with 9 steps and 3 distinct resources will yield a ratio of $\frac{1}{3}$, less than that of path 4) but does not reflect the least attacking effort (e.g., the aforementioned attack path will require more effort than path 4 since it has more distinct resources).
- Finally, yet another option is to pick the shortest path that minimizes both the number of distinct resources (path 2 and 4) and the above ratio $\frac{\# \, of \, resources}{\# \, of \, steps}$ (path 4). While this may seem to be the most reasonable choice, a closer look will reveal that, although path 4 does represent the least attacking effort, it does not represent the maximum amount of potential improvement in diversity, because once we start to diversify path 4, the shortest path may change to be path 1 or 2.

Based on these discussions, we define the network diversity by combining the first two options above. Specifically, the network diversity is defined as the ratio between the minimum number of distinct resources on a path and the minimum number of steps on a path (note these can be different paths). Going back to our running example above, we find path 2 and 4 to have the minimum number of distinct resources (two), and also path 1 and 2 to have the minimum number of steps (three), so the network diversity in this example is equal to $\frac{2}{3}$ (note that it is a simple fact that this ratio will never exceed 1). Intuitively, the numerator 2 denotes the network's current level of robustness against zero day exploits (no more than 2 different attacks), whereas the denominator 3 denotes the network's maximum potential of robustness (tolerating no more than 3 different attacks) by increasing the amount of diversity (from $\frac{2}{3}$ to 1). More formally, we introduce our second network diversity metric in Definition 5 (note that, for simplicity, we only consider a single goal condition for representing the given critical asset, which is not a limitation since multiple goal conditions can be easily handled through adding a few dummy conditions [20]).

---

[1] Note that, although we will refer to the number of distinct resources for simplicity, it is to be understood that this can be replaced by the effective richness concept in Definition 2.

Definition 5 (d_2-**Diversity**). *Given a resource graph $G(E \cup C, R_r \cup R_i)$ and a goal condition $c_g \in C$, for each $c \in C$ and $q \in seq(c)$, denote $R(q)$ for $\{r : r \in R, r$ appears in $q\}$, the network diversity is defined as (where $min(.)$ returns the minimum value in a set)*

$$d_2 = \frac{min_{q \in seq(c_g)} \mid R(q) \mid}{min_{q' \in seq(c_g)} \mid q' \mid}$$

3.2   The Complexity and Algorithm

Since the problem of finding the shortest paths (in terms of the number of exploits) in an attack graph (which is syntactically equivalent to a resource graph) is known to be intractable [18], not surprisingly, the problem of determining the network diversity d_2 is also intractable, as stated in Theorem 1. However, we note that, for a specific network, the two problems are not necessarily comparable in terms of their relative hardness. For example, in a network with all resources being distinct, it is trivial that $d_2 = 1$, whereas the shortest paths (in terms of the number of steps) may not be easy to find. On the other hand, the proof of Theorem 1 is based on special cases where finding the shortest paths is trivial, whereas determining the network diversity is still intractable.

Theorem 1. *Given a resource graph $G(E \cup C, R_r \cup R_i)$, determining the network diversity d_2 is NP-hard.*

Proof: The NP-complete Minimum Set Covering (MSC) problem [21] can be reduced to this problem through a construction similar to that in [22]. Specifically, the MSC problem is to determine that, given a finite set $S = \{c_1, c_2, \ldots, c_n\}$ and a collection $SC = \{r_1, r_2, \ldots, r_m\}$ where $r_i \subseteq S (1 \le i \le m)$, whether there exists a minimum $SC' \subseteq SC$ satisfying that every $c_i \in S$ is a member of some $r_j \in SC'$. For any given MSC instance, we construct a special resource graph $G(E \cup C, R_r \cup R_i)$ in which we let $C = S \cup \{s, d\}$, where s denotes an initial condition and d the goal condition, and whenever $c_i \in r_j$ is true, we create an exploit that involves resource r_j, with pre-condition c_{i-1} (or s for $i = 1$) and post-condition c_i. Finally, we add an additional exploit that involves an extra resource r_0, with pre-condition c_n and post-condition d. Since every attack path q in this special resource graph has the same length $\mid q \mid = n + 1$, we need to find a path q that minimizes the set of distinct resources involved in q, denoted as $R(q)$ (which also minimizes $\mid R(q) \mid / \mid q \mid$). Moreover, a path that minimizes $\mid R(q) \mid$ clearly provides a solution to the MSC problem. Therefore, we can determine the network diversity d_2 if and only if we can solve the MSC problem, which concludes the proof. □

Although determining network diversity is computationally infeasible in general, in most cases the network diversity of a given network may still be computed or estimated within a reasonable time using heuristics. In particular, Algorithm *Heuristic_Diversity* shown in Figure 3 employs the heuristic of only maintaining a limited number of local optima at each step in order to keep the complexity manageable. Specifically, the algorithm starts by marking all exploits and conditions as unprocessed (lines 1-2) and all initial conditions as processed (line 3-4). Functions $\sigma()$ and $\sigma'()$ represent two collections of attack paths (as sets of exploits, since the order of exploits is unimportant here) leading to an exploit or condition, to be used to calculate the minimum number of resources and steps, respectively. Therefore, for each initial condition c, such collections $\sigma()$ and $\sigma'()$ are both initialized as empty sets (line 5).

Procedure *Heuristic_Diversity*
Input: Resource graph $G(E \cup C, R_r \cup R_i)$, goal condition c_g, parameter k
Output: d_2
Method:
1. **For each** $e \in E$ and $c \in C \setminus C_I$
2.   **Mark** e and c as unprocessed
3. **For each** $c \in C_I$
4.   **Mark** c as processed
5.   **Let** $\sigma(c) = \sigma'(c) = \phi$
6. **While** $(\exists e \in E)(e$ is unprocessed$)$ and $(\forall c \in C)((c,e) \in R_r \Rightarrow c$ is processed$)$
7.   **Let** $\{c \in C : (c,e) \in R_r\} = \{c_1, c_2, \ldots, c_n\}$
8.   **Let** $\sigma(e) = ShortestK(\{q_1 \cup q_2 \cup \ldots \cup q_n \cup \{e\} : q_i \in \sigma(c_i), 1 \le i \le n\}, k)$
9.   **Let** $\sigma'(e) = ShortestK'(\{q_1 \cup q_2 \cup \ldots \cup q_n \cup \{e\} : q_i \in \sigma(c_i), 1 \le i \le n\}, k)$
10.   **Mark** e as processed
11.   **For each** c s.t. $(e,c) \in R_i$
12.   **If** $(\forall e' \in E)((e',c) \in R_i \Rightarrow e'$ is processed$)$ **Then**
13.   **Let** $\sigma(c) = ShortestK(\bigcup_{e' \text{ s.t. } (e',c) \in R_i} \sigma(e'), k)$
14.   **Let** $\sigma'(c) = ShortestK'(\bigcup_{e' \text{ s.t. } (e',c) \in R_i} \sigma(e'), k)$
15.   **Mark** c as processed
16. **Return** $\dfrac{min_{q \in seq(c_g)} |R(q)|}{min_{q' \in seq(c_g)} |q'|}$

Fig. 3. A Heuristic Algorithm for Computing the Network Diversity d_2

The main loop cycles through each unprocessed exploit whose pre-conditions have all been processed (line 6). For each such exploit e, all of its pre-conditions are first placed in a set (line 7). The collection of attack paths $\sigma(e)$ (and $\sigma'(e)$) is then constructed from the attack paths of those pre-conditions (line 8 and 9). Specifically, since the exploit e requires all the pre-conditions to be satisfied, an attack path leading to e must be the union of n attack paths $(q_1 \cup q_2 \cup \ldots \cup q_n$, each of which leads to one of the pre-conditions $(q_i \in \sigma(c_i))$. The function $ShortestK()$ simply picks the top k solutions, that is, the k paths with the minimum number of distinct resources ($ShortestK'()$ for paths with the minimum number of steps). After this, the exploit e is marked as processed (line 10). Next, the inner loop cycles through each post-condition of e (line 11-15) in a similar way (the differences arise from the fact that a condition c may be satisfied by any of the exploits implying it alone). The final result is calculated based on the two collections of attack paths leading to the goal condition (line 16).

The complexity of the algorithm is dominated by the main loop (lines 6-15). The outer loop will execute at most $\mid E \mid$ times since it only cycles through unprocessed exploits while each cycle will mark one exploit as processed. The inner loop executes at most $\mid C \mid$ times, and its complexity is dominated by line 13 and 14 which calculate the union over at most k paths leading to each of the $\mid E \mid$ or less exploits. Considering the maximum length of each path $\mid E \mid$, the complexity of the inner loop is thus $\mid C \mid$ $\cdot \mid E \mid^2 \cdot k$. However, this complexity is actually dominated by line 8 and 9, in which at most k paths may lead to every one of the $\mid C \mid$ or less conditions, and this results in at most $k^{\mid C \mid}$ candidates for $ShortestK()$ (and $ShortestK'()$) to choose from. Therefore, heuristics will be needed in designing the $ShortestK()$ (and $ShortestK'()$) function such that it only evaluates a limited number of candidates in picking the top k solutions. However, in practice, the number of pre-conditions of most exploits is expected to be a constant (compared to the size of the resource graph), and hence the overall complexity $\mid E \mid \cdot (\mid C \mid \cdot \mid E \mid^2 \cdot k + k^{\mid C \mid})$ would still be manageable.

4   Probabilistic Network Diversity

In Section 2.1, we have shown that the least attacking effort-based metric only provides a partial picture of the threat and is insufficient by itself. In this section, we develop a metric to capture the average attacking effort by combining all attack paths. For this purpose, we take a probabilistic approach to modeling network diversity. More specifically, we define network diversity as the conditional probability p that, given that an attacker can compromise a given critical asset in the network, he/she would still be able to do so even if all the resources were to be made different (i.e., every type of resource would appear at most once). This probability p represents the level of diversity currently present in the network, and a higher value means higher diversity (in the special case of $p = 1$, the network is already perfectly diverse, since further diversification effort will not reduce the attack likelihood with respect to the given critical asset).

Clearly, the aforementioned conditional probability is equal to the ratio between two probabilities, the probability that an attacker may compromise the given critical asset when all resource instances in the network are different, and the probability that he/she can do so in the current network. Both probabilities represent the *attack likelihood* with respect to the goal condition, and can be modeled using a Bayesian network constructed based on the resource graph (a similar approach using attack graph is given in [23]).

Definition 6 formally introduces network diversity following this intuition. In the definition, the first set of conditional probabilities represent the probability that an exploit e can be successfully executed, given that all its pre-conditions are already satisfied. The second and third set together represent the simple fact that an exploit cannot be executed unless all its pre-conditions are already satisfied, whereas a condition can be satisfied as the post-condition of one or more executed exploits. Finally, the fourth set represents the conditional probability that an exploit e_2 may be executed by an attacker who has already successfully executed another exploit e_1 which involves the same resource (i.e., the attack likelihood while reusing a previous exploit).

Definition 6 (d_3 **Diversity**). *Given a resource graph $G(E \cup C, R_r \cup R_i)$, and*

1. *for each $e \in E$, a given conditional probability $P(e \mid \bigwedge_{\{c:\langle c,e \rangle \in R_r\}} c = TRUE)$,*
2. *conditional probabilities $P(e \mid \bigwedge_{\{c:\langle c,e \rangle \in R_r\}} c = FALSE) = 0$,*
3. *conditional probabilities $P(c \mid e = TRUE \wedge \langle e,c \rangle \in R_i) = 1$, and*
4. *for any $e_1, e_2 \in E$ involving the same resource r, conditional probabilities $P(e_1 \mid e_2 = TRUE \wedge (\bigwedge_{\{c:\langle c,e_1 \rangle \in R_r\}} c) = TRUE)$ (and $P(e_2 \mid e_1 = TRUE \wedge \bigwedge_{\{c:\langle c,e_2 \rangle \in R_r\}} c = TRUE)$),*

Given any $c_g \in C$, the network diversity d_3 is defined as $d_3 = \frac{p'}{p}$ where p denotes the conditional probability of c_g being satisfied given that all the initial conditions are true, and p' denotes the probability of c_g being satisfied given that all initial conditions are true and the above fourth set of probabilities not given (i.e., without considering the effect of reusing any exploit).

Figure 4 demonstrates the proposed metric model using our running example, by assuming all resource instances to be different (even if they may be under the same name) except the $http$ service, which is the same on three different hosts. In the figure, on the left side is the case when the effect of reusing an exploit is not considered in the above definition, and on the right side the case when the same effect is considered. In the figure, each number inside the box represents the first set of given conditional probabilities (assigned with arbitrary values in this example). The dotted lines in the right figure show the last set of given conditional probabilities. The number beside each exploit or condition represents the probability calculated through statistical inferences using the Bayesian network. Finally, we show part of the two conditional probability tables (CPTs) to illustrate the difference between not considering the effect of reusing the $http$ exploit (e.g., probability 0.5 in the left CPT), and considering it (e.g., probability 0.9 in the right CPT). The diversity in this case will be calculated as $d_3 = \frac{0.007}{0.0103}$.

To instantiate the above model, we need to obtain the first and last set of conditional probabilities in Definition 6. For the former, we can adopt the simple approach in [23] to base the probability on the Common Vulnerability Scoring System (CVSS) [24] scores (available in public databases [25]). For zero day exploits, we can assign a nominal value as follows. Since a zero day vulnerability is commonly interpreted as a vulnerability not publicly known or announced, we can interpret this using the CVSS base metrics [24], as a vulnerability with a remediation level *unavailable*, a report confidence *unconfirmed*, and a maximum overall base score (and hence produce a conservative metric value). We therefore obtain a nominal value of 0.8, converting to a probability of 0.08 (for reference purpose, the lowest existing CVSS score in [25] is currently 1.7). Finally, the last set of conditional probabilities models the attack likelihood while reusing an exploit on different machines and therefore can be assigned with a higher value than the corresponding attack probability in the first set.

5 Simulation

In this section, we study the performance of our proposed heuristic algorithm and briefly compare the three proposed metrics via simulations, while leaving more detailed comparative studies of those metrics to future work. All simulation results are collected using a computer equipped with a 3.0 GHz CPU and 8GB RAM in the Python environment under Ubuntu 12.04 LTS. We calculate the Bayesian network-based metric using OpenBayes [26]. To generate a large number of resource graphs, we first construct a small number of seed graphs based on real networks, and then we obtain larger graphs from these seed graphs by injecting new hosts and assigning resources in a random but realistic fashion (e.g., we vary the number of pre-conditions of each exploit within a small range since real world exploits usually have a few pre-conditions).

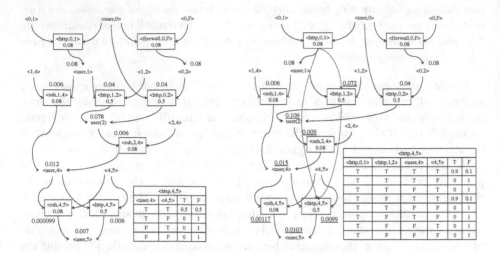

Fig. 4. Modeling Network Diversity Using Bayesian Networks

The objective of the first two simulations is to evaluate the accuracy (approximation ratio between the result obtained using our algorithm and that using brute force) of our heuristic algorithm (in Figure 3). The left-hand side of Figure 5 shows the approximation ratio in increasing k (the parameter of the algorithm that represents the number of local optima stored at each step). We also examine the results under different in-degrees (i.e., the maximum number of pre-conditions of any exploit). We can see that the approximate ratios increase with the in-degrees, and they decrease to an acceptable level (lower than 1.03) when k reaches about 4, and the trends stay flatten when $k > 6$ (almost equal to 1). Therefore, k can be chosen as around 5 in practice. The right-hand side of Figure 5 shows that the approximation ratio grows when the resource graph gets larger, which is expected (with a fixed parameter k, the relative amount of local optima stored at each step will decrease when the size of resource graphs increases, and hence worse performance). We only show k up to 3 since from the previous simulation it is clear that the approximation ratio will be close to 1 when k is 4 or greater.

The objective of next simulation is to evaluate the processing time of the heuristic algorithm. Since the approximation ratio will stay flatten when $k \geq 6$, we only show the processing time for $k \leq 6$. The left-hand side of Figure 6 shows that the processing time is still acceptable (about 10 seconds) when $k = 6$ with around 1000 nodes. For in-degrees of 3 and 4, the trend is much closer to linear. Although it is well known that inference using Bayesian networks is intractable in general, the right-hand side of Figure 6 shows that our processing time for computing the Bayesian network-based metrics (using OpenBayes [26]) exhibits an acceptable trend (mostly due to the special structure of resource graphs).

The last two simulations compare the results of all three metrics proposed in this paper. To convert the Bayesian network-based metric d_3 to a comparable scale of the other

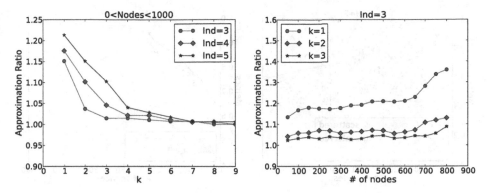

Fig. 5. Approximation Ratio in k under Different In-degrees (Left) and in Graph Size under Different k (Right)

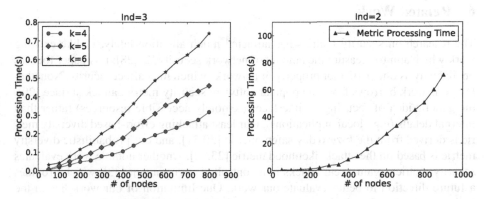

Fig. 6. Processing Time for Computing d_2 in Graph Size under Different k (Left) and Processing Time for Computing d_3

two, we use $\frac{\log_{0.08}(p')}{\log_{0.08}(p)}$ (i.e., the ratio based on equivalent numbers of zero day exploits) instead of d_3. In the left-hand side of Figure 7, the scatter points marked with X in the red color are the individual values of d_2. The blue points marked with Y are the values of d_3 (converted as above). Also shown are their average values, and the average value of the effective richness-based metric d_1. While all three metrics follow a similar trend (diversity will decrease in larger graphs since there will be more duplicated resources), the Bayesian network-based metric d_3 somehow reflects an intermediate result between the two other extremes (d_1 can be considered as the average over all resources, whereas d_2 only depends on the shortest path). The right-hand side of Figure 7 shows the average value of the three metrics in increasing number of distinct resources for resource graphs of a fixed size. All three metrics capture the same effect of increasing diversity, and their relationships are similar to that in the previous simulation.

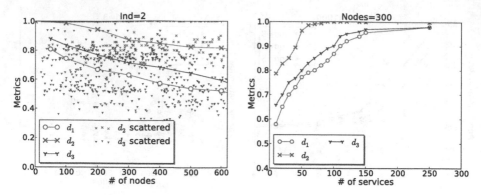

Fig. 7. Comparison of Metrics (Left) and the Effect of Increasing Diversity (Right)

6 Related Work

The research on security metrics has attracted much attention lately. Unlike existing work which aim to measure the amount of network security [27,28], this paper focuses on diversity as one particular property of networks which may affect security. Nonetheless, our work borrows from the popular software security metric, attack surface [29], the general idea of focusing on interfaces (remotely accessible resources) rather than internal details (e.g., local applications). Our least attacking effort-based diversity metric is derived from the k-zero day safety metric [30,31], and our probabilistic diversity metric is based on the attack likelihood metric [23,32]. Another notable work evaluates security metrics against real attacks in a controlled environment [33], which provides a future direction to better evaluate our work. One limitation of our work lies in the high complexity of analyzing a resource graph; high level models of resource dependencies [34] may provide coarser but more efficient solutions to modeling diversity.

The idea of using design diversity for fault tolerance has been investigated for a long time. The N-version programming approach generates $N \geq 2$ functionally equivalent programs and compares their results to determine a faulty version [35], with metrics defined for measuring the diversity of software and faults [36]. The main limitation of design diversity lies in the high complexity of creating different versions, which may not justify the benefit [37]. The use of design diversity as a security mechanism has also attracted much attention [38]. The general principles of design diversity is shown to be applicable to security as well in [2]. The N-Variant system extends the idea of N-version programming to detect intrusions [3], and the concept of behavioral distance takes it beyond output voting [4]. Different randomization techniques have been used to automatically generate diversity [7,9,8,10].

In addition to design diversity and generated diversity, recent work employ opportunistic diversity which already exists among different software systems. The practicality of employing OS diversity for intrusion tolerance is evaluated in [6] and the feasibility of using opportunistic diversity already existing between different OSes to tolerate intrusions is demonstrated. Diversity has also been applied to intrusion tolerant systems which usually implement some kinds of Byzantine Fault Tolerant (BFT) replication as fault tolerance solutions. Considering single-machine environments based on multiple cores and virtualization, diversified replications are employed as a method to offer Byzantine-fault tolerance to software attacks [5]. A generic architecture for implementing intrusion-tolerant Web servers based on redundancy and diversification principles is introduced using redundant proxies and diversified application servers with redundancy levels selected according to threat levels [39]. Components-off-the-shelf (COTS) diversity is employed to provide an implicit reference model, instead of the explicit model usually required, for anomaly detection in Web servers [40].

7 Conclusion

In this paper, we have taken a first step towards formally modeling network diversity as a security metric for evaluating networks' robustness against zero day attacks. We first devised an effective richness-based metric based on the counterpart in ecology. We then proposed a least attacking effort-based metric to address causal relationships between resources and a probabilistic metric to reflect the average attacking effort. Finally, we evaluated our algorithms and metrics through simulations.

The main limitations of this work are the following.

- First, our models depend on the availability and accuracy of many inputs, such as the modeling of resources and their relationships (to form the resource graph), the degree of difference and similarity between different types of resources (to calculate the effective richness), which may be challenging to characterize in practice.
- Second, we have employed simulations to evaluate our models, although it is certainly ideal to conduct experiments with real-world networks and attacks. Unfortunately, there does not currently exist any publicly available benchmark dataset containing a significant number of representative real networks, and with both vulnerabilities and attack information.
- Third, we have focused on modeling diversity, but did not address other factors that may also affect decisions regarding diversity, such as the cost (in terms of deployment and maintenance) and impact to functionality.
- Fourth, we regard all resources as equally likely to have zero day vulnerabilities, which can easily be extended by assigning different weights to resources, when their likelihood of having vulnerabilities can be estimated from past experiences.

As future work, we will address those limitations by refining and extending the models, employing real vulnerabilities for experiments and case studies, and studying various applications of the proposed diversity metrics.

Acknowledgements. The authors thank the anonymous reviewers for their valuable comments. The work of Sushil Jajodia and Massimiliano Albanese was partially supported by the Army Research Office under grants W911NF-13-1-0421, W911NF-09-1-0525, and W911NF-13-1-0317, and by the Office of Naval Research under grants N00014-12-1-0461 and N00014-13-1-0703. The work of Sushil Jajodia and Lingyu Wang was also supported by the National Institute of Standards and Technology under the grant 60NANB14D060. The work of Lingyu Wang and Mengyuan Zhang was also supported by Natural Sciences and Engineering Research Council of Canada under Discovery Grant N01035. Commercial products are identified in order to adequately specify certain procedures. In no case does such identification imply recommendation or endorsement by the National Institute of Standards and Technology, nor does it imply that the identified products are necessarily the best available for the purpose.

References

1. Falliere, N., Murchu, L.O., Chien, E.: W32.stuxnet dossier. Symantec Security Response (2011)
2. Littlewood, B., Strigini, L.: Redundancy and diversity in security. In: Samarati, P., Ryan, P.Y.A., Gollmann, D., Molva, R. (eds.) ESORICS 2004. LNCS, vol. 3193, pp. 423–438. Springer, Heidelberg (2004)
3. Cox, B., Evans, D., Filipi, A., Rowanhill, J., Hu, W., Davidson, J., Knight, J., Nguyen-Tuong, A., Hiser, J.: N-variant systems: A secretless framework for security through diversity. Defense Technical Information Center (2006)
4. Gao, D., Reiter, M.K., Song, D.: Behavioral distance measurement using hidden markov models. In: Zamboni, D., Kruegel, C. (eds.) RAID 2006. LNCS, vol. 4219, pp. 19–40. Springer, Heidelberg (2006)
5. Chun, B., Maniatis, P., Shenker, S.: Diverse replication for single-machine byzantine-fault tolerance. In: USENIX Annual Technical Conference, pp. 287–292 (2008)
6. Garcia, M., Bessani, A., Gashi, I., Neves, N., Obelheiro, R.: OS diversity for intrusion tolerance: Myth or reality? In: 2011 IEEE/IFIP 41st International Conference on Dependable Systems & Networks (DSN), pp. 383–394 (2011)
7. Bhatkar, S., DuVarney, D., Sekar, R.: Address obfuscation: An efficient approach to combat a broad range of memory error exploits. In: Proceedings of the 12th USENIX Security Symposium, Washington, DC, vol. 120 (2003)
8. Team, T.P.: PaX address space layout randomization, http://pax.grsecurity.net/
9. Kc, G., Keromytis, A., Prevelakis, V.: Countering code-injection attacks with instruction-set randomization. In: Proceedings of the 10th ACM Conference on Computer and Communications Security, pp. 272–280. ACM (2003)
10. Bhatkar, S., Sekar, R.: Data space randomization. In: Zamboni, D. (ed.) DIMVA 2008. LNCS, vol. 5137, pp. 1–22. Springer, Heidelberg (2008)
11. Jajodia, S., Ghosh, A., Swarup, V., Wang, C., Wang, X.: Moving Target Defense: Creating Asymmetric Uncertainty for Cyber Threats, 1st edn. Springer (2011)
12. Yang, Y., Zhu, S., Cao, G.: Improving sensor network immunity under worm attacks: a software diversity approach. In: Proceedings of the 9th ACM International Symposium on Mobile ad hoc Networking and Computing, pp. 149–158. ACM (2008)
13. Caballero, J., Kampouris, T., Song, D., Wang, J.: Would diversity really increase the robustness of the routing infrastructure against software defects? In: Proceedings of the Network and Distributed System Security Symposium (2008)
14. Elton, C.: The ecology of invasion by animals and plants. University of Chicago Press, Chicago (1958)
15. Pielou, E.: Ecological diversity. Wiley, New York (1975)
16. Hill, M.: Diversity and evenness: a unifying notation and its consequences. Ecology 54(2), 427–432 (1973)
17. Leinster, T., Cobbold, C.: Measuring diversity: the importance of species similarity. Ecology 93(3), 477–489 (2012)
18. Sheyner, O., Haines, J., Jha, S., Lippmann, R., Wing, J.: Automated generation and analysis of attack graphs. In: Proceedings of the 2002 IEEE Symposium on Security and Privacy (2002)

19. Ammann, P., Wijesekera, D., Kaushik, S.: Scalable, graph-based network vulnerability analysis. In: Proceedings of ACM CCS 2002 (2002)
20. Albanese, M., Jajodia, S., Noel, S.: A time-efficient approach to cost-effective network hardening using attack graphs. In: Proceedings of the 42nd Annual IEEE/IFIP International Conference on Dependable Systems and Networks (DSN 2012), pp. 1–12 (2012)
21. Garey, M., Johnson, D.: Computers and intractability: A guide to the theory of NP-Completeness. W.H. Freeman, San Francisco (1979)
22. Yuan, S., Varma, S., Jue, J.: Minimum-color path problems for reliability in mesh networks. In: 24th Annual Joint Conference of the IEEE Computer and Communications Societies (INFOCOM), pp. 2658–2669 (2005)
23. Frigault, M., Wang, L., Singhal, A., Jajodia, S.: Measuring network security using dynamic bayesian network. In: Proceedings of 4th ACM QoP (2008)
24. Mell, P., Scarfone, K., Romanosky, S.: Common vulnerability scoring system. IEEE Security & Privacy 4(6), 85–89 (2006)
25. National vulnerability database, http://www.nvd.org (May 9, 2008)
26. Gaitanis, K., Cohen, E.: Open bayes 0.1.0 (2013), https://pypi.python.org/pypi/OpenBayes
27. Idika, N., Bhargava, B.: Extending attack graph-based security metrics and aggregating their application. IEEE Transactions on Dependable and Secure Computing 9, 75–85 (2012)
28. Wang, L., Singhal, A., Jajodia, S.: Toward measuring network security using attack graphs. In: Proceedings of 3rd ACM QoP (2007)
29. Manadhata, P., Wing, J.: An attack surface metric. IEEE Trans. Softw. Eng. 37(3), 371–386 (2011)
30. Wang, L., Jajodia, S., Singhal, A., Noel, S.: k-zero day safety: Measuring the security risk of networks against unknown attacks. In: Gritzalis, D., Preneel, B., Theoharidou, M. (eds.) ESORICS 2010. LNCS, vol. 6345, pp. 573–587. Springer, Heidelberg (2010)
31. Wang, L., Jajodia, S., Singhal, A., Cheng, P., Noel, S.: k-zero day safety: A network security metric for measuring the risk of unknown vulnerabilities. IEEE Transactions on Dependable and Secure Computing 11(1), 30–44 (2013)
32. Wang, L., Singhal, A., Jajodia, S.: Measuring the overall security of network configurations using attack graphs. In: Barker, S., Ahn, G.-J. (eds.) Data and Applications Security 2007. LNCS, vol. 4602, pp. 98–112. Springer, Heidelberg (2007)
33. Holm, H., Ekstedt, M., Andersson, D.: Empirical analysis of system-level vulnerability metrics through actual attacks. IEEE Trans. Dependable Secur. Comput. 9(6), 825–837 (2012)
34. Kheir, N., Cuppens-Boulahia, N., Cuppens, F., Debar, H.: A service dependency model for cost-sensitive intrusion response. In: Gritzalis, D., Preneel, B., Theoharidou, M. (eds.) ESORICS 2010. LNCS, vol. 6345, pp. 626–642. Springer, Heidelberg (2010)
35. Avizienis, A., Chen, L.: On the implementation of n-version programming for software fault tolerance during execution. In: Proc. IEEE COMPSAC., vol. 77, pp. 149–155 (1977)
36. Mitra, S., Saxena, N., McCluskey, E.: A design diversity metric and analysis of redundant systems. IEEE Trans. Comput. 51(5), 498–510 (2002)
37. Littlewood, B., Popov, P., Strigini, L.: Modeling software design diversity: A review. ACM Comput. Surv. 33(2), 177–208 (2001)
38. Maxion, R.: Use of diversity as a defense mechanism. In: Proceedings of the 2005 Workshop on New Security Paradigms, NSPW 2005, pp. 21–22. ACM, New York (2005)
39. Saïdane, A., Nicomette, V., Deswarte, Y.: The design of a generic intrusion-tolerant architecture for web servers. IEEE Trans. Dependable Sec. Comput. 6(1), 45–58 (2009)
40. Totel, E., Majorczyk, F., Mé, L.: Cots diversity based intrusion detection and application to web servers. In: Valdes, A., Zamboni, D. (eds.) RAID 2005. LNCS, vol. 3858, pp. 43–62. Springer, Heidelberg (2006)

Author Index